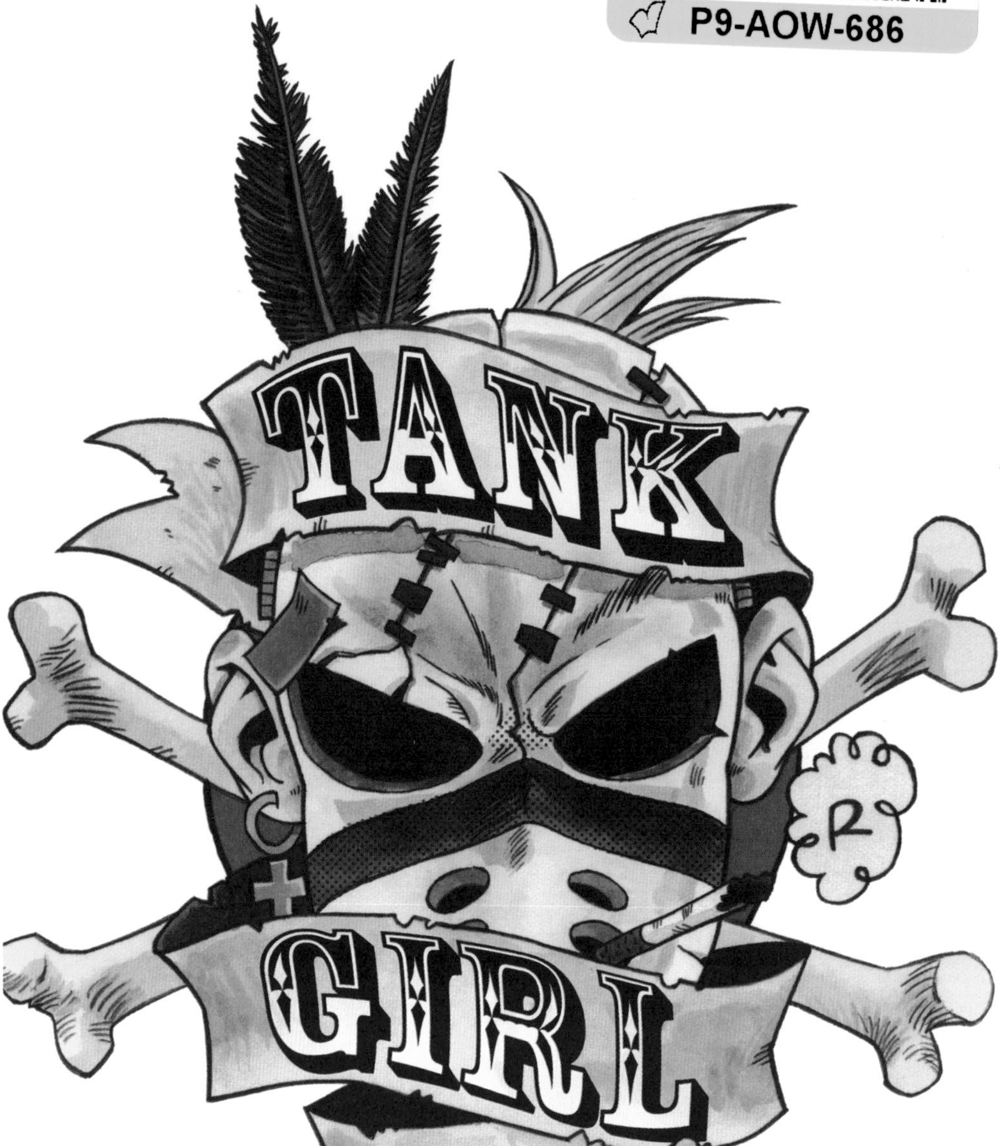
TANK
GIRL
R

THE COSMIC BEAM FROM OUTER-SPACE

"Every time you wank, the stars move." - Dr. Booga

Okay, here's the score - in our current state, right now, as the human race is at this present moment in time...

WE ARE WELL AND TRULY FUCKED. Too many people, not enough space, not enough water, food-mountains growing while whole populations starve, pollution, war, paranoia, greed, rain forests being stripped to make way for cattle grazing so that fat fuckers can get their cheap burgers, four-wheel-drive SUVs being driven by one skinny little cunt for ten miles just so that he can get a new doo-hicky for his whatsname WHICH WAS A USELESS PIECE OF SHIT IN THE FIRST PLACE.

How can you argue with facts like that?

Is the human race a success?

NO. WE HAVE FUCKED UP ROYALLY. There is no way that we can change our ways in time to save the planet because we are all too fucking brainwashed into this mindset by huge, gormless companies that are making too much money and holding too much power. And it's not the fault of the government either, it's everybody's fault.

WE ARE ALL FUCKING IDIOTS. I don't envy the governments that have to try and keep all of this shit afloat. Man, the best that they can possibly do is to juggle with the cash and debts and populations and all that mind-boggling crap that is spiralling out of anyone's control, and try to keep some sort of equilibrium until the last moment when it all implodes and the shit of mankind's stupidity hits the fan of nature's wrath. You're probably thinking that this all sounds pretty fucking dark and bleak, yeah?

WELL, JUST YOU HOLD ON THERE, BOOBY. I know something you don't. And I heard this in a pub, so it's got to be true. Listen...

EVERYTHING IS GONNA BE ALRIGHT, OKAY, YEAH? There's this thing that's gonna happen, it's difficult to explain because nothing like it has happened in thousands of years, not since the days of Atlantis and ancient cool civilizations and all that shit. But it's coming our way. Think of a massive, planet-wide beam of light, full of rainbow colours, ghostly strands, glowing spheres and glittery bits, trawling its way across the galaxy.

THAT'S WHAT I'M TALKING ABOUT. You won't be able to see it through a telescope because it's invisible to the human eye. None of the world's scientific apparatus will pick it up on their sensors because it's got nothing to do with the kind of things that scientists are interested in.

THIS IS TRIPPY COSMIC SHIT. OKAY? Only the most freaked out amongst you will know where I'm coming from, man. Booga understands, but that's because he's fried his brain to a level of understanding that can only be achieved with over a decade of abuse. Okay then. So when this beam thing gets here and passes across the planet, touching everyone and everything to the very core of every atom...

THAT'S WHEN EVERYTHING WILL CHANGE FOREVER AND LOTS OF TRIPPED-OUT MAGIC STUFF WILL START TO HAPPEN. You see, it's not anything that a single man or group of men are gonna do that will save Earth. It's out of our hands, we've already fucked it beyond belief, so what the hell else can we do to ease the situation? Nature is sending its own remedy - a dose so awesomely powerful that all germs will be eradicated, once and for all. Keep your hands in your pockets and stop fiddling with the planet. We've already taken it to the brink of total annihilation, no amount of sticking plasters and quick fixes are gonna make amends.

WE'VE KICKED IT SO HARD IN THE BOLLOCKS, WE CAN NEVER KISS IT BETTER.
So there it is, in a nutshell. We've fucked up the planet and a cosmic beam is coming from across the universe to sort the shit out. Although, the beam was on its way anyway - some sort of cyclical-universal-renewal thing that it does. And we probably couldn't have played it any other way either - it's deep in our pre-programming that we should make such a pig's ear of paradise.

ALL WE HAVE TO DO NOW IS STAY ALIVE AND SANE LONG ENOUGH FOR THE DAMN THING TO GET HERE. And not everyone has got a free bus pass onto the survival coach, oh no. You can't just stick your head up your bum and wait to be rescued, that's not what this is about at all. Only those that are painfully aware of the situation will have a chance of getting through.

YOU MUST BE AWAKE. YOU MUST BE AWARE. WATCH FOR SIGNS AND SIGNALS AND SHIT.
If you keep your wits about you and follow our simple instructions, you can rest assured that you will still be alive and well in ten years time, and will be able to fully appreciate the full-on trippy-ness of the new, crispy...

GOLDEN AGE OF COSMIC FAR-OUT-NESS.
Alright?

I'm not even gonna try and explain what it's gonna be like, we are not yet of mature enough minds that we could comprehend the joy and splendour of how great it's all gonna be. Just trust me, I know what I'm talking about. And besides, what the fuck else have you got to put your faith in these days?

THIS IS THE NEXT EVOLUTIONARY STEP FOR MANKIND.
Just remember that.

We are about to make a giant leap forwards. And, as always, it's got nothing to do with what our turd-brained scientists, politicians or great leaders and thinkers have been doing.

SIT BACK.
STRAP YOURSELF IN.
START LOOKING REAL SCARED.
HANG ON TO THIS BOOK.

THE TRIP STARTS RIGHT NOW.

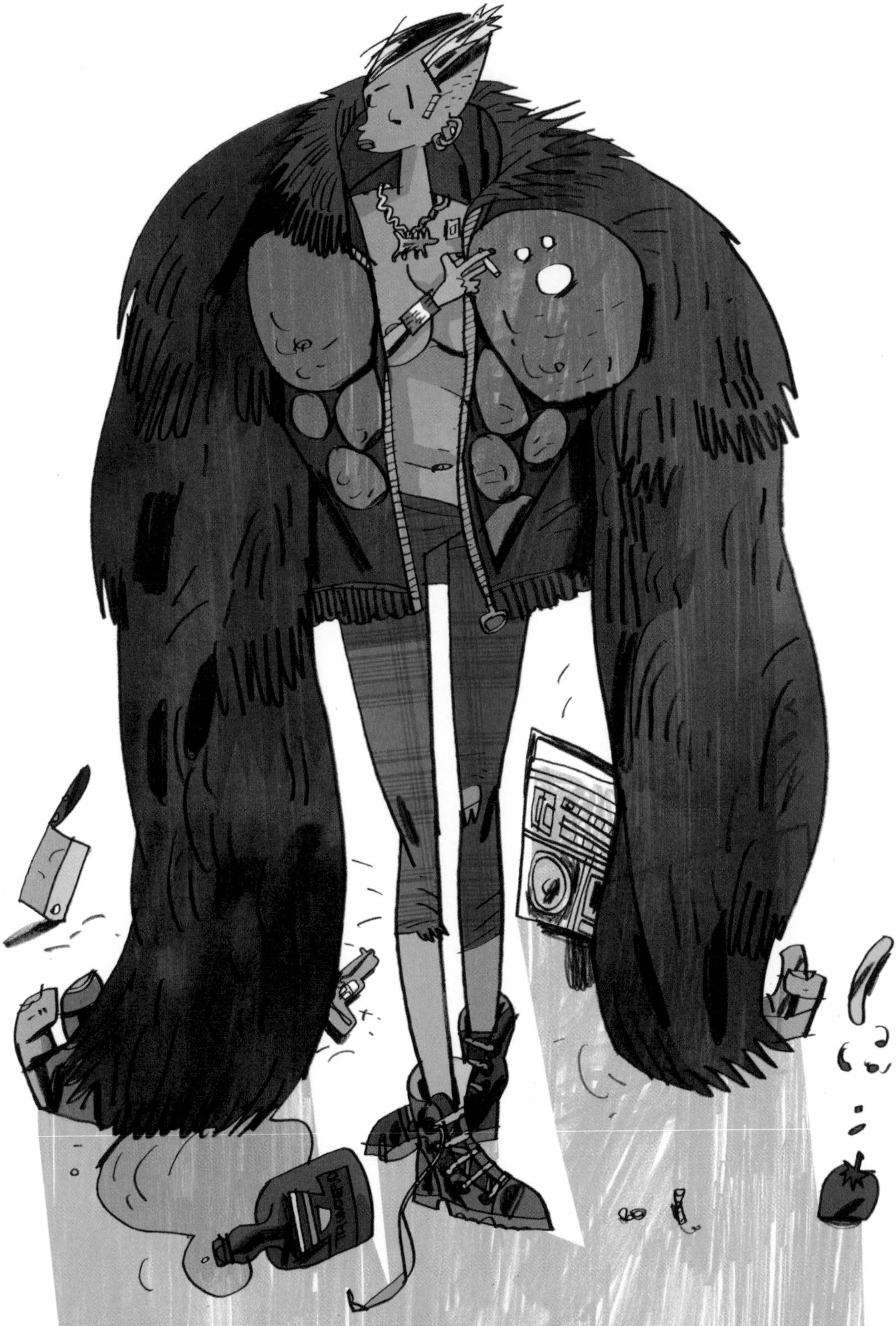

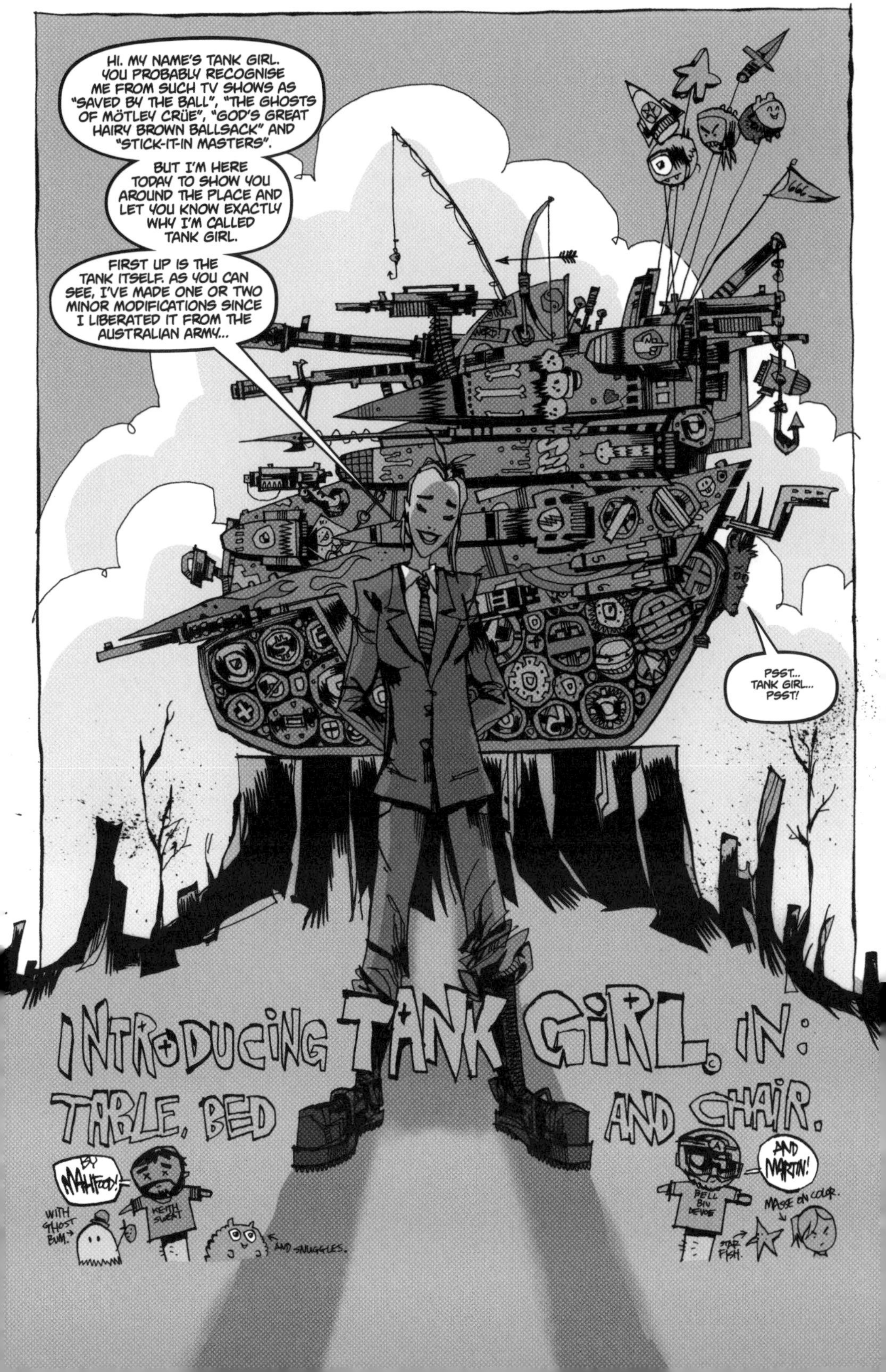
HI. MY NAME'S TANK GIRL. YOU PROBABLY RECOGNISE ME FROM SUCH TV SHOWS AS "SAVED BY THE BALL", "THE GHOSTS OF MÖTLEY CRÜE", "GOD'S GREAT HAIRY BROWN BALLSACK" AND "STICK-IT-IN MASTERS".
BUT I'M HERE TODAY TO SHOW YOU AROUND THE PLACE AND LET YOU KNOW EXACTLY WHY I'M CALLED TANK GIRL.
FIRST UP IS THE TANK ITSELF. AS YOU CAN SEE, I'VE MADE ONE OR TWO MINOR MODIFICATIONS SINCE I LIBERATED IT FROM THE AUSTRALIAN ARMY...
PSST... TANK GIRL... PSST!
INTRODUCING TANK GIRL IN:
TABLE, BED AND CHAIR.
BY MAHFOOD!
AND MARTIN!
WITH GHOST BUM.
KEITH SWEAT
AND SNUGGLES.
BELL BIV DEVOE
MASSE ON COLOR.
STAR FISH.

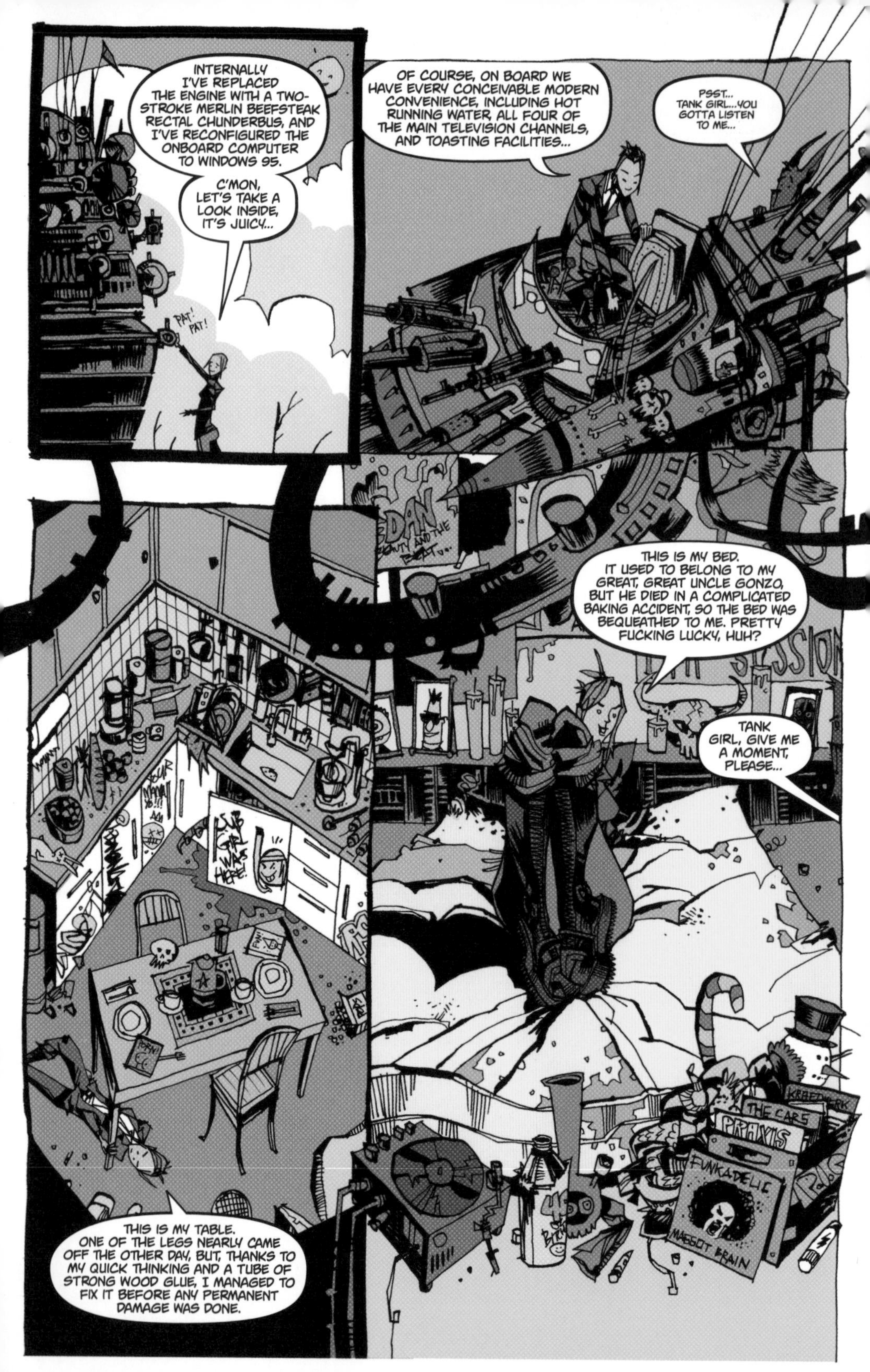
INTERNALLY I'VE REPLACED THE ENGINE WITH A TWO-STROKE MERLIN BEEFSTEAK RECTAL CHUNDERBUS, AND I'VE RECONFIGURED THE ONBOARD COMPUTER TO WINDOWS 95.
C'MON, LET'S TAKE A LOOK INSIDE, IT'S JUICY...
PAT! PAT!
OF COURSE, ON BOARD WE HAVE EVERY CONCEIVABLE MODERN CONVENIENCE, INCLUDING HOT RUNNING WATER, ALL FOUR OF THE MAIN TELEVISION CHANNELS, AND TOASTING FACILITIES...
PSST... TANK GIRL...YOU GOTTA LISTEN TO ME...
THIS IS MY BED. IT USED TO BELONG TO MY GREAT, GREAT UNCLE GONZO, BUT HE DIED IN A COMPLICATED BAKING ACCIDENT, SO THE BED WAS BEQUEATHED TO ME. PRETTY FUCKING LUCKY, HUH?
TANK GIRL, GIVE ME A MOMENT, PLEASE...
SUB GIRL WAS HERE!
THE CARS
PRAXIS
FUNKADELIC
MAGGOT BRAIN
THIS IS MY TABLE. ONE OF THE LEGS NEARLY CAME OFF THE OTHER DAY, BUT, THANKS TO MY QUICK THINKING AND A TUBE OF STRONG WOOD GLUE, I MANAGED TO FIX IT BEFORE ANY PERMANENT DAMAGE WAS DONE.

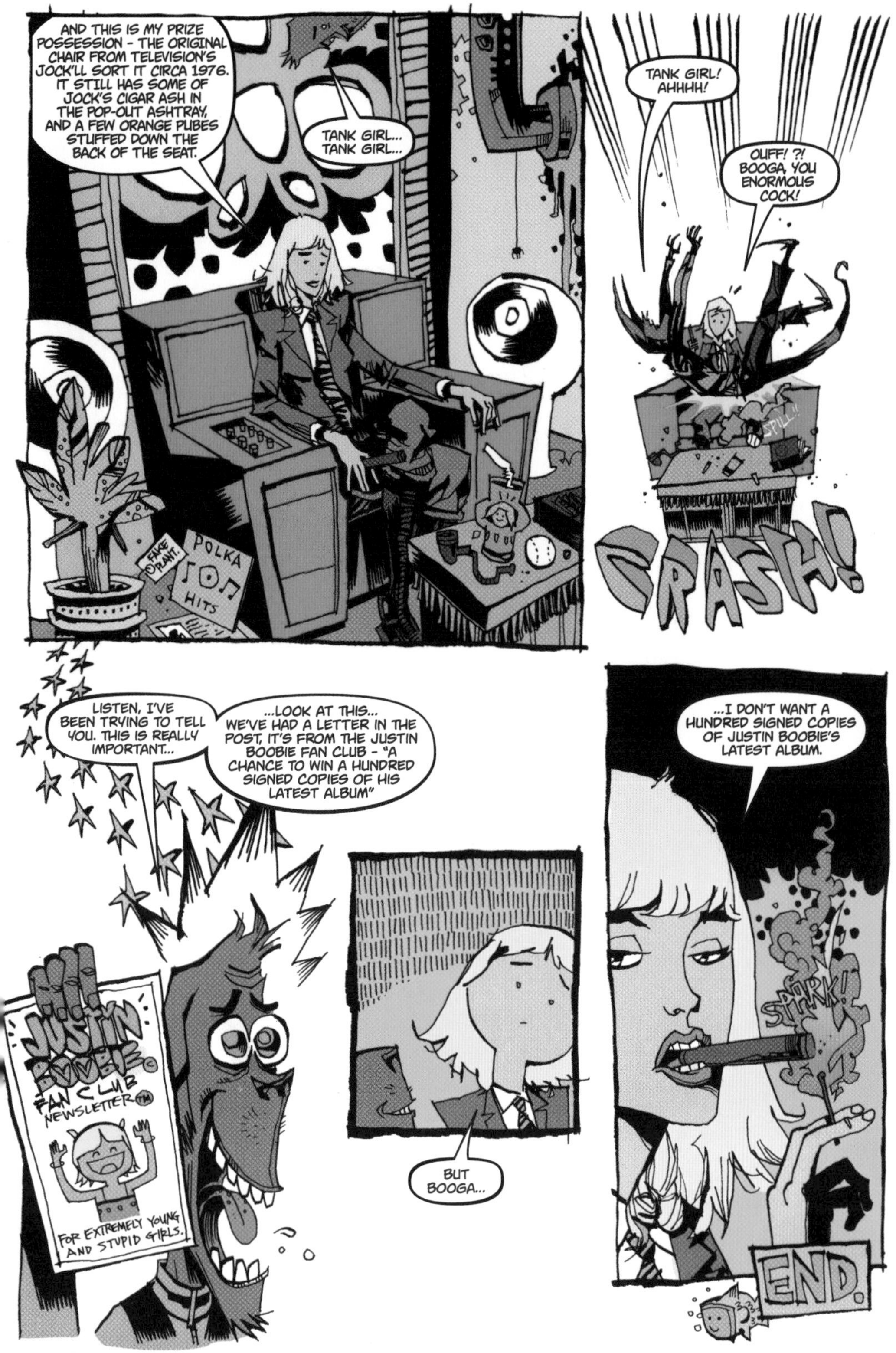
AND THIS IS MY PRIZE POSSESSION - THE ORIGINAL CHAIR FROM TELEVISION'S JOCK'LL SORT IT CIRCA 1976. IT STILL HAS SOME OF JOCK'S CIGAR ASH IN THE POP-OUT ASHTRAY, AND A FEW ORANGE PUBES STUFFED DOWN THE BACK OF THE SEAT.
TANK GIRL... TANK GIRL...
FAKE PLANT.
POLKA HITS
TANK GIRL! AHHHH!
OUFF! ?! BOOGA, YOU ENORMOUS COCK!
SPILL!!
CRASH!
LISTEN, I'VE BEEN TRYING TO TELL YOU. THIS IS REALLY IMPORTANT...
...LOOK AT THIS... WE'VE HAD A LETTER IN THE POST, IT'S FROM THE JUSTIN BOOBIE FAN CLUB - "A CHANCE TO WIN A HUNDRED SIGNED COPIES OF HIS LATEST ALBUM"
JUSTIN BOOBIE FAN CLUB NEWSLETTER™
FOR EXTREMELY YOUNG AND STUPID GIRLS.
BUT BOOGA...
...I DON'T WANT A HUNDRED SIGNED COPIES OF JUSTIN BOOBIE'S LATEST ALBUM.
SPARK!
END.

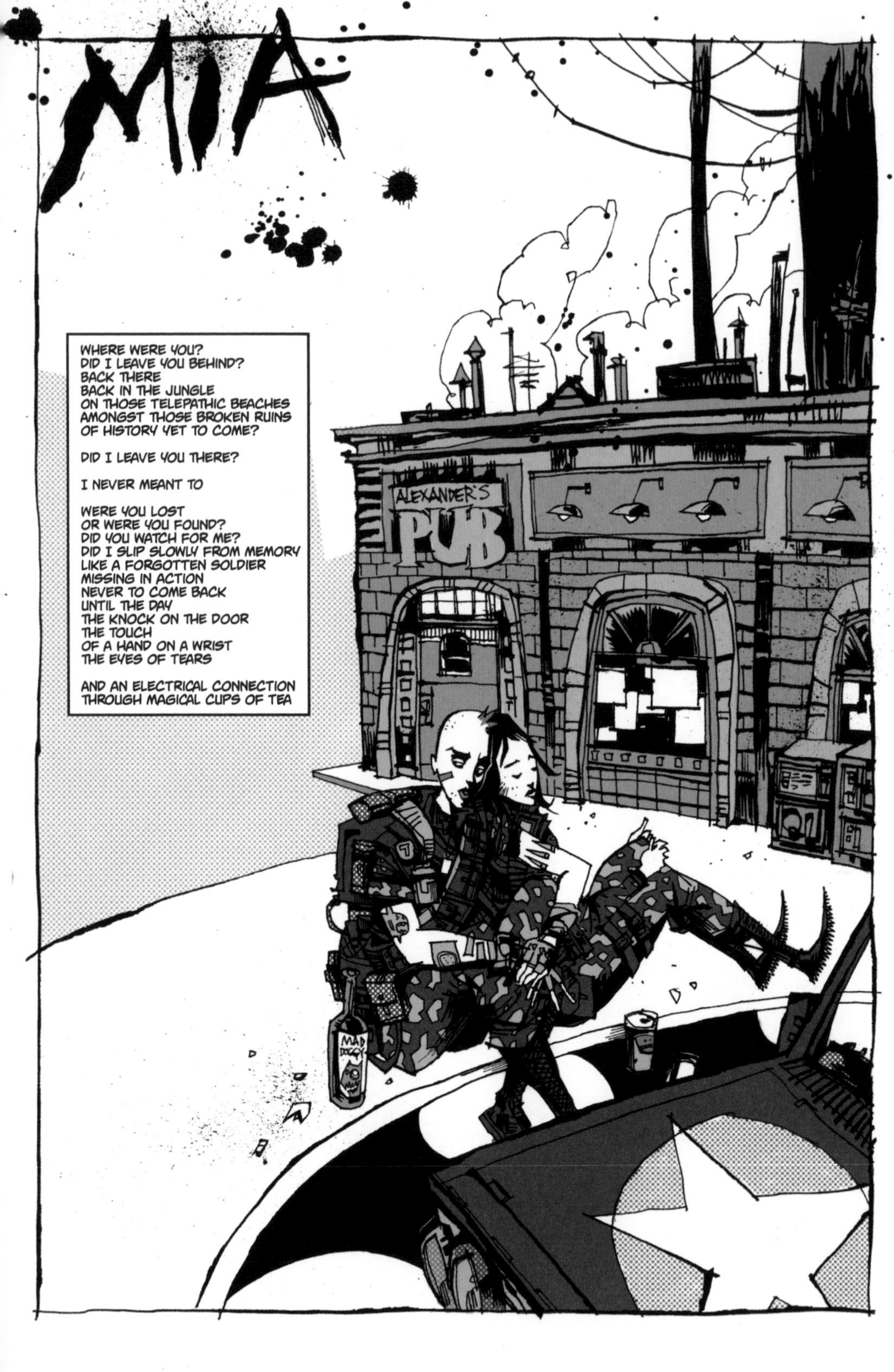
MIA
WHERE WERE YOU?
DID I LEAVE YOU BEHIND?
BACK THERE
BACK IN THE JUNGLE
ON THOSE TELEPATHIC BEACHES
AMONGST THOSE BROKEN RUINS
OF HISTORY YET TO COME?

DID I LEAVE YOU THERE?

I NEVER MEANT TO

WERE YOU LOST
OR WERE YOU FOUND?
DID YOU WATCH FOR ME?
DID I SLIP SLOWLY FROM MEMORY
LIKE A FORGOTTEN SOLDIER
MISSING IN ACTION
NEVER TO COME BACK
UNTIL THE DAY
THE KNOCK ON THE DOOR
THE TOUCH
OF A HAND ON A WRIST
THE EYES OF TEARS

AND AN ELECTRICAL CONNECTION
THROUGH MAGICAL CUPS OF TEA
ALEXANDER'S
PUB

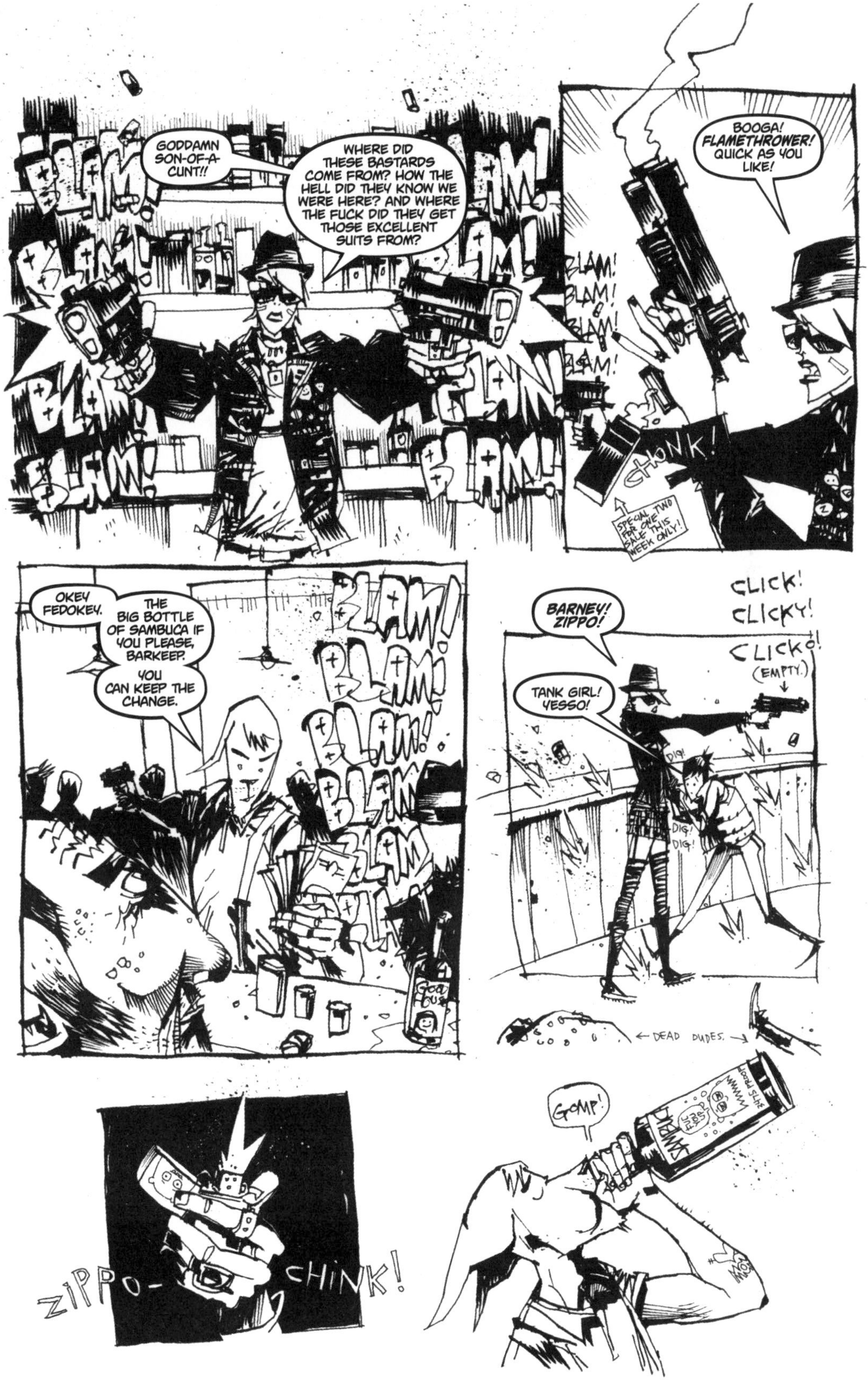
BLAM! BLAM! BLAM! BLAM!
GODDAMN SON-OF-A-CUNT!!
WHERE DID THESE BASTARDS COME FROM? HOW THE HELL DID THEY KNOW WE WERE HERE? AND WHERE THE FUCK DID THEY GET THOSE EXCELLENT SUITS FROM?
BLAM! BLAM! BLAM!
BOOGA! FLAMETHROWER! QUICK AS YOU LIKE!
BLAM! BLAM! BLAM! BLAM!
CHONK!
SPECIAL TWO FOR ONE SALE THIS WEEK ONLY!
OKEY FEDOKEY.
THE BIG BOTTLE OF SAMBUCA IF YOU PLEASE, BARKEEP.
YOU CAN KEEP THE CHANGE.
BLAM! BLAM! BLAM! BLAM! BLAM!
BARNEY! ZIPPO!
CLICK! CLICKY! CLICK!
(EMPTY.)
TANK GIRL! YESSO!
DIG! DIG! DIG!
← DEAD DUDES. →
ZIPPO-CHINK!
GOMP!

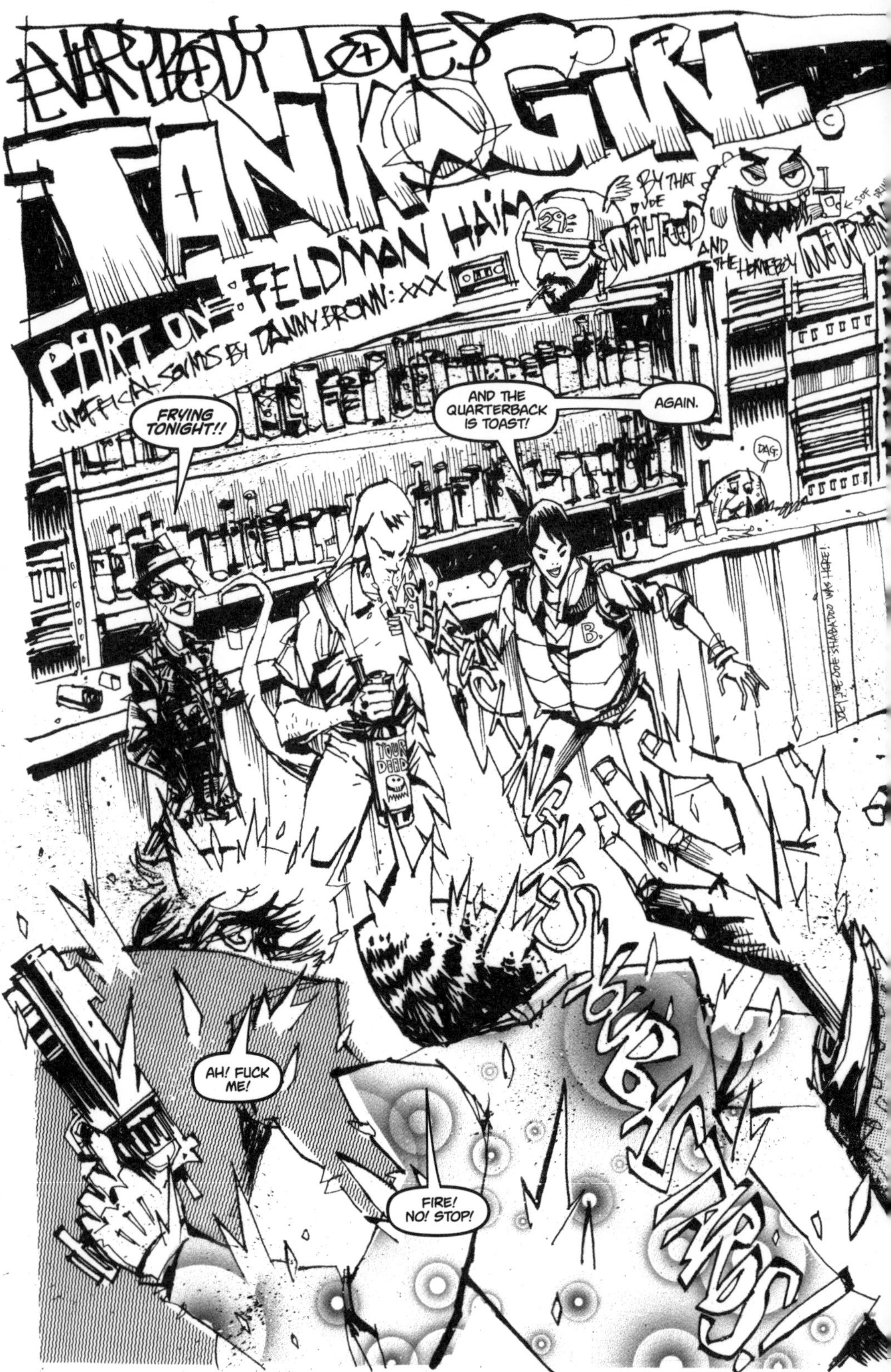

EVERYBODY LOVES TANK GIRL
BY THAT DUDE WAHFOOD AND THE HOMEBOY MARTIN
PART ONE: FELDMAN HAIM
UNOFFICIAL SOUNDS BY DANNY BROWN: XXX
FRYING TONIGHT!!
AND THE QUARTERBACK IS TOAST!
AGAIN.
DAG.
JOEY JOE JOE SHABADOO WAS HERE!
AH! FUCK ME!
FIRE! NO! STOP!

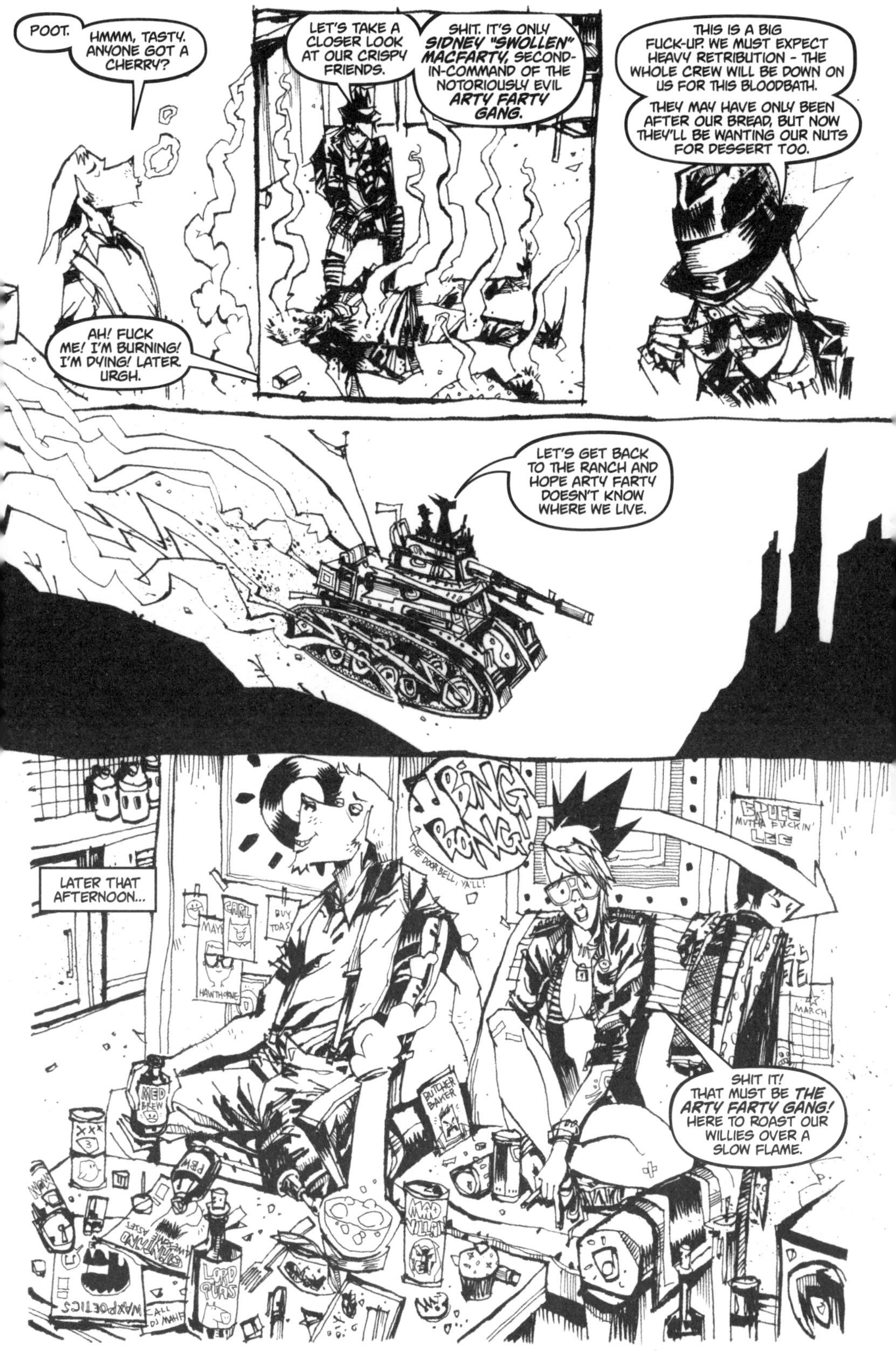

POOT.
HMMM, TASTY. ANYONE GOT A CHERRY?
AH! FUCK ME! I'M BURNING! I'M DYING! LATER. URGH.
LET'S TAKE A CLOSER LOOK AT OUR CRISPY FRIENDS.
SHIT. IT'S ONLY SIDNEY "SWOLLEN" MACFARTY, SECOND-IN-COMMAND OF THE NOTORIOUSLY EVIL ARTY FARTY GANG.
THIS IS A BIG FUCK-UP. WE MUST EXPECT HEAVY RETRIBUTION - THE WHOLE CREW WILL BE DOWN ON US FOR THIS BLOODBATH.
THEY MAY HAVE ONLY BEEN AFTER OUR BREAD, BUT NOW THEY'LL BE WANTING OUR NUTS FOR DESSERT TOO.
LET'S GET BACK TO THE RANCH AND HOPE ARTY FARTY DOESN'T KNOW WHERE WE LIVE.
LATER THAT AFTERNOON...
BING BONG!
THE DOOR BELL, YA'LL!
BRUCE MUTHA FUCKIN' LEE
SHIT IT! THAT MUST BE THE ARTY FARTY GANG! HERE TO ROAST OUR WILLIES OVER A SLOW FLAME.

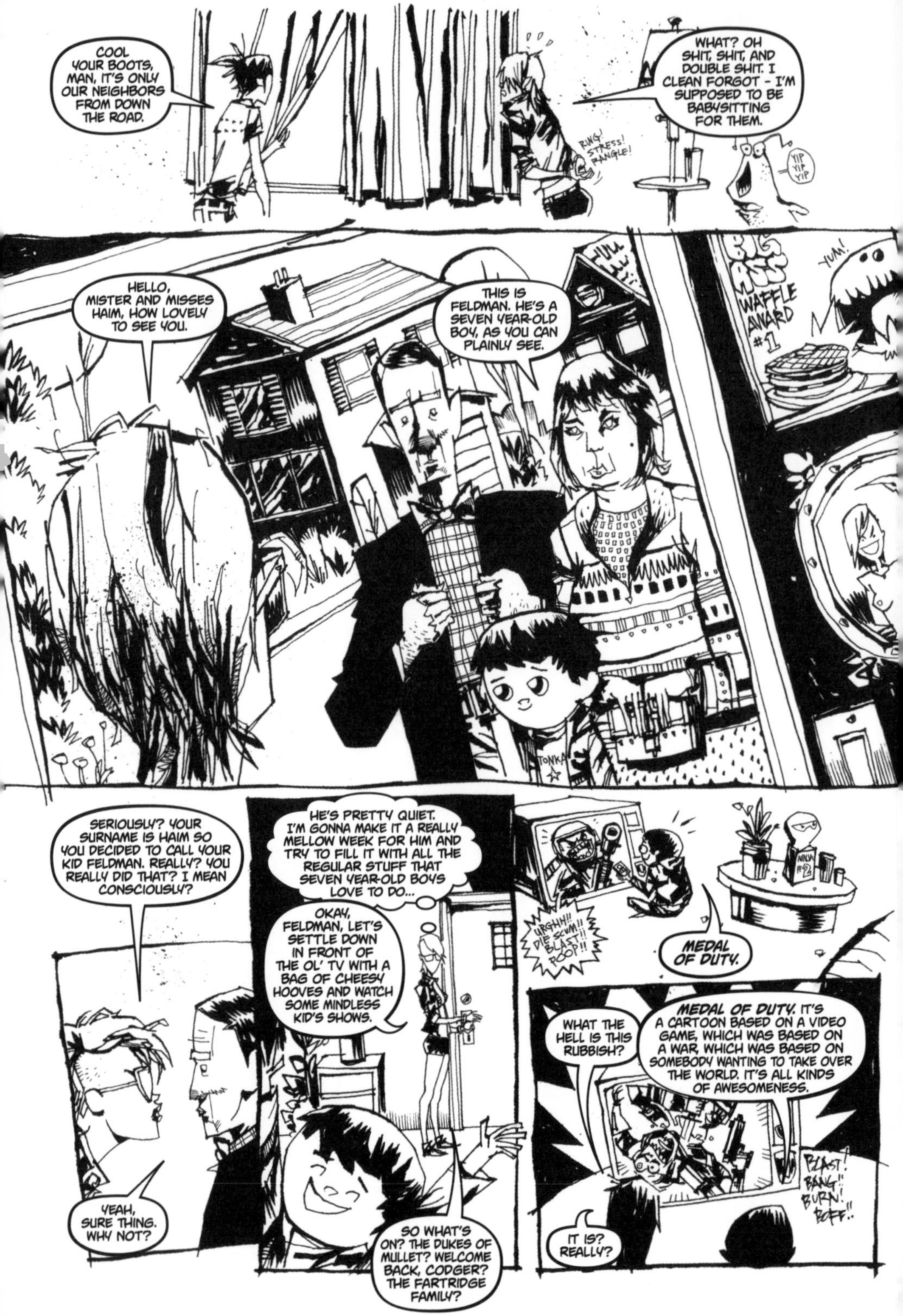
COOL YOUR BOOTS, MAN, IT'S ONLY OUR NEIGHBORS FROM DOWN THE ROAD.
RING! STRESS! RANGLE!
WHAT? OH SHIT, SHIT, AND DOUBLE SHIT. I CLEAN FORGOT - I'M SUPPOSED TO BE BABYSITTING FOR THEM.
YIP YIP YIP
HELLO, MISTER AND MISSES HAIM, HOW LOVELY TO SEE YOU.
THIS IS FELDMAN. HE'S A SEVEN YEAR-OLD BOY, AS YOU CAN PLAINLY SEE.
WAFFLE AWARD #1
YUM!
TONKA
SERIOUSLY? YOUR SURNAME IS HAIM SO YOU DECIDED TO CALL YOUR KID FELDMAN. REALLY? YOU REALLY DID THAT? I MEAN CONSCIOUSLY?
YEAH, SURE THING. WHY NOT?
HE'S PRETTY QUIET. I'M GONNA MAKE IT A REALLY MELLOW WEEK FOR HIM AND TRY TO FILL IT WITH ALL THE REGULAR STUFF THAT SEVEN YEAR-OLD BOYS LOVE TO DO...
OKAY, FELDMAN, LET'S SETTLE DOWN IN FRONT OF THE OL' TV WITH A BAG OF CHEESY HOOVES AND WATCH SOME MINDLESS KID'S SHOWS.
SO WHAT'S ON? THE DUKES OF MULLET? WELCOME BACK, CODGER? THE FARTRIDGE FAMILY?
URGHH!! DIE SCUM!! BLAST!! POOP!!
NINJA #2
MEDAL OF DUTY.
WHAT THE HELL IS THIS RUBBISH?
MEDAL OF DUTY. IT'S A CARTOON BASED ON A VIDEO GAME, WHICH WAS BASED ON A WAR, WHICH WAS BASED ON SOMEBODY WANTING TO TAKE OVER THE WORLD. IT'S ALL KINDS OF AWESOMENESS.
BLAST! BANG!! BURN! BOFF!!
IT IS? REALLY?

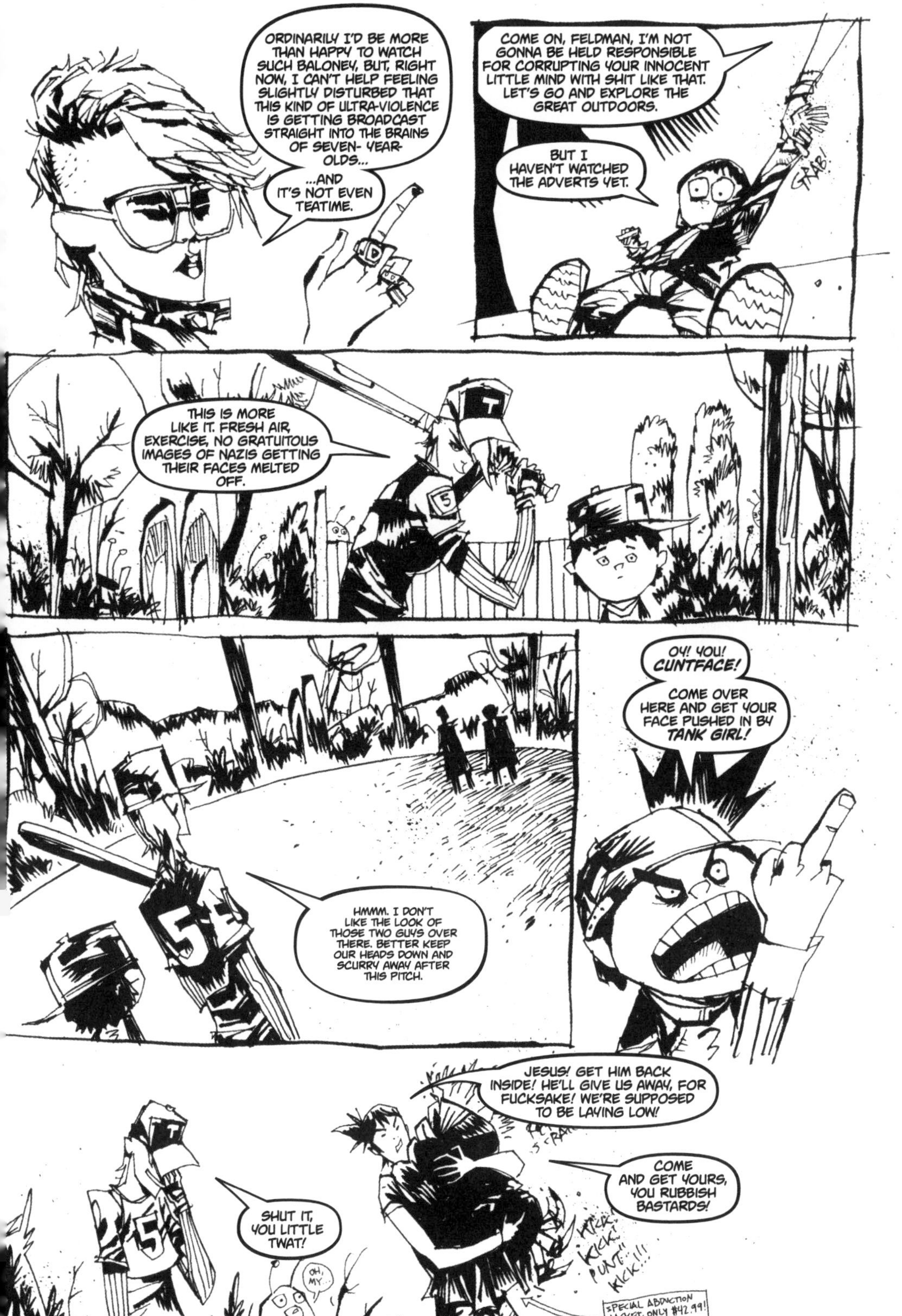
ORDINARILY I'D BE MORE THAN HAPPY TO WATCH SUCH BALONEY, BUT, RIGHT NOW, I CAN'T HELP FEELING SLIGHTLY DISTURBED THAT THIS KIND OF ULTRA-VIOLENCE IS GETTING BROADCAST STRAIGHT INTO THE BRAINS OF SEVEN- YEAR-OLDS...
...AND IT'S NOT EVEN TEATIME.
COME ON, FELDMAN, I'M NOT GONNA BE HELD RESPONSIBLE FOR CORRUPTING YOUR INNOCENT LITTLE MIND WITH SHIT LIKE THAT. LET'S GO AND EXPLORE THE GREAT OUTDOORS.
BUT I HAVEN'T WATCHED THE ADVERTS YET.
GRAB!
THIS IS MORE LIKE IT. FRESH AIR, EXERCISE, NO GRATUITOUS IMAGES OF NAZIS GETTING THEIR FACES MELTED OFF.
HMMM. I DON'T LIKE THE LOOK OF THOSE TWO GUYS OVER THERE. BETTER KEEP OUR HEADS DOWN AND SCURRY AWAY AFTER THIS PITCH.
OY! YOU! CUNTFACE!
COME OVER HERE AND GET YOUR FACE PUSHED IN BY TANK GIRL!
SHUT IT, YOU LITTLE TWAT!
JESUS! GET HIM BACK INSIDE! HE'LL GIVE US AWAY, FOR FUCKSAKE! WE'RE SUPPOSED TO BE LAYING LOW!
COME AND GET YOURS, YOU RUBBISH BASTARDS!
OH, MY...
KICK! KICK! PUNT! KICK!!!
SPECIAL ABDUCTION JACKET. ONLY #42.99! BUY NOW!

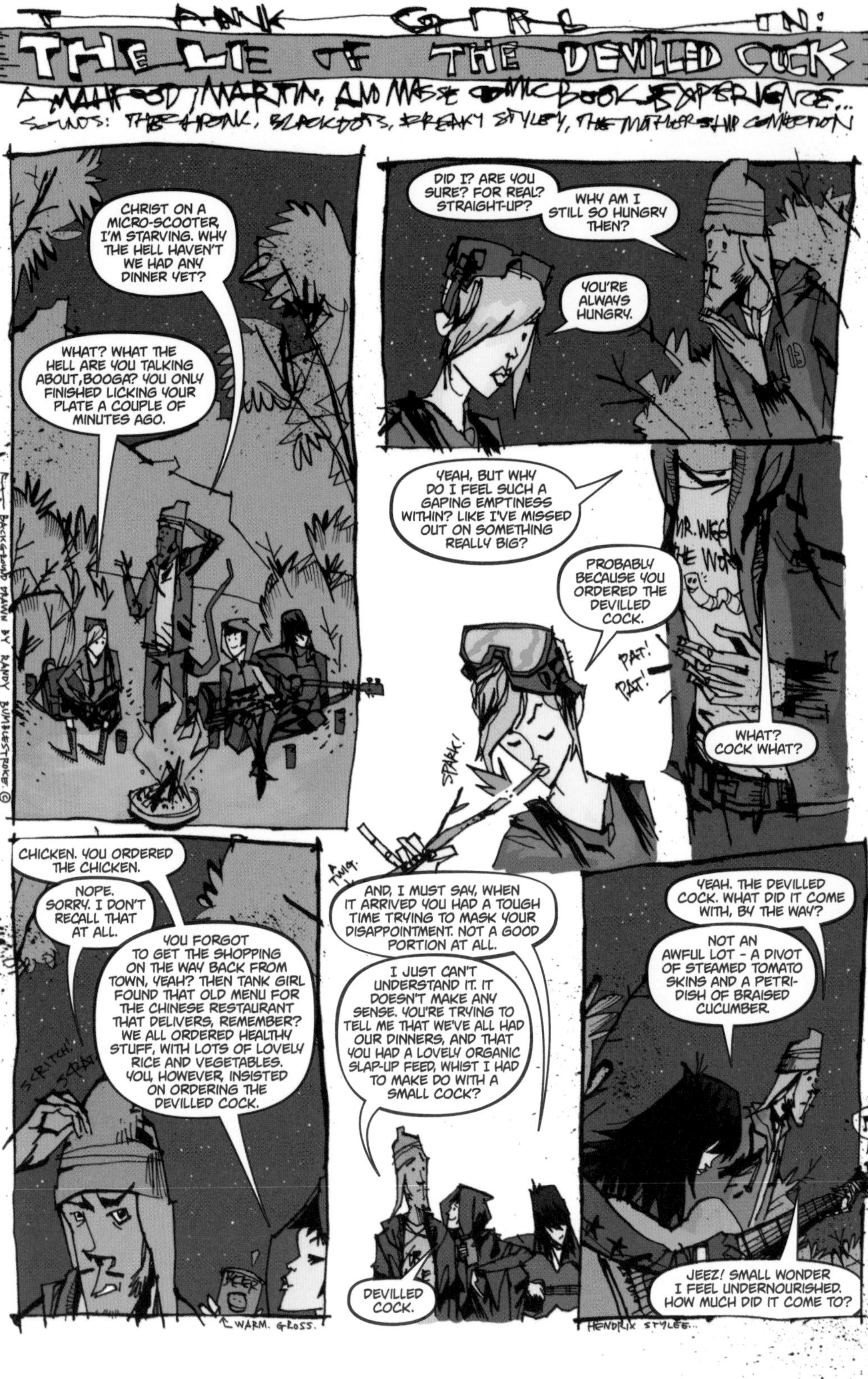
TANK GIRL IN:
THE LIE OF THE DEVILLED COCK
A MAHFOOD, MARTIN, AND MASSE COMIC BOOK EXPERIENCE...
CHRIST ON A MICRO-SCOOTER, I'M STARVING. WHY THE HELL HAVEN'T WE HAD ANY DINNER YET?
WHAT? WHAT THE HELL ARE YOU TALKING ABOUT, BOOGA? YOU ONLY FINISHED LICKING YOUR PLATE A COUPLE OF MINUTES AGO.
BACKGROUND DRAWN BY RANDY BUMBLESTROKE ©
DID I? ARE YOU SURE? FOR REAL? STRAIGHT-UP?
WHY AM I STILL SO HUNGRY THEN?
YOU'RE ALWAYS HUNGRY.
YEAH, BUT WHY DO I FEEL SUCH A GAPING EMPTINESS WITHIN? LIKE I'VE MISSED OUT ON SOMETHING REALLY BIG?
PROBABLY BECAUSE YOU ORDERED THE DEVILLED COCK.
PAT! PAT!
WHAT? COCK WHAT?
SPARK!
A TWIG.
CHICKEN. YOU ORDERED THE CHICKEN.
NOPE. SORRY. I DON'T RECALL THAT AT ALL.
YOU FORGOT TO GET THE SHOPPING ON THE WAY BACK FROM TOWN, YEAH? THEN TANK GIRL FOUND THAT OLD MENU FOR THE CHINESE RESTAURANT THAT DELIVERS, REMEMBER? WE ALL ORDERED HEALTHY STUFF, WITH LOTS OF LOVELY RICE AND VEGETABLES. YOU, HOWEVER, INSISTED ON ORDERING THE DEVILLED COCK.
SCRITCH!
BEER
WARM. GROSS.
AND, I MUST SAY, WHEN IT ARRIVED YOU HAD A TOUGH TIME TRYING TO MASK YOUR DISAPPOINTMENT. NOT A GOOD PORTION AT ALL.
I JUST CAN'T UNDERSTAND IT. IT DOESN'T MAKE ANY SENSE. YOU'RE TRYING TO TELL ME THAT WE'VE ALL HAD OUR DINNERS, AND THAT YOU HAD A LOVELY ORGANIC SLAP-UP FEED, WHIST I HAD TO MAKE DO WITH A SMALL COCK?
DEVILLED COCK.
YEAH. THE DEVILLED COCK. WHAT DID IT COME WITH, BY THE WAY?
NOT AN AWFUL LOT - A DIVOT OF STEAMED TOMATO SKINS AND A PETRI-DISH OF BRAISED CUCUMBER.
JEEZ! SMALL WONDER I FEEL UNDERNOURISHED. HOW MUCH DID IT COME TO?
HENDRIX STYLEE...

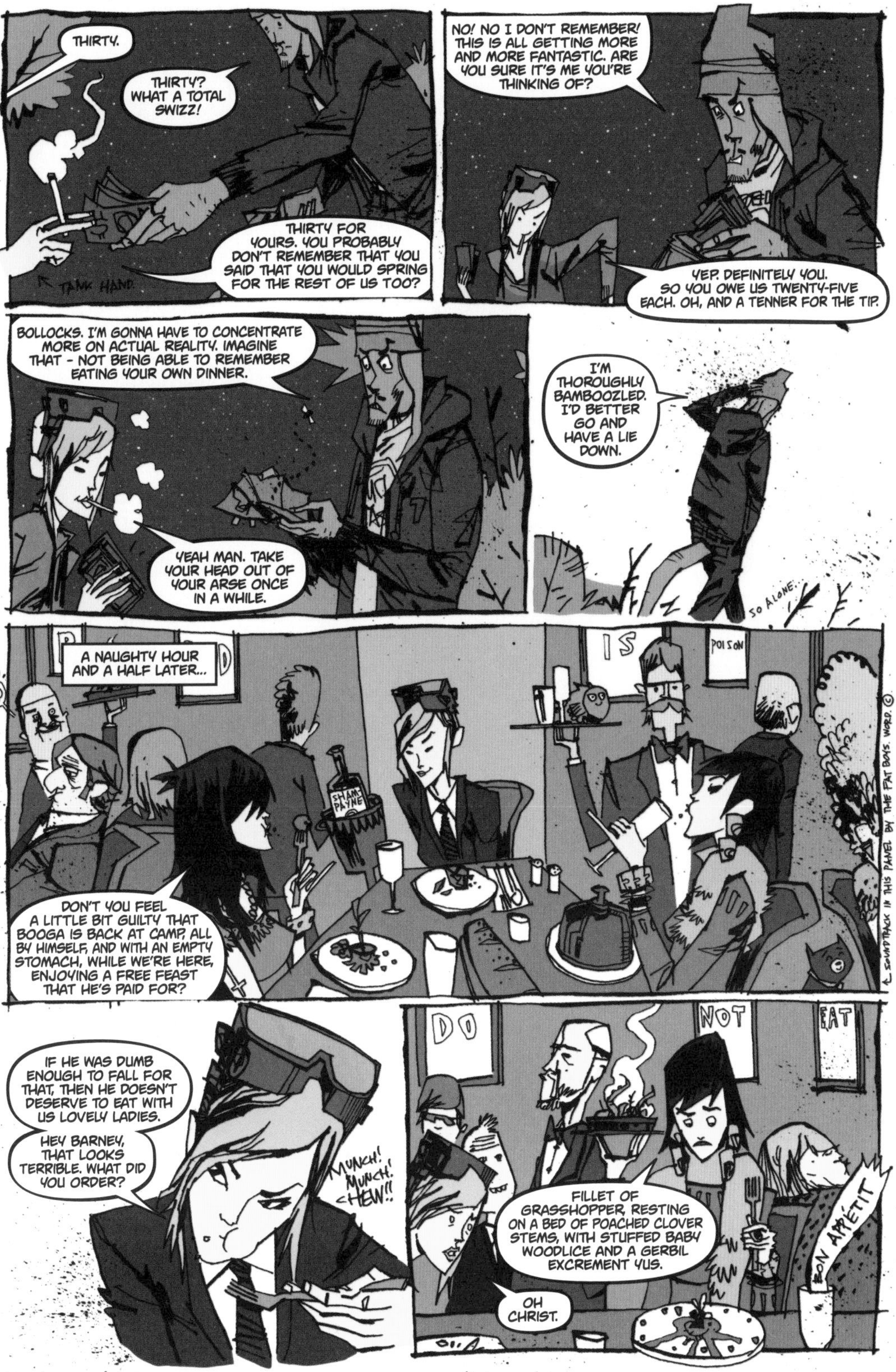
THIRTY.
THIRTY? WHAT A TOTAL SWIZZ!
THIRTY FOR YOURS. YOU PROBABLY DON'T REMEMBER THAT YOU SAID THAT YOU WOULD SPRING FOR THE REST OF US TOO?
TANK HAND
NO! NO I DON'T REMEMBER! THIS IS ALL GETTING MORE AND MORE FANTASTIC. ARE YOU SURE IT'S ME YOU'RE THINKING OF?
YEP. DEFINITELY YOU. SO YOU OWE US TWENTY-FIVE EACH. OH, AND A TENNER FOR THE TIP.
BOLLOCKS. I'M GONNA HAVE TO CONCENTRATE MORE ON ACTUAL REALITY. IMAGINE THAT - NOT BEING ABLE TO REMEMBER EATING YOUR OWN DINNER.
YEAH MAN. TAKE YOUR HEAD OUT OF YOUR ARSE ONCE IN A WHILE.
I'M THOROUGHLY BAMBOOZLED. I'D BETTER GO AND HAVE A LIE DOWN.
SO ALONE...
A NAUGHTY HOUR AND A HALF LATER...
IS
POISON
SHAM-PAYNE
DON'T YOU FEEL A LITTLE BIT GUILTY THAT BOOGA IS BACK AT CAMP, ALL BY HIMSELF, AND WITH AN EMPTY STOMACH, WHILE WE'RE HERE, ENJOYING A FREE FEAST THAT HE'S PAID FOR?
SOUNDTRACK IN THIS PANEL BY THE FAT BOYS. WORD. ©
IF HE WAS DUMB ENOUGH TO FALL FOR THAT, THEN HE DOESN'T DESERVE TO EAT WITH US LOVELY LADIES.
HEY BARNEY, THAT LOOKS TERRIBLE. WHAT DID YOU ORDER?
MUNCH! MUNCH! CHEW!!
DO
NOT
EAT
FILLET OF GRASSHOPPER, RESTING ON A BED OF POACHED CLOVER STEMS, WITH STUFFED BABY WOODLICE AND A GERBIL EXCREMENT JUS.
BON APPÉTIT
OH CHRIST.

COUNTRY BOLLOCKS

YOU TOOK ME TO THE CONCERT
YOU TOOK ME TO THE BAR
YOU PLAYED IT ON THE JUKEBOX
YOU PLAYED IT IN YOUR CAR

I SAW YOU WITH THAT OTHER GIRL
YOU'D WRITTEN HER THAT SONG
AND ALL THAT YOU HAD LEFT FOR ME
WAS COUNTRY MUSIC ALL DAY LONG

I CAN'T LISTEN TO WILLIE OR DOLLY
EMMYLOU OR PEGGY SUE
I USED TO THINK ALL COUNTRY WAS BOLLOCKS
BUT NOW I KNOW IT'S JUST YOU

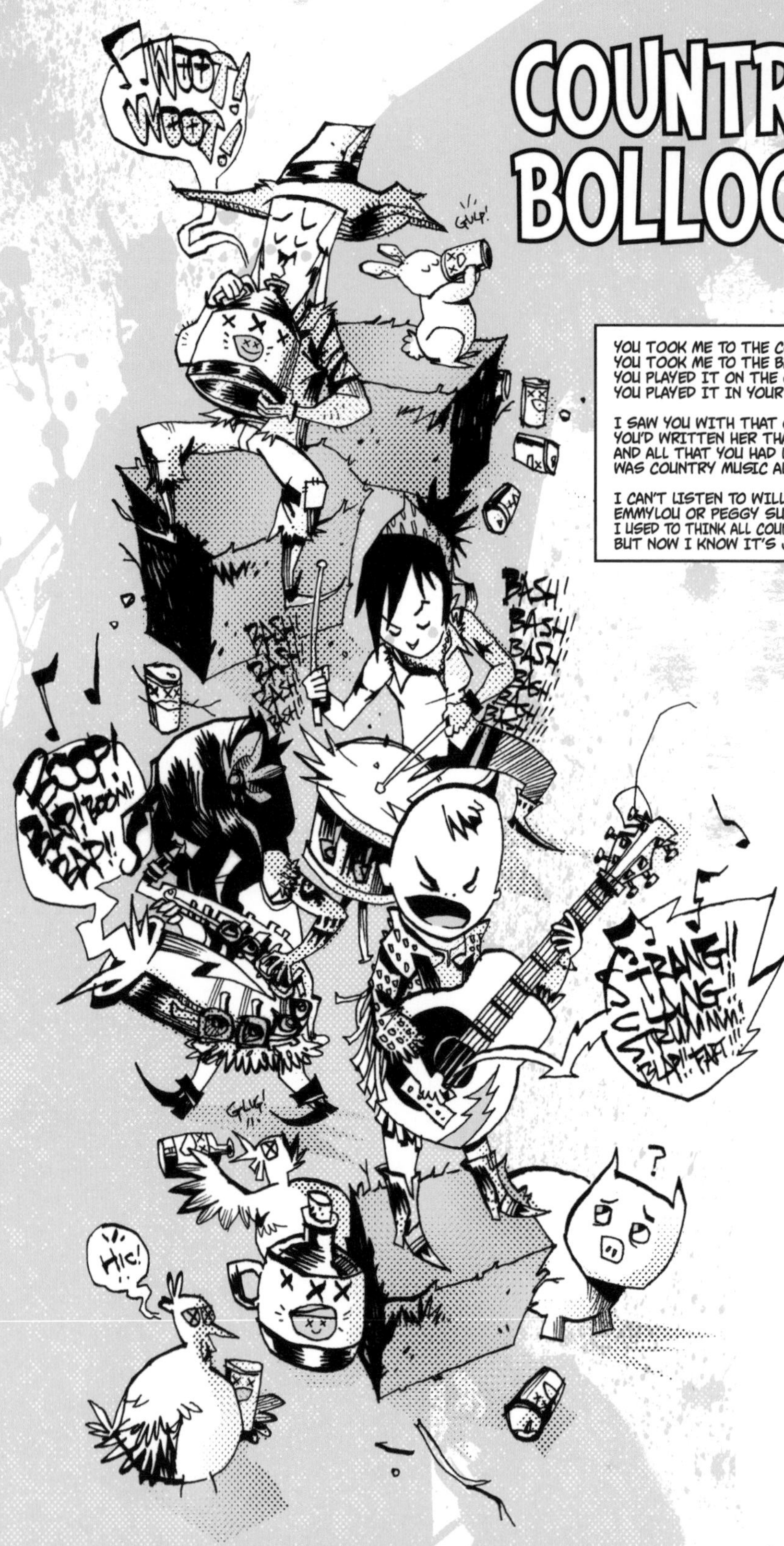
WOOT! WOOT!
GULP!
BASH BASH BASH
GULP!
HIC!
?

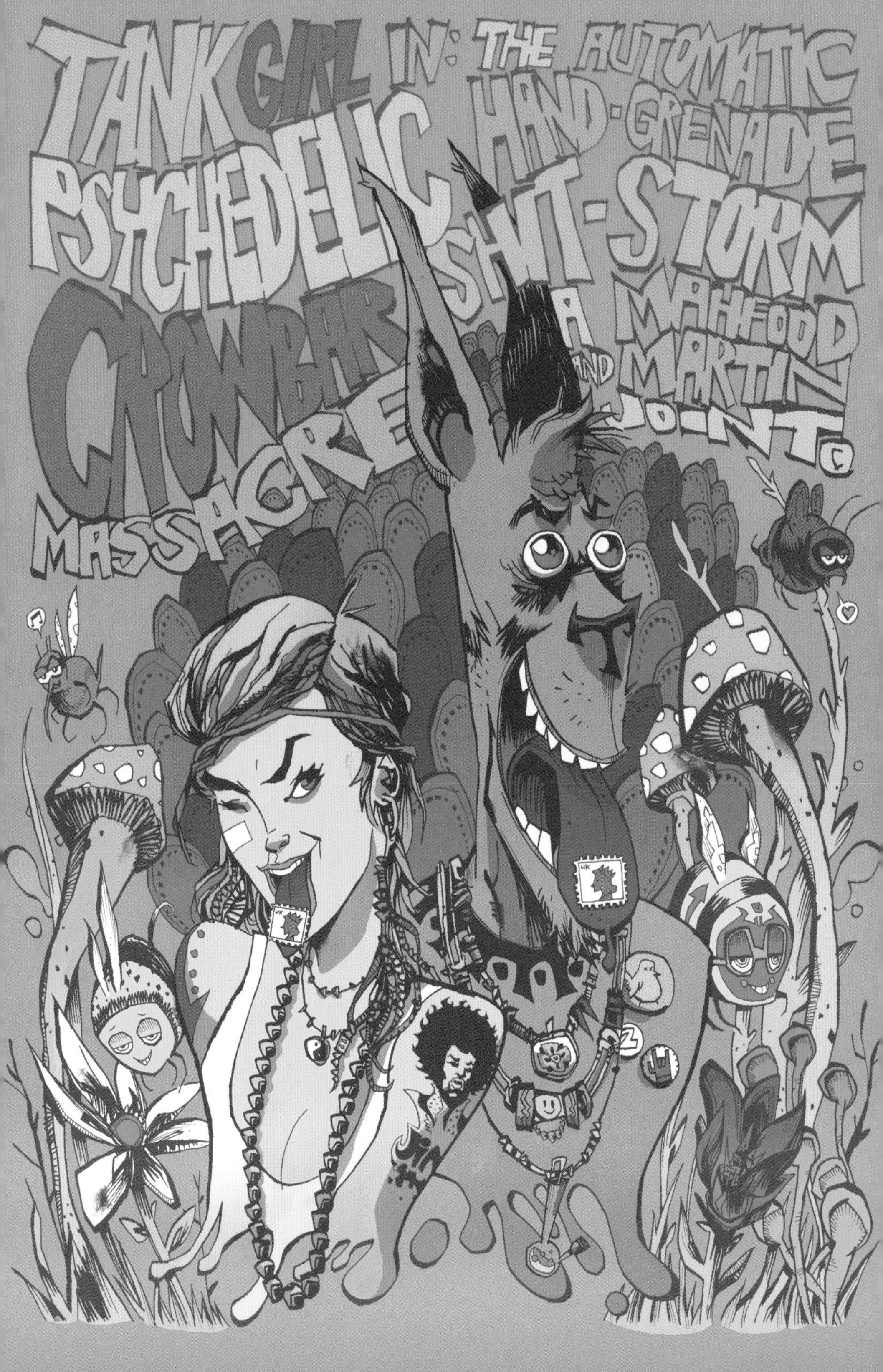
TANK GIRL IN: THE AUTOMATIC PSYCHEDELIC HAND-GRENADE SHIT-STORM CROWBAR MASSACRE
A MAHFOOD AND MARTIN JOINT ©

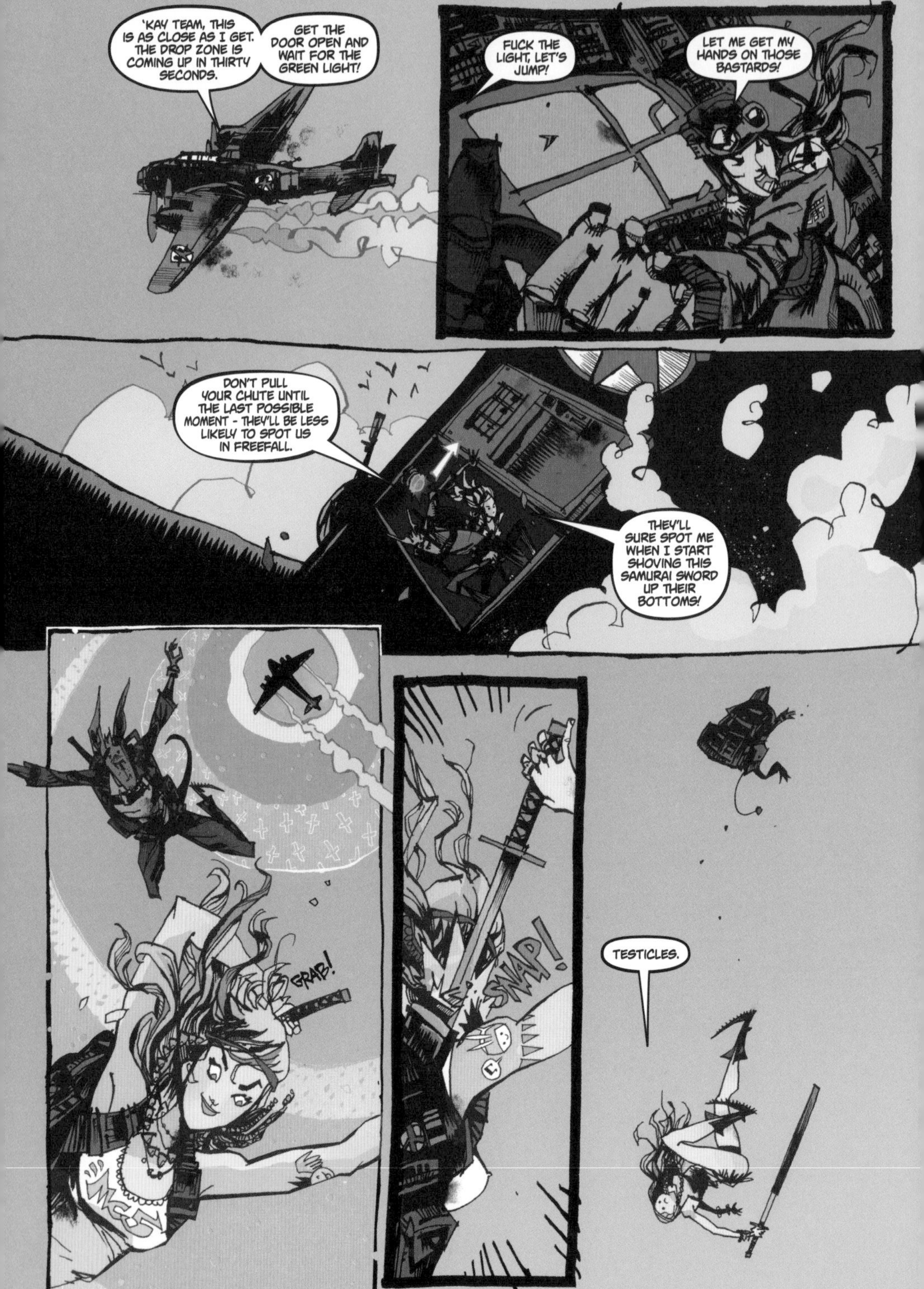
'KAY TEAM, THIS IS AS CLOSE AS I GET. THE DROP ZONE IS COMING UP IN THIRTY SECONDS.
GET THE DOOR OPEN AND WAIT FOR THE GREEN LIGHT!
FUCK THE LIGHT, LET'S JUMP!
LET ME GET MY HANDS ON THOSE BASTARDS!
DON'T PULL YOUR CHUTE UNTIL THE LAST POSSIBLE MOMENT - THEY'LL BE LESS LIKELY TO SPOT US IN FREEFALL.
THEY'LL SURE SPOT ME WHEN I START SHOVING THIS SAMURAI SWORD UP THEIR BOTTOMS!
GRAB!
SNAP!
TESTICLES.

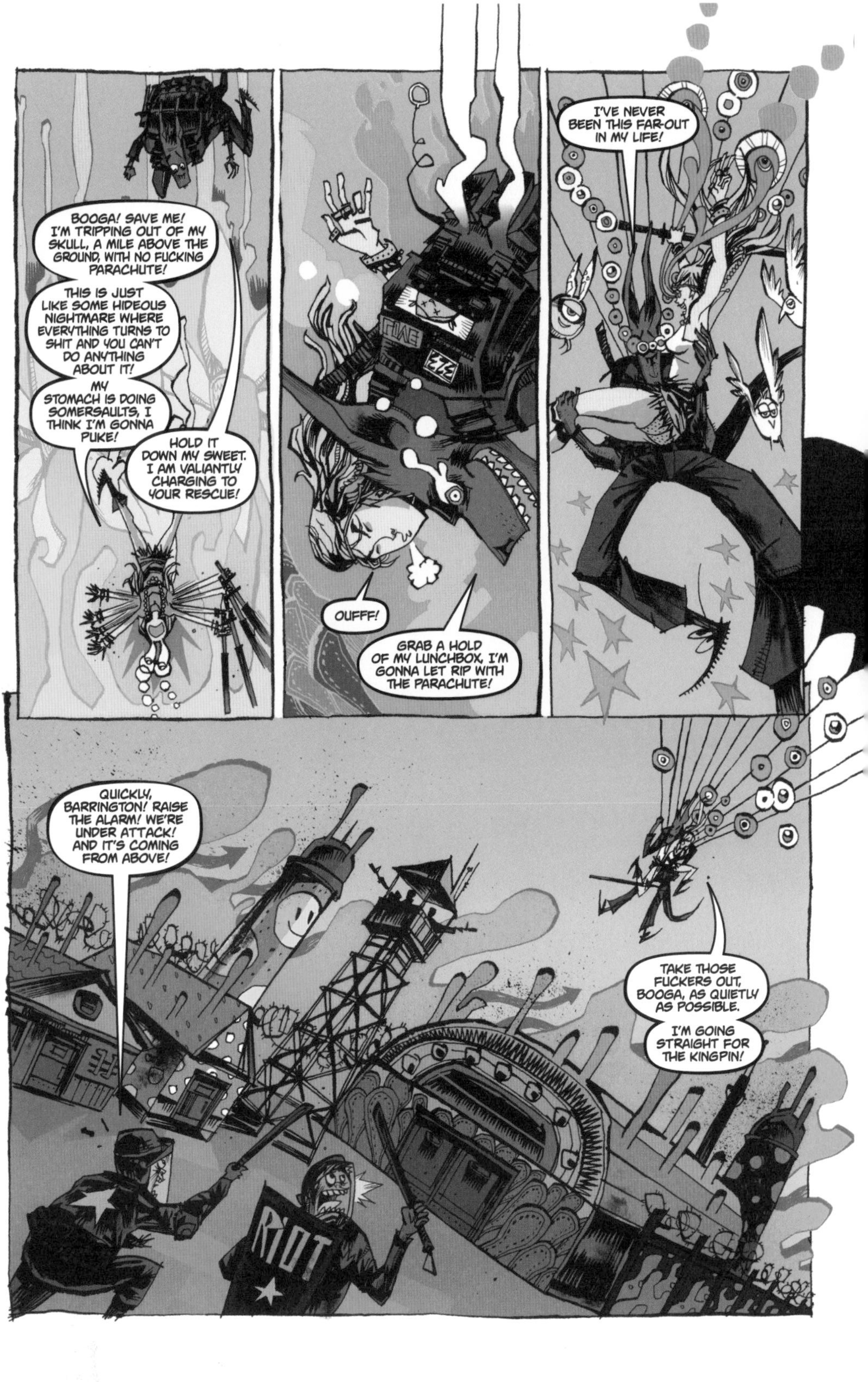
BOOGA! SAVE ME! I'M TRIPPING OUT OF MY SKULL, A MILE ABOVE THE GROUND, WITH NO FUCKING PARACHUTE!
THIS IS JUST LIKE SOME HIDEOUS NIGHTMARE WHERE EVERYTHING TURNS TO SHIT AND YOU CAN'T DO ANYTHING ABOUT IT!
MY STOMACH IS DOING SOMERSAULTS, I THINK I'M GONNA PUKE!
HOLD IT DOWN MY SWEET. I AM VALIANTLY CHARGING TO YOUR RESCUE!
OUFFF!
GRAB A HOLD OF MY LUNCHBOX, I'M GONNA LET RIP WITH THE PARACHUTE!
I'VE NEVER BEEN THIS FAR-OUT IN MY LIFE!
QUICKLY, BARRINGTON! RAISE THE ALARM! WE'RE UNDER ATTACK! AND IT'S COMING FROM ABOVE!
TAKE THOSE FUCKERS OUT, BOOGA, AS QUIETLY AS POSSIBLE.
I'M GOING STRAIGHT FOR THE KINGPIN!
RIOT

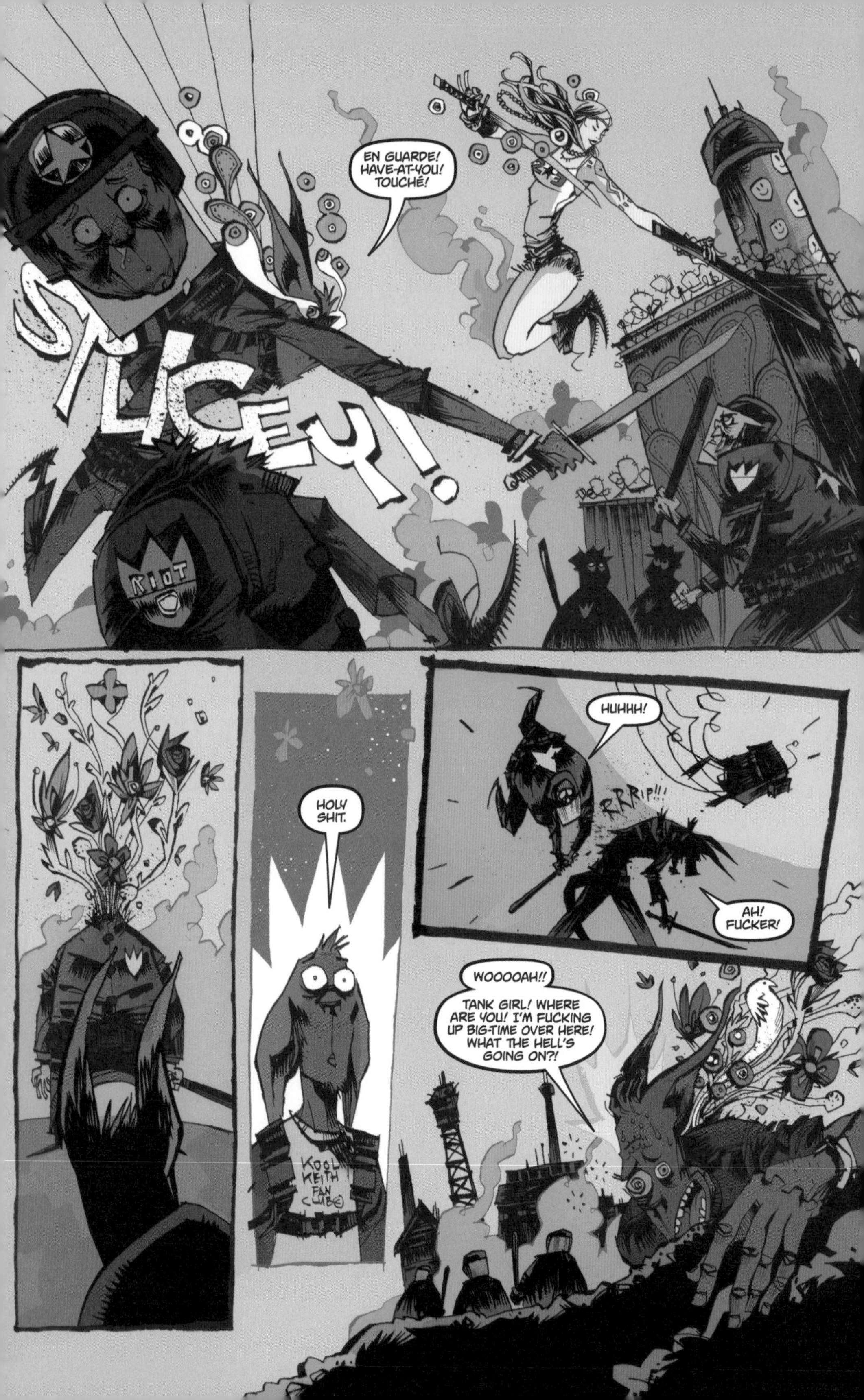
EN GUARDE! HAVE-AT-YOU! TOUCHÉ!
SLICEY!
RIOT
HOLY SHIT.
KOOL KEITH FAN CLUB
HUHHH!
RRRIP!!!
AH! FUCKER!
WOOOOAH!!
TANK GIRL! WHERE ARE YOU! I'M FUCKING UP BIG-TIME OVER HERE! WHAT THE HELL'S GOING ON?!

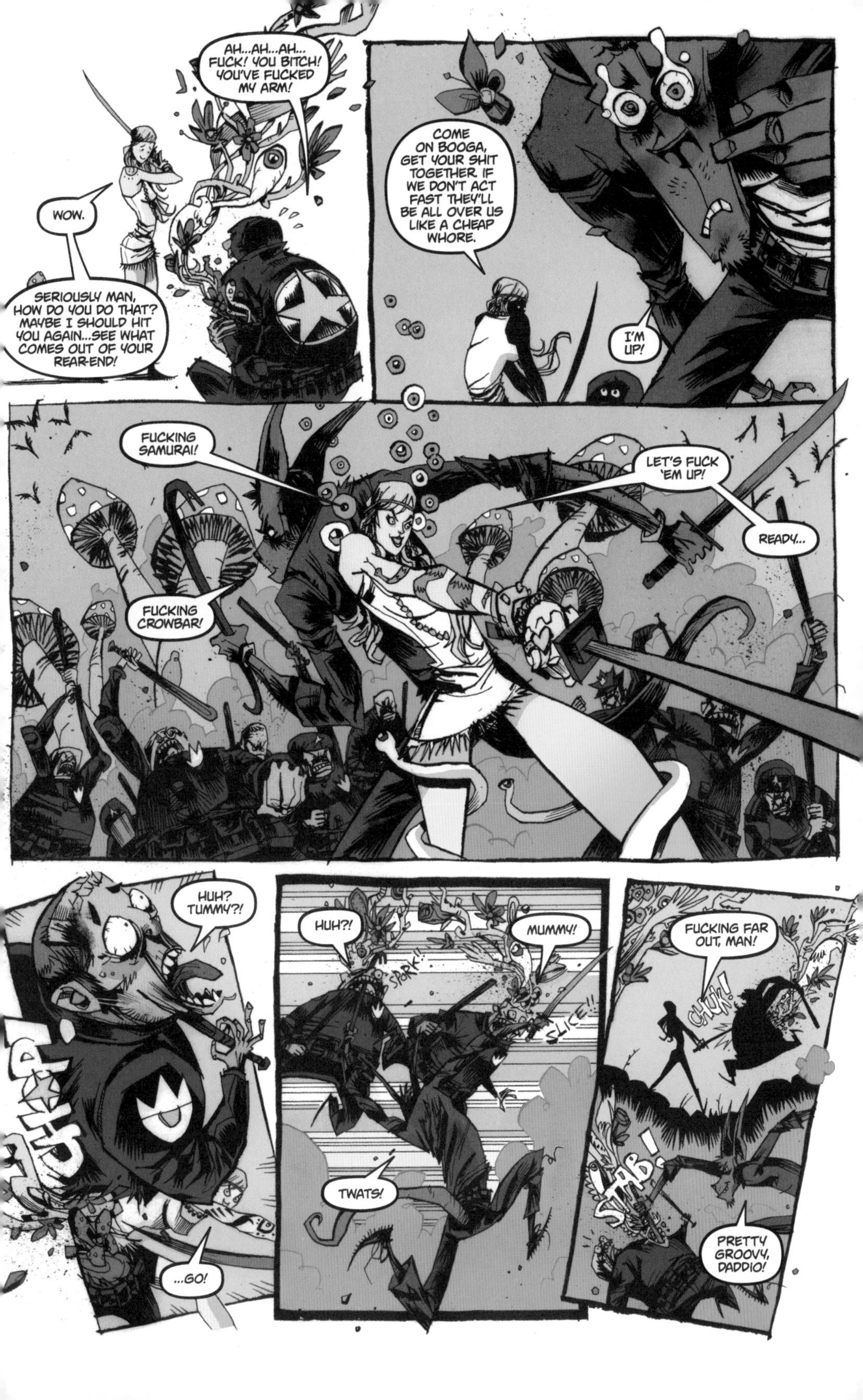
AH...AH...AH... FUCK! YOU BITCH! YOU'VE FUCKED MY ARM!
WOW.
SERIOUSLY MAN, HOW DO YOU DO THAT? MAYBE I SHOULD HIT YOU AGAIN...SEE WHAT COMES OUT OF YOUR REAR-END!
COME ON BOOGA, GET YOUR SHIT TOGETHER. IF WE DON'T ACT FAST THEY'LL BE ALL OVER US LIKE A CHEAP WHORE.
I'M UP!
FUCKING SAMURAI!
LET'S FUCK 'EM UP!
READY...
FUCKING CROWBAR!
HUH? TUMMY?!
...GO!
HUH?!
SPORK!
MUMMY!
SLICE!!
TWATS!
FUCKING FAR OUT, MAN!
CHUK!
STAB!
PRETTY GROOVY, DADDIO!

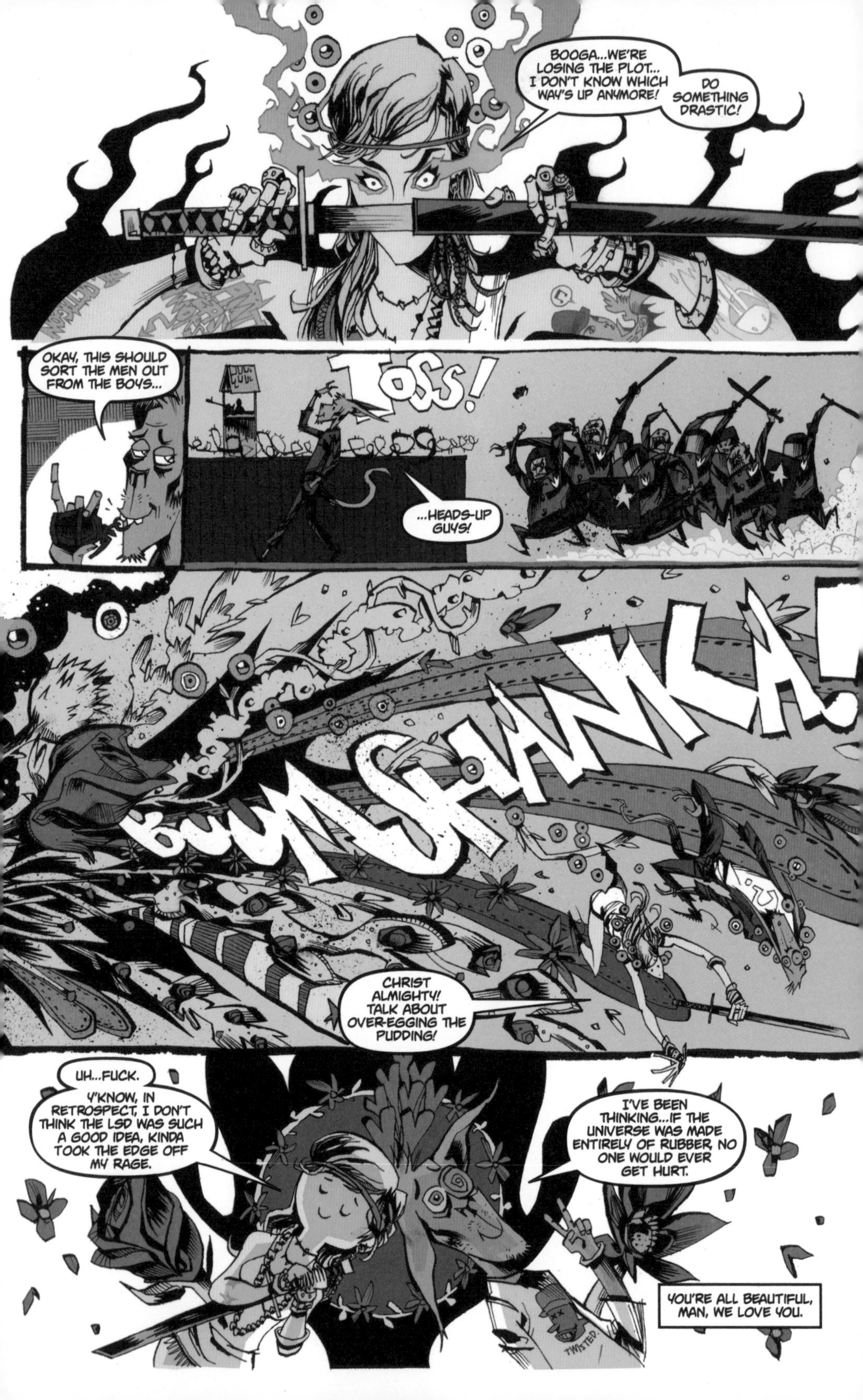
BOOGA...WE'RE LOSING THE PLOT... I DON'T KNOW WHICH WAY'S UP ANYMORE!
DO SOMETHING DRASTIC!
OKAY, THIS SHOULD SORT THE MEN OUT FROM THE BOYS...
TOSS!
...HEADS-UP GUYS!
BOOM SHAWKLA!
CHRIST ALMIGHTY! TALK ABOUT OVER-EGGING THE PUDDING!
UH...FUCK.
Y'KNOW, IN RETROSPECT, I DON'T THINK THE LSD WAS SUCH A GOOD IDEA, KINDA TOOK THE EDGE OFF MY RAGE.
I'VE BEEN THINKING...IF THE UNIVERSE WAS MADE ENTIRELY OF RUBBER, NO ONE WOULD EVER GET HURT.
YOU'RE ALL BEAUTIFUL, MAN, WE LOVE YOU.

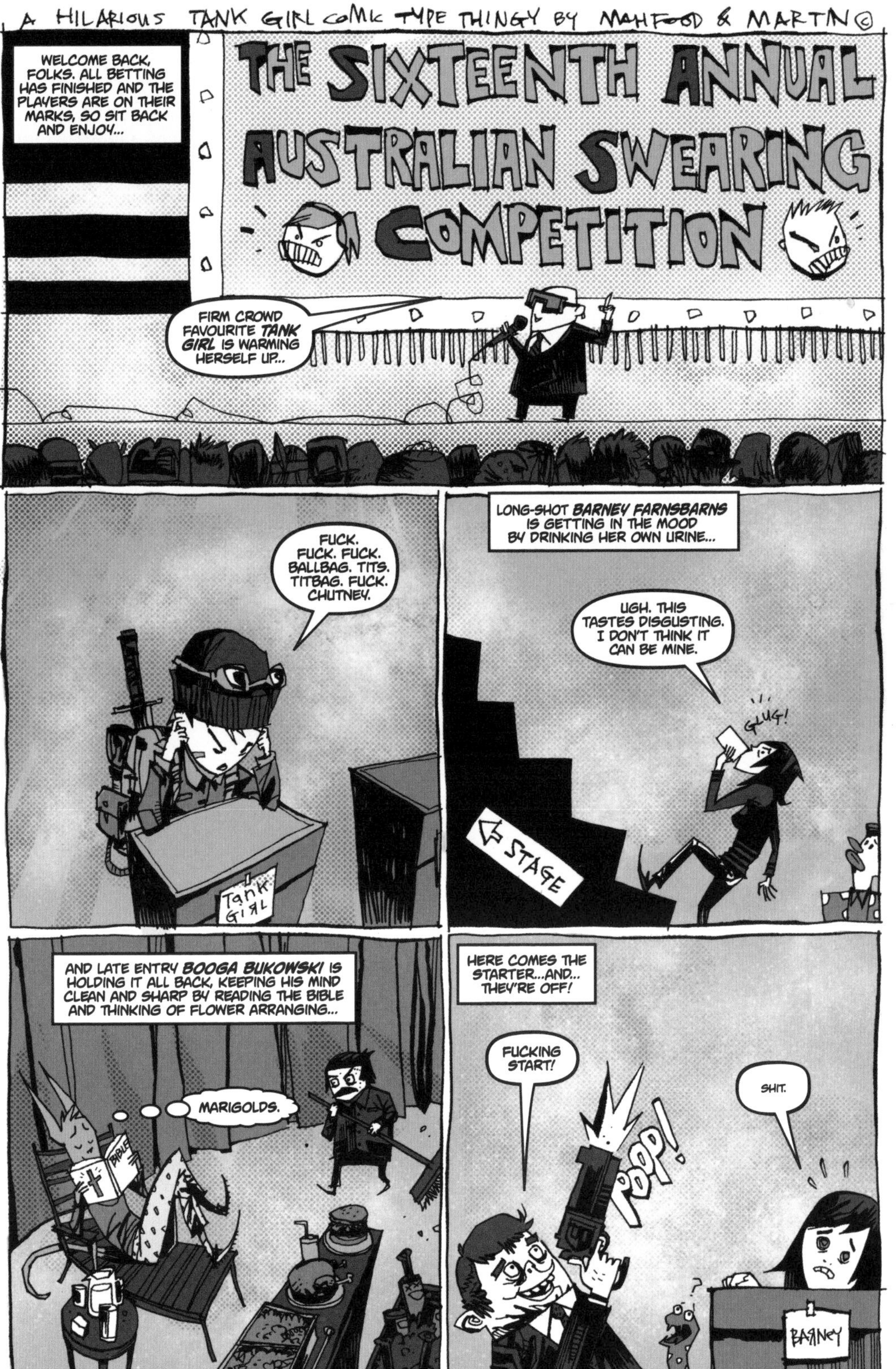

A HILARIOUS TANK GIRL COMIC TYPE THINGY BY MAHFOOD & MARTIN ©
WELCOME BACK, FOLKS. ALL BETTING HAS FINISHED AND THE PLAYERS ARE ON THEIR MARKS, SO SIT BACK AND ENJOY...
THE SIXTEENTH ANNUAL AUSTRALIAN SWEARING COMPETITION
FIRM CROWD FAVOURITE TANK GIRL IS WARMING HERSELF UP...
FUCK. FUCK. FUCK. BALLBAG. TITS. TITBAG. FUCK. CHUTNEY.
TANK GIRL
LONG-SHOT BARNEY FARNSBARNS IS GETTING IN THE MOOD BY DRINKING HER OWN URINE...
UGH. THIS TASTES DISGUSTING. I DON'T THINK IT CAN BE MINE.
GLUG!
STAGE
AND LATE ENTRY BOOGA BUKOWSKI IS HOLDING IT ALL BACK, KEEPING HIS MIND CLEAN AND SHARP BY READING THE BIBLE AND THINKING OF FLOWER ARRANGING...
MARIGOLDS.
BIBLE
HERE COMES THE STARTER...AND... THEY'RE OFF!
FUCKING START!
SHIT.
POOP!
BARNEY

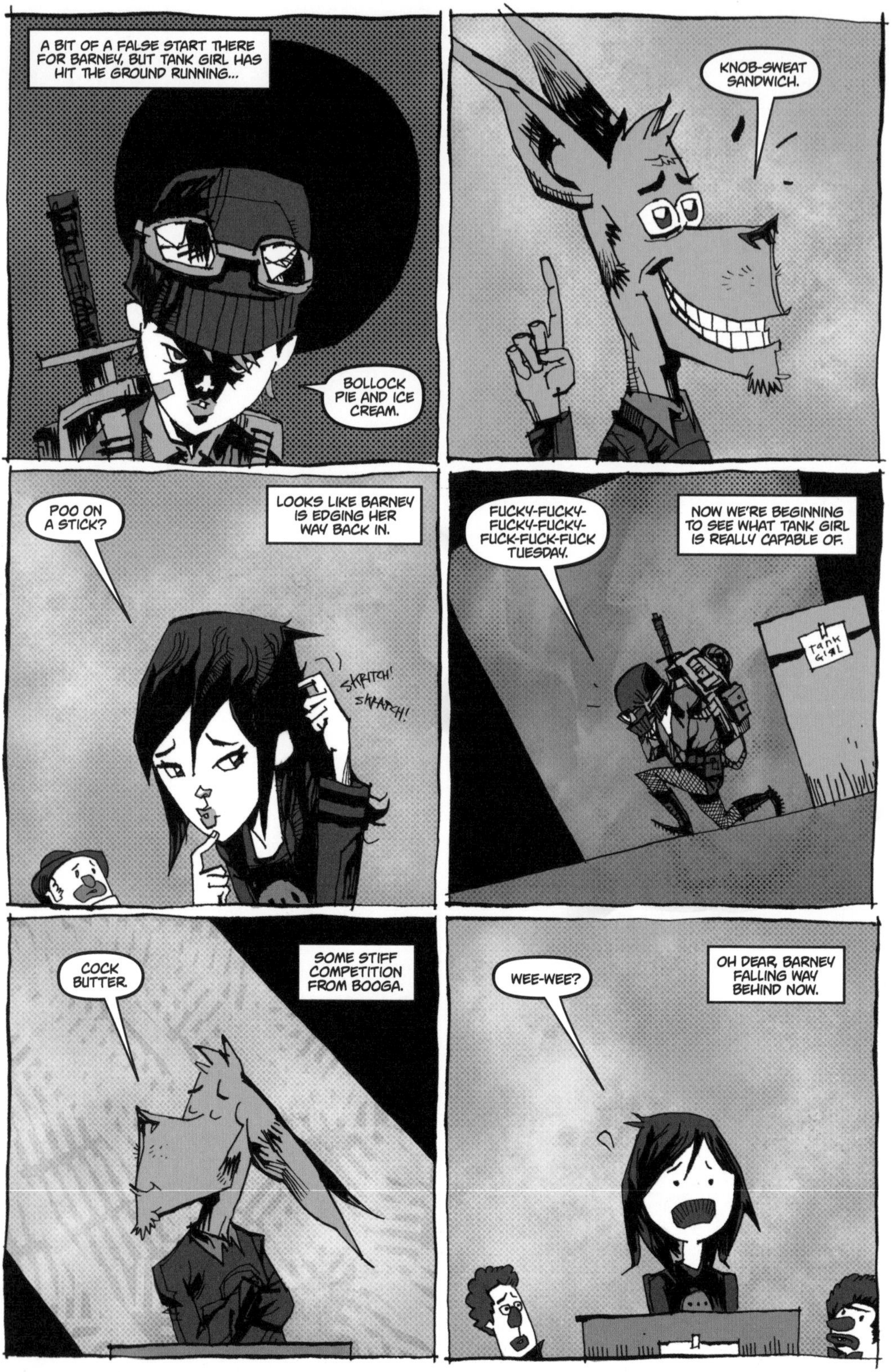
A BIT OF A FALSE START THERE FOR BARNEY, BUT TANK GIRL HAS HIT THE GROUND RUNNING...
BOLLOCK PIE AND ICE CREAM.
KNOB-SWEAT SANDWICH.
POO ON A STICK?
LOOKS LIKE BARNEY IS EDGING HER WAY BACK IN.
SKRITCH!
SHAARCH!
FUCKY-FUCKY-FUCKY-FUCKY-FUCK-FUCK-FUCK TUESDAY.
NOW WE'RE BEGINNING TO SEE WHAT TANK GIRL IS REALLY CAPABLE OF.
TANK GIRL
COCK BUTTER.
SOME STIFF COMPETITION FROM BOOGA.
WEE-WEE?
OH DEAR, BARNEY FALLING WAY BEHIND NOW.

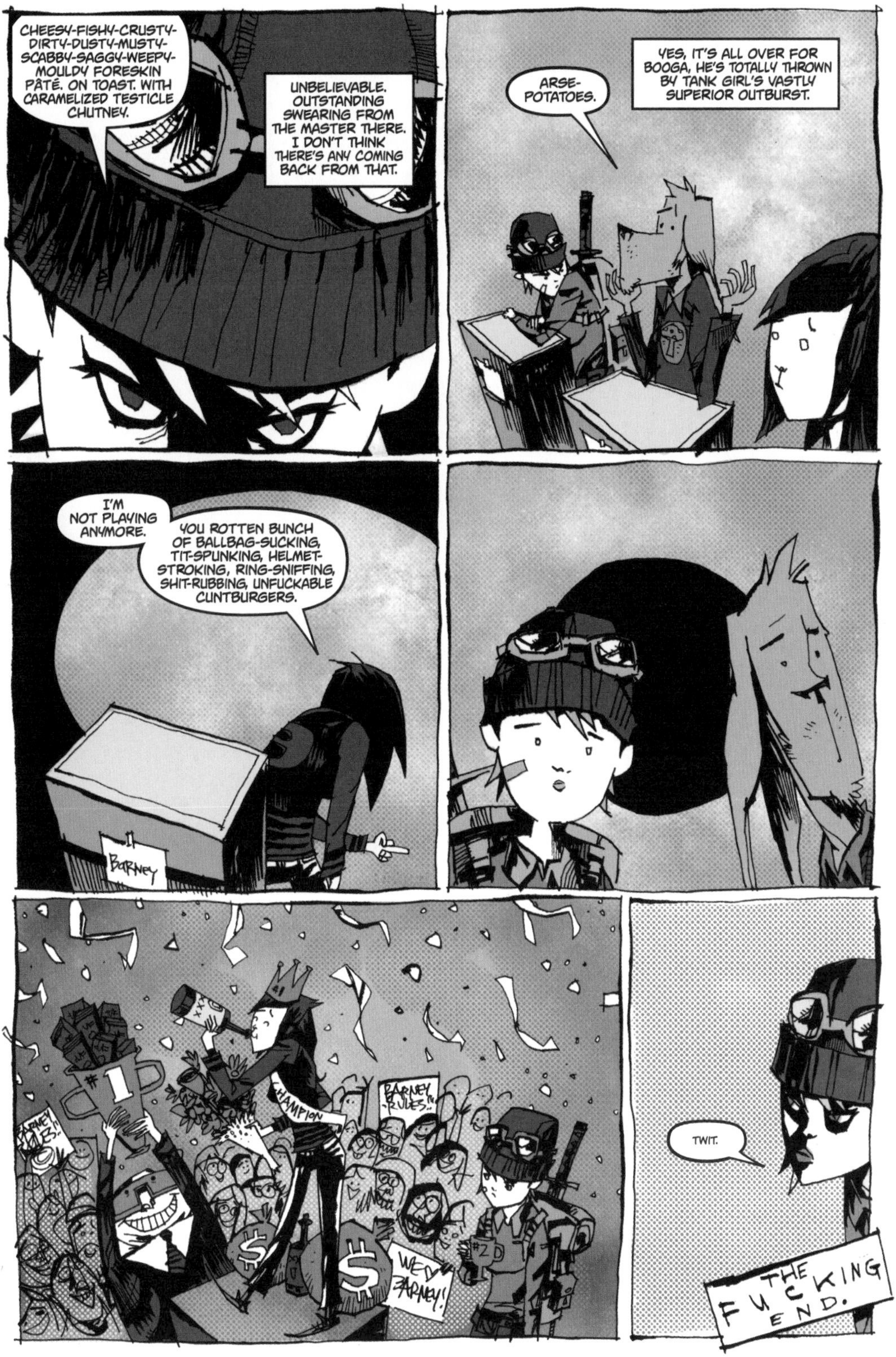
CHEESY-FISHY-CRUSTY-DIRTY-DUSTY-MUSTY-SCABBY-SAGGY-WEEPY-MOULDY FORESKIN PÂTÉ. ON TOAST. WITH CARAMELIZED TESTICLE CHUTNEY.
UNBELIEVABLE. OUTSTANDING SWEARING FROM THE MASTER THERE. I DON'T THINK THERE'S ANY COMING BACK FROM THAT.
ARSE-POTATOES.
YES, IT'S ALL OVER FOR BOOGA, HE'S TOTALLY THROWN BY TANK GIRL'S VASTLY SUPERIOR OUTBURST.
I'M NOT PLAYING ANYMORE.
YOU ROTTEN BUNCH OF BALLBAG-SUCKING, TIT-SPUNKING, HELMET-STROKING, RING-SNIFFING, SHIT-RUBBING, UNFUCKABLE CUNTBURGERS.
BARNEY
#1
CHAMPION
BARNEY RULES!!
BARNEY RULES!!
WE ♥ BARNEY!
#2
TWIT.
THE FUCKING END.

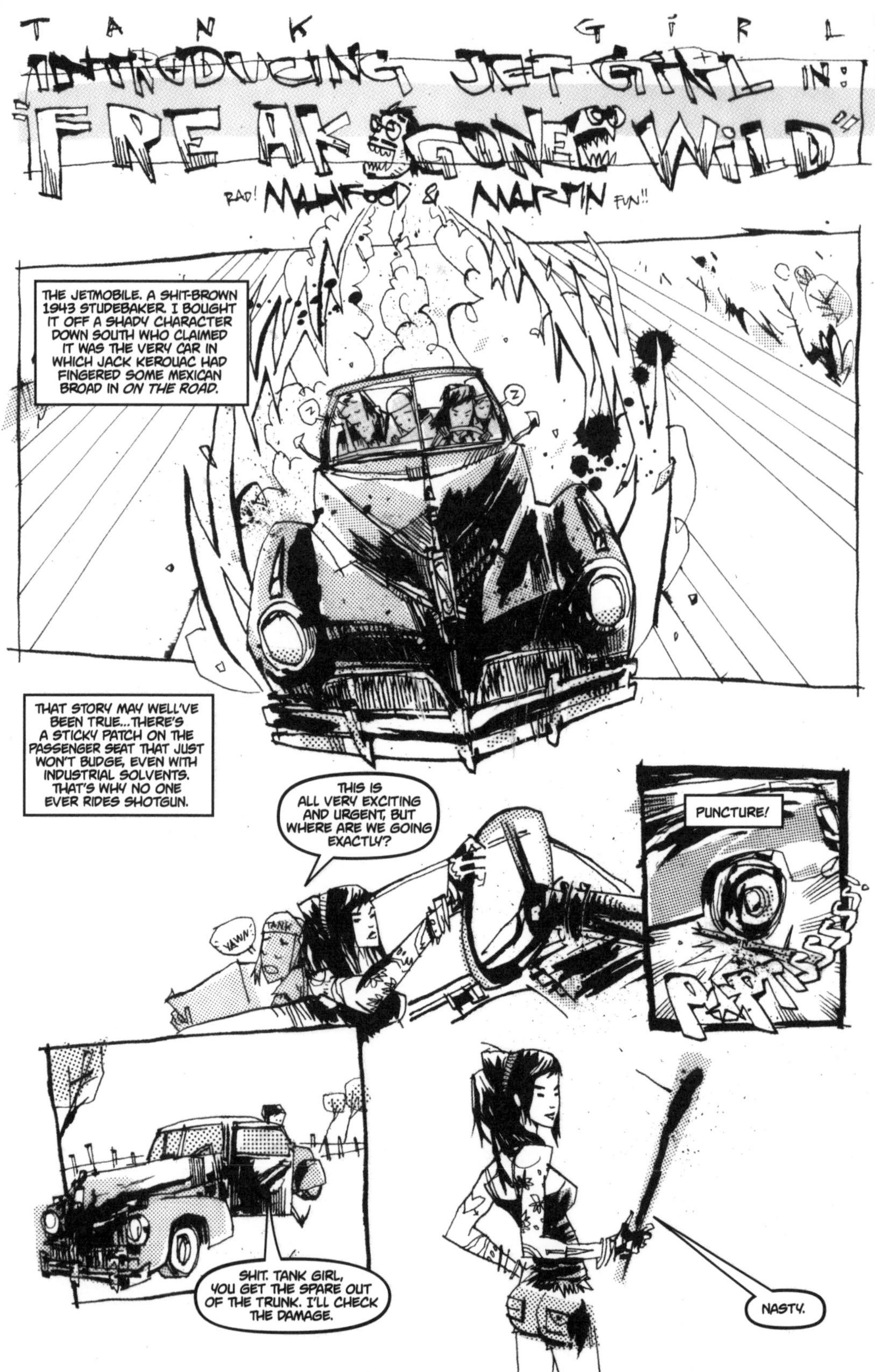
TANK GIRL
INTRODUCING JET GIRL IN:
FREAK GONE WILD
RAD! MAHFOOD & MARTIN FUN!!
THE JETMOBILE. A SHIT-BROWN 1943 STUDEBAKER. I BOUGHT IT OFF A SHADY CHARACTER DOWN SOUTH WHO CLAIMED IT WAS THE VERY CAR IN WHICH JACK KEROUAC HAD FINGERED SOME MEXICAN BROAD IN *ON THE ROAD*.
Z
Z
THAT STORY MAY WELL'VE BEEN TRUE...THERE'S A STICKY PATCH ON THE PASSENGER SEAT THAT JUST WON'T BUDGE, EVEN WITH INDUSTRIAL SOLVENTS. THAT'S WHY NO ONE EVER RIDES SHOTGUN.
THIS IS ALL VERY EXCITING AND URGENT, BUT WHERE ARE WE GOING EXACTLY?
YAWN!
PUNCTURE!
SHIT. TANK GIRL, YOU GET THE SPARE OUT OF THE TRUNK. I'LL CHECK THE DAMAGE.
NASTY.

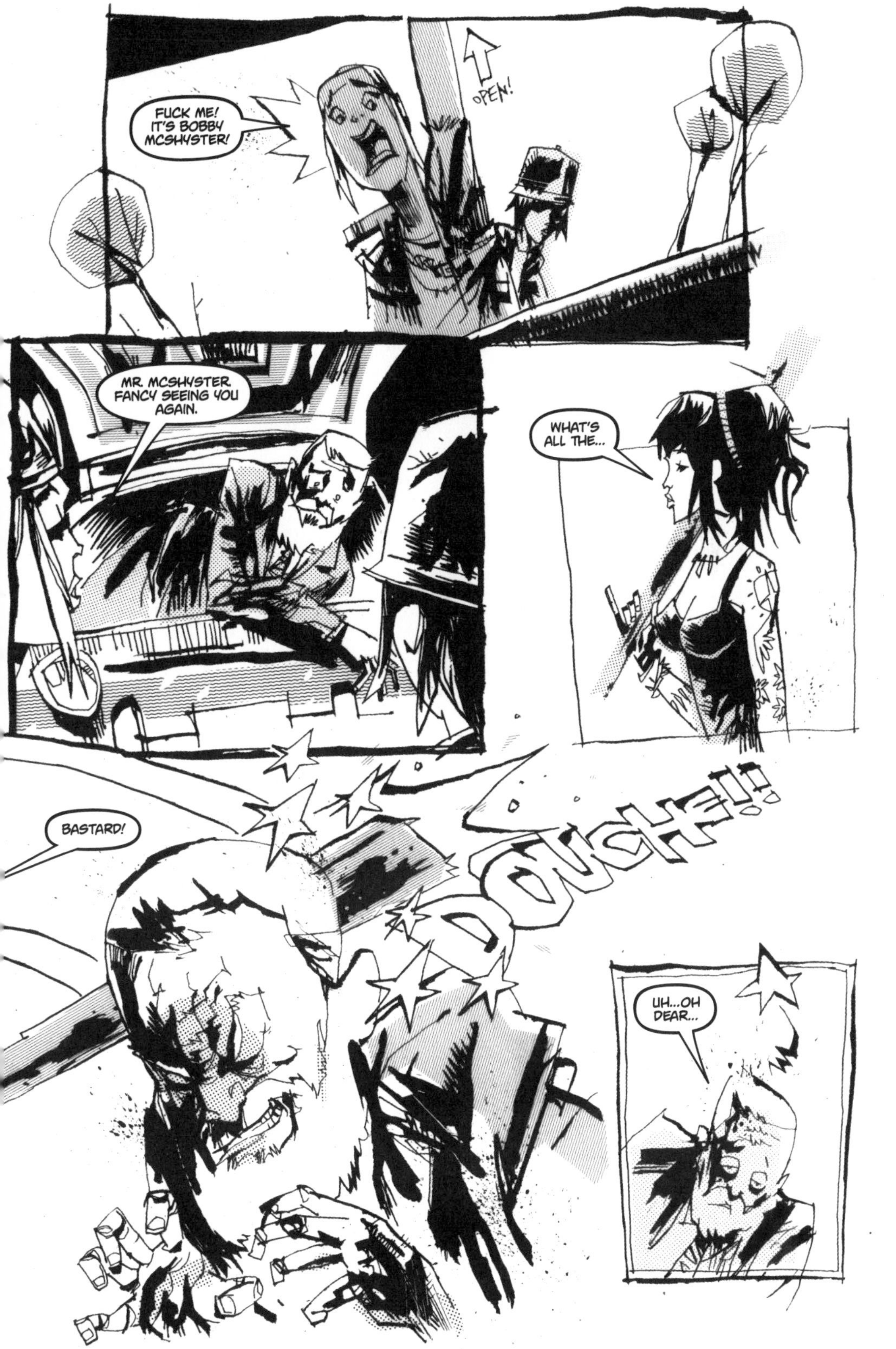
FUCK ME! IT'S BOBBY MCSHYSTER!
OPEN!
MR. MCSHYSTER. FANCY SEEING YOU AGAIN.
WHAT'S ALL THE...
BASTARD!
DOUCHE!!!
UH...OH DEAR...

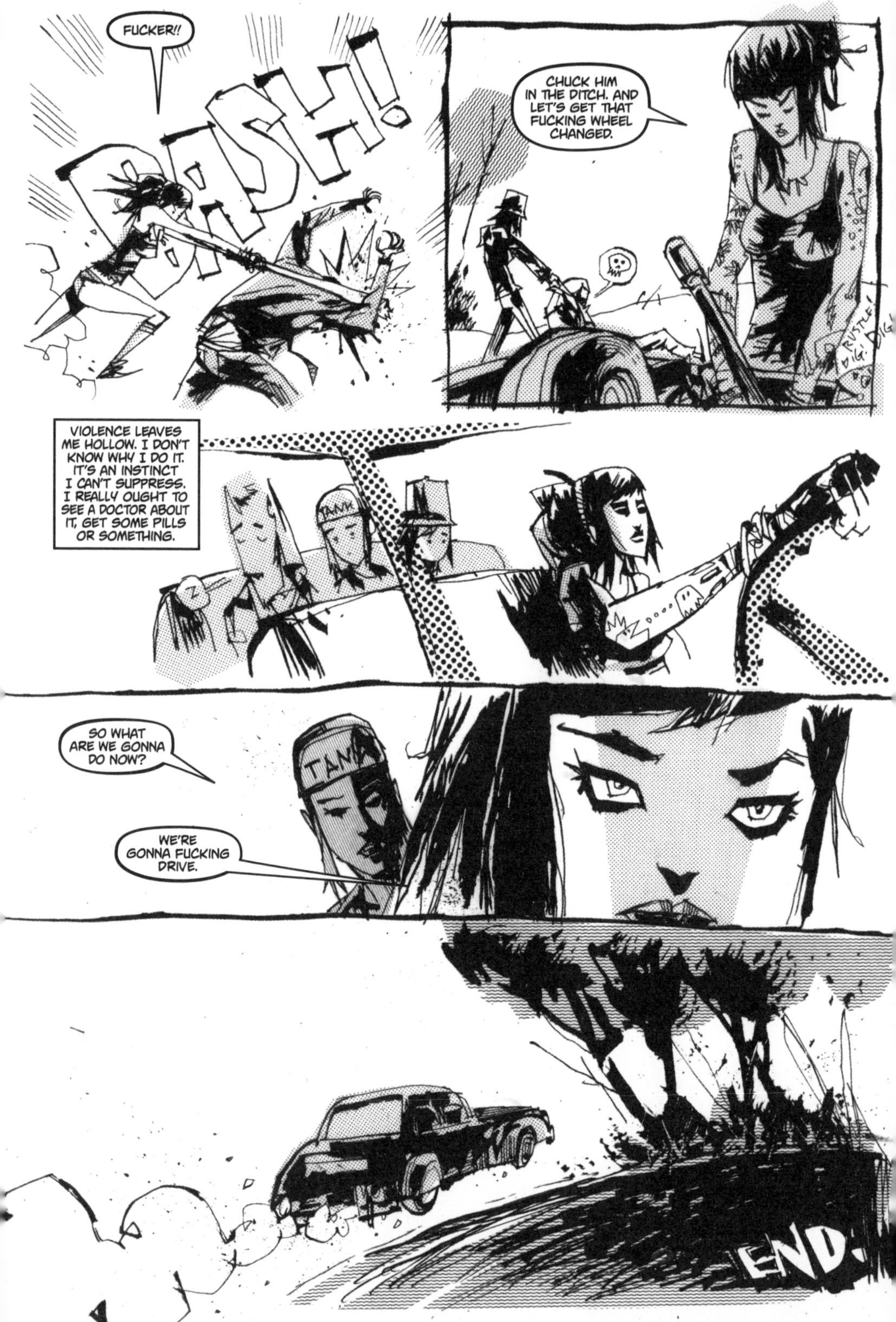
FUCKER!!
BASH!
CHUCK HIM IN THE DITCH. AND LET'S GET THAT FUCKING WHEEL CHANGED.
RUSTLE! DIG! DIG!
VIOLENCE LEAVES ME HOLLOW. I DON'T KNOW WHY I DO IT. IT'S AN INSTINCT I CAN'T SUPPRESS. I REALLY OUGHT TO SEE A DOCTOR ABOUT IT, GET SOME PILLS OR SOMETHING.
SO WHAT ARE WE GONNA DO NOW?
WE'RE GONNA FUCKING DRIVE.
END.

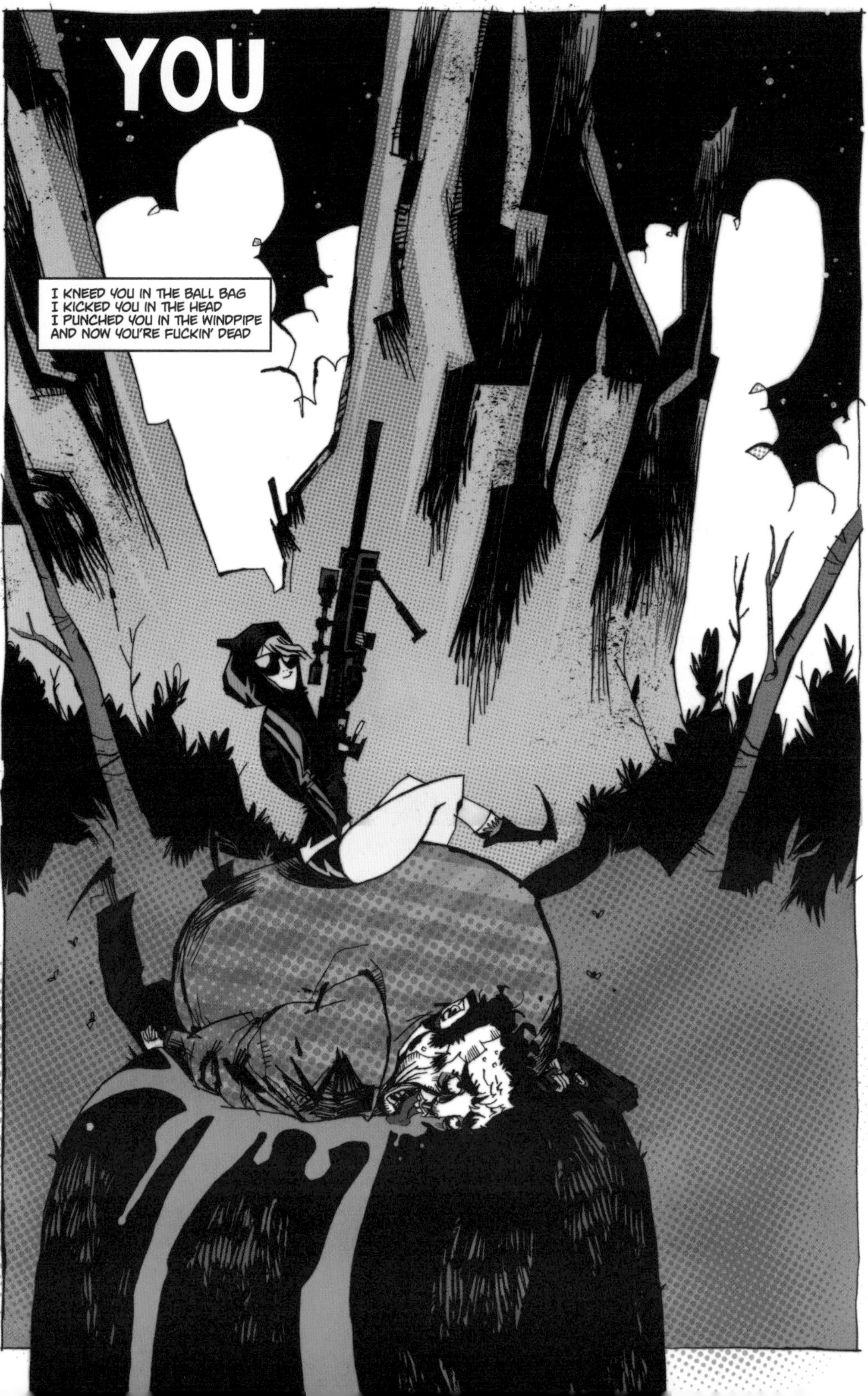
YOU
I KNEED YOU IN THE BALL BAG
I KICKED YOU IN THE HEAD
I PUNCHED YOU IN THE WINDPIPE
AND NOW YOU'RE FUCKIN' DEAD

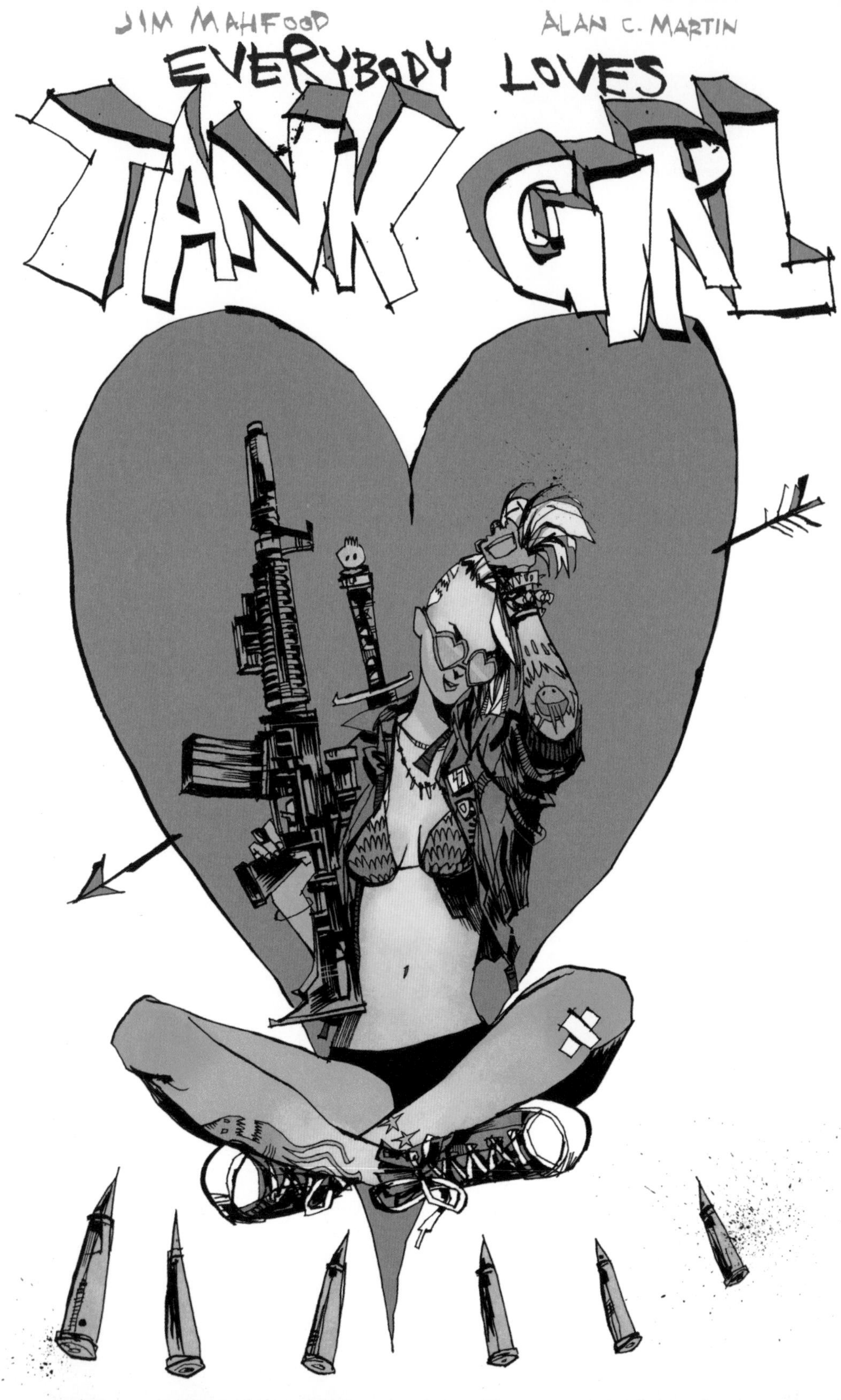
JIM MAHFOOD
ALAN C. MARTIN
EVERYBODY LOVES
TANK GIRL

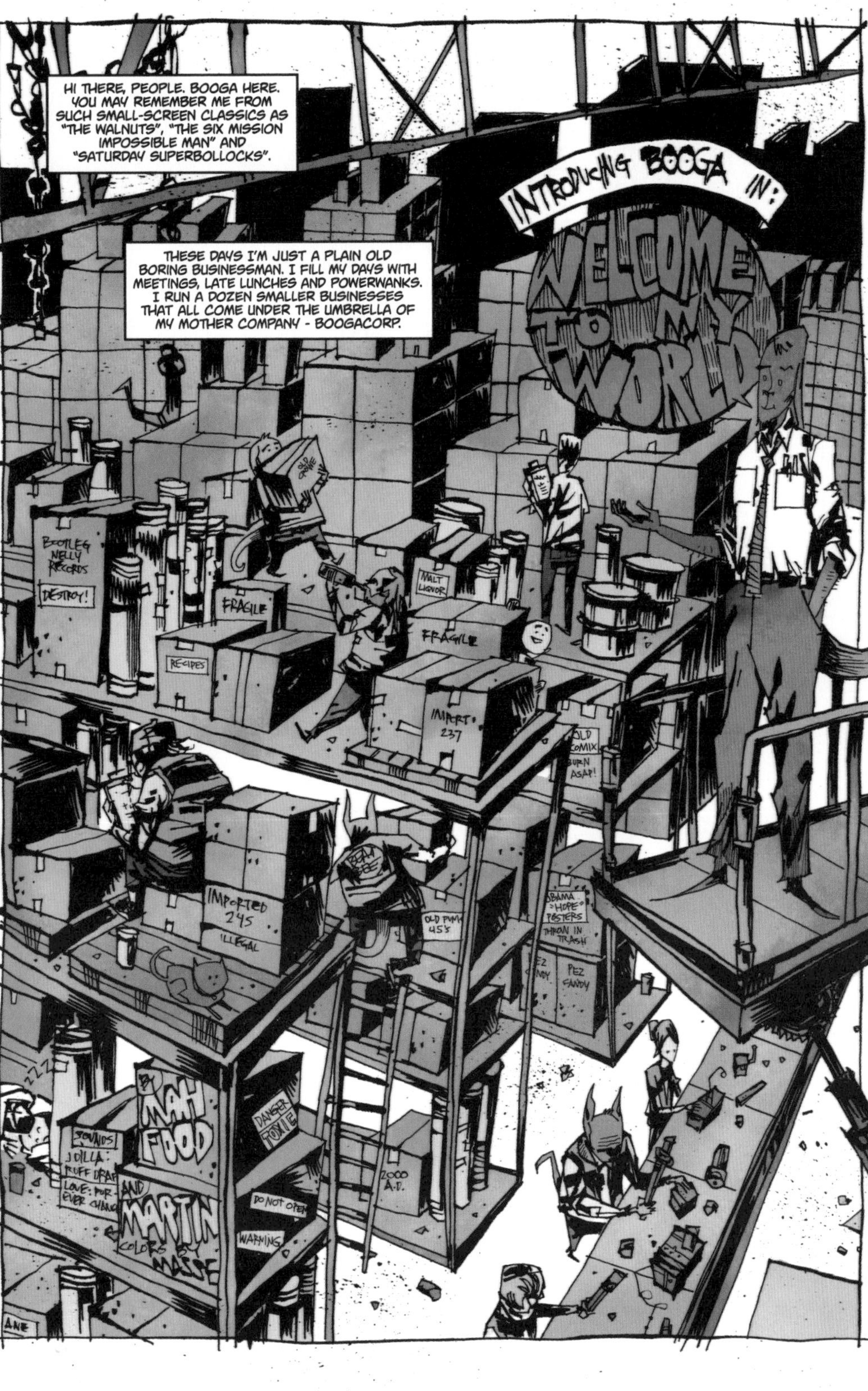
HI THERE, PEOPLE. BOOGA HERE. YOU MAY REMEMBER ME FROM SUCH SMALL-SCREEN CLASSICS AS "THE WALNUTS", "THE SIX MISSION IMPOSSIBLE MAN" AND "SATURDAY SUPERBOLLOCKS".
INTRODUCING BOOGA IN:
WELCOME TO MY WORLD
THESE DAYS I'M JUST A PLAIN OLD BORING BUSINESSMAN. I FILL MY DAYS WITH MEETINGS, LATE LUNCHES AND POWERWANKS. I RUN A DOZEN SMALLER BUSINESSES THAT ALL COME UNDER THE UMBRELLA OF MY MOTHER COMPANY - BOOGACORP.
BOOTLEG NELLY RECORDS
DESTROY!
FRAGILE
RECIPES
MALT LIQUOR
FRAGILE
IMPORT 237
OLD COMIX BURN ASAP!
IMPORTED 245
ILLEGAL
OLD PUNK 45'S
OBAMA "HOPE" POSTERS THROW IN TRASH
PEZ CANDY
DANGER TOXIC
DO NOT OPEN
WARNING
2000 A.D.

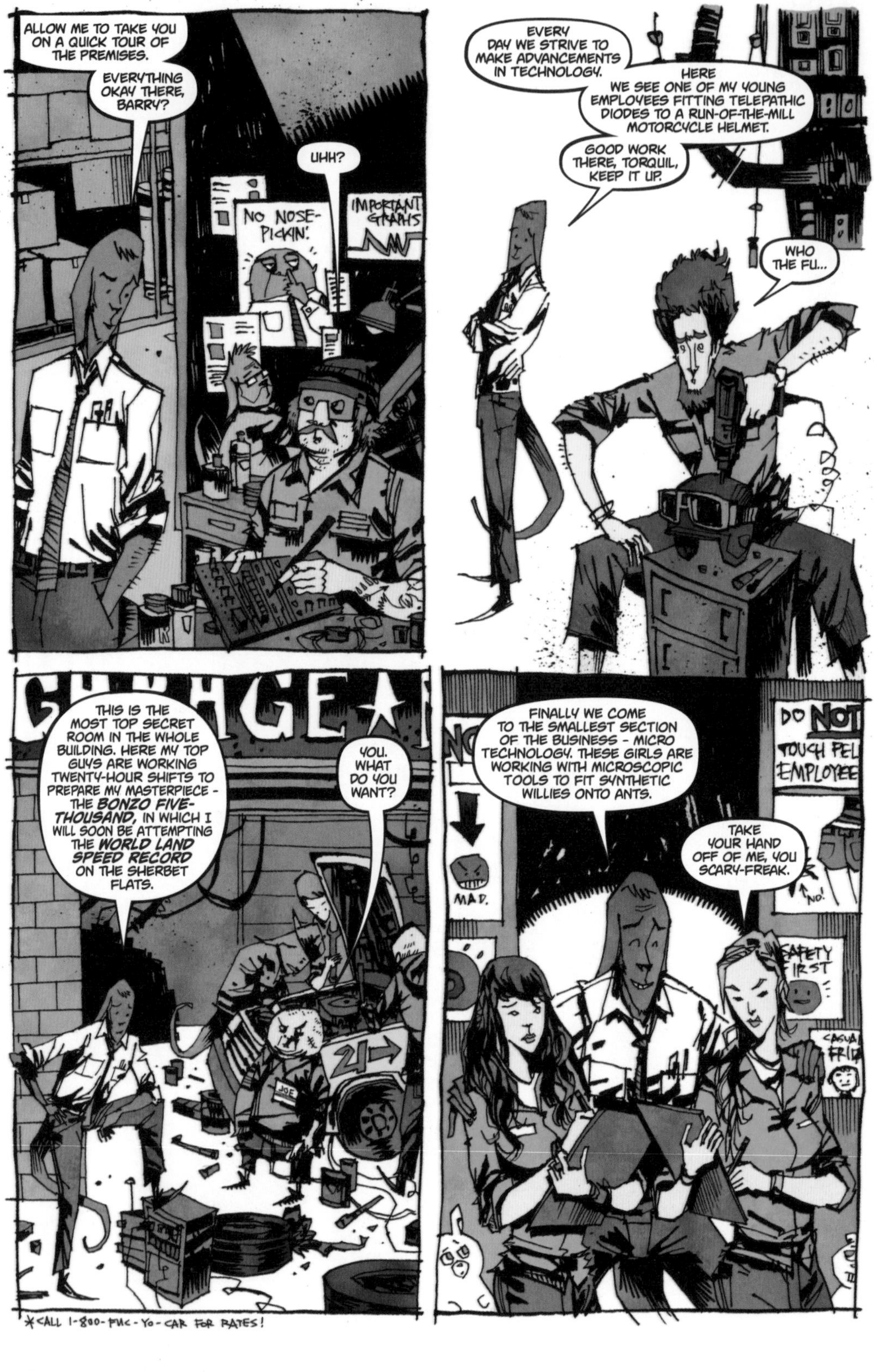
ALLOW ME TO TAKE YOU ON A QUICK TOUR OF THE PREMISES.
EVERYTHING OKAY THERE, BARRY?
UHH?
NO NOSE-PICKIN'.
IMPORTANT GRAPHS
EVERY DAY WE STRIVE TO MAKE ADVANCEMENTS IN TECHNOLOGY.
HERE WE SEE ONE OF MY YOUNG EMPLOYEES FITTING TELEPATHIC DIODES TO A RUN-OF-THE-MILL MOTORCYCLE HELMET.
GOOD WORK THERE, TORQUIL, KEEP IT UP.
WHO THE FU...
THIS IS THE MOST TOP SECRET ROOM IN THE WHOLE BUILDING. HERE MY TOP GUYS ARE WORKING TWENTY-HOUR SHIFTS TO PREPARE MY MASTERPIECE - THE ***BONZO FIVE-THOUSAND,*** IN WHICH I WILL SOON BE ATTEMPTING THE ***WORLD LAND SPEED RECORD*** ON THE SHERBET FLATS.
YOU. WHAT DO YOU WANT?
JOE
FINALLY WE COME TO THE SMALLEST SECTION OF THE BUSINESS - MICRO TECHNOLOGY. THESE GIRLS ARE WORKING WITH MICROSCOPIC TOOLS TO FIT SYNTHETIC WILLIES ONTO ANTS.
TAKE YOUR HAND OFF OF ME, YOU SCARY-FREAK.
MAD.
NO!

*CALL 1-800-FUK-YO-CAR FOR RATES!

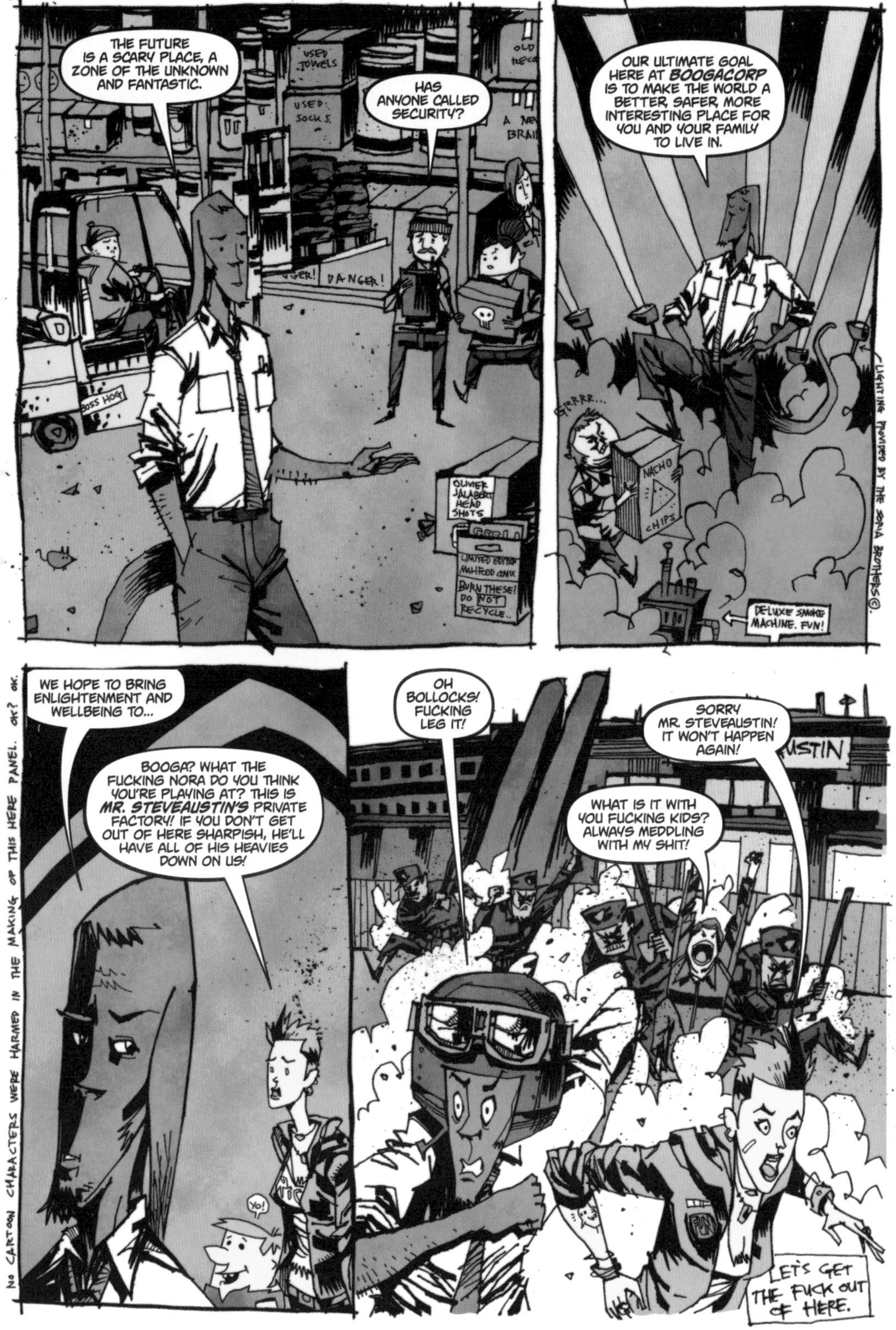
THE FUTURE IS A SCARY PLACE, A ZONE OF THE UNKNOWN AND FANTASTIC.
USED TOWELS
USED: SOCKS
HAS ANYONE CALLED SECURITY?
DANGER!
BOSS HOG
OLIVIER JALABERT HEAD SHOTS
LIMITED EDITION MAHFOOD COMIX
BURN THESE! DO NOT RECYCLE.
OUR ULTIMATE GOAL HERE AT BOOGACORP IS TO MAKE THE WORLD A BETTER, SAFER, MORE INTERESTING PLACE FOR YOU AND YOUR FAMILY TO LIVE IN.
GRRRR...
NACHO CHIPS
DELUXE SMOKE MACHINE. FUN!
LIGHTING PROVIDED BY THE SONIA BROTHERS ©.
WE HOPE TO BRING ENLIGHTENMENT AND WELLBEING TO...
BOOGA? WHAT THE FUCKING NORA DO YOU THINK YOU'RE PLAYING AT? THIS IS MR. STEVEAUSTIN'S PRIVATE FACTORY! IF YOU DON'T GET OUT OF HERE SHARPISH, HE'LL HAVE ALL OF HIS HEAVIES DOWN ON US!
YO!
NO CARTOON CHARACTERS WERE HARMED IN THE MAKING OF THIS HERE PANEL. OK? OK.
OH BOLLOCKS! FUCKING LEG IT!
SORRY MR. STEVEAUSTIN! IT WON'T HAPPEN AGAIN!
WHAT IS IT WITH YOU FUCKING KIDS? ALWAYS MEDDLING WITH MY SHIT!
LET'S GET THE FUCK OUT OF HERE.

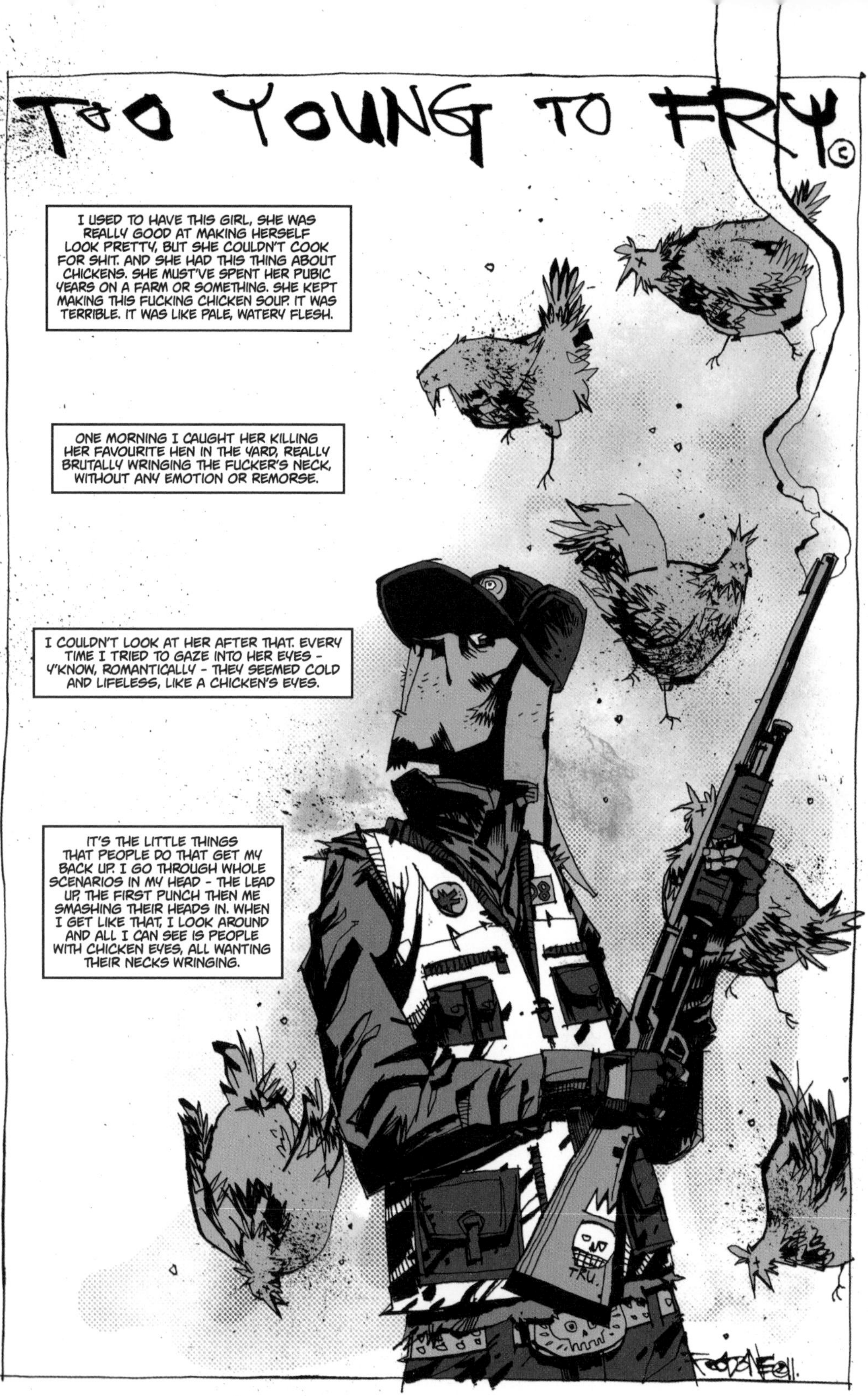
TOO YOUNG TO FRY ©
I USED TO HAVE THIS GIRL, SHE WAS REALLY GOOD AT MAKING HERSELF LOOK PRETTY, BUT SHE COULDN'T COOK FOR SHIT. AND SHE HAD THIS THING ABOUT CHICKENS. SHE MUST'VE SPENT HER PUBIC YEARS ON A FARM OR SOMETHING. SHE KEPT MAKING THIS FUCKING CHICKEN SOUP. IT WAS TERRIBLE. IT WAS LIKE PALE, WATERY FLESH.
ONE MORNING I CAUGHT HER KILLING HER FAVOURITE HEN IN THE YARD, REALLY BRUTALLY WRINGING THE FUCKER'S NECK, WITHOUT ANY EMOTION OR REMORSE.
I COULDN'T LOOK AT HER AFTER THAT. EVERY TIME I TRIED TO GAZE INTO HER EYES - Y'KNOW, ROMANTICALLY - THEY SEEMED COLD AND LIFELESS, LIKE A CHICKEN'S EYES.
IT'S THE LITTLE THINGS THAT PEOPLE DO THAT GET MY BACK UP. I GO THROUGH WHOLE SCENARIOS IN MY HEAD - THE LEAD UP, THE FIRST PUNCH THEN ME SMASHING THEIR HEADS IN. WHEN I GET LIKE THAT, I LOOK AROUND AND ALL I CAN SEE IS PEOPLE WITH CHICKEN EYES, ALL WANTING THEIR NECKS WRINGING.
TRU.

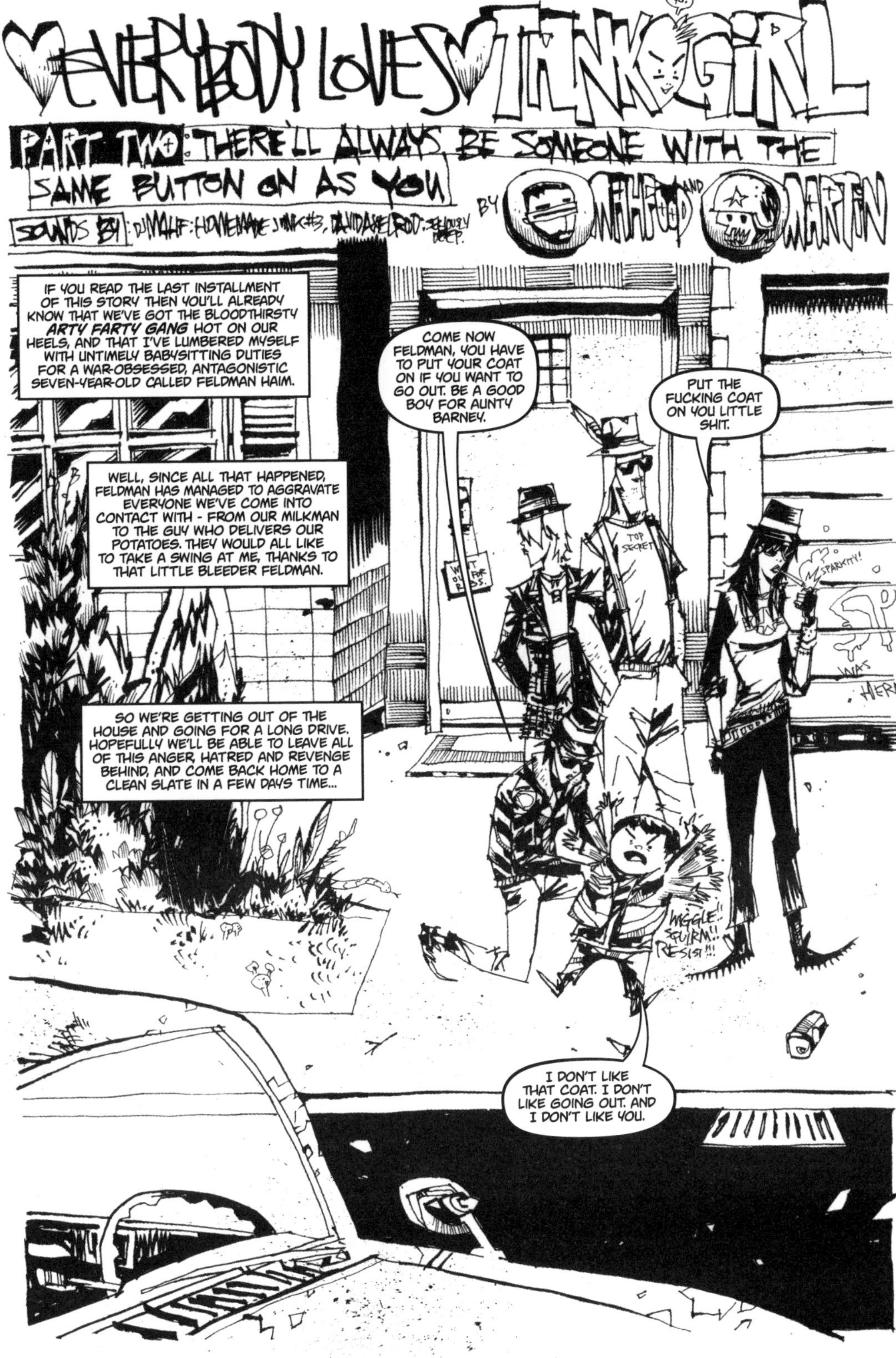
EVERYBODY LOVES TANK GIRL
YO!
PART TWO: THERE'LL ALWAYS BE SOMEONE WITH THE SAME BUTTON ON AS YOU
SOUNDS BY: DJ MAHF: HOMEMADE JUNK #3, DAVID AXELROD: SERIOUSLY DEEP.
IF YOU READ THE LAST INSTALLMENT OF THIS STORY THEN YOU'LL ALREADY KNOW THAT WE'VE GOT THE BLOODTHIRSTY ARTY FARTY GANG HOT ON OUR HEELS, AND THAT I'VE LUMBERED MYSELF WITH UNTIMELY BABYSITTING DUTIES FOR A WAR-OBSESSED, ANTAGONISTIC SEVEN-YEAR-OLD CALLED FELDMAN HAIM.
WELL, SINCE ALL THAT HAPPENED, FELDMAN HAS MANAGED TO AGGRAVATE EVERYONE WE'VE COME INTO CONTACT WITH - FROM OUR MILKMAN TO THE GUY WHO DELIVERS OUR POTATOES. THEY WOULD ALL LIKE TO TAKE A SWING AT ME, THANKS TO THAT LITTLE BLEEDER FELDMAN.
SO WE'RE GETTING OUT OF THE HOUSE AND GOING FOR A LONG DRIVE. HOPEFULLY WE'LL BE ABLE TO LEAVE ALL OF THIS ANGER, HATRED AND REVENGE BEHIND, AND COME BACK HOME TO A CLEAN SLATE IN A FEW DAYS TIME...
COME NOW FELDMAN, YOU HAVE TO PUT YOUR COAT ON IF YOU WANT TO GO OUT. BE A GOOD BOY FOR AUNTY BARNEY.
PUT THE FUCKING COAT ON YOU LITTLE SHIT.
TOP SECRET
STARKITY!
WAS HERE
WIGGLE!! SQUIRM!! RESIST!!!
I DON'T LIKE THAT COAT. I DON'T LIKE GOING OUT. AND I DON'T LIKE YOU.

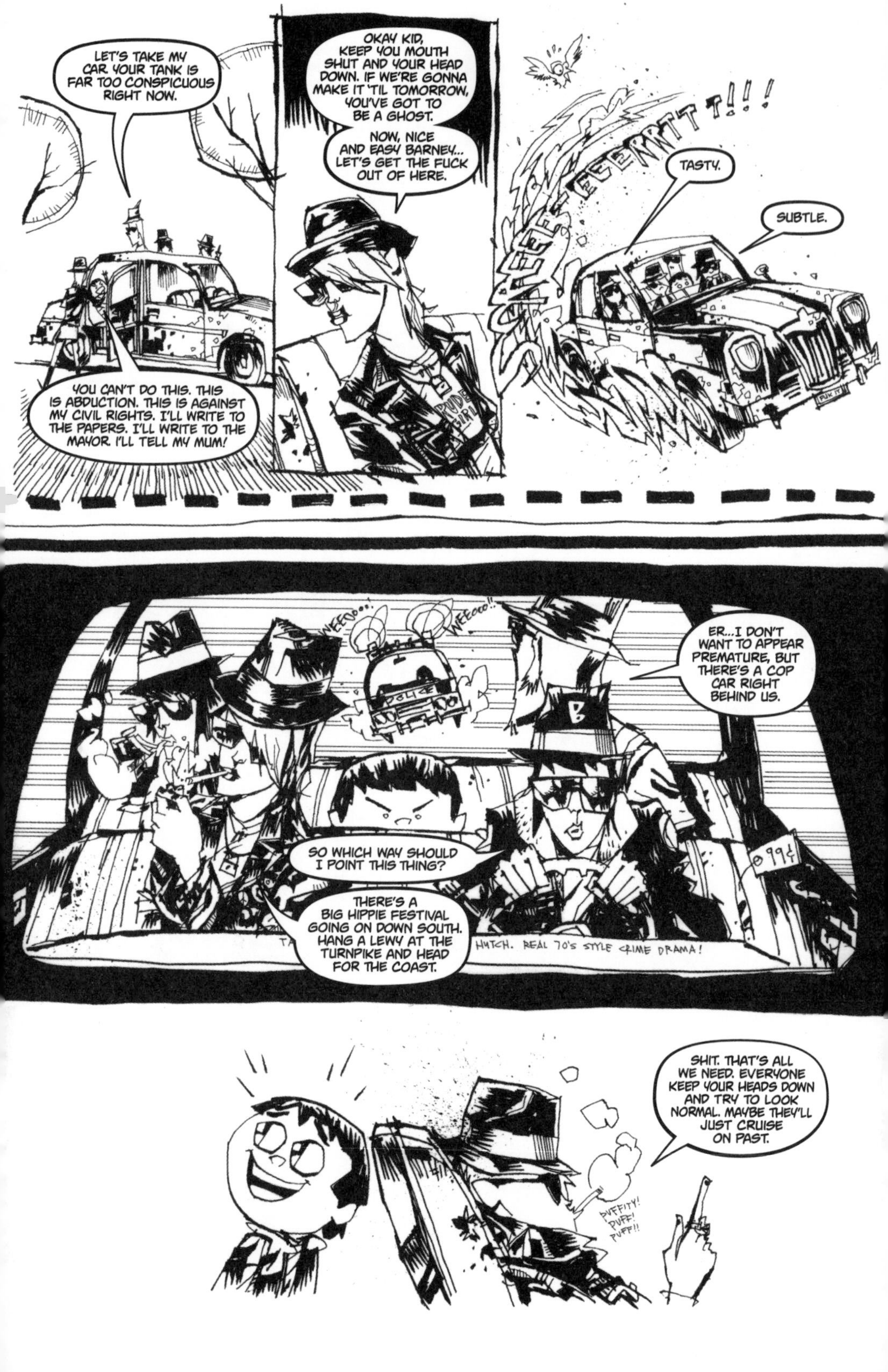
LET'S TAKE MY CAR. YOUR TANK IS FAR TOO CONSPICUOUS RIGHT NOW.
YOU CAN'T DO THIS. THIS IS ABDUCTION. THIS IS AGAINST MY CIVIL RIGHTS. I'LL WRITE TO THE PAPERS. I'LL WRITE TO THE MAYOR. I'LL TELL MY MUM!
OKAY KID, KEEP YOU MOUTH SHUT AND YOUR HEAD DOWN. IF WE'RE GONNA MAKE IT 'TIL TOMORROW, YOU'VE GOT TO BE A GHOST.
NOW, NICE AND EASY BARNEY... LET'S GET THE FUCK OUT OF HERE.
TASTY.
SUBTLE.
POLICE
ER...I DON'T WANT TO APPEAR PREMATURE, BUT THERE'S A COP CAR RIGHT BEHIND US.
SO WHICH WAY SHOULD I POINT THIS THING?
THERE'S A BIG HIPPIE FESTIVAL GOING ON DOWN SOUTH. HANG A LEWY AT THE TURNPIKE AND HEAD FOR THE COAST.
HUTCH. REAL 70'S STYLE CRIME DRAMA!
99¢
SHIT. THAT'S ALL WE NEED. EVERYONE KEEP YOUR HEADS DOWN AND TRY TO LOOK NORMAL. MAYBE THEY'LL JUST CRUISE ON PAST.
PUFFITY! PUFF! PUFF!!

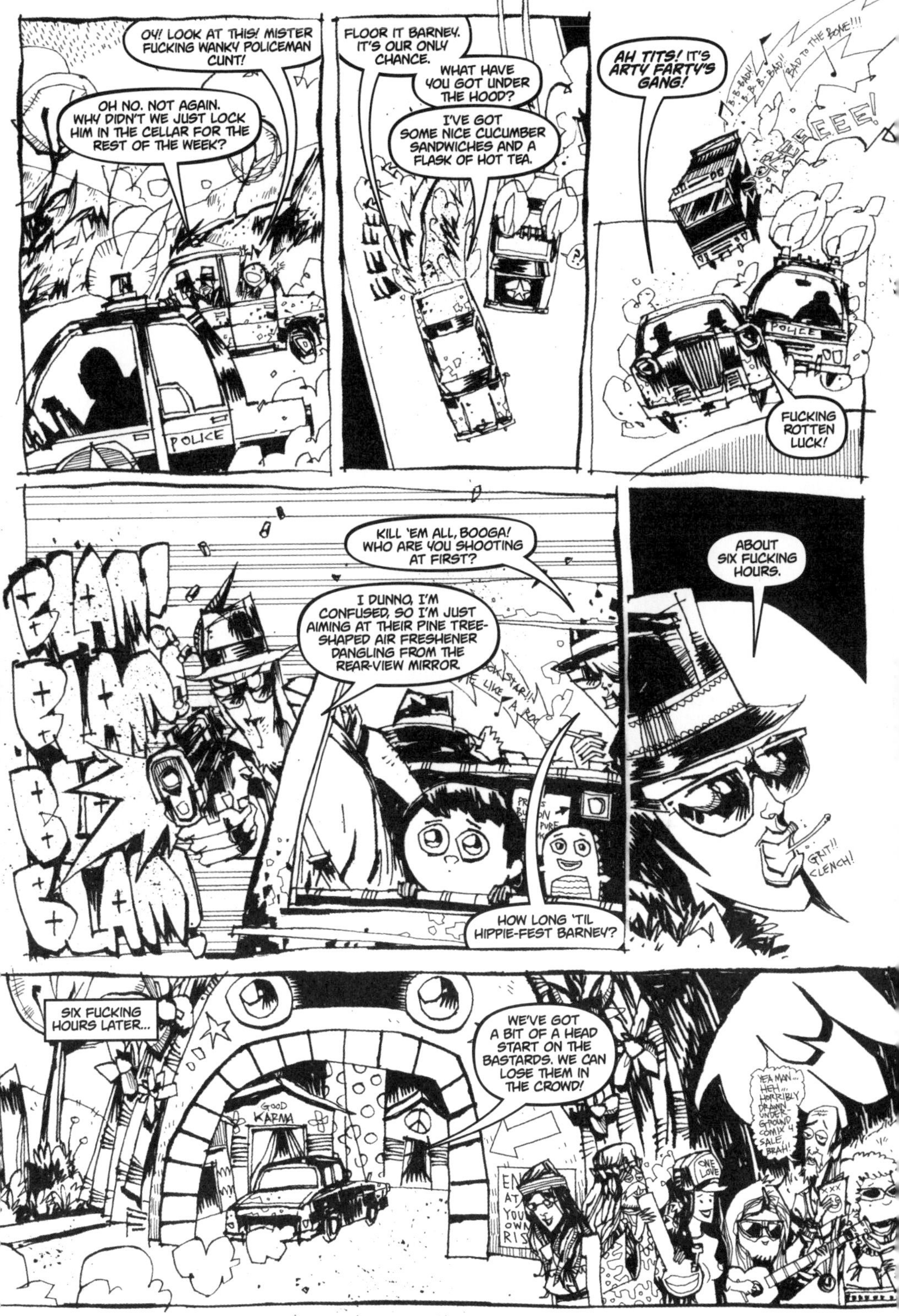

OY! LOOK AT THIS! MISTER FUCKING WANKY POLICEMAN CUNT!
OH NO. NOT AGAIN. WHY DIDN'T WE JUST LOCK HIM IN THE CELLAR FOR THE REST OF THE WEEK?
POLICE
FLOOR IT BARNEY. IT'S OUR ONLY CHANCE.
WHAT HAVE YOU GOT UNDER THE HOOD?
I'VE GOT SOME NICE CUCUMBER SANDWICHES AND A FLASK OF HOT TEA.
AH TITS! IT'S ARTY FARTY'S GANG!
B-B-BAD!! B-B-B-BAD!! BAD TO THE BONE!!!
EEEE!
POLICE
FUCKING ROTTEN LUCK!
BLAM! BLAM! BLAM! BLAM! BLAM!
KILL 'EM ALL, BOOGA! WHO ARE YOU SHOOTING AT FIRST?
I DUNNO, I'M CONFUSED, SO I'M JUST AIMING AT THEIR PINE TREE-SHAPED AIR FRESHENER DANGLING FROM THE REAR-VIEW MIRROR.
LIKE A ROC
STAR!!
HOW LONG 'TIL HIPPIE-FEST BARNEY?
ABOUT SIX FUCKING HOURS.
GRIT!! CLENCH!
SIX FUCKING HOURS LATER...
WE'VE GOT A BIT OF A HEAD START ON THE BASTARDS. WE CAN LOSE THEM IN THE CROWD!
GOOD KARMA
ONE LOVE
YEA MAN... HEH... HORRIBLY DRAWN UNDER-GROUND COMIX 4 SALE, BRAH!

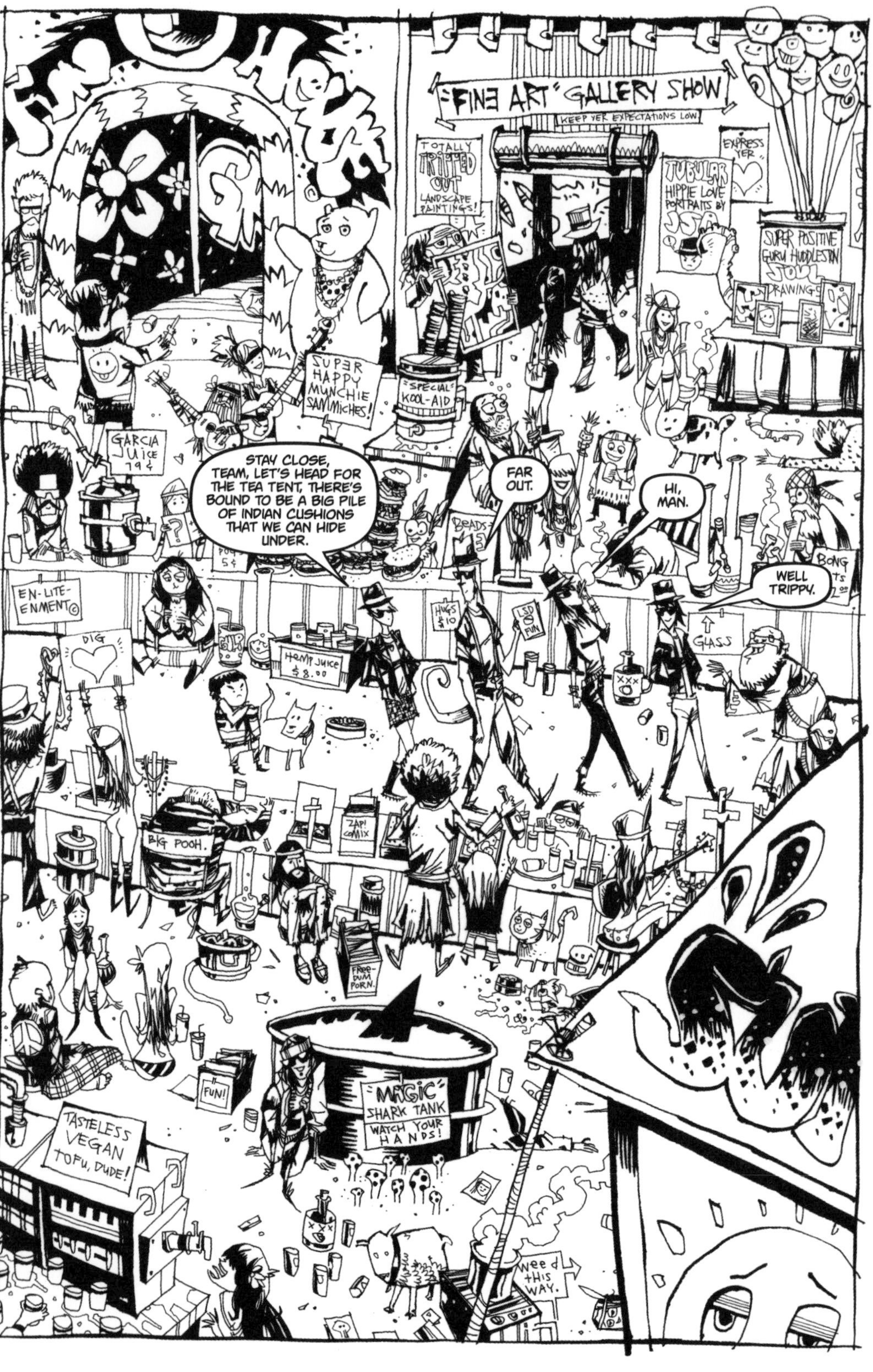
FINE ART GALLERY SHOW
KEEP YER EXPECTATIONS LOW.
TOTALLY TRIPPED OUT LANDSCAPE PAINTINGS!
TUBULAR HIPPIE LOVE PORTRAITS BY JSA
EXPRESS YER
SUPER POSITIVE GURU HUDDLESTON SOUL DRAWINGS
SUPER HAPPY MUNCHIE SAMMICHES!
SPECIAL KOOL-AID
GARCIA JUICE 79¢
STAY CLOSE, TEAM, LET'S HEAD FOR THE TEA TENT, THERE'S BOUND TO BE A BIG PILE OF INDIAN CUSHIONS THAT WE CAN HIDE UNDER.
FAR OUT.
HI, MAN.
BEADS
WELL TRIPPY.
EN-LITE-ENMENT©
DIG
HEMP JUICE $8.00
HUGS $10
LSD FUN
GLASS
BIG POOH.
ZAP! COMIX
FREE-DUM PORN.
FUN!
MAGIC SHARK TANK WATCH YOUR HANDS!
TASTELESS VEGAN TOFU, DUDE!
weed THIS WAY.

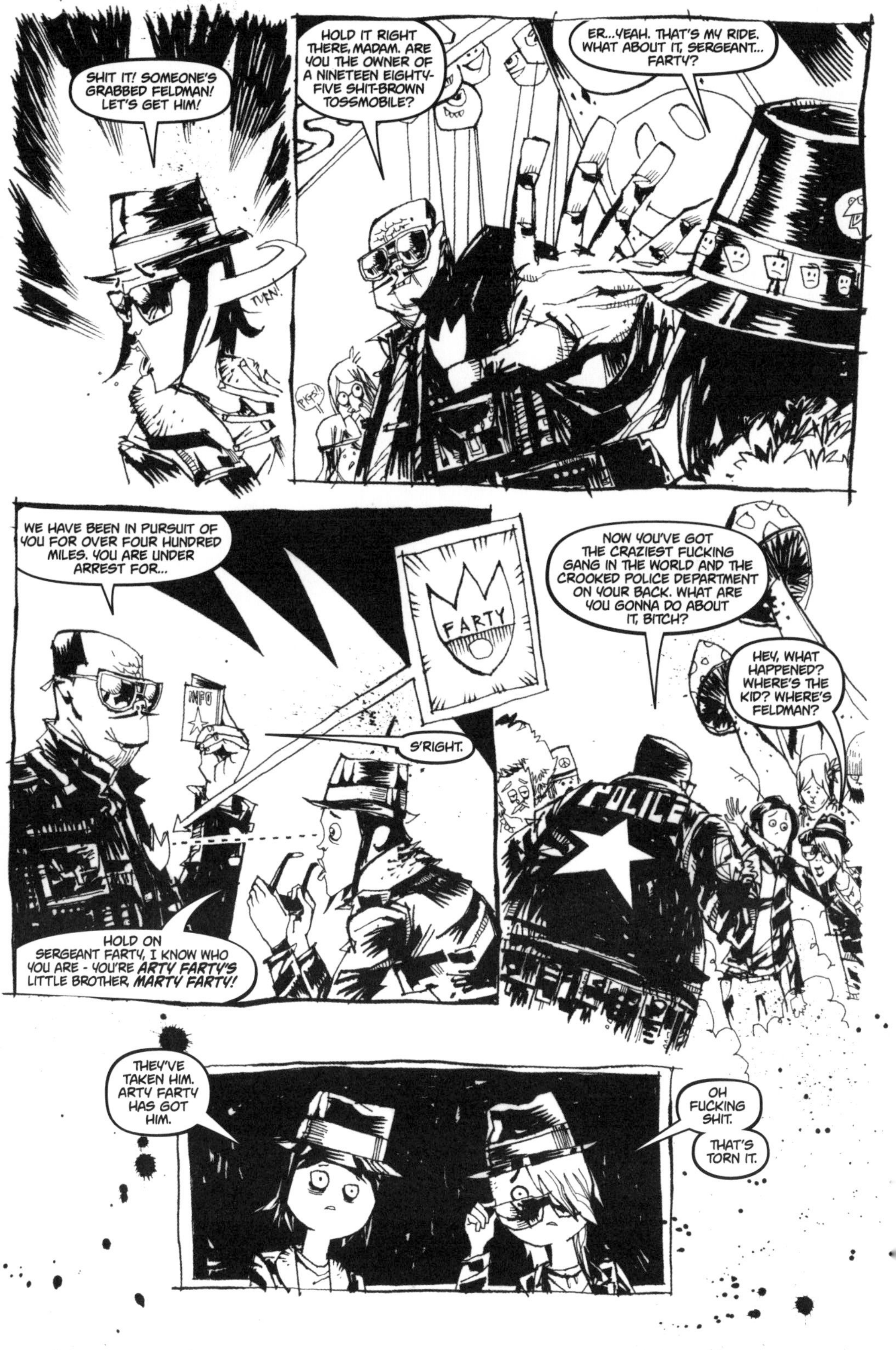
SHIT IT! SOMEONE'S GRABBED FELDMAN! LET'S GET HIM!
TURN!
HOLD IT RIGHT THERE, MADAM. ARE YOU THE OWNER OF A NINETEEN EIGHTY-FIVE SHIT-BROWN TOSSMOBILE?
PIGS!!
ER...YEAH. THAT'S MY RIDE. WHAT ABOUT IT, SERGEANT... FARTY?
WE HAVE BEEN IN PURSUIT OF YOU FOR OVER FOUR HUNDRED MILES. YOU ARE UNDER ARREST FOR...
INFO
FARTY
S'RIGHT.
HOLD ON SERGEANT FARTY, I KNOW WHO YOU ARE - YOU'RE ARTY FARTY'S LITTLE BROTHER, MARTY FARTY!
NOW YOU'VE GOT THE CRAZIEST FUCKING GANG IN THE WORLD AND THE CROOKED POLICE DEPARTMENT ON YOUR BACK. WHAT ARE YOU GONNA DO ABOUT IT, BITCH?
HEY, WHAT HAPPENED? WHERE'S THE KID? WHERE'S FELDMAN?
POLICE
THEY'VE TAKEN HIM. ARTY FARTY HAS GOT HIM.
OH FUCKING SHIT.
THAT'S TORN IT.

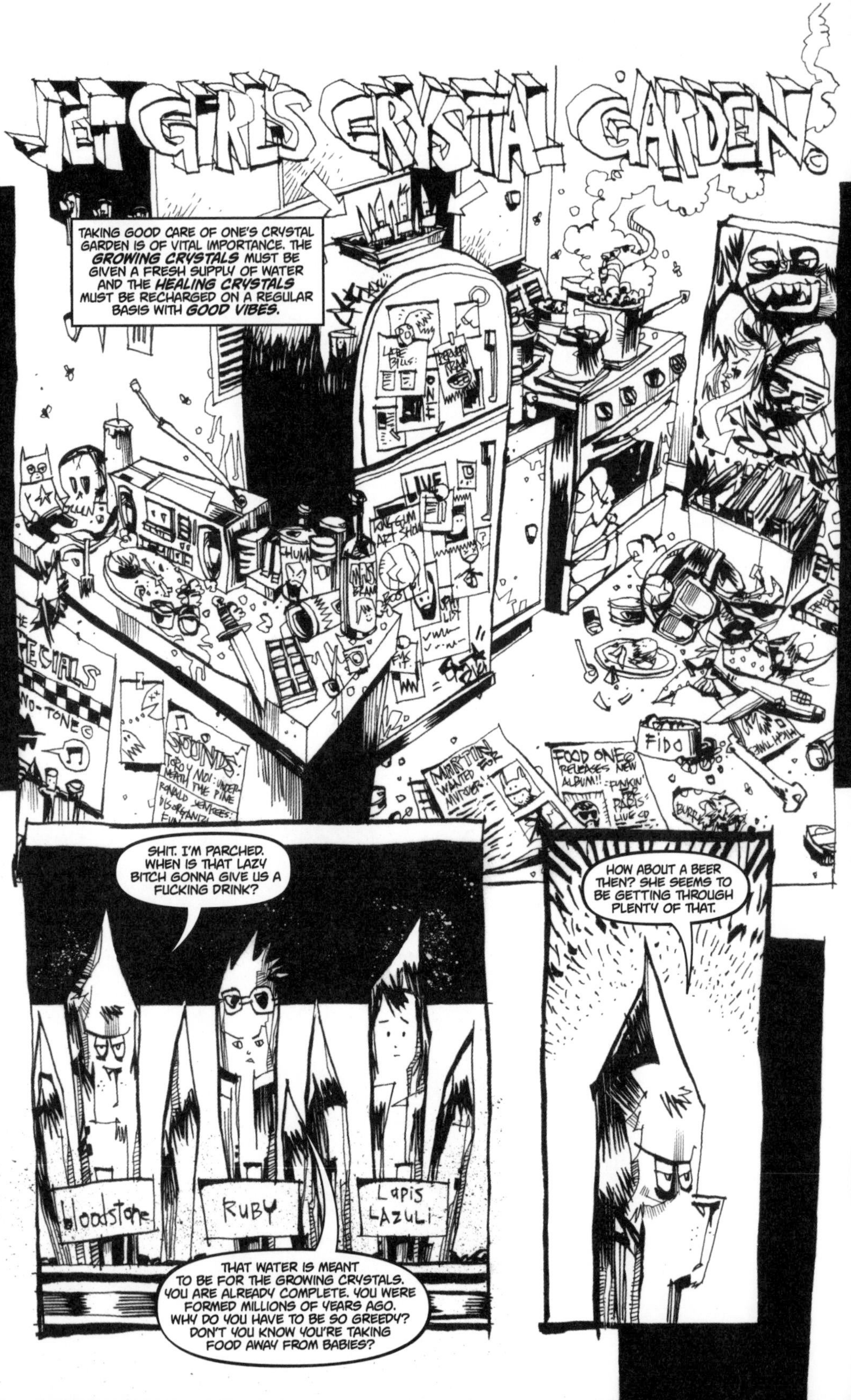
JET GIRL'S CRYSTAL GARDEN!
TAKING GOOD CARE OF ONE'S CRYSTAL GARDEN IS OF VITAL IMPORTANCE. THE GROWING CRYSTALS MUST BE GIVEN A FRESH SUPPLY OF WATER AND THE HEALING CRYSTALS MUST BE RECHARGED ON A REGULAR BASIS WITH GOOD VIBES.
FIDO
SHIT. I'M PARCHED. WHEN IS THAT LAZY BITCH GONNA GIVE US A FUCKING DRINK?
bloodstone
RUBY
Lapis LAZULI
THAT WATER IS MEANT TO BE FOR THE GROWING CRYSTALS. YOU ARE ALREADY COMPLETE. YOU WERE FORMED MILLIONS OF YEARS AGO. WHY DO YOU HAVE TO BE SO GREEDY? DON'T YOU KNOW YOU'RE TAKING FOOD AWAY FROM BABIES?
HOW ABOUT A BEER THEN? SHE SEEMS TO BE GETTING THROUGH PLENTY OF THAT.

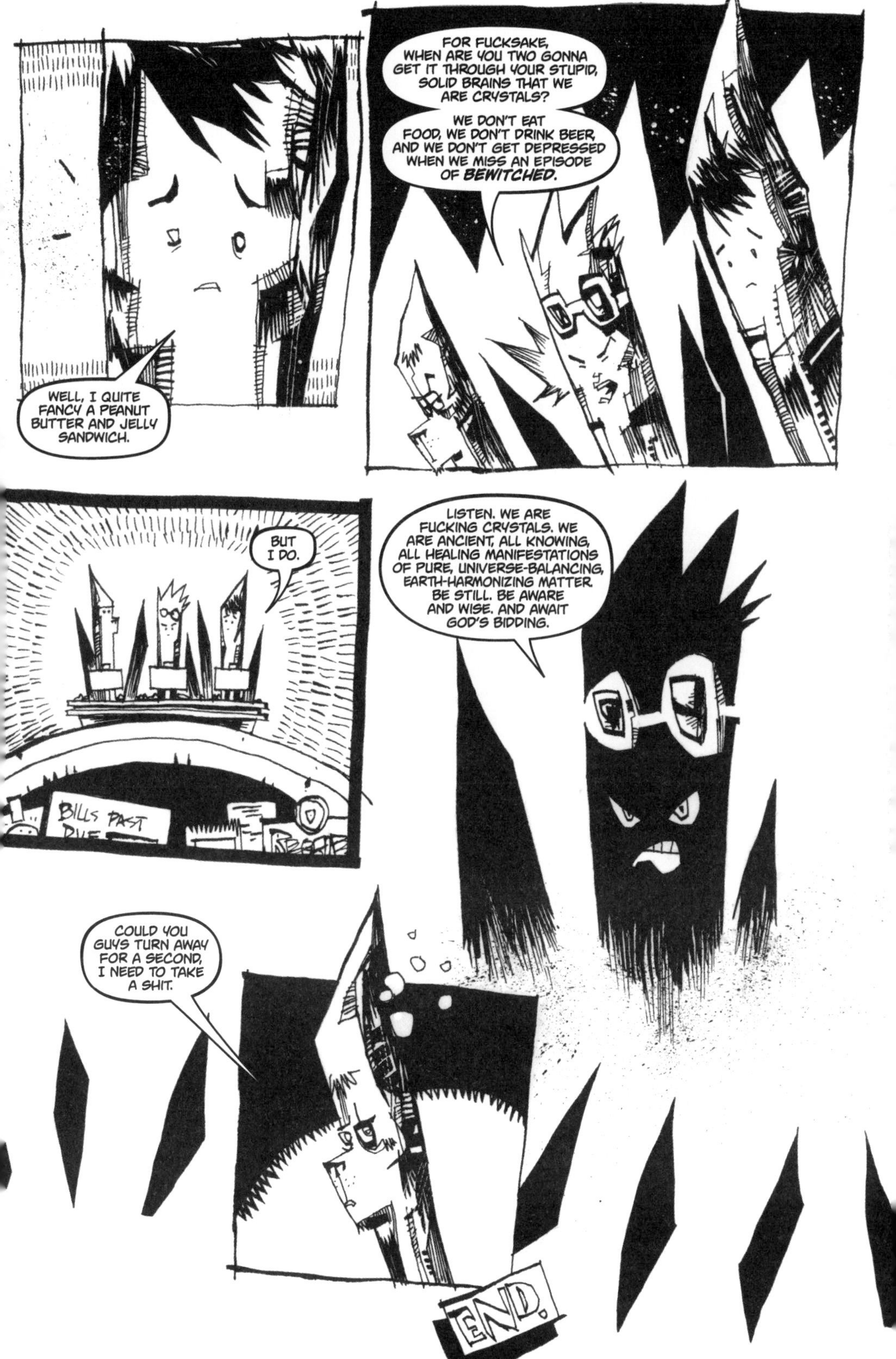
WELL, I QUITE FANCY A PEANUT BUTTER AND JELLY SANDWICH.
FOR FUCKSAKE, WHEN ARE YOU TWO GONNA GET IT THROUGH YOUR STUPID, SOLID BRAINS THAT WE ARE CRYSTALS?
WE DON'T EAT FOOD, WE DON'T DRINK BEER, AND WE DON'T GET DEPRESSED WHEN WE MISS AN EPISODE OF *BEWITCHED*.
BUT I DO.
BILLS PAST DUE
LISTEN. WE ARE FUCKING CRYSTALS. WE ARE ANCIENT, ALL KNOWING, ALL HEALING MANIFESTATIONS OF PURE, UNIVERSE-BALANCING, EARTH-HARMONIZING MATTER. BE STILL. BE AWARE AND WISE. AND AWAIT GOD'S BIDDING.
COULD YOU GUYS TURN AWAY FOR A SECOND, I NEED TO TAKE A SHIT.
END.

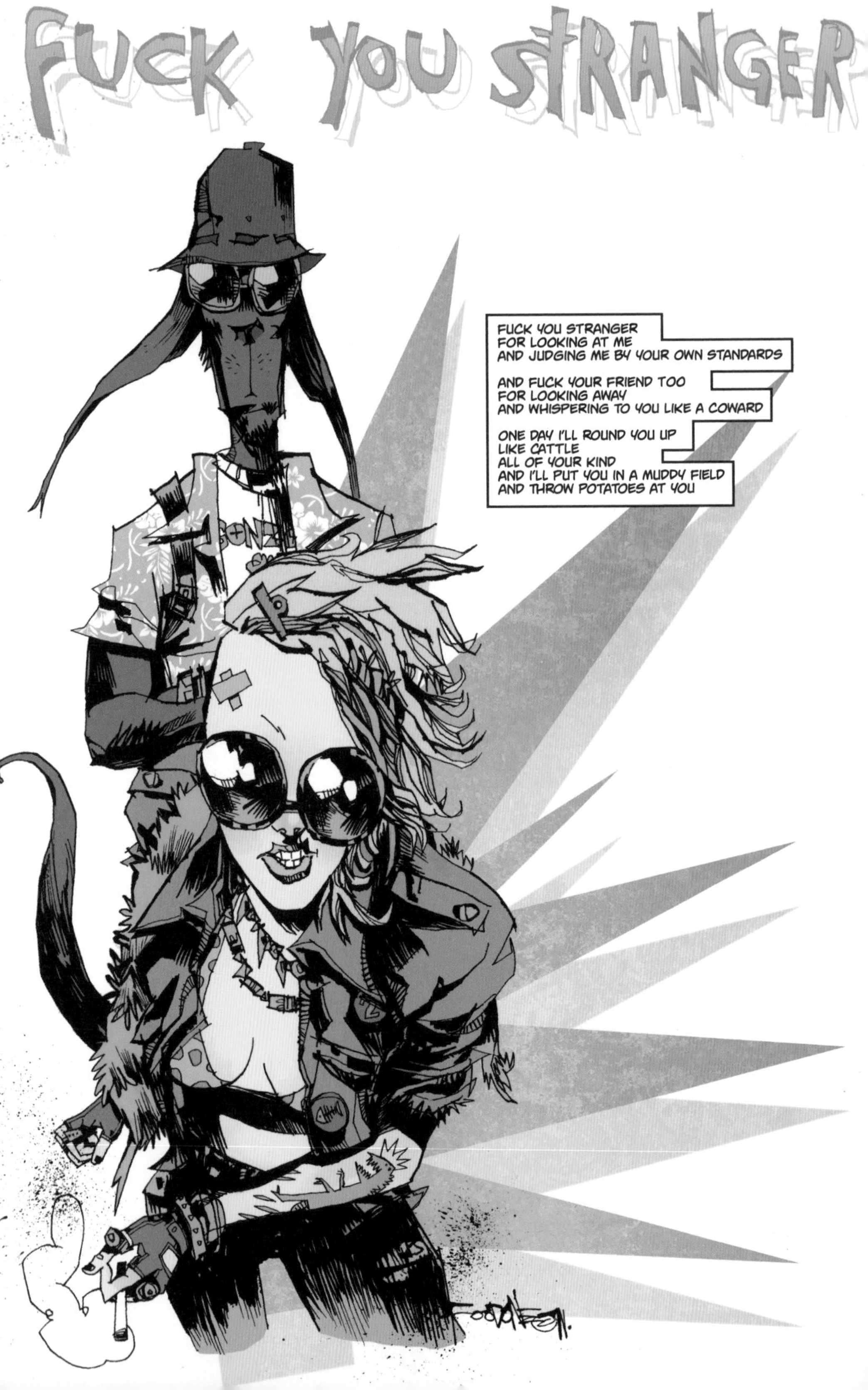
FUCK YOU STRANGER
FUCK YOU STRANGER
FOR LOOKING AT ME
AND JUDGING ME BY YOUR OWN STANDARDS
AND FUCK YOUR FRIEND TOO
FOR LOOKING AWAY
AND WHISPERING TO YOU LIKE A COWARD
ONE DAY I'LL ROUND YOU UP
LIKE CATTLE
ALL OF YOUR KIND
AND I'LL PUT YOU IN A MUDDY FIELD
AND THROW POTATOES AT YOU

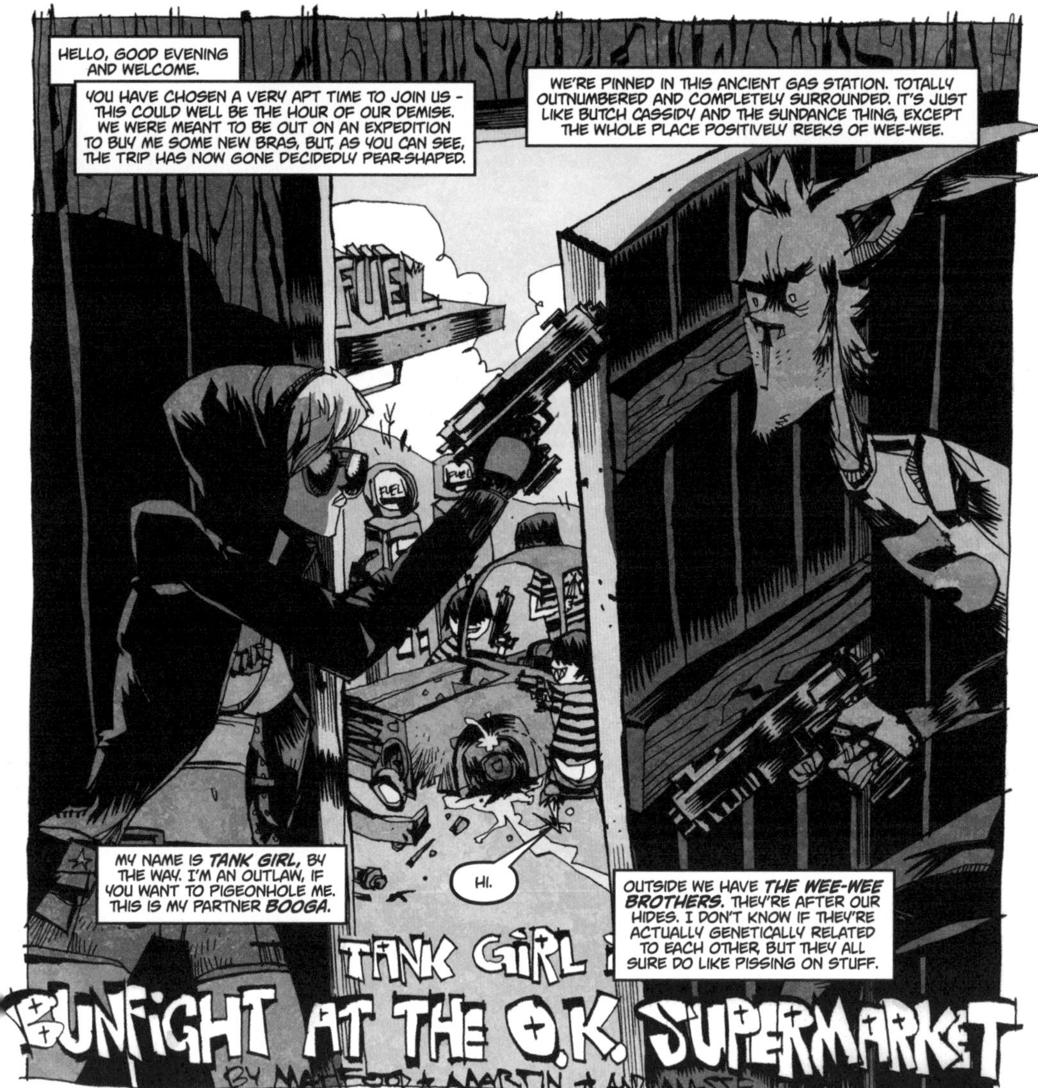

HELLO, GOOD EVENING AND WELCOME.
YOU HAVE CHOSEN A VERY APT TIME TO JOIN US - THIS COULD WELL BE THE HOUR OF OUR DEMISE. WE WERE MEANT TO BE OUT ON AN EXPEDITION TO BUY ME SOME NEW BRAS, BUT, AS YOU CAN SEE, THE TRIP HAS NOW GONE DECIDEDLY PEAR-SHAPED.
WE'RE PINNED IN THIS ANCIENT GAS STATION. TOTALLY OUTNUMBERED AND COMPLETELY SURROUNDED. IT'S JUST LIKE BUTCH CASSIDY AND THE SUNDANCE THING, EXCEPT THE WHOLE PLACE POSITIVELY REEKS OF WEE-WEE.
FUEL
MY NAME IS ***TANK GIRL***, BY THE WAY. I'M AN OUTLAW, IF YOU WANT TO PIGEONHOLE ME. THIS IS MY PARTNER ***BOOGA***.
HI.
OUTSIDE WE HAVE ***THE WEE-WEE BROTHERS***. THEY'RE AFTER OUR HIDES. I DON'T KNOW IF THEY'RE ACTUALLY GENETICALLY RELATED TO EACH OTHER, BUT THEY ALL SURE DO LIKE PISSING ON STUFF.
TANK GIRL
BUNFIGHT AT THE O.K. SUPERMARKET

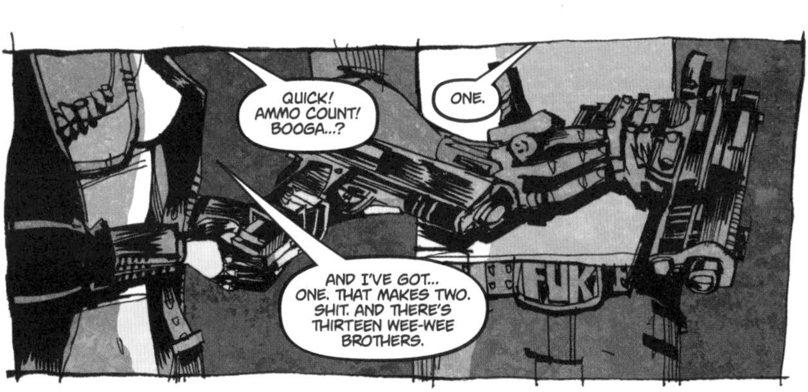

QUICK! AMMO COUNT! BOOGA...?
ONE.
AND I'VE GOT... ONE. THAT MAKES TWO. SHIT. AND THERE'S THIRTEEN WEE-WEE BROTHERS.
FUK

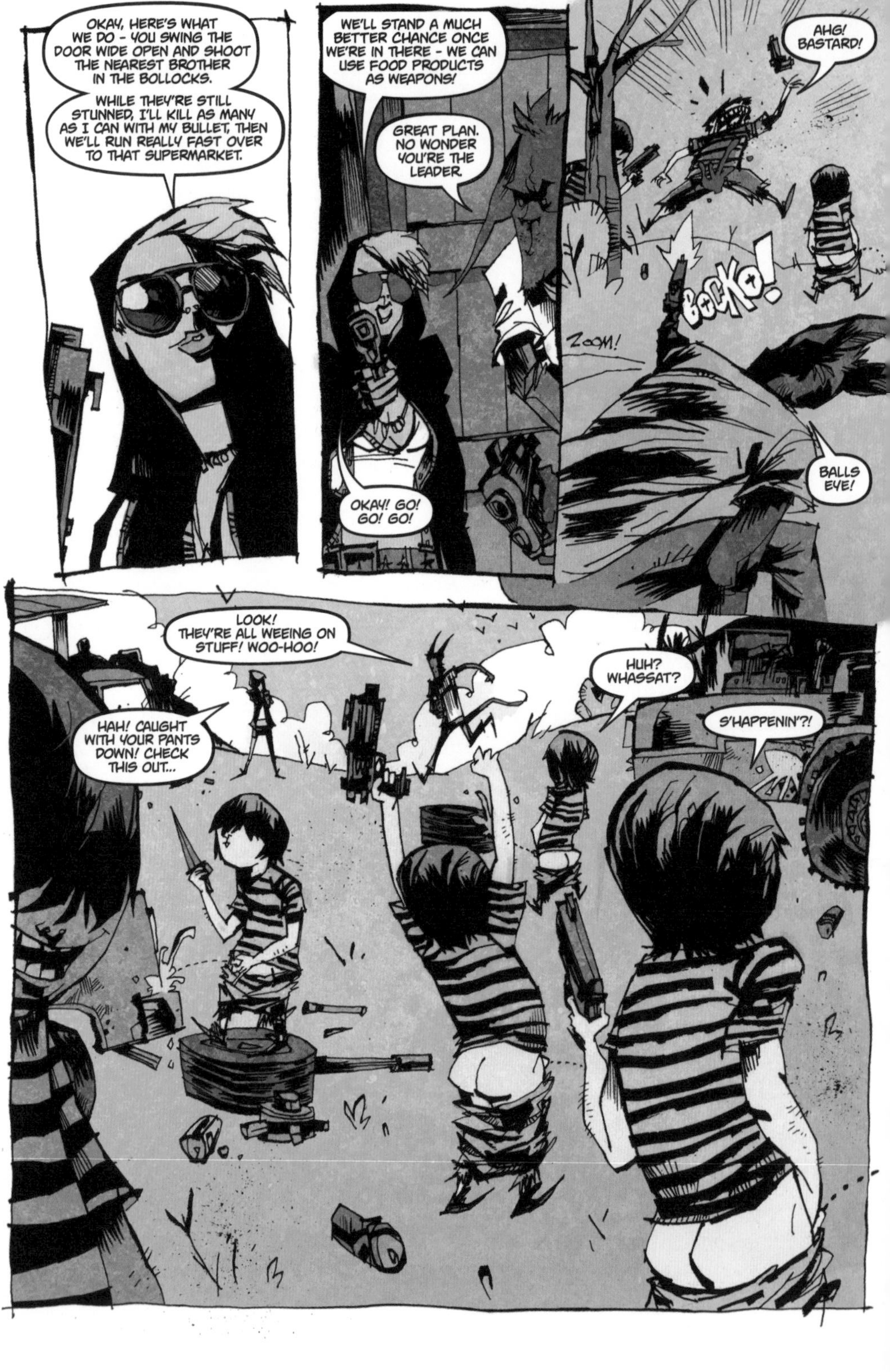
OKAY, HERE'S WHAT WE DO - YOU SWING THE DOOR WIDE OPEN AND SHOOT THE NEAREST BROTHER IN THE BOLLOCKS.
WHILE THEY'RE STILL STUNNED, I'LL KILL AS MANY AS I CAN WITH MY BULLET, THEN WE'LL RUN REALLY FAST OVER TO THAT SUPERMARKET.
WE'LL STAND A MUCH BETTER CHANCE ONCE WE'RE IN THERE - WE CAN USE FOOD PRODUCTS AS WEAPONS!
GREAT PLAN. NO WONDER YOU'RE THE LEADER.
OKAY! GO! GO! GO!
AHG! BASTARD!
BOCKO!
ZOOM!
BALLS EYE!
LOOK! THEY'RE ALL WEEING ON STUFF! WOO-HOO!
HAH! CAUGHT WITH YOUR PANTS DOWN! CHECK THIS OUT...
HUH? WHASSAT?
S'HAPPENIN'?!

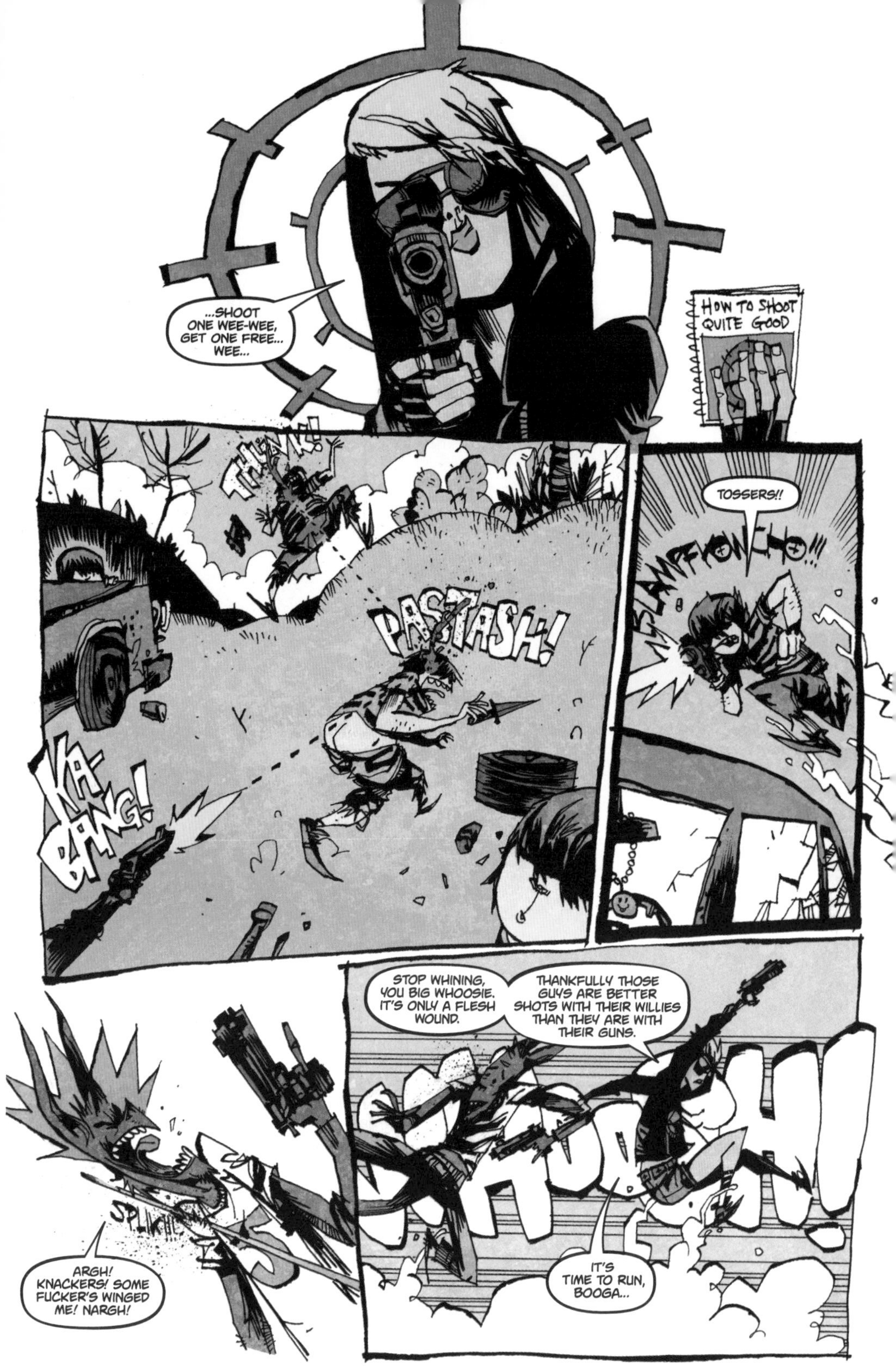
...SHOOT ONE WEE-WEE, GET ONE FREE... WEE...
HOW TO SHOOT QUITE GOOD
PASTASH!
KA-BANG!
TOSSERS!!
STOP WHINING, YOU BIG WHOOSIE. IT'S ONLY A FLESH WOUND.
THANKFULLY THOSE GUYS ARE BETTER SHOTS WITH THEIR WILLIES THAN THEY ARE WITH THEIR GUNS.
ARGH! KNACKERS! SOME FUCKER'S WINGED ME! NARGH!
IT'S TIME TO RUN, BOOGA...

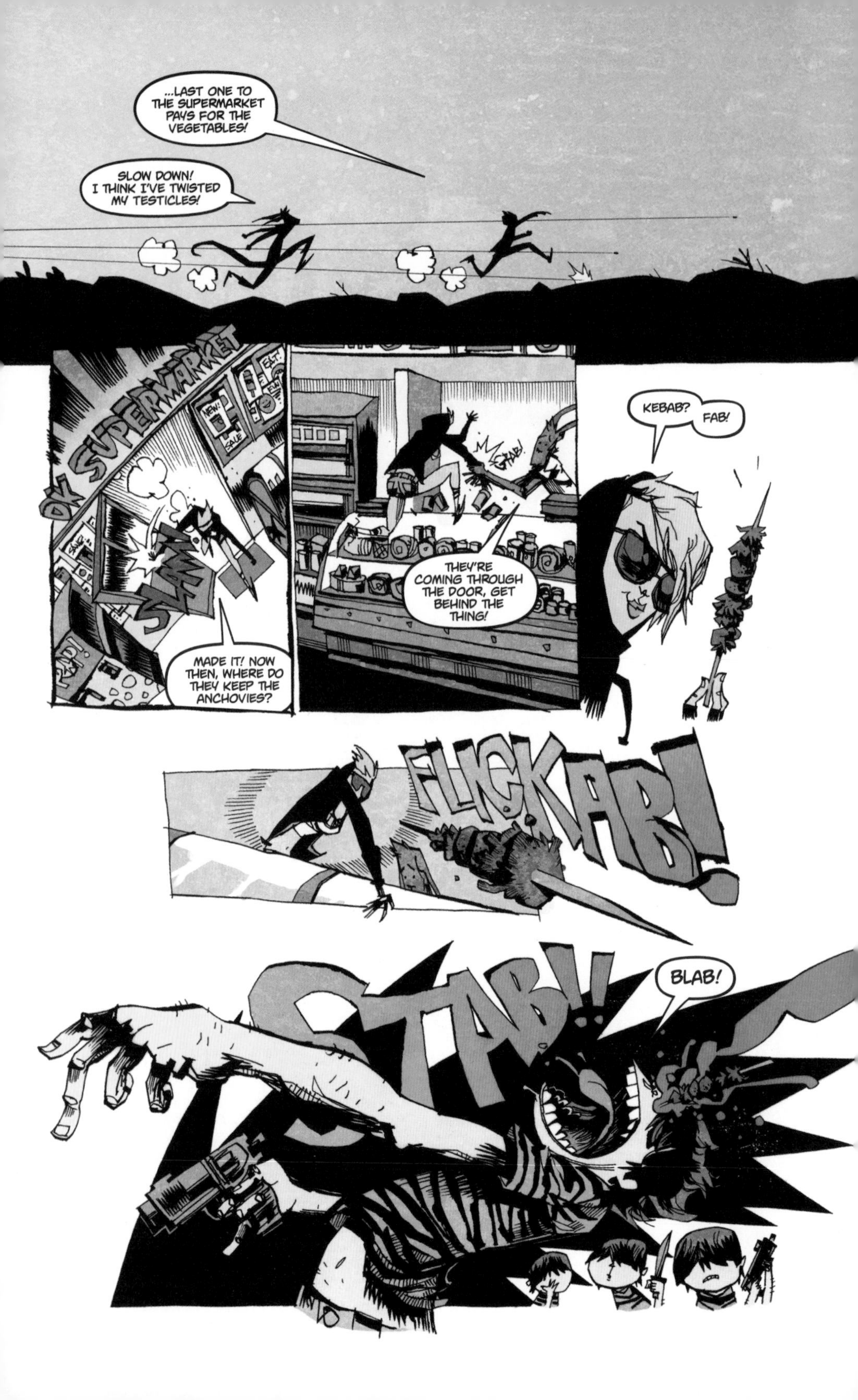
...LAST ONE TO THE SUPERMARKET PAYS FOR THE VEGETABLES!
SLOW DOWN! I THINK I'VE TWISTED MY TESTICLES!
SUPERMARKET
SLAM!
MADE IT! NOW THEN, WHERE DO THEY KEEP THE ANCHOVIES?
STAB!
THEY'RE COMING THROUGH THE DOOR, GET BEHIND THE THING!
KEBAB?
FAB!
FLICKAB!
STAB!!
BLAB!

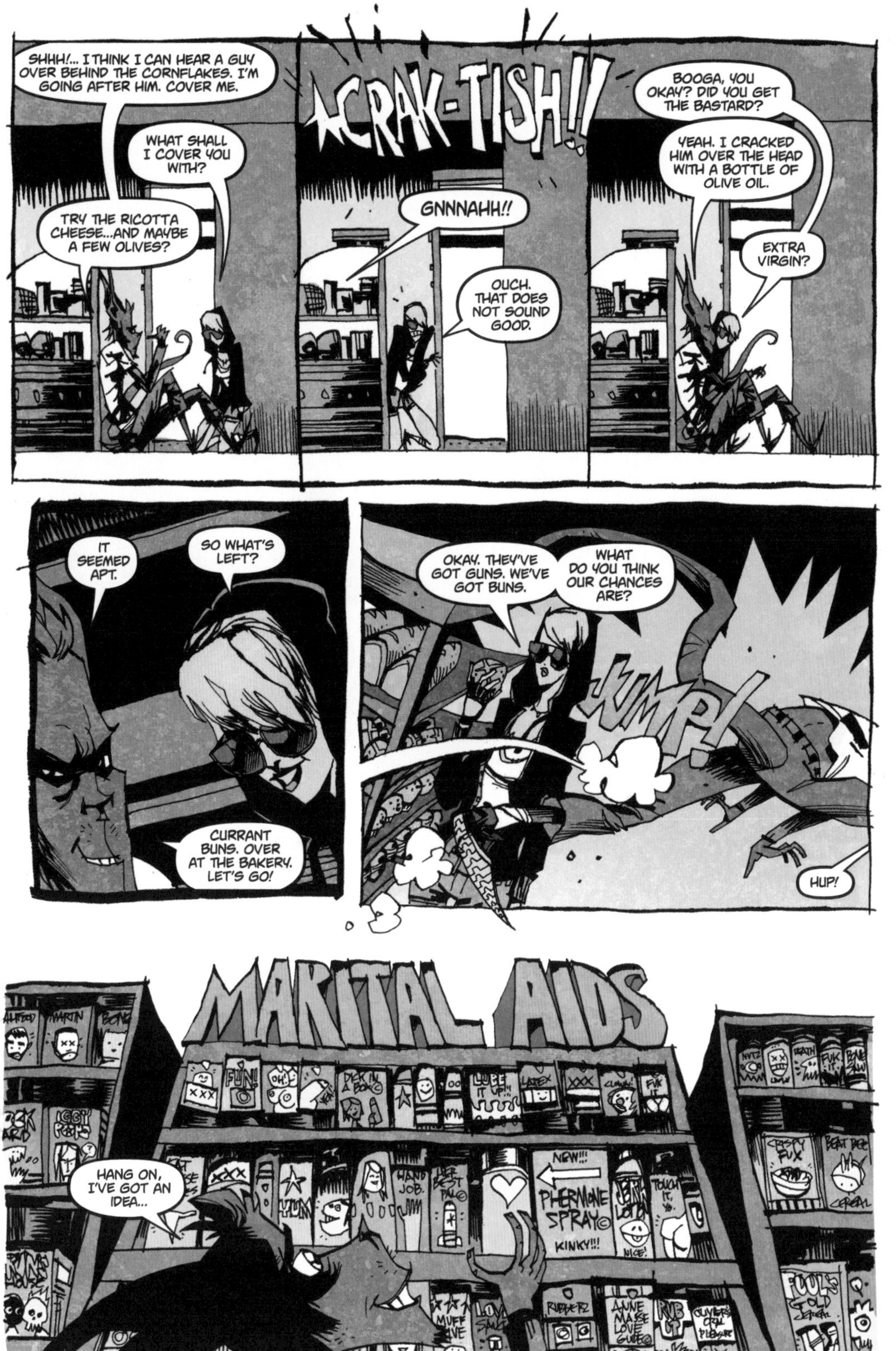
SHHH!... I THINK I CAN HEAR A GUY OVER BEHIND THE CORNFLAKES. I'M GOING AFTER HIM. COVER ME.
WHAT SHALL I COVER YOU WITH?
TRY THE RICOTTA CHEESE...AND MAYBE A FEW OLIVES?
CRAK-TISH!!
GNNNAHH!!
OUCH. THAT DOES NOT SOUND GOOD.
BOOGA, YOU OKAY? DID YOU GET THE BASTARD?
YEAH. I CRACKED HIM OVER THE HEAD WITH A BOTTLE OF OLIVE OIL.
EXTRA VIRGIN?
IT SEEMED APT.
SO WHAT'S LEFT?
CURRANT BUNS. OVER AT THE BAKERY. LET'S GO!
OKAY. THEY'VE GOT GUNS. WE'VE GOT BUNS.
WHAT DO YOU THINK OUR CHANCES ARE?
JUMP!
HUP!
MARITAL AIDS
HANG ON, I'VE GOT AN IDEA...
NEW!!!
PHERMONE SPRAY
KINKY!!!

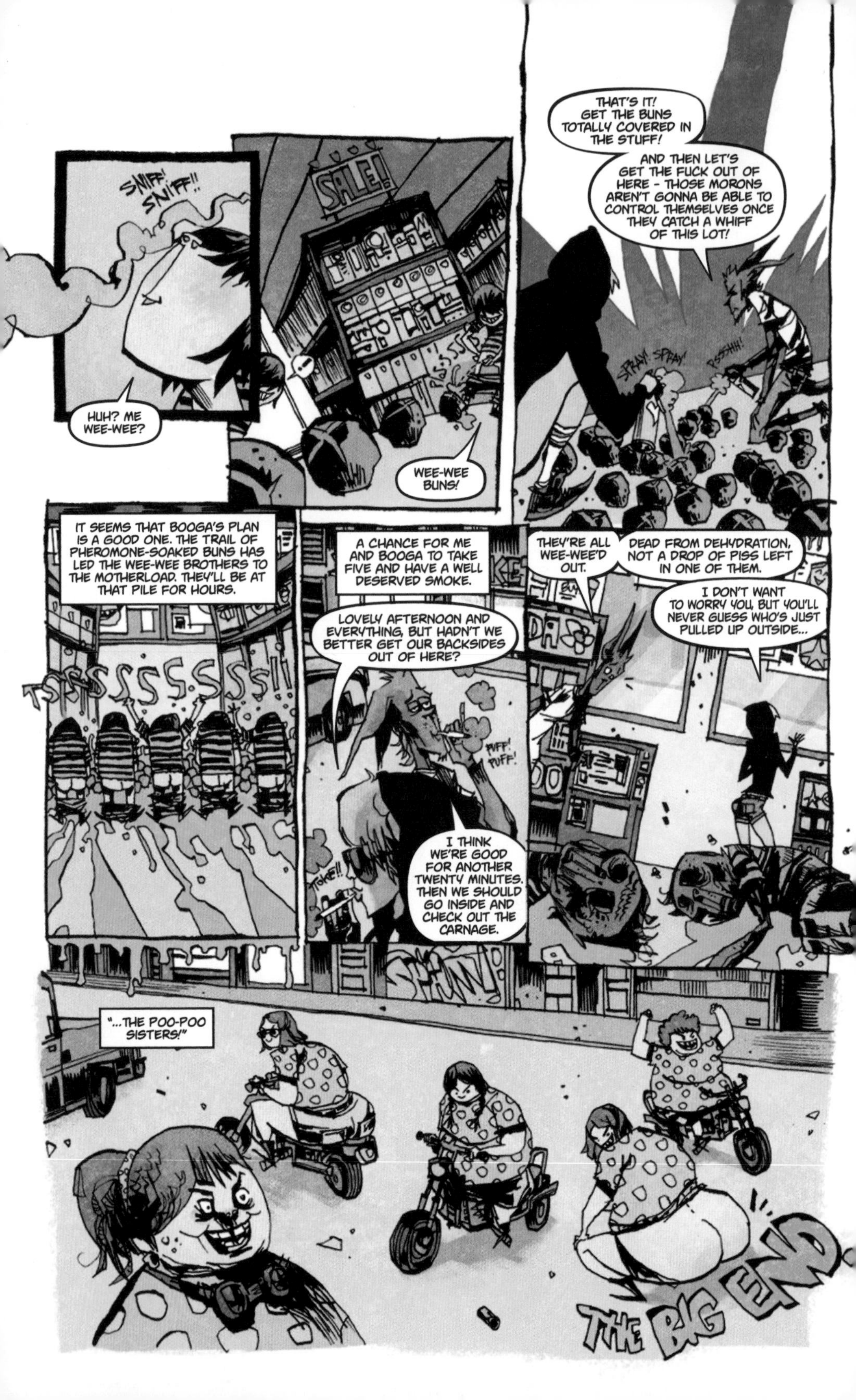
SNIFF! SNIFF!!
HUH? ME WEE-WEE?
SALE!
WEE-WEE BUNS!
THAT'S IT! GET THE BUNS TOTALLY COVERED IN THE STUFF!
AND THEN LET'S GET THE FUCK OUT OF HERE - THOSE MORONS AREN'T GONNA BE ABLE TO CONTROL THEMSELVES ONCE THEY CATCH A WHIFF OF THIS LOT!
SPRAY! SPRAY!
PSSSHH!
IT SEEMS THAT BOOGA'S PLAN IS A GOOD ONE. THE TRAIL OF PHEROMONE-SOAKED BUNS HAS LED THE WEE-WEE BROTHERS TO THE MOTHERLOAD. THEY'LL BE AT THAT PILE FOR HOURS.
TSSSSSSSSSHH!
A CHANCE FOR ME AND BOOGA TO TAKE FIVE AND HAVE A WELL DESERVED SMOKE.
LOVELY AFTERNOON AND EVERYTHING, BUT HADN'T WE BETTER GET OUR BACKSIDES OUT OF HERE?
PUFF! PUFF!
TOKE!!
I THINK WE'RE GOOD FOR ANOTHER TWENTY MINUTES. THEN WE SHOULD GO INSIDE AND CHECK OUT THE CARNAGE.
THEY'RE ALL WEE-WEE'D OUT.
DEAD FROM DEHYDRATION, NOT A DROP OF PISS LEFT IN ONE OF THEM.
I DON'T WANT TO WORRY YOU, BUT YOU'LL NEVER GUESS WHO'S JUST PULLED UP OUTSIDE...
"...THE POO-POO SISTERS!"
THE BIG END.

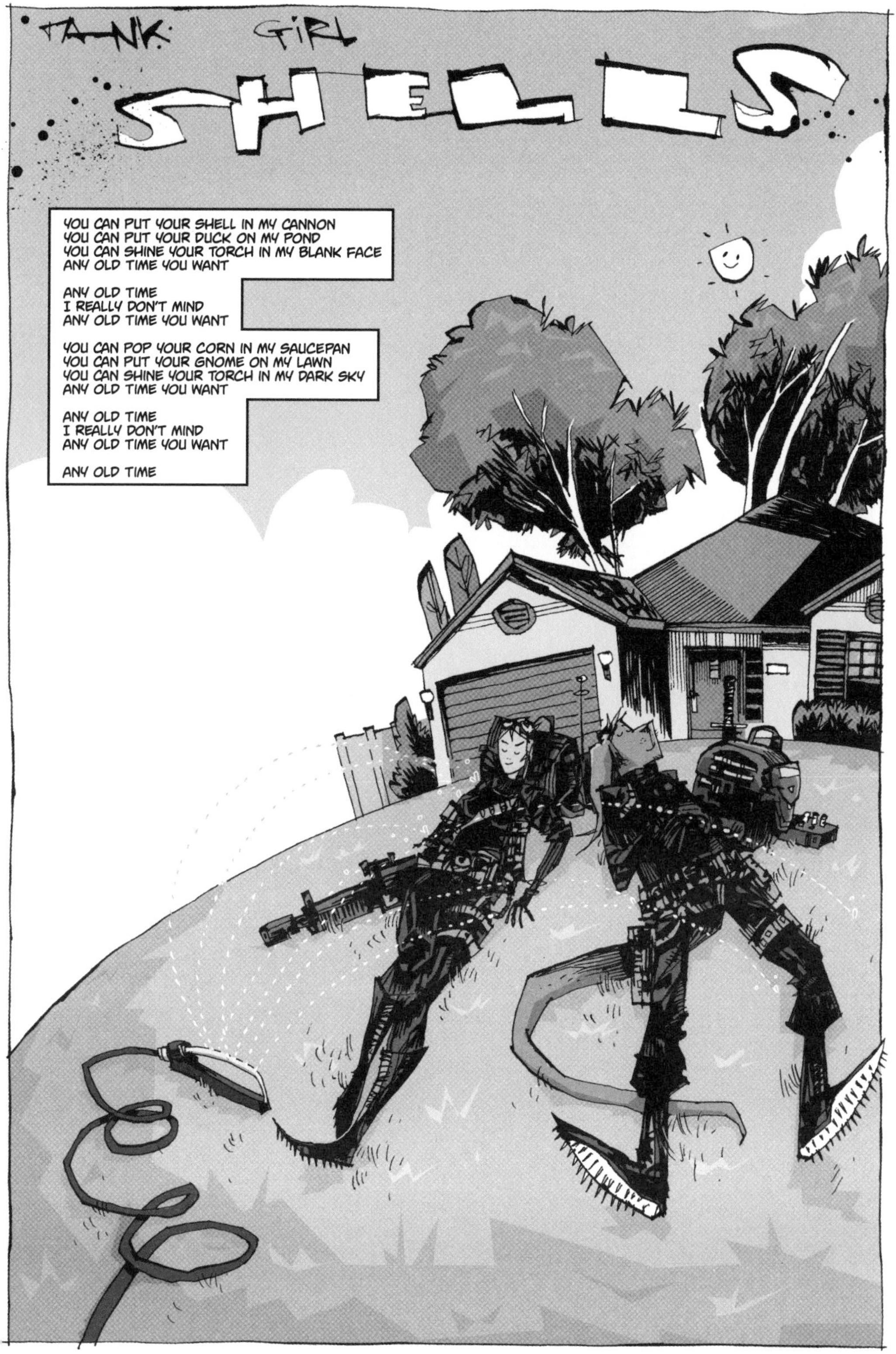
TANK GIRL
SHELLS
YOU CAN PUT YOUR SHELL IN MY CANNON
YOU CAN PUT YOUR DUCK ON MY POND
YOU CAN SHINE YOUR TORCH IN MY BLANK FACE
ANY OLD TIME YOU WANT
ANY OLD TIME
I REALLY DON'T MIND
ANY OLD TIME YOU WANT
YOU CAN POP YOUR CORN IN MY SAUCEPAN
YOU CAN PUT YOUR GNOME ON MY LAWN
YOU CAN SHINE YOUR TORCH IN MY DARK SKY
ANY OLD TIME YOU WANT
ANY OLD TIME
I REALLY DON'T MIND
ANY OLD TIME YOU WANT
ANY OLD TIME

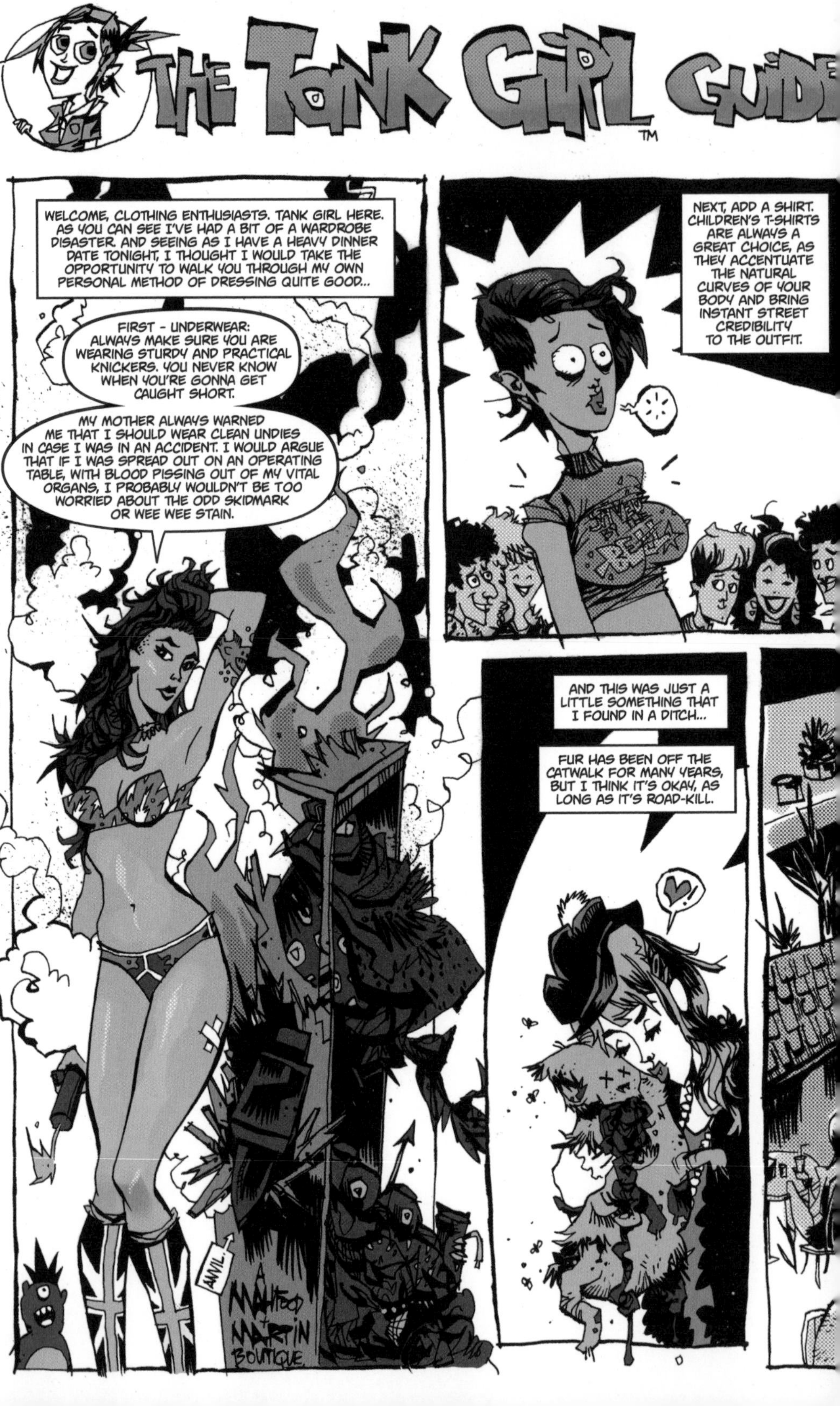
THE TANK GIRL GUIDE
TM
WELCOME, CLOTHING ENTHUSIASTS. TANK GIRL HERE. AS YOU CAN SEE I'VE HAD A BIT OF A WARDROBE DISASTER, AND SEEING AS I HAVE A HEAVY DINNER DATE TONIGHT, I THOUGHT I WOULD TAKE THE OPPORTUNITY TO WALK YOU THROUGH MY OWN PERSONAL METHOD OF DRESSING QUITE GOOD...
FIRST - UNDERWEAR: ALWAYS MAKE SURE YOU ARE WEARING STURDY AND PRACTICAL KNICKERS. YOU NEVER KNOW WHEN YOU'RE GONNA GET CAUGHT SHORT.
MY MOTHER ALWAYS WARNED ME THAT I SHOULD WEAR CLEAN UNDIES IN CASE I WAS IN AN ACCIDENT. I WOULD ARGUE THAT IF I WAS SPREAD OUT ON AN OPERATING TABLE, WITH BLOOD PISSING OUT OF MY VITAL ORGANS, I PROBABLY WOULDN'T BE TOO WORRIED ABOUT THE ODD SKIDMARK OR WEE WEE STAIN.
ANVIL.
MAHFOOD + MARTIN BOUTIQUE
NEXT, ADD A SHIRT. CHILDREN'S T-SHIRTS ARE ALWAYS A GREAT CHOICE, AS THEY ACCENTUATE THE NATURAL CURVES OF YOUR BODY AND BRING INSTANT STREET CREDIBILITY TO THE OUTFIT.
AND THIS WAS JUST A LITTLE SOMETHING THAT I FOUND IN A DITCH...
FUR HAS BEEN OFF THE CATWALK FOR MANY YEARS, BUT I THINK IT'S OKAY, AS LONG AS IT'S ROAD-KILL.

HOW TO DRESS QUITE GOOD ©

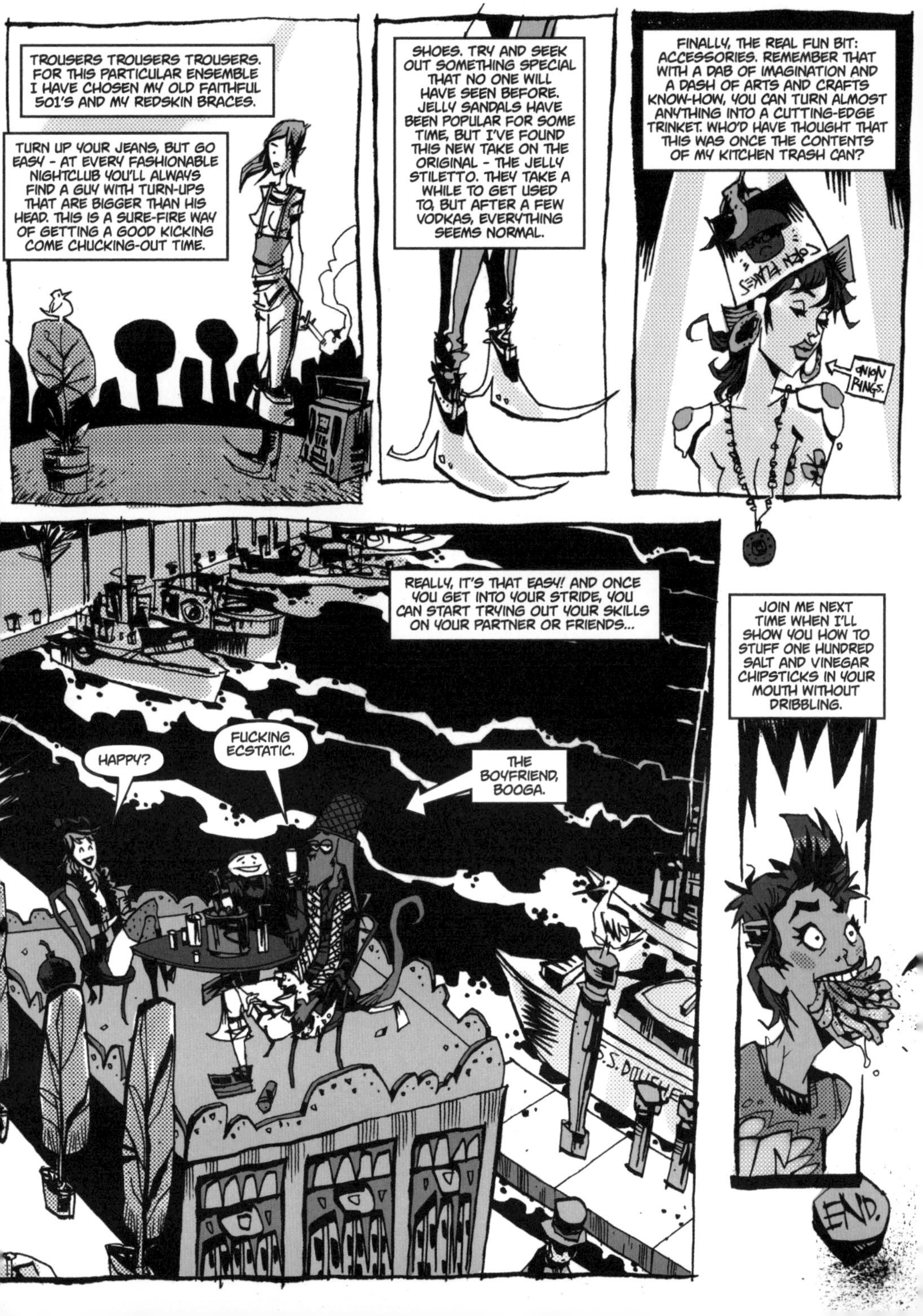

TROUSERS TROUSERS TROUSERS. FOR THIS PARTICULAR ENSEMBLE I HAVE CHOSEN MY OLD FAITHFUL 501'S AND MY REDSKIN BRACES.
TURN UP YOUR JEANS, BUT GO EASY - AT EVERY FASHIONABLE NIGHTCLUB YOU'LL ALWAYS FIND A GUY WITH TURN-UPS THAT ARE BIGGER THAN HIS HEAD. THIS IS A SURE-FIRE WAY OF GETTING A GOOD KICKING COME CHUCKING-OUT TIME.
SHOES. TRY AND SEEK OUT SOMETHING SPECIAL THAT NO ONE WILL HAVE SEEN BEFORE. JELLY SANDALS HAVE BEEN POPULAR FOR SOME TIME, BUT I'VE FOUND THIS NEW TAKE ON THE ORIGINAL - THE JELLY STILETTO. THEY TAKE A WHILE TO GET USED TO, BUT AFTER A FEW VODKAS, EVERYTHING SEEMS NORMAL.
FINALLY, THE REAL FUN BIT: ACCESSORIES. REMEMBER THAT WITH A DAB OF IMAGINATION AND A DASH OF ARTS AND CRAFTS KNOW-HOW, YOU CAN TURN ALMOST ANYTHING INTO A CUTTING-EDGE TRINKET. WHO'D HAVE THOUGHT THAT THIS WAS ONCE THE CONTENTS OF MY KITCHEN TRASH CAN?
ONION RINGS.
REALLY, IT'S THAT EASY! AND ONCE YOU GET INTO YOUR STRIDE, YOU CAN START TRYING OUT YOUR SKILLS ON YOUR PARTNER OR FRIENDS...
HAPPY?
FUCKING ECSTATIC.
THE BOYFRIEND, BOOGA.
JOIN ME NEXT TIME WHEN I'LL SHOW YOU HOW TO STUFF ONE HUNDRED SALT AND VINEGAR CHIPSTICKS IN YOUR MOUTH WITHOUT DRIBBLING.
END.

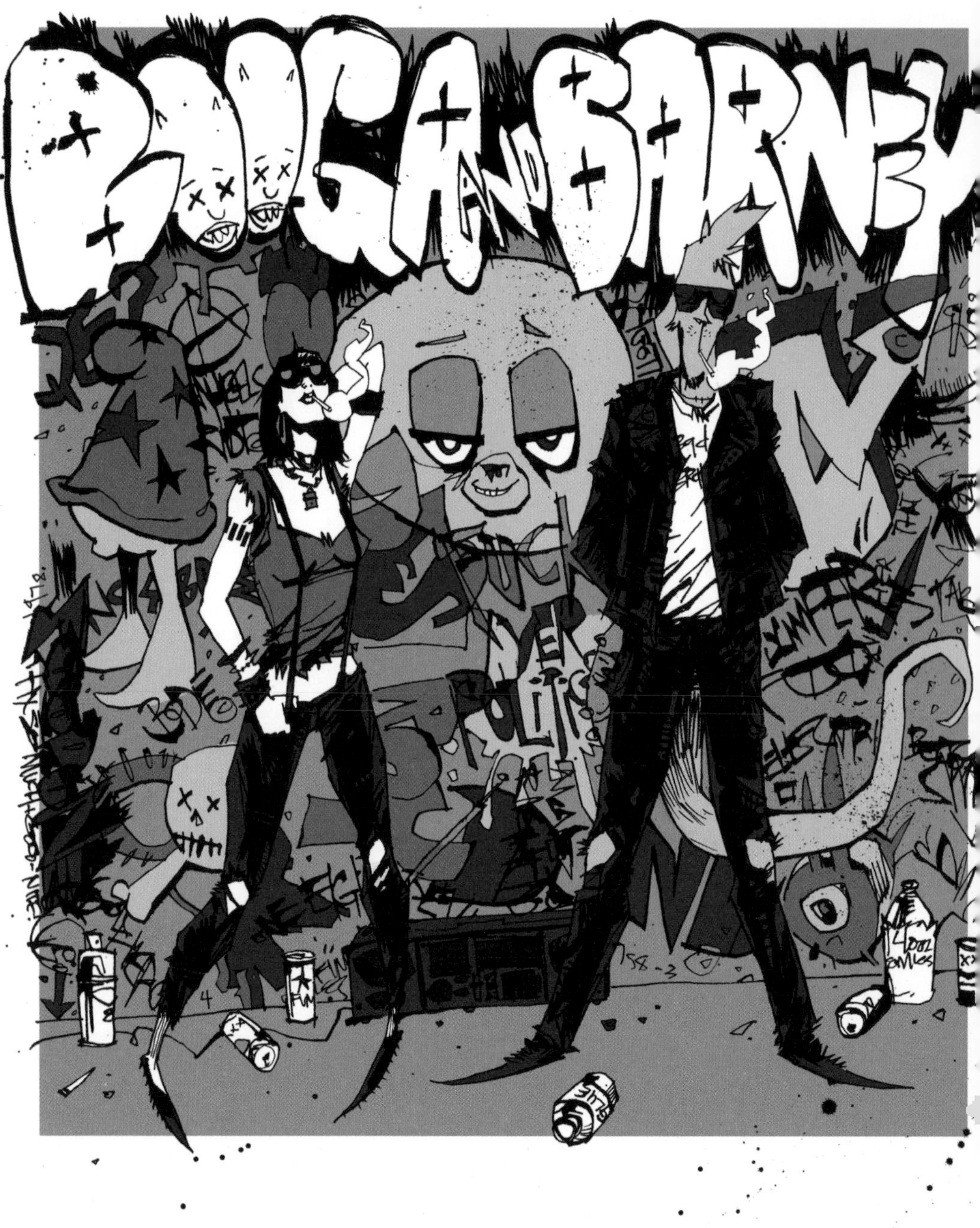
BOOGA AND BARNEY

THEY WERE ALMOST AN ITEM ONCE. BOOGA AND BARNEY. BOOGA HAD FUCKED ME OFF TO THE POINT WHERE I HAD TO LEAVE HIM TO IT FOR A FEW DAYS. IT DIDN'T TAKE LONG FOR HIM TO TOTALLY FORGET HE WAS MEANT TO BE WITH ME AND HIS DICK STARTED TWITCHING IN BARNEY'S DIRECTION. AS YOU MAY WELL KNOW, SHE IS A WOMAN OF VERY LOW MORAL STANDARDS, SO SHE HARDLY EVEN NOTICED WHEN HE STARTED RUBBING UP AGAINST HER LEG LIKE A RANDY DOG. I CAME HOME TO FIND THEM HALF-NAKED ON THE SOFA, ABOUT TO ENGAGE IN SOME KIND OF MINDLESS COPULATION. I POURED HALF A KEG OF ICE-COLD BEER OVER THEM AND THEY SOON SNAPPED OUT OF THEIR STUPOR. SOMETIMES I WISH I'D DRUNK THE BEER INSTEAD.

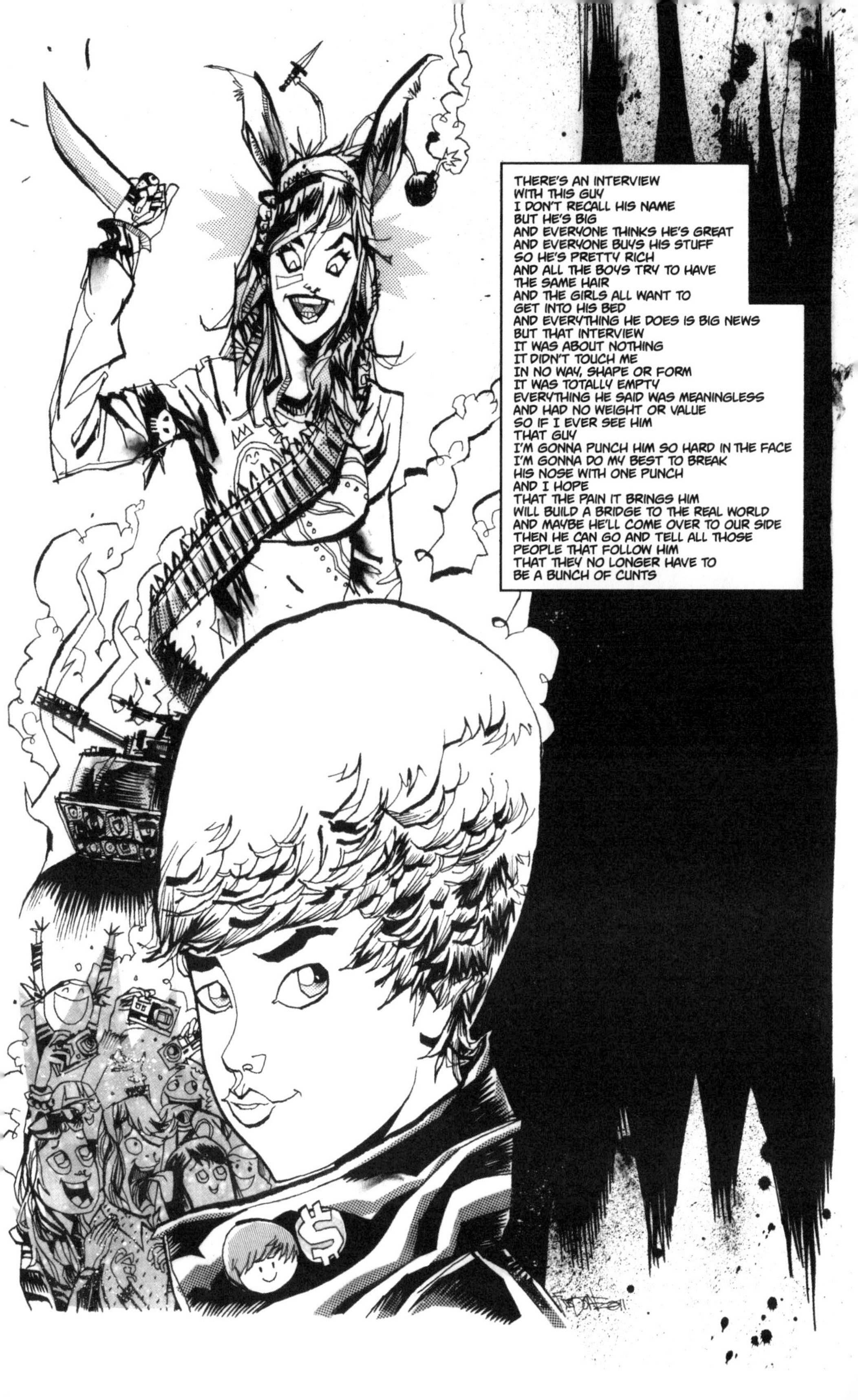
THERE'S AN INTERVIEW
WITH THIS GUY
I DON'T RECALL HIS NAME
BUT HE'S BIG
AND EVERYONE THINKS HE'S GREAT
AND EVERYONE BUYS HIS STUFF
SO HE'S PRETTY RICH
AND ALL THE BOYS TRY TO HAVE
THE SAME HAIR
AND THE GIRLS ALL WANT TO
GET INTO HIS BED
AND EVERYTHING HE DOES IS BIG NEWS
BUT THAT INTERVIEW
IT WAS ABOUT NOTHING
IT DIDN'T TOUCH ME
IN NO WAY, SHAPE OR FORM
IT WAS TOTALLY EMPTY
EVERYTHING HE SAID WAS MEANINGLESS
AND HAD NO WEIGHT OR VALUE
SO IF I EVER SEE HIM
THAT GUY
I'M GONNA PUNCH HIM SO HARD IN THE FACE
I'M GONNA DO MY BEST TO BREAK
HIS NOSE WITH ONE PUNCH
AND I HOPE
THAT THE PAIN IT BRINGS HIM
WILL BUILD A BRIDGE TO THE REAL WORLD
AND MAYBE HE'LL COME OVER TO OUR SIDE
THEN HE CAN GO AND TELL ALL THOSE
PEOPLE THAT FOLLOW HIM
THAT THEY NO LONGER HAVE TO
BE A BUNCH OF CUNTS

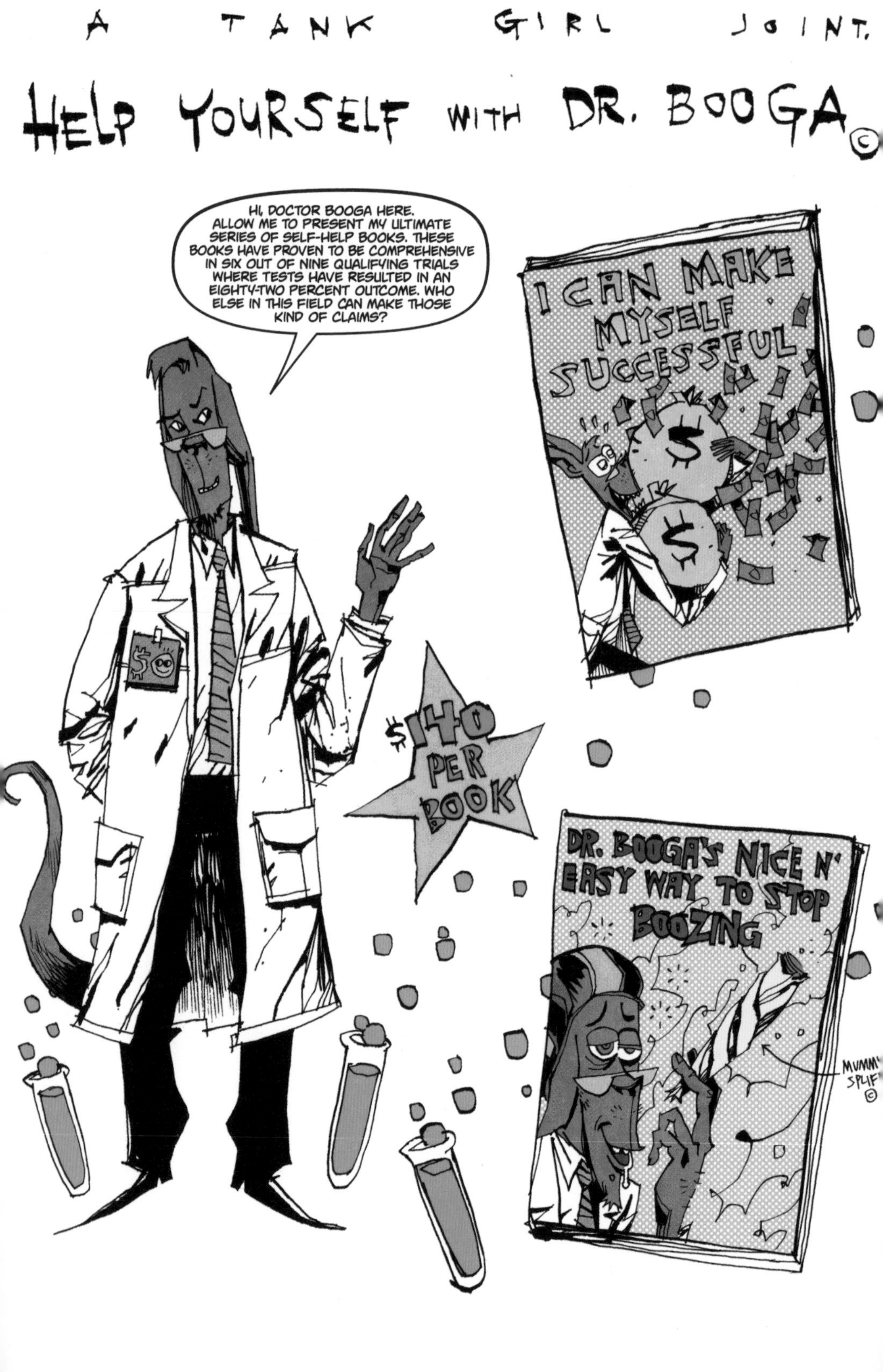
A TANK GIRL JOINT.
HELP YOURSELF WITH DR. BOOGA ©
HI, DOCTOR BOOGA HERE. ALLOW ME TO PRESENT MY ULTIMATE SERIES OF SELF-HELP BOOKS. THESE BOOKS HAVE PROVEN TO BE COMPREHENSIVE IN SIX OUT OF NINE QUALIFYING TRIALS WHERE TESTS HAVE RESULTED IN AN EIGHTY-TWO PERCENT OUTCOME. WHO ELSE IN THIS FIELD CAN MAKE THOSE KIND OF CLAIMS?
I CAN MAKE MYSELF SUCCESSFUL
$140 PER BOOK
DR. BOOGA'S NICE N' EASY WAY TO STOP BOOZING

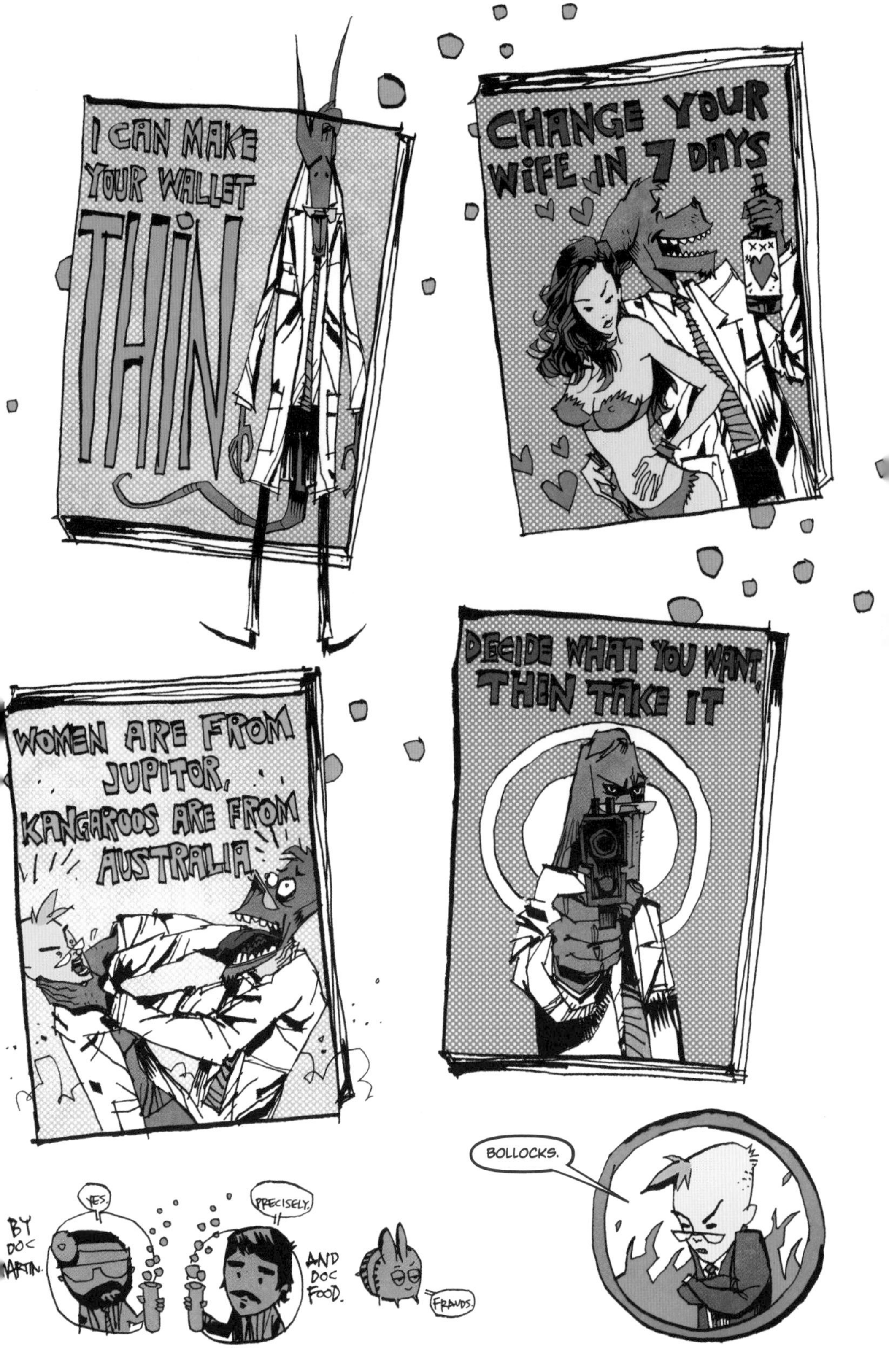
I CAN MAKE YOUR WALLET THIN
CHANGE YOUR WIFE IN 7 DAYS
WOMEN ARE FROM JUPITOR, KANGAROOS ARE FROM AUSTRALIA
DECIDE WHAT YOU WANT, THEN TAKE IT
BOLLOCKS.
BY DOC MARTIN.
YES.
PRECISELY.
AND DOC FOOD.
FRANDS.

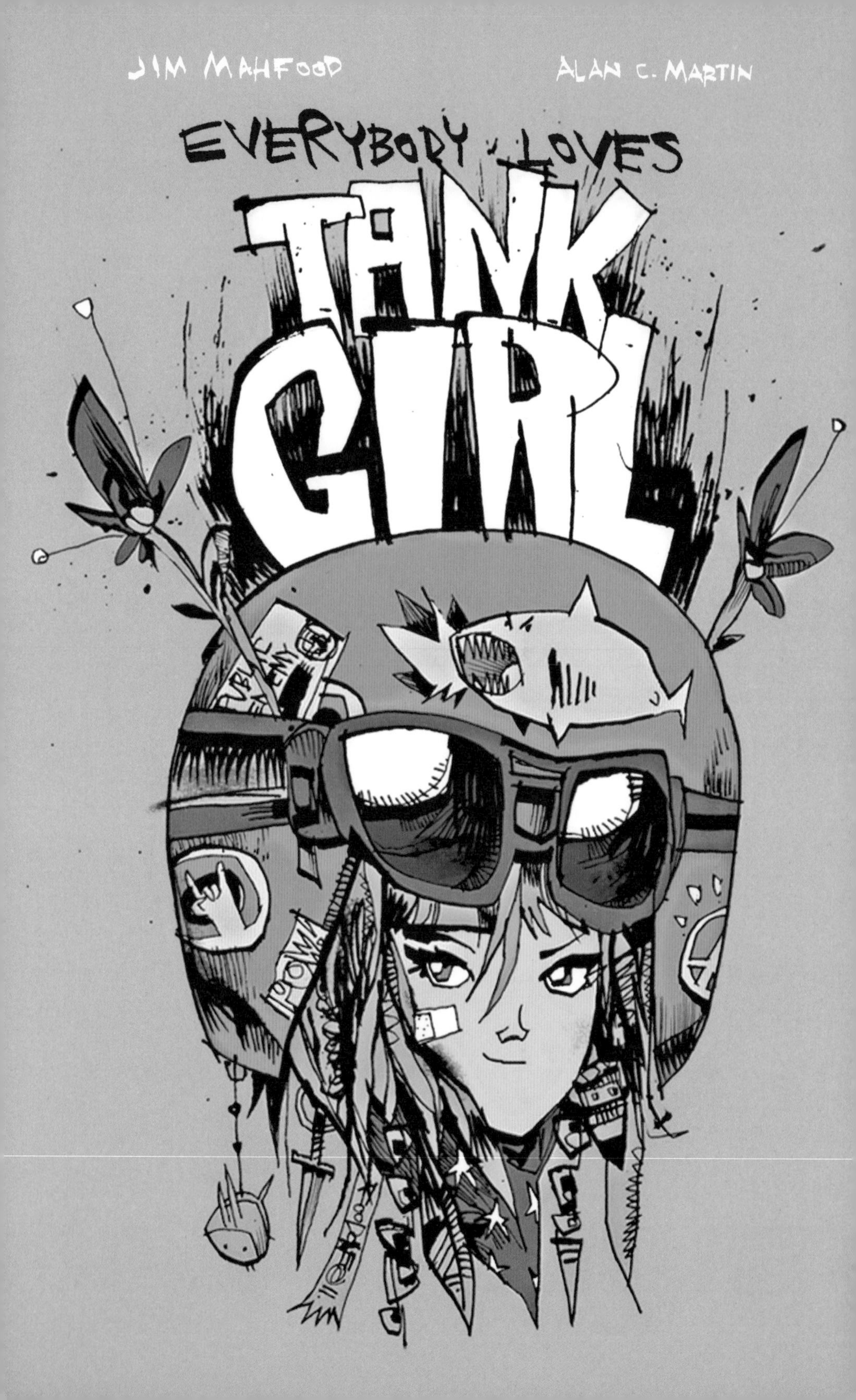
JIM MAHFOOD
ALAN C. MARTIN
EVERYBODY LOVES
TANK GIRL
POW!

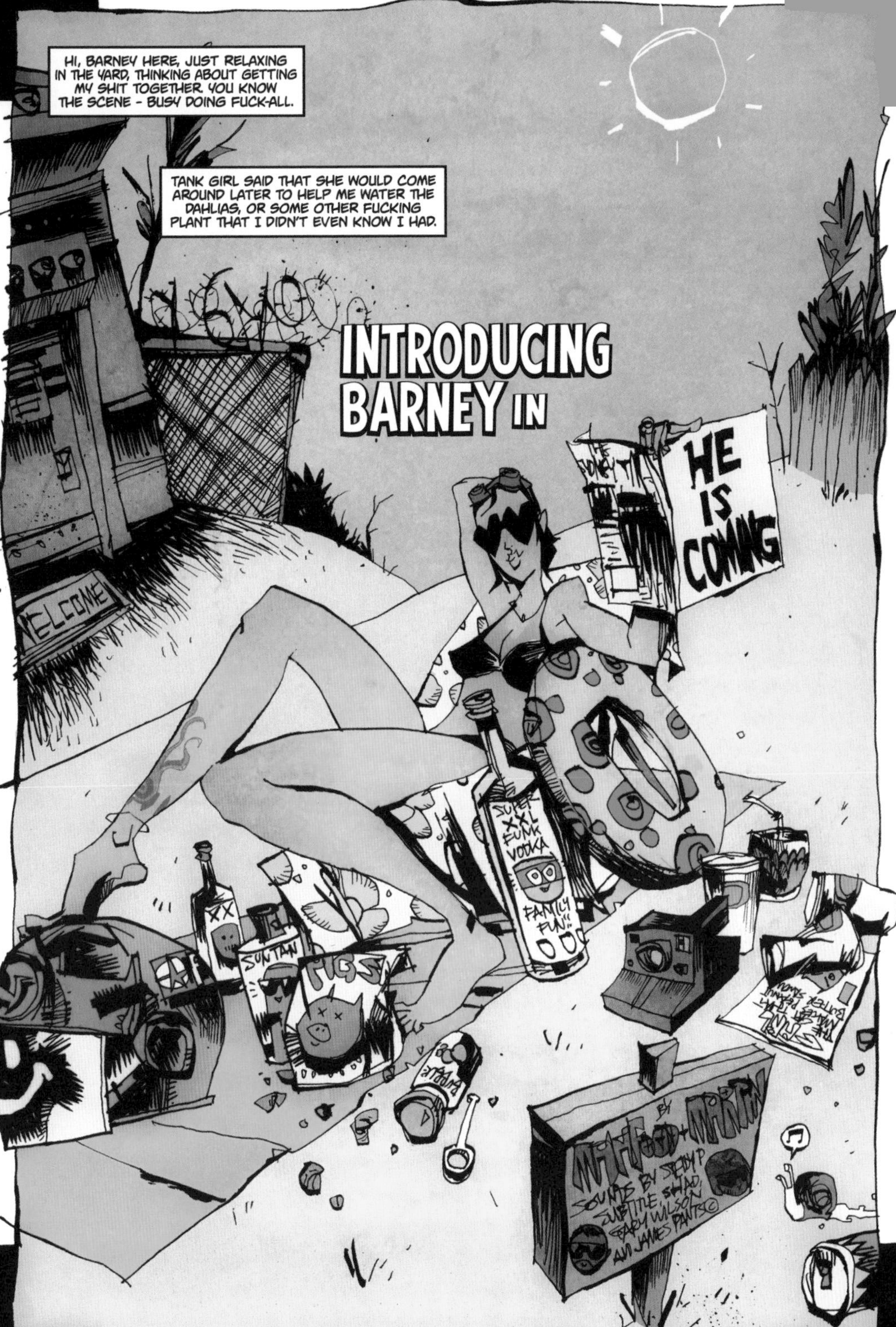
HI, BARNEY HERE, JUST RELAXING IN THE YARD, THINKING ABOUT GETTING MY SHIT TOGETHER. YOU KNOW THE SCENE – BUSY DOING FUCK-ALL.
TANK GIRL SAID THAT SHE WOULD COME AROUND LATER TO HELP ME WATER THE DAHLIAS, OR SOME OTHER FUCKING PLANT THAT I DIDN'T EVEN KNOW I HAD.
INTRODUCING BARNEY IN
HE IS COMING
WELCOME
SUPER XXL FUNK VODKA
FAMILY FUN!!
SUNTAN
PIGS
BY
SOUNDS BY STEADY P
SUBTITLE, SHAD,
GARY WILSON
AND JAMES PANTS©

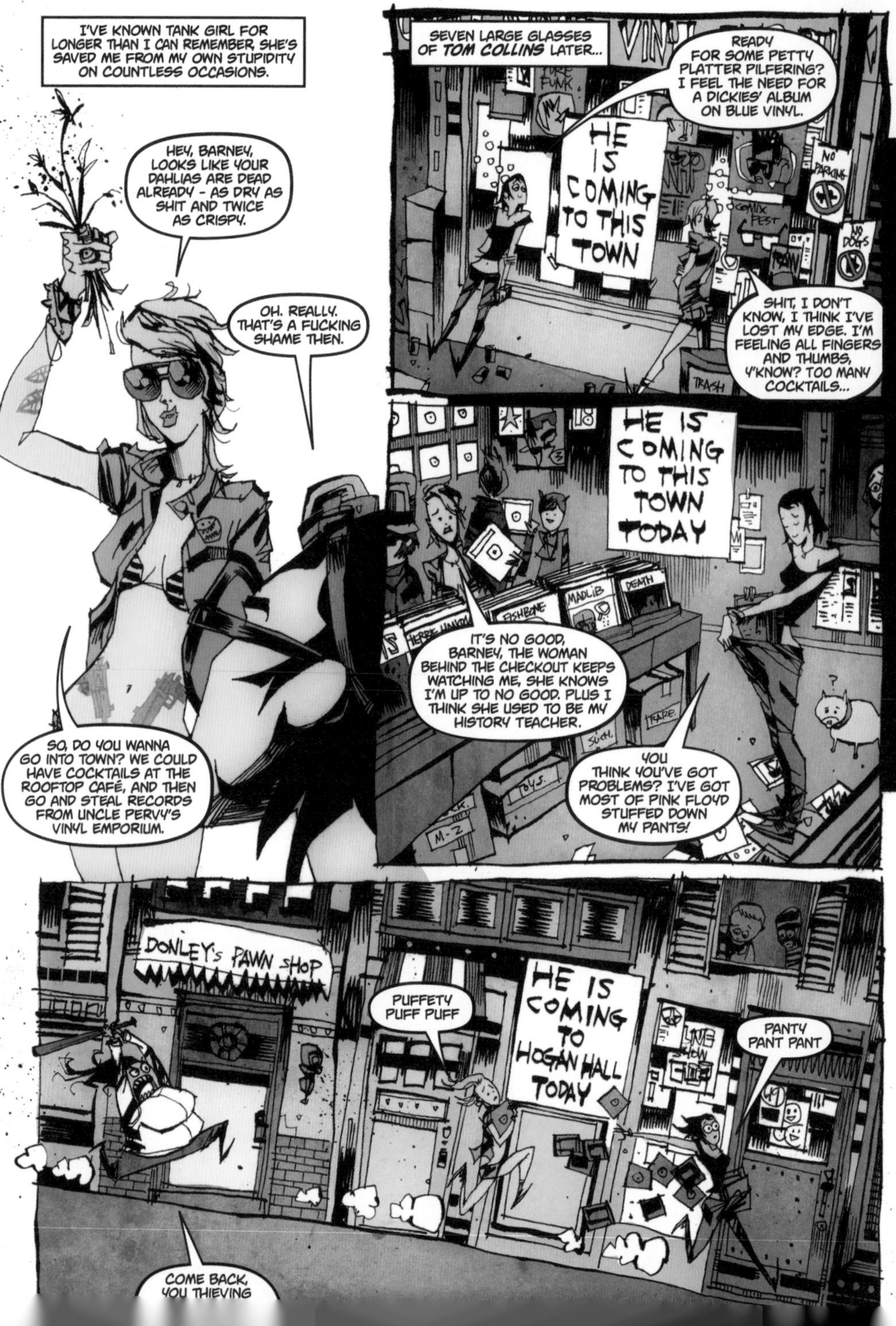
I'VE KNOWN TANK GIRL FOR LONGER THAN I CAN REMEMBER, SHE'S SAVED ME FROM MY OWN STUPIDITY ON COUNTLESS OCCASIONS.
HEY, BARNEY, LOOKS LIKE YOUR DAHLIAS ARE DEAD ALREADY - AS DRY AS SHIT AND TWICE AS CRISPY.
OH. REALLY. THAT'S A FUCKING SHAME THEN.
SO, DO YOU WANNA GO INTO TOWN? WE COULD HAVE COCKTAILS AT THE ROOFTOP CAFÉ, AND THEN GO AND STEAL RECORDS FROM UNCLE PERVY'S VINYL EMPORIUM.
SEVEN LARGE GLASSES OF TOM COLLINS LATER...
HE IS COMING TO THIS TOWN
READY FOR SOME PETTY PLATTER PILFERING? I FEEL THE NEED FOR A DICKIES' ALBUM ON BLUE VINYL.
NO PARKING
COMIX FEST
NO DOGS
SHIT, I DON'T KNOW, I THINK I'VE LOST MY EDGE. I'M FEELING ALL FINGERS AND THUMBS, Y'KNOW? TOO MANY COCKTAILS...
TRASH
HE IS COMING TO THIS TOWN TODAY
FISHBONE
MADLIB
DEATH
IT'S NO GOOD, BARNEY, THE WOMAN BEHIND THE CHECKOUT KEEPS WATCHING ME, SHE KNOWS I'M UP TO NO GOOD. PLUS I THINK SHE USED TO BE MY HISTORY TEACHER.
RARE
TOYS
M-2
YOU THINK YOU'VE GOT PROBLEMS? I'VE GOT MOST OF PINK FLOYD STUFFED DOWN MY PANTS!
DONLEY'S PAWN SHOP
HE IS COMING TO HOGAN HALL TODAY
PUFFETY PUFF PUFF
PANTY PANT PANT
COME BACK, YOU THIEVING

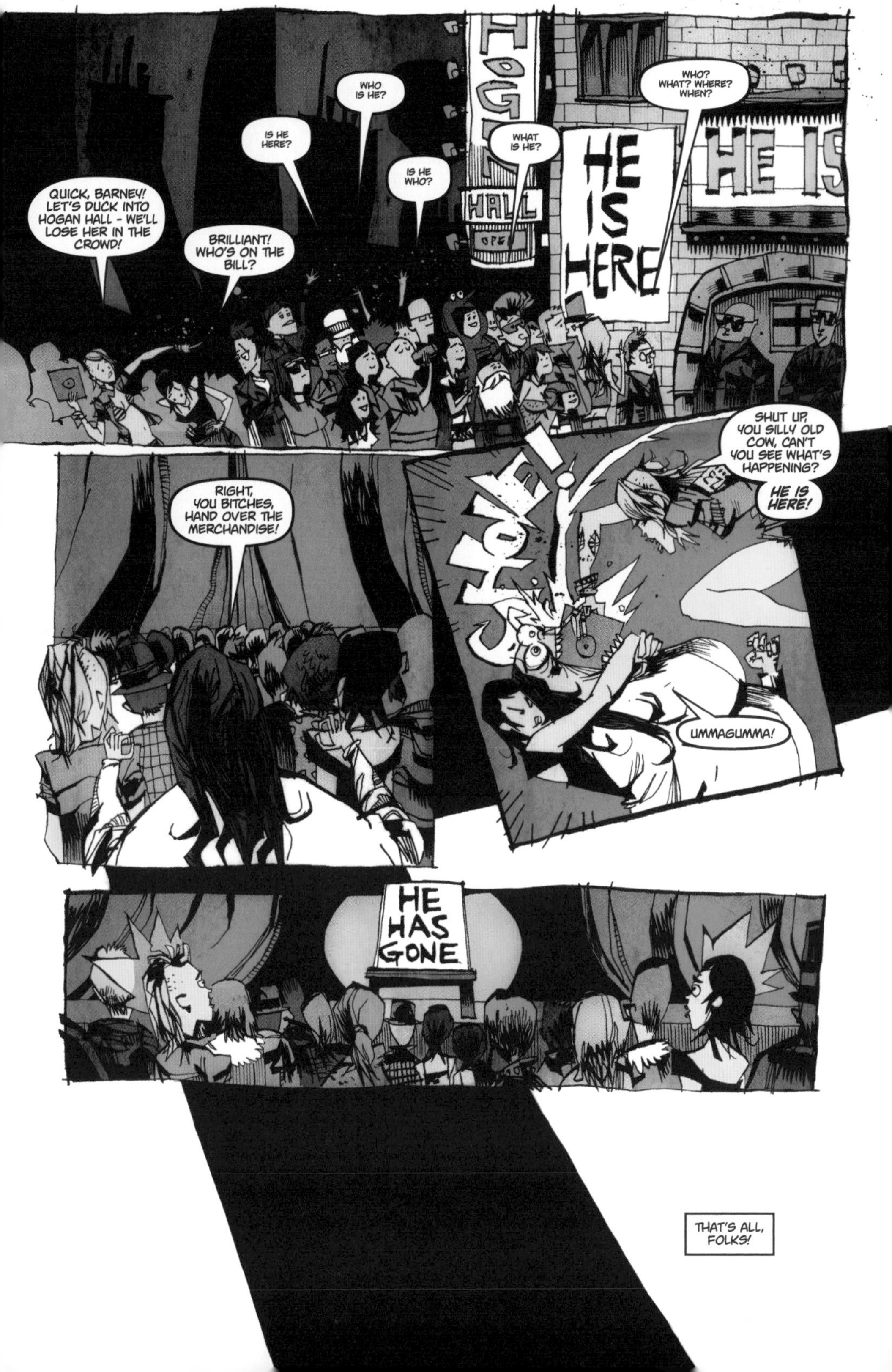
QUICK, BARNEY! LET'S DUCK INTO HOGAN HALL - WE'LL LOSE HER IN THE CROWD!
BRILLIANT! WHO'S ON THE BILL?
IS HE HERE?
WHO IS HE?
IS HE WHO?
HOGAN HALL
WHAT IS HE?
HE IS HERE
WHO? WHAT? WHERE? WHEN?
HE IS
RIGHT, YOU BITCHES, HAND OVER THE MERCHANDISE!
SHUT UP, YOU SILLY OLD COW, CAN'T YOU SEE WHAT'S HAPPENING?
HE IS HERE!
UMMAGUMMA!
HE HAS GONE
THAT'S ALL, FOLKS!

YOURS AYE

I AM

COMPLETELY
UTTERLY
DEVASTATINGLY
BRILLIANTLY
HOPELESSLY
ENDLESSLY
CRAZILY
STEADFASTLY
ROBOTICALLY
RESOLUTELY
REMOTELY
IMMEASURABLY
MADLY
CONSTANTLY
FANTASTICALLY
ABSOLUTELY
STUPIDLY

TRULY

FUCKING

YOURS

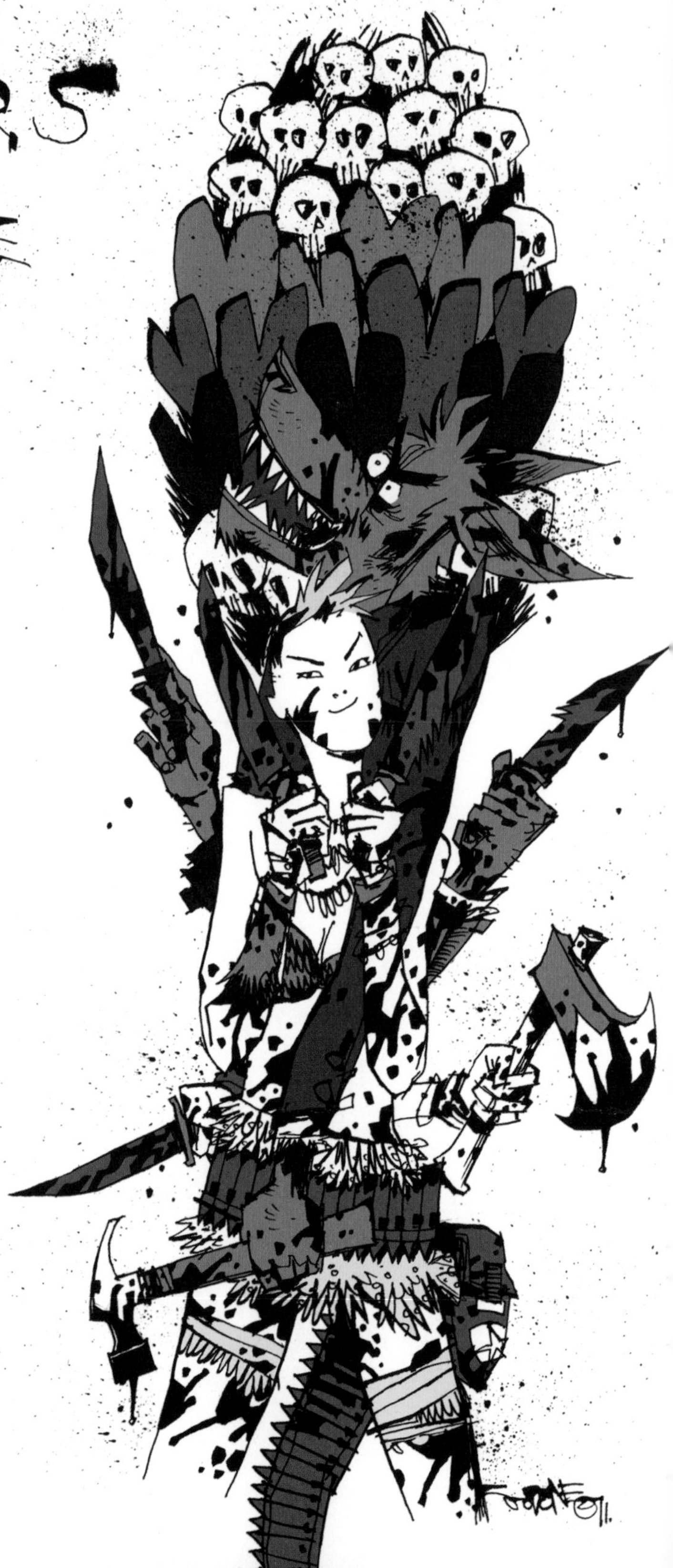

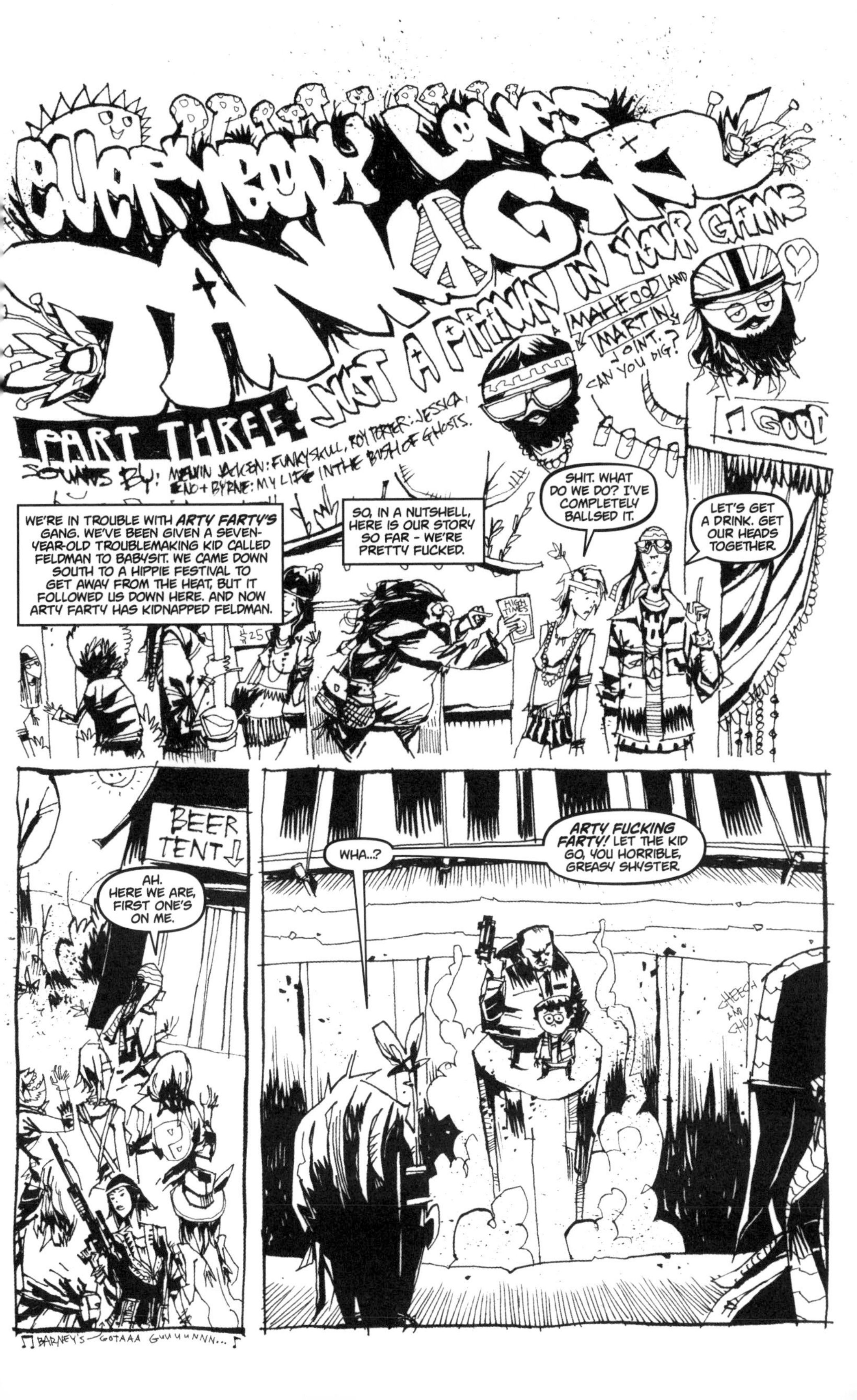

EVERYBODY LOVES TANK GIRL
PART THREE: JUST A PINION IN YOUR GAME
A MAHFOOD AND MARTIN JOINT. CAN YOU DIG?
SOUNDS BY: MELVIN JACKSON: FUNKYSKULL, ROY PORTER: JESSICA. ENO + BYRNE: MY LIFE IN THE BUSH OF GHOSTS.
GOOD
WE'RE IN TROUBLE WITH ARTY FARTY'S GANG. WE'VE BEEN GIVEN A SEVEN-YEAR-OLD TROUBLEMAKING KID CALLED FELDMAN TO BABYSIT. WE CAME DOWN SOUTH TO A HIPPIE FESTIVAL TO GET AWAY FROM THE HEAT, BUT IT FOLLOWED US DOWN HERE. AND NOW ARTY FARTY HAS KIDNAPPED FELDMAN.
SO, IN A NUTSHELL, HERE IS OUR STORY SO FAR - WE'RE PRETTY FUCKED.
HIGH TIMES
SHIT. WHAT DO WE DO? I'VE COMPLETELY BALLSED IT.
LET'S GET A DRINK. GET OUR HEADS TOGETHER.
BEER TENT
AH. HERE WE ARE, FIRST ONE'S ON ME.
BARNEY'S GOTAAA GUUUUNNN...
WHA...?
ARTY FUCKING FARTY! LET THE KID GO, YOU HORRIBLE, GREASY SHYSTER.

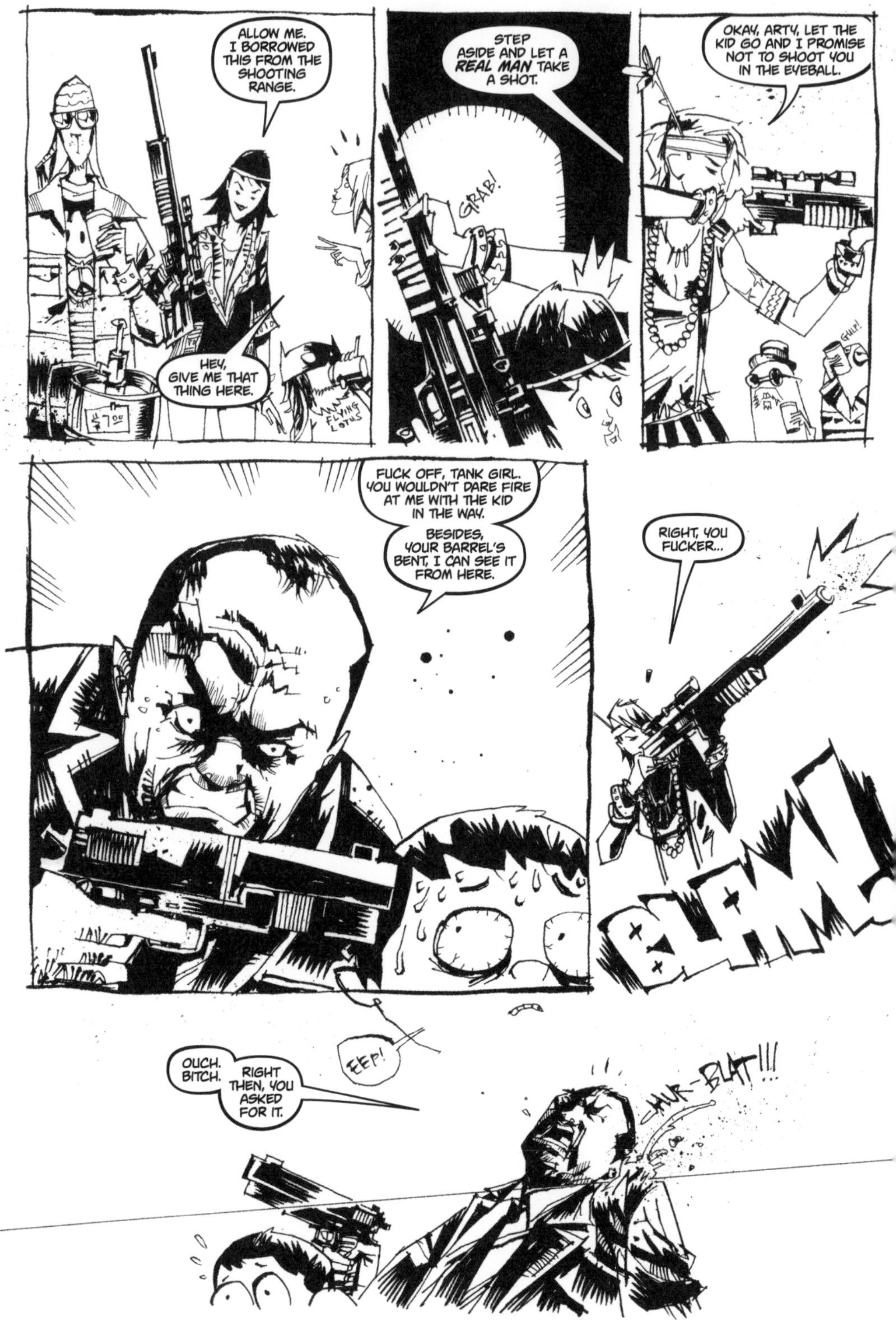
ALLOW ME. I BORROWED THIS FROM THE SHOOTING RANGE.
HEY, GIVE ME THAT THING HERE.
FLYING LOTUS
STEP ASIDE AND LET A REAL MAN TAKE A SHOT.
GRAB!
OKAY, ARTY, LET THE KID GO AND I PROMISE NOT TO SHOOT YOU IN THE EYEBALL.
GULP!
FUCK OFF, TANK GIRL. YOU WOULDN'T DARE FIRE AT ME WITH THE KID IN THE WAY.
BESIDES, YOUR BARREL'S BENT, I CAN SEE IT FROM HERE.
RIGHT, YOU FUCKER...
OUCH. BITCH.
RIGHT THEN, YOU ASKED FOR IT.
EEP!
CHUR-BLAT!!!

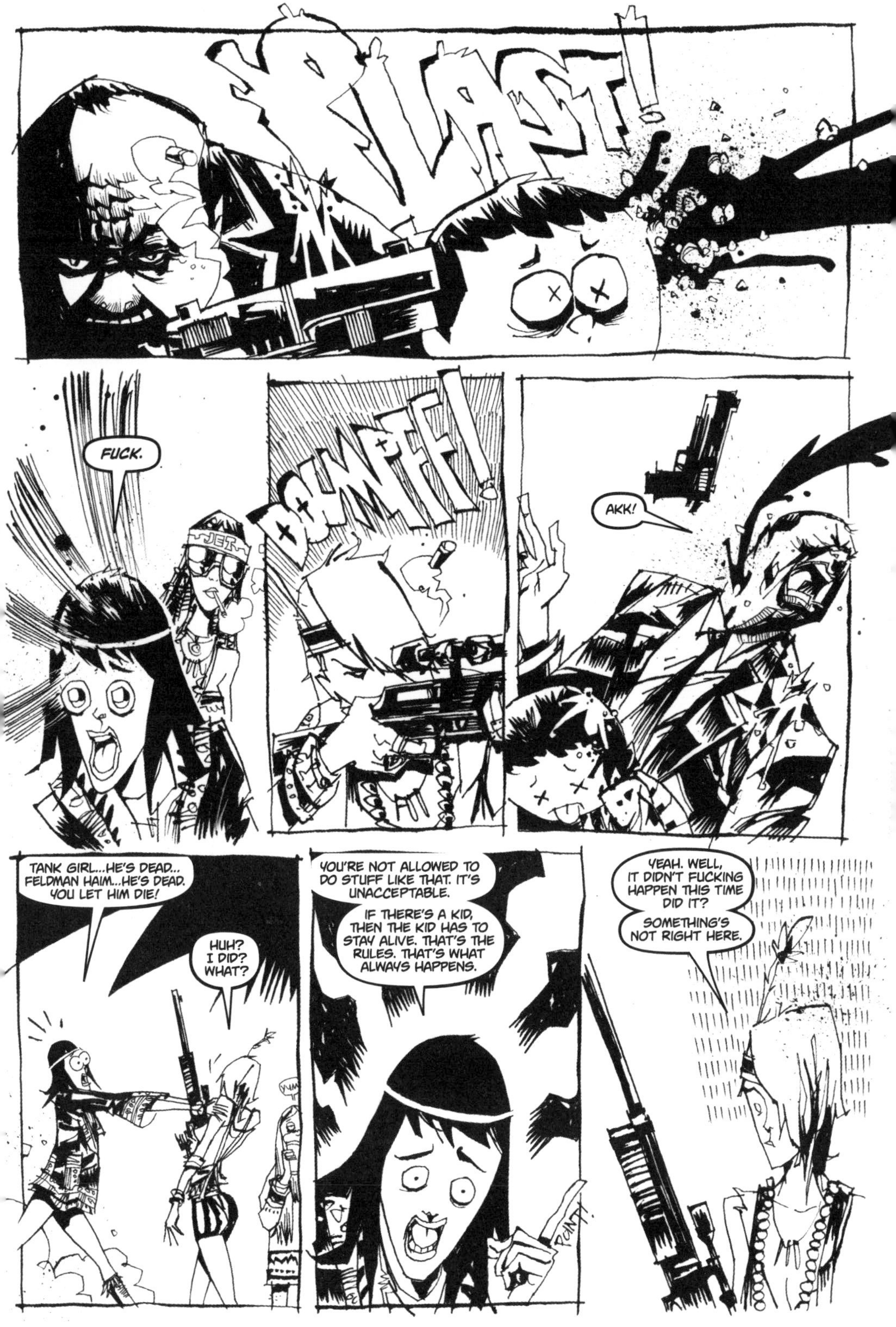
BLAST!
FUCK.
AKK!
TANK GIRL...HE'S DEAD... FELDMAN HAIM...HE'S DEAD. YOU LET HIM DIE!
HUH? I DID? WHAT?
YOU'RE NOT ALLOWED TO DO STUFF LIKE THAT. IT'S UNACCEPTABLE.
IF THERE'S A KID, THEN THE KID HAS TO STAY ALIVE. THAT'S THE RULES. THAT'S WHAT ALWAYS HAPPENS.
POINT!
YEAH. WELL, IT DIDN'T FUCKING HAPPEN THIS TIME DID IT?
SOMETHING'S NOT RIGHT HERE.

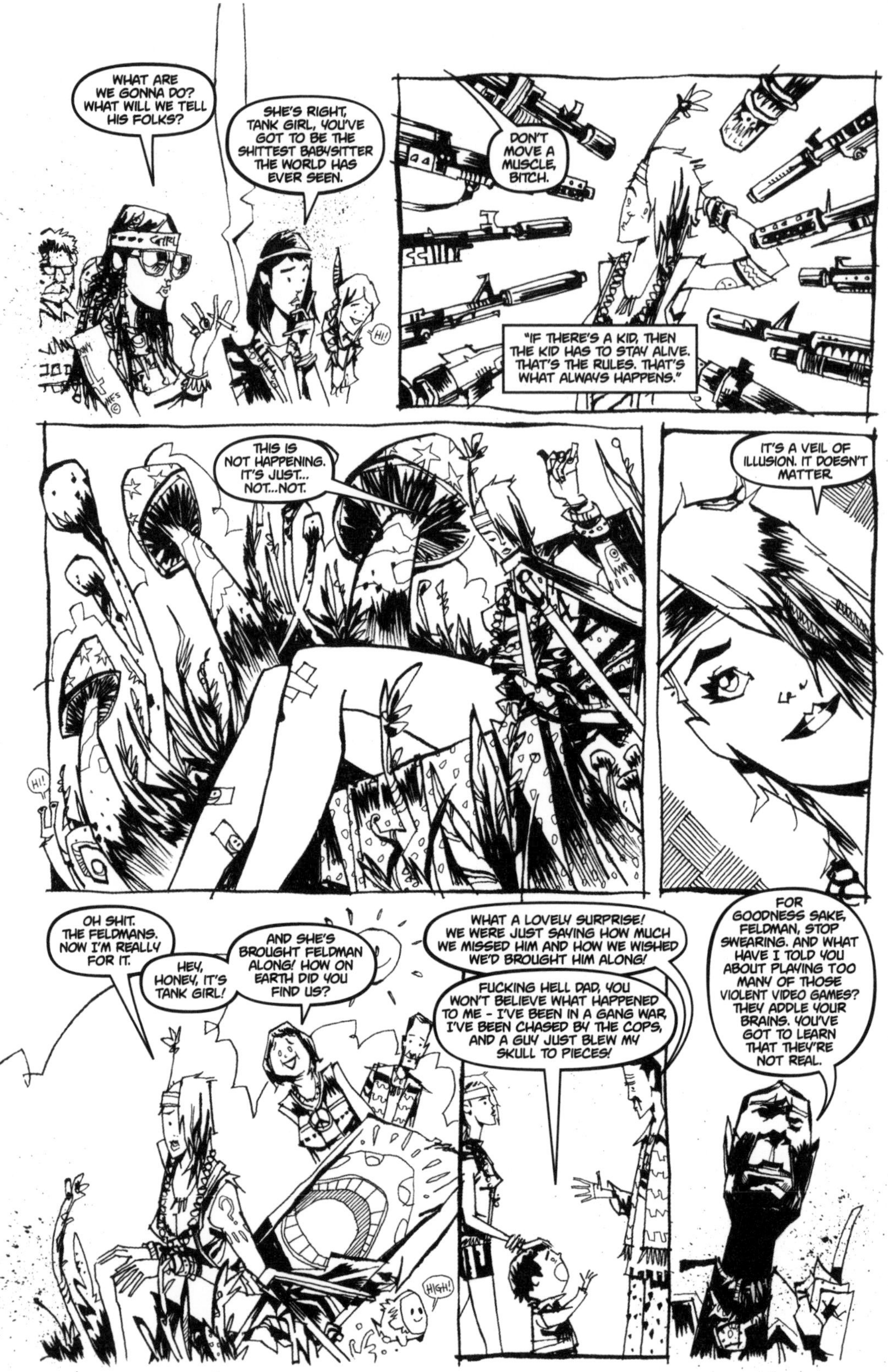
WHAT ARE WE GONNA DO? WHAT WILL WE TELL HIS FOLKS?
SHE'S RIGHT, TANK GIRL, YOU'VE GOT TO BE THE SHITTEST BABYSITTER THE WORLD HAS EVER SEEN.
HI!
DON'T MOVE A MUSCLE, BITCH.
"IF THERE'S A KID, THEN THE KID HAS TO STAY ALIVE. THAT'S THE RULES. THAT'S WHAT ALWAYS HAPPENS."
THIS IS NOT HAPPENING. IT'S JUST... NOT...NOT.
HI!
IT'S A VEIL OF ILLUSION. IT DOESN'T MATTER
OH SHIT. THE FELDMANS. NOW I'M REALLY FOR IT.
HEY, HONEY, IT'S TANK GIRL!
AND SHE'S BROUGHT FELDMAN ALONG! HOW ON EARTH DID YOU FIND US?
HIGH!
WHAT A LOVELY SURPRISE! WE WERE JUST SAYING HOW MUCH WE MISSED HIM AND HOW WE WISHED WE'D BROUGHT HIM ALONG!
FUCKING HELL DAD, YOU WON'T BELIEVE WHAT HAPPENED TO ME - I'VE BEEN IN A GANG WAR, I'VE BEEN CHASED BY THE COPS, AND A GUY JUST BLEW MY SKULL TO PIECES!
FOR GOODNESS SAKE, FELDMAN, STOP SWEARING. AND WHAT HAVE I TOLD YOU ABOUT PLAYING TOO MANY OF THOSE VIOLENT VIDEO GAMES? THEY ADDLE YOUR BRAINS. YOU'VE GOT TO LEARN THAT THEY'RE NOT REAL.

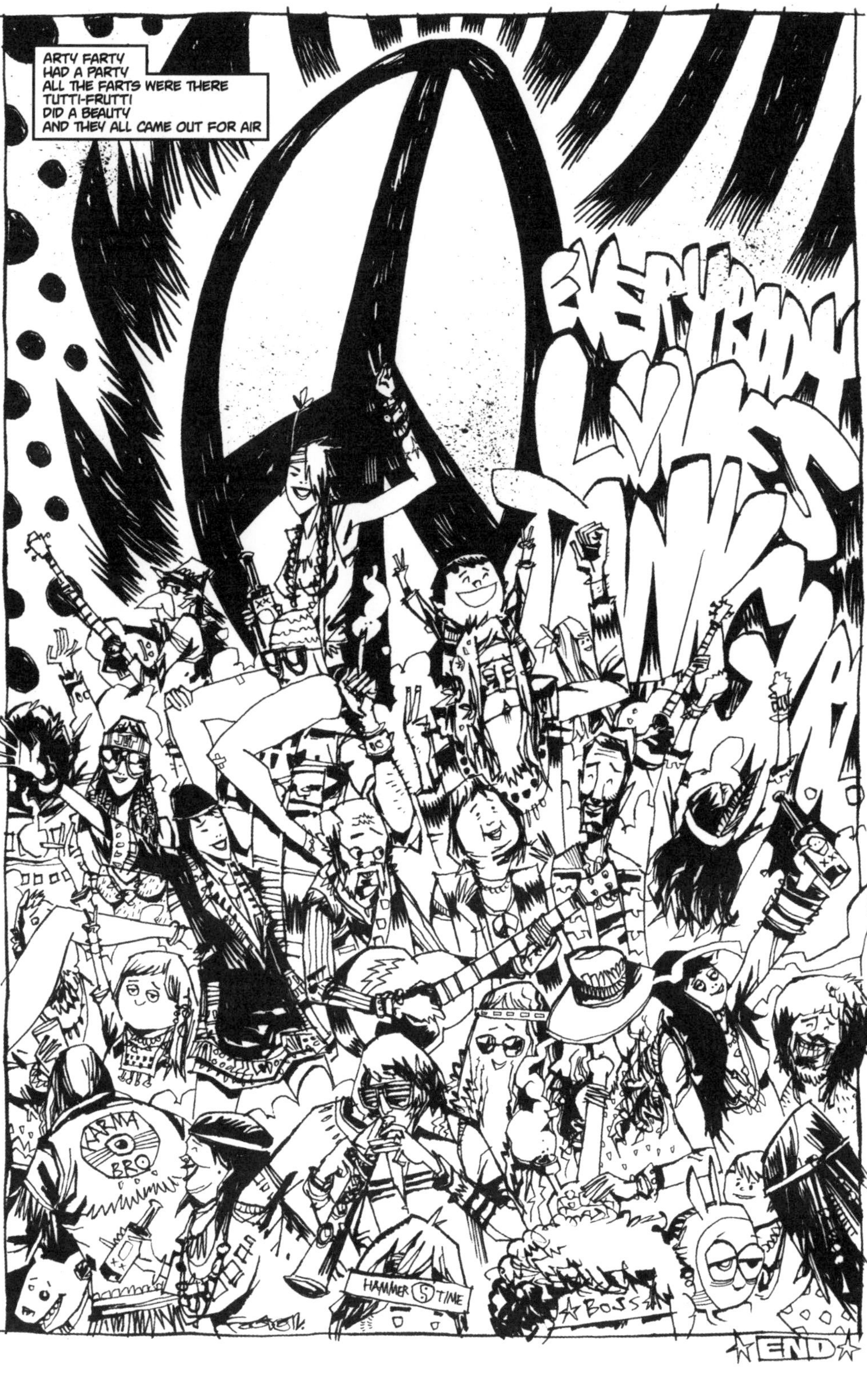
ARTY FARTY
HAD A PARTY
ALL THE FARTS WERE THERE
TUTTI-FRUTTI
DID A BEAUTY
AND THEY ALL CAME OUT FOR AIR
EVERYBODY
HAMMER TIME
BOSS
END

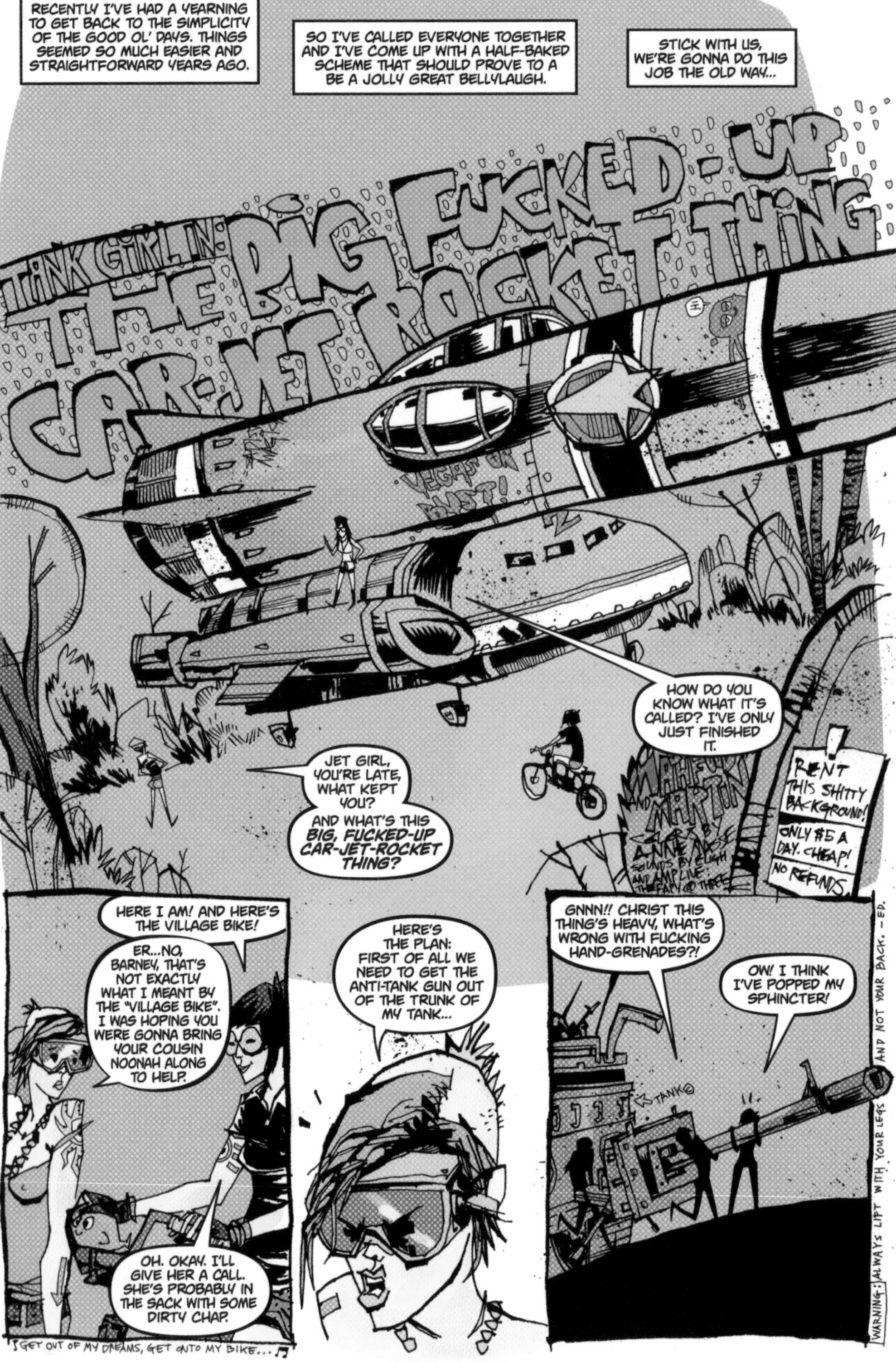
RECENTLY I'VE HAD A YEARNING TO GET BACK TO THE SIMPLICITY OF THE GOOD OL' DAYS. THINGS SEEMED SO MUCH EASIER AND STRAIGHTFORWARD YEARS AGO.
SO I'VE CALLED EVERYONE TOGETHER AND I'VE COME UP WITH A HALF-BAKED SCHEME THAT SHOULD PROVE TO A BE A JOLLY GREAT BELLYLAUGH.
STICK WITH US, WE'RE GONNA DO THIS JOB THE OLD WAY...
TANK GIRL IN: THE BIG FUCKED-UP CAR-JET-ROCKET THING
VEGAS OR BUST!
JET GIRL, YOU'RE LATE, WHAT KEPT YOU? AND WHAT'S THIS *BIG, FUCKED-UP CAR-JET-ROCKET THING?*
HOW DO YOU KNOW WHAT IT'S CALLED? I'VE ONLY JUST FINISHED IT.
AND MARTIN
SOUNDS BY ELIGH AND AMPLIVE
RENT THIS SHITTY BACKGROUND! ONLY $5 A DAY. CHEAP! NO REFUNDS.
HERE I AM! AND HERE'S THE VILLAGE BIKE!
ER...NO, BARNEY, THAT'S NOT EXACTLY WHAT I MEANT BY THE "VILLAGE BIKE". I WAS HOPING YOU WERE GONNA BRING YOUR COUSIN NOONAH ALONG TO HELP.
OH. OKAY. I'LL GIVE HER A CALL. SHE'S PROBABLY IN THE SACK WITH SOME DIRTY CHAP.
♪ GET OUT OF MY DREAMS, GET ONTO MY BIKE... ♫
HERE'S THE PLAN: FIRST OF ALL WE NEED TO GET THE ANTI-TANK GUN OUT OF THE TRUNK OF MY TANK...
GNNN!! CHRIST THIS THING'S HEAVY, WHAT'S WRONG WITH FUCKING HAND-GRENADES?!
OW! I THINK I'VE POPPED MY SPHINCTER!
TANK©
WARNING: ALWAYS LIFT WITH YOUR LEGS AND NOT YOUR BACK. —ED.

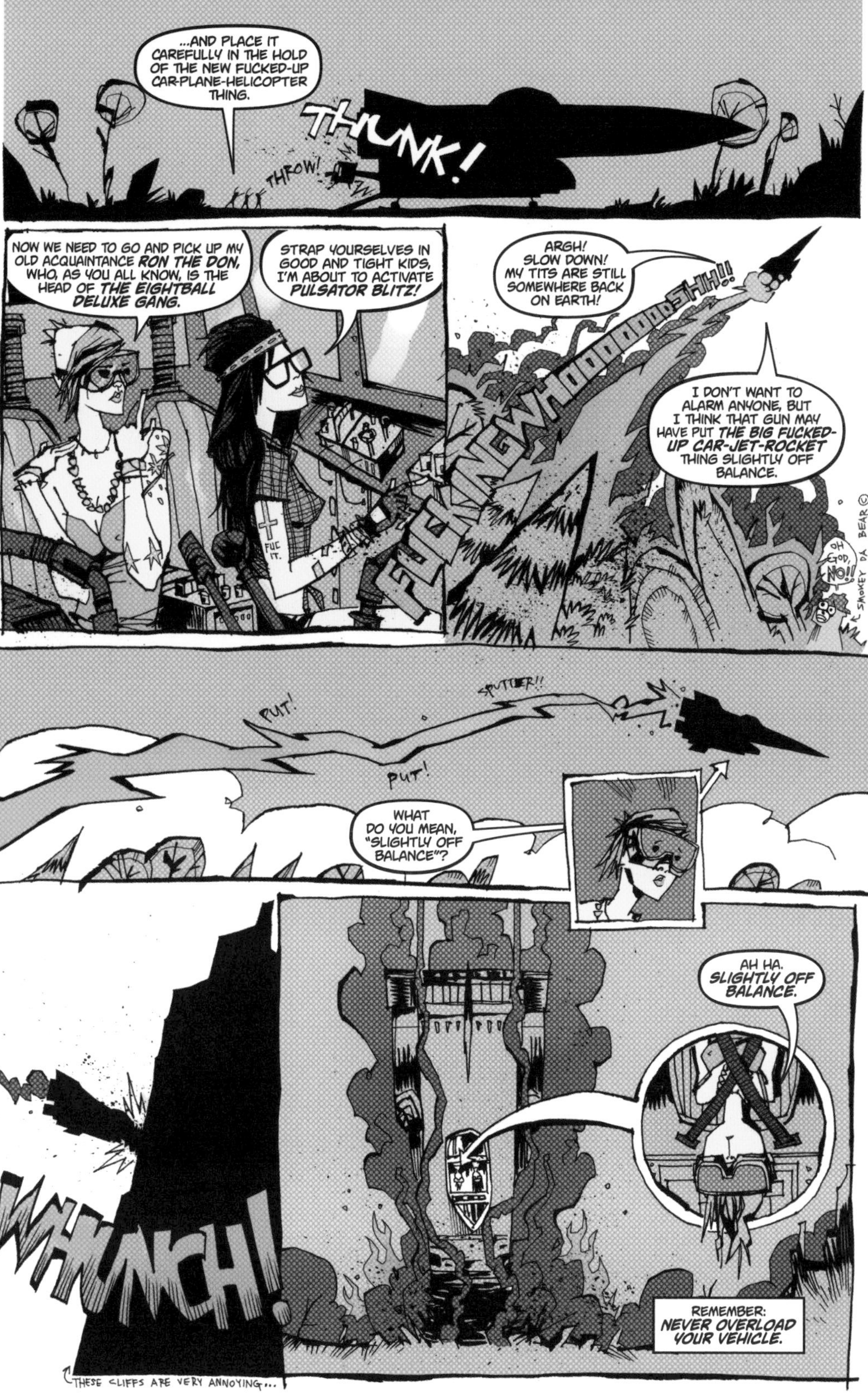

...AND PLACE IT CAREFULLY IN THE HOLD OF THE NEW FUCKED-UP CAR-PLANE-HELICOPTER THING.
THROW!
THUNK!
NOW WE NEED TO GO AND PICK UP MY OLD ACQUAINTANCE RON THE DON, WHO, AS YOU ALL KNOW, IS THE HEAD OF THE EIGHTBALL DELUXE GANG.
STRAP YOURSELVES IN GOOD AND TIGHT KIDS, I'M ABOUT TO ACTIVATE PULSATOR BLITZ!
FUC IT.
FUCKINGWHOOOOOOOSHH!!
ARGH! SLOW DOWN! MY TITS ARE STILL SOMEWHERE BACK ON EARTH!
I DON'T WANT TO ALARM ANYONE, BUT I THINK THAT GUN MAY HAVE PUT THE BIG FUCKED-UP CAR-JET-ROCKET THING SLIGHTLY OFF BALANCE.
OH GOD, NO!!
SMOKEY DA BEAR ©
PUT!
SPUTTER!!
PUT!
WHAT DO YOU MEAN, "SLIGHTLY OFF BALANCE"?
WHUNCH!
THESE CLIFFS ARE VERY ANNOYING...
AH HA. SLIGHTLY OFF BALANCE.
REMEMBER: NEVER OVERLOAD YOUR VEHICLE.

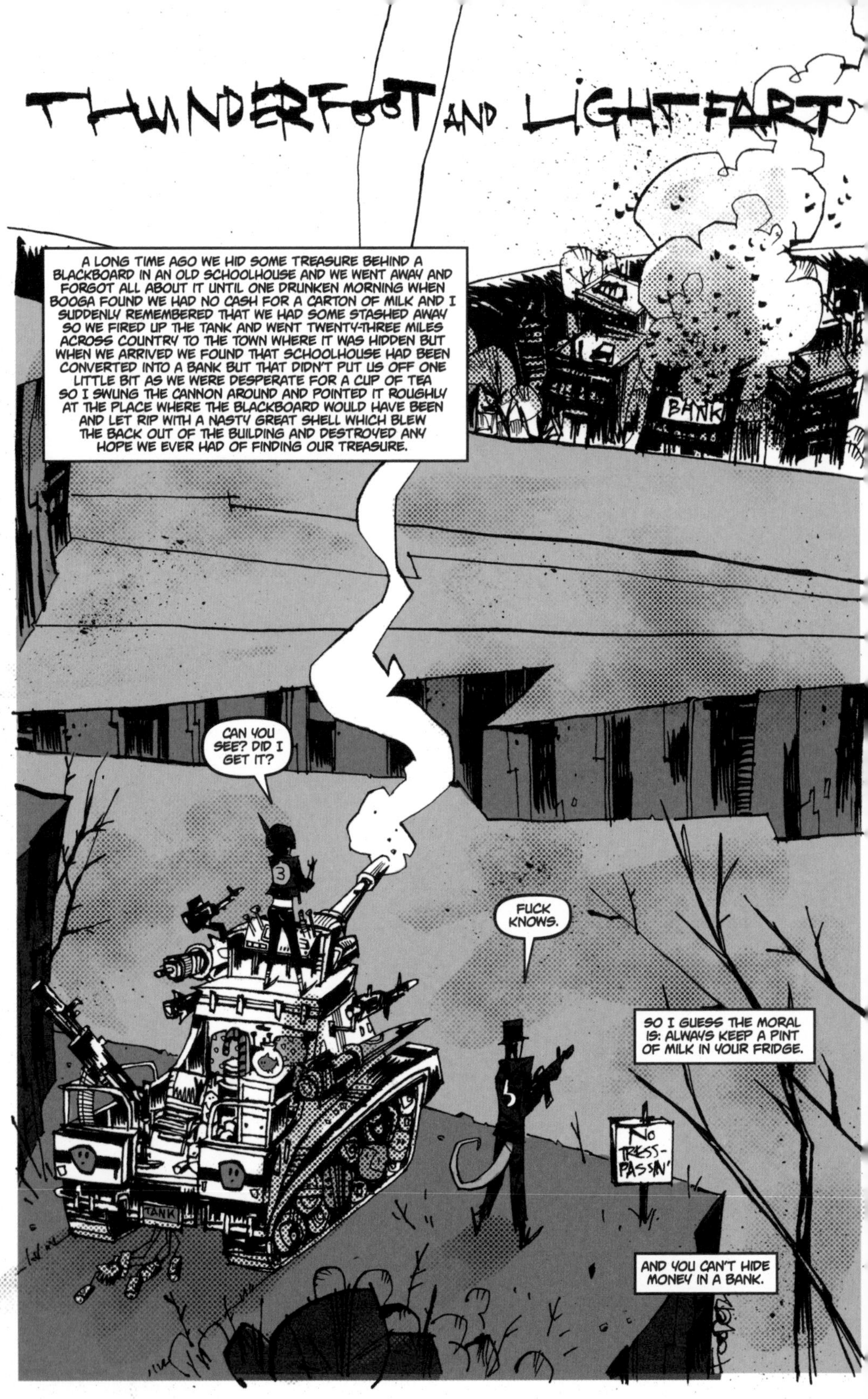
THUNDERFOOT AND LIGHTFART
A LONG TIME AGO WE HID SOME TREASURE BEHIND A BLACKBOARD IN AN OLD SCHOOLHOUSE AND WE WENT AWAY AND FORGOT ALL ABOUT IT UNTIL ONE DRUNKEN MORNING WHEN BOOGA FOUND WE HAD NO CASH FOR A CARTON OF MILK AND I SUDDENLY REMEMBERED THAT WE HAD SOME STASHED AWAY SO WE FIRED UP THE TANK AND WENT TWENTY-THREE MILES ACROSS COUNTRY TO THE TOWN WHERE IT WAS HIDDEN BUT WHEN WE ARRIVED WE FOUND THAT SCHOOLHOUSE HAD BEEN CONVERTED INTO A BANK BUT THAT DIDN'T PUT US OFF ONE LITTLE BIT AS WE WERE DESPERATE FOR A CUP OF TEA SO I SWUNG THE CANNON AROUND AND POINTED IT ROUGHLY AT THE PLACE WHERE THE BLACKBOARD WOULD HAVE BEEN AND LET RIP WITH A NASTY GREAT SHELL WHICH BLEW THE BACK OUT OF THE BUILDING AND DESTROYED ANY HOPE WE EVER HAD OF FINDING OUR TREASURE.
BANK
CAN YOU SEE? DID I GET IT?
FUCK KNOWS.
SO I GUESS THE MORAL IS: ALWAYS KEEP A PINT OF MILK IN YOUR FRIDGE.
NO TRESS-PASSIN'
TANK
AND YOU CAN'T HIDE MONEY IN A BANK.

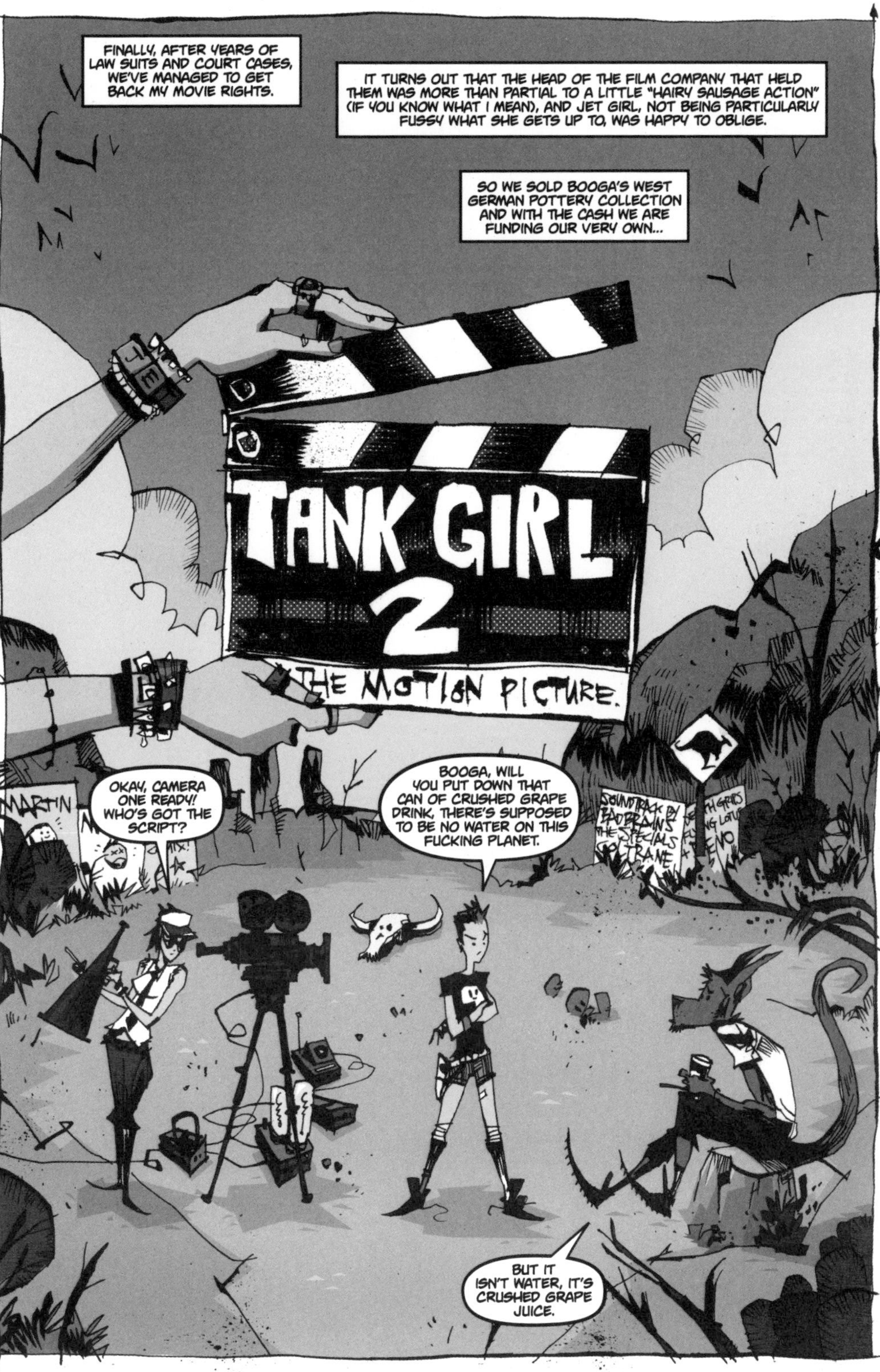
FINALLY, AFTER YEARS OF LAW SUITS AND COURT CASES, WE'VE MANAGED TO GET BACK MY MOVIE RIGHTS.
IT TURNS OUT THAT THE HEAD OF THE FILM COMPANY THAT HELD THEM WAS MORE THAN PARTIAL TO A LITTLE "HAIRY SAUSAGE ACTION" (IF YOU KNOW WHAT I MEAN), AND JET GIRL, NOT BEING PARTICULARLY FUSSY WHAT SHE GETS UP TO, WAS HAPPY TO OBLIGE.
SO WE SOLD BOOGA'S WEST GERMAN POTTERY COLLECTION AND WITH THE CASH WE ARE FUNDING OUR VERY OWN...
TANK GIRL 2
THE MOTION PICTURE.
MARTIN
OKAY, CAMERA ONE READY! WHO'S GOT THE SCRIPT?
BOOGA, WILL YOU PUT DOWN THAT CAN OF CRUSHED GRAPE DRINK, THERE'S SUPPOSED TO BE NO WATER ON THIS FUCKING PLANET.
BUT IT ISN'T WATER, IT'S CRUSHED GRAPE JUICE.

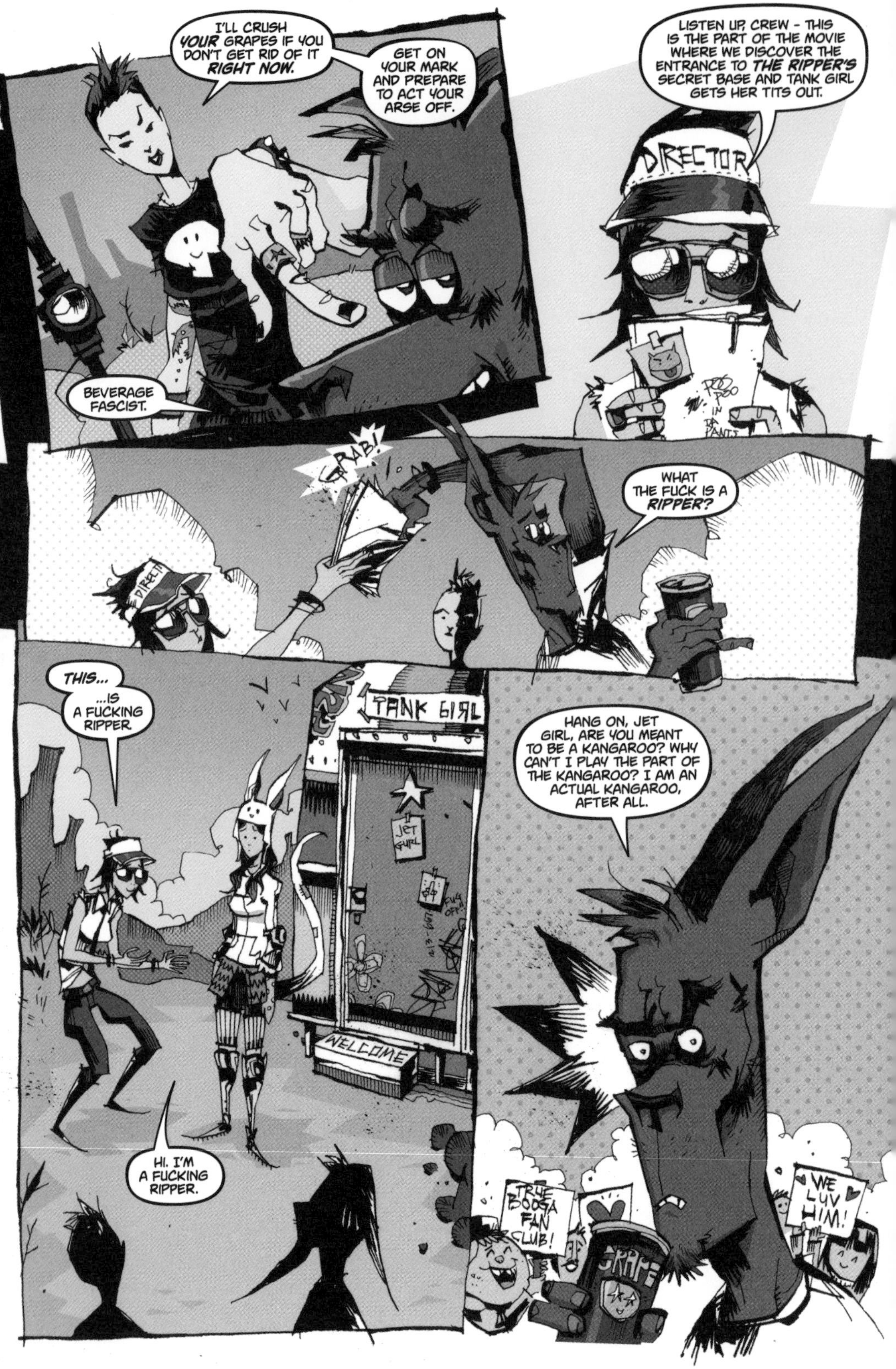
I'LL CRUSH *YOUR* GRAPES IF YOU DON'T GET RID OF IT *RIGHT NOW.*
GET ON YOUR MARK AND PREPARE TO ACT YOUR ARSE OFF.
BEVERAGE FASCIST.
LISTEN UP, CREW - THIS IS THE PART OF THE MOVIE WHERE WE DISCOVER THE ENTRANCE TO *THE RIPPER'S* SECRET BASE AND TANK GIRL GETS HER TITS OUT.
DIRECTOR
GRAB!
WHAT THE FUCK IS A *RIPPER?*
THIS...
...IS A FUCKING RIPPER.
TANK GIRL
JET GIRL
FUG OFF!!
WELCOME
HI. I'M A FUCKING RIPPER.
HANG ON, JET GIRL, ARE YOU MEANT TO BE A KANGAROO? WHY CAN'T I PLAY THE PART OF THE KANGAROO? I AM AN ACTUAL KANGAROO, AFTER ALL.
TRUE BOOGA FAN CLUB!
GRAPE
WE LUV HIM!

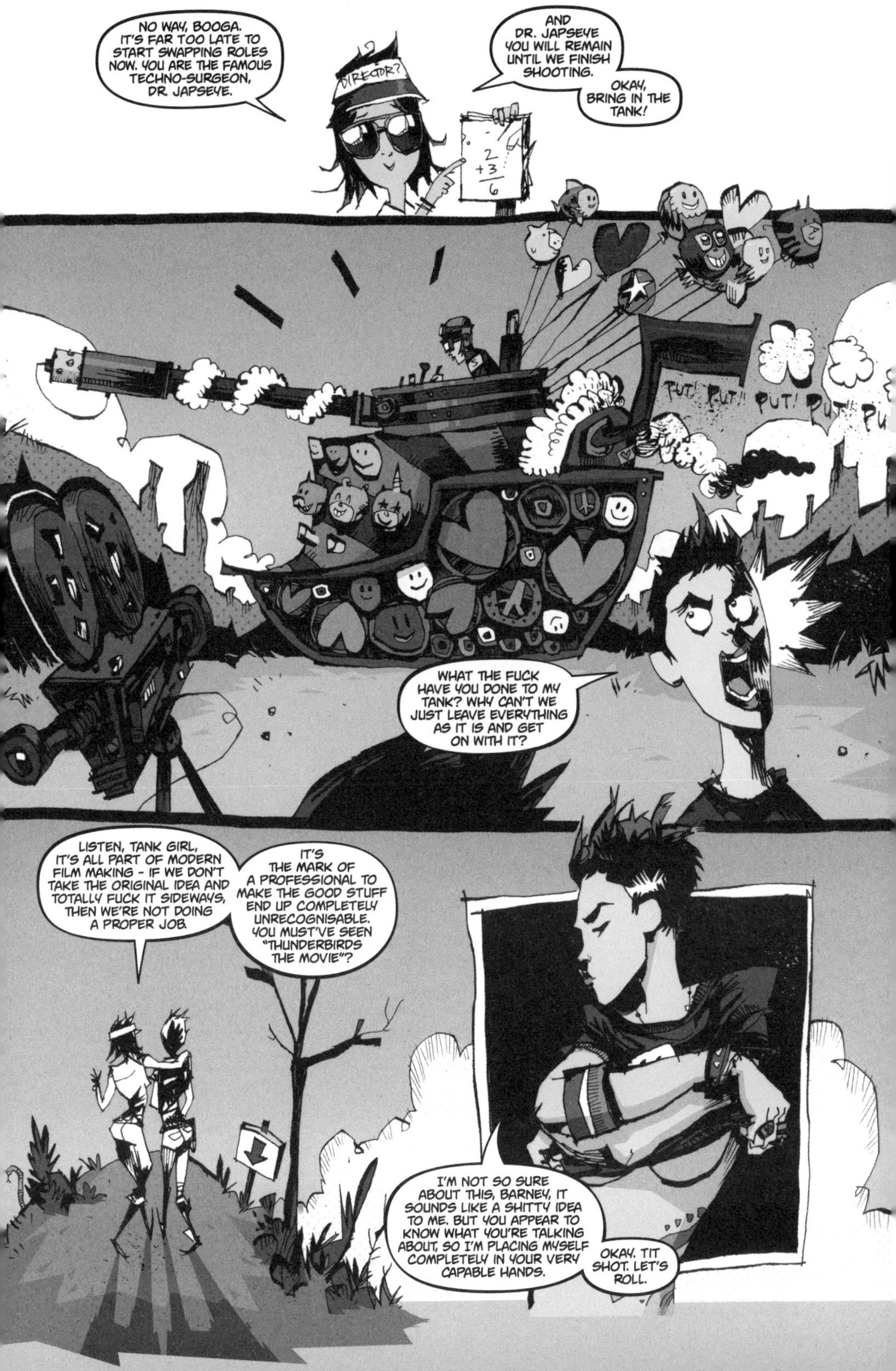
NO WAY, BOOGA. IT'S FAR TOO LATE TO START SWAPPING ROLES NOW. YOU ARE THE FAMOUS TECHNO-SURGEON, DR. JAPSEYE.
AND DR. JAPSEYE YOU WILL REMAIN UNTIL WE FINISH SHOOTING.
OKAY, BRING IN THE TANK!
DIRECTOR?
2
+3
6
PUT! PUT! PUT!
WHAT THE FUCK HAVE YOU DONE TO MY TANK? WHY CAN'T WE JUST LEAVE EVERYTHING AS IT IS AND GET ON WITH IT?
LISTEN, TANK GIRL, IT'S ALL PART OF MODERN FILM MAKING - IF WE DON'T TAKE THE ORIGINAL IDEA AND TOTALLY FUCK IT SIDEWAYS, THEN WE'RE NOT DOING A PROPER JOB.
IT'S THE MARK OF A PROFESSIONAL TO MAKE THE GOOD STUFF END UP COMPLETELY UNRECOGNISABLE. YOU MUST'VE SEEN "THUNDERBIRDS THE MOVIE"?
I'M NOT SO SURE ABOUT THIS, BARNEY, IT SOUNDS LIKE A SHITTY IDEA TO ME. BUT YOU APPEAR TO KNOW WHAT YOU'RE TALKING ABOUT, SO I'M PLACING MYSELF COMPLETELY IN YOUR VERY CAPABLE HANDS.
OKAY. TIT SHOT. LET'S ROLL.

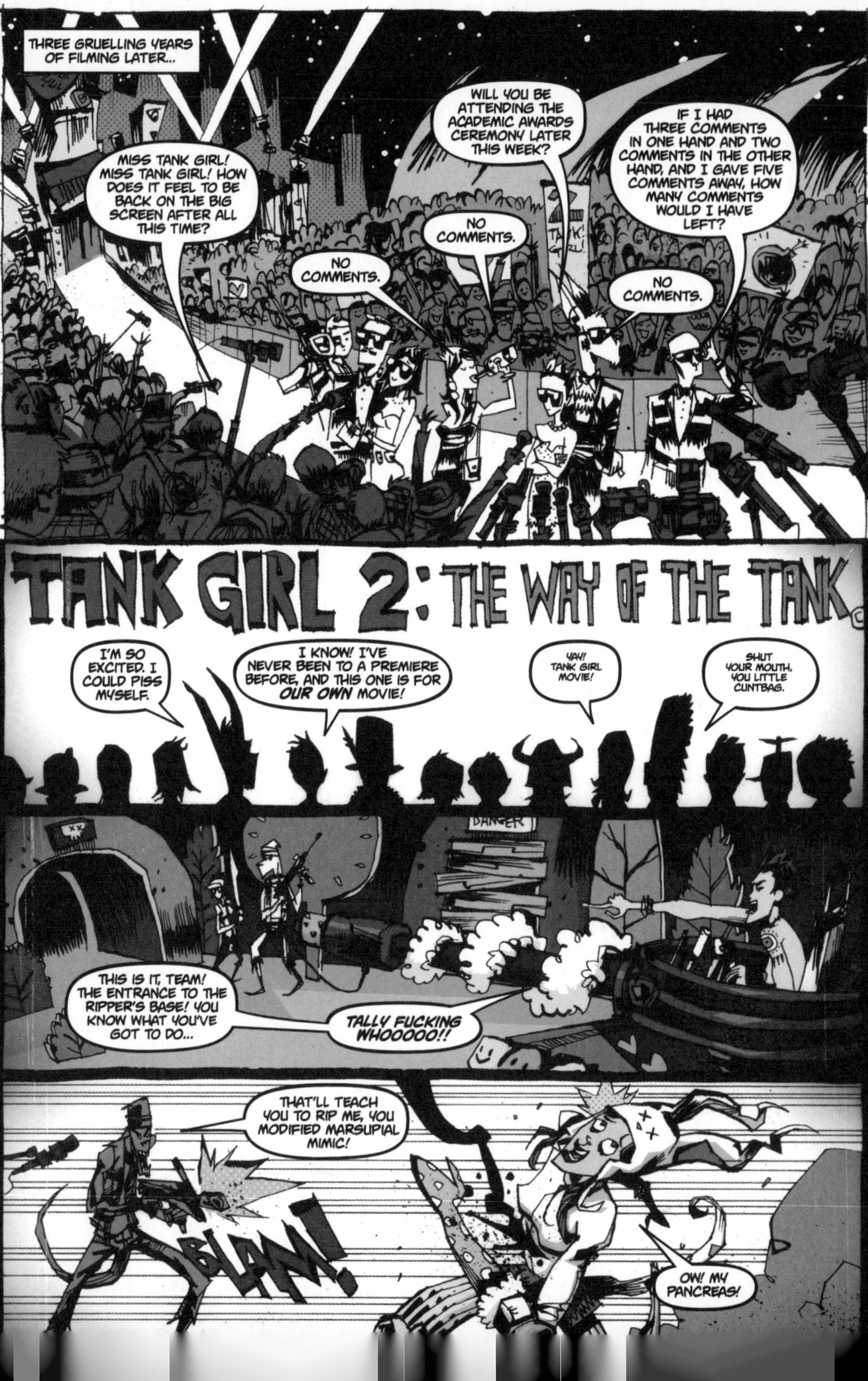
THREE GRUELLING YEARS OF FILMING LATER...
MISS TANK GIRL! MISS TANK GIRL! HOW DOES IT FEEL TO BE BACK ON THE BIG SCREEN AFTER ALL THIS TIME?
NO COMMENTS.
WILL YOU BE ATTENDING THE ACADEMIC AWARDS CEREMONY LATER THIS WEEK?
NO COMMENTS.
IF I HAD THREE COMMENTS IN ONE HAND AND TWO COMMENTS IN THE OTHER HAND, AND I GAVE FIVE COMMENTS AWAY, HOW MANY COMMENTS WOULD I HAVE LEFT?
NO COMMENTS.
TANK GIRL 2: THE WAY OF THE TANK
I'M SO EXCITED. I COULD PISS MYSELF.
I KNOW! I'VE NEVER BEEN TO A PREMIERE BEFORE, AND THIS ONE IS FOR OUR OWN MOVIE!
YAY! TANK GIRL MOVIE!
SHUT YOUR MOUTH, YOU LITTLE CUNTBAG.
DANGER
THIS IS IT, TEAM! THE ENTRANCE TO THE RIPPER'S BASE! YOU KNOW WHAT YOU'VE GOT TO DO...
TALLY FUCKING WHOOOOO!!
THAT'LL TEACH YOU TO RIP ME, YOU MODIFIED MARSUPIAL MIMIC!
BLAM!
OW! MY PANCREAS!

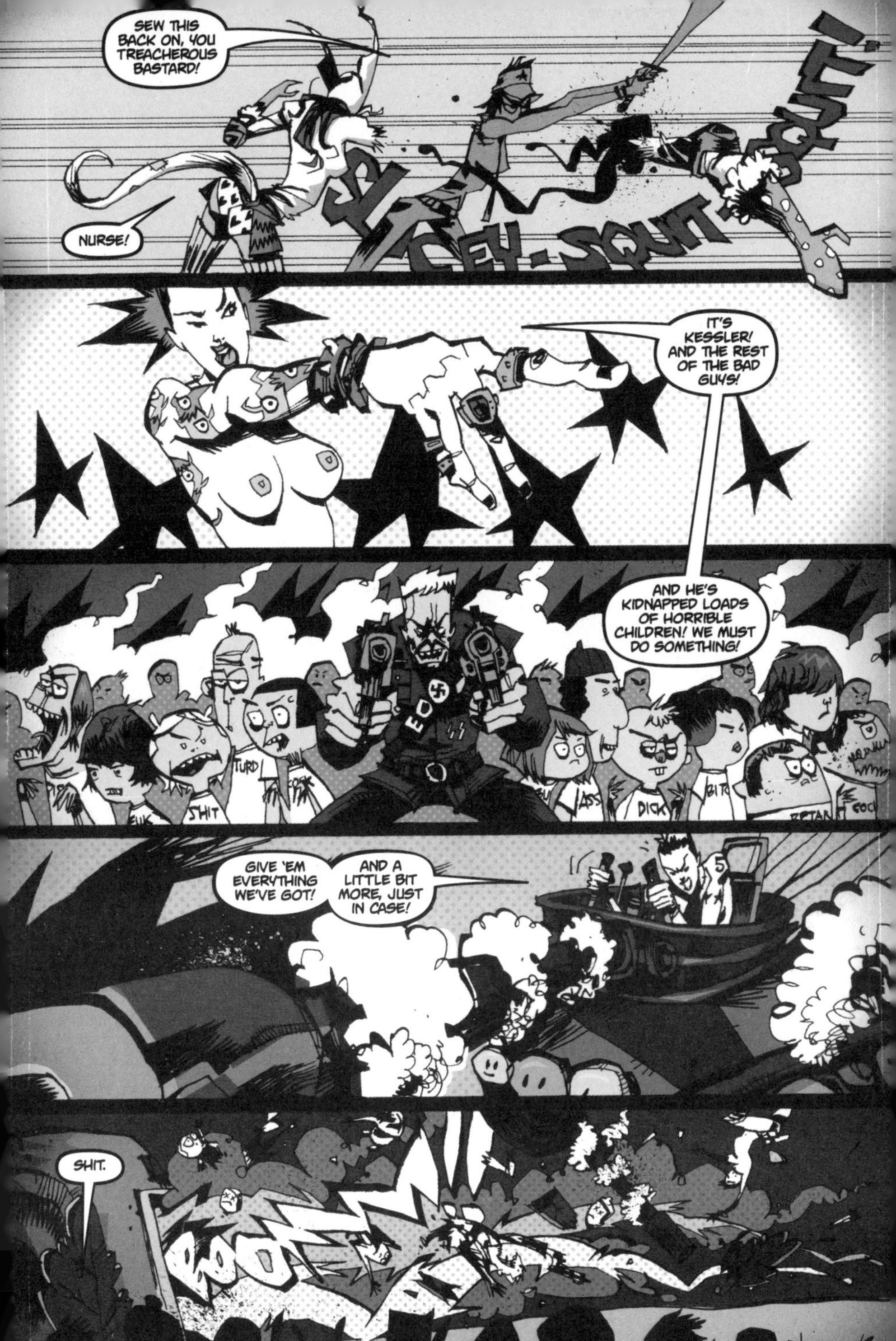
SEW THIS BACK ON, YOU TREACHEROUS BASTARD!
NURSE!
SLICEY-SQUIT-SQUIT!
IT'S KESSLER! AND THE REST OF THE BAD GUYS!
AND HE'S KIDNAPPED LOADS OF HORRIBLE CHILDREN! WE MUST DO SOMETHING!
GIVE 'EM EVERYTHING WE'VE GOT!
AND A LITTLE BIT MORE, JUST IN CASE!
SHIT.

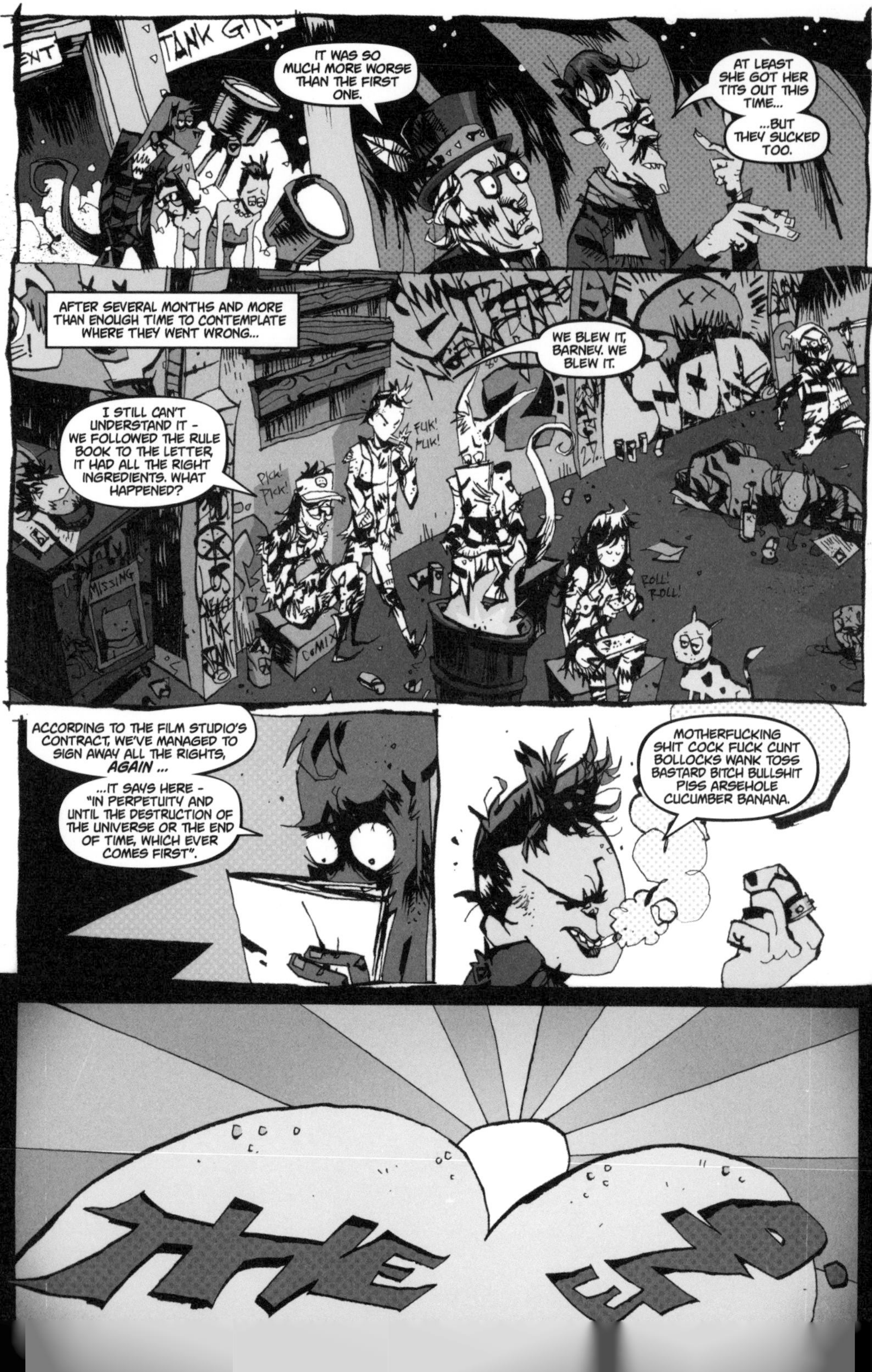
EXIT
TANK GIRL
IT WAS SO MUCH MORE WORSE THAN THE FIRST ONE.
AT LEAST SHE GOT HER TITS OUT THIS TIME...
...BUT THEY SUCKED TOO.
AFTER SEVERAL MONTHS AND MORE THAN ENOUGH TIME TO CONTEMPLATE WHERE THEY WENT WRONG...
WE BLEW IT, BARNEY. WE BLEW IT.
I STILL CAN'T UNDERSTAND IT - WE FOLLOWED THE RULE BOOK TO THE LETTER, IT HAD ALL THE RIGHT INGREDIENTS. WHAT HAPPENED?
FUK! FUK!
PICK! PICK!
ROLL! ROLL!
MISSING
COMIX
ACCORDING TO THE FILM STUDIO'S CONTRACT, WE'VE MANAGED TO SIGN AWAY ALL THE RIGHTS, ***AGAIN*** ...
...IT SAYS HERE - "IN PERPETUITY AND UNTIL THE DESTRUCTION OF THE UNIVERSE OR THE END OF TIME, WHICH EVER COMES FIRST".
MOTHERFUCKING SHIT COCK FUCK CUNT BOLLOCKS WANK TOSS BASTARD BITCH BULLSHIT PISS ARSEHOLE CUCUMBER BANANA.
THE END.

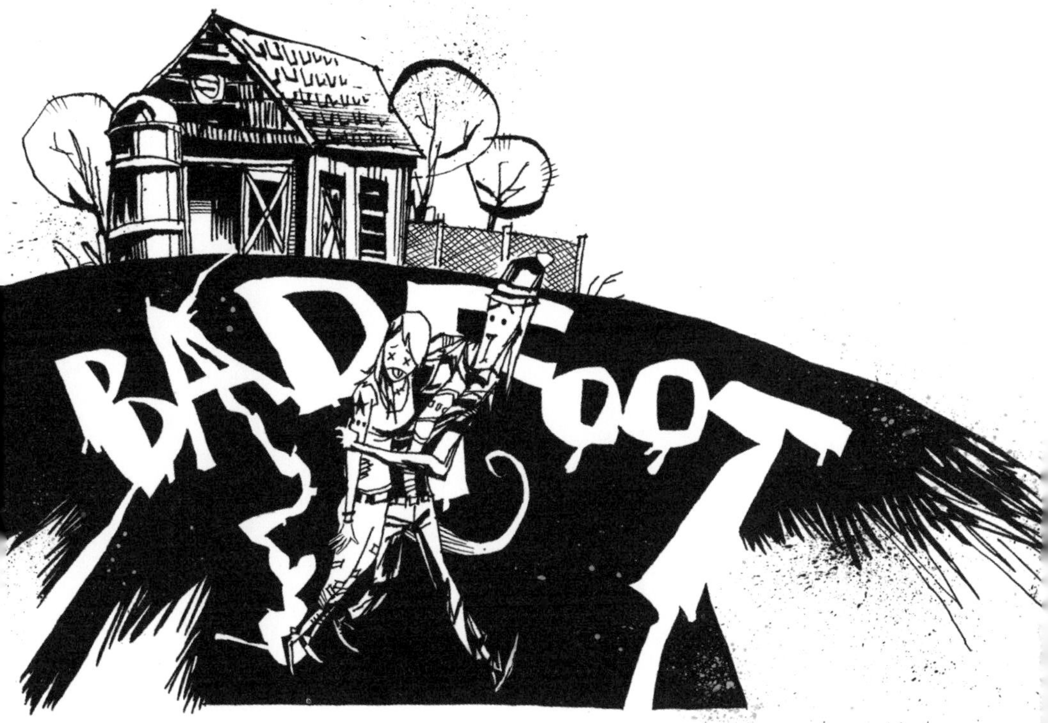
BAD FOOT

THERE'S A WHOLE LOTTA SWEARIN' GOIN' ON...

"FUCK. FUCK. FUCK. FUCK. FUCK. FUCK. FUCK. FUCK. FUCK. FUCK. FUCKIN' HELL. SHIT. FUCKIN' SHIT. FUCKIN' SHIT IN HELL. FUCKER. BLOODY SHITTING FUCKER. FUCKY FUCKY FUCK FUCK. TITS. SHITTY TIT FUCKER. BALL-SHITTER. FUCKING SHIT-SPITTER."

PLEASE EXCUSE MY UNUSUALLY PROFANE OUTBURST, BUT I'VE TOTALLY FUCKED MYSELF UP.

OH MAN. OH FUCK.

I WAS RESHAPING MY STEEL TOECAPS AFTER GIVING MY TANK A GOOD KICKING WHEN I ACCIDENTALLY KNOCKED THE ANVIL OFF OF ITS PLINTH. THE FUCKING BASTARD THING LANDED SQUARELY ON MY FUCKING FOOT.

SHIT.

OH FUCK.

I'VE REALLY MASHED IT THIS TIME. I'VE NEVER KNOWN PAIN QUITE LIKE IT. THERE'S A WHOLE CHOIR OF BANSHEES SQUEALING THEIR AWFUL HYMN TO AGONY RIGHT IN THE FRONT OF MY SKULL. AND MY NERVOUS SYSTEM IS BEING WRUNG THROUGH A SANDPAPER-LINED MANGLE AND HAMMERED BLOODY WITH A RUSTY POKER AS IT COMES OUT THE OTHER END.

WHAT A FUCKING TWAT I AM.

HERE COMES BOOGA. BOOGA IS MY BOYFRIEND, HAS BEEN FOR SEVERAL YEARS NOW. HE LOVES ME AND I LOVE HIM, EVEN THOUGH HE'S A KANGAROO AND A BIT OF A DICK.

HE LOOKS DOWN AT ME AS I HALF-PROP MYSELF AGAINST A HORSEBOX BY THE DOOR OF THE BARN. "WHAT HAVE YOU DONE TO YOURSELF NOW, MY LITTLE MITTEN?" HE ASKS IN AN ANNOYINGLY DOTING PARENTAL TONE.

"ARGH...FUCKIN'...DROPPED...ANVIL...FOOT...FUCKED IT..." I GRUMBLE THROUGH GRITTED TEETH, "...CAN'T...FUCKIN'...WALK... BOLLOCKS..."

"DO YOU WANT ME TO KISS IT BETTER?"

I LOOK AT HIM THROUGH SLANTY, TEAR-FILLED EYES. "DO YOU THINK IT'LL HELP?" I WHISPER.

"ALWAYS USED TO WORK FOR ME," HE REPLIES IN AN OFF-THE-CUFF MANNER, "IF I'D INJURED MYSELF WHEN I WAS A KID MOTHER WOULD ALWAYS KISS ME ON THE SPOT WHERE IT HURT THE MOST."

"THAT'S JUST GREAT," I REMARK, "THE NEXT TIME WE GO ROUND HER HOUSE FOR TEA, REMIND ME TO KICK YOU REALLY HARD IN THE COCK."

BOOGA CROUCHES DOWN AND PUTS HIS BIG OL' MARSUPIAL HANDS UNDER MY ARMPITS. "CAN YOU STAND UP?"

"YEAH," I SNAP SARCASTICALLY, "BUT I'LL FALL STRAIGHT-BACK-FUCKIN'-DOWN AGAIN."

"LET'S GIVE IT A GO," HE SAYS, LIFTING ME EASILY WITH HIS POWERFUL ARMS, "THERE, NOT A CHALLENGE."

I'M HANGING THERE BY HIS SUPPORT, MY FEET DANGLING JUST ABOVE THE GROUND LIKE A MARIONETTE. THE RELIEF FROM THE PAIN IS MAKING ME FEEL LIKE FAINTING.

"NOW, LET'S SEE YOU TAKE A FEW STEPS..." HE SAYS WITH ASSURANCE. SUDDENLY HIS HANDS ARE PULLED AWAY FROM UNDER MY ARMS AND I LAND WITH MY FULL WEIGHT ON MY FEET.

"FUCKING HELL!!!!"

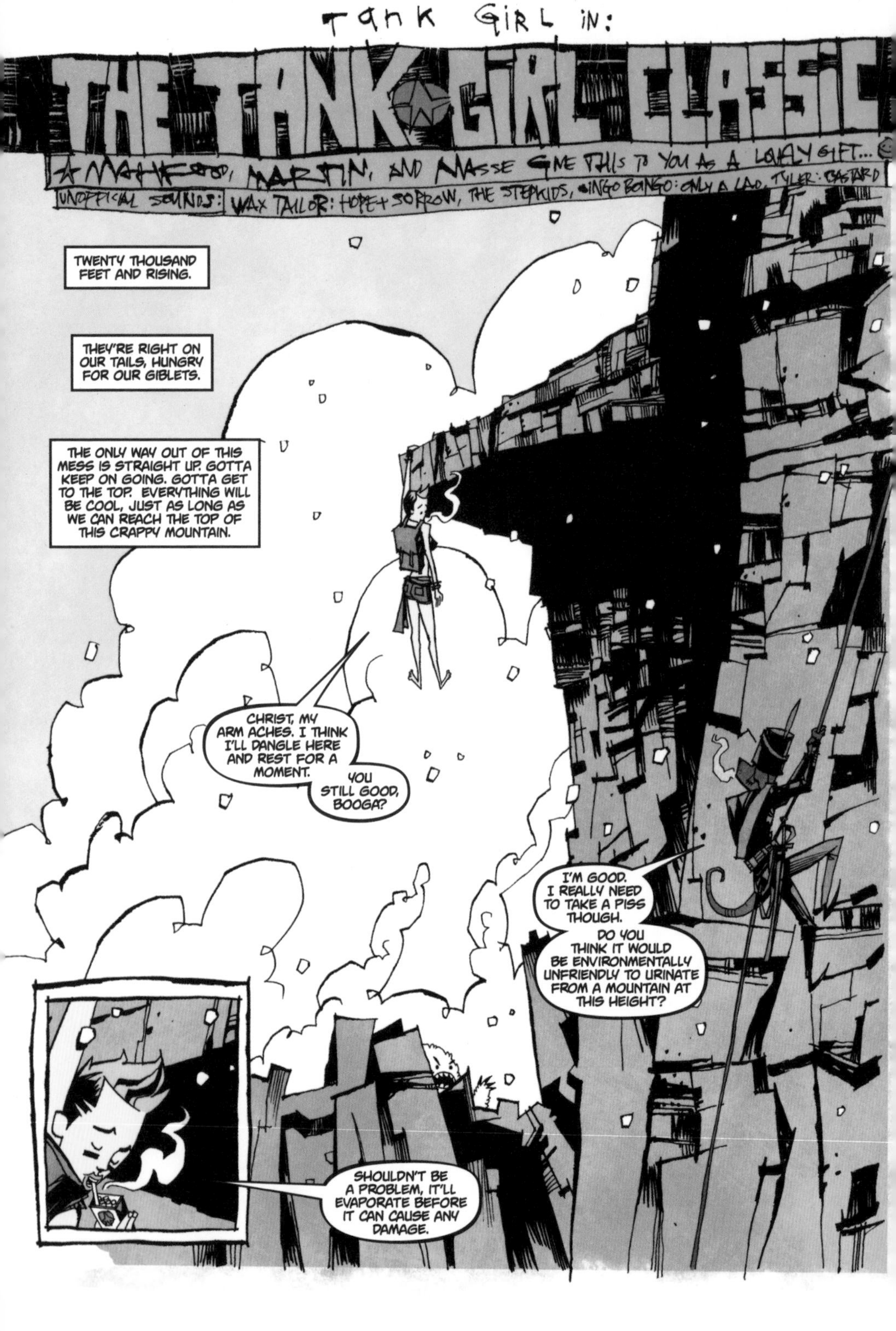
TANK GIRL IN:
THE TANK GIRL CLASSIC
MARTIN, AND MASSE GIVE THIS TO YOU AS A LOVELY GIFT...
UNOFFICIAL SOUNDS: WAX TAILOR: HOPE + SORROW, THE STEPKIDS, OINGO BOINGO: ONLY A LAD, TYLER: BASTARD
TWENTY THOUSAND FEET AND RISING.
THEY'RE RIGHT ON OUR TAILS, HUNGRY FOR OUR GIBLETS.
THE ONLY WAY OUT OF THIS MESS IS STRAIGHT UP. GOTTA KEEP ON GOING. GOTTA GET TO THE TOP. EVERYTHING WILL BE COOL, JUST AS LONG AS WE CAN REACH THE TOP OF THIS CRAPPY MOUNTAIN.
CHRIST, MY ARM ACHES. I THINK I'LL DANGLE HERE AND REST FOR A MOMENT.
YOU STILL GOOD, BOOGA?
I'M GOOD. I REALLY NEED TO TAKE A PISS THOUGH.
DO YOU THINK IT WOULD BE ENVIRONMENTALLY UNFRIENDLY TO URINATE FROM A MOUNTAIN AT THIS HEIGHT?
SHOULDN'T BE A PROBLEM, IT'LL EVAPORATE BEFORE IT CAN CAUSE ANY DAMAGE.

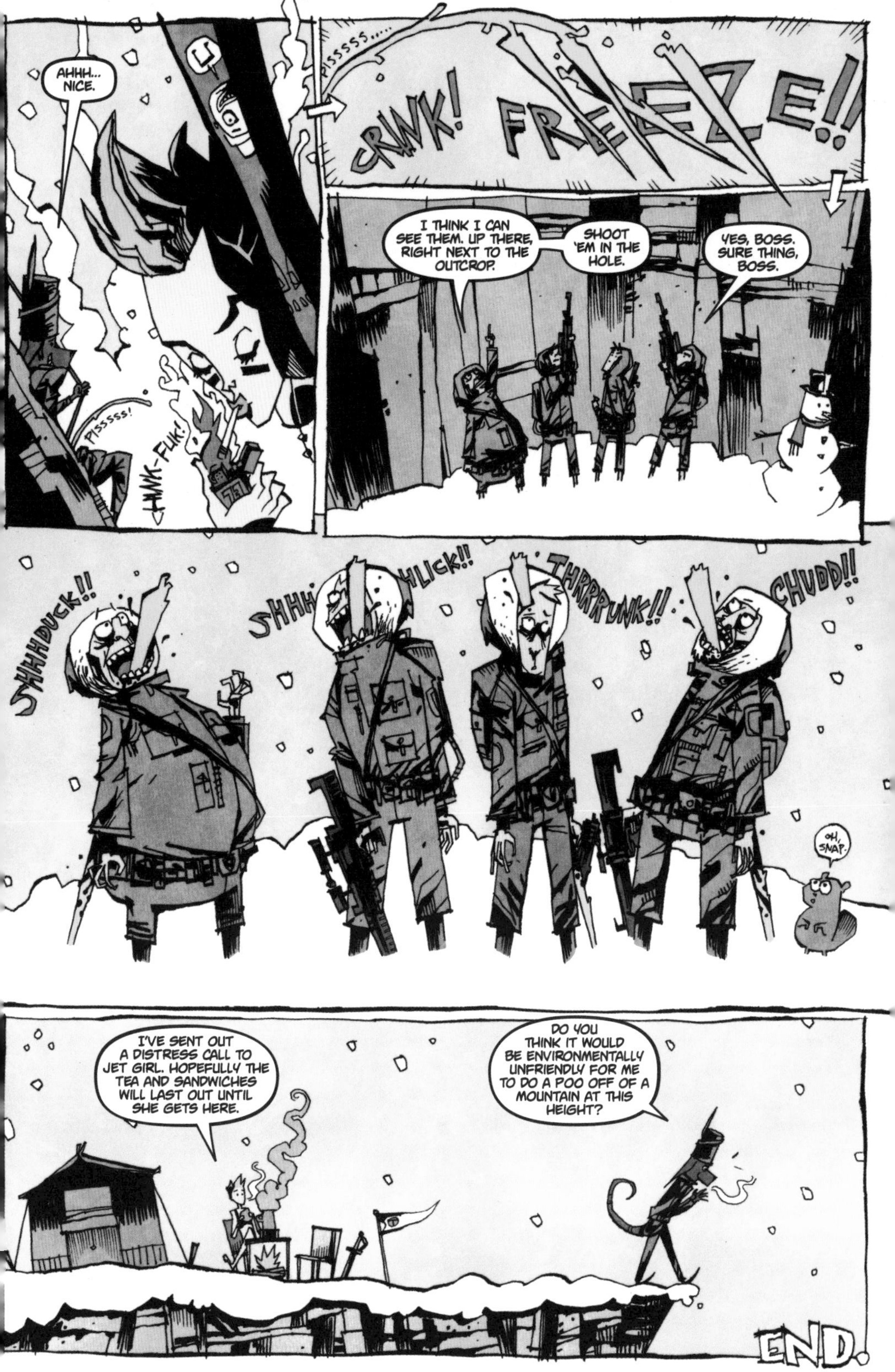
AHHH... NICE.
PISSSSS!
HNK-FLIK!
PISSSSS.....
CRINK! FREEZE!!
I THINK I CAN SEE THEM. UP THERE, RIGHT NEXT TO THE OUTCROP.
SHOOT 'EM IN THE HOLE.
YES, BOSS. SURE THING, BOSS.
SHHHDUCK!!
SHHHHLICK!!
THRRRUNK!!
CHUDD!!
OH, SNAP.
I'VE SENT OUT A DISTRESS CALL TO JET GIRL. HOPEFULLY THE TEA AND SANDWICHES WILL LAST OUT UNTIL SHE GETS HERE.
DO YOU THINK IT WOULD BE ENVIRONMENTALLY UNFRIENDLY FOR ME TO DO A POO OFF OF A MOUNTAIN AT THIS HEIGHT?
END.

NOT AS MUCH FUN AS IT LOOKS

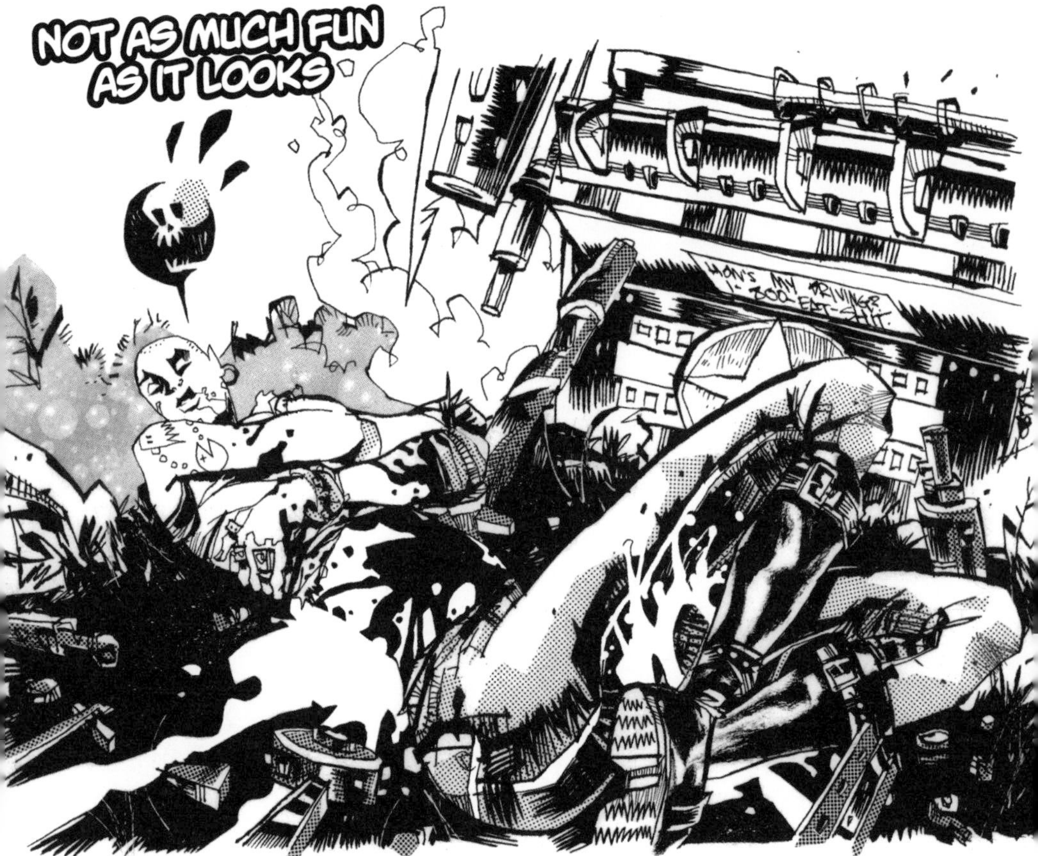
HOW'S MY DRIVING?
1-800-EAT-SHIT.

I'VE BEEN LOSING A LOT OF BLOOD. PINTS OF THE STUFF. IT'S THERE, ALL OVER MY KHAKI TROUSERS AND WHITE SHIRT. THE HEAT OF THE MIDDAY SUN HAS DRIED IT OUT AND TURNED IT INTO A KIND OF STICKY, RED TOFFEE. BUT THAT HASN'T HELPED, AND STILL IT KEEPS ON COMING. I CAN'T STOP IT; THE WOUND IS TOO BIG. THE BULLET ENTERED MY BACK, JUST ABOVE MY PELVIS, AND I CAN FEEL THE BLOOD CAKED ON TO THE BACK OF MY PANTS, BUT IT'S THE EXIT WOUND THAT'S GIVING ME THE REAL TROUBLE. IT MUST'VE BEEN A FUCKING HUGE CALIBRE BULLET; GOD KNOWS WHAT IT'S DONE TO MY INSIDES.

I MUST TRY AND DRINK SOMETHING - ANYTHING - BUT I LITERALLY CANNOT MOVE. THERE IS NOT AN OUNCE OF ENERGY LEFT IN ME.

MY TANK IS BELLY-UP IN A DRY DIRT DITCH AND I'M TUCKED AWAY AT THE BACK-END OF IT, KEEPING MY HEAD DOWN. I'M MANAGING TO FIRE OFF A ROUND FROM MY PISTOL EVERY COUPLE OF MINUTES AS A WARNING TO ANYONE WHO MIGHT BE THINKING THAT THE COAST IS CLEAR.

I AM ALONE. I'M PRETTY CERTAIN THAT WITHOUT SERIOUS MEDICAL ATTENTION, I WILL BE DEAD WITHIN FIFTEEN MINUTES.

THERE IS NOTHING LEFT FOR ME TO DO BUT SIT TIGHT AND WAIT, AS THE WORLD SLOWLY FOGS OVER AND RECEDES FROM VIEW.

GOODBYE EVERYONE.

GOODBYE MUM, THANKS FOR MAKING ME EAT MY GREENS AND IRONING MY SCHOOL UNIFORM.

THANKS FOR FUCKING EVERYTHING, DAD, YOU BASTARD.

AND BOOGA, HOW CAN I SAY GOODBYE TO YOU? THE ONE REAL MAN IN MY LIFE. I KNOW YOU'LL BE THERE, WAITING TO CATCH ME, WHEREVER I GO.

SOMETHING'S MOVING OUT THERE, JUST BEYOND THE OTHER END OF THE TANK. I'VE GOT TO PULL MY TRIGGER, GOT TO MAKE A SCARY BANG.

BANG!

"AH! AH! OH FUCK!! OH FUCKING HELL!! YOU STUPID FUCKING COW!!" I'VE SHOT MYSELF IN THE LEG. NOW THAT'S REALLY FUCKED IT. LUCKILY THE BULLET IN MY BACK HAS CUT OFF THE NERVES FROM MY LEG, SO I'M FEELING NOTHING. BUT NOW I'M LETTING OUT BLOOD AT AN ALARMING RATE.

THE DARK SHROUD OF DEATH IS RACING TOWARDS ME LIKE THE SHADOW OF A RAIN CLOUD ACROSS A ROLLING PASTURE.

HELLO.

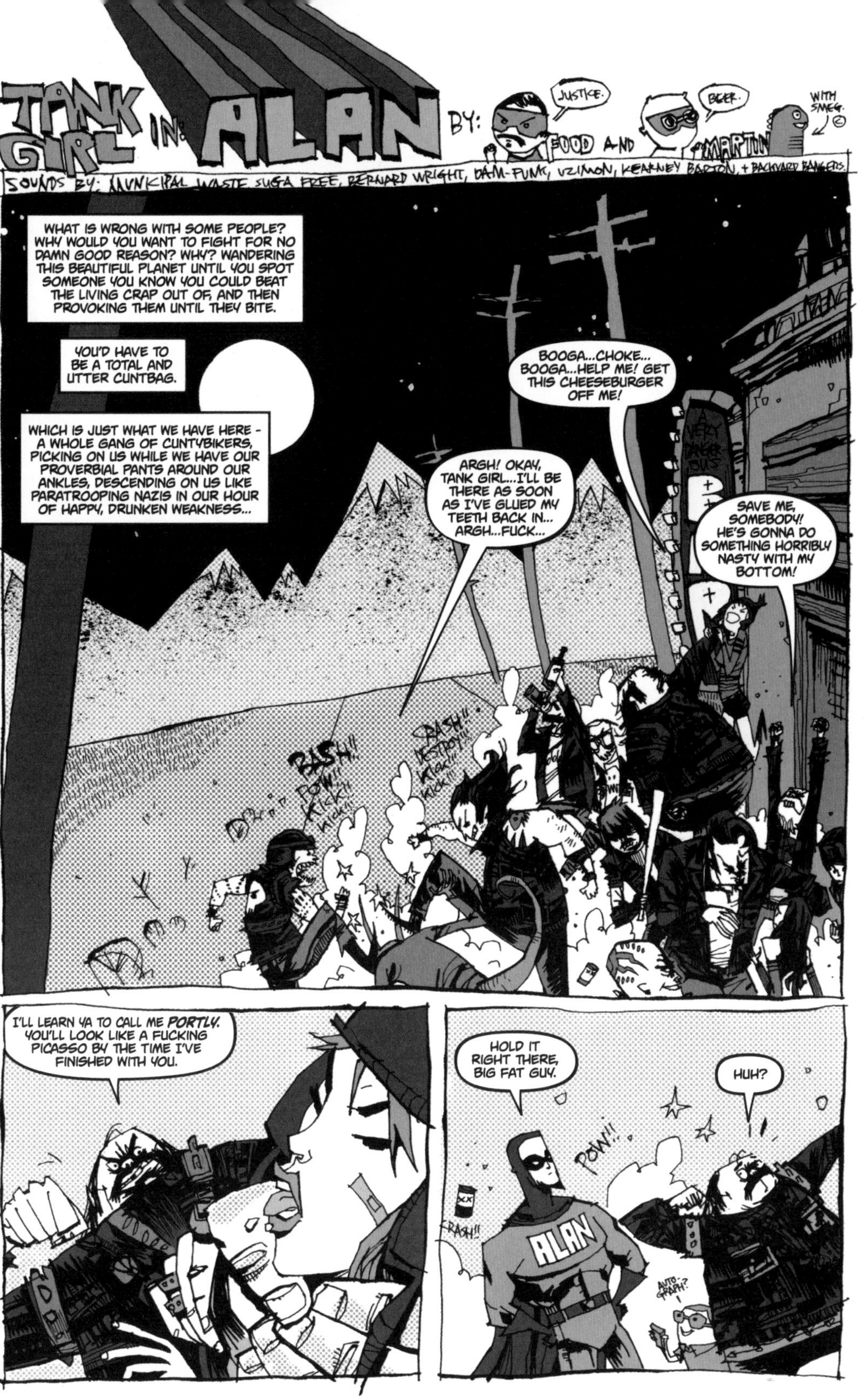
TANK GIRL IN: ALAN
BY:
JUSTICE.
FOOD AND
BEER.
MARTIN
WITH SMEG. ©
SOUNDS BY: MUNICIPAL WASTE, SUGA FREE, BERNARD WRIGHT, DAM-FUNK, UZIMON, KEARNEY BARTON, + BACKYARD BANGERS.
WHAT IS WRONG WITH SOME PEOPLE? WHY WOULD YOU WANT TO FIGHT FOR NO DAMN GOOD REASON? WHY? WANDERING THIS BEAUTIFUL PLANET UNTIL YOU SPOT SOMEONE YOU KNOW YOU COULD BEAT THE LIVING CRAP OUT OF, AND THEN PROVOKING THEM UNTIL THEY BITE.
YOU'D HAVE TO BE A TOTAL AND UTTER CUNTBAG.
WHICH IS JUST WHAT WE HAVE HERE - A WHOLE GANG OF CUNTYBIKERS, PICKING ON US WHILE WE HAVE OUR PROVERBIAL PANTS AROUND OUR ANKLES, DESCENDING ON US LIKE PARATROOPING NAZIS IN OUR HOUR OF HAPPY, DRUNKEN WEAKNESS...
BOOGA...CHOKE... BOOGA...HELP ME! GET THIS CHEESEBURGER OFF ME!
ARGH! OKAY, TANK GIRL...I'LL BE THERE AS SOON AS I'VE GLUED MY TEETH BACK IN... ARGH...FUCK...
SAVE ME, SOMEBODY! HE'S GONNA DO SOMETHING HORRIBLY NASTY WITH MY BOTTOM!
A VERY DANGEROUS
BASH!! POW!! KICK!! KICK!!
CRASH!! DESTROY!! KICK!! KICK!!
I'LL LEARN YA TO CALL ME *PORTLY*. YOU'LL LOOK LIKE A FUCKING PICASSO BY THE TIME I'VE FINISHED WITH YOU.
HOLD IT RIGHT THERE, BIG FAT GUY.
HUH?
POW!!
CRASH!!
XX
ALAN
AUTO-GRAPH?

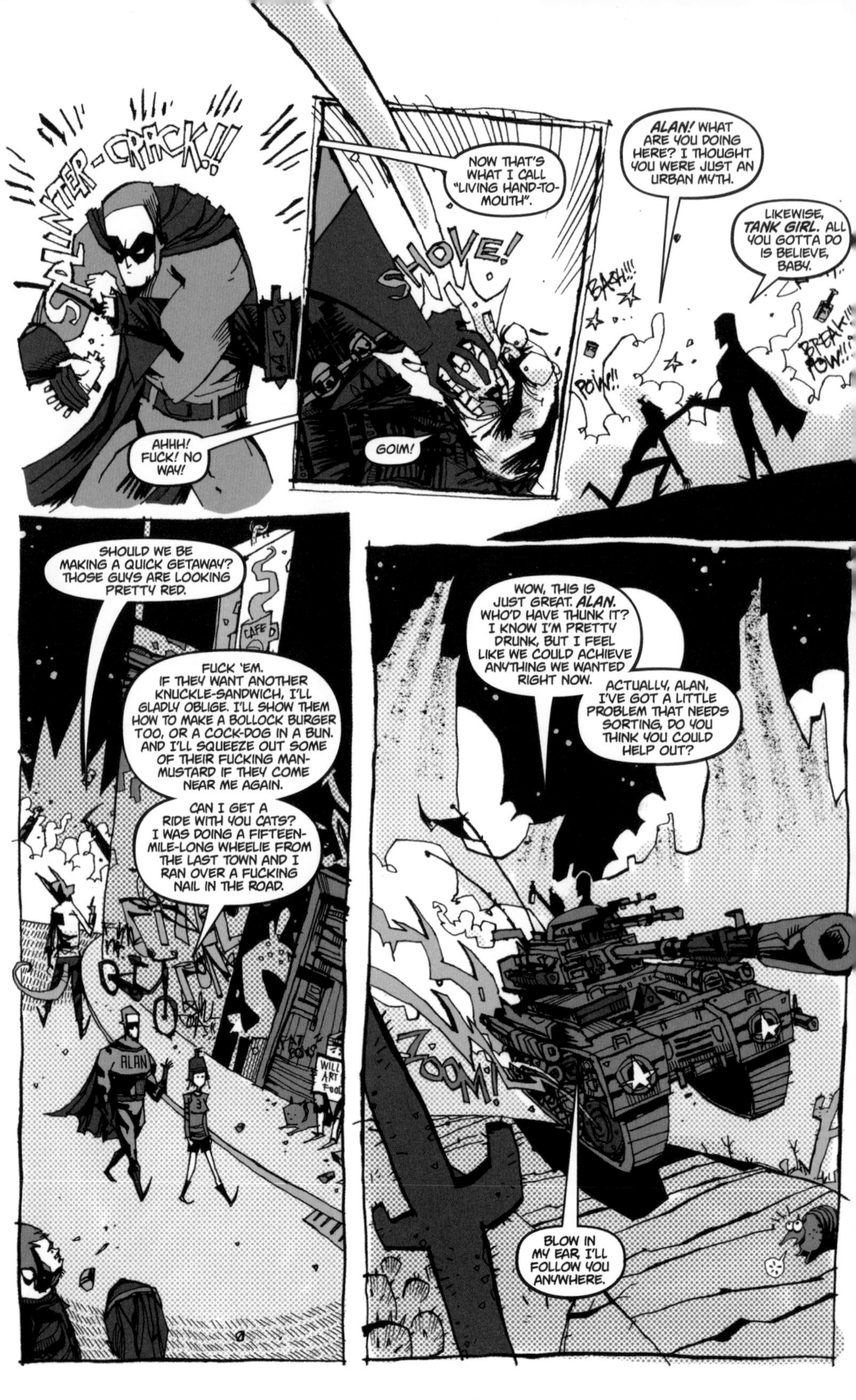
SPLINTER-CRACK!!
AHHH! FUCK! NO WAY!
NOW THAT'S WHAT I CALL "LIVING HAND-TO-MOUTH".
SHOVE!
GOIM!
ALAN! WHAT ARE YOU DOING HERE? I THOUGHT YOU WERE JUST AN URBAN MYTH.
LIKEWISE, TANK GIRL. ALL YOU GOTTA DO IS BELIEVE, BABY.
BASH!!!
POW!!
BREAK!
POW!!!
SHOULD WE BE MAKING A QUICK GETAWAY? THOSE GUYS ARE LOOKING PRETTY RED.
FUCK 'EM. IF THEY WANT ANOTHER KNUCKLE-SANDWICH, I'LL GLADLY OBLIGE. I'LL SHOW THEM HOW TO MAKE A BOLLOCK BURGER TOO, OR A COCK-DOG IN A BUN. AND I'LL SQUEEZE OUT SOME OF THEIR FUCKING MAN-MUSTARD IF THEY COME NEAR ME AGAIN.
CAN I GET A RIDE WITH YOU CATS? I WAS DOING A FIFTEEN-MILE-LONG WHEELIE FROM THE LAST TOWN AND I RAN OVER A FUCKING NAIL IN THE ROAD.
CAFE
ALAN
WILL ART FOOD
WOW, THIS IS JUST GREAT. ALAN. WHO'D HAVE THUNK IT? I KNOW I'M PRETTY DRUNK, BUT I FEEL LIKE WE COULD ACHIEVE ANYTHING WE WANTED RIGHT NOW.
ACTUALLY, ALAN, I'VE GOT A LITTLE PROBLEM THAT NEEDS SORTING, DO YOU THINK YOU COULD HELP OUT?
ZOOM!
BLOW IN MY EAR, I'LL FOLLOW YOU ANYWHERE.

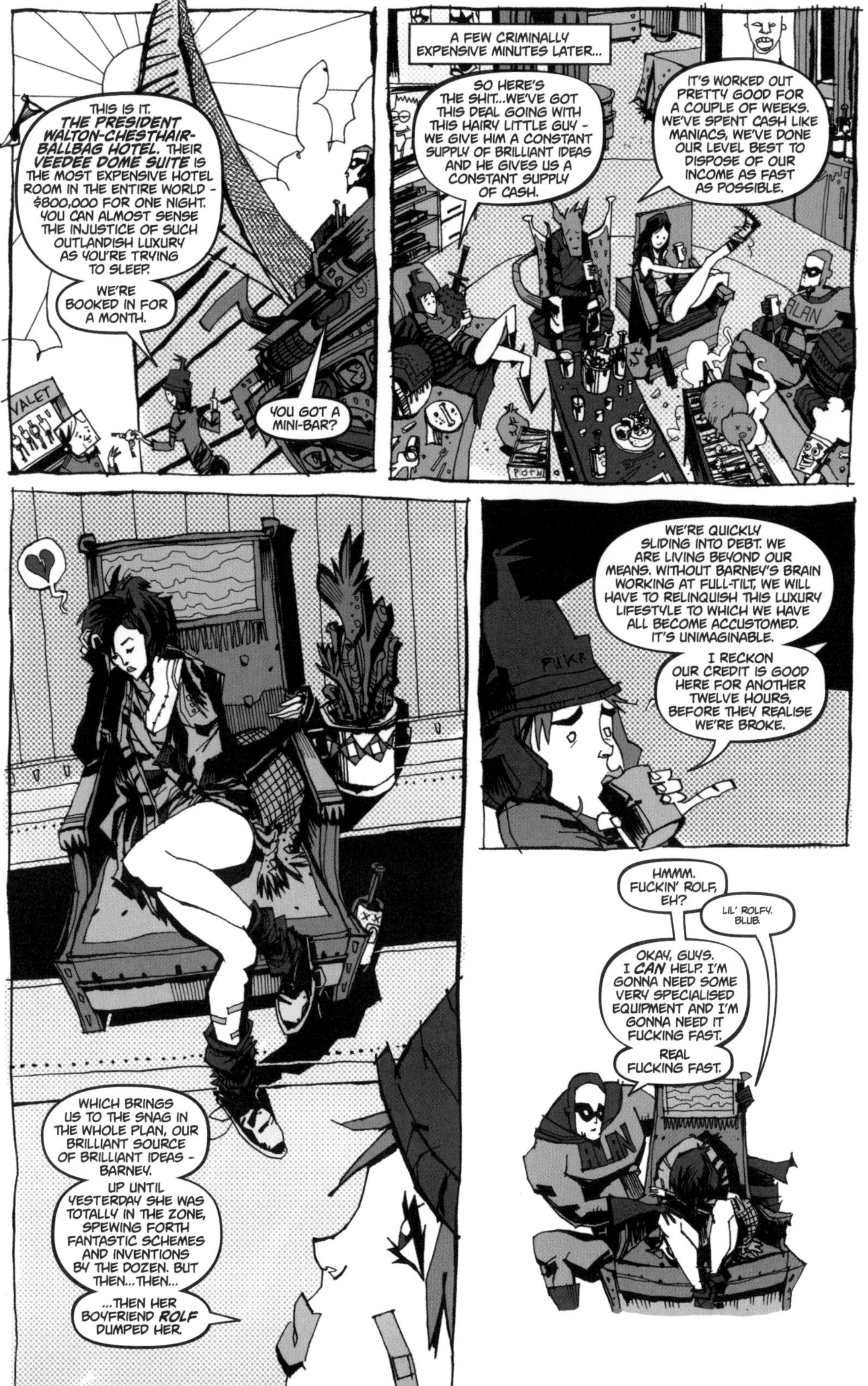
THIS IS IT. THE PRESIDENT WALTON-CHESTHAIR-BALLBAG HOTEL. THEIR VEEDEE DOME SUITE IS THE MOST EXPENSIVE HOTEL ROOM IN THE ENTIRE WORLD - $800,000 FOR ONE NIGHT. YOU CAN ALMOST SENSE THE INJUSTICE OF SUCH OUTLANDISH LUXURY AS YOU'RE TRYING TO SLEEP.
WE'RE BOOKED IN FOR A MONTH.
VALET
YOU GOT A MINI-BAR?
A FEW CRIMINALLY EXPENSIVE MINUTES LATER...
SO HERE'S THE SHIT...WE'VE GOT THIS DEAL GOING WITH THIS HAIRY LITTLE GUY - WE GIVE HIM A CONSTANT SUPPLY OF BRILLIANT IDEAS AND HE GIVES US A CONSTANT SUPPLY OF CASH.
IT'S WORKED OUT PRETTY GOOD FOR A COUPLE OF WEEKS. WE'VE SPENT CASH LIKE MANIACS, WE'VE DONE OUR LEVEL BEST TO DISPOSE OF OUR INCOME AS FAST AS POSSIBLE.
WHICH BRINGS US TO THE SNAG IN THE WHOLE PLAN, OUR BRILLIANT SOURCE OF BRILLIANT IDEAS - BARNEY.
UP UNTIL YESTERDAY SHE WAS TOTALLY IN THE ZONE, SPEWING FORTH FANTASTIC SCHEMES AND INVENTIONS BY THE DOZEN. BUT THEN...THEN...
...THEN HER BOYFRIEND ROLF DUMPED HER.
WE'RE QUICKLY SLIDING INTO DEBT. WE ARE LIVING BEYOND OUR MEANS. WITHOUT BARNEY'S BRAIN WORKING AT FULL-TILT, WE WILL HAVE TO RELINQUISH THIS LUXURY LIFESTYLE TO WHICH WE HAVE ALL BECOME ACCUSTOMED. IT'S UNIMAGINABLE.
I RECKON OUR CREDIT IS GOOD HERE FOR ANOTHER TWELVE HOURS, BEFORE THEY REALISE WE'RE BROKE.
HMMM. FUCKIN' ROLF, EH?
LIL' ROLFY. BLUB.
OKAY, GUYS. I CAN HELP. I'M GONNA NEED SOME VERY SPECIALISED EQUIPMENT AND I'M GONNA NEED IT FUCKING FAST.
REAL FUCKING FAST.

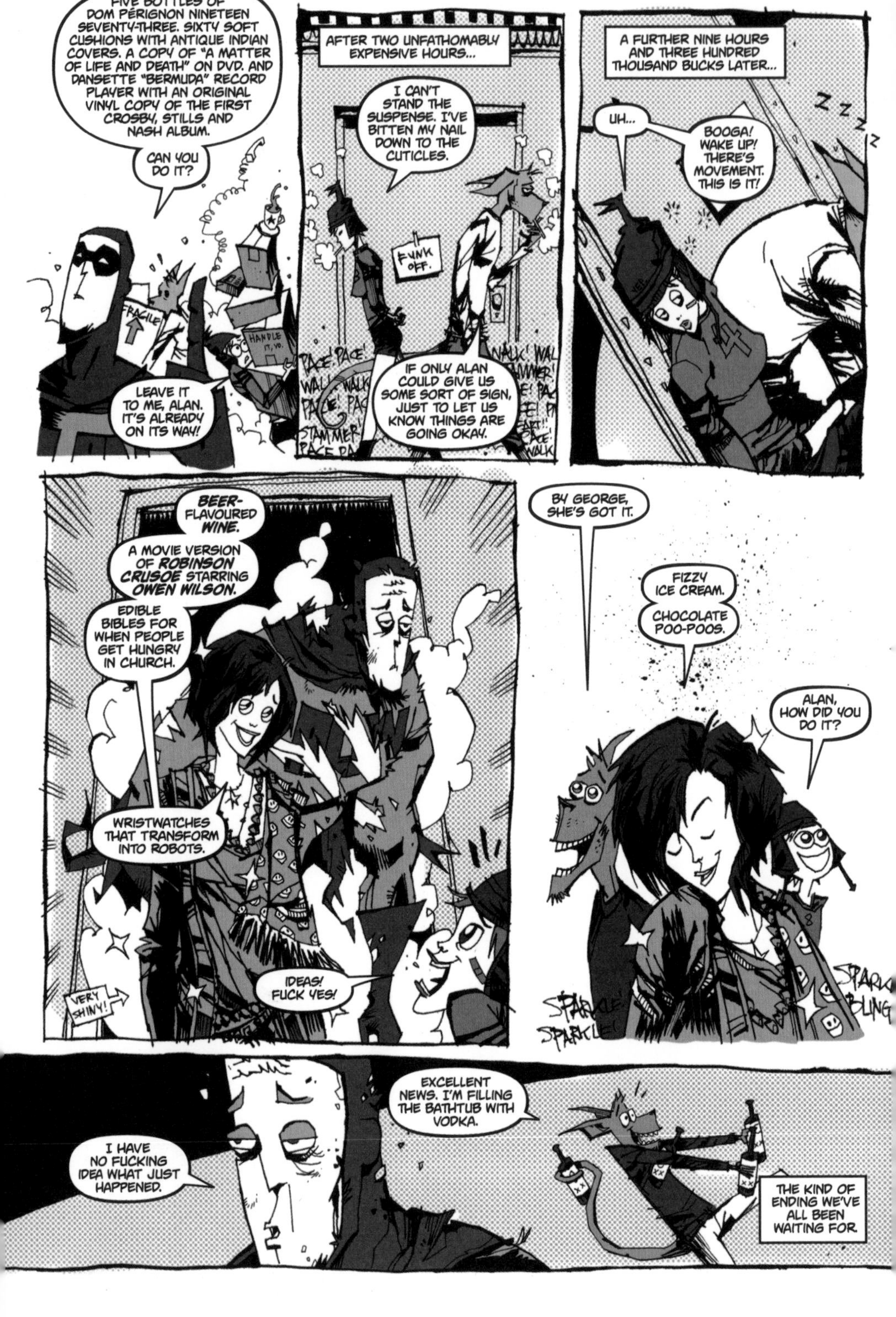
FIVE BOTTLES OF DOM PÉRIGNON NINETEEN SEVENTY-THREE. SIXTY SOFT CUSHIONS WITH ANTIQUE INDIAN COVERS. A COPY OF "A MATTER OF LIFE AND DEATH" ON DVD. AND DANSETTE "BERMUDA" RECORD PLAYER WITH AN ORIGINAL VINYL COPY OF THE FIRST CROSBY, STILLS AND NASH ALBUM.
CAN YOU DO IT?
FRAGILE
HANDLE IT, YO.
LEAVE IT TO ME, ALAN. IT'S ALREADY ON ITS WAY!
AFTER TWO UNFATHOMABLY EXPENSIVE HOURS...
I CAN'T STAND THE SUSPENSE. I'VE BITTEN MY NAIL DOWN TO THE CUTICLES.
FUNK OFF.
IF ONLY ALAN COULD GIVE US SOME SORT OF SIGN, JUST TO LET US KNOW THINGS ARE GOING OKAY.
A FURTHER NINE HOURS AND THREE HUNDRED THOUSAND BUCKS LATER...
Z Z Z Z
UH...
BOOGA! WAKE UP! THERE'S MOVEMENT. THIS IS IT!
BEER-FLAVOURED WINE.
A MOVIE VERSION OF ROBINSON CRUSOE STARRING OWEN WILSON.
EDIBLE BIBLES FOR WHEN PEOPLE GET HUNGRY IN CHURCH.
WRISTWATCHES THAT TRANSFORM INTO ROBOTS.
VERY SHINY!
IDEAS! FUCK YES!
BY GEORGE, SHE'S GOT IT.
FIZZY ICE CREAM.
CHOCOLATE POO-POOS.
ALAN, HOW DID YOU DO IT?
SPARKLE SPARKLE
BLING
I HAVE NO FUCKING IDEA WHAT JUST HAPPENED.
EXCELLENT NEWS. I'M FILLING THE BATHTUB WITH VODKA.
THE KIND OF ENDING WE'VE ALL BEEN WAITING FOR.

ALAN MARTIN RUFUS DAYGLO

TANK GIRL

BAD WIND RISING

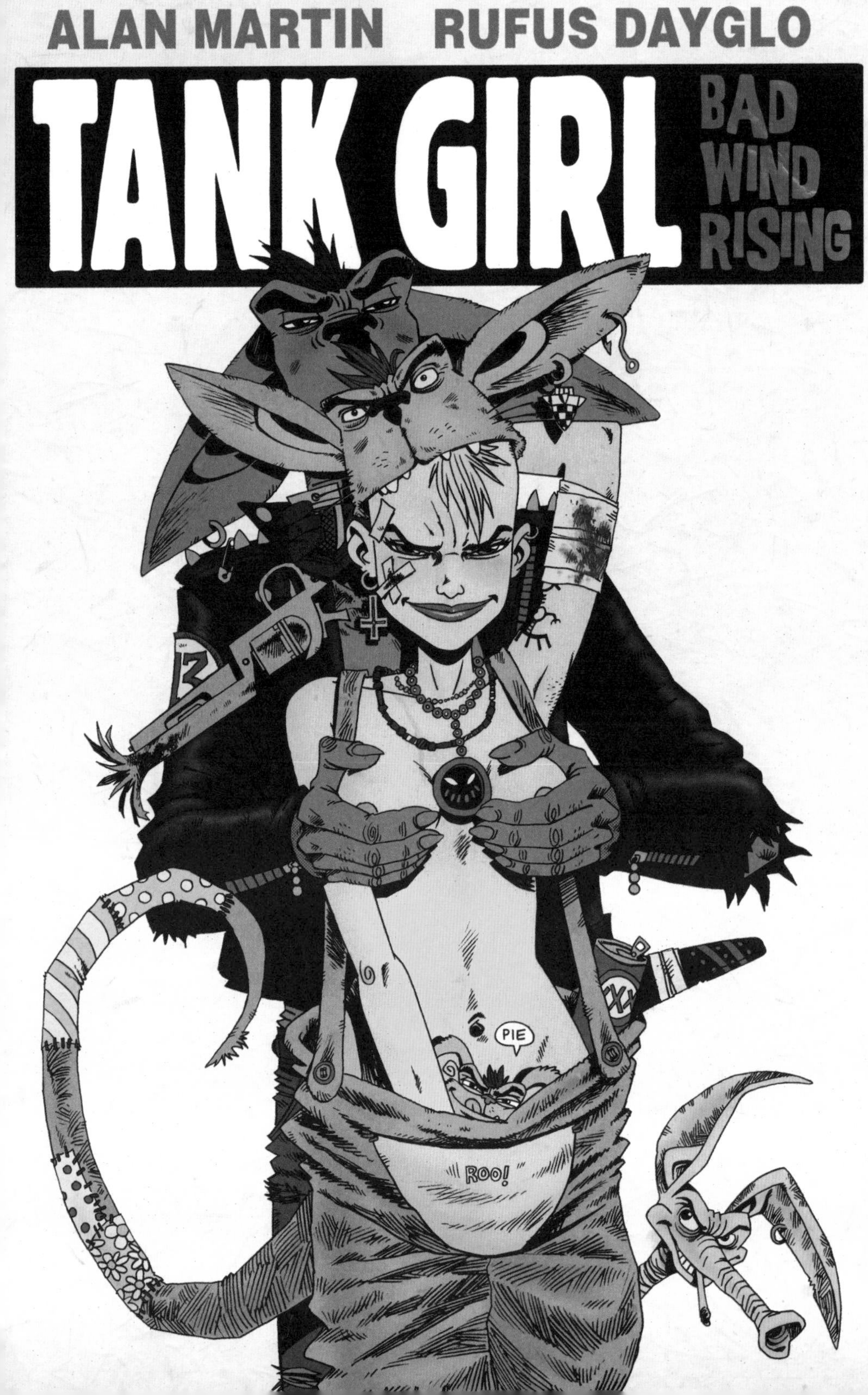
PIE
ROO!

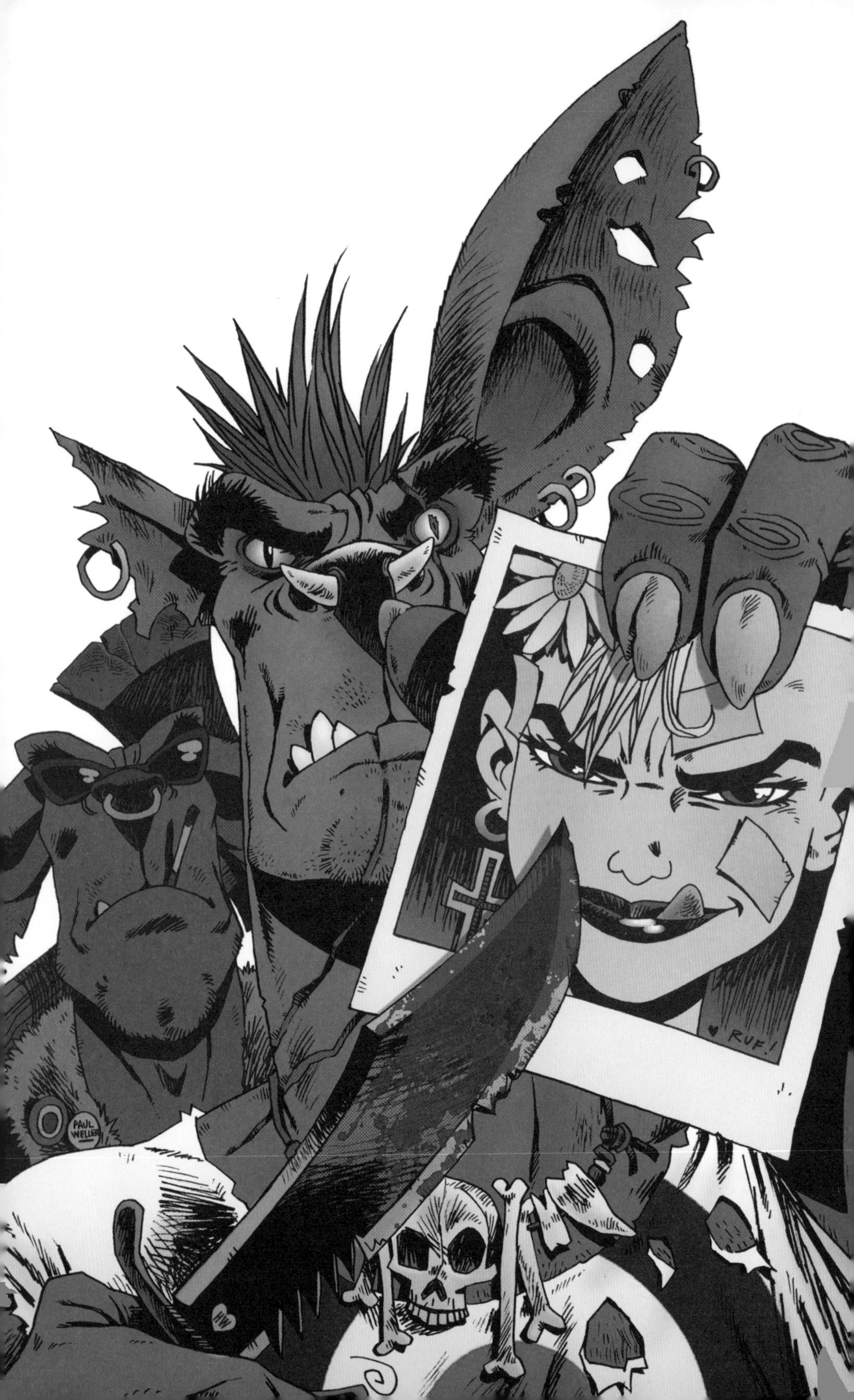
PAUL WELLER
RUF!

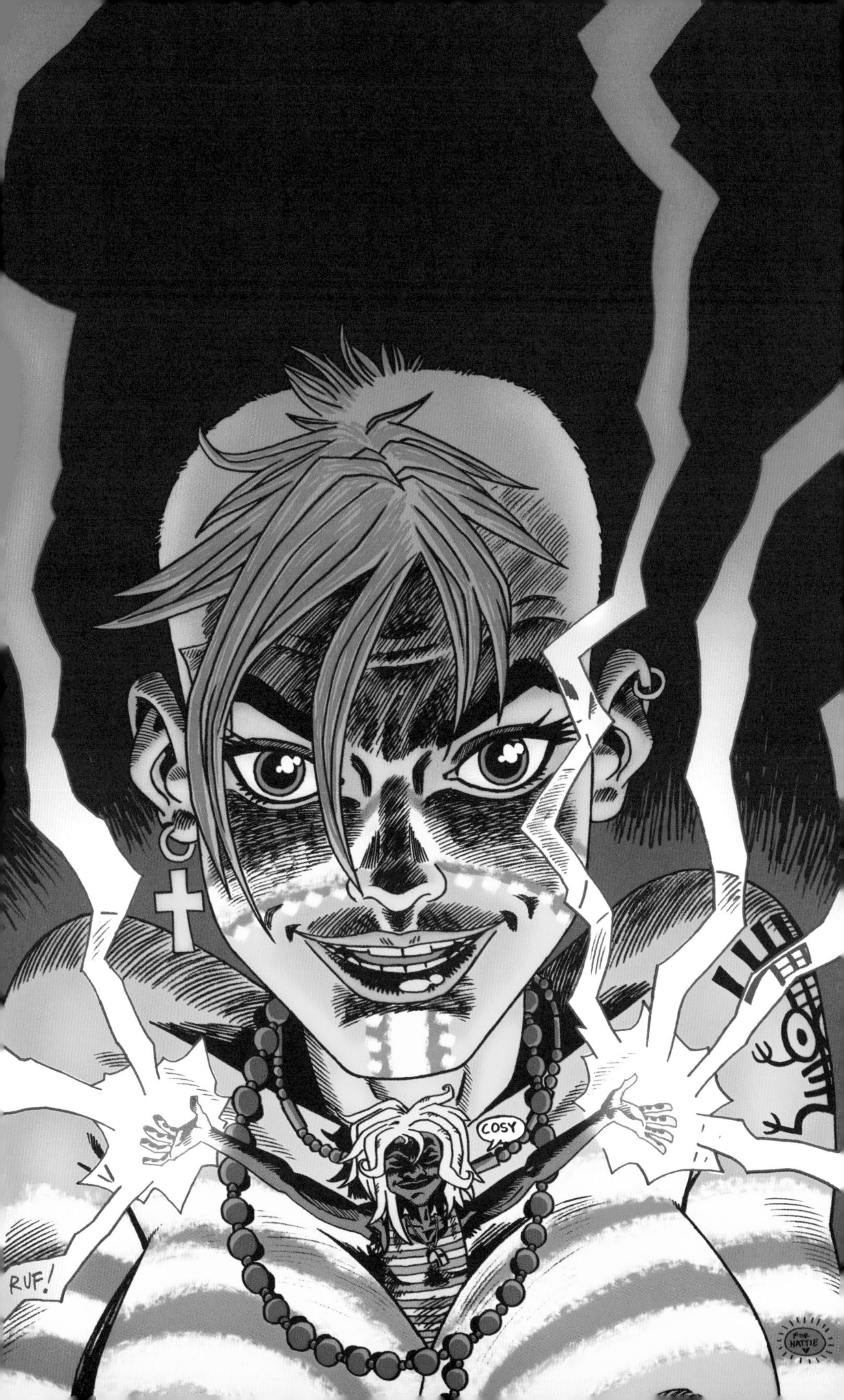
COSY
RUF!
FOR HATTIE

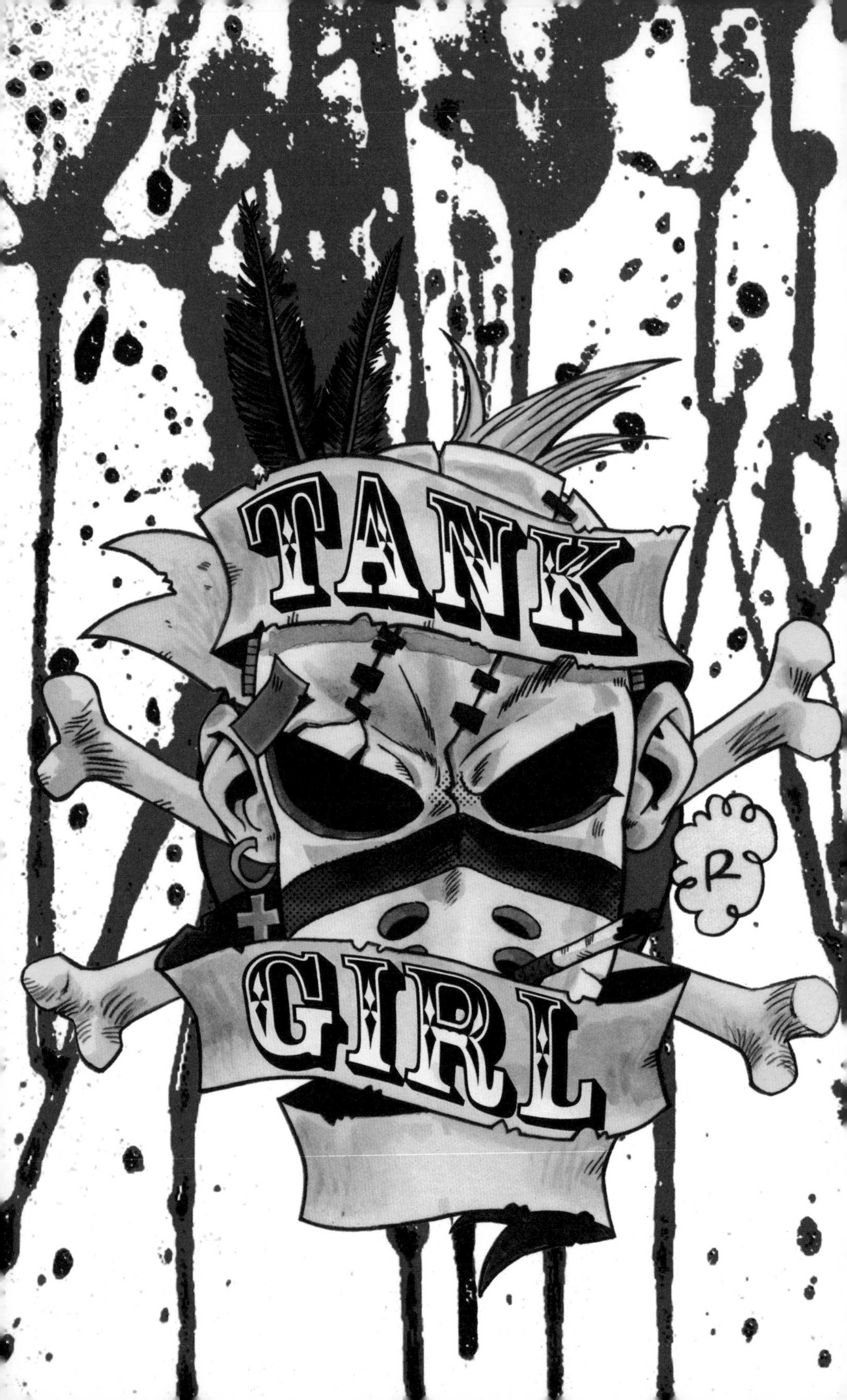
TANK
GIRL

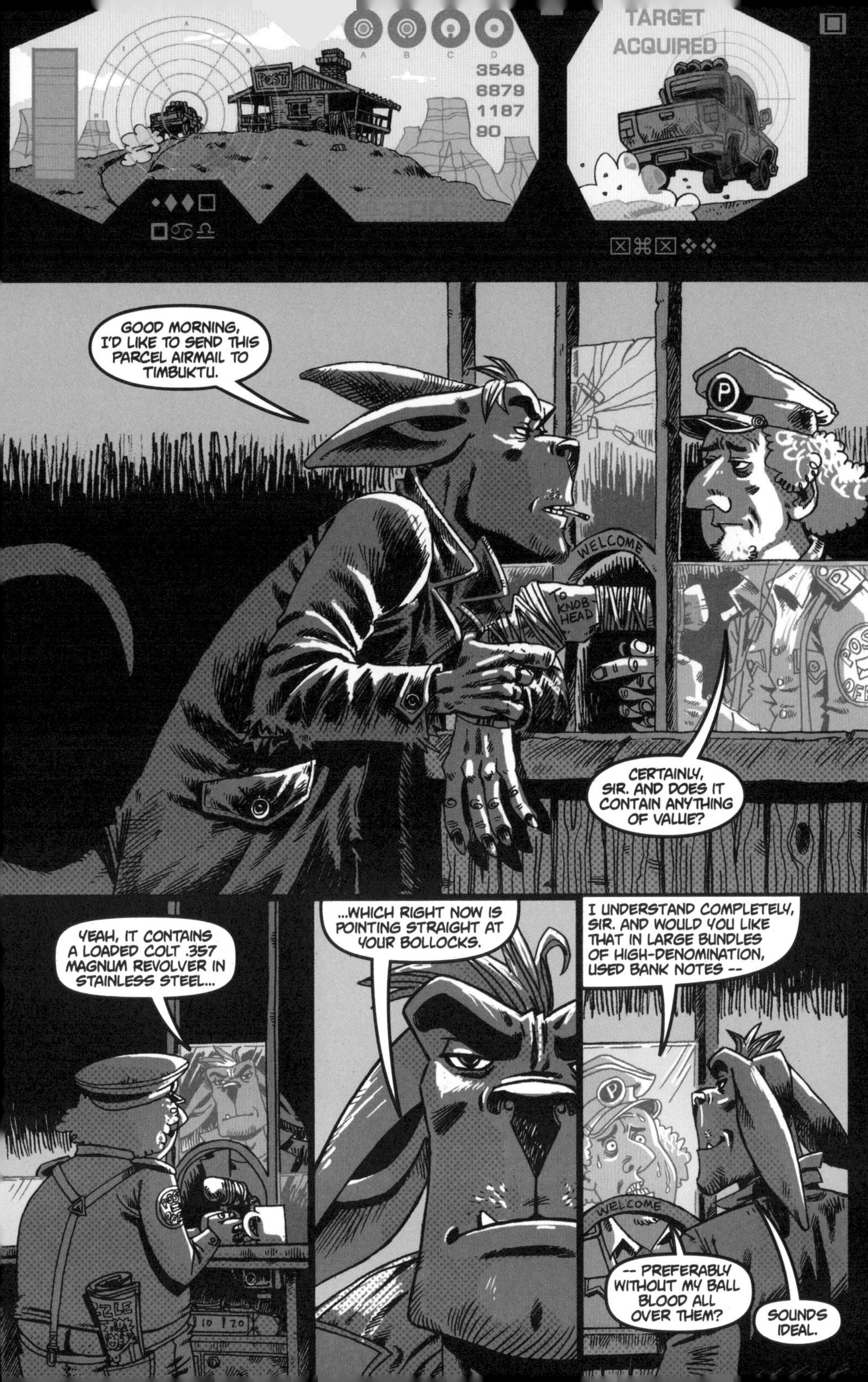
3546
6879
1187
90
TARGET ACQUIRED
POST
GOOD MORNING, I'D LIKE TO SEND THIS PARCEL AIRMAIL TO TIMBUKTU.
WELCOME
TO KNOB HEAD
CERTAINLY, SIR. AND DOES IT CONTAIN ANYTHING OF VALUE?
YEAH, IT CONTAINS A LOADED COLT .357 MAGNUM REVOLVER IN STAINLESS STEEL...
...WHICH RIGHT NOW IS POINTING STRAIGHT AT YOUR BOLLOCKS.
I UNDERSTAND COMPLETELY, SIR. AND WOULD YOU LIKE THAT IN LARGE BUNDLES OF HIGH-DENOMINATION, USED BANK NOTES --
WELCOME
-- PREFERABLY WITHOUT MY BALL BLOOD ALL OVER THEM?
SOUNDS IDEAL.

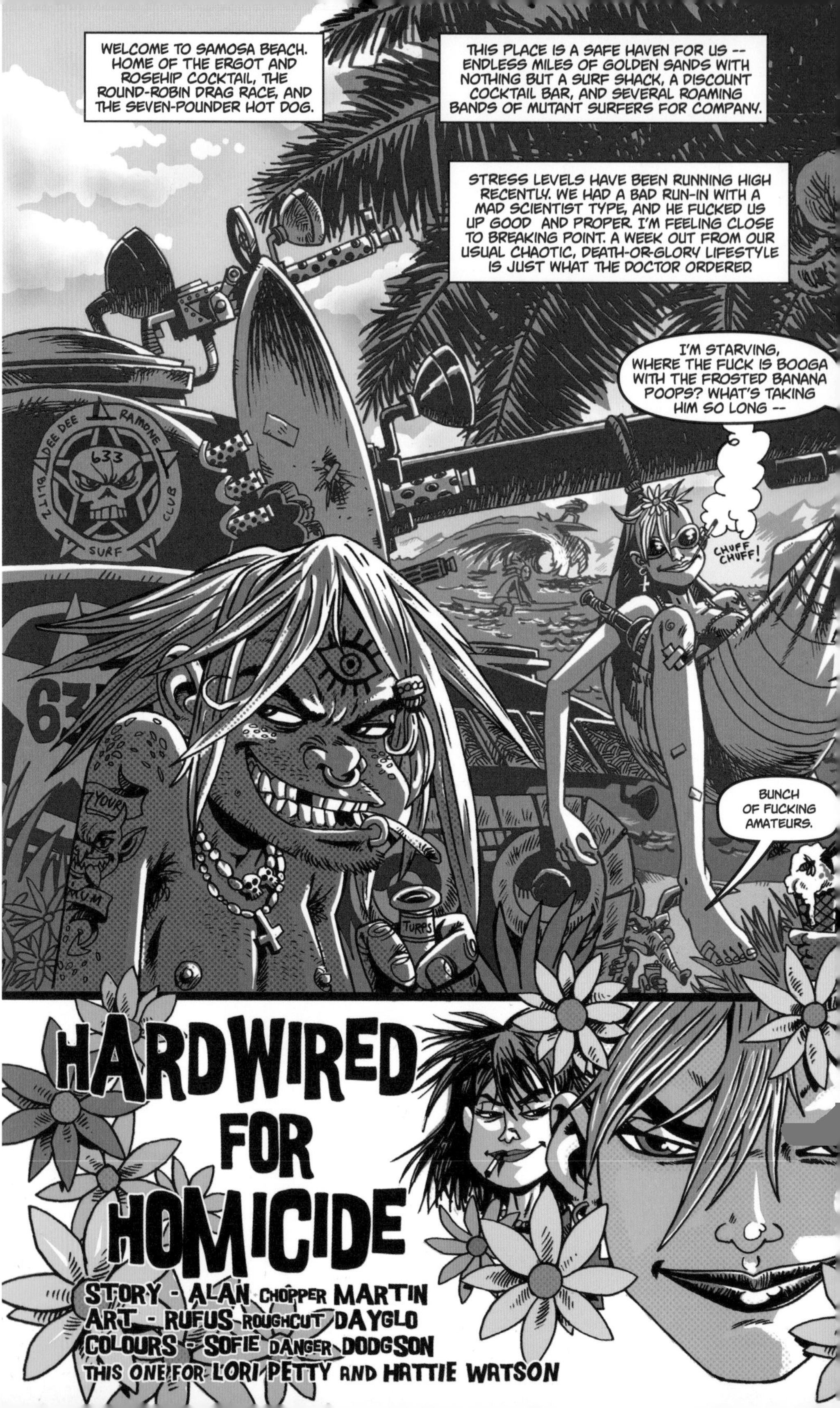
WELCOME TO SAMOSA BEACH. HOME OF THE ERGOT AND ROSEHIP COCKTAIL, THE ROUND-ROBIN DRAG RACE, AND THE SEVEN-POUNDER HOT DOG.
THIS PLACE IS A SAFE HAVEN FOR US -- ENDLESS MILES OF GOLDEN SANDS WITH NOTHING BUT A SURF SHACK, A DISCOUNT COCKTAIL BAR, AND SEVERAL ROAMING BANDS OF MUTANT SURFERS FOR COMPANY.
STRESS LEVELS HAVE BEEN RUNNING HIGH RECENTLY. WE HAD A BAD RUN-IN WITH A MAD SCIENTIST TYPE, AND HE FUCKED US UP GOOD AND PROPER. I'M FEELING CLOSE TO BREAKING POINT. A WEEK OUT FROM OUR USUAL CHAOTIC, DEATH-OR-GLORY LIFESTYLE IS JUST WHAT THE DOCTOR ORDERED.
DEE DEE RAMONE BLITZ SURF CLUB 633
I'M STARVING, WHERE THE FUCK IS BOOGA WITH THE FROSTED BANANA POOPS? WHAT'S TAKING HIM SO LONG --
CHUFF CHUFF!
YOUR MUM
TURPS
BUNCH OF FUCKING AMATEURS.
HARDWIRED FOR HOMICIDE
STORY - ALAN CHOPPER MARTIN
ART - RUFUS ROUGHCUT DAYGLO
COLOURS - SOFIE DANGER DODGSON
THIS ONE FOR LORI PETTY AND HATTIE WATSON

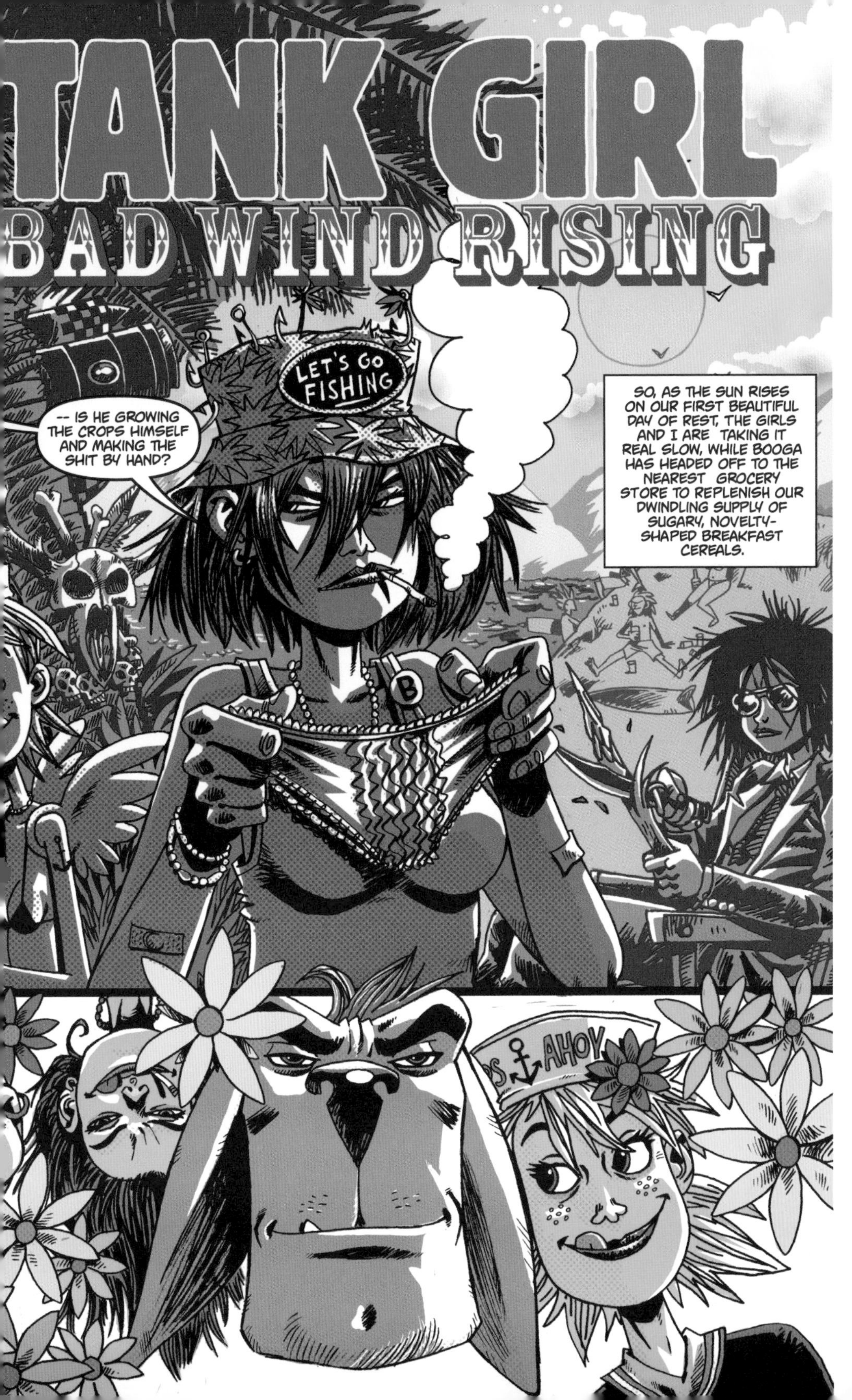
TANK GIRL
BAD WIND RISING
LET'S GO FISHING
-- IS HE GROWING THE CROPS HIMSELF AND MAKING THE SHIT BY HAND?
SO, AS THE SUN RISES ON OUR FIRST BEAUTIFUL DAY OF REST, THE GIRLS AND I ARE TAKING IT REAL SLOW, WHILE BOOGA HAS HEADED OFF TO THE NEAREST GROCERY STORE TO REPLENISH OUR DWINDLING SUPPLY OF SUGARY, NOVELTY-SHAPED BREAKFAST CEREALS.
AHOY

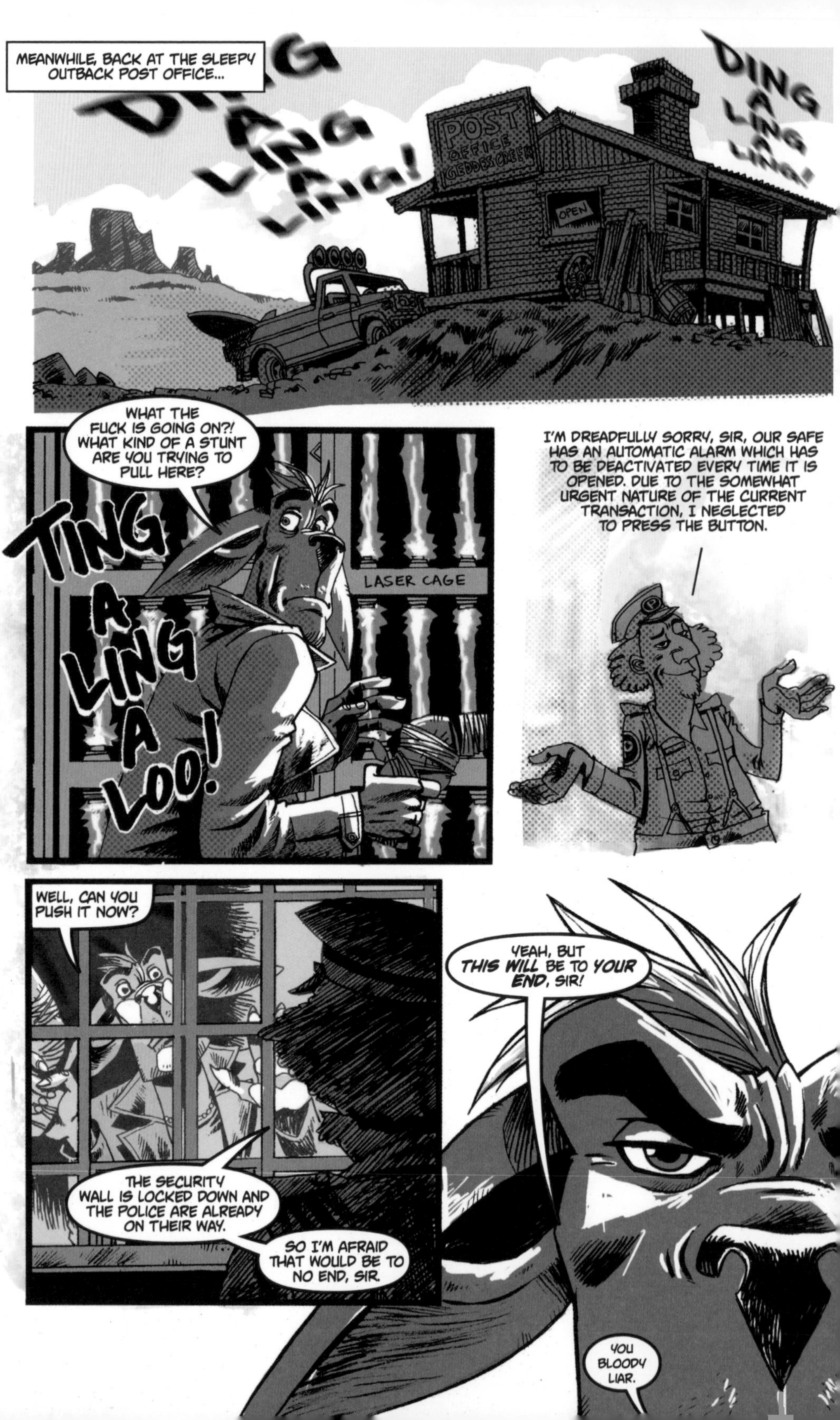
MEANWHILE, BACK AT THE SLEEPY OUTBACK POST OFFICE...
DING A LING A LING!
DING A LING A LING!
POST OFFICE GEDDES CREEK
OPEN
WHAT THE FUCK IS GOING ON?! WHAT KIND OF A STUNT ARE YOU TRYING TO PULL HERE?
TING A LING A LOO!
LASER CAGE
I'M DREADFULLY SORRY, SIR, OUR SAFE HAS AN AUTOMATIC ALARM WHICH HAS TO BE DEACTIVATED EVERY TIME IT IS OPENED. DUE TO THE SOMEWHAT URGENT NATURE OF THE CURRENT TRANSACTION, I NEGLECTED TO PRESS THE BUTTON.
WELL, CAN YOU PUSH IT NOW?
THE SECURITY WALL IS LOCKED DOWN AND THE POLICE ARE ALREADY ON THEIR WAY.
SO I'M AFRAID THAT WOULD BE TO NO END, SIR.
YEAH, BUT THIS WILL BE TO YOUR END, SIR!
YOU BLOODY LIAR.

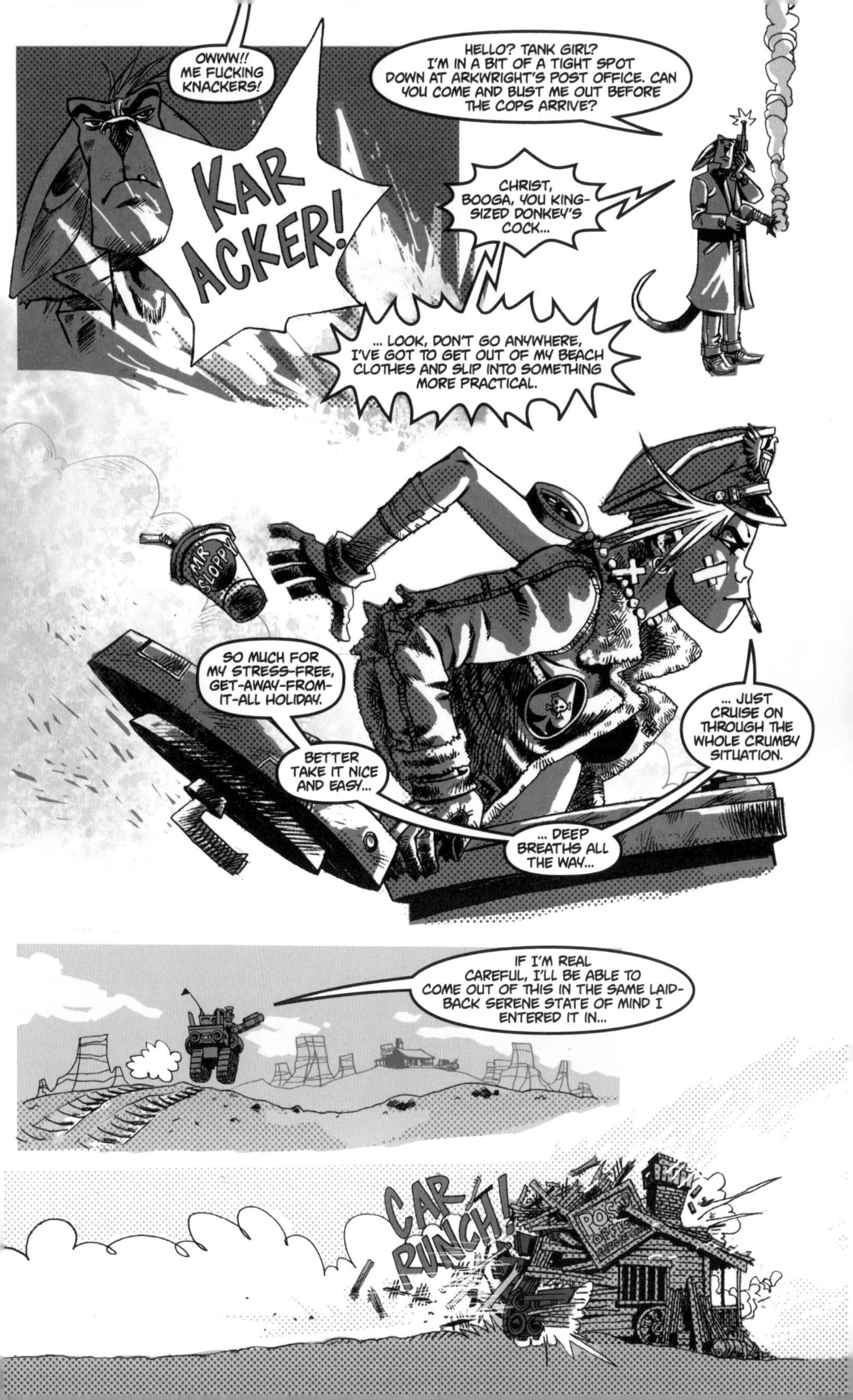
OWWW!! ME FUCKING KNACKERS!
KAR ACKER!
HELLO? TANK GIRL? I'M IN A BIT OF A TIGHT SPOT DOWN AT ARKWRIGHT'S POST OFFICE. CAN YOU COME AND BUST ME OUT BEFORE THE COPS ARRIVE?
CHRIST, BOOGA, YOU KING-SIZED DONKEY'S COCK...
... LOOK, DON'T GO ANYWHERE, I'VE GOT TO GET OUT OF MY BEACH CLOTHES AND SLIP INTO SOMETHING MORE PRACTICAL.
MR SLOPPY
SO MUCH FOR MY STRESS-FREE, GET-AWAY-FROM-IT-ALL HOLIDAY.
BETTER TAKE IT NICE AND EASY...
... JUST CRUISE ON THROUGH THE WHOLE CRUMBY SITUATION.
... DEEP BREATHS ALL THE WAY...
IF I'M REAL CAREFUL, I'LL BE ABLE TO COME OUT OF THIS IN THE SAME LAID-BACK SERENE STATE OF MIND I ENTERED IT IN...
CAR RUNCH!

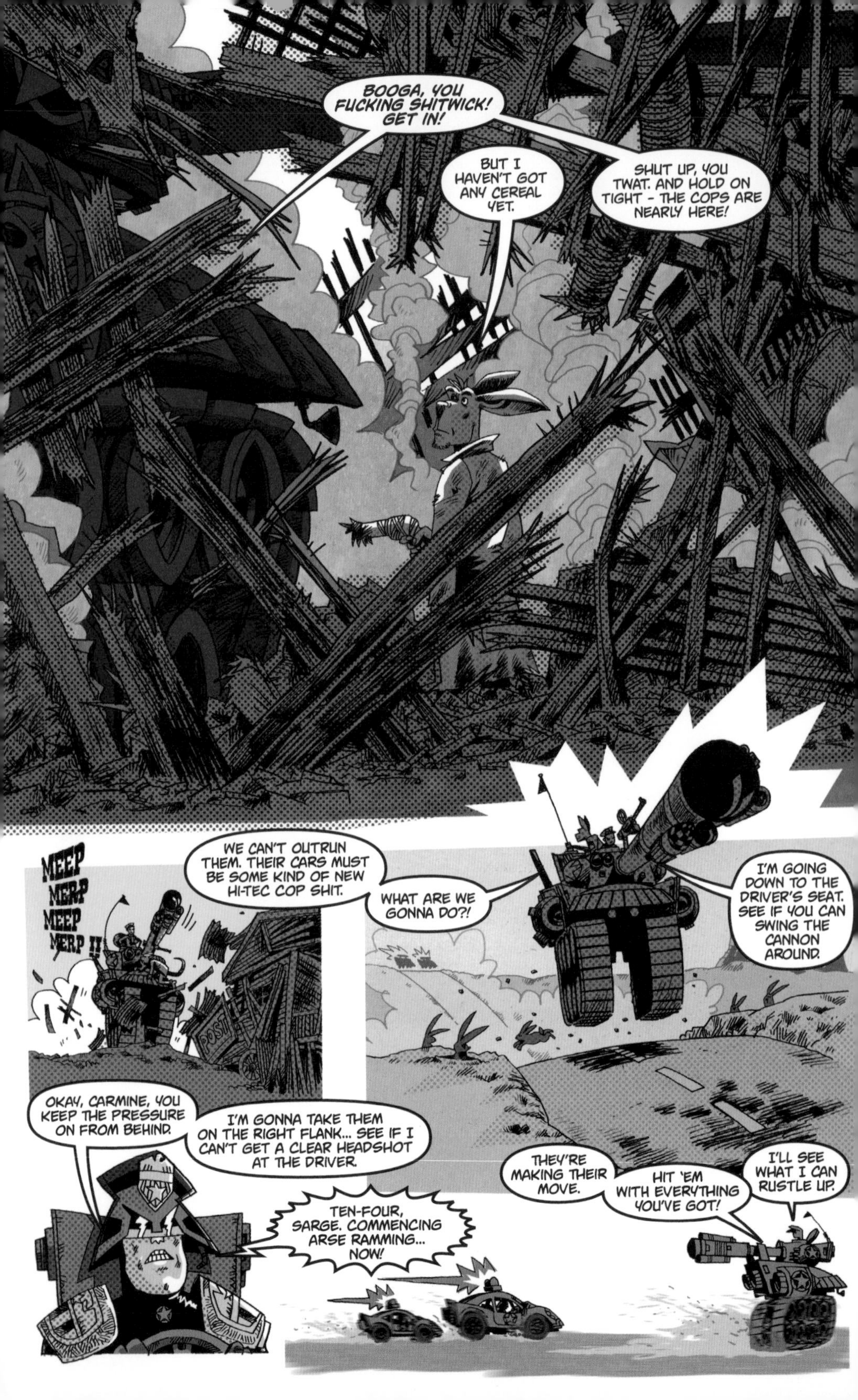
BOOGA, YOU FUCKING SHITWICK! GET IN!
BUT I HAVEN'T GOT ANY CEREAL YET.
SHUT UP, YOU TWAT. AND HOLD ON TIGHT - THE COPS ARE NEARLY HERE!
MEEP MERP MEEP MERP !!
WE CAN'T OUTRUN THEM. THEIR CARS MUST BE SOME KIND OF NEW HI-TEC COP SHIT.
WHAT ARE WE GONNA DO?!
I'M GOING DOWN TO THE DRIVER'S SEAT. SEE IF YOU CAN SWING THE CANNON AROUND.
POST
OKAY, CARMINE, YOU KEEP THE PRESSURE ON FROM BEHIND.
I'M GONNA TAKE THEM ON THE RIGHT FLANK... SEE IF I CAN'T GET A CLEAR HEADSHOT AT THE DRIVER.
TEN-FOUR, SARGE. COMMENCING ARSE RAMMING... NOW!
THEY'RE MAKING THEIR MOVE.
HIT 'EM WITH EVERYTHING YOU'VE GOT!
I'LL SEE WHAT I CAN RUSTLE UP.

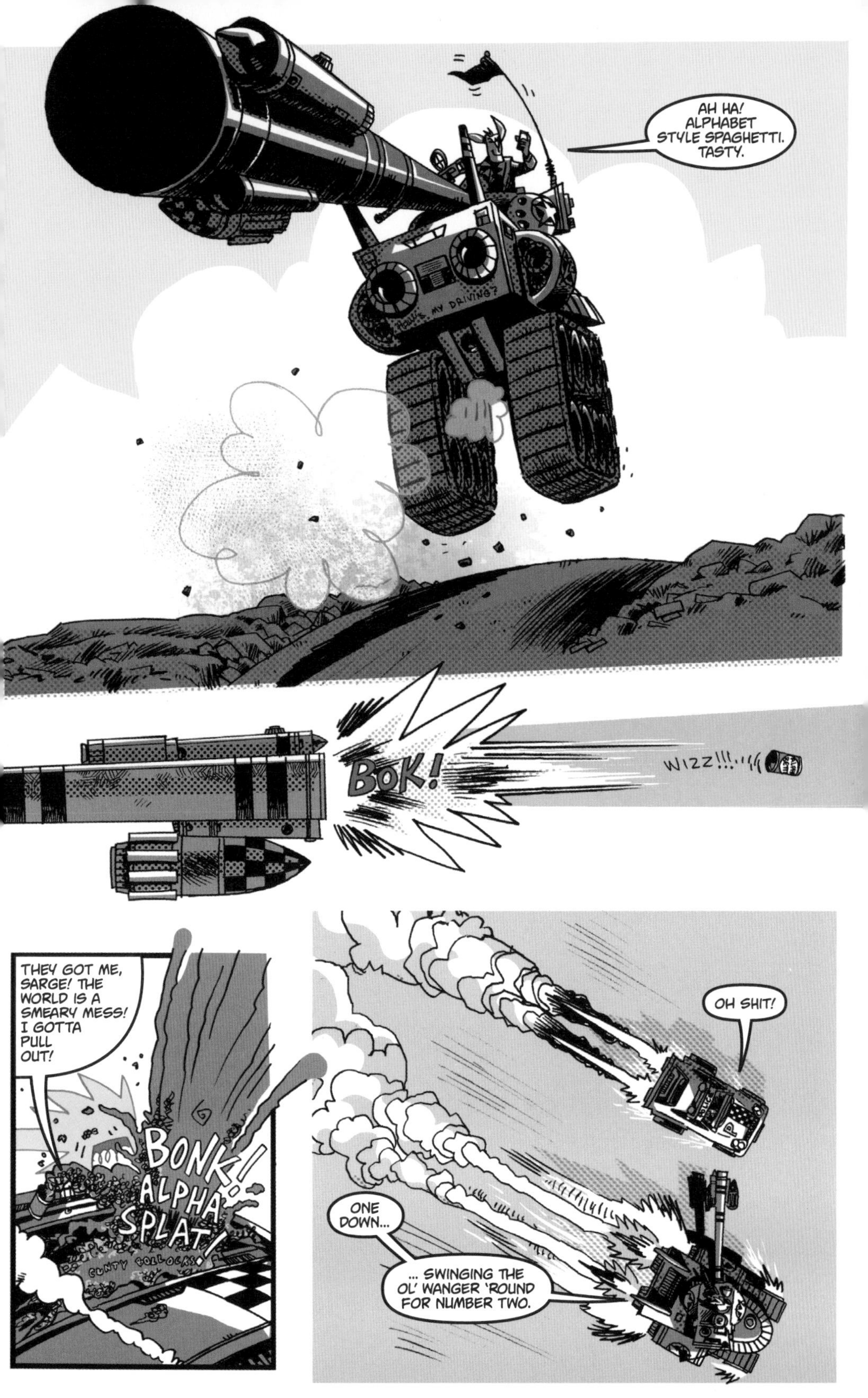
AH HA! ALPHABET STYLE SPAGHETTI. TASTY.
BOK!
WIZZ!!!
THEY GOT ME, SARGE! THE WORLD IS A SMEARY MESS! I GOTTA PULL OUT!
BONK! ALPHA SPLAT!
OH SHIT!
ONE DOWN...
... SWINGING THE OL' WANGER 'ROUND FOR NUMBER TWO.

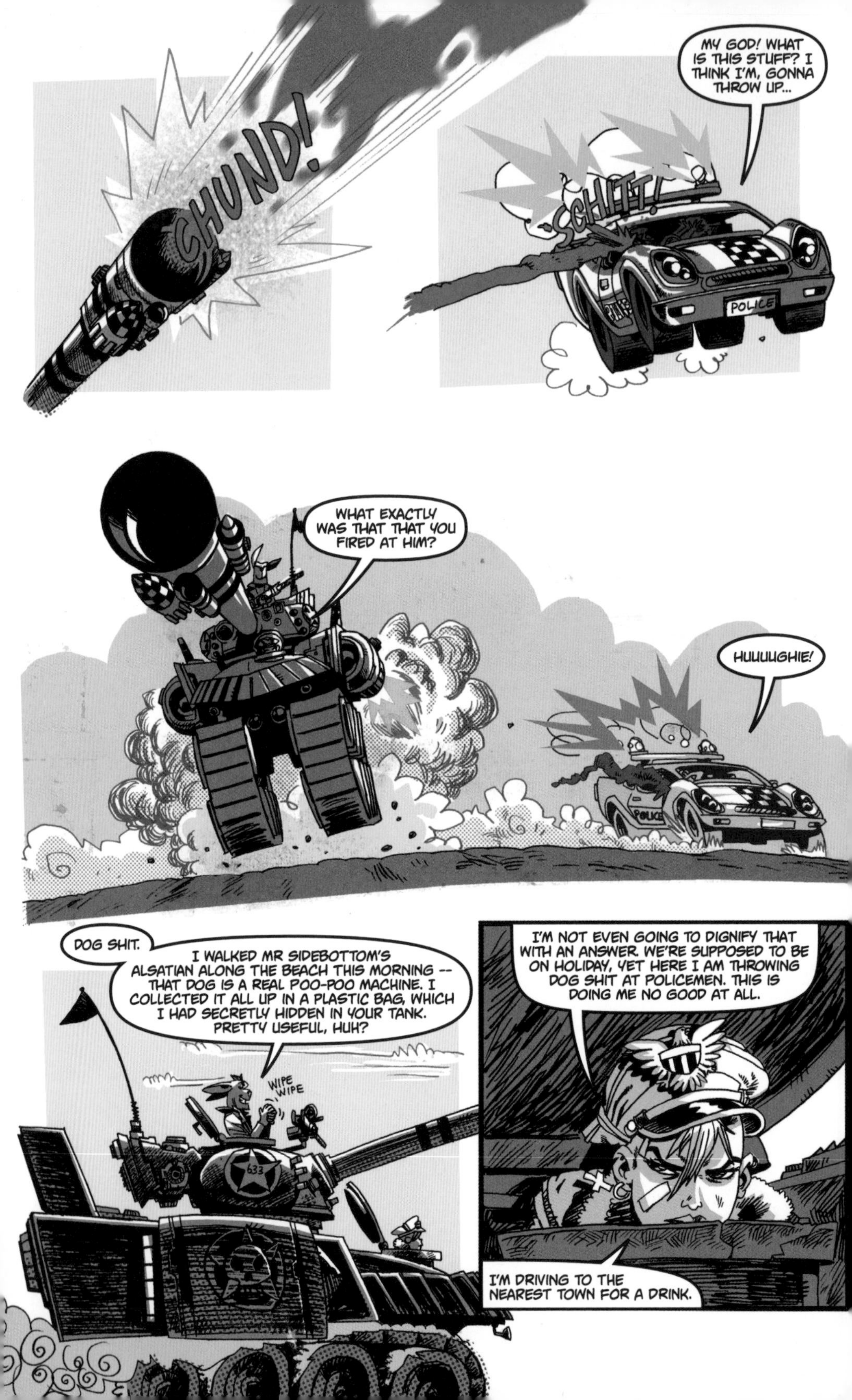
CHUND!
MY GOD! WHAT IS THIS STUFF? I THINK I'M, GONNA THROW UP...
SCHITT!
POLICE
WHAT EXACTLY WAS THAT THAT YOU FIRED AT HIM?
HUUUUGHIE!
DOG SHIT.
I WALKED MR SIDEBOTTOM'S ALSATIAN ALONG THE BEACH THIS MORNING -- THAT DOG IS A REAL POO-POO MACHINE. I COLLECTED IT ALL UP IN A PLASTIC BAG, WHICH I HAD SECRETLY HIDDEN IN YOUR TANK. PRETTY USEFUL, HUH?
WIPE WIPE
I'M NOT EVEN GOING TO DIGNIFY THAT WITH AN ANSWER. WE'RE SUPPOSED TO BE ON HOLIDAY, YET HERE I AM THROWING DOG SHIT AT POLICEMEN. THIS IS DOING ME NO GOOD AT ALL.
I'M DRIVING TO THE NEAREST TOWN FOR A DRINK.

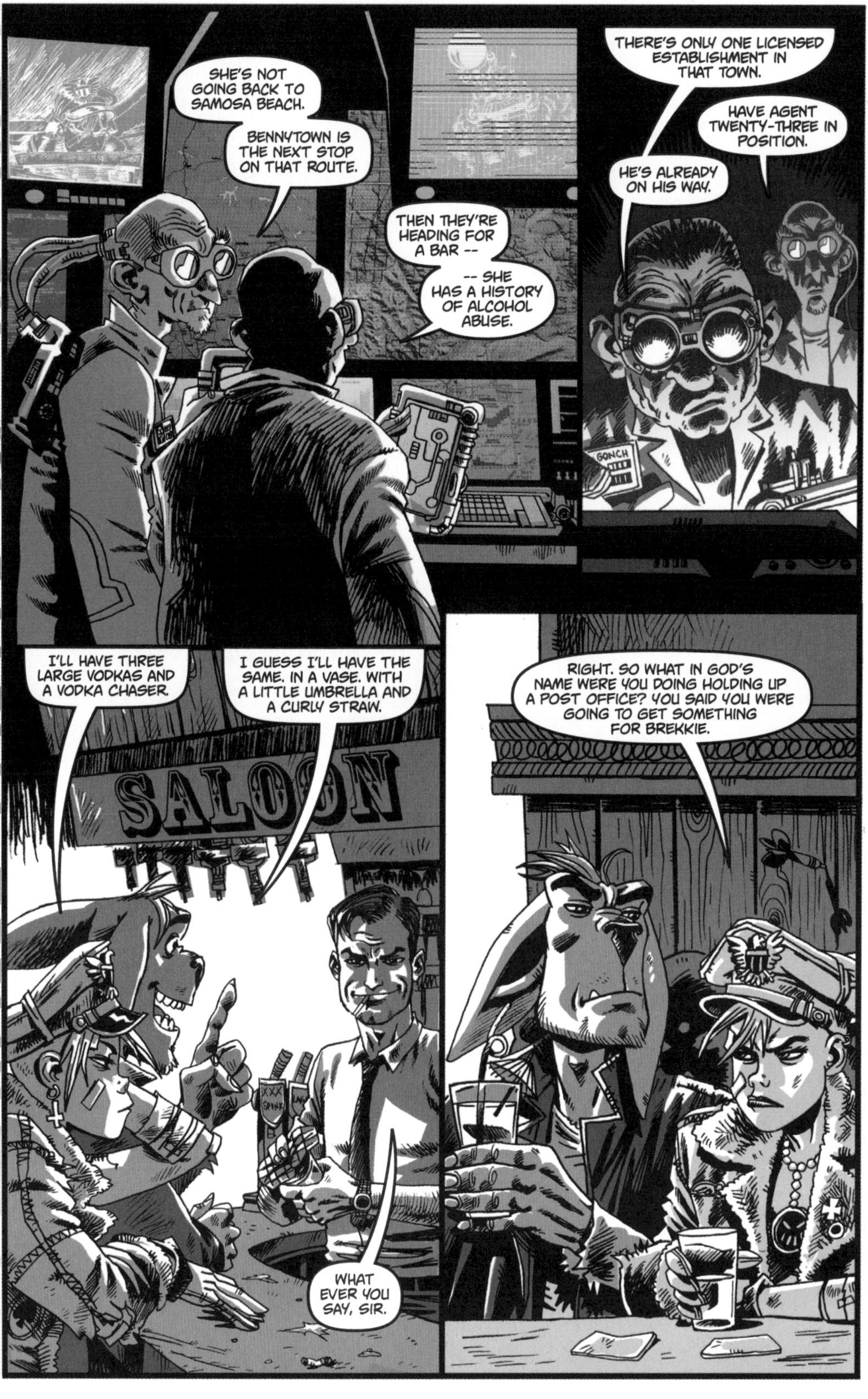
SHE'S NOT GOING BACK TO SAMOSA BEACH.
BENNYTOWN IS THE NEXT STOP ON THAT ROUTE.
THEN THEY'RE HEADING FOR A BAR --
-- SHE HAS A HISTORY OF ALCOHOL ABUSE.
THERE'S ONLY ONE LICENSED ESTABLISHMENT IN THAT TOWN.
HAVE AGENT TWENTY-THREE IN POSITION.
HE'S ALREADY ON HIS WAY.
GONCH
I'LL HAVE THREE LARGE VODKAS AND A VODKA CHASER.
I GUESS I'LL HAVE THE SAME. IN A VASE. WITH A LITTLE UMBRELLA AND A CURLY STRAW.
SALOON
WHAT EVER YOU SAY, SIR.
RIGHT. SO WHAT IN GOD'S NAME WERE YOU DOING HOLDING UP A POST OFFICE? YOU SAID YOU WERE GOING TO GET SOMETHING FOR BREKKIE.

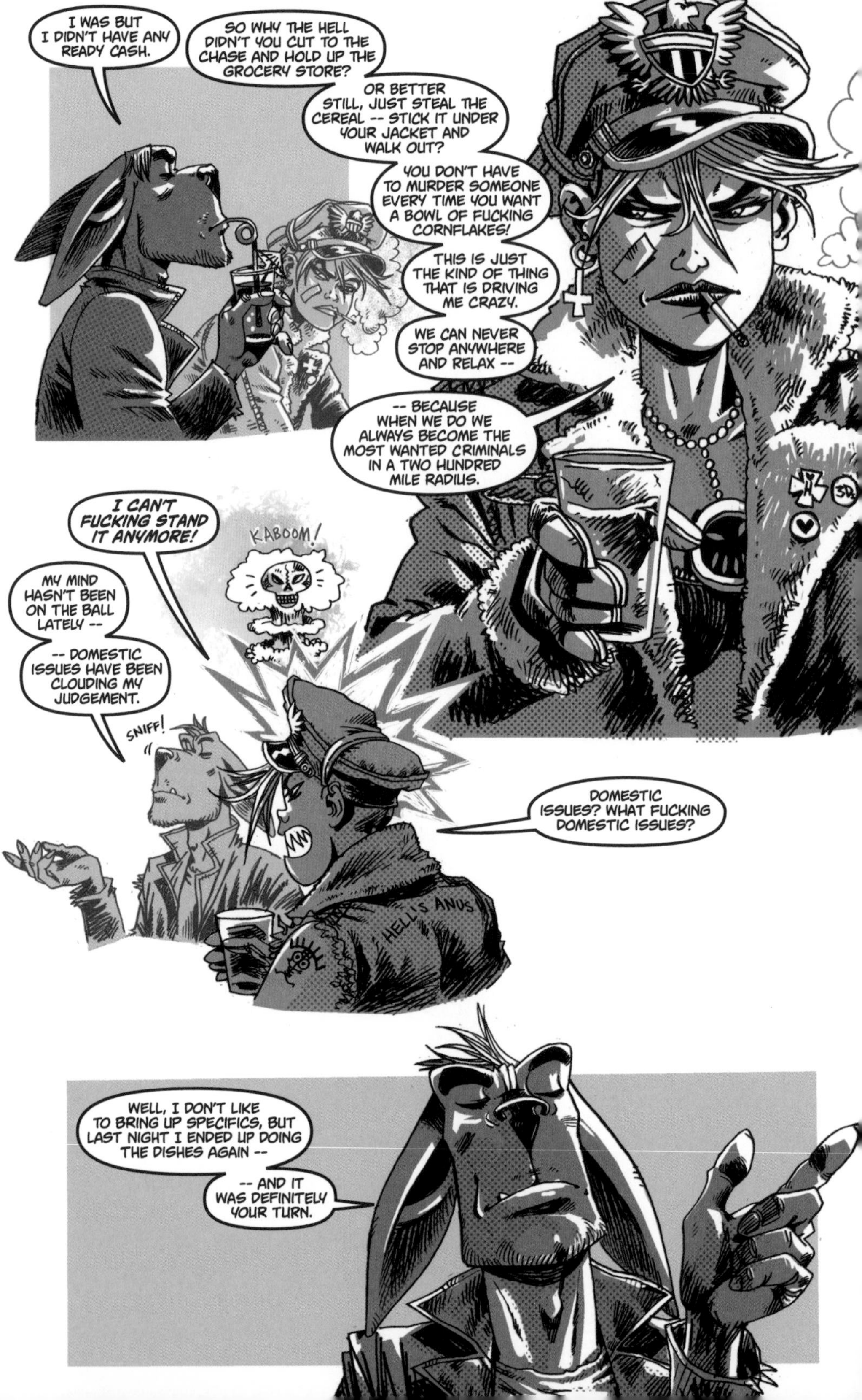
I WAS BUT I DIDN'T HAVE ANY READY CASH.
SO WHY THE HELL DIDN'T YOU CUT TO THE CHASE AND HOLD UP THE GROCERY STORE?
OR BETTER STILL, JUST STEAL THE CEREAL -- STICK IT UNDER YOUR JACKET AND WALK OUT?
YOU DON'T HAVE TO MURDER SOMEONE EVERY TIME YOU WANT A BOWL OF FUCKING CORNFLAKES!
THIS IS JUST THE KIND OF THING THAT IS DRIVING ME CRAZY.
WE CAN NEVER STOP ANYWHERE AND RELAX --
-- BECAUSE WHEN WE DO WE ALWAYS BECOME THE MOST WANTED CRIMINALS IN A TWO HUNDRED MILE RADIUS.
I CAN'T FUCKING STAND IT ANYMORE!
KABOOM!
MY MIND HASN'T BEEN ON THE BALL LATELY --
-- DOMESTIC ISSUES HAVE BEEN CLOUDING MY JUDGEMENT.
SNIFF!
DOMESTIC ISSUES? WHAT FUCKING DOMESTIC ISSUES?
HELL'S ANUS
WELL, I DON'T LIKE TO BRING UP SPECIFICS, BUT LAST NIGHT I ENDED UP DOING THE DISHES AGAIN --
-- AND IT WAS DEFINITELY YOUR TURN.

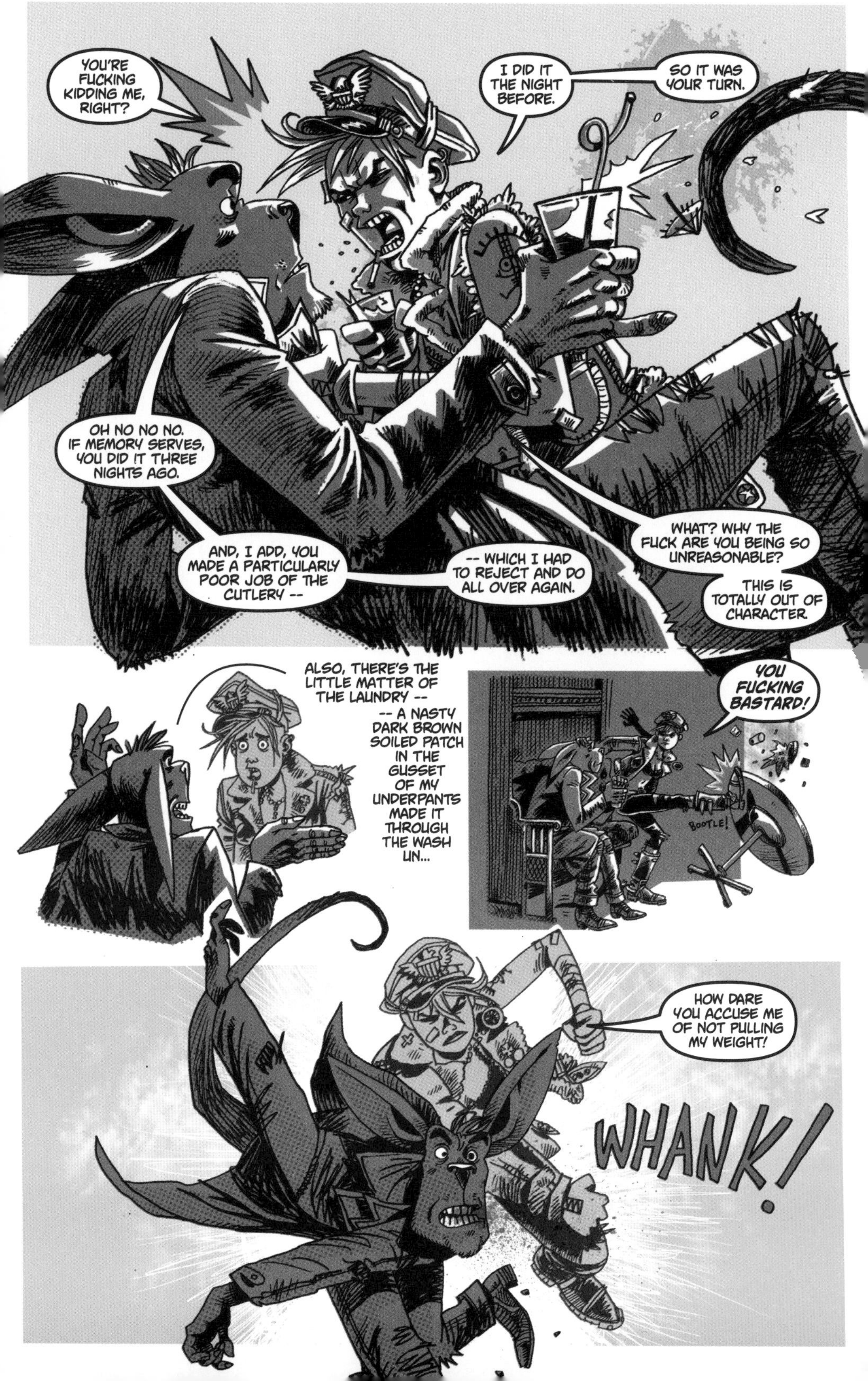
YOU'RE FUCKING KIDDING ME, RIGHT?
I DID IT THE NIGHT BEFORE.
SO IT WAS YOUR TURN.
OH NO NO NO. IF MEMORY SERVES, YOU DID IT THREE NIGHTS AGO.
AND, I ADD, YOU MADE A PARTICULARLY POOR JOB OF THE CUTLERY --
-- WHICH I HAD TO REJECT AND DO ALL OVER AGAIN.
WHAT? WHY THE FUCK ARE YOU BEING SO UNREASONABLE?
THIS IS TOTALLY OUT OF CHARACTER.
ALSO, THERE'S THE LITTLE MATTER OF THE LAUNDRY --
-- A NASTY DARK BROWN SOILED PATCH IN THE GUSSET OF MY UNDERPANTS MADE IT THROUGH THE WASH UN...
YOU FUCKING BASTARD!
BOOTLE!
HOW DARE YOU ACCUSE ME OF NOT PULLING MY WEIGHT!
WHANK!

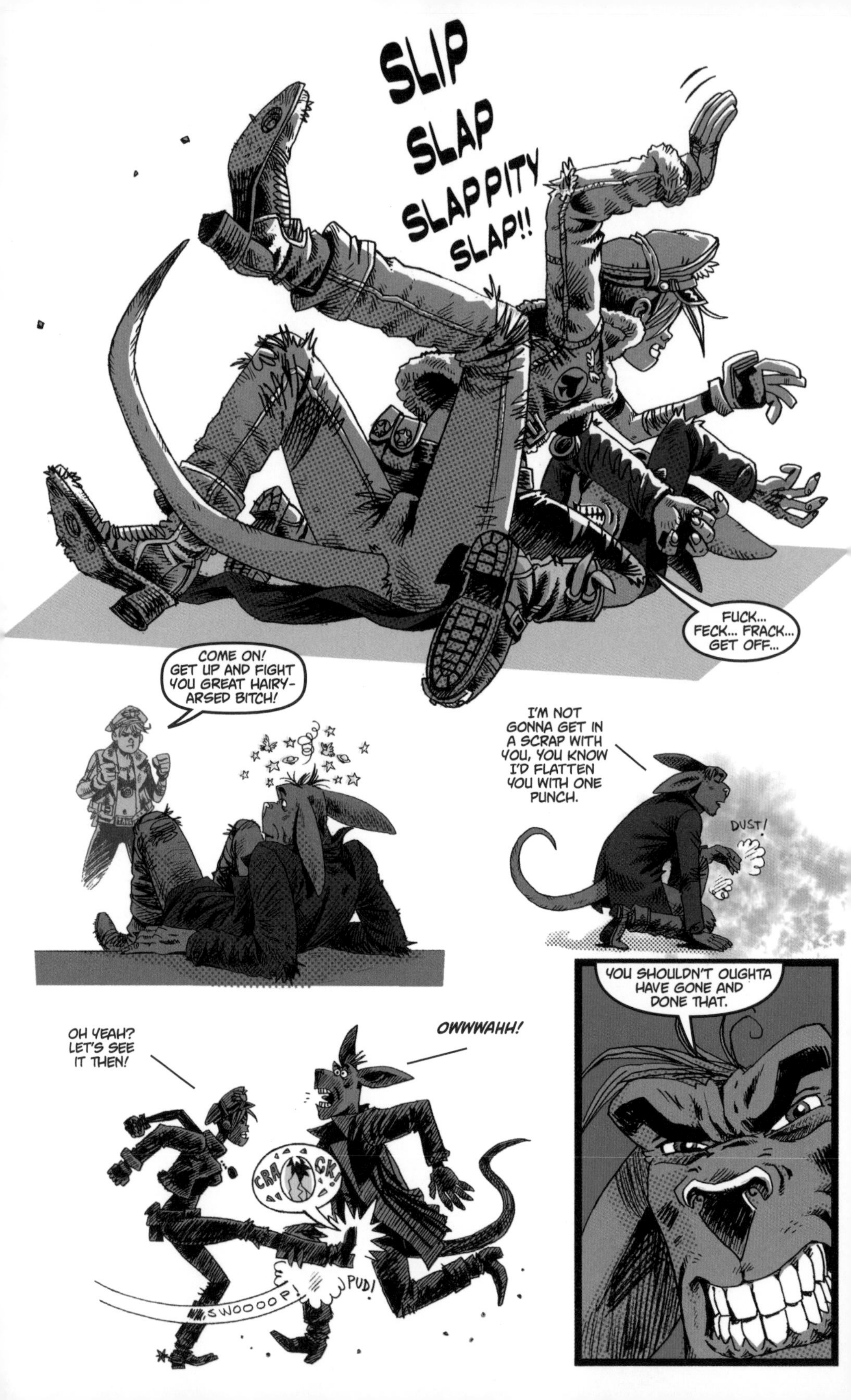
SLIP
SLAP
SLAPPITY
SLAP!!
FUCK... FECK... FRACK... GET OFF...
COME ON! GET UP AND FIGHT YOU GREAT HAIRY-ARSED BITCH!
I'M NOT GONNA GET IN A SCRAP WITH YOU, YOU KNOW I'D FLATTEN YOU WITH ONE PUNCH.
DUST!
OH YEAH? LET'S SEE IT THEN!
OWWWAHH!
CRACK!
SWOOOOP!
PUD!
YOU SHOULDN'T OUGHTA HAVE GONE AND DONE THAT.

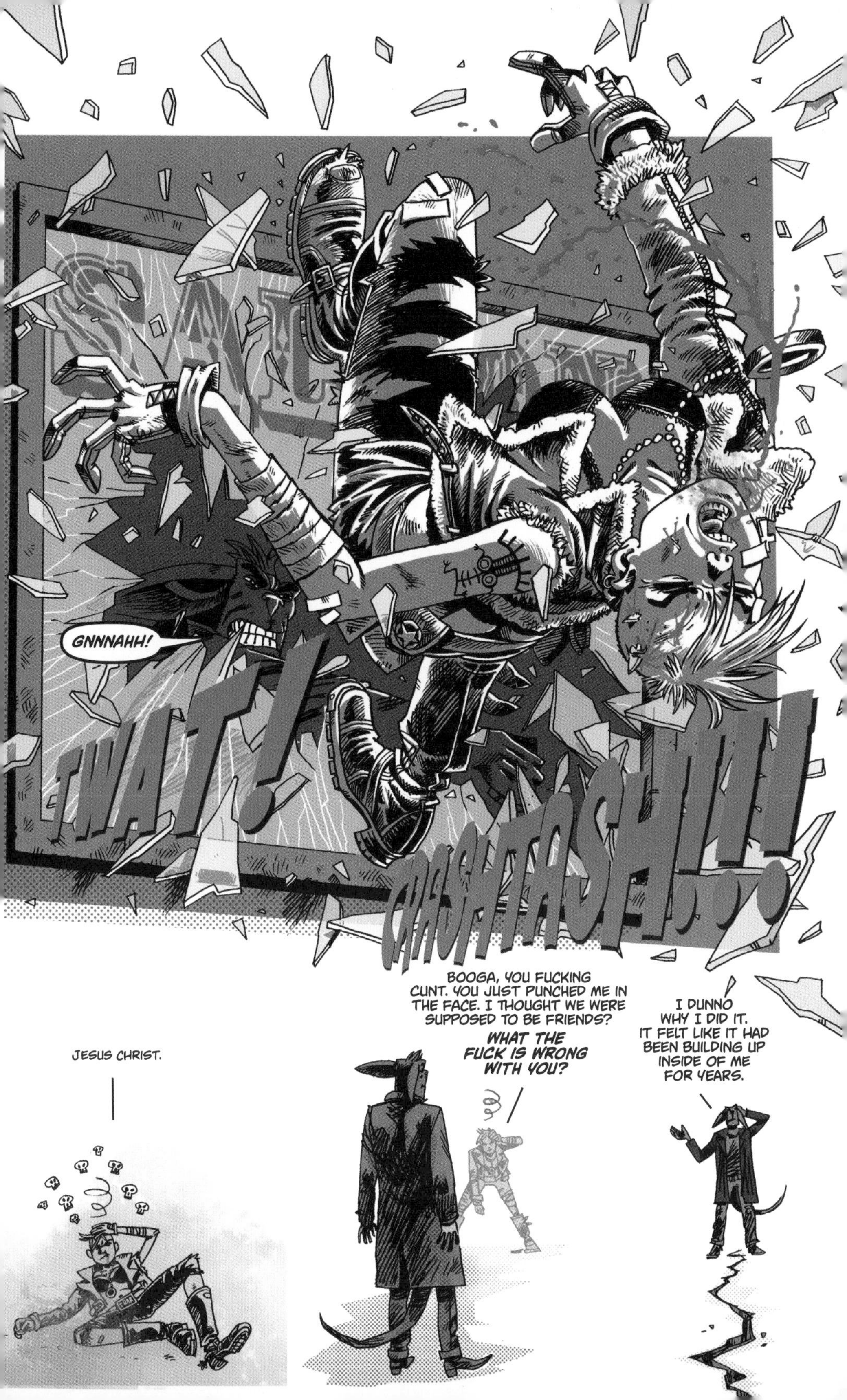
GNNNAHH!
TWAT!!
CRASHTASH!!!...
JESUS CHRIST.
BOOGA, YOU FUCKING CUNT. YOU JUST PUNCHED ME IN THE FACE. I THOUGHT WE WERE SUPPOSED TO BE FRIENDS?
WHAT THE FUCK IS WRONG WITH YOU?
I DUNNO WHY I DID IT. IT FELT LIKE IT HAD BEEN BUILDING UP INSIDE OF ME FOR YEARS.

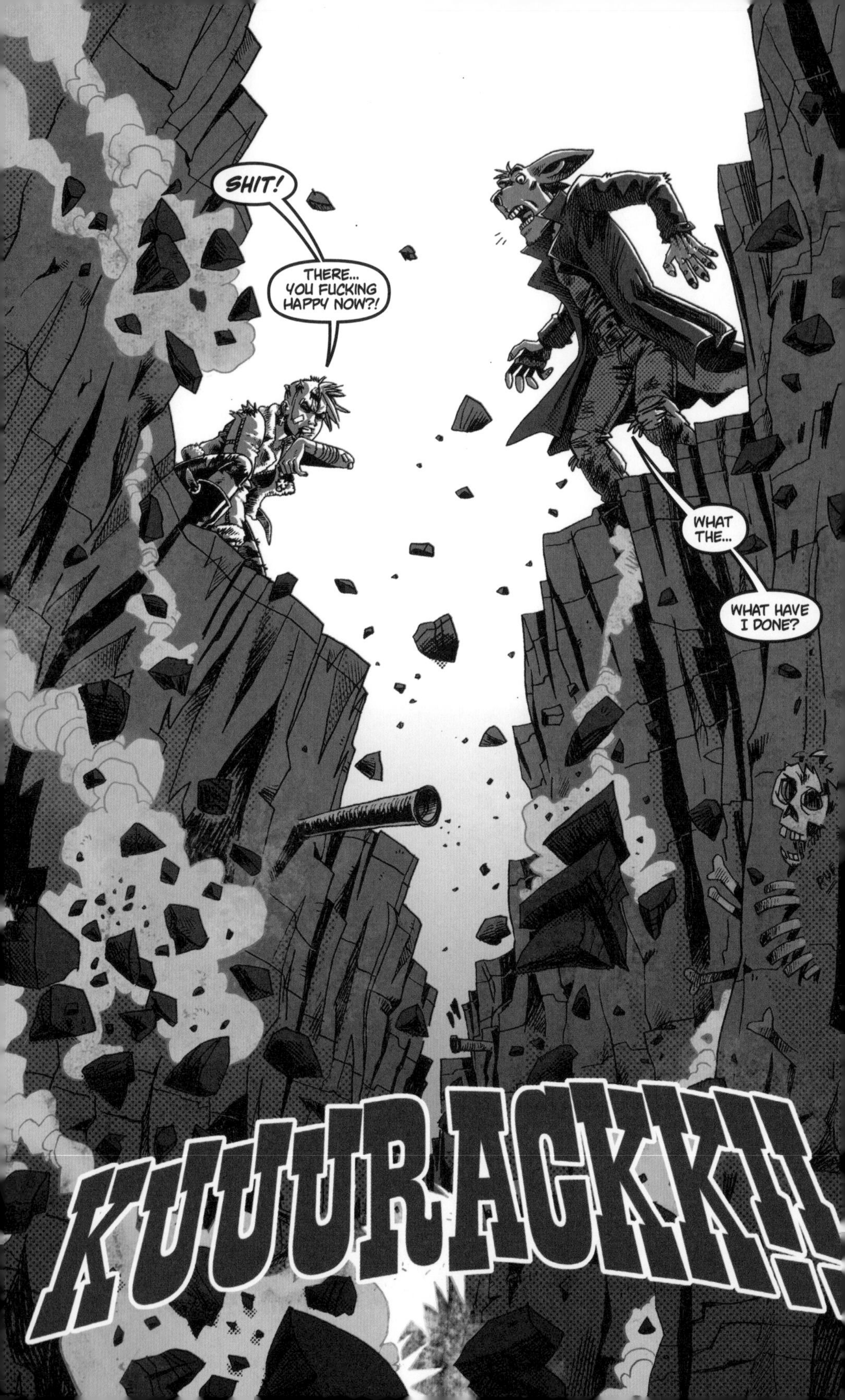
SHIT!
THERE... YOU FUCKING HAPPY NOW?!
WHAT THE...
WHAT HAVE I DONE?
KUUURACKK!!

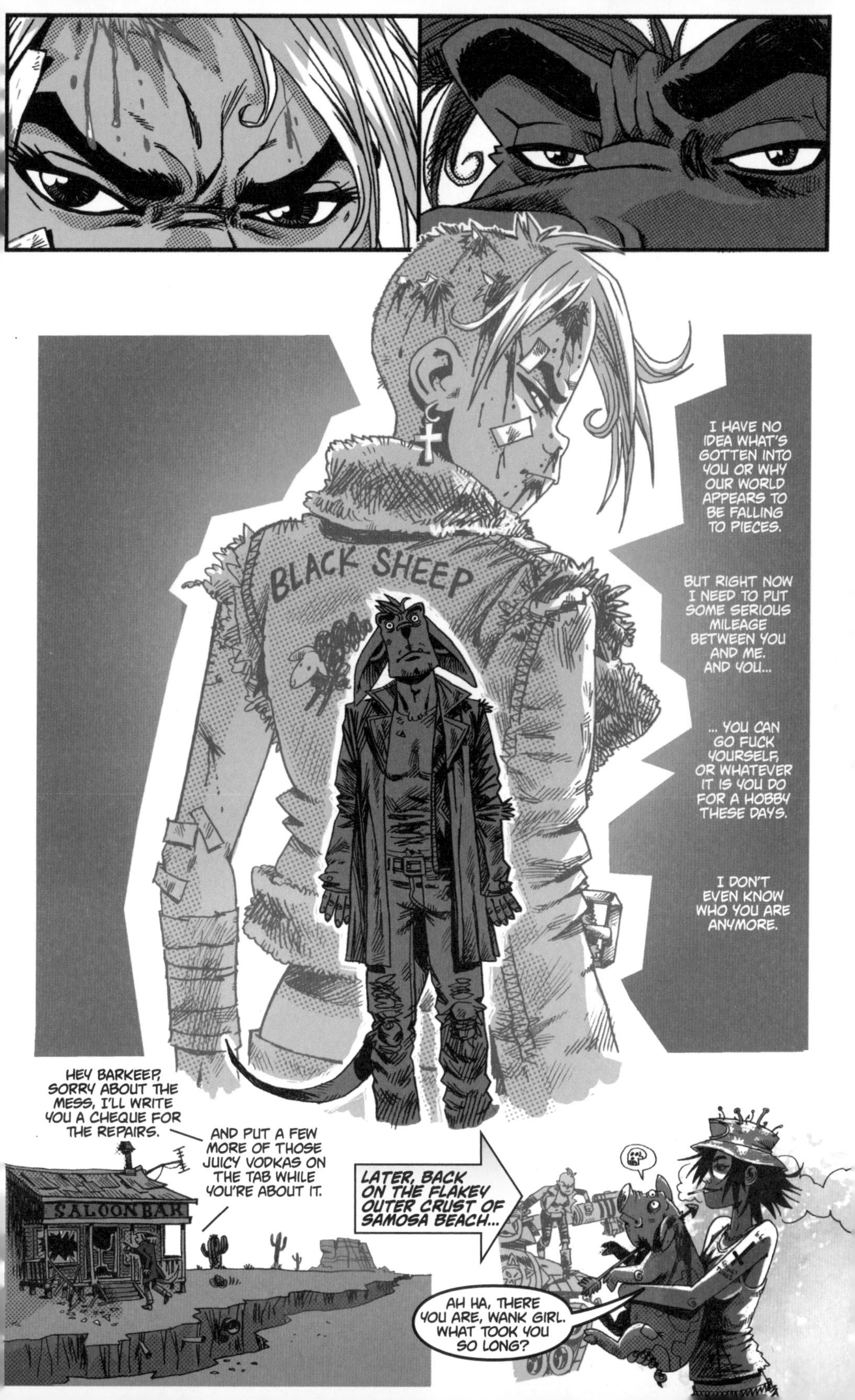
BLACK SHEEP
I HAVE NO IDEA WHAT'S GOTTEN INTO YOU OR WHY OUR WORLD APPEARS TO BE FALLING TO PIECES.
BUT RIGHT NOW I NEED TO PUT SOME SERIOUS MILEAGE BETWEEN YOU AND ME. AND YOU...
... YOU CAN GO FUCK YOURSELF, OR WHATEVER IT IS YOU DO FOR A HOBBY THESE DAYS.
I DON'T EVEN KNOW WHO YOU ARE ANYMORE.
HEY BARKEEP, SORRY ABOUT THE MESS, I'LL WRITE YOU A CHEQUE FOR THE REPAIRS.
AND PUT A FEW MORE OF THOSE JUICY VODKAS ON THE TAB WHILE YOU'RE ABOUT IT.
SALOONBAR
LATER, BACK ON THE FLAKEY OUTER CRUST OF SAMOSA BEACH...
AH HA, THERE YOU ARE, WANK GIRL. WHAT TOOK YOU SO LONG?

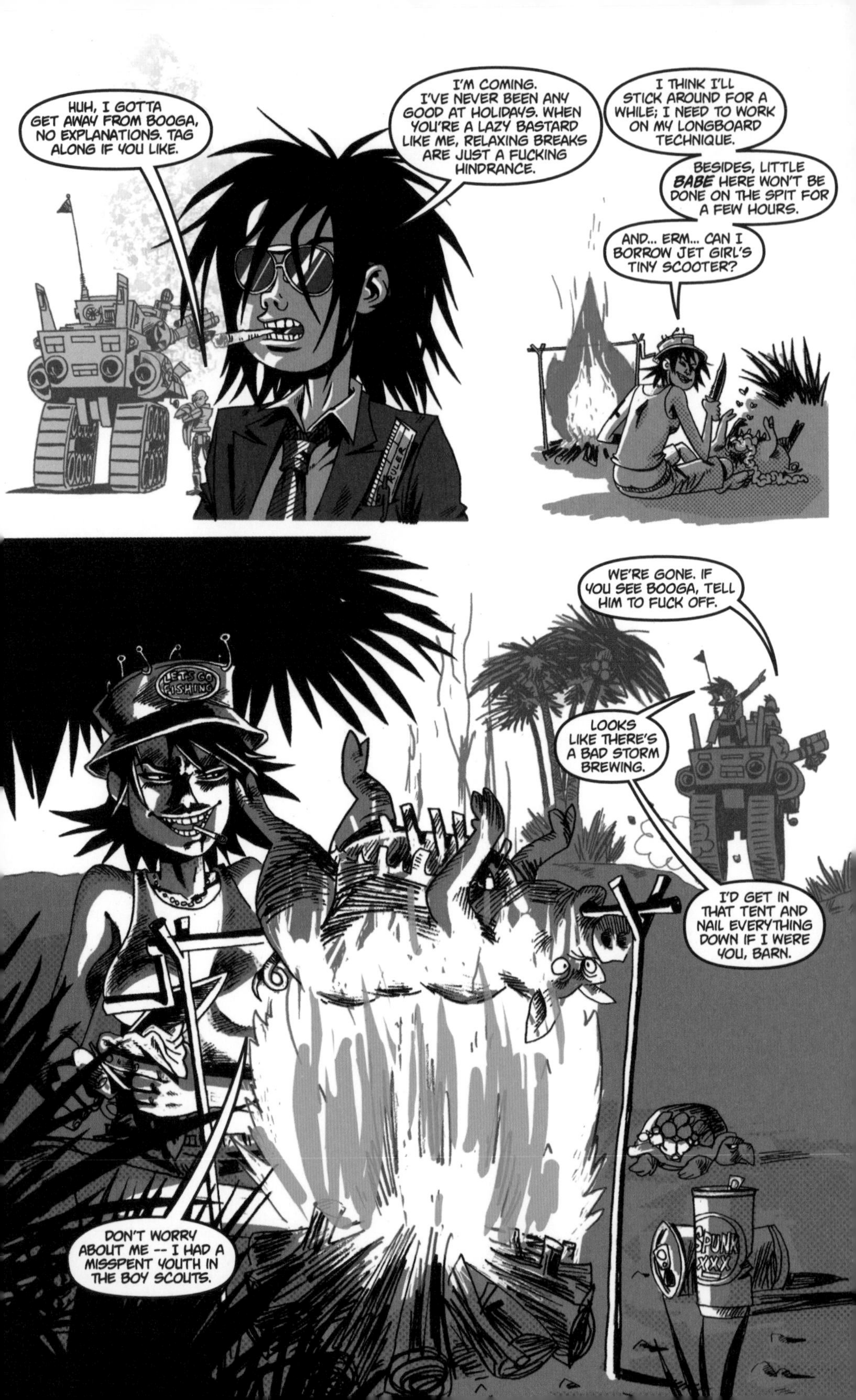

HUH, I GOTTA GET AWAY FROM BOOGA, NO EXPLANATIONS. TAG ALONG IF YOU LIKE.
I'M COMING. I'VE NEVER BEEN ANY GOOD AT HOLIDAYS. WHEN YOU'RE A LAZY BASTARD LIKE ME, RELAXING BREAKS ARE JUST A FUCKING HINDRANCE.
RULER
I THINK I'LL STICK AROUND FOR A WHILE; I NEED TO WORK ON MY LONGBOARD TECHNIQUE.
BESIDES, LITTLE BABE HERE WON'T BE DONE ON THE SPIT FOR A FEW HOURS.
AND... ERM... CAN I BORROW JET GIRL'S TINY SCOOTER?
WE'RE GONE. IF YOU SEE BOOGA, TELL HIM TO FUCK OFF.
LOOKS LIKE THERE'S A BAD STORM BREWING.
I'D GET IN THAT TENT AND NAIL EVERYTHING DOWN IF I WERE YOU, BARN.
LET'S GO FISHING
DON'T WORRY ABOUT ME -- I HAD A MISSPENT YOUTH IN THE BOY SCOUTS.
SPUNK XXX

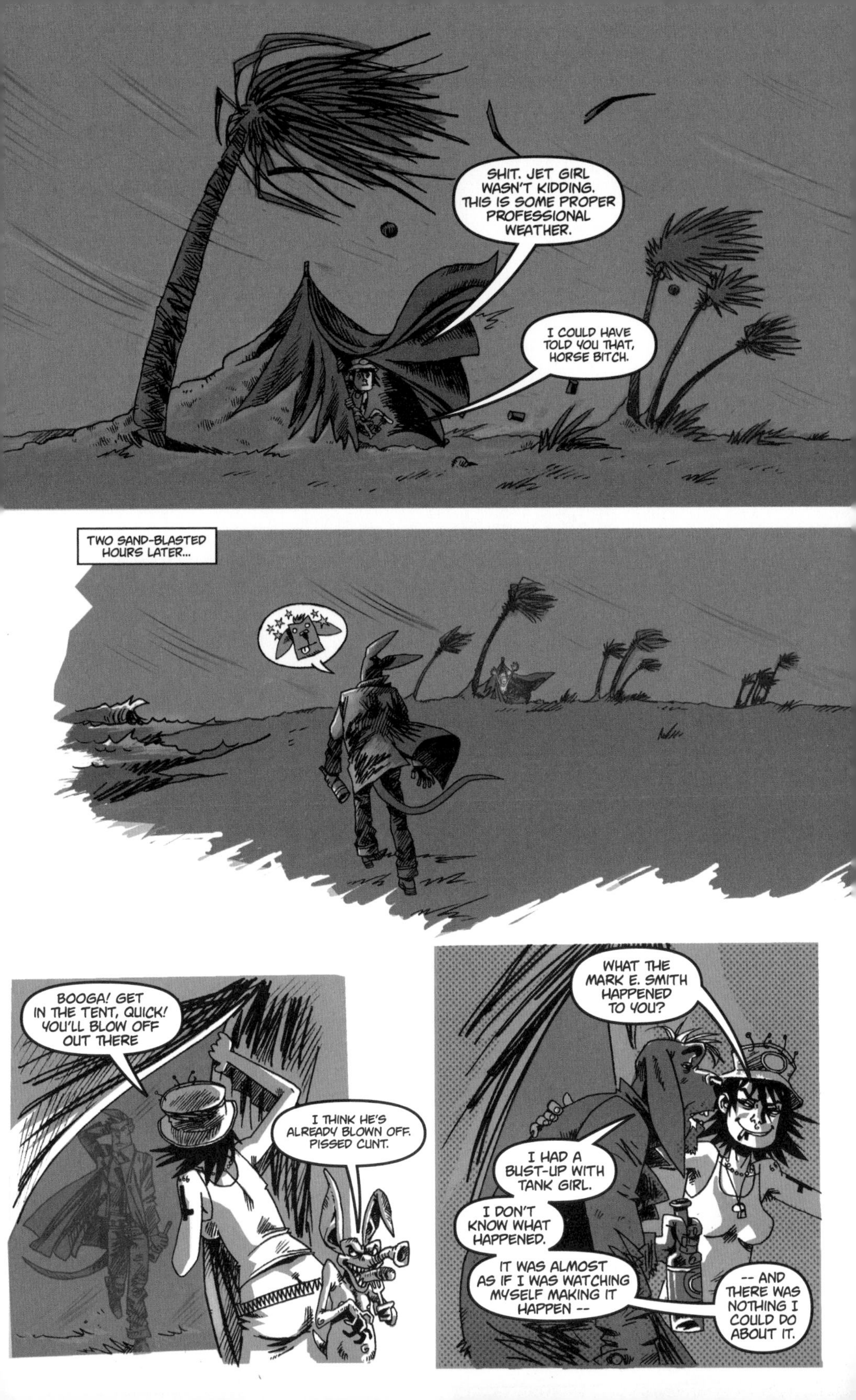
SHIT. JET GIRL WASN'T KIDDING. THIS IS SOME PROPER PROFESSIONAL WEATHER.
I COULD HAVE TOLD YOU THAT, HORSE BITCH.
TWO SAND-BLASTED HOURS LATER...
BOOGA! GET IN THE TENT, QUICK! YOU'LL BLOW OFF OUT THERE
I THINK HE'S ALREADY BLOWN OFF. PISSED CUNT.
WHAT THE MARK E. SMITH HAPPENED TO YOU?
I HAD A BUST-UP WITH TANK GIRL.
I DON'T KNOW WHAT HAPPENED.
IT WAS ALMOST AS IF I WAS WATCHING MYSELF MAKING IT HAPPEN --
-- AND THERE WAS NOTHING I COULD DO ABOUT IT.

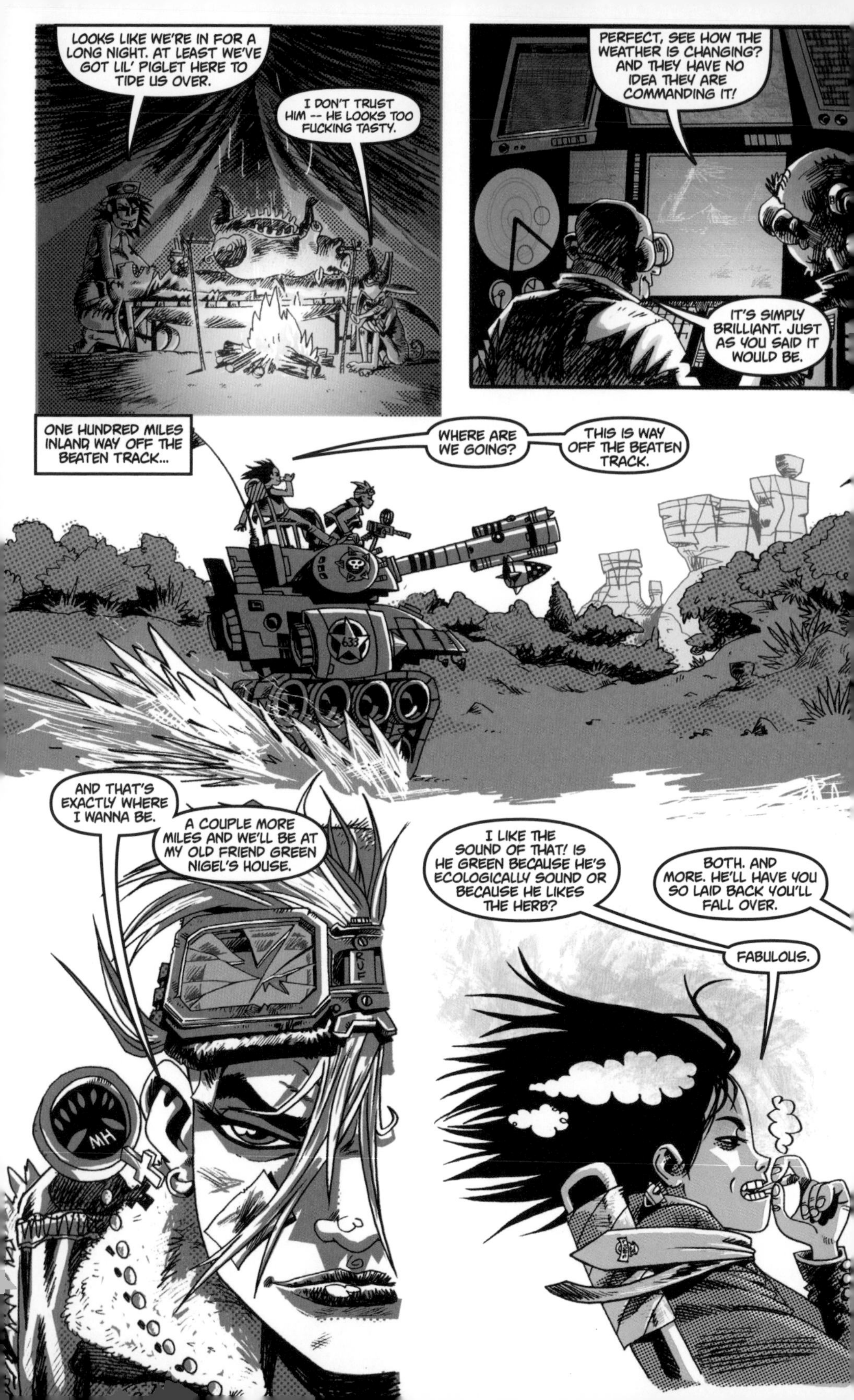
LOOKS LIKE WE'RE IN FOR A LONG NIGHT. AT LEAST WE'VE GOT LIL' PIGLET HERE TO TIDE US OVER.
I DON'T TRUST HIM -- HE LOOKS TOO FUCKING TASTY.
PERFECT, SEE HOW THE WEATHER IS CHANGING? AND THEY HAVE NO IDEA THEY ARE COMMANDING IT!
IT'S SIMPLY BRILLIANT. JUST AS YOU SAID IT WOULD BE.
ONE HUNDRED MILES INLAND, WAY OFF THE BEATEN TRACK...
WHERE ARE WE GOING?
THIS IS WAY OFF THE BEATEN TRACK.
AND THAT'S EXACTLY WHERE I WANNA BE.
A COUPLE MORE MILES AND WE'LL BE AT MY OLD FRIEND GREEN NIGEL'S HOUSE.
I LIKE THE SOUND OF THAT! IS HE GREEN BECAUSE HE'S ECOLOGICALLY SOUND OR BECAUSE HE LIKES THE HERB?
BOTH. AND MORE. HE'LL HAVE YOU SO LAID BACK YOU'LL FALL OVER.
FABULOUS.

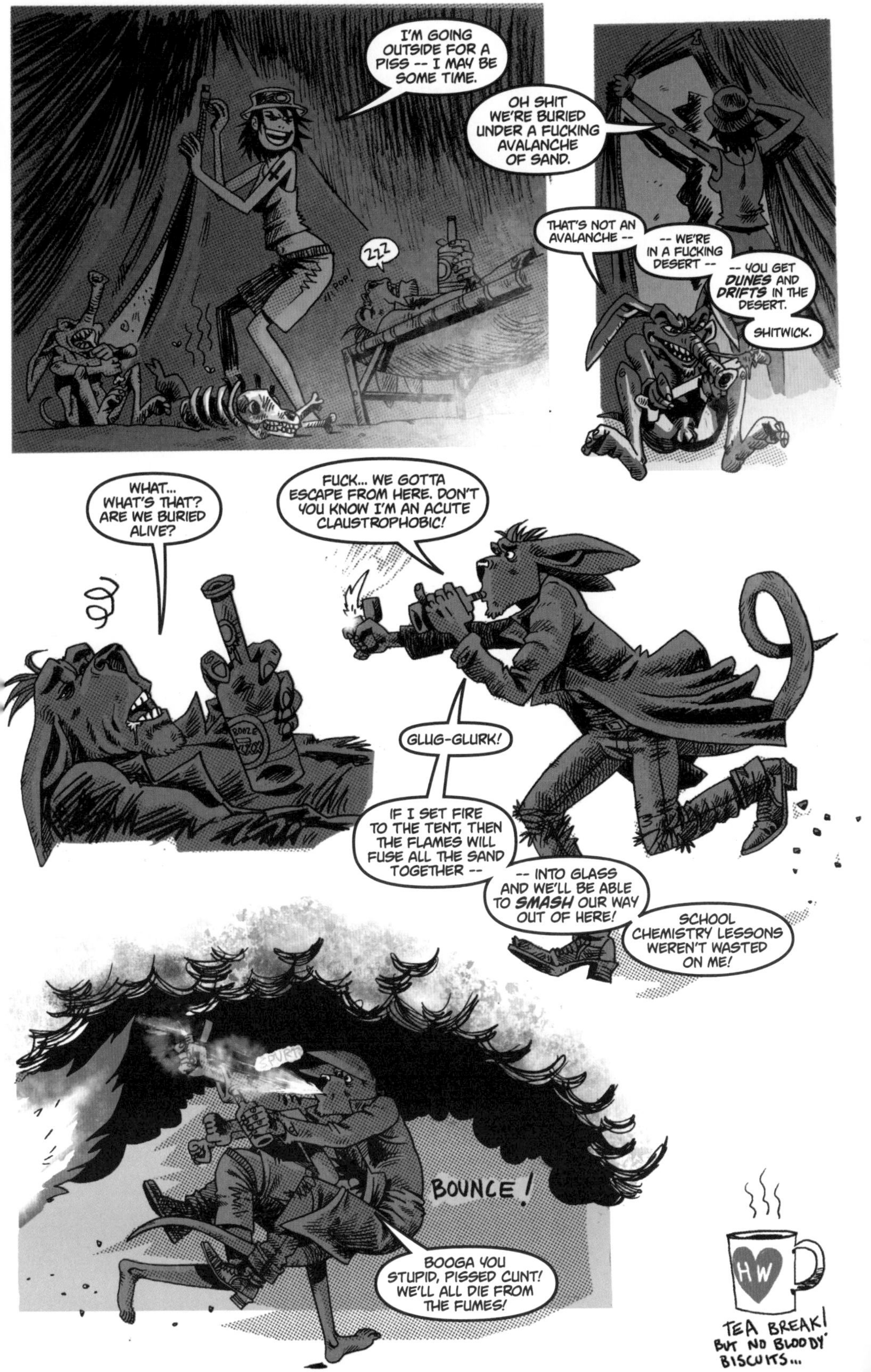
I'M GOING OUTSIDE FOR A PISS -- I MAY BE SOME TIME.
POP!
ZZZ
OH SHIT WE'RE BURIED UNDER A FUCKING AVALANCHE OF SAND.
THAT'S NOT AN AVALANCHE --
-- WE'RE IN A FUCKING DESERT --
-- YOU GET DUNES AND DRIFTS IN THE DESERT.
SHITWICK.
WHAT... WHAT'S THAT? ARE WE BURIED ALIVE?
BOOZE
FUCK... WE GOTTA ESCAPE FROM HERE. DON'T YOU KNOW I'M AN ACUTE CLAUSTROPHOBIC!
GLUG-GLURK!
IF I SET FIRE TO THE TENT, THEN THE FLAMES WILL FUSE ALL THE SAND TOGETHER --
-- INTO GLASS AND WE'LL BE ABLE TO SMASH OUR WAY OUT OF HERE!
SCHOOL CHEMISTRY LESSONS WEREN'T WASTED ON ME!
SPURT!
BOUNCE!
BOOGA YOU STUPID, PISSED CUNT! WE'LL ALL DIE FROM THE FUMES!
HW
TEA BREAK! BUT NO BLOODY BISCUITS...

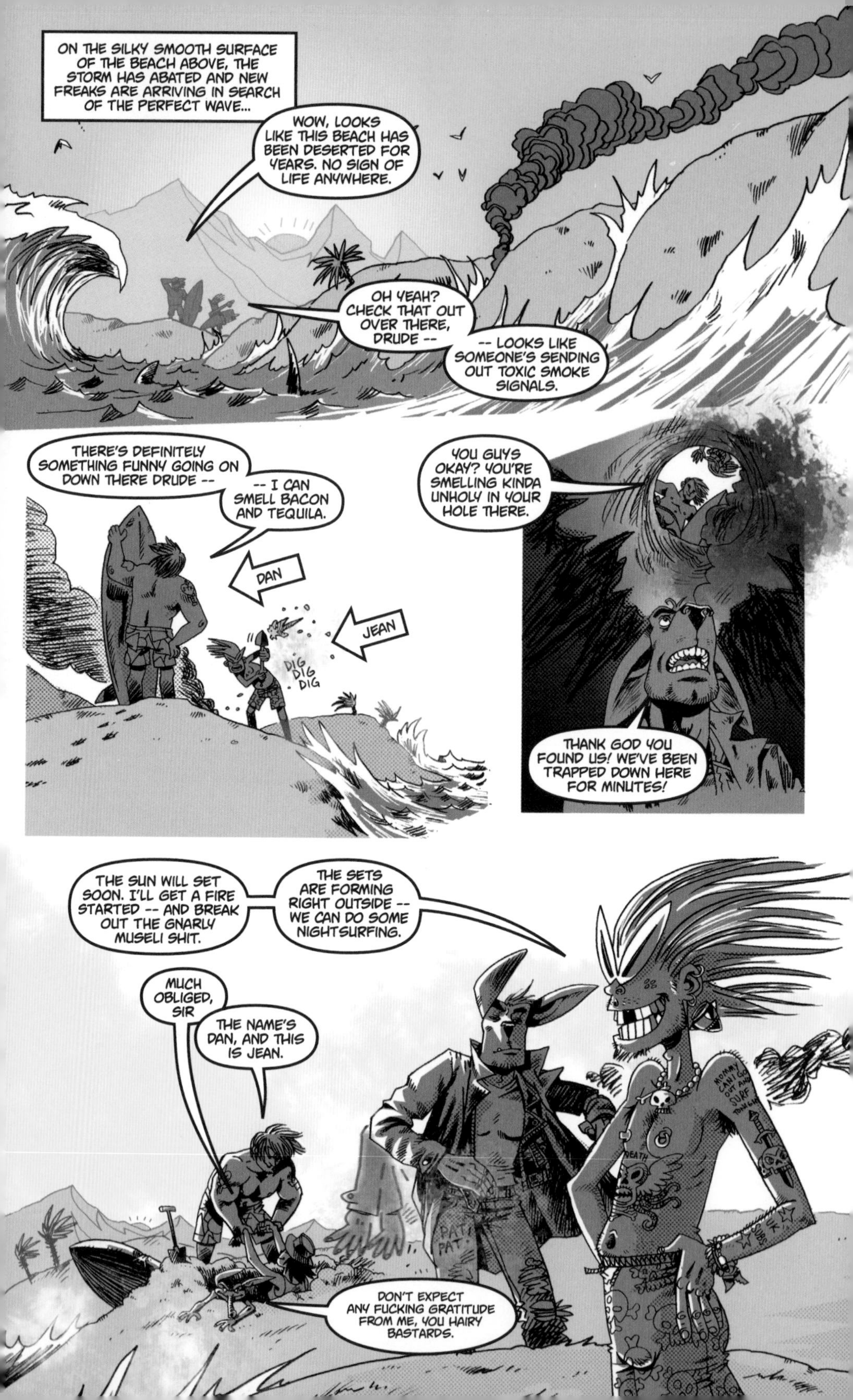
ON THE SILKY SMOOTH SURFACE OF THE BEACH ABOVE, THE STORM HAS ABATED AND NEW FREAKS ARE ARRIVING IN SEARCH OF THE PERFECT WAVE...
WOW, LOOKS LIKE THIS BEACH HAS BEEN DESERTED FOR YEARS. NO SIGN OF LIFE ANYWHERE.
OH YEAH? CHECK THAT OUT OVER THERE, DRUDE --
-- LOOKS LIKE SOMEONE'S SENDING OUT TOXIC SMOKE SIGNALS.
THERE'S DEFINITELY SOMETHING FUNNY GOING ON DOWN THERE DRUDE --
-- I CAN SMELL BACON AND TEQUILA.
DAN
JEAN
DIG DIG DIG
YOU GUYS OKAY? YOU'RE SMELLING KINDA UNHOLY IN YOUR HOLE THERE.
THANK GOD YOU FOUND US! WE'VE BEEN TRAPPED DOWN HERE FOR MINUTES!
THE SUN WILL SET SOON. I'LL GET A FIRE STARTED -- AND BREAK OUT THE GNARLY MUSELI SHIT.
THE SETS ARE FORMING RIGHT OUTSIDE -- WE CAN DO SOME NIGHTSURFING.
MUCH OBLIGED, SIR
THE NAME'S DAN, AND THIS IS JEAN.
PAT PAT
DON'T EXPECT ANY FUCKING GRATITUDE FROM ME, YOU HAIRY BASTARDS.

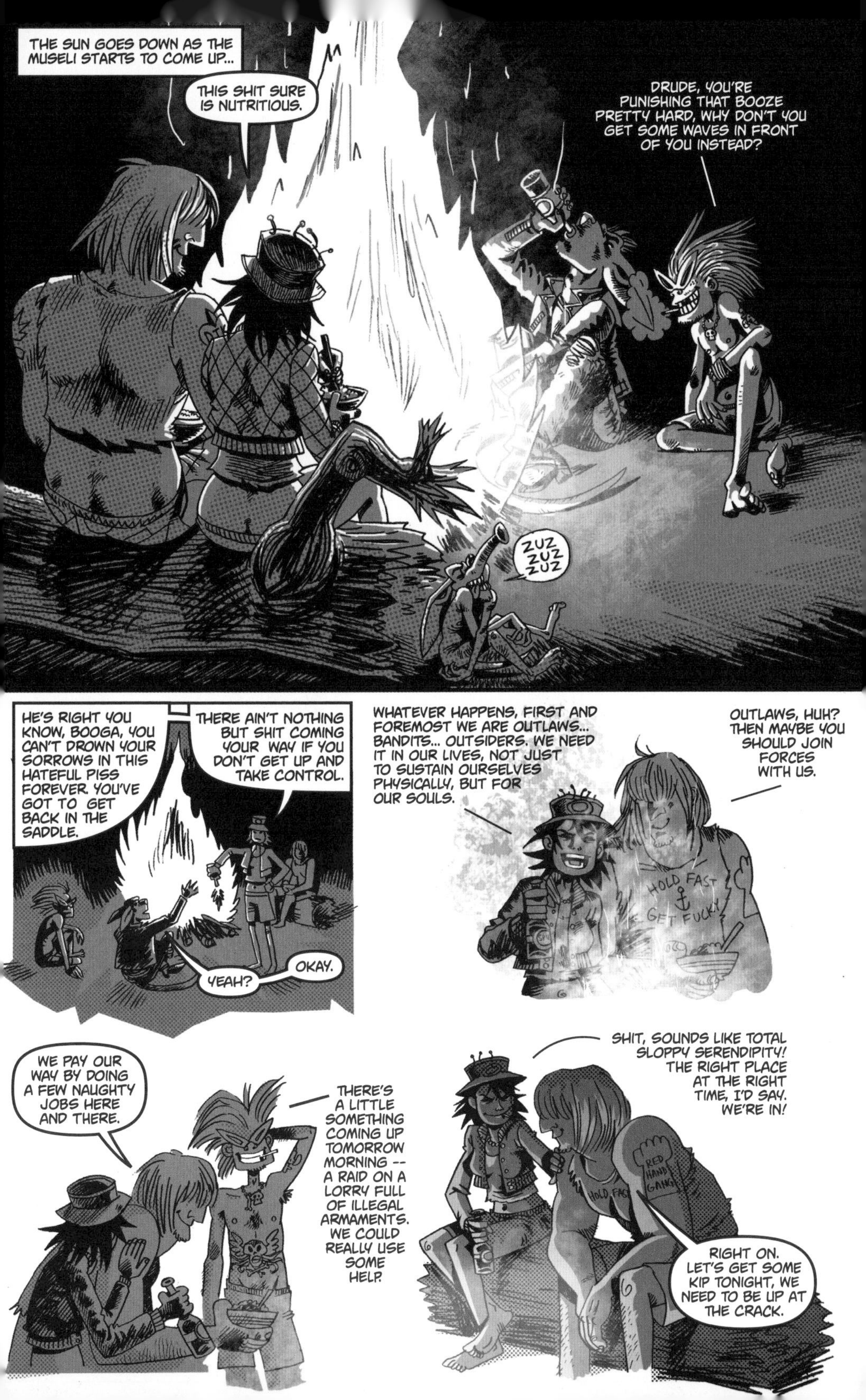
THE SUN GOES DOWN AS THE MUSELI STARTS TO COME UP...
THIS SHIT SURE IS NUTRITIOUS.
DRUDE, YOU'RE PUNISHING THAT BOOZE PRETTY HARD, WHY DON'T YOU GET SOME WAVES IN FRONT OF YOU INSTEAD?
ZUZ ZUZ ZUZ
HE'S RIGHT YOU KNOW, BOOGA, YOU CAN'T DROWN YOUR SORROWS IN THIS HATEFUL PISS FOREVER. YOU'VE GOT TO GET BACK IN THE SADDLE.
THERE AIN'T NOTHING BUT SHIT COMING YOUR WAY IF YOU DON'T GET UP AND TAKE CONTROL.
YEAH?
OKAY.
WHATEVER HAPPENS, FIRST AND FOREMOST WE ARE OUTLAWS... BANDITS... OUTSIDERS. WE NEED IT IN OUR LIVES, NOT JUST TO SUSTAIN OURSELVES PHYSICALLY, BUT FOR OUR SOULS.
OUTLAWS, HUH? THEN MAYBE YOU SHOULD JOIN FORCES WITH US.
HOLD FAST
GET FUCKY
WE PAY OUR WAY BY DOING A FEW NAUGHTY JOBS HERE AND THERE.
THERE'S A LITTLE SOMETHING COMING UP TOMORROW MORNING -- A RAID ON A LORRY FULL OF ILLEGAL ARMAMENTS. WE COULD REALLY USE SOME HELP.
SHIT, SOUNDS LIKE TOTAL SLOPPY SERENDIPITY! THE RIGHT PLACE AT THE RIGHT TIME, I'D SAY. WE'RE IN!
RED HAND GANG
HOLD FAST
RIGHT ON. LET'S GET SOME KIP TONIGHT, WE NEED TO BE UP AT THE CRACK.

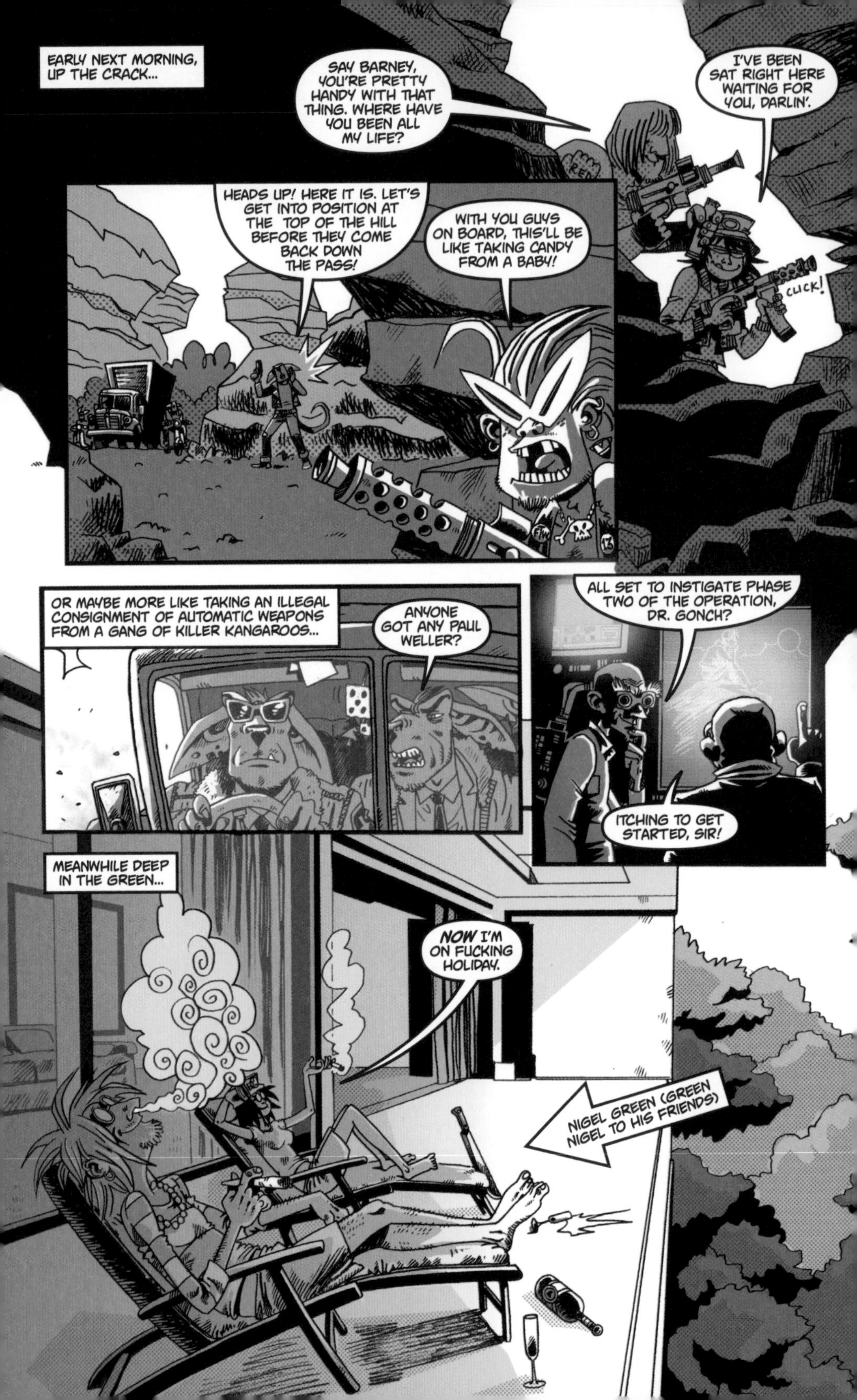
EARLY NEXT MORNING, UP THE CRACK...
SAY BARNEY, YOU'RE PRETTY HANDY WITH THAT THING. WHERE HAVE YOU BEEN ALL MY LIFE?
I'VE BEEN SAT RIGHT HERE WAITING FOR YOU, DARLIN'.
CLICK!
HEADS UP! HERE IT IS. LET'S GET INTO POSITION AT THE TOP OF THE HILL BEFORE THEY COME BACK DOWN THE PASS!
WITH YOU GUYS ON BOARD, THIS'LL BE LIKE TAKING CANDY FROM A BABY!
OR MAYBE MORE LIKE TAKING AN ILLEGAL CONSIGNMENT OF AUTOMATIC WEAPONS FROM A GANG OF KILLER KANGAROOS...
ANYONE GOT ANY PAUL WELLER?
ALL SET TO INSTIGATE PHASE TWO OF THE OPERATION, DR. GONCH?
ITCHING TO GET STARTED, SIR!
MEANWHILE DEEP IN THE GREEN...
NOW I'M ON FUCKING HOLIDAY.
NIGEL GREEN (GREEN NIGEL TO HIS FRIENDS)

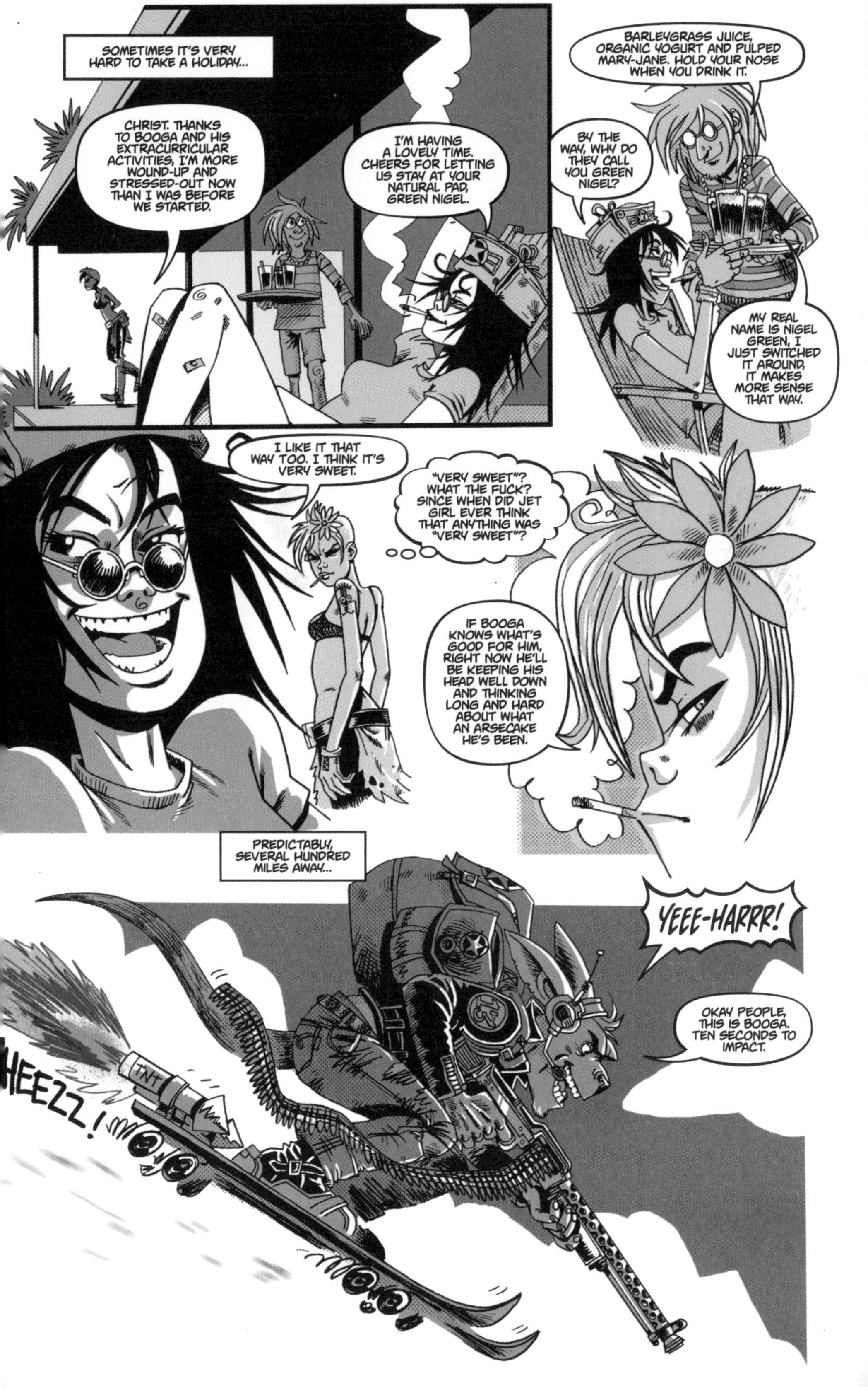
SOMETIMES IT'S VERY HARD TO TAKE A HOLIDAY...
CHRIST. THANKS TO BOOGA AND HIS EXTRACURRICULAR ACTIVITIES, I'M MORE WOUND-UP AND STRESSED-OUT NOW THAN I WAS BEFORE WE STARTED.
I'M HAVING A LOVELY TIME. CHEERS FOR LETTING US STAY AT YOUR NATURAL PAD, GREEN NIGEL.
BARLEYGRASS JUICE, ORGANIC YOGURT AND PULPED MARY-JANE. HOLD YOUR NOSE WHEN YOU DRINK IT.
BY THE WAY, WHY DO THEY CALL YOU GREEN NIGEL?
MY REAL NAME IS NIGEL GREEN, I JUST SWITCHED IT AROUND, IT MAKES MORE SENSE THAT WAY.
I LIKE IT THAT WAY TOO. I THINK IT'S VERY SWEET.
"VERY SWEET"? WHAT THE FUCK? SINCE WHEN DID JET GIRL EVER THINK THAT ANYTHING WAS "VERY SWEET"?
IF BOOGA KNOWS WHAT'S GOOD FOR HIM, RIGHT NOW HE'LL BE KEEPING HIS HEAD WELL DOWN AND THINKING LONG AND HARD ABOUT WHAT AN ARSECAKE HE'S BEEN.
PREDICTABLY, SEVERAL HUNDRED MILES AWAY...
YEEE-HARRR!
OKAY PEOPLE, THIS IS BOOGA. TEN SECONDS TO IMPACT.
HEEZZ!
TNT

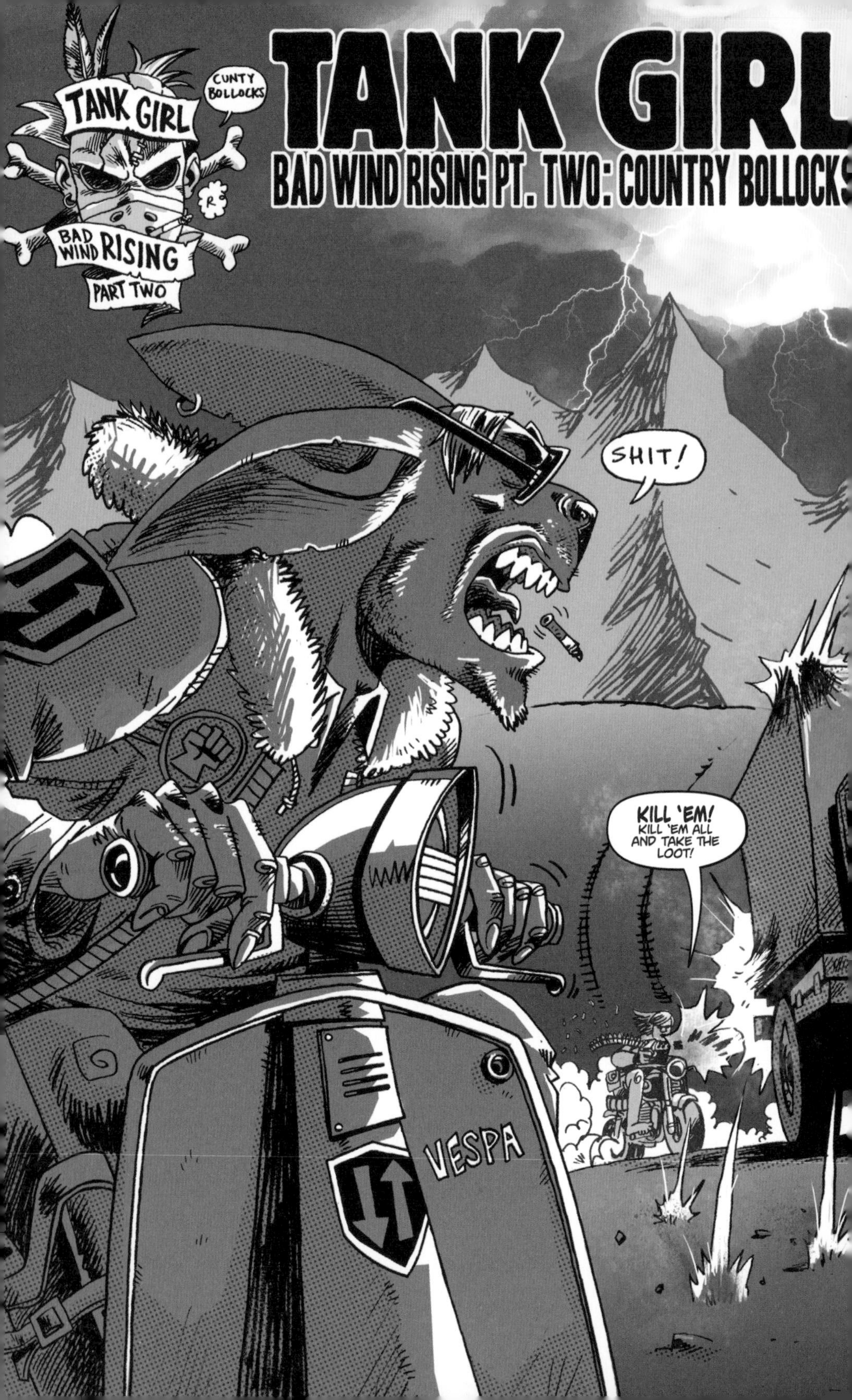
TANK GIRL
BAD WIND RISING PT. TWO: COUNTRY BOLLOCKS
TANK GIRL
CUNTY BOLLOCKS
BAD WIND RISING
PART TWO
SHIT!
KILL 'EM! KILL 'EM ALL AND TAKE THE LOOT!
VESPA

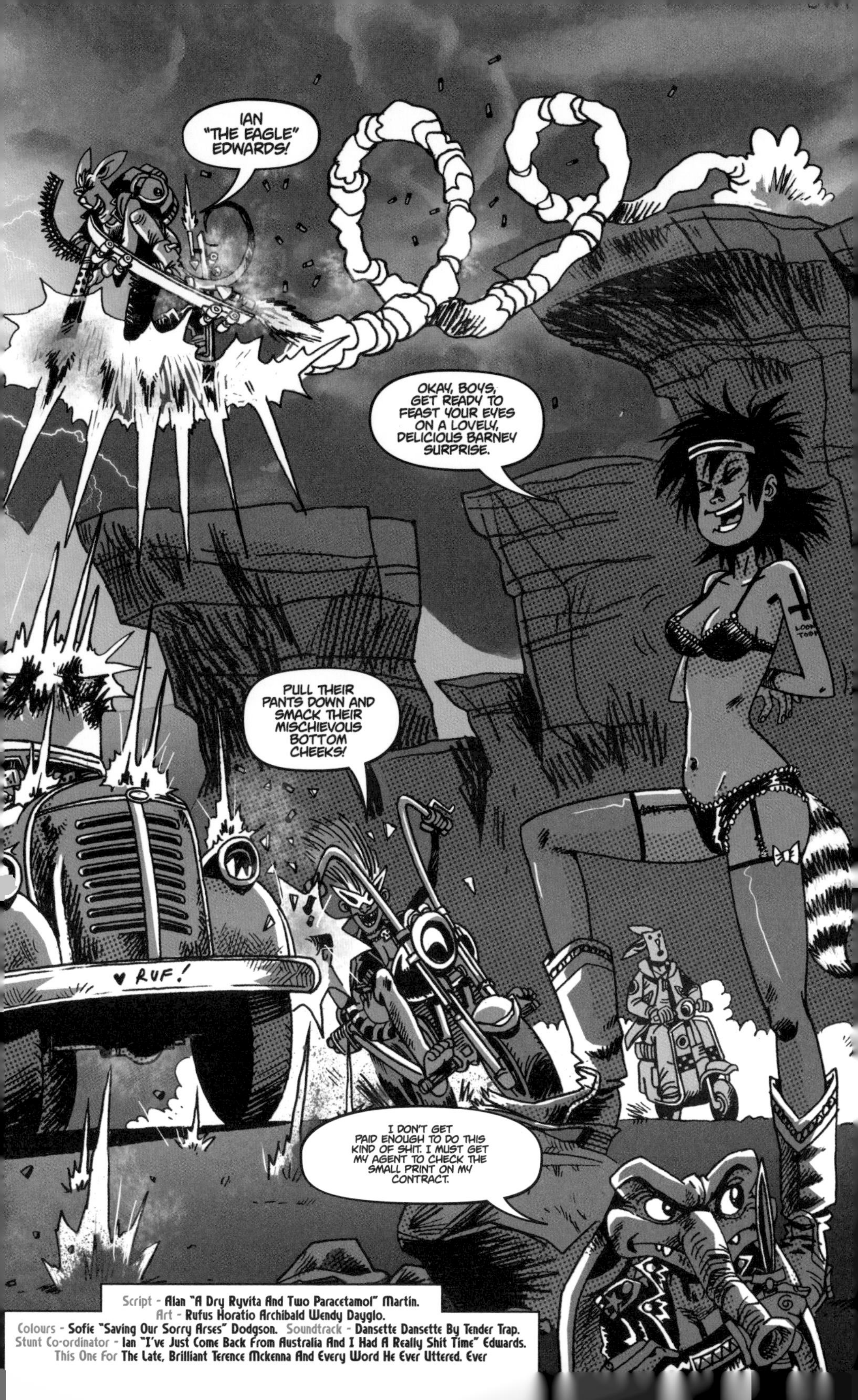
IAN "THE EAGLE" EDWARDS!
OKAY, BOYS, GET READY TO FEAST YOUR EYES ON A LOVELY, DELICIOUS BARNEY SURPRISE.
PULL THEIR PANTS DOWN AND SMACK THEIR MISCHIEVOUS BOTTOM CHEEKS!
RUF!
I DON'T GET PAID ENOUGH TO DO THIS KIND OF SHIT. I MUST GET MY AGENT TO CHECK THE SMALL PRINT ON MY CONTRACT.
Script - Alan "A Dry Ryvita And Two Paracetamol" Martin.
Art - Rufus Horatio Archibald Wendy Dayglo.
Colours - Sofie "Saving Our Sorry Arses" Dodgson. Soundtrack - Dansette Dansette By Tender Trap.
Stunt Co-ordinator - Ian "I've Just Come Back From Australia And I Had A Really Shit Time" Edwards.
This One For The Late, Brilliant Terence Mckenna And Every Word He Ever Uttered. Ever

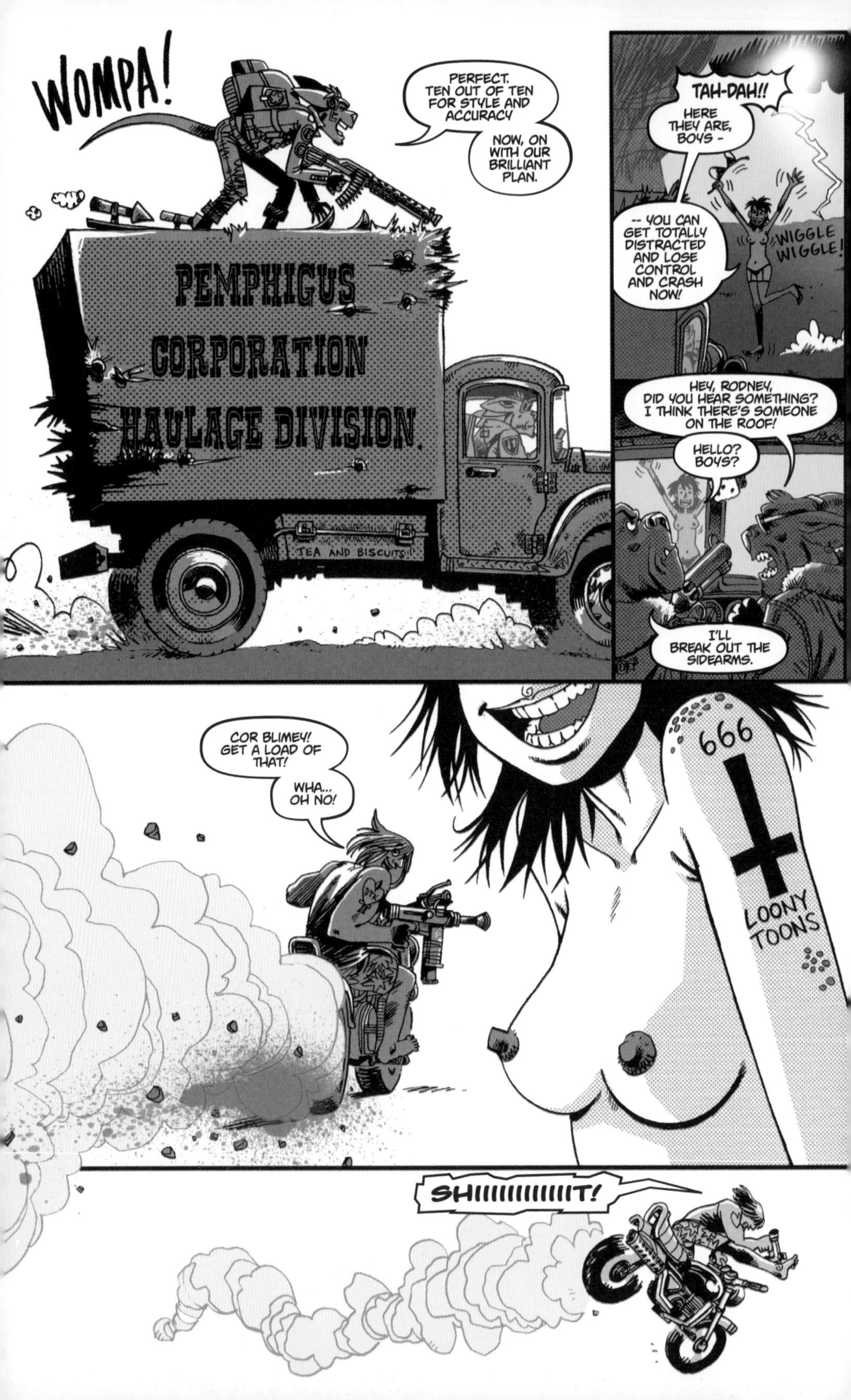
WOMPA!
PERFECT. TEN OUT OF TEN FOR STYLE AND ACCURACY
NOW, ON WITH OUR BRILLIANT PLAN.
PEMPHIGUS CORPORATION HAULAGE DIVISION
TEA AND BISCUITS
TAH-DAH!!
HERE THEY ARE, BOYS -
-- YOU CAN GET TOTALLY DISTRACTED AND LOSE CONTROL AND CRASH NOW!
WIGGLE WIGGLE!
HEY, RODNEY, DID YOU HEAR SOMETHING? I THINK THERE'S SOMEONE ON THE ROOF!
HELLO? BOYS?
I'LL BREAK OUT THE SIDEARMS.
COR BLIMEY! GET A LOAD OF THAT!
WHA... OH NO!
666
LOONY TOONS
SHIIIIIIIIIIIIT!

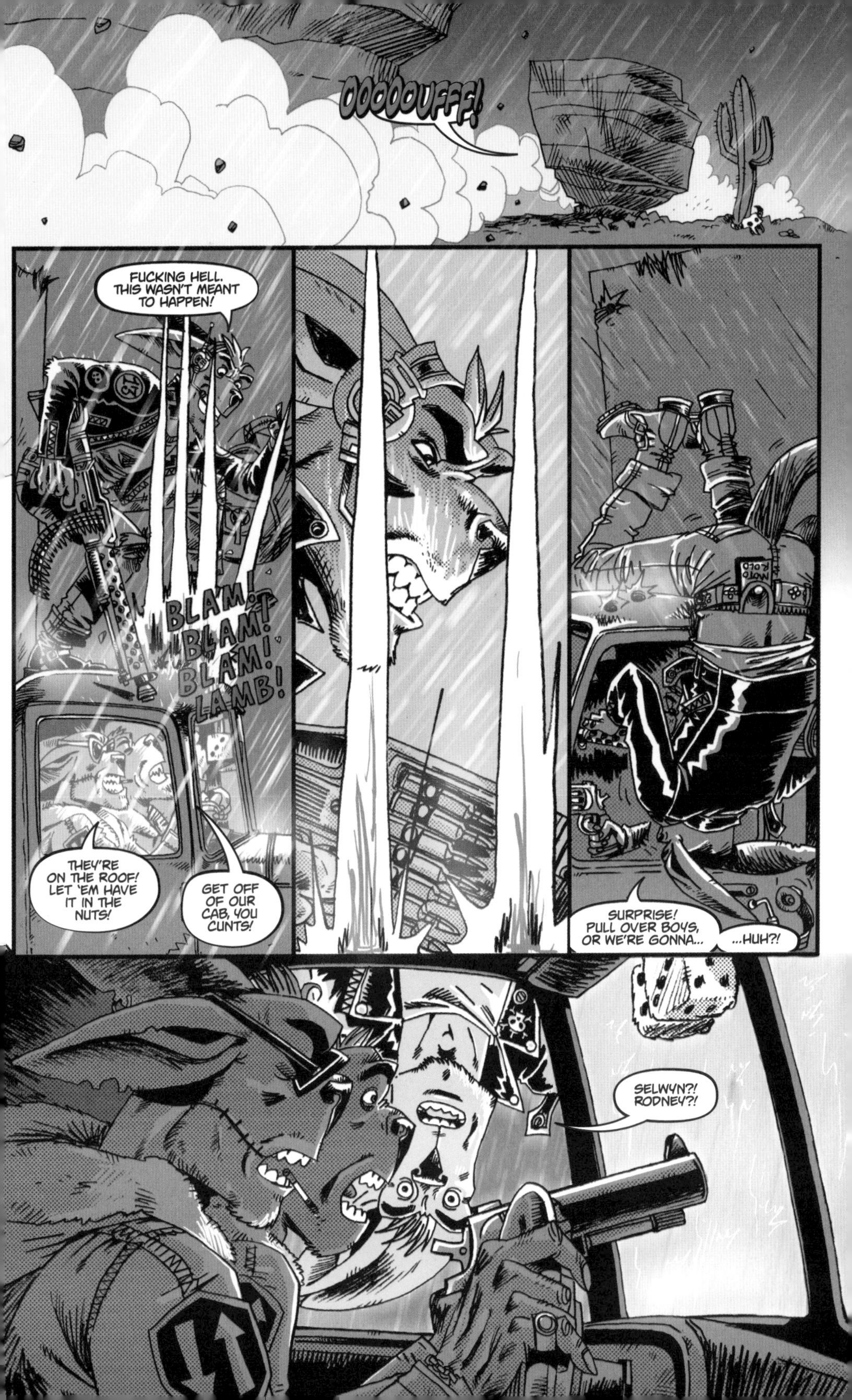
OOOOOOUFFF!
FUCKING HELL. THIS WASN'T MEANT TO HAPPEN!
BLAM! BLAM! BLAM! LAMB!
THEY'RE ON THE ROOF! LET 'EM HAVE IT IN THE NUTS!
GET OFF OF OUR CAB, YOU CUNTS!
MOTO ROLO
SURPRISE! PULL OVER BOYS, OR WE'RE GONNA...
...HUH?!
SELWYN?! RODNEY?!

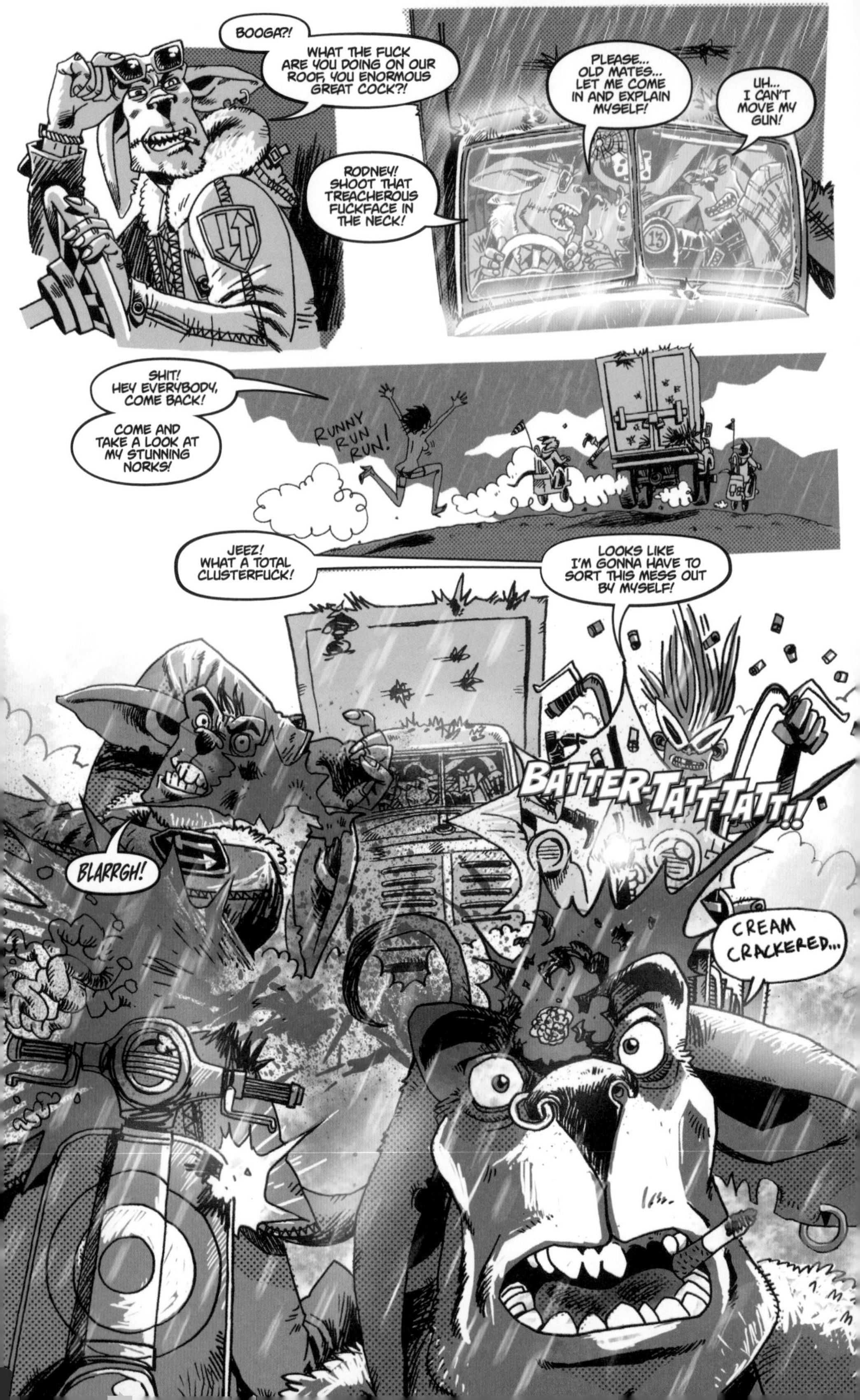
BOOGA?!
WHAT THE FUCK ARE YOU DOING ON OUR ROOF, YOU ENORMOUS GREAT COCK?!
PLEASE... OLD MATES... LET ME COME IN AND EXPLAIN MYSELF!
UH... I CAN'T MOVE MY GUN!
RODNEY! SHOOT THAT TREACHEROUS FUCKFACE IN THE NECK!
SHIT! HEY EVERYBODY, COME BACK!
COME AND TAKE A LOOK AT MY STUNNING NORKS!
RUNNY RUN RUN!
JEEZ! WHAT A TOTAL CLUSTERFUCK!
LOOKS LIKE I'M GONNA HAVE TO SORT THIS MESS OUT BY MYSELF!
BATTER-TATT-TATT!!
BLARRGH!
CREAM CRACKERED...

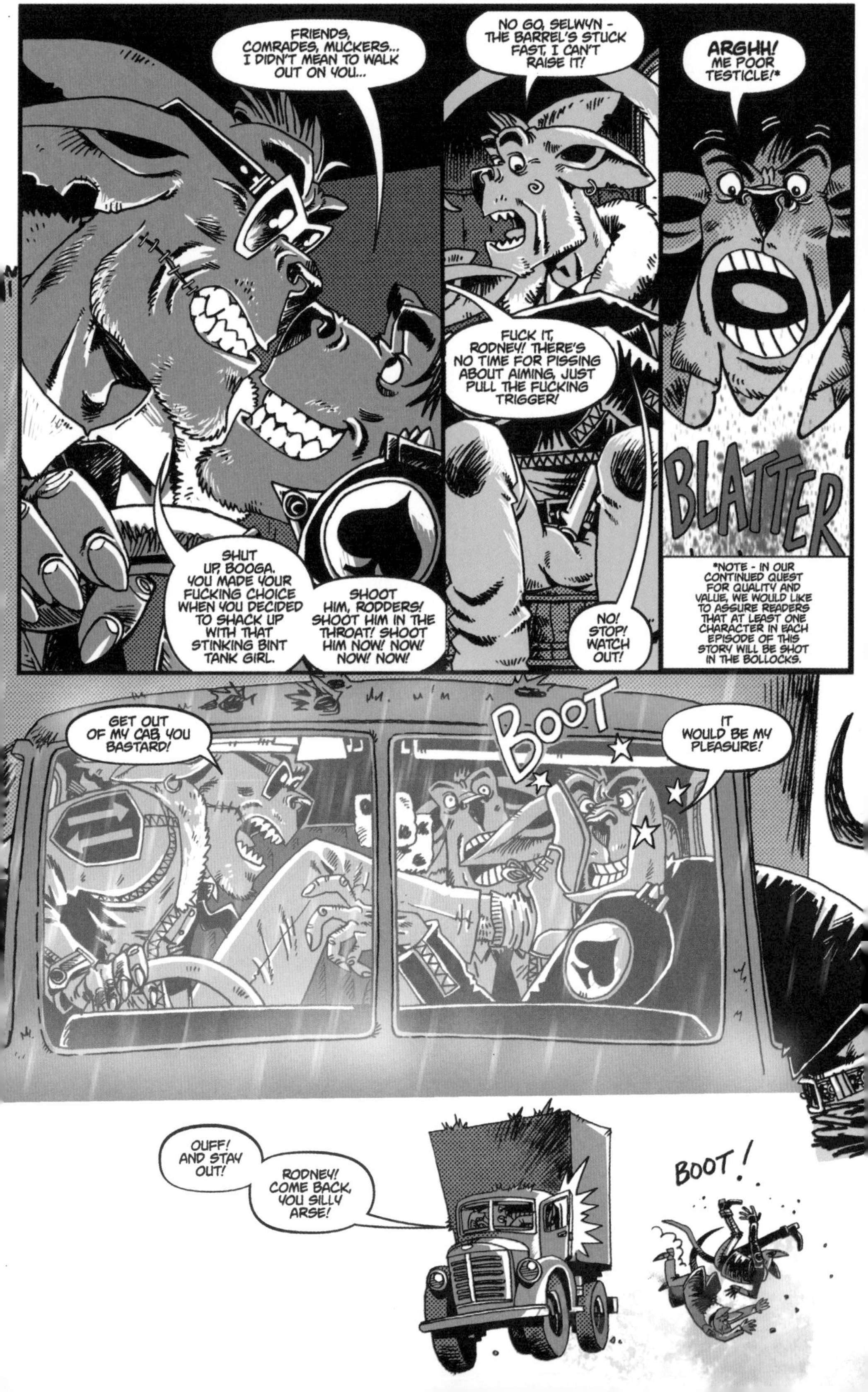
FRIENDS, COMRADES, MUCKERS... I DIDN'T MEAN TO WALK OUT ON YOU...
SHUT UP, BOOGA. YOU MADE YOUR FUCKING CHOICE WHEN YOU DECIDED TO SHACK UP WITH THAT STINKING BINT TANK GIRL.
SHOOT HIM, RODDERS! SHOOT HIM IN THE THROAT! SHOOT HIM NOW! NOW! NOW! NOW!
NO GO, SELWYN - THE BARREL'S STUCK FAST, I CAN'T RAISE IT!
FUCK IT, RODNEY! THERE'S NO TIME FOR PISSING ABOUT AIMING, JUST PULL THE FUCKING TRIGGER!
NO! STOP! WATCH OUT!
ARGHH! ME POOR TESTICLE!*
BLATTER
*NOTE - IN OUR CONTINUED QUEST FOR QUALITY AND VALUE, WE WOULD LIKE TO ASSURE READERS THAT AT LEAST ONE CHARACTER IN EACH EPISODE OF THIS STORY WILL BE SHOT IN THE BOLLOCKS.
GET OUT OF MY CAB, YOU BASTARD!
BOOT
IT WOULD BE MY PLEASURE!
OUFF! AND STAY OUT!
RODNEY! COME BACK, YOU SILLY ARSE!
BOOT!

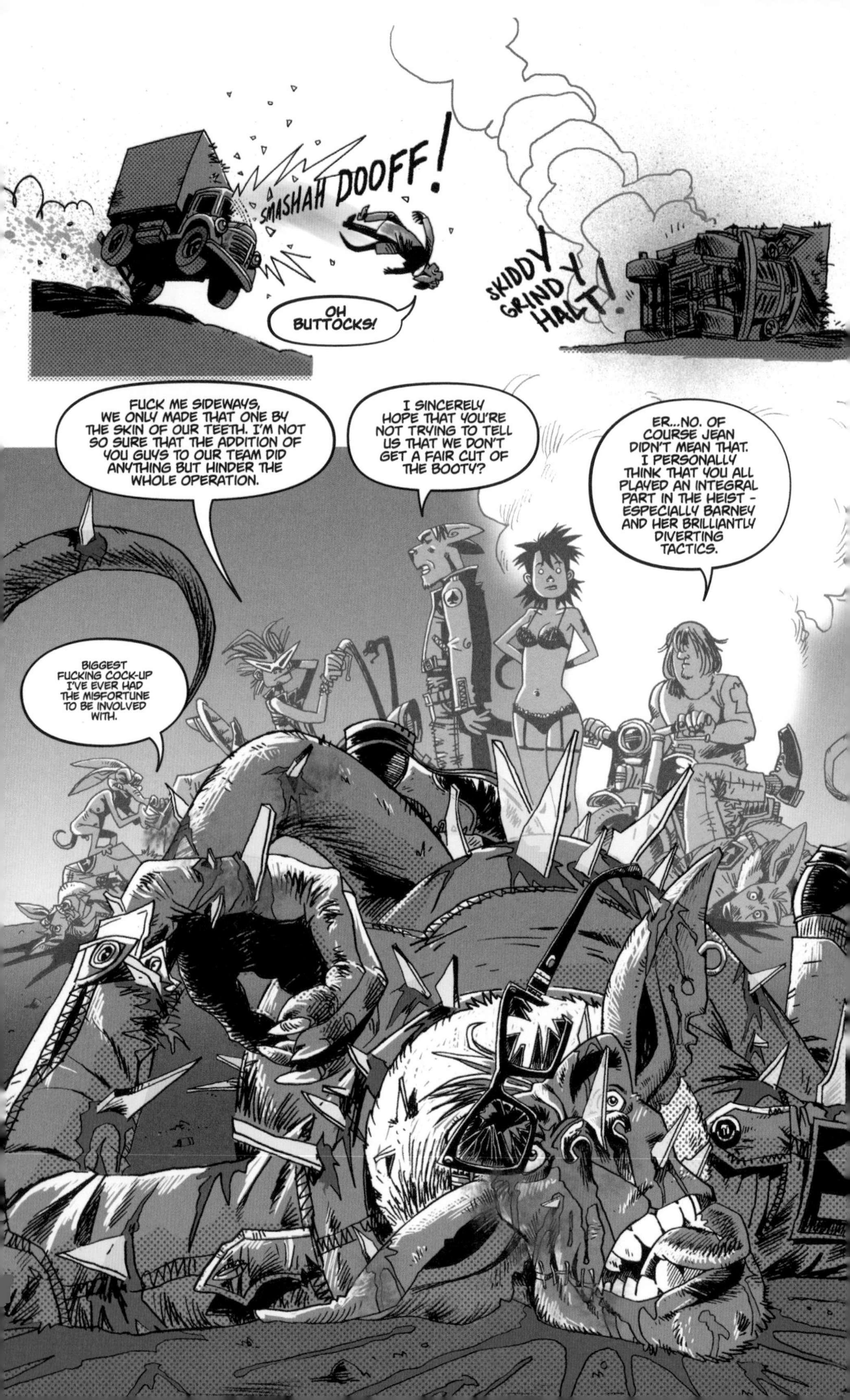
SMASHAH DOOFF!
OH BUTTOCKS!
SKIDDY GRINDY HALT!
FUCK ME SIDEWAYS, WE ONLY MADE THAT ONE BY THE SKIN OF OUR TEETH. I'M NOT SO SURE THAT THE ADDITION OF YOU GUYS TO OUR TEAM DID ANYTHING BUT HINDER THE WHOLE OPERATION.
I SINCERELY HOPE THAT YOU'RE NOT TRYING TO TELL US THAT WE DON'T GET A FAIR CUT OF THE BOOTY?
ER...NO. OF COURSE JEAN DIDN'T MEAN THAT. I PERSONALLY THINK THAT YOU ALL PLAYED AN INTEGRAL PART IN THE HEIST - ESPECIALLY BARNEY AND HER BRILLIANTLY DIVERTING TACTICS.
BIGGEST FUCKING COCK-UP I'VE EVER HAD THE MISFORTUNE TO BE INVOLVED WITH.

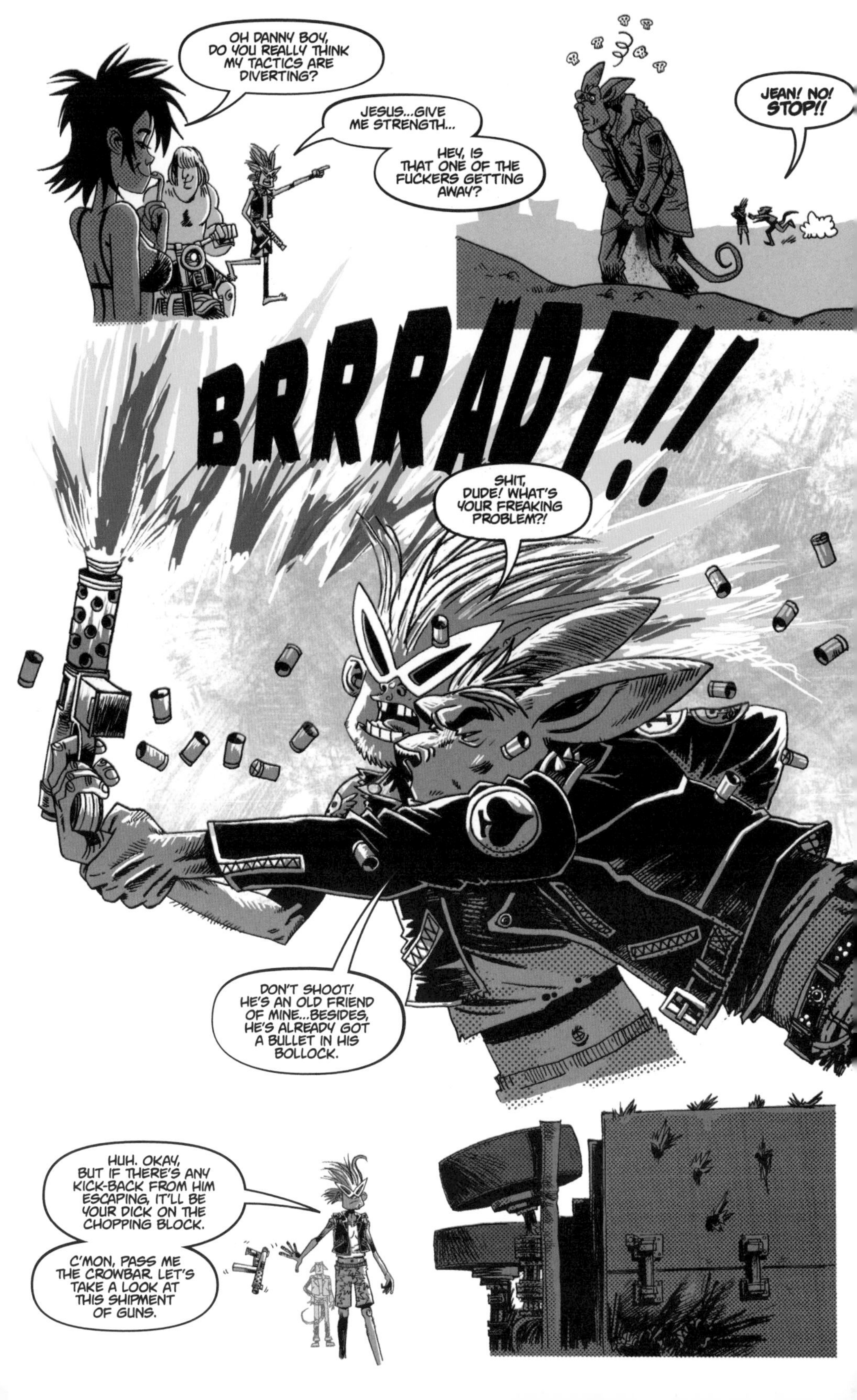
OH DANNY BOY, DO YOU REALLY THINK MY TACTICS ARE DIVERTING?
JESUS...GIVE ME STRENGTH...
HEY, IS THAT ONE OF THE FUCKERS GETTING AWAY?
JEAN! NO! STOP!!
BRRRAPT!!
SHIT, DUDE! WHAT'S YOUR FREAKING PROBLEM?!
DON'T SHOOT! HE'S AN OLD FRIEND OF MINE...BESIDES, HE'S ALREADY GOT A BULLET IN HIS BOLLOCK.
HUH. OKAY, BUT IF THERE'S ANY KICK-BACK FROM HIM ESCAPING, IT'LL BE YOUR DICK ON THE CHOPPING BLOCK.
C'MON, PASS ME THE CROWBAR. LET'S TAKE A LOOK AT THIS SHIPMENT OF GUNS.

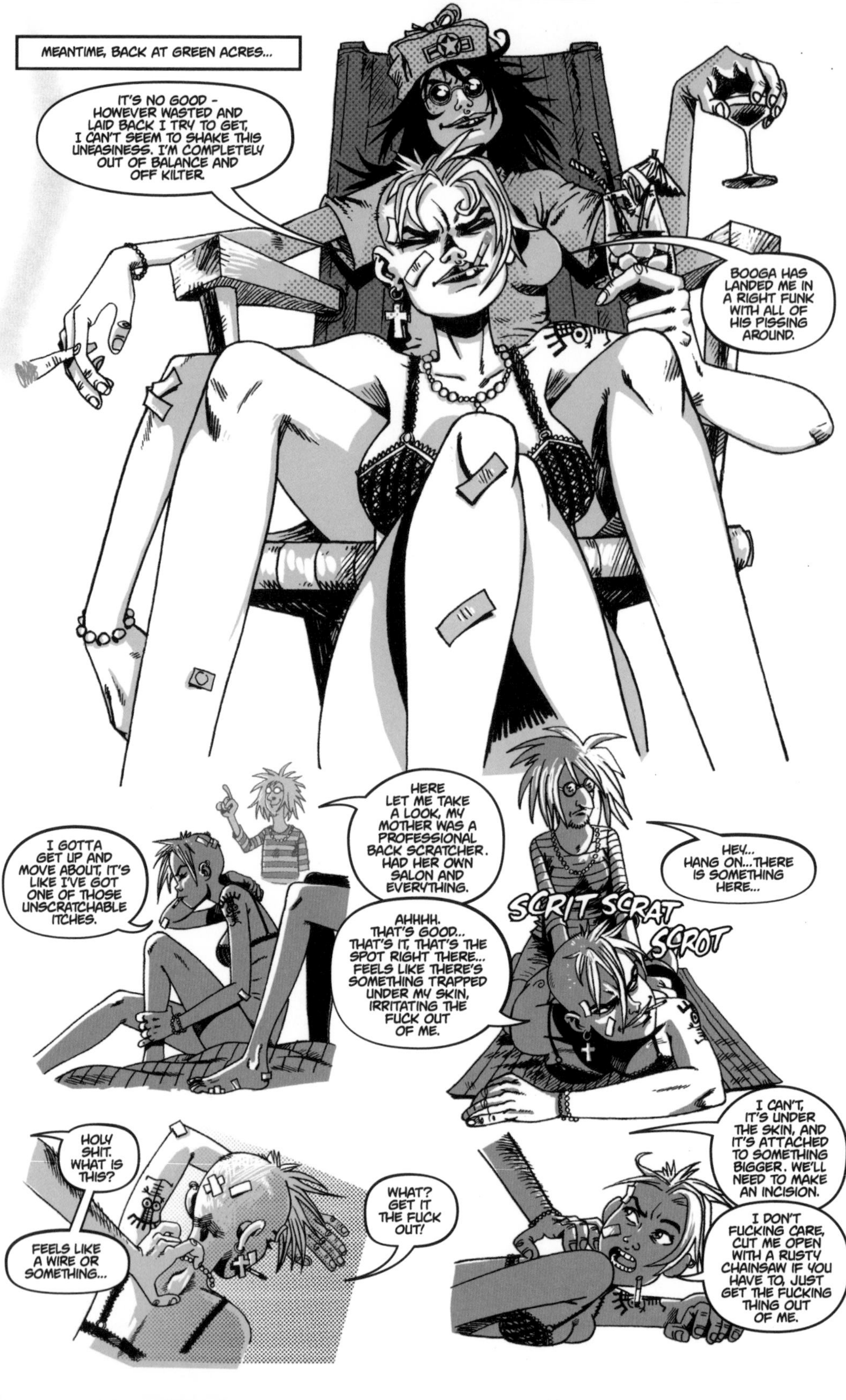

MEANTIME, BACK AT GREEN ACRES...
IT'S NO GOOD - HOWEVER WASTED AND LAID BACK I TRY TO GET, I CAN'T SEEM TO SHAKE THIS UNEASINESS. I'M COMPLETELY OUT OF BALANCE AND OFF KILTER.
BOOGA HAS LANDED ME IN A RIGHT FUNK WITH ALL OF HIS PISSING AROUND.
I GOTTA GET UP AND MOVE ABOUT, IT'S LIKE I'VE GOT ONE OF THOSE UNSCRATCHABLE ITCHES.
HERE LET ME TAKE A LOOK, MY MOTHER WAS A PROFESSIONAL BACK SCRATCHER. HAD HER OWN SALON AND EVERYTHING.
AHHHH. THAT'S GOOD... THAT'S IT, THAT'S THE SPOT RIGHT THERE... FEELS LIKE THERE'S SOMETHING TRAPPED UNDER MY SKIN, IRRITATING THE FUCK OUT OF ME.
SCRIT SCRAT SCROT
HEY... HANG ON... THERE IS SOMETHING HERE...
HOLY SHIT. WHAT IS THIS?
FEELS LIKE A WIRE OR SOMETHING...
WHAT? GET IT THE FUCK OUT!
I CAN'T, IT'S UNDER THE SKIN, AND IT'S ATTACHED TO SOMETHING BIGGER. WE'LL NEED TO MAKE AN INCISION.
I DON'T FUCKING CARE, CUT ME OPEN WITH A RUSTY CHAINSAW IF YOU HAVE TO, JUST GET THE FUCKING THING OUT OF ME.

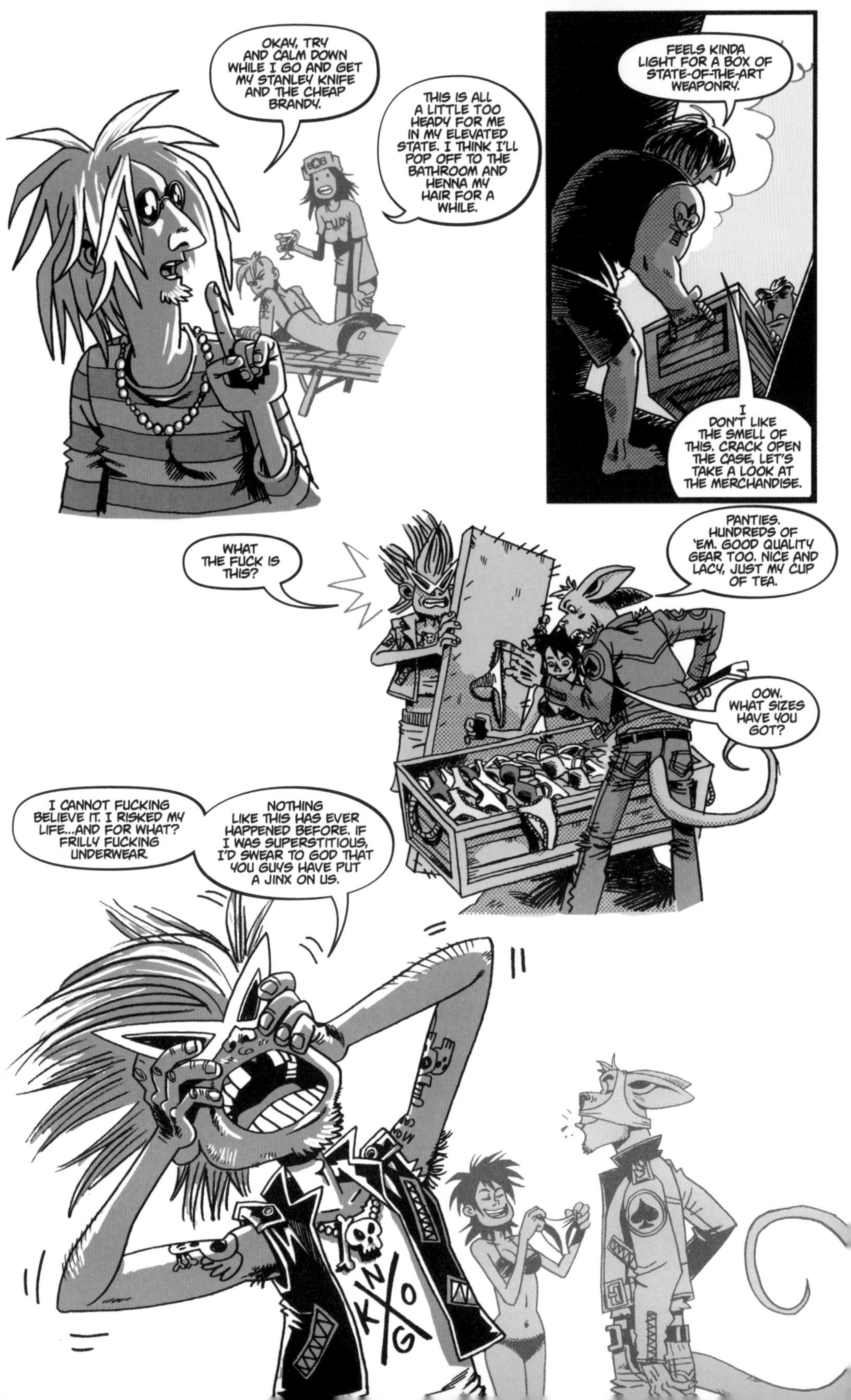
OKAY, TRY AND CALM DOWN WHILE I GO AND GET MY STANLEY KNIFE AND THE CHEAP BRANDY.
THIS IS ALL A LITTLE TOO HEADY FOR ME IN MY ELEVATED STATE. I THINK I'LL POP OFF TO THE BATHROOM AND HENNA MY HAIR FOR A WHILE.
FEELS KINDA LIGHT FOR A BOX OF STATE-OF-THE-ART WEAPONRY.
I DON'T LIKE THE SMELL OF THIS. CRACK OPEN THE CASE, LET'S TAKE A LOOK AT THE MERCHANDISE.
WHAT THE FUCK IS THIS?
PANTIES. HUNDREDS OF 'EM. GOOD QUALITY GEAR TOO. NICE AND LACY, JUST MY CUP OF TEA.
OOW. WHAT SIZES HAVE YOU GOT?
I CANNOT FUCKING BELIEVE IT. I RISKED MY LIFE...AND FOR WHAT? FRILLY FUCKING UNDERWEAR.
NOTHING LIKE THIS HAS EVER HAPPENED BEFORE. IF I WAS SUPERSTITIOUS, I'D SWEAR TO GOD THAT YOU GUYS HAVE PUT A JINX ON US.

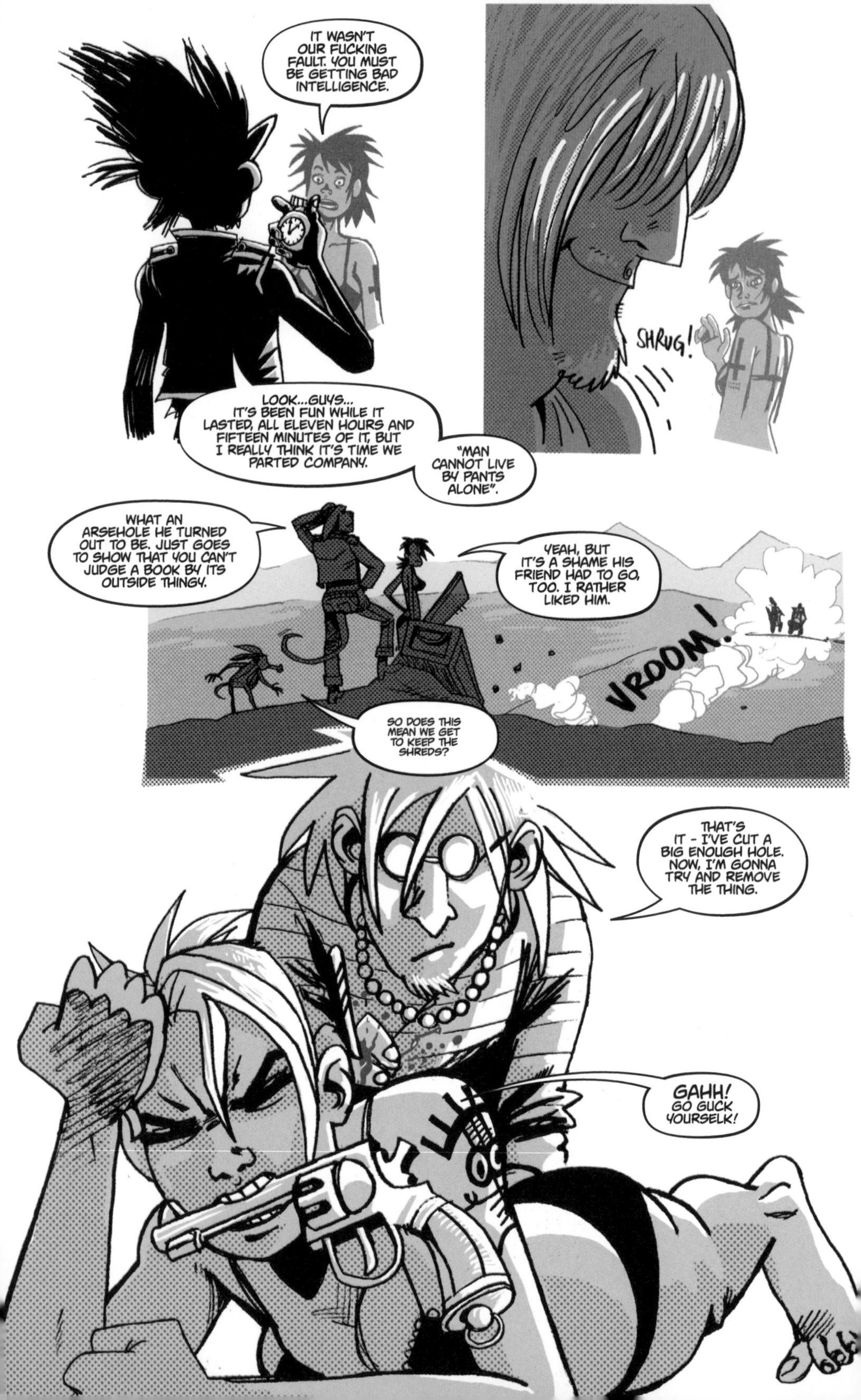
IT WASN'T OUR FUCKING FAULT. YOU MUST BE GETTING BAD INTELLIGENCE.
SHRUG!
LOOK...GUYS... IT'S BEEN FUN WHILE IT LASTED, ALL ELEVEN HOURS AND FIFTEEN MINUTES OF IT, BUT I REALLY THINK IT'S TIME WE PARTED COMPANY.
"MAN CANNOT LIVE BY PANTS ALONE".
WHAT AN ARSEHOLE HE TURNED OUT TO BE. JUST GOES TO SHOW THAT YOU CAN'T JUDGE A BOOK BY ITS OUTSIDE THINGY.
YEAH, BUT IT'S A SHAME HIS FRIEND HAD TO GO, TOO. I RATHER LIKED HIM.
VROOM!
SO DOES THIS MEAN WE GET TO KEEP THE SHREDS?
THAT'S IT - I'VE CUT A BIG ENOUGH HOLE. NOW, I'M GONNA TRY AND REMOVE THE THING.
GAHH! GO GUCK YOURSELK!

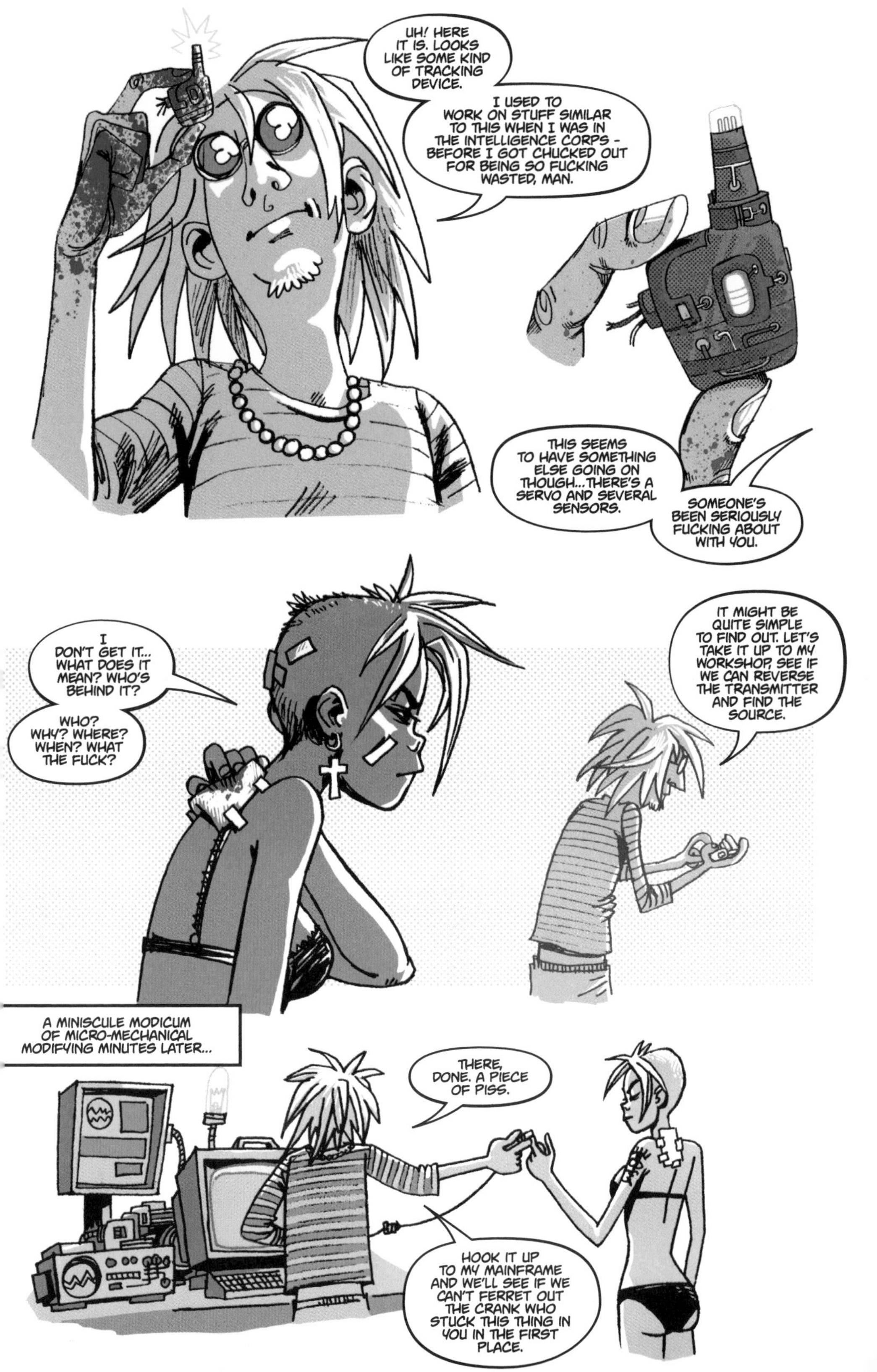

UH! HERE IT IS. LOOKS LIKE SOME KIND OF TRACKING DEVICE.
I USED TO WORK ON STUFF SIMILAR TO THIS WHEN I WAS IN THE INTELLIGENCE CORPS - BEFORE I GOT CHUCKED OUT FOR BEING SO FUCKING WASTED, MAN.
THIS SEEMS TO HAVE SOMETHING ELSE GOING ON THOUGH... THERE'S A SERVO AND SEVERAL SENSORS.
SOMEONE'S BEEN SERIOUSLY FUCKING ABOUT WITH YOU.
I DON'T GET IT... WHAT DOES IT MEAN? WHO'S BEHIND IT?
WHO? WHY? WHERE? WHEN? WHAT THE FUCK?
IT MIGHT BE QUITE SIMPLE TO FIND OUT. LET'S TAKE IT UP TO MY WORKSHOP, SEE IF WE CAN REVERSE THE TRANSMITTER AND FIND THE SOURCE.
A MINISCULE MODICUM OF MICRO-MECHANICAL MODIFYING MINUTES LATER...
THERE, DONE. A PIECE OF PISS.
HOOK IT UP TO MY MAINFRAME AND WE'LL SEE IF WE CAN'T FERRET OUT THE CRANK WHO STUCK THIS THING IN YOU IN THE FIRST PLACE.

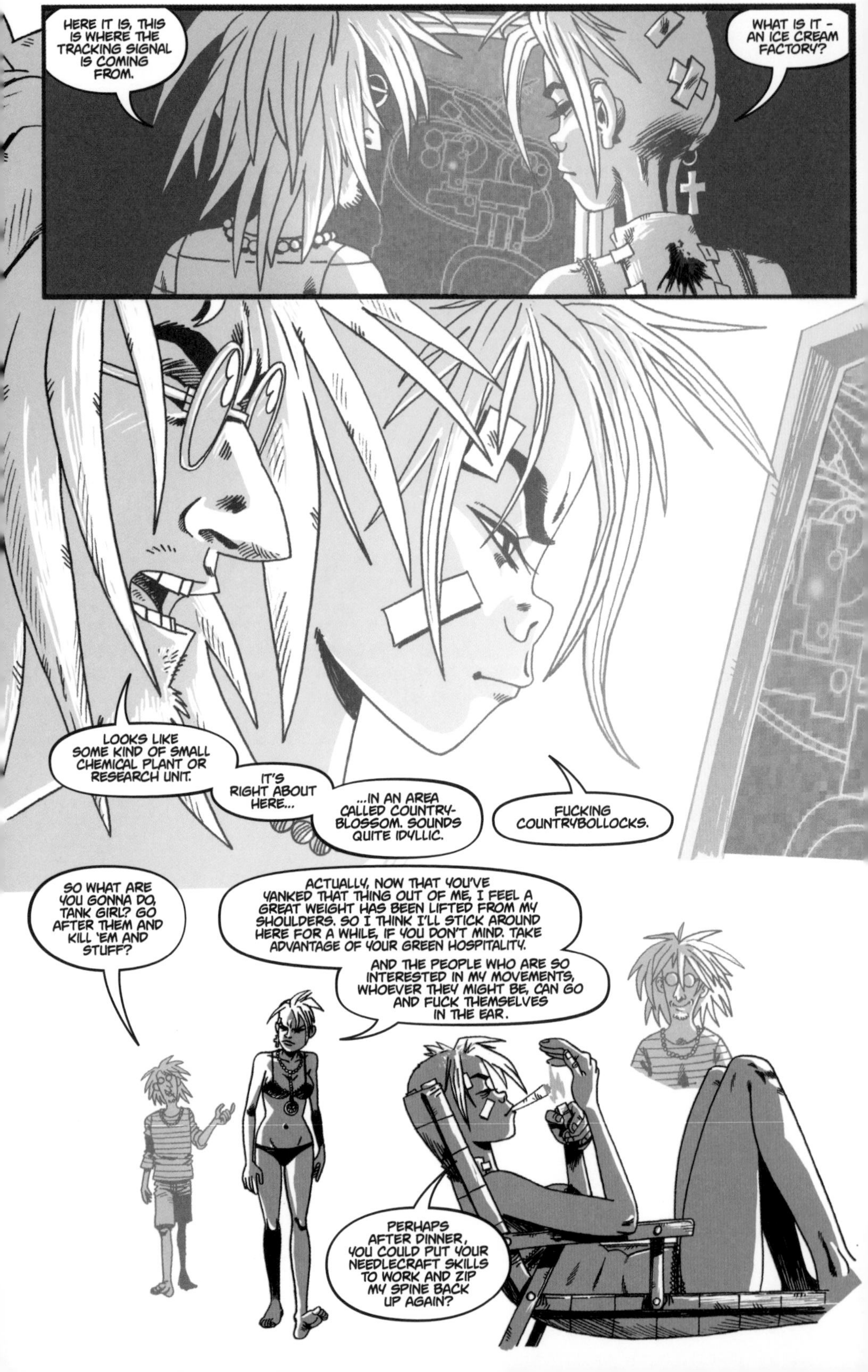
HERE IT IS, THIS IS WHERE THE TRACKING SIGNAL IS COMING FROM.
WHAT IS IT - AN ICE CREAM FACTORY?
LOOKS LIKE SOME KIND OF SMALL CHEMICAL PLANT OR RESEARCH UNIT.
IT'S RIGHT ABOUT HERE...
...IN AN AREA CALLED COUNTRY-BLOSSOM. SOUNDS QUITE IDYLLIC.
FUCKING COUNTRYBOLLOCKS.
SO WHAT ARE YOU GONNA DO, TANK GIRL? GO AFTER THEM AND KILL 'EM AND STUFF?
ACTUALLY, NOW THAT YOU'VE YANKED THAT THING OUT OF ME, I FEEL A GREAT WEIGHT HAS BEEN LIFTED FROM MY SHOULDERS. SO I THINK I'LL STICK AROUND HERE FOR A WHILE, IF YOU DON'T MIND. TAKE ADVANTAGE OF YOUR GREEN HOSPITALITY.
AND THE PEOPLE WHO ARE SO INTERESTED IN MY MOVEMENTS, WHOEVER THEY MIGHT BE, CAN GO AND FUCK THEMSELVES IN THE EAR.
PERHAPS AFTER DINNER, YOU COULD PUT YOUR NEEDLECRAFT SKILLS TO WORK AND ZIP MY SPINE BACK UP AGAIN?

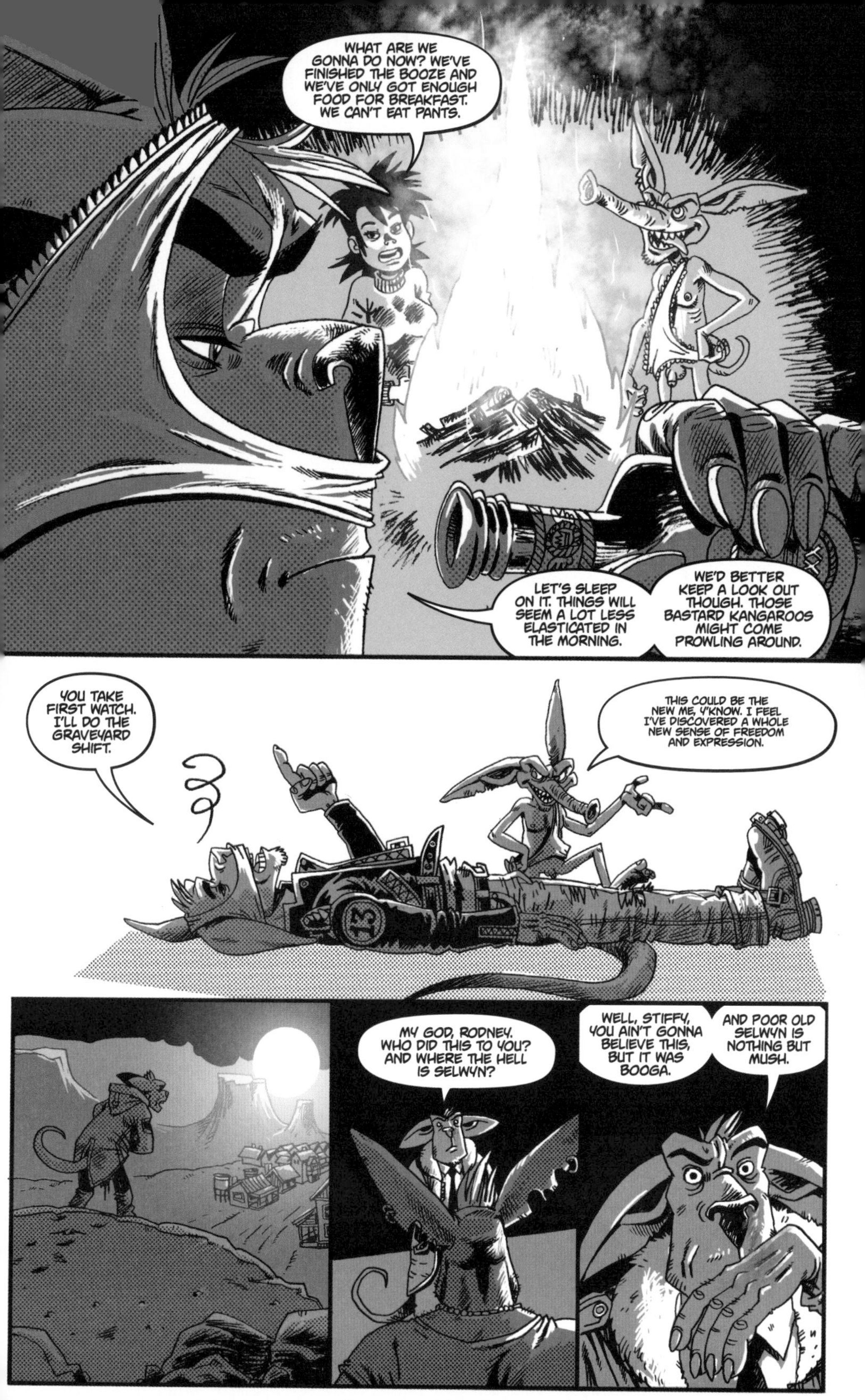
WHAT ARE WE GONNA DO NOW? WE'VE FINISHED THE BOOZE AND WE'VE ONLY GOT ENOUGH FOOD FOR BREAKFAST. WE CAN'T EAT PANTS.
LET'S SLEEP ON IT. THINGS WILL SEEM A LOT LESS ELASTICATED IN THE MORNING.
WE'D BETTER KEEP A LOOK OUT THOUGH. THOSE BASTARD KANGAROOS MIGHT COME PROWLING AROUND.
YOU TAKE FIRST WATCH. I'LL DO THE GRAVEYARD SHIFT.
THIS COULD BE THE NEW ME, Y'KNOW. I FEEL I'VE DISCOVERED A WHOLE NEW SENSE OF FREEDOM AND EXPRESSION.
13
MY GOD, RODNEY. WHO DID THIS TO YOU? AND WHERE THE HELL IS SELWYN?
WELL, STIFFY, YOU AIN'T GONNA BELIEVE THIS, BUT IT WAS BOOGA.
AND POOR OLD SELWYN IS NOTHING BUT MUSH.

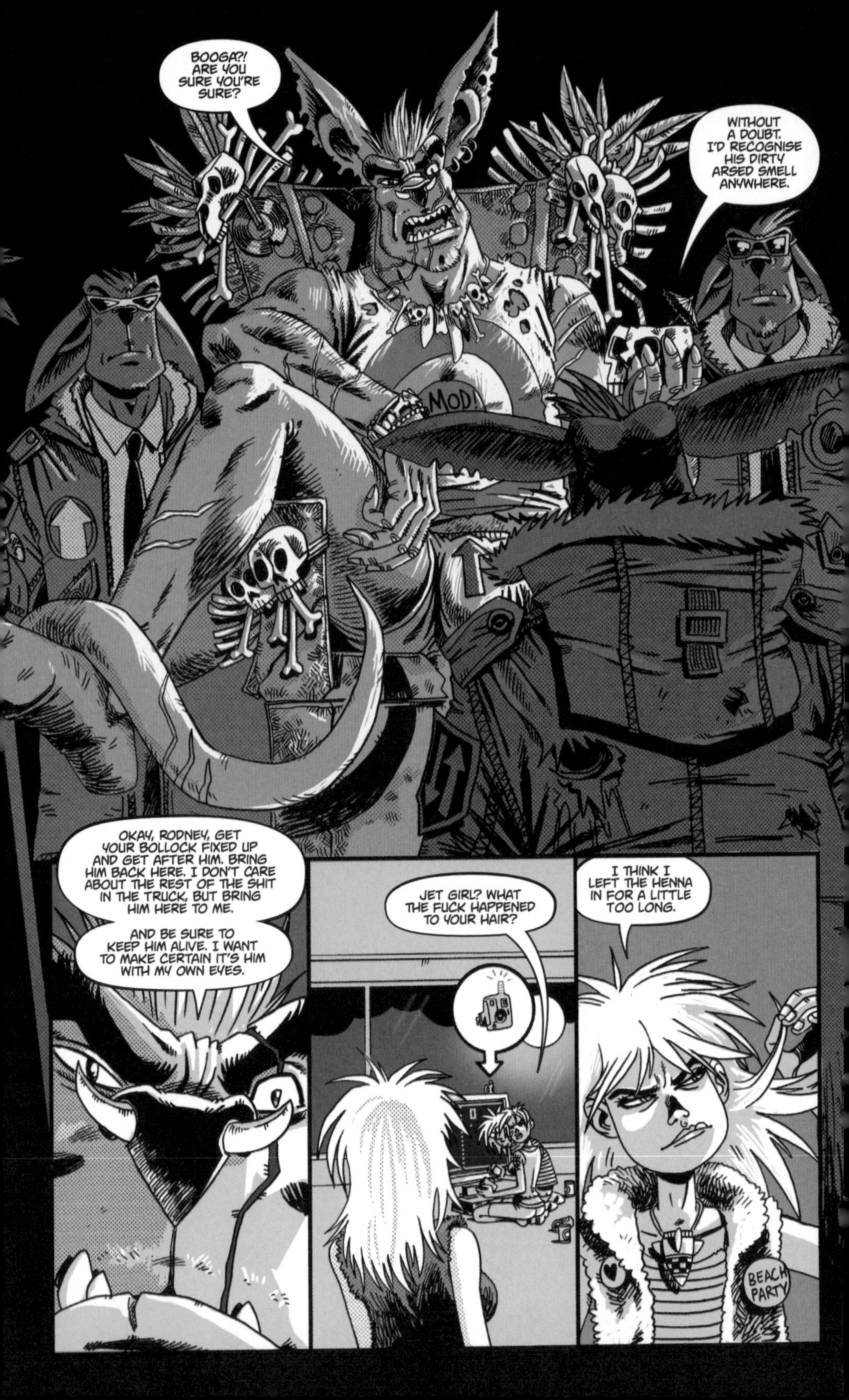
BOOGA?! ARE YOU SURE YOU'RE SURE?
WITHOUT A DOUBT. I'D RECOGNISE HIS DIRTY ARSED SMELL ANYWHERE.
MOD!
OKAY, RODNEY, GET YOUR BOLLOCK FIXED UP AND GET AFTER HIM. BRING HIM BACK HERE. I DON'T CARE ABOUT THE REST OF THE SHIT IN THE TRUCK, BUT BRING HIM HERE TO ME.
AND BE SURE TO KEEP HIM ALIVE. I WANT TO MAKE CERTAIN IT'S HIM WITH MY OWN EYES.
JET GIRL? WHAT THE FUCK HAPPENED TO YOUR HAIR?
I THINK I LEFT THE HENNA IN FOR A LITTLE TOO LONG.
BEACH PARTY

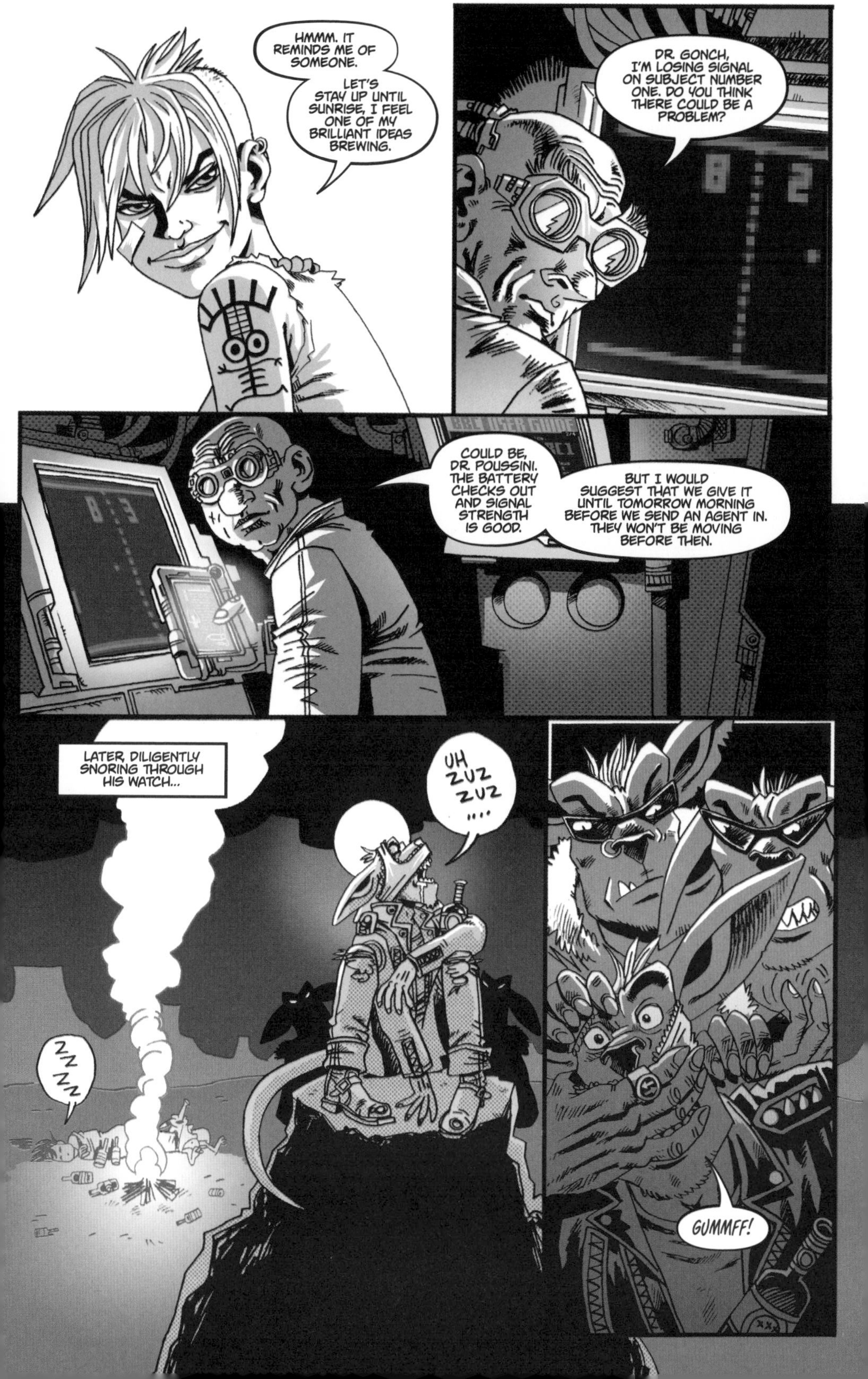
HMMM. IT REMINDS ME OF SOMEONE.
LET'S STAY UP UNTIL SUNRISE, I FEEL ONE OF MY BRILLIANT IDEAS BREWING.
DR. GONCH, I'M LOSING SIGNAL ON SUBJECT NUMBER ONE. DO YOU THINK THERE COULD BE A PROBLEM?
COULD BE, DR. POUSSINI. THE BATTERY CHECKS OUT AND SIGNAL STRENGTH IS GOOD.
BUT I WOULD SUGGEST THAT WE GIVE IT UNTIL TOMORROW MORNING BEFORE WE SEND AN AGENT IN. THEY WON'T BE MOVING BEFORE THEN.
LATER, DILIGENTLY SNORING THROUGH HIS WATCH...
UH ZUZ ZUZ ....
Z Z Z Z
GUMMFF!

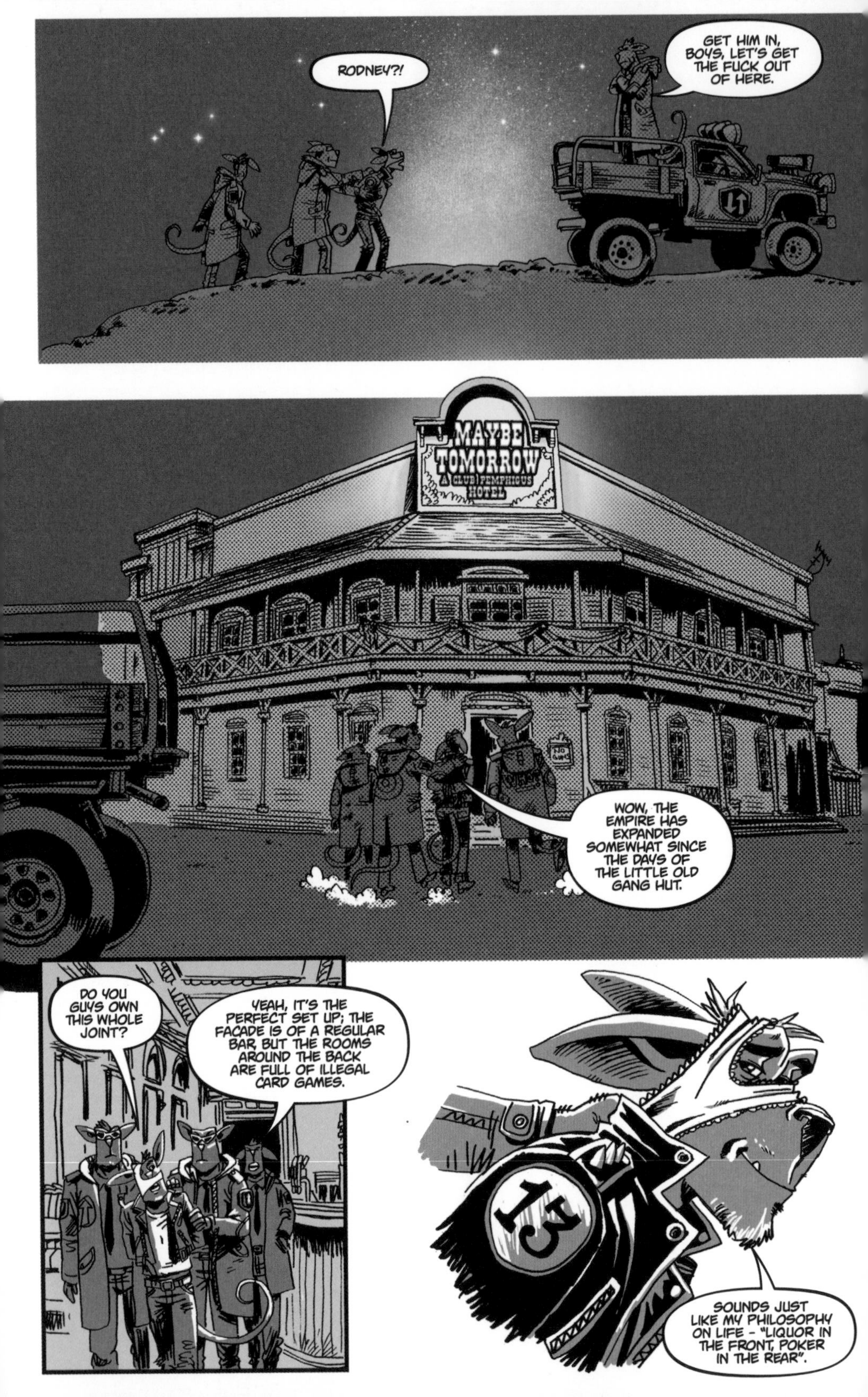
RODNEY?!
GET HIM IN, BOYS, LET'S GET THE FUCK OUT OF HERE.
MAYBE TOMORROW
A CLUB PEMPHIGUS HOTEL
WOW, THE EMPIRE HAS EXPANDED SOMEWHAT SINCE THE DAYS OF THE LITTLE OLD GANG HUT.
DO YOU GUYS OWN THIS WHOLE JOINT?
YEAH, IT'S THE PERFECT SET UP; THE FACADE IS OF A REGULAR BAR, BUT THE ROOMS AROUND THE BACK ARE FULL OF ILLEGAL CARD GAMES.
13
SOUNDS JUST LIKE MY PHILOSOPHY ON LIFE - "LIQUOR IN THE FRONT, POKER IN THE REAR".

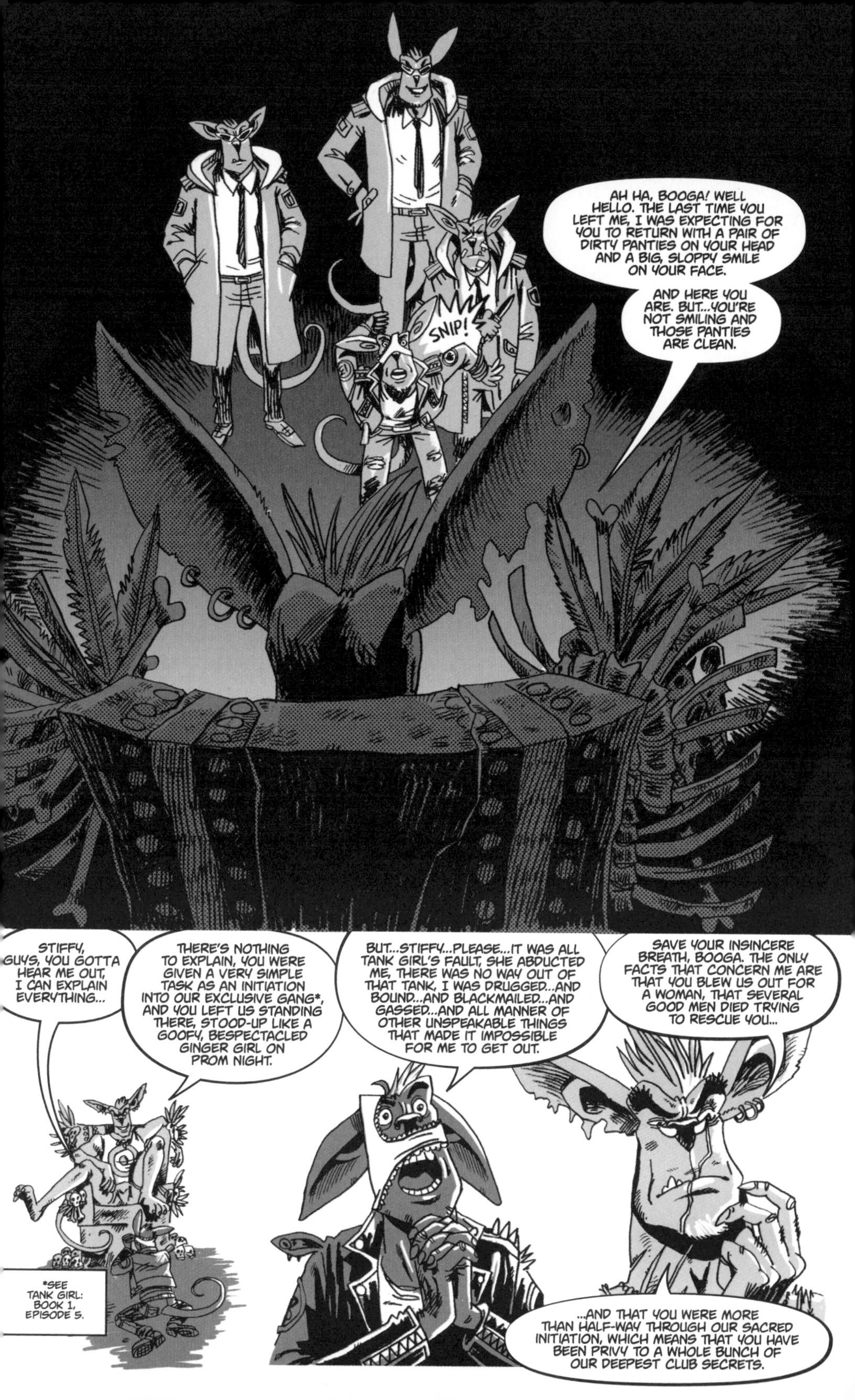
AH HA, BOOGA! WELL HELLO. THE LAST TIME YOU LEFT ME, I WAS EXPECTING FOR YOU TO RETURN WITH A PAIR OF DIRTY PANTIES ON YOUR HEAD AND A BIG, SLOPPY SMILE ON YOUR FACE.
AND HERE YOU ARE. BUT...YOU'RE NOT SMILING AND THOSE PANTIES ARE CLEAN.
SNIP!
STIFFY, GUYS, YOU GOTTA HEAR ME OUT, I CAN EXPLAIN EVERYTHING...
THERE'S NOTHING TO EXPLAIN, YOU WERE GIVEN A VERY SIMPLE TASK AS AN INITIATION INTO OUR EXCLUSIVE GANG*, AND YOU LEFT US STANDING THERE, STOOD-UP LIKE A GOOFY, BESPECTACLED GINGER GIRL ON PROM NIGHT.
BUT...STIFFY...PLEASE...IT WAS ALL TANK GIRL'S FAULT, SHE ABDUCTED ME, THERE WAS NO WAY OUT OF THAT TANK, I WAS DRUGGED...AND BOUND...AND BLACKMAILED...AND GASSED...AND ALL MANNER OF OTHER UNSPEAKABLE THINGS THAT MADE IT IMPOSSIBLE FOR ME TO GET OUT.
SAVE YOUR INSINCERE BREATH, BOOGA. THE ONLY FACTS THAT CONCERN ME ARE THAT YOU BLEW US OUT FOR A WOMAN, THAT SEVERAL GOOD MEN DIED TRYING TO RESCUE YOU...
*SEE TANK GIRL: BOOK 1, EPISODE 5.
...AND THAT YOU WERE MORE THAN HALF-WAY THROUGH OUR SACRED INITIATION, WHICH MEANS THAT YOU HAVE BEEN PRIVY TO A WHOLE BUNCH OF OUR DEEPEST CLUB SECRETS.

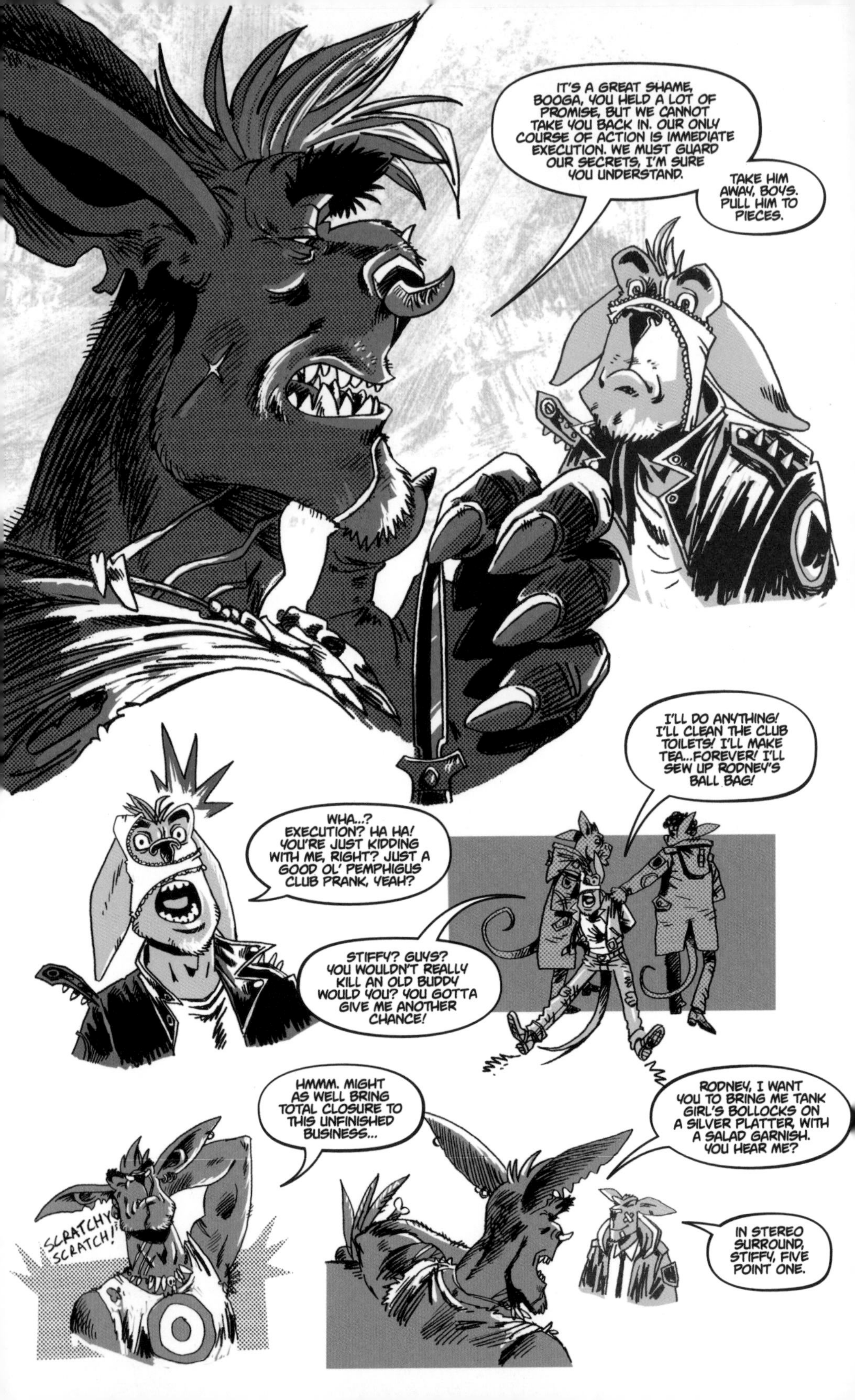
IT'S A GREAT SHAME, BOOGA, YOU HELD A LOT OF PROMISE, BUT WE CANNOT TAKE YOU BACK IN. OUR ONLY COURSE OF ACTION IS IMMEDIATE EXECUTION. WE MUST GUARD OUR SECRETS, I'M SURE YOU UNDERSTAND.
TAKE HIM AWAY, BOYS. PULL HIM TO PIECES.
WHA...? EXECUTION? HA HA! YOU'RE JUST KIDDING WITH ME, RIGHT? JUST A GOOD OL' PEMPHIGUS CLUB PRANK, YEAH?
I'LL DO ANYTHING! I'LL CLEAN THE CLUB TOILETS! I'LL MAKE TEA...FOREVER! I'LL SEW UP RODNEY'S BALL BAG!
STIFFY? GUYS? YOU WOULDN'T REALLY KILL AN OLD BUDDY WOULD YOU? YOU GOTTA GIVE ME ANOTHER CHANCE!
HMMM. MIGHT AS WELL BRING TOTAL CLOSURE TO THIS UNFINISHED BUSINESS...
SCRATCHY SCRATCH!
RODNEY, I WANT YOU TO BRING ME TANK GIRL'S BOLLOCKS ON A SILVER PLATTER, WITH A SALAD GARNISH. YOU HEAR ME?
IN STEREO SURROUND, STIFFY, FIVE POINT ONE.

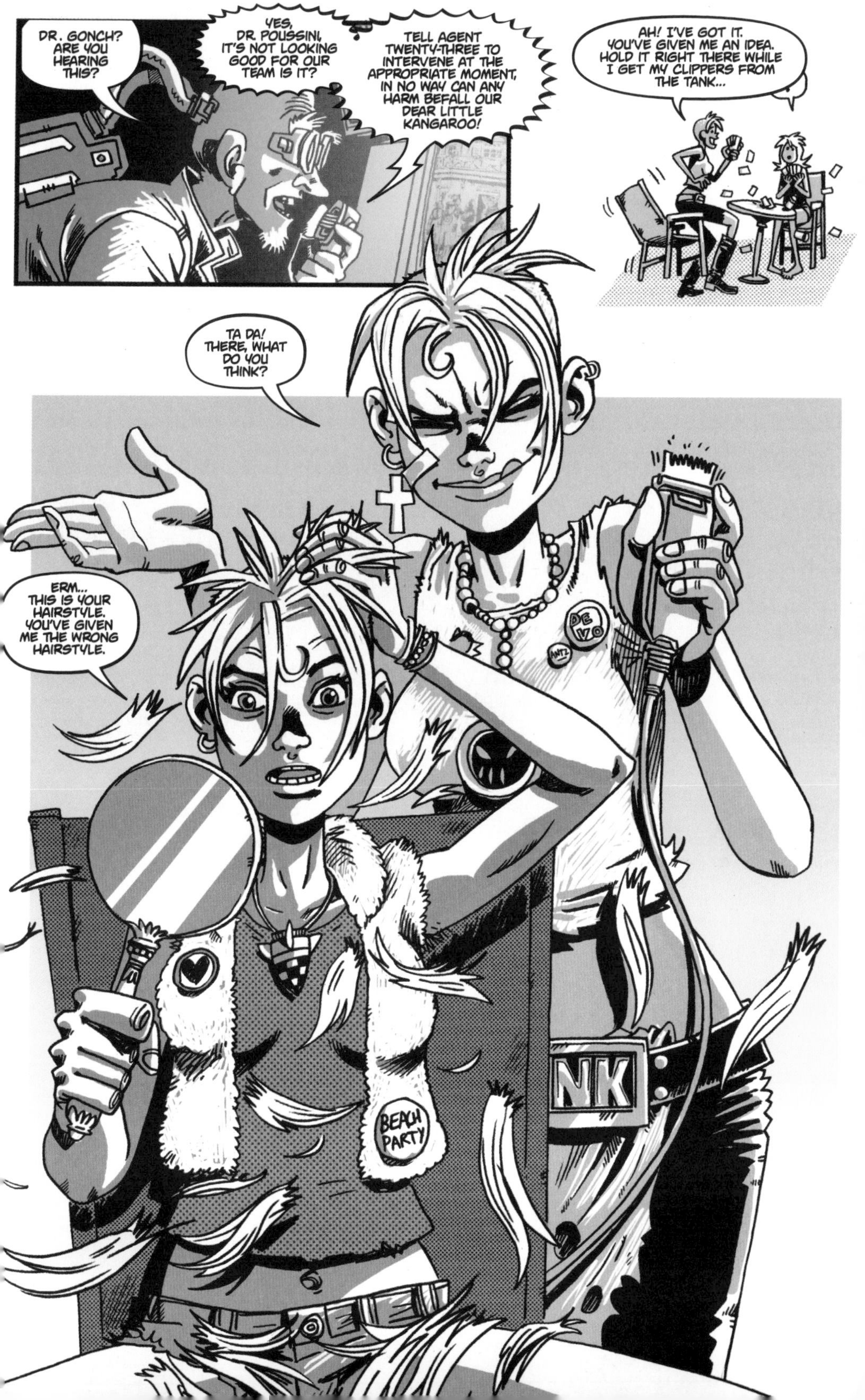
DR. GONCH? ARE YOU HEARING THIS?
YES, DR. POUSSINI, IT'S NOT LOOKING GOOD FOR OUR TEAM IS IT?
TELL AGENT TWENTY-THREE TO INTERVENE AT THE APPROPRIATE MOMENT, IN NO WAY CAN ANY HARM BEFALL OUR DEAR LITTLE KANGAROO!
AH! I'VE GOT IT. YOU'VE GIVEN ME AN IDEA. HOLD IT RIGHT THERE WHILE I GET MY CLIPPERS FROM THE TANK...
TA DA! THERE, WHAT DO YOU THINK?
ERM... THIS IS YOUR HAIRSTYLE. YOU'VE GIVEN ME THE WRONG HAIRSTYLE.
DEVO
BEACH PARTY
NK

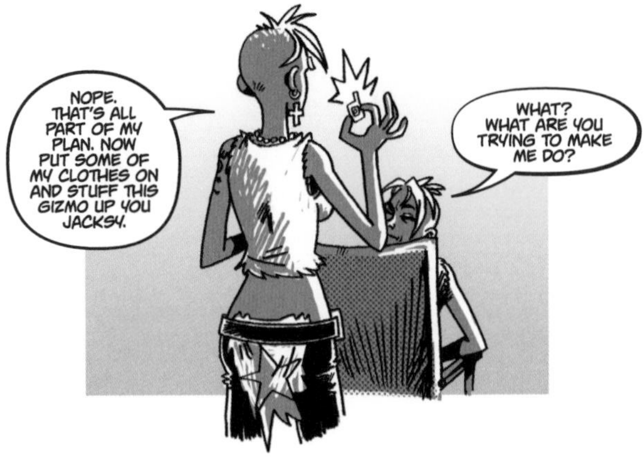
NOPE. THAT'S ALL PART OF MY PLAN. NOW PUT SOME OF MY CLOTHES ON AND STUFF THIS GIZMO UP YOU JACKSY.
WHAT? WHAT ARE YOU TRYING TO MAKE ME DO?

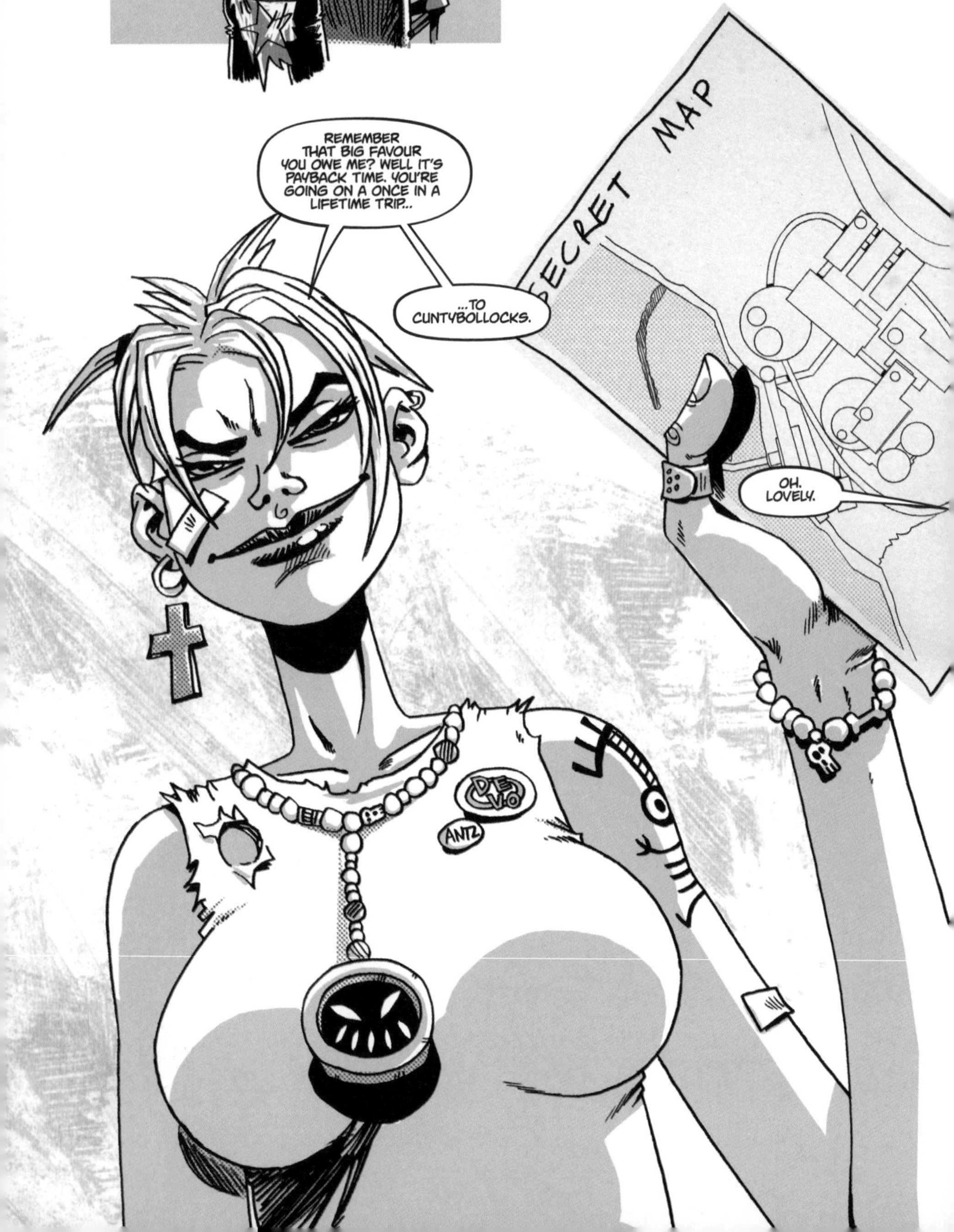
REMEMBER THAT BIG FAVOUR YOU OWE ME? WELL IT'S PAYBACK TIME. YOU'RE GOING ON A ONCE IN A LIFETIME TRIP...
...TO CUNTYBOLLOCKS.
SECRET MAP
OH. LOVELY.
DEVO
ANTZ

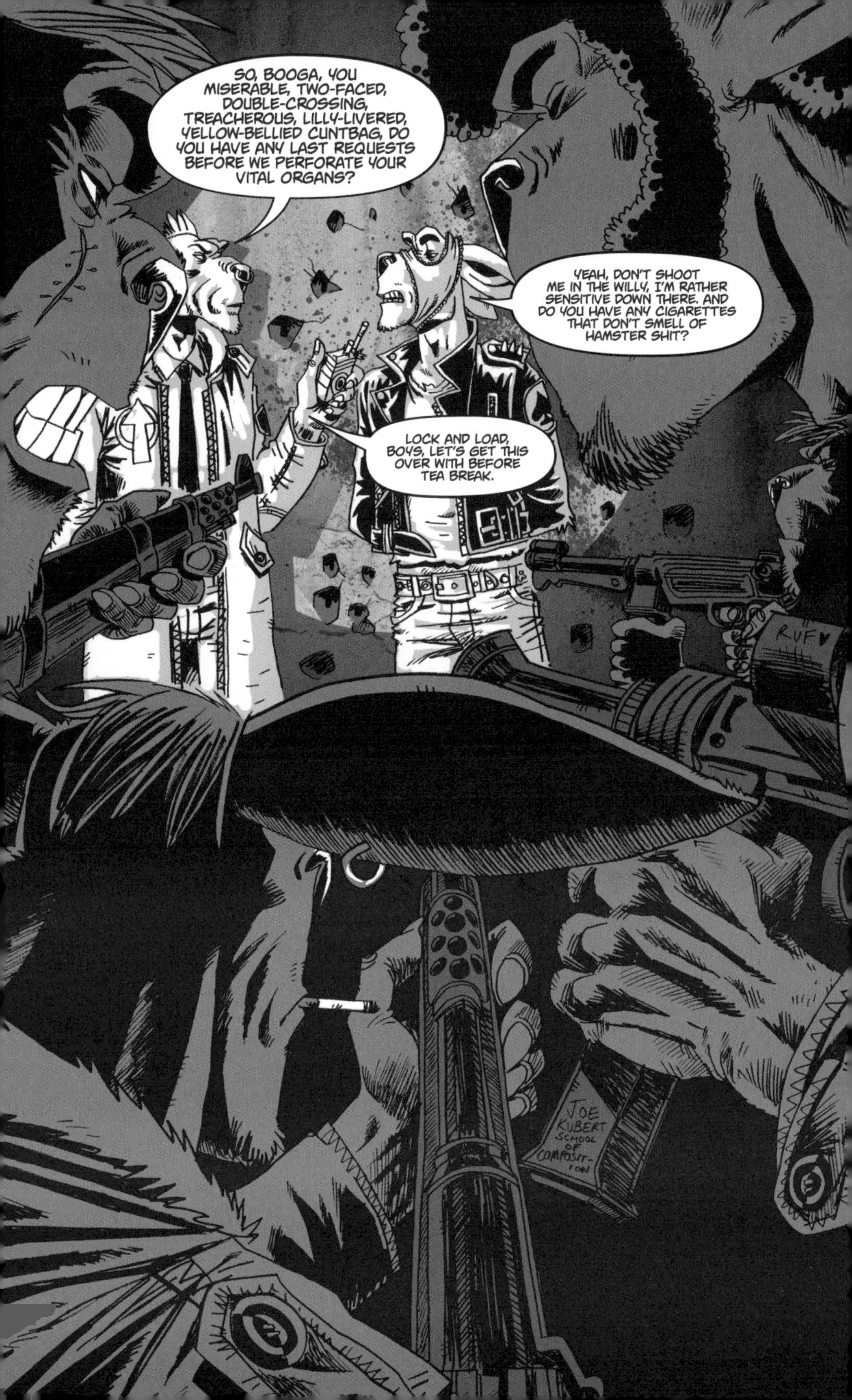
SO, BOOGA, YOU MISERABLE, TWO-FACED, DOUBLE-CROSSING, TREACHEROUS, LILLY-LIVERED, YELLOW-BELLIED CUNTBAG, DO YOU HAVE ANY LAST REQUESTS BEFORE WE PERFORATE YOUR VITAL ORGANS?
YEAH, DON'T SHOOT ME IN THE WILLY, I'M RATHER SENSITIVE DOWN THERE. AND DO YOU HAVE ANY CIGARETTES THAT DON'T SMELL OF HAMSTER SHIT?
LOCK AND LOAD, BOYS, LET'S GET THIS OVER WITH BEFORE TEA BREAK.
JOE KUBERT SCHOOL OF COMPOSIT-ION

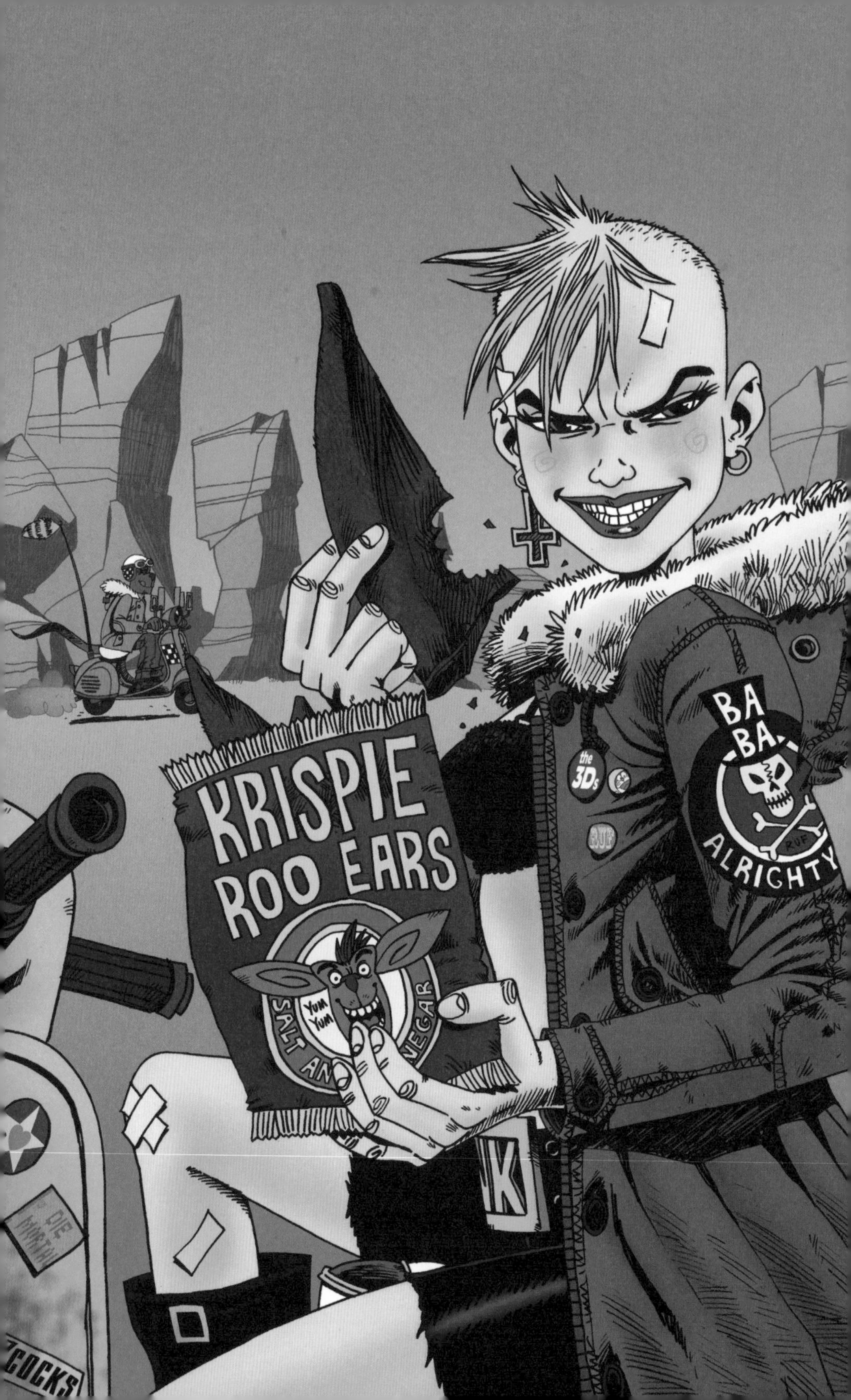

KRISPIE
ROO EARS
YUM YUM
the 3Ds
RUF
BA BA
ALRIGHTY

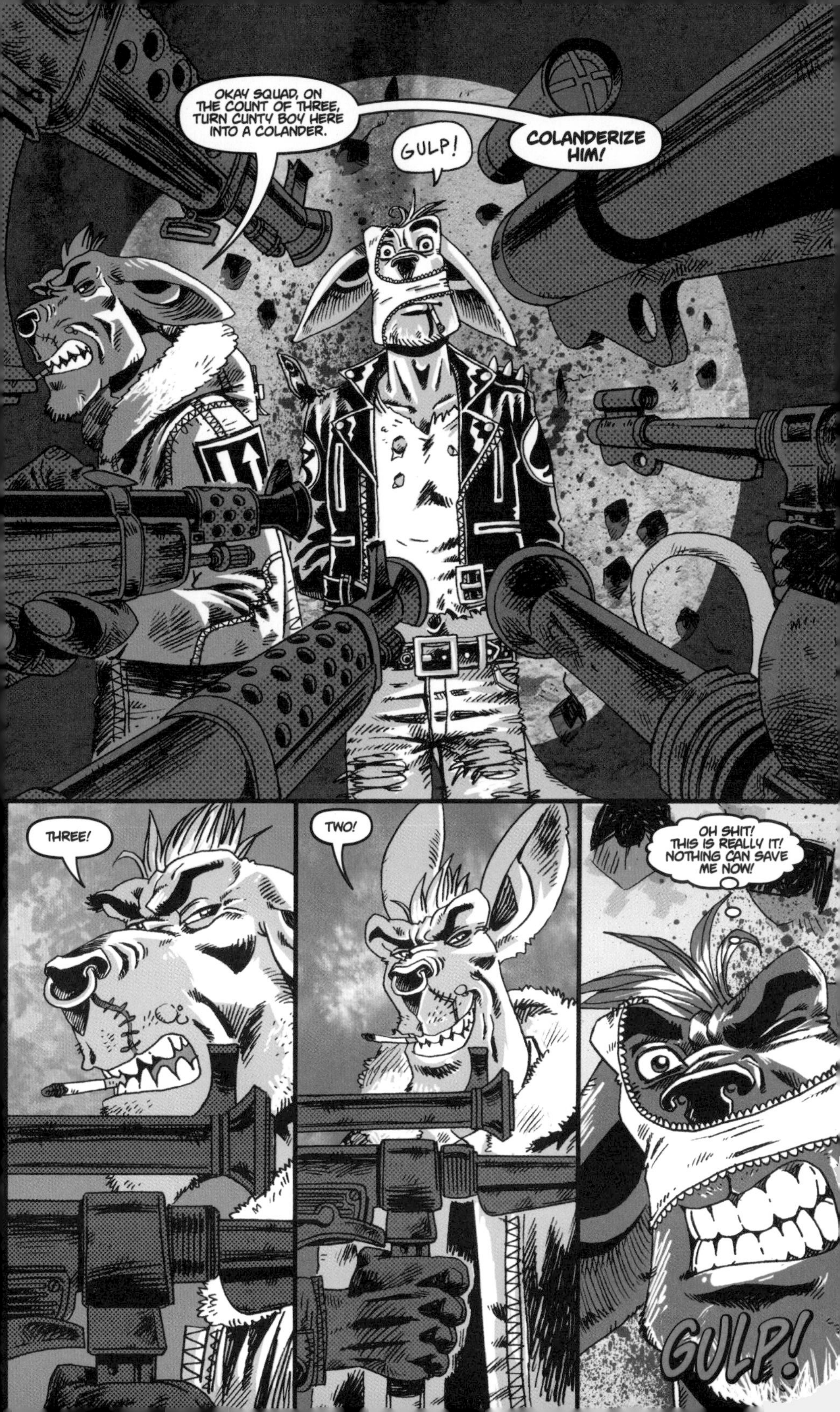
OKAY SQUAD, ON THE COUNT OF THREE, TURN CUNTY BOY HERE INTO A COLANDER.
GULP!
COLANDERIZE HIM!
THREE!
TWO!
OH SHIT! THIS IS REALLY IT! NOTHING CAN SAVE ME NOW!
GULP!

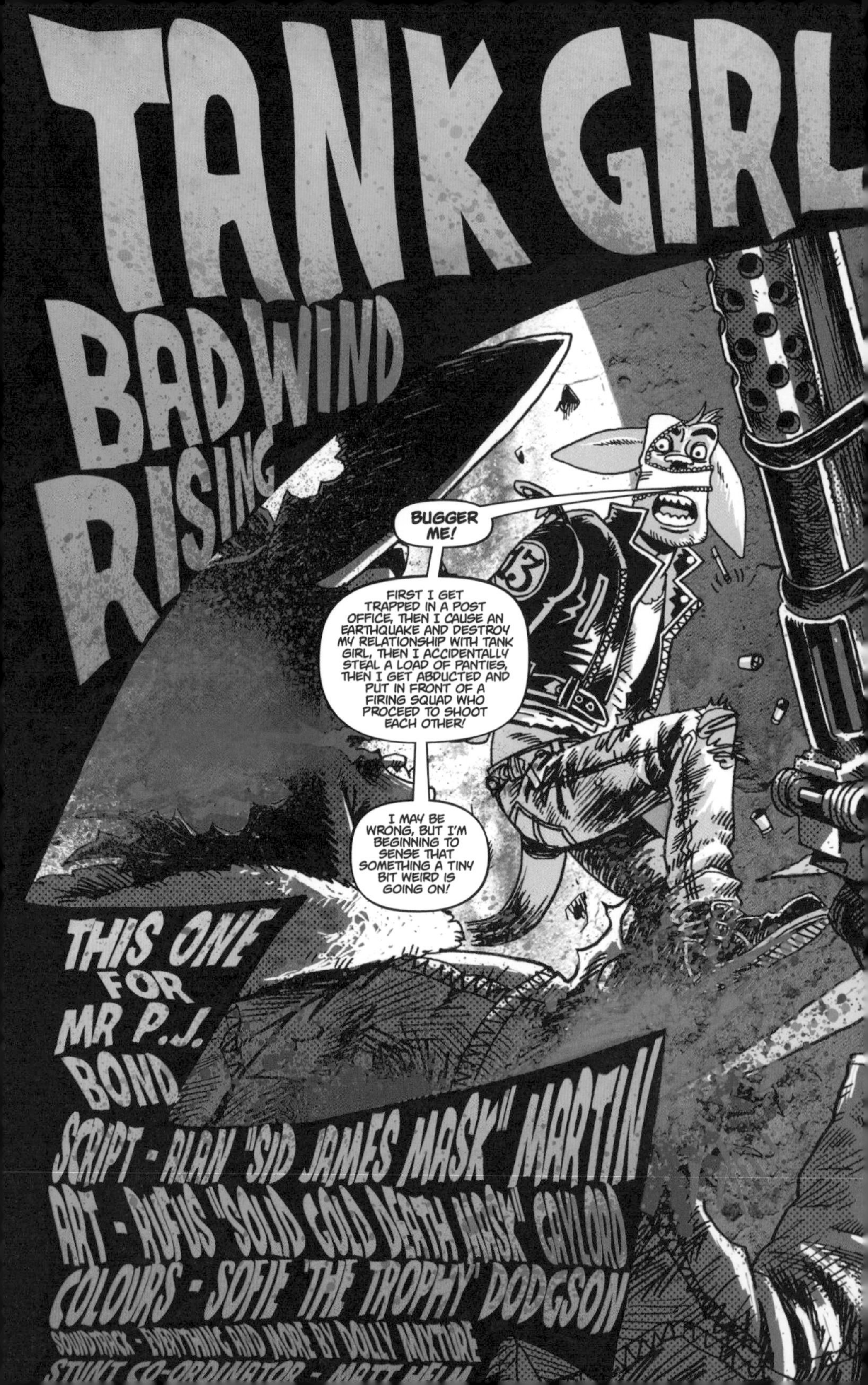
TANK GIRL
BAD WIND RISING
BUGGER ME!
FIRST I GET TRAPPED IN A POST OFFICE, THEN I CAUSE AN EARTHQUAKE AND DESTROY MY RELATIONSHIP WITH TANK GIRL, THEN I ACCIDENTALLY STEAL A LOAD OF PANTIES, THEN I GET ABDUCTED AND PUT IN FRONT OF A FIRING SQUAD WHO PROCEED TO SHOOT EACH OTHER!
I MAY BE WRONG, BUT I'M BEGINNING TO SENSE THAT SOMETHING A TINY BIT WEIRD IS GOING ON!
THIS ONE FOR MR P.J. BOND
SCRIPT - ALAN "SID JAMES MASK" MARTIN
ART - RUFUS "SOLID GOLD DEATH MASK" GAYLORD
COLOURS - SOFIE 'THE TROPHY' DODGSON
SOUNDTRACK - EVERYTHING AND MORE BY DOLLY MIXTURE
STUNT CO-ORDINATOR -

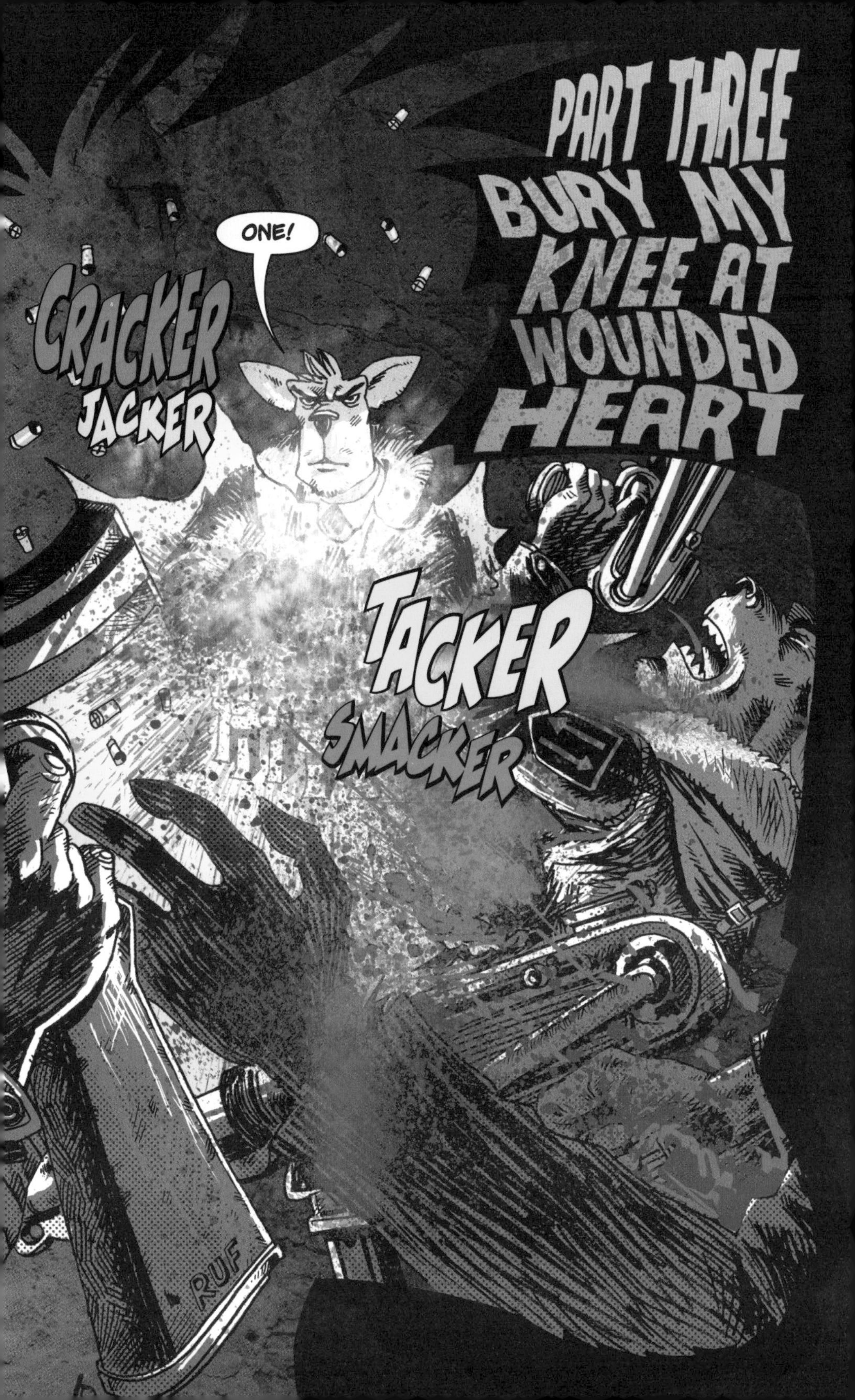
PART THREE
BURY MY KNEE AT WOUNDED HEART
ONE!
CRACKER
JACKER
TACKER
SMACKER
RUF

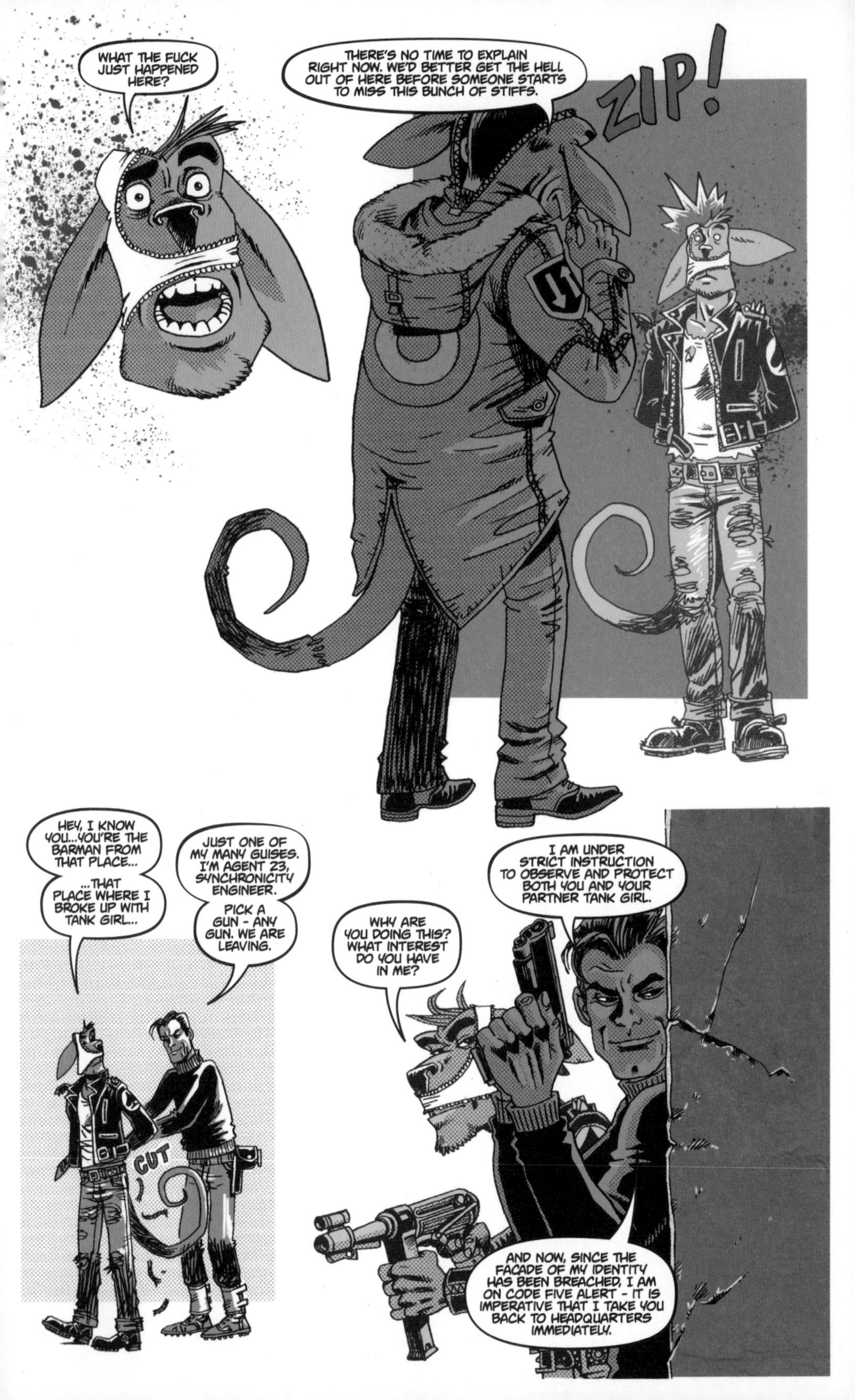
WHAT THE FUCK JUST HAPPENED HERE?
THERE'S NO TIME TO EXPLAIN RIGHT NOW. WE'D BETTER GET THE HELL OUT OF HERE BEFORE SOMEONE STARTS TO MISS THIS BUNCH OF STIFFS.
ZIP!
HEY, I KNOW YOU...YOU'RE THE BARMAN FROM THAT PLACE...
...THAT PLACE WHERE I BROKE UP WITH TANK GIRL...
JUST ONE OF MY MANY GUISES. I'M AGENT 23, SYNCHRONICITY ENGINEER.
PICK A GUN - ANY GUN. WE ARE LEAVING.
CUT
WHY ARE YOU DOING THIS? WHAT INTEREST DO YOU HAVE IN ME?
I AM UNDER STRICT INSTRUCTION TO OBSERVE AND PROTECT BOTH YOU AND YOUR PARTNER TANK GIRL.
AND NOW, SINCE THE FACADE OF MY IDENTITY HAS BEEN BREACHED, I AM ON CODE FIVE ALERT - IT IS IMPERATIVE THAT I TAKE YOU BACK TO HEADQUARTERS IMMEDIATELY.

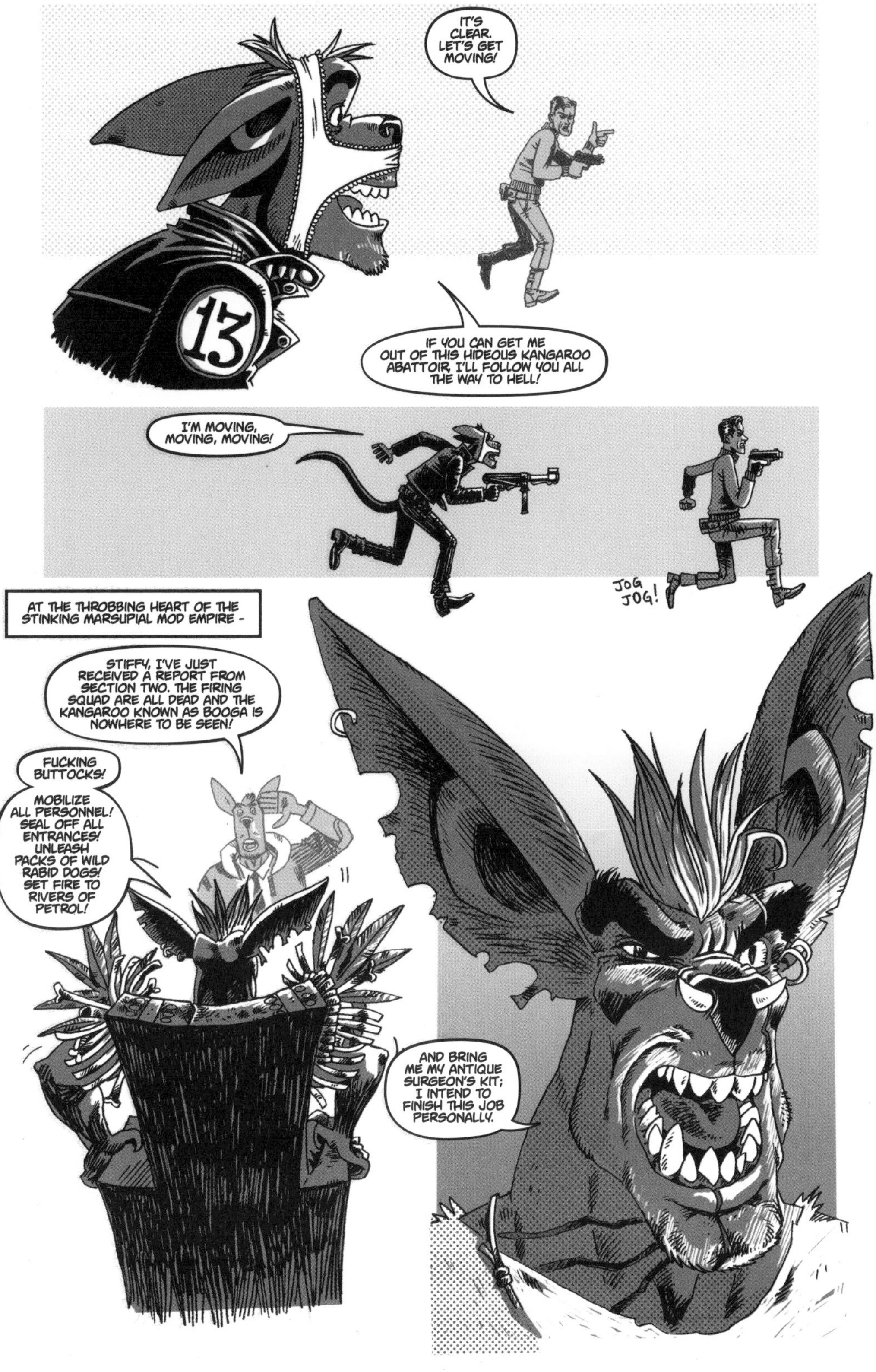
IT'S CLEAR. LET'S GET MOVING!
IF YOU CAN GET ME OUT OF THIS HIDEOUS KANGAROO ABATTOIR, I'LL FOLLOW YOU ALL THE WAY TO HELL!
I'M MOVING, MOVING, MOVING!
JOG JOG!
AT THE THROBBING HEART OF THE STINKING MARSUPIAL MOD EMPIRE -
STIFFY, I'VE JUST RECEIVED A REPORT FROM SECTION TWO. THE FIRING SQUAD ARE ALL DEAD AND THE KANGAROO KNOWN AS BOOGA IS NOWHERE TO BE SEEN!
FUCKING BUTTOCKS!
MOBILIZE ALL PERSONNEL! SEAL OFF ALL ENTRANCES! UNLEASH PACKS OF WILD RABID DOGS! SET FIRE TO RIVERS OF PETROL!
AND BRING ME MY ANTIQUE SURGEON'S KIT; I INTEND TO FINISH THIS JOB PERSONALLY.

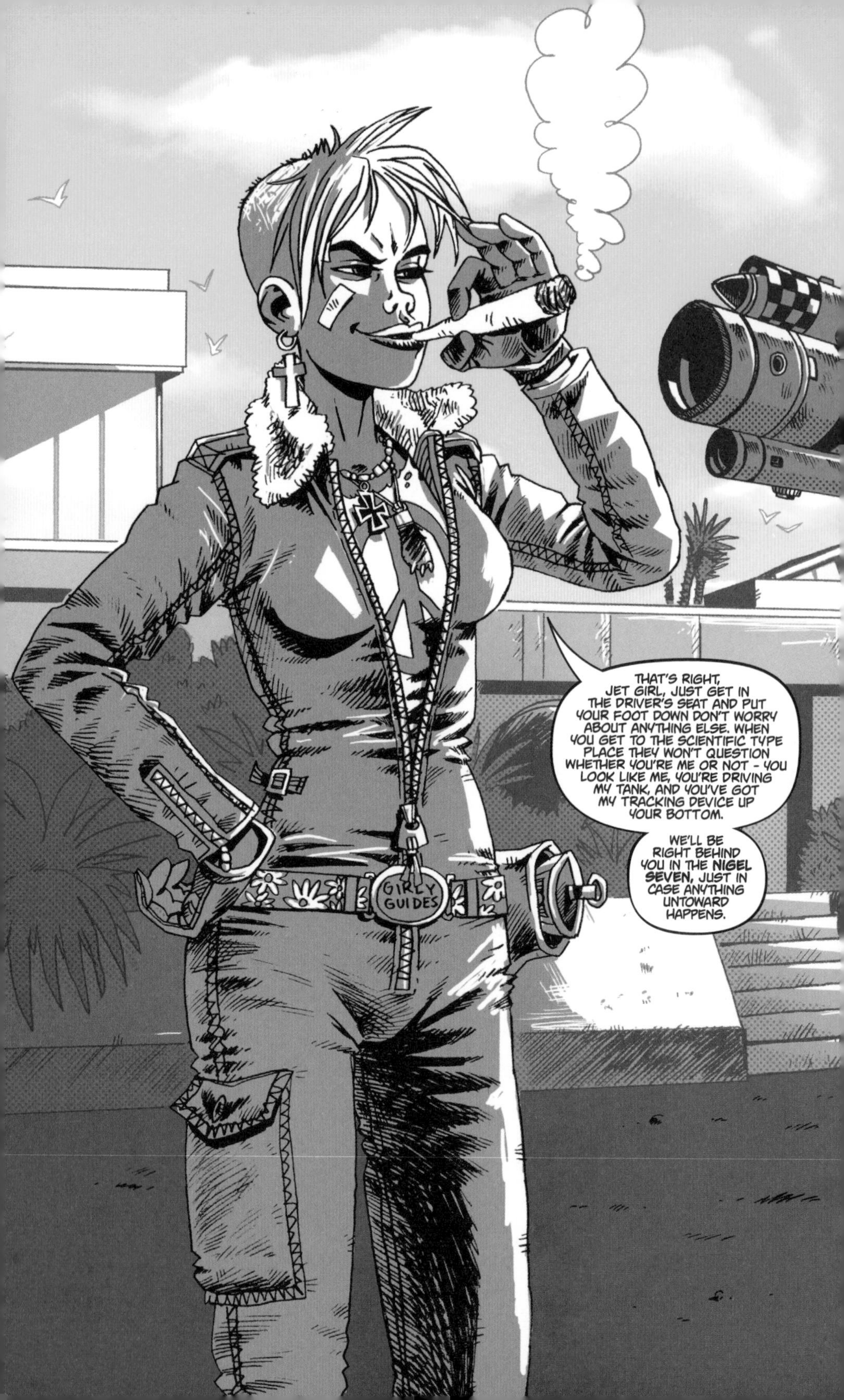
GIRLY GUIDES
THAT'S RIGHT, JET GIRL, JUST GET IN THE DRIVER'S SEAT AND PUT YOUR FOOT DOWN DON'T WORRY ABOUT ANYTHING ELSE. WHEN YOU GET TO THE SCIENTIFIC TYPE PLACE THEY WON'T QUESTION WHETHER YOU'RE ME OR NOT - YOU LOOK LIKE ME, YOU'RE DRIVING MY TANK, AND YOU'VE GOT MY TRACKING DEVICE UP YOUR BOTTOM.
WE'LL BE RIGHT BEHIND YOU IN THE NIGEL SEVEN, JUST IN CASE ANYTHING UNTOWARD HAPPENS.

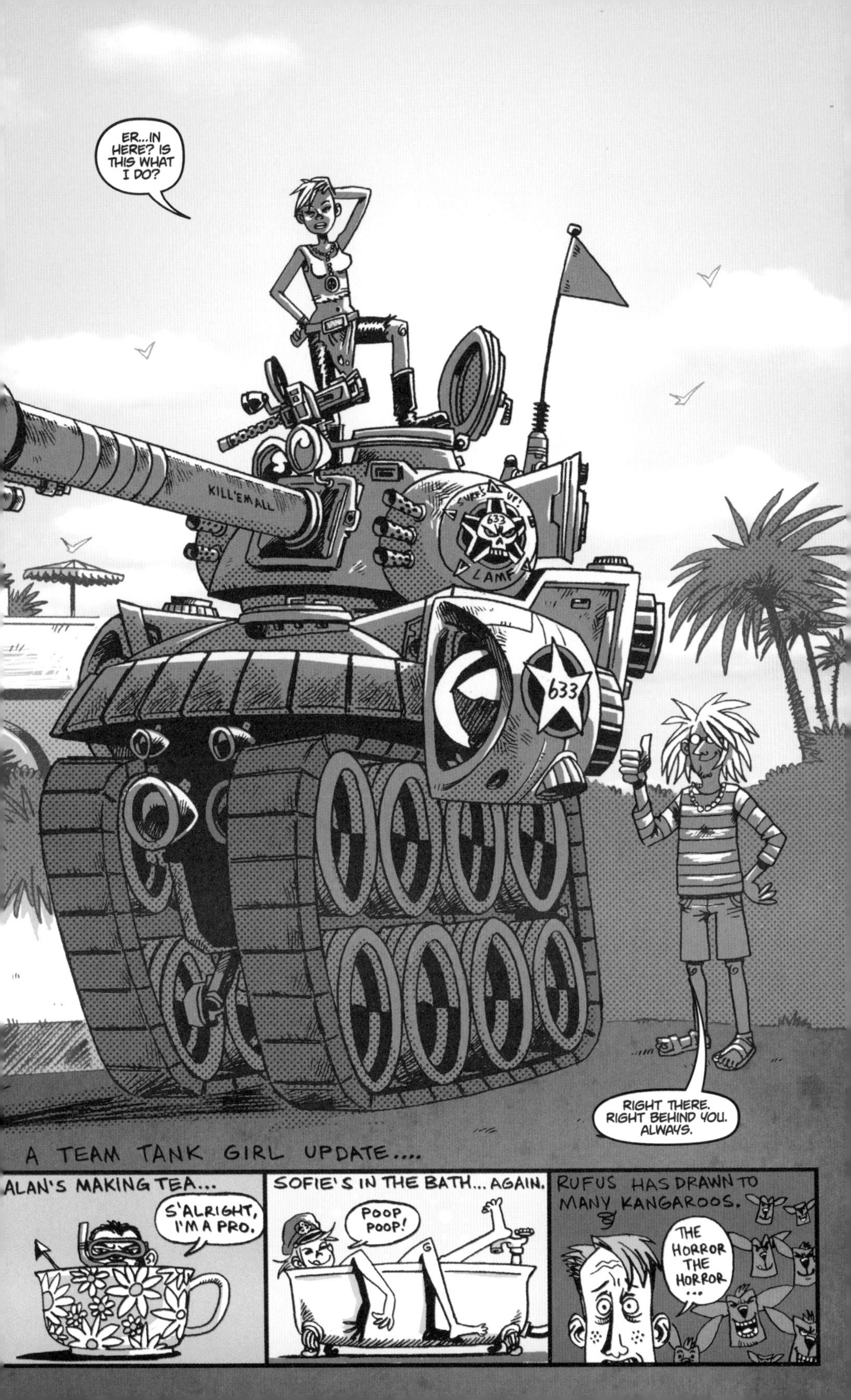
ER...IN HERE? IS THIS WHAT I DO?
KILL'EM ALL
633
LAMF
633
RIGHT THERE. RIGHT BEHIND YOU. ALWAYS.
A TEAM TANK GIRL UPDATE....
ALAN'S MAKING TEA...
S'ALRIGHT, I'M A PRO.
SOFIE'S IN THE BATH... AGAIN.
POOP POOP!
RUFUS HAS DRAWN TO MANY KANGAROOS.
THE HORROR THE HORROR ...

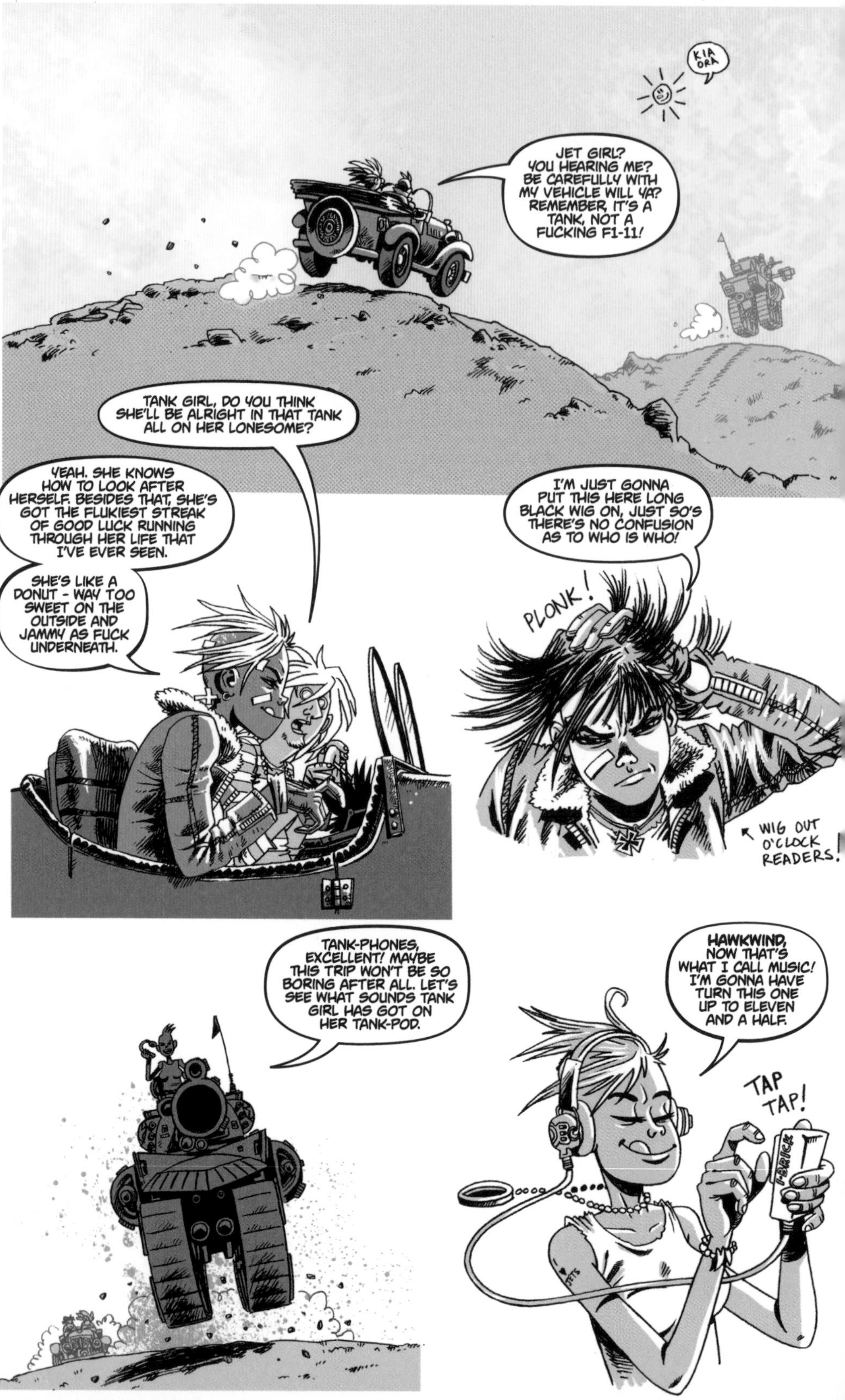
KIA ORA
JET GIRL? YOU HEARING ME? BE CAREFULLY WITH MY VEHICLE WILL YA? REMEMBER, IT'S A TANK, NOT A FUCKING F1-11!
TANK GIRL, DO YOU THINK SHE'LL BE ALRIGHT IN THAT TANK ALL ON HER LONESOME?
YEAH. SHE KNOWS HOW TO LOOK AFTER HERSELF. BESIDES THAT, SHE'S GOT THE FLUKIEST STREAK OF GOOD LUCK RUNNING THROUGH HER LIFE THAT I'VE EVER SEEN.
SHE'S LIKE A DONUT - WAY TOO SWEET ON THE OUTSIDE AND JAMMY AS FUCK UNDERNEATH.
I'M JUST GONNA PUT THIS HERE LONG BLACK WIG ON, JUST SO'S THERE'S NO CONFUSION AS TO WHO IS WHO!
PLONK!
WIG OUT O'CLOCK READERS!
TANK-PHONES, EXCELLENT! MAYBE THIS TRIP WON'T BE SO BORING AFTER ALL. LET'S SEE WHAT SOUNDS TANK GIRL HAS GOT ON HER TANK-POD.
HAWKWIND, NOW THAT'S WHAT I CALL MUSIC! I'M GONNA HAVE TURN THIS ONE UP TO ELEVEN AND A HALF.
TAP TAP!

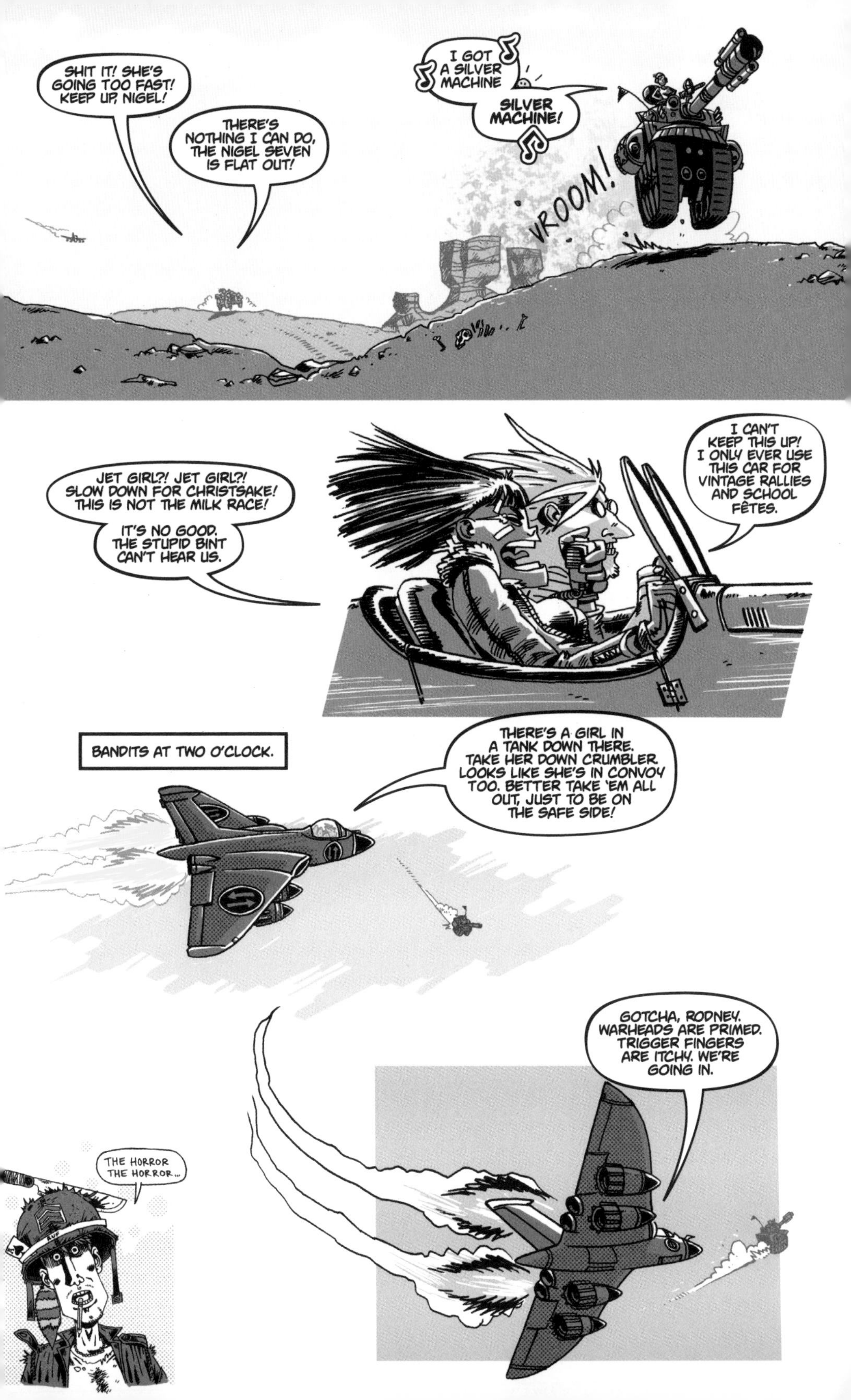
SHIT IT! SHE'S GOING TOO FAST! KEEP UP, NIGEL!
THERE'S NOTHING I CAN DO, THE NIGEL SEVEN IS FLAT OUT!
I GOT A SILVER MACHINE
SILVER MACHINE!
VROOM!
JET GIRL?! JET GIRL?! SLOW DOWN FOR CHRISTSAKE! THIS IS NOT THE MILK RACE!
IT'S NO GOOD. THE STUPID BINT CAN'T HEAR US.
I CAN'T KEEP THIS UP! I ONLY EVER USE THIS CAR FOR VINTAGE RALLIES AND SCHOOL FÊTES.
BANDITS AT TWO O'CLOCK.
THERE'S A GIRL IN A TANK DOWN THERE. TAKE HER DOWN CRUMBLER. LOOKS LIKE SHE'S IN CONVOY TOO. BETTER TAKE 'EM ALL OUT, JUST TO BE ON THE SAFE SIDE!
GOTCHA, RODNEY. WARHEADS ARE PRIMED. TRIGGER FINGERS ARE ITCHY. WE'RE GOING IN.
THE HORROR THE HORROR...

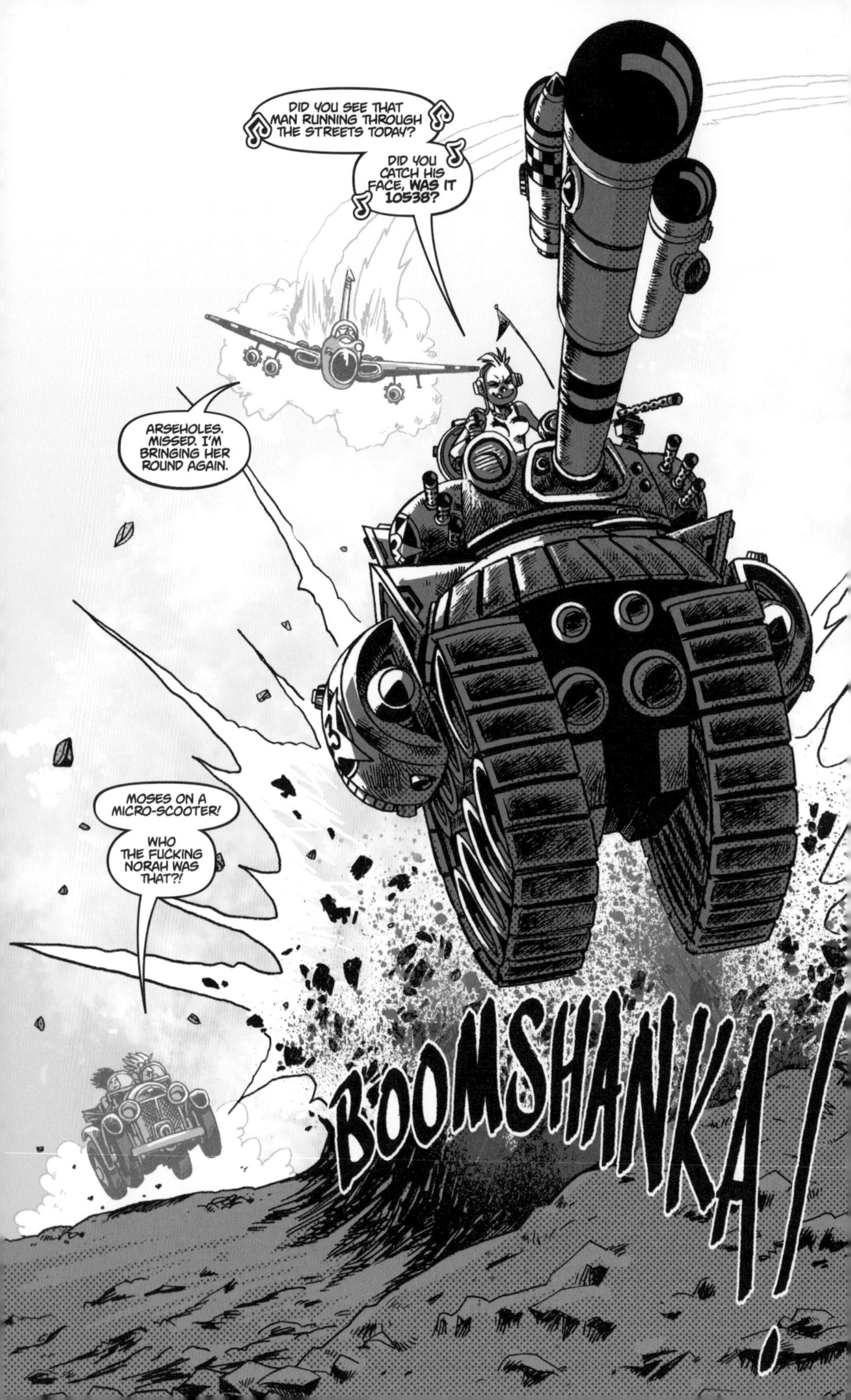
DID YOU SEE THAT MAN RUNNING THROUGH THE STREETS TODAY?
DID YOU CATCH HIS FACE, WAS IT 10538?
ARSEHOLES. MISSED. I'M BRINGING HER ROUND AGAIN.
MOSES ON A MICRO-SCOOTER!
WHO THE FUCKING NORAH WAS THAT?!
BOOMSHANKA!!

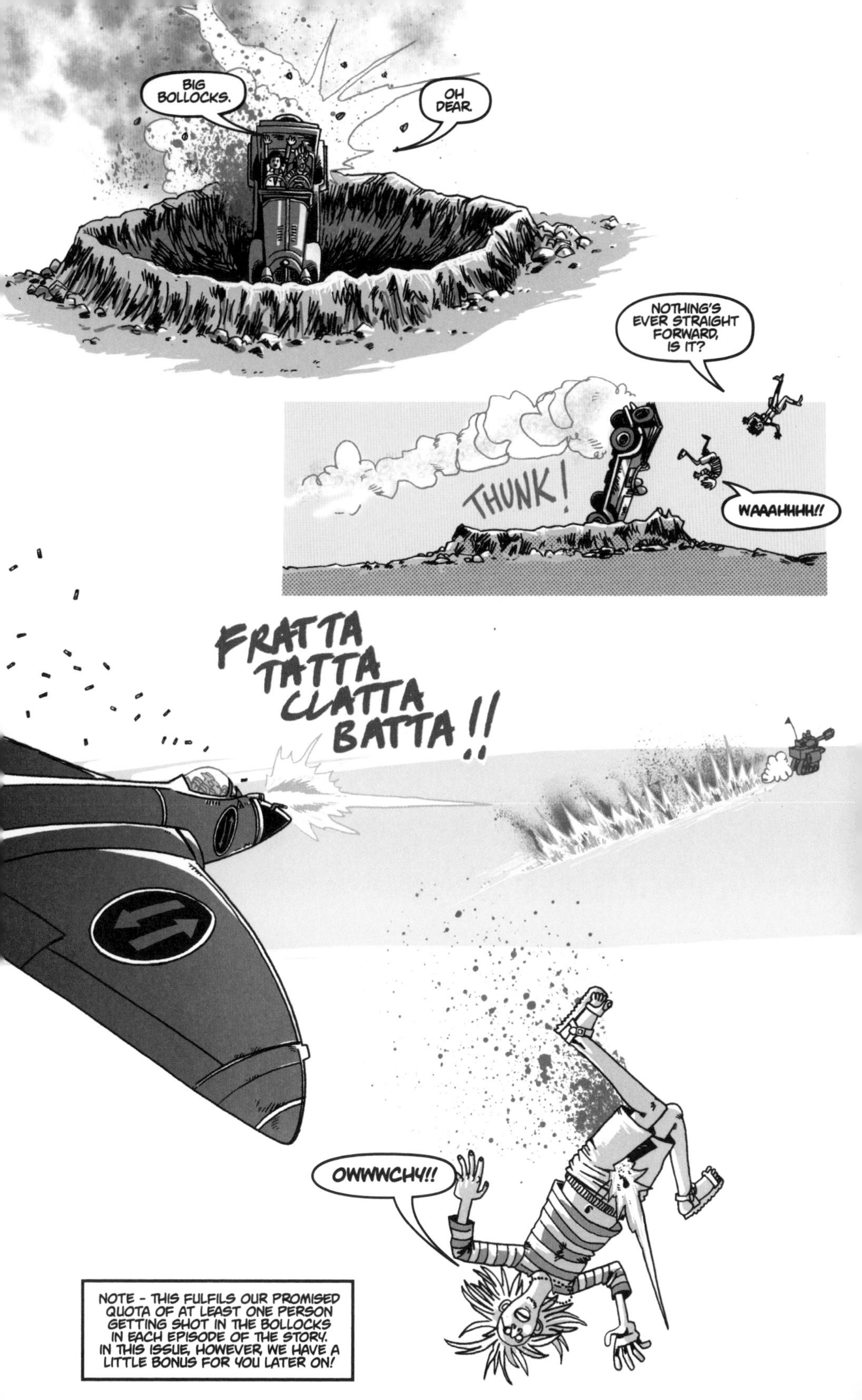
BIG BOLLOCKS.
OH DEAR.
NOTHING'S EVER STRAIGHT FORWARD, IS IT?
THUNK!
WAAAHHHH!!
FRATTA TATTA CLATTA BATTA!!
OWWWCHY!!
NOTE - THIS FULFILS OUR PROMISED QUOTA OF AT LEAST ONE PERSON GETTING SHOT IN THE BOLLOCKS IN EACH EPISODE OF THE STORY. IN THIS ISSUE, HOWEVER, WE HAVE A LITTLE BONUS FOR YOU LATER ON!

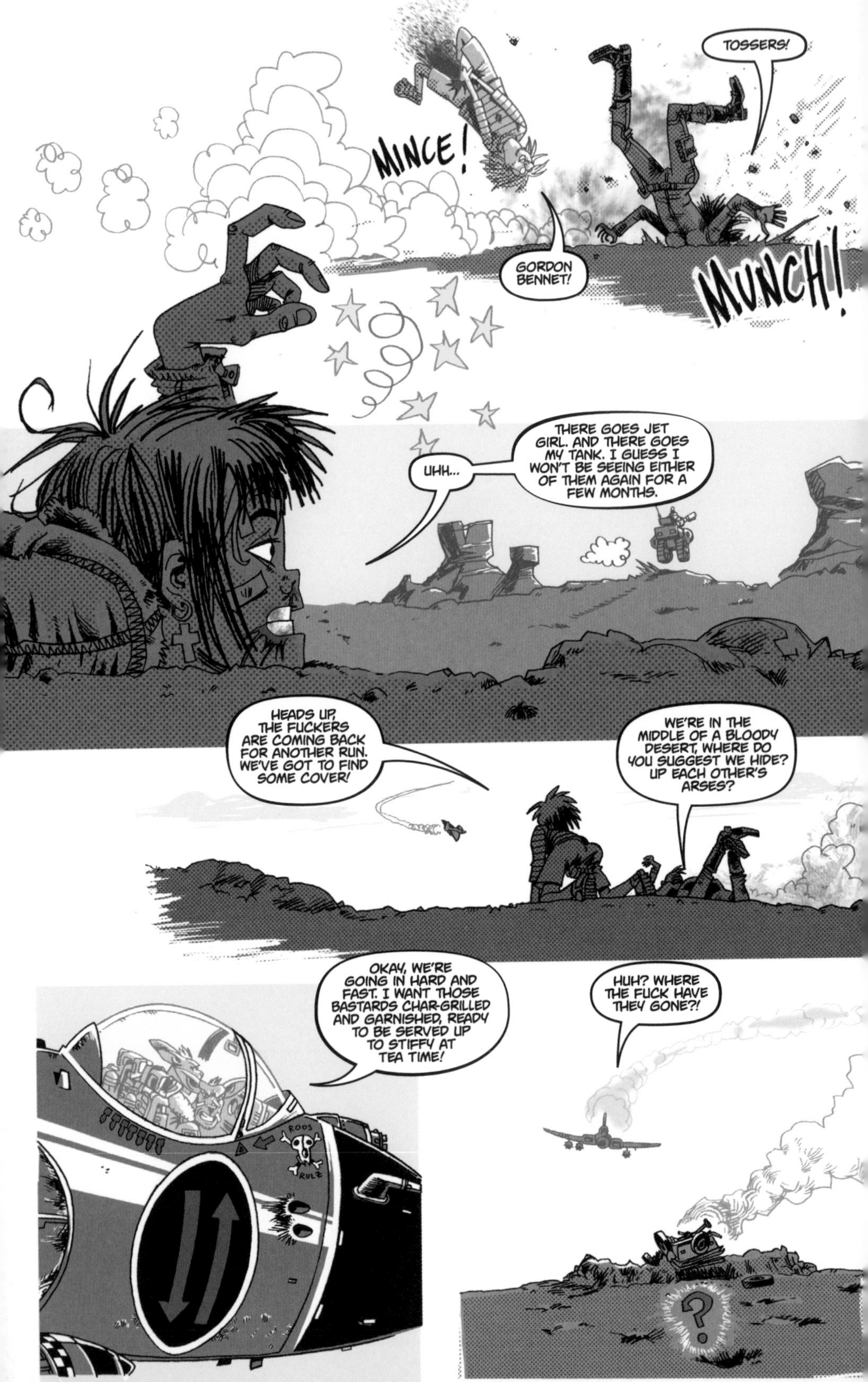
TOSSERS!
MINCE!
GORDON BENNET!
MUNCH!
UHH...
THERE GOES JET GIRL. AND THERE GOES MY TANK. I GUESS I WON'T BE SEEING EITHER OF THEM AGAIN FOR A FEW MONTHS.
HEADS UP, THE FUCKERS ARE COMING BACK FOR ANOTHER RUN. WE'VE GOT TO FIND SOME COVER!
WE'RE IN THE MIDDLE OF A BLOODY DESERT, WHERE DO YOU SUGGEST WE HIDE? UP EACH OTHER'S ARSES?
OKAY, WE'RE GOING IN HARD AND FAST. I WANT THOSE BASTARDS CHAR-GRILLED AND GARNISHED, READY TO BE SERVED UP TO STIFFY AT TEA TIME!
ROOS RULZ
HUH? WHERE THE FUCK HAVE THEY GONE?!
?

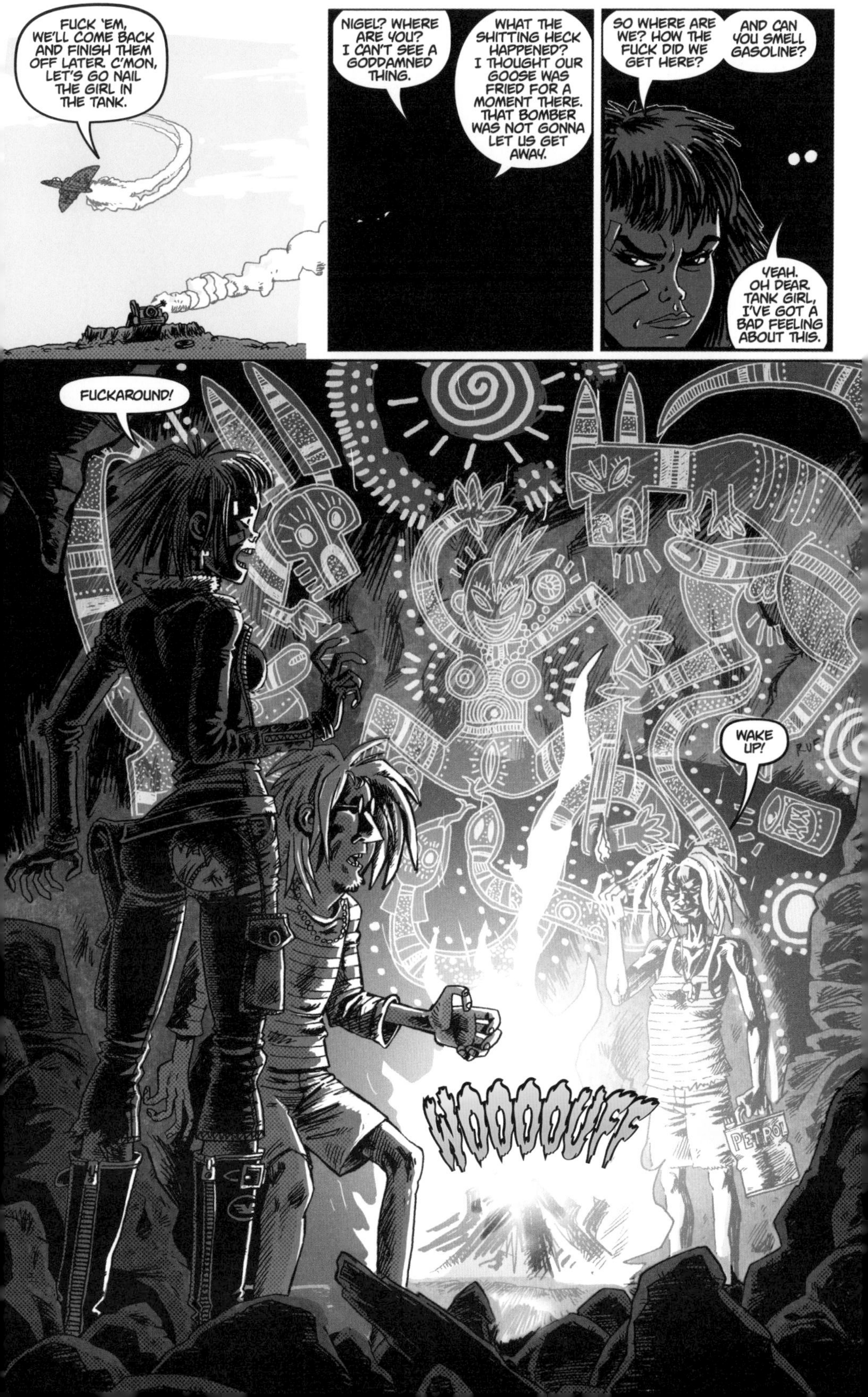

FUCK 'EM, WE'LL COME BACK AND FINISH THEM OFF LATER. C'MON, LET'S GO NAIL THE GIRL IN THE TANK.
NIGEL? WHERE ARE YOU? I CAN'T SEE A GODDAMNED THING.
WHAT THE SHITTING HECK HAPPENED? I THOUGHT OUR GOOSE WAS FRIED FOR A MOMENT THERE. THAT BOMBER WAS NOT GONNA LET US GET AWAY.
SO WHERE ARE WE? HOW THE FUCK DID WE GET HERE?
AND CAN YOU SMELL GASOLINE?
YEAH. OH DEAR. TANK GIRL, I'VE GOT A BAD FEELING ABOUT THIS.
FUCKAROUND!
WAKE UP!
WOOOOOUFF
PETROL

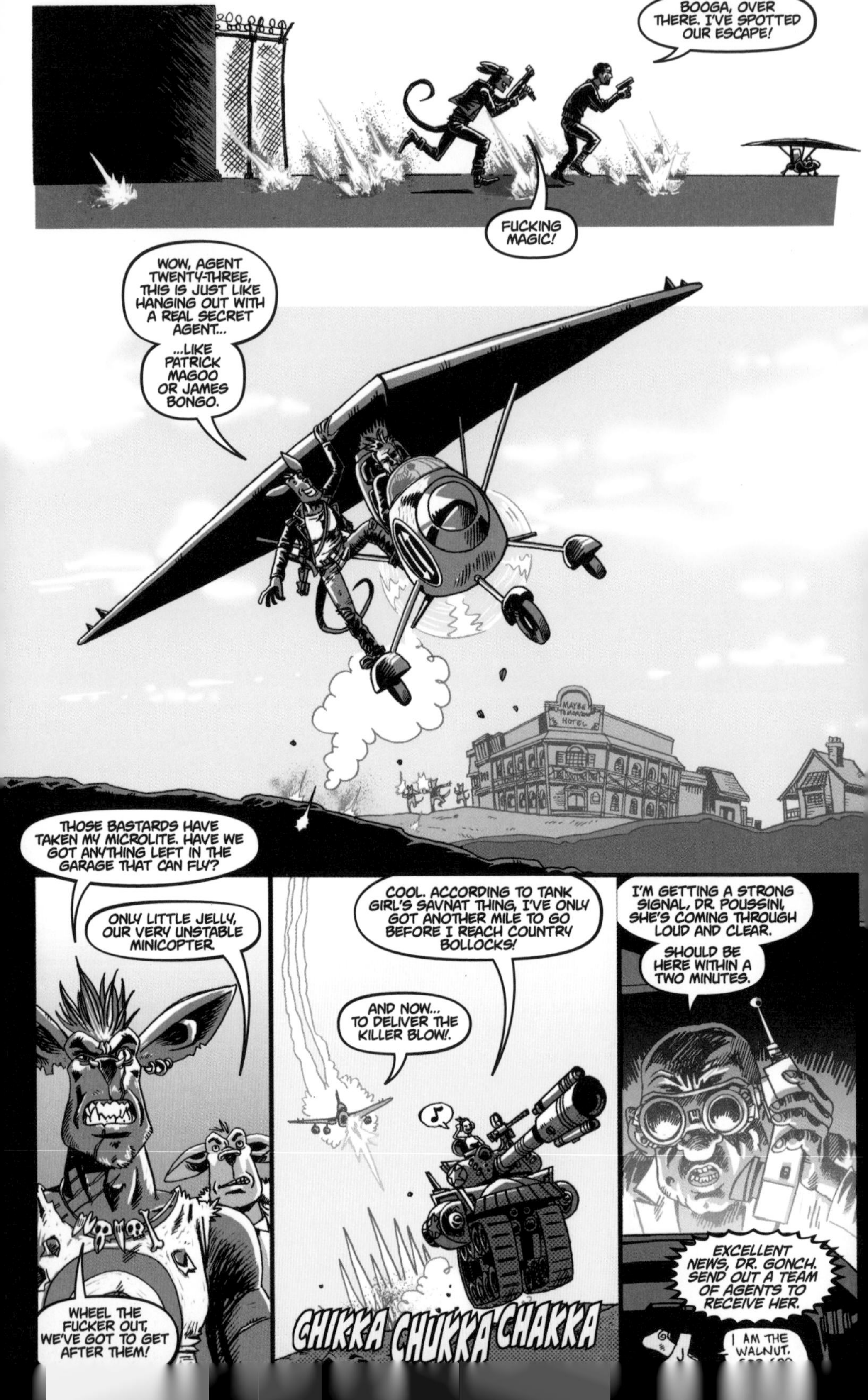

BOOGA, OVER THERE. I'VE SPOTTED OUR ESCAPE!
FUCKING MAGIC!
WOW, AGENT TWENTY-THREE, THIS IS JUST LIKE HANGING OUT WITH A REAL SECRET AGENT...
...LIKE PATRICK MAGOO OR JAMES BONGO.
MAYBE TOMORROW HOTEL
THOSE BASTARDS HAVE TAKEN MY MICROLITE. HAVE WE GOT ANYTHING LEFT IN THE GARAGE THAT CAN FLY?
ONLY LITTLE JELLY, OUR VERY UNSTABLE MINICOPTER.
WHEEL THE FUCKER OUT, WE'VE GOT TO GET AFTER THEM!
COOL. ACCORDING TO TANK GIRL'S SAVNAT THING, I'VE ONLY GOT ANOTHER MILE TO GO BEFORE I REACH COUNTRY BOLLOCKS!
AND NOW... TO DELIVER THE KILLER BLOW!.
CHIKKA CHUKKA CHAKKA
I'M GETTING A STRONG SIGNAL, DR. POUSSINI, SHE'S COMING THROUGH LOUD AND CLEAR.
SHOULD BE HERE WITHIN A TWO MINUTES.
EXCELLENT NEWS, DR. GONCH. SEND OUT A TEAM OF AGENTS TO RECEIVE HER.
I AM THE WALNUT.

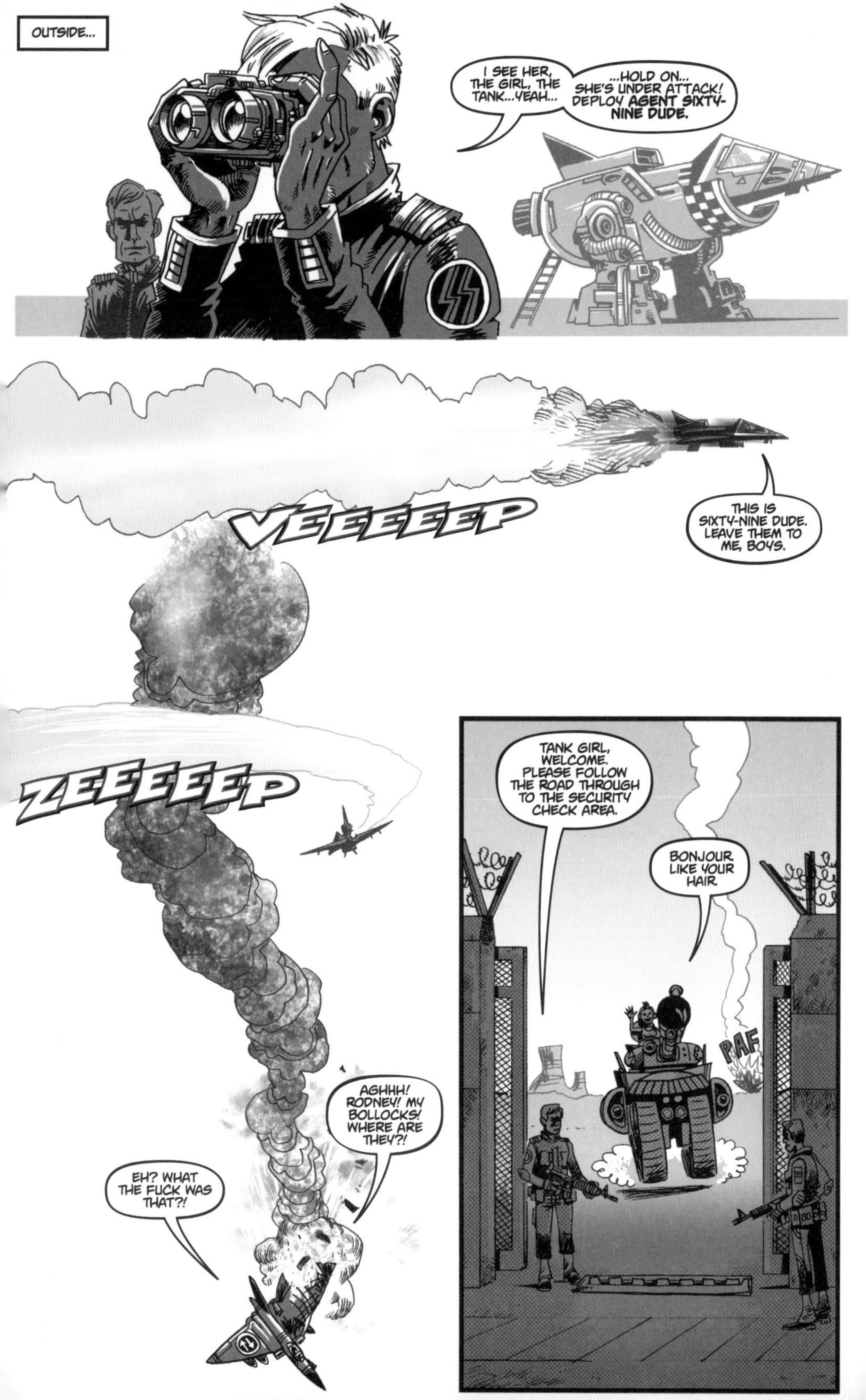
OUTSIDE...
I SEE HER, THE GIRL, THE TANK...YEAH...
...HOLD ON... SHE'S UNDER ATTACK! DEPLOY AGENT SIXTY-NINE DUDE.
THIS IS SIXTY-NINE DUDE. LEAVE THEM TO ME, BOYS.
VEEEEEP
ZEEEEEP
AGHHH! RODNEY! MY BOLLOCKS! WHERE ARE THEY?!
EH? WHAT THE FUCK WAS THAT?!
TANK GIRL, WELCOME. PLEASE FOLLOW THE ROAD THROUGH TO THE SECURITY CHECK AREA.
BONJOUR. LIKE YOUR HAIR.
PAF

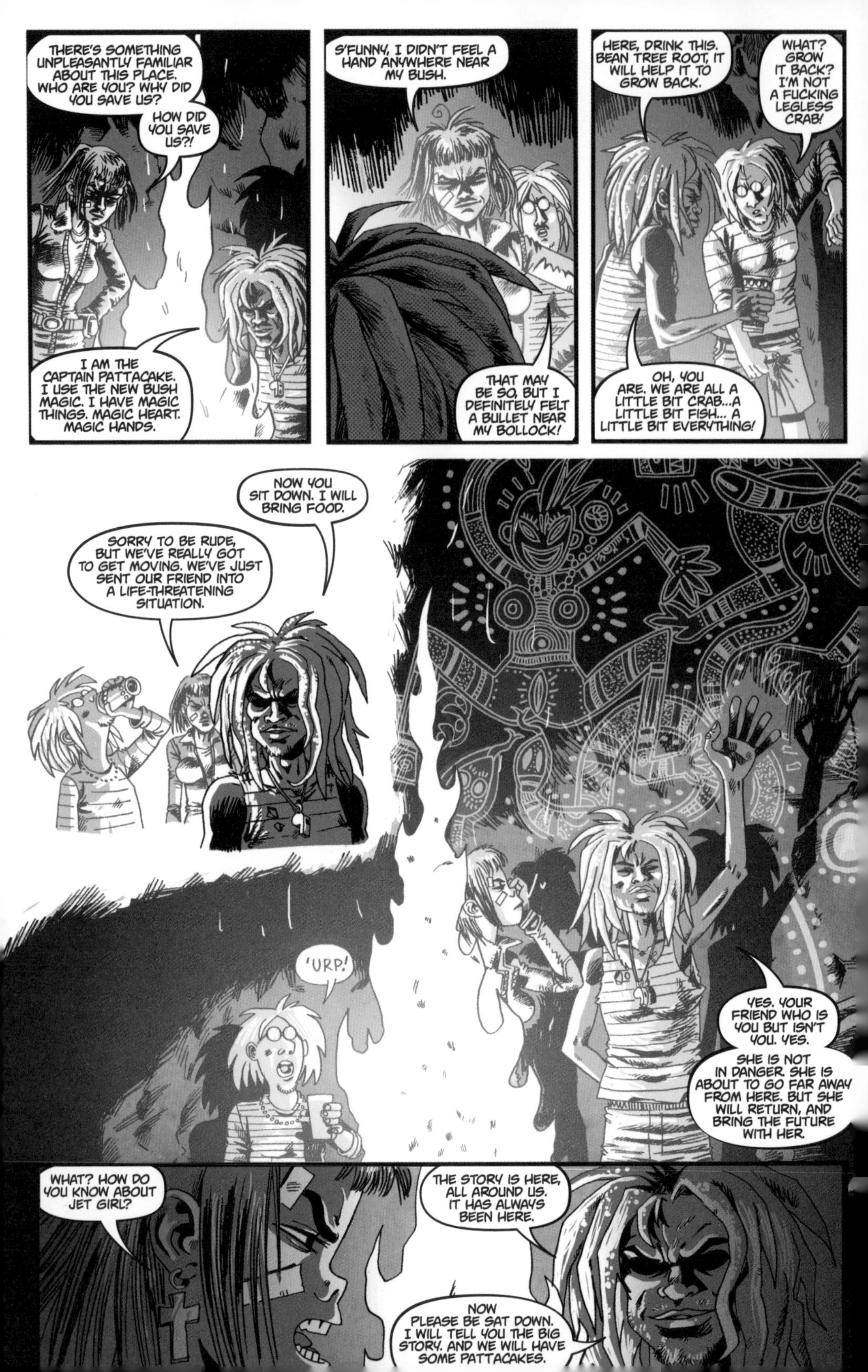
THERE'S SOMETHING UNPLEASANTLY FAMILIAR ABOUT THIS PLACE. WHO ARE YOU? WHY DID YOU SAVE US?
HOW DID YOU SAVE US?!
I AM THE CAPTAIN PATTACAKE. I USE THE NEW BUSH MAGIC. I HAVE MAGIC THINGS. MAGIC HEART. MAGIC HANDS.
S'FUNNY, I DIDN'T FEEL A HAND ANYWHERE NEAR MY BUSH.
THAT MAY BE SO, BUT I DEFINITELY FELT A BULLET NEAR MY BOLLOCK!
HERE, DRINK THIS. BEAN TREE ROOT, IT WILL HELP IT TO GROW BACK.
WHAT? GROW IT BACK? I'M NOT A FUCKING LEGLESS CRAB!
OH, YOU ARE. WE ARE ALL A LITTLE BIT CRAB...A LITTLE BIT FISH... A LITTLE BIT EVERYTHING!
SORRY TO BE RUDE, BUT WE'VE REALLY GOT TO GET MOVING. WE'VE JUST SENT OUR FRIEND INTO A LIFE-THREATENING SITUATION.
NOW YOU SIT DOWN. I WILL BRING FOOD.
'URP!
YES. YOUR FRIEND WHO IS YOU BUT ISN'T YOU. YES.
SHE IS NOT IN DANGER. SHE IS ABOUT TO GO FAR AWAY FROM HERE. BUT SHE WILL RETURN, AND BRING THE FUTURE WITH HER.
WHAT? HOW DO YOU KNOW ABOUT JET GIRL?
THE STORY IS HERE, ALL AROUND US. IT HAS ALWAYS BEEN HERE.
NOW PLEASE BE SAT DOWN. I WILL TELL YOU THE BIG STORY. AND WE WILL HAVE SOME PATTACAKES.

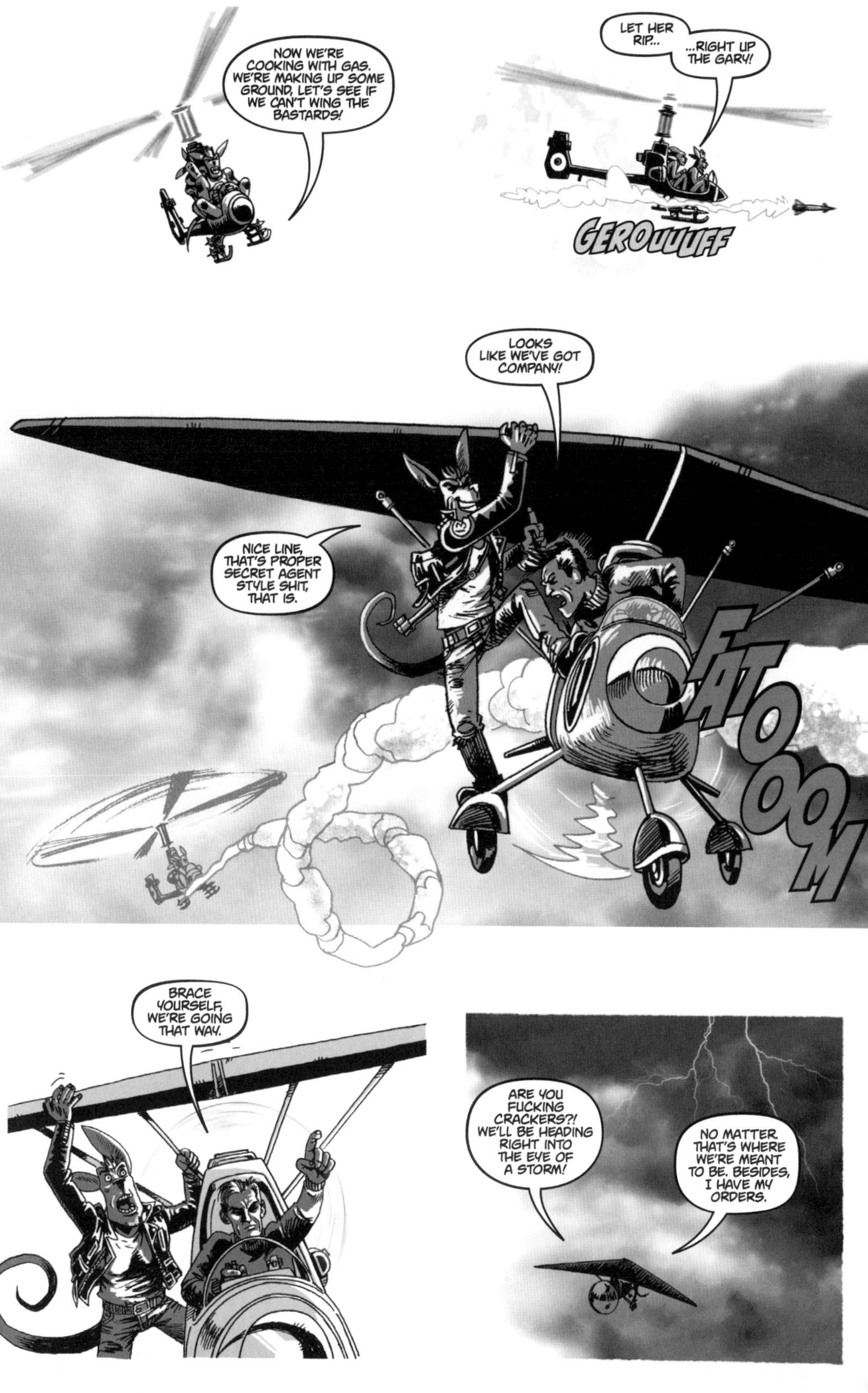
NOW WE'RE COOKING WITH GAS. WE'RE MAKING UP SOME GROUND, LET'S SEE IF WE CAN'T WING THE BASTARDS!
LET HER RIP...
...RIGHT UP THE GARY!
GEROUUUFF
LOOKS LIKE WE'VE GOT COMPANY!
NICE LINE, THAT'S PROPER SECRET AGENT STYLE SHIT, THAT IS.
FATOOOM
BRACE YOURSELF, WE'RE GOING THAT WAY.
ARE YOU FUCKING CRACKERS?! WE'LL BE HEADING RIGHT INTO THE EYE OF A STORM!
NO MATTER. THAT'S WHERE WE'RE MEANT TO BE. BESIDES, I HAVE MY ORDERS.

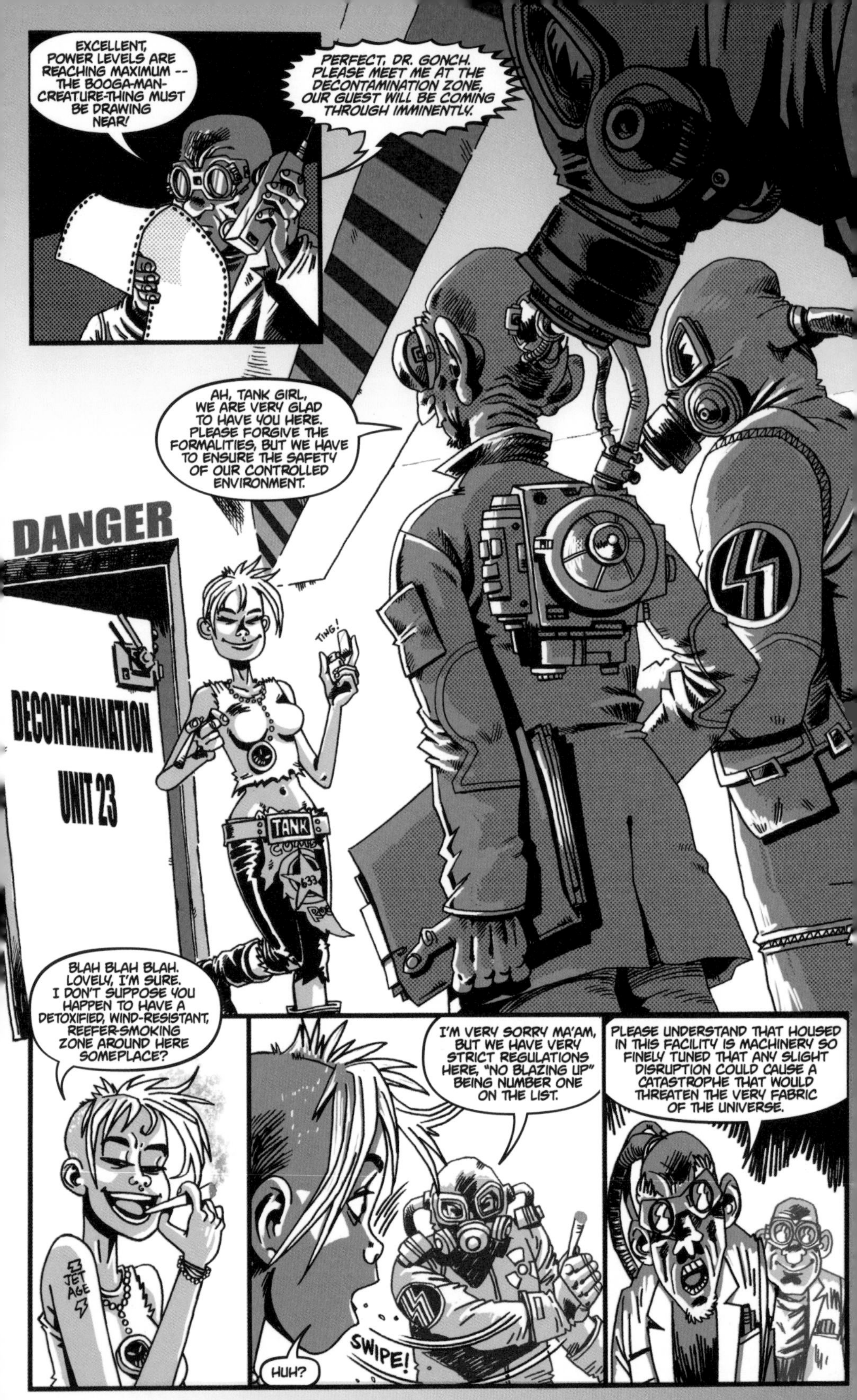

EXCELLENT, POWER LEVELS ARE REACHING MAXIMUM -- THE BOOGA-MAN-CREATURE-THING MUST BE DRAWING NEAR!
PERFECT, DR. GONCH. PLEASE MEET ME AT THE DECONTAMINATION ZONE, OUR GUEST WILL BE COMING THROUGH IMMINENTLY.
AH, TANK GIRL, WE ARE VERY GLAD TO HAVE YOU HERE. PLEASE FORGIVE THE FORMALITIES, BUT WE HAVE TO ENSURE THE SAFETY OF OUR CONTROLLED ENVIRONMENT.
DANGER
DECONTAMINATION
UNIT 23
TING!
TANK
BLAH BLAH BLAH. LOVELY, I'M SURE. I DON'T SUPPOSE YOU HAPPEN TO HAVE A DETOXIFIED, WIND-RESISTANT, REEFER-SMOKING ZONE AROUND HERE SOMEPLACE?
JET AGE
I'M VERY SORRY MA'AM, BUT WE HAVE VERY STRICT REGULATIONS HERE, "NO BLAZING UP" BEING NUMBER ONE ON THE LIST.
SWIPE!
HUH?
PLEASE UNDERSTAND THAT HOUSED IN THIS FACILITY IS MACHINERY SO FINELY TUNED THAT ANY SLIGHT DISRUPTION COULD CAUSE A CATASTROPHE THAT WOULD THREATEN THE VERY FABRIC OF THE UNIVERSE.

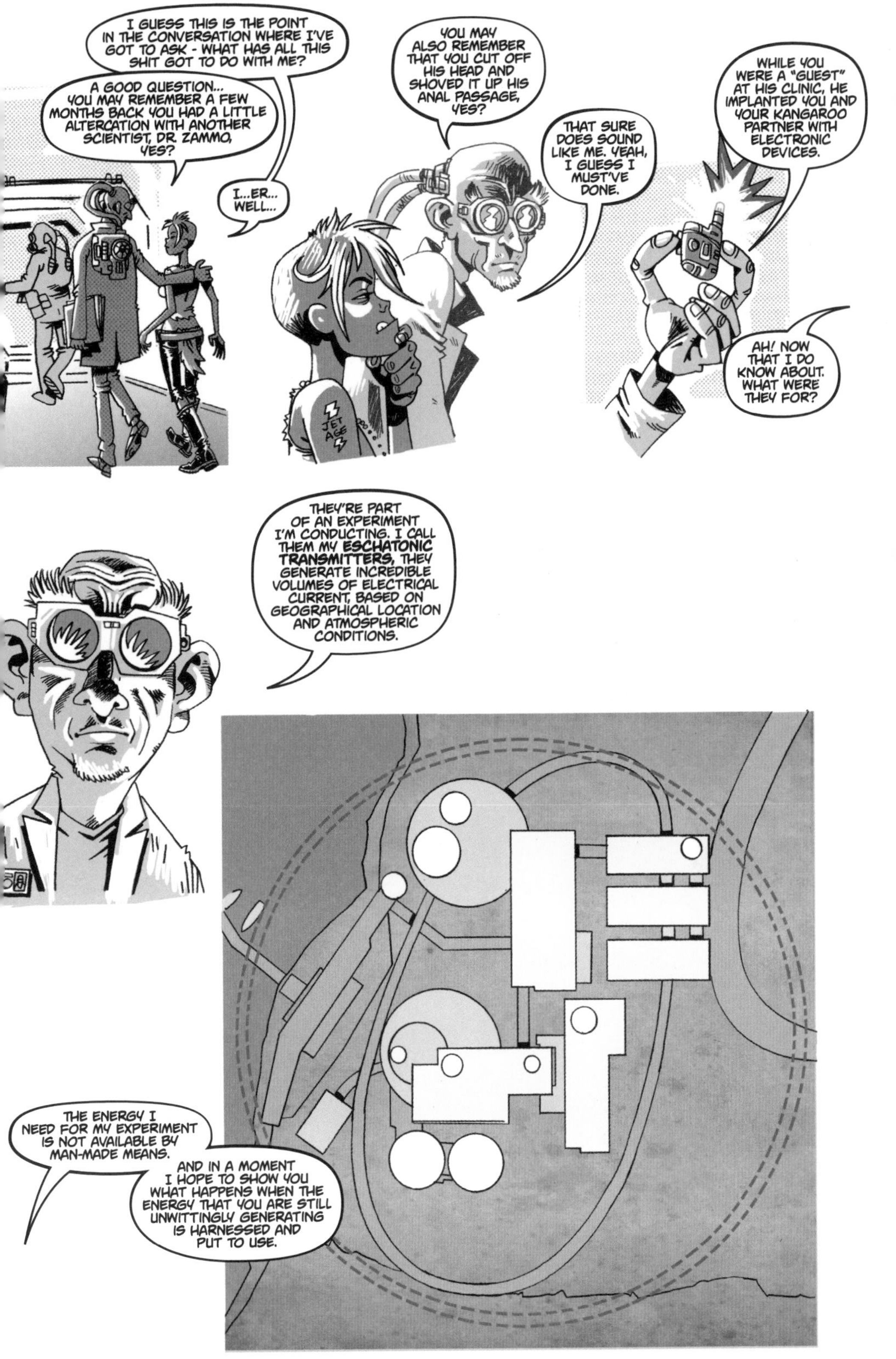
I GUESS THIS IS THE POINT IN THE CONVERSATION WHERE I'VE GOT TO ASK - WHAT HAS ALL THIS SHIT GOT TO DO WITH ME?
A GOOD QUESTION... YOU MAY REMEMBER A FEW MONTHS BACK YOU HAD A LITTLE ALTERCATION WITH ANOTHER SCIENTIST, DR ZAMMO, YES?
I...ER... WELL...
YOU MAY ALSO REMEMBER THAT YOU CUT OFF HIS HEAD AND SHOVED IT UP HIS ANAL PASSAGE, YES?
THAT SURE DOES SOUND LIKE ME. YEAH, I GUESS I MUST'VE DONE.
JET AGE
WHILE YOU WERE A "GUEST" AT HIS CLINIC, HE IMPLANTED YOU AND YOUR KANGAROO PARTNER WITH ELECTRONIC DEVICES.
AH! NOW THAT I DO KNOW ABOUT. WHAT WERE THEY FOR?
THEY'RE PART OF AN EXPERIMENT I'M CONDUCTING. I CALL THEM MY ESCHATONIC TRANSMITTERS, THEY GENERATE INCREDIBLE VOLUMES OF ELECTRICAL CURRENT, BASED ON GEOGRAPHICAL LOCATION AND ATMOSPHERIC CONDITIONS.
THE ENERGY I NEED FOR MY EXPERIMENT IS NOT AVAILABLE BY MAN-MADE MEANS.
AND IN A MOMENT I HOPE TO SHOW YOU WHAT HAPPENS WHEN THE ENERGY THAT YOU ARE STILL UNWITTINGLY GENERATING IS HARNESSED AND PUT TO USE.

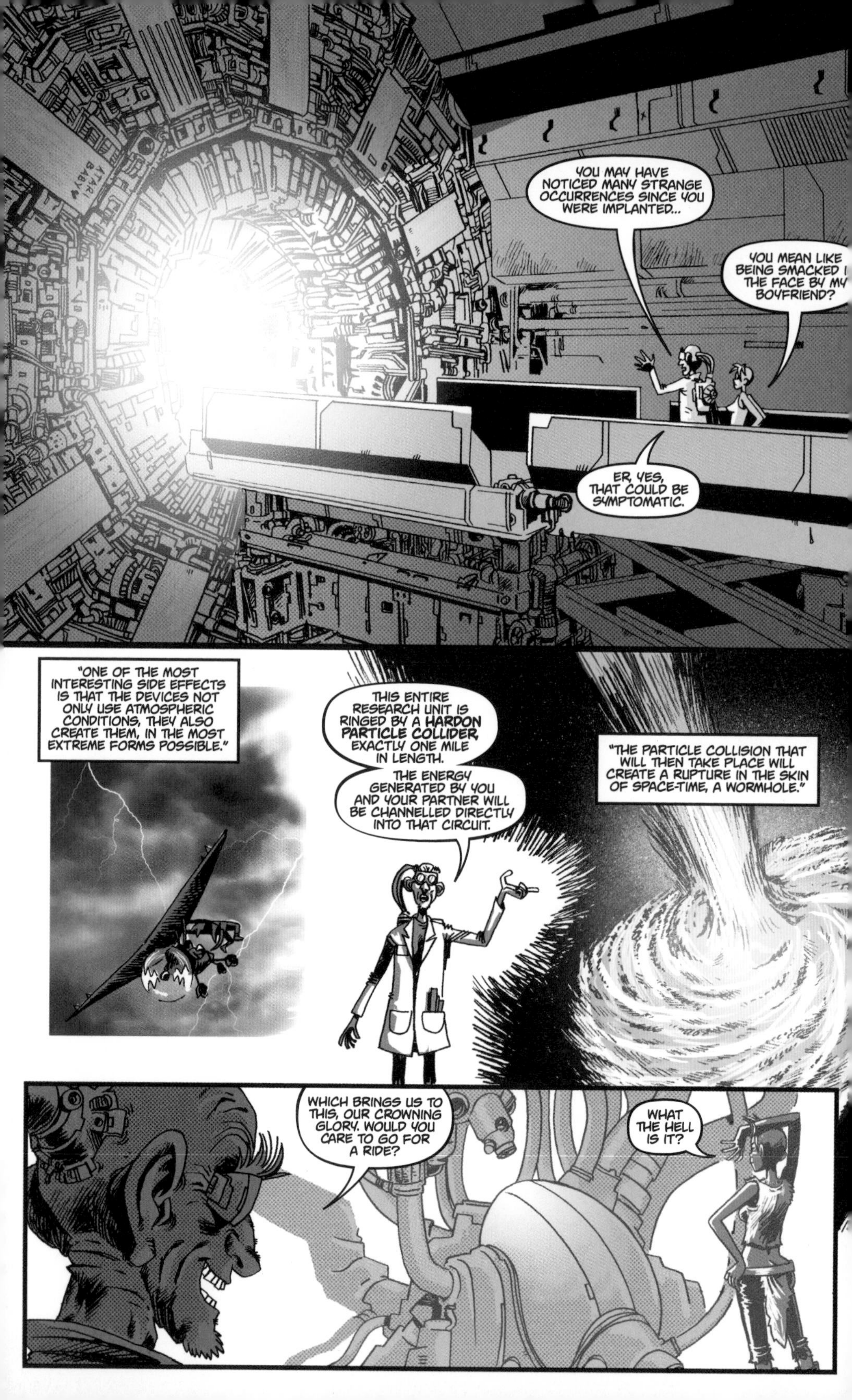
ATARI BABY
YOU MAY HAVE NOTICED MANY STRANGE OCCURRENCES SINCE YOU WERE IMPLANTED...
YOU MEAN LIKE BEING SMACKED I THE FACE BY MY BOYFRIEND?
ER, YES, THAT COULD BE SYMPTOMATIC.
"ONE OF THE MOST INTERESTING SIDE EFFECTS IS THAT THE DEVICES NOT ONLY USE ATMOSPHERIC CONDITIONS, THEY ALSO CREATE THEM, IN THE MOST EXTREME FORMS POSSIBLE."
THIS ENTIRE RESEARCH UNIT IS RINGED BY A HARDON PARTICLE COLLIDER, EXACTLY ONE MILE IN LENGTH.
THE ENERGY GENERATED BY YOU AND YOUR PARTNER WILL BE CHANNELLED DIRECTLY INTO THAT CIRCUIT.
"THE PARTICLE COLLISION THAT WILL THEN TAKE PLACE WILL CREATE A RUPTURE IN THE SKIN OF SPACE-TIME, A WORMHOLE."
WHICH BRINGS US TO THIS, OUR CROWNING GLORY. WOULD YOU CARE TO GO FOR A RIDE?
WHAT THE HELL IS IT?

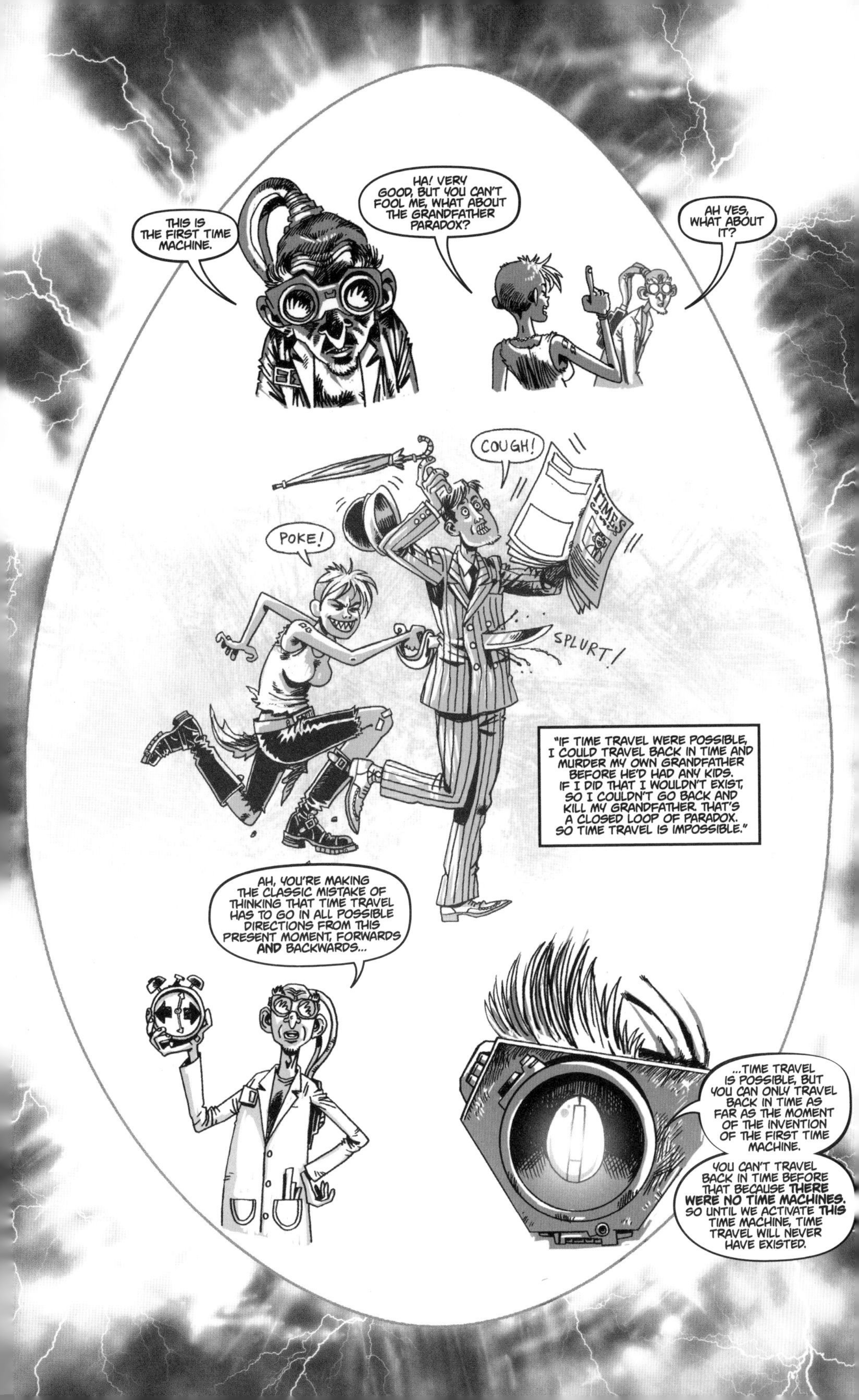
THIS IS THE FIRST TIME MACHINE.
HA! VERY GOOD, BUT YOU CAN'T FOOL ME, WHAT ABOUT THE GRANDFATHER PARADOX?
AH YES, WHAT ABOUT IT?
COUGH!
POKE!
SPLURT!
"IF TIME TRAVEL WERE POSSIBLE, I COULD TRAVEL BACK IN TIME AND MURDER MY OWN GRANDFATHER BEFORE HE'D HAD ANY KIDS. IF I DID THAT I WOULDN'T EXIST, SO I COULDN'T GO BACK AND KILL MY GRANDFATHER. THAT'S A CLOSED LOOP OF PARADOX. SO TIME TRAVEL IS IMPOSSIBLE."
AH, YOU'RE MAKING THE CLASSIC MISTAKE OF THINKING THAT TIME TRAVEL HAS TO GO IN ALL POSSIBLE DIRECTIONS FROM THIS PRESENT MOMENT, FORWARDS AND BACKWARDS...
...TIME TRAVEL IS POSSIBLE, BUT YOU CAN ONLY TRAVEL BACK IN TIME AS FAR AS THE MOMENT OF THE INVENTION OF THE FIRST TIME MACHINE.
YOU CAN'T TRAVEL BACK IN TIME BEFORE THAT BECAUSE THERE WERE NO TIME MACHINES. SO UNTIL WE ACTIVATE THIS TIME MACHINE, TIME TRAVEL WILL NEVER HAVE EXISTED.

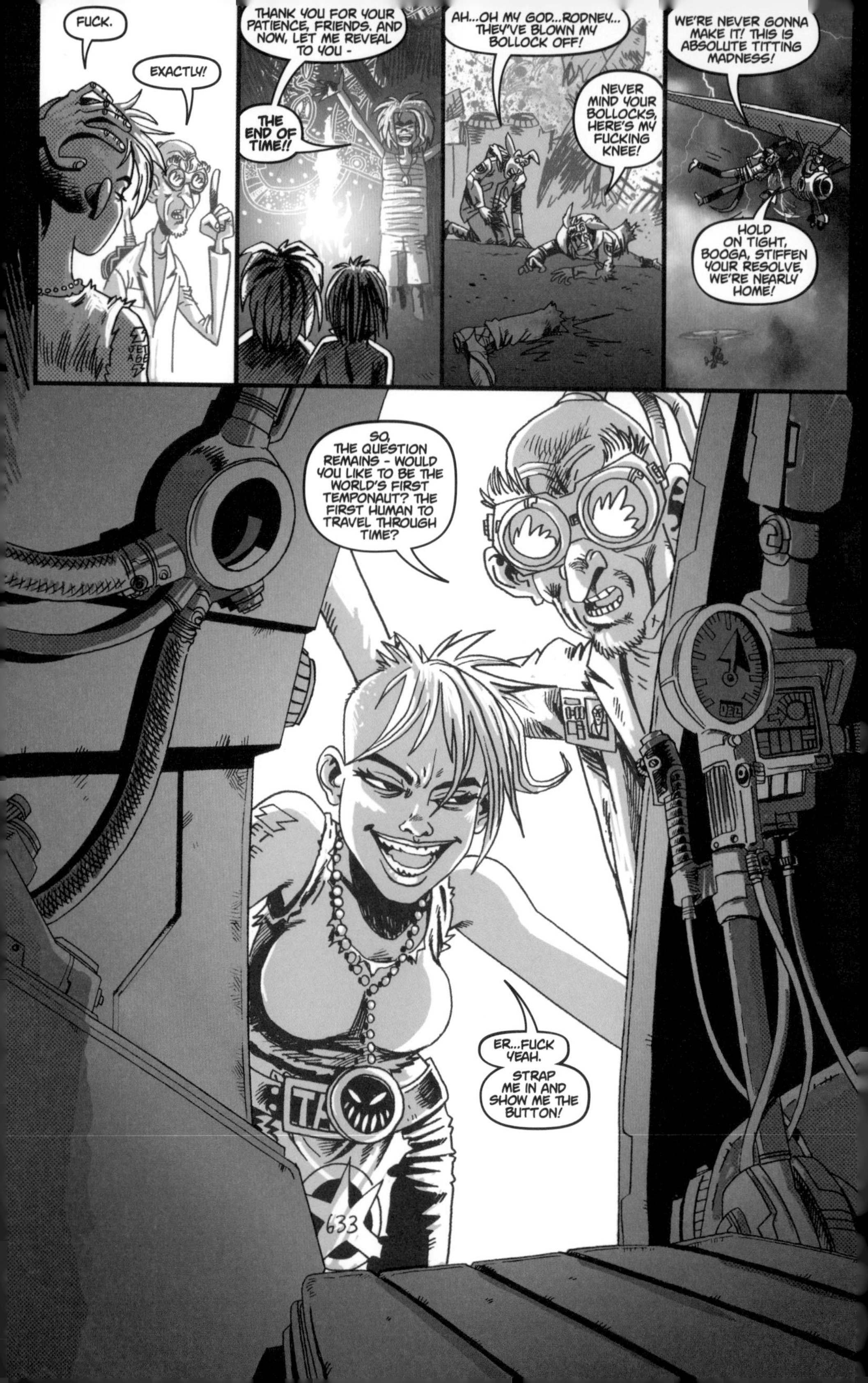
FUCK.
EXACTLY!
THANK YOU FOR YOUR PATIENCE, FRIENDS. AND NOW, LET ME REVEAL TO YOU -
THE END OF TIME!!
AH...OH MY GOD...RODNEY... THEY'VE BLOWN MY BOLLOCK OFF!
NEVER MIND YOUR BOLLOCKS, HERE'S MY FUCKING KNEE!
WE'RE NEVER GONNA MAKE IT! THIS IS ABSOLUTE TITTING MADNESS!
HOLD ON TIGHT, BOOGA, STIFFEN YOUR RESOLVE, WE'RE NEARLY HOME!
SO, THE QUESTION REMAINS - WOULD YOU LIKE TO BE THE WORLD'S FIRST TEMPONAUT? THE FIRST HUMAN TO TRAVEL THROUGH TIME?
ER...FUCK YEAH.
STRAP ME IN AND SHOW ME THE BUTTON!
633

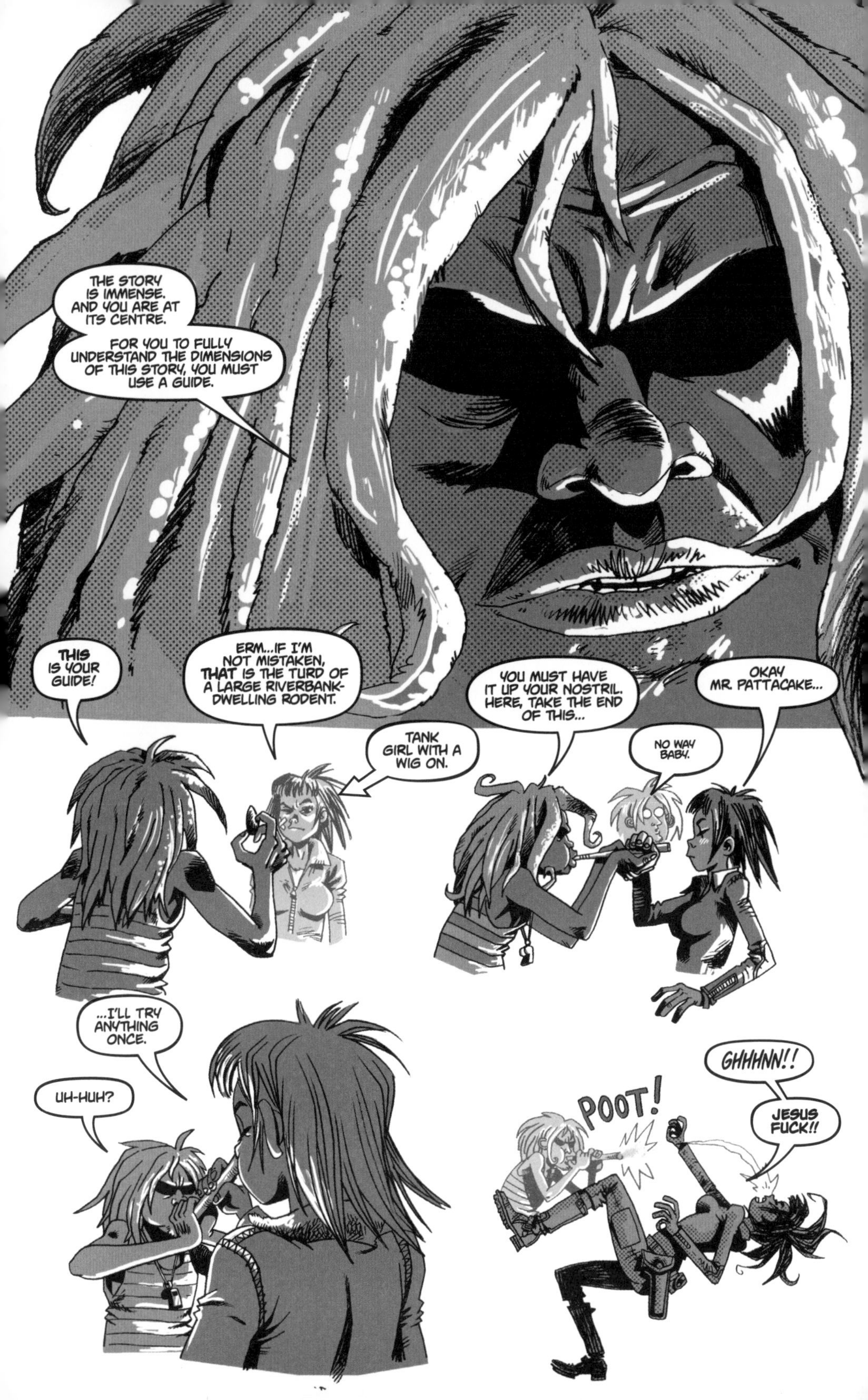

THE STORY IS IMMENSE. AND YOU ARE AT ITS CENTRE.
FOR YOU TO FULLY UNDERSTAND THE DIMENSIONS OF THIS STORY, YOU MUST USE A GUIDE.
THIS IS YOUR GUIDE!
ERM...IF I'M NOT MISTAKEN, THAT IS THE TURD OF A LARGE RIVERBANK-DWELLING RODENT.
TANK GIRL WITH A WIG ON.
YOU MUST HAVE IT UP YOUR NOSTRIL. HERE, TAKE THE END OF THIS...
NO WAY BABY.
OKAY MR. PATTACAKE...
...I'LL TRY ANYTHING ONCE.
UH-HUH?
POOT!
GHHHNN!!
JESUS FUCK!!

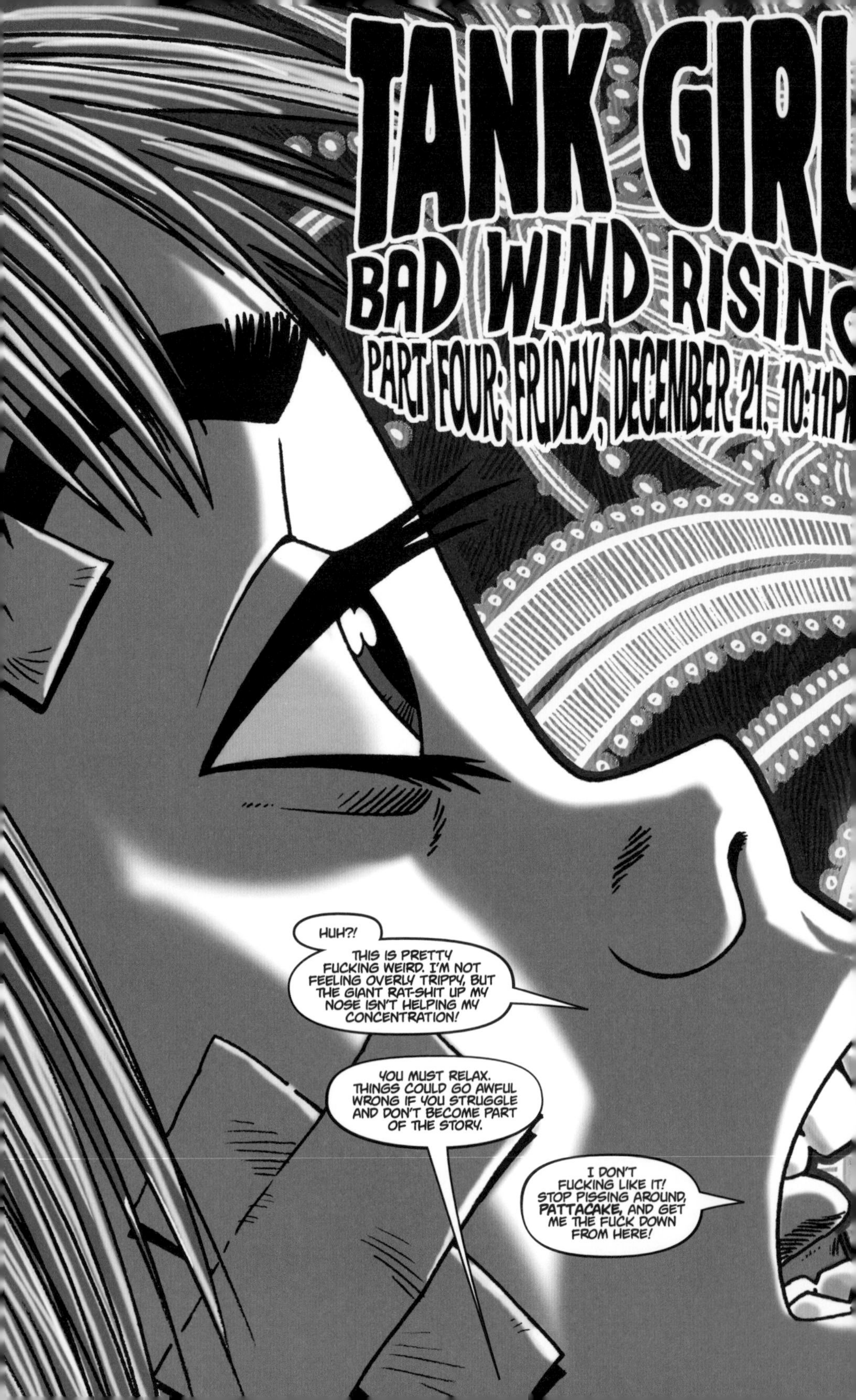
TANK GIRL
BAD WIND RISING
PART FOUR: FRIDAY, DECEMBER 21, 10:11PM
HUH?!
THIS IS PRETTY FUCKING WEIRD. I'M NOT FEELING OVERLY TRIPPY, BUT THE GIANT RAT-SHIT UP MY NOSE ISN'T HELPING MY CONCENTRATION!
YOU MUST RELAX. THINGS COULD GO AWFUL WRONG IF YOU STRUGGLE AND DON'T BECOME PART OF THE STORY.
I DON'T FUCKING LIKE IT! STOP PISSING AROUND, PATTACAKE, AND GET ME THE FUCK DOWN FROM HERE!

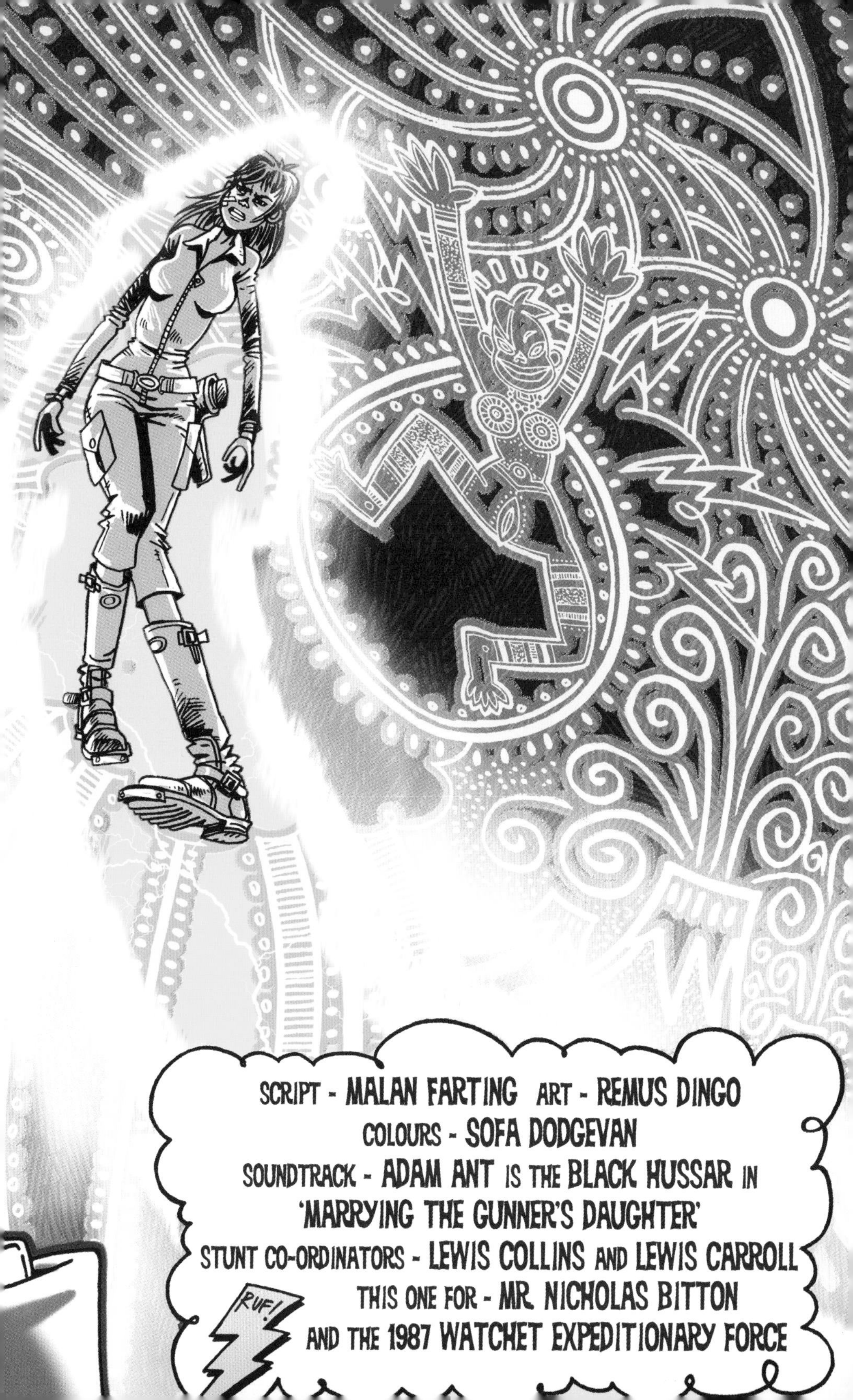
SCRIPT - MALAN FARTING ART - REMUS DINGO
COLOURS - SOFA DODGEVAN
SOUNDTRACK - ADAM ANT IS THE BLACK HUSSAR IN
'MARRYING THE GUNNER'S DAUGHTER'
STUNT CO-ORDINATORS - LEWIS COLLINS AND LEWIS CARROLL
THIS ONE FOR - MR. NICHOLAS BITTON
AND THE 1987 WATCHET EXPEDITIONARY FORCE
RUF!

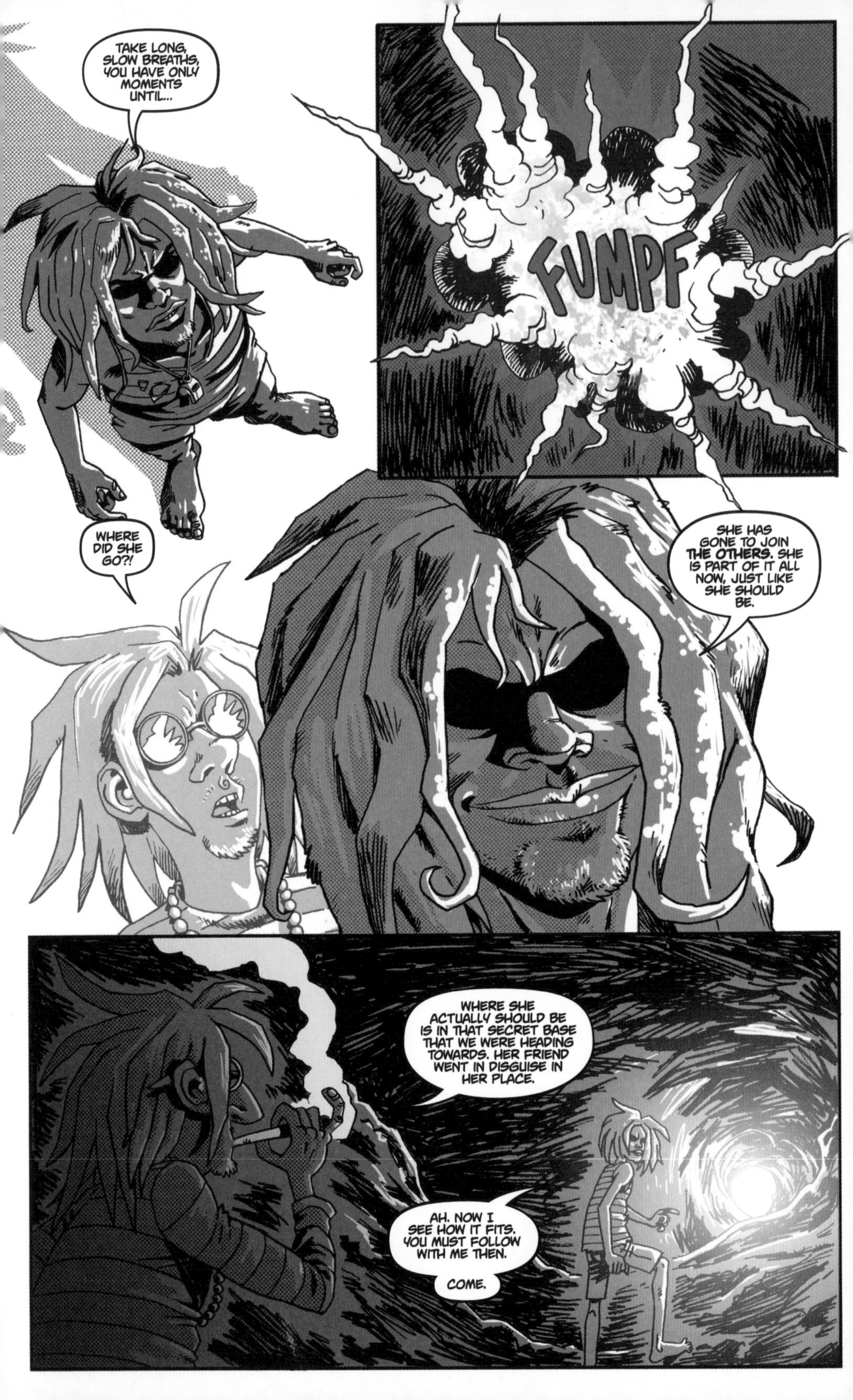
TAKE LONG, SLOW BREATHS, YOU HAVE ONLY MOMENTS UNTIL...
FUMPF
WHERE DID SHE GO?!
SHE HAS GONE TO JOIN THE OTHERS. SHE IS PART OF IT ALL NOW, JUST LIKE SHE SHOULD BE.
WHERE SHE ACTUALLY SHOULD BE IS IN THAT SECRET BASE THAT WE WERE HEADING TOWARDS. HER FRIEND WENT IN DISGUISE IN HER PLACE.
AH. NOW I SEE HOW IT FITS. YOU MUST FOLLOW WITH ME THEN.
COME.

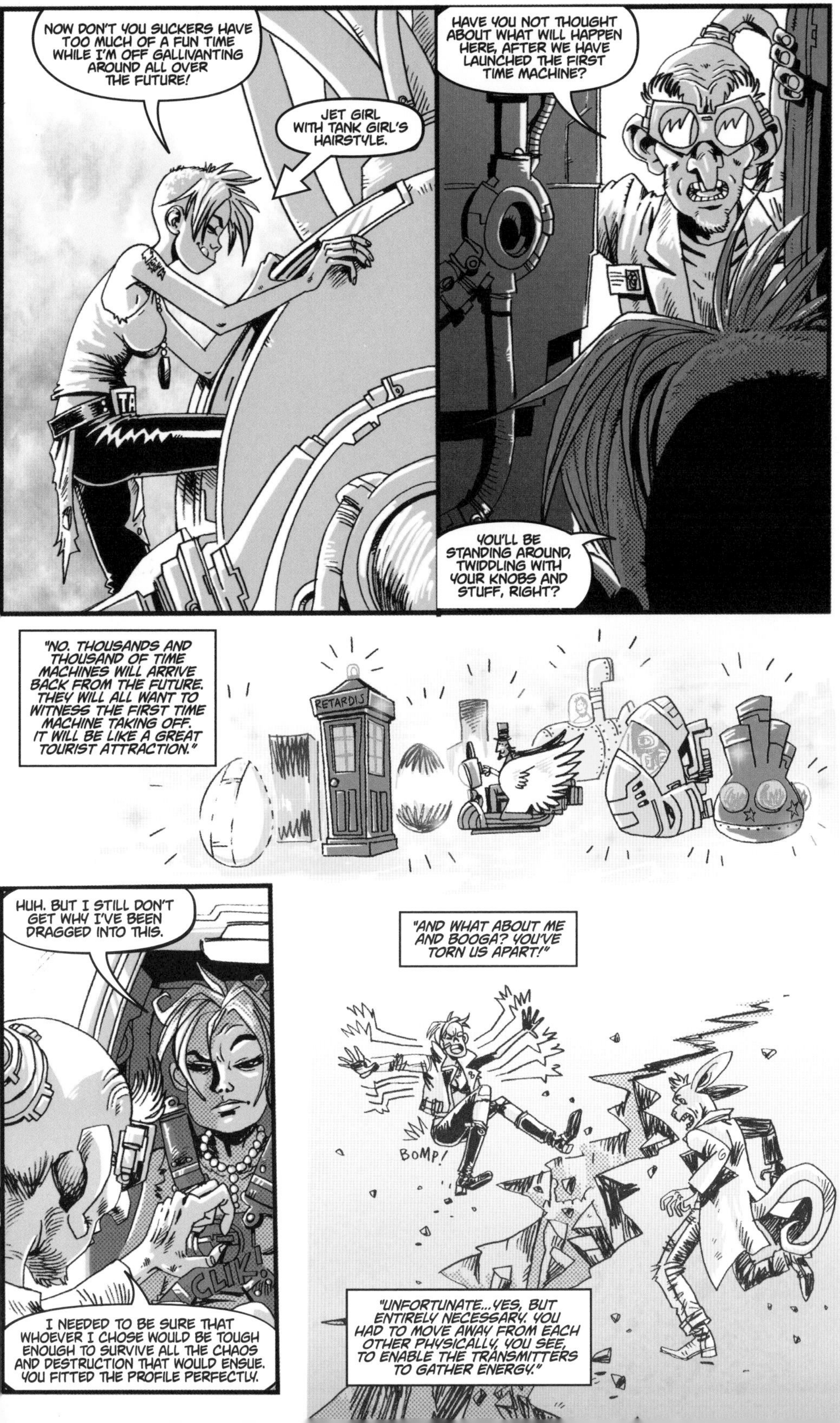
NOW DON'T YOU SUCKERS HAVE TOO MUCH OF A FUN TIME WHILE I'M OFF GALLIVANTING AROUND ALL OVER THE FUTURE!
JET GIRL WITH TANK GIRL'S HAIRSTYLE.
HAVE YOU NOT THOUGHT ABOUT WHAT WILL HAPPEN HERE, AFTER WE HAVE LAUNCHED THE FIRST TIME MACHINE?
YOU'LL BE STANDING AROUND, TWIDDLING WITH YOUR KNOBS AND STUFF, RIGHT?
"NO. THOUSANDS AND THOUSAND OF TIME MACHINES WILL ARRIVE BACK FROM THE FUTURE. THEY WILL ALL WANT TO WITNESS THE FIRST TIME MACHINE TAKING OFF. IT WILL BE LIKE A GREAT TOURIST ATTRACTION."
RETARDIS
HUH. BUT I STILL DON'T GET WHY I'VE BEEN DRAGGED INTO THIS.
CLIK!
I NEEDED TO BE SURE THAT WHOEVER I CHOSE WOULD BE TOUGH ENOUGH TO SURVIVE ALL THE CHAOS AND DESTRUCTION THAT WOULD ENSUE. YOU FITTED THE PROFILE PERFECTLY.
"AND WHAT ABOUT ME AND BOOGA? YOU'VE TORN US APART!"
BOMP!
"UNFORTUNATE...YES, BUT ENTIRELY NECESSARY. YOU HAD TO MOVE AWAY FROM EACH OTHER PHYSICALLY, YOU SEE, TO ENABLE THE TRANSMITTERS TO GATHER ENERGY."

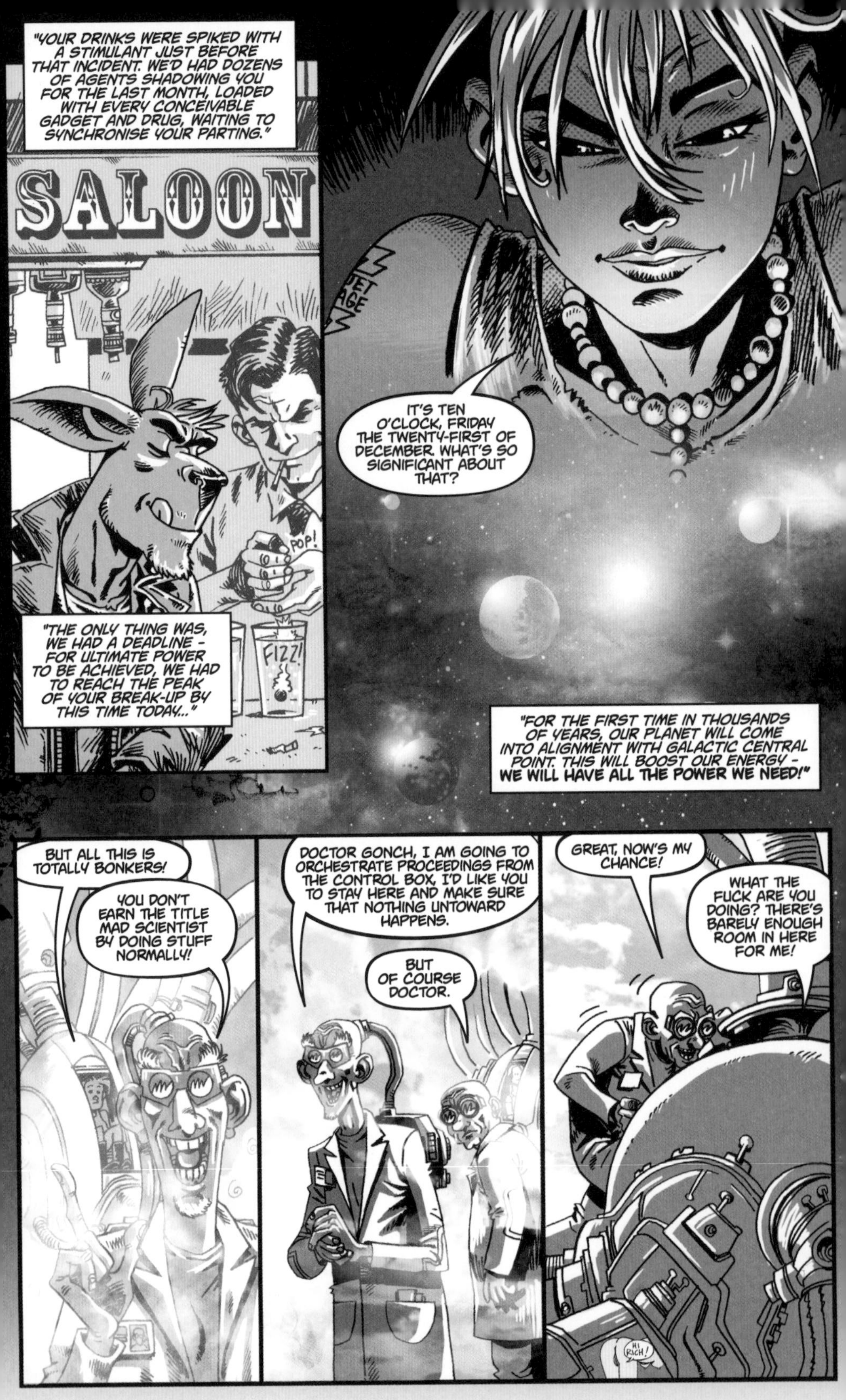
"YOUR DRINKS WERE SPIKED WITH A STIMULANT JUST BEFORE THAT INCIDENT. WE'D HAD DOZENS OF AGENTS SHADOWING YOU FOR THE LAST MONTH, LOADED WITH EVERY CONCEIVABLE GADGET AND DRUG, WAITING TO SYNCHRONISE YOUR PARTING."
SALOON
POP!
FIZZ!
"THE ONLY THING WAS, WE HAD A DEADLINE - FOR ULTIMATE POWER TO BE ACHIEVED, WE HAD TO REACH THE PEAK OF YOUR BREAK-UP BY THIS TIME TODAY..."
IT'S TEN O'CLOCK, FRIDAY THE TWENTY-FIRST OF DECEMBER. WHAT'S SO SIGNIFICANT ABOUT THAT?
"FOR THE FIRST TIME IN THOUSANDS OF YEARS, OUR PLANET WILL COME INTO ALIGNMENT WITH GALACTIC CENTRAL POINT. THIS WILL BOOST OUR ENERGY - **WE WILL HAVE ALL THE POWER WE NEED!"**
BUT ALL THIS IS TOTALLY BONKERS!
YOU DON'T EARN THE TITLE MAD SCIENTIST BY DOING STUFF NORMALLY!
DOCTOR GONCH, I AM GOING TO ORCHESTRATE PROCEEDINGS FROM THE CONTROL BOX, I'D LIKE YOU TO STAY HERE AND MAKE SURE THAT NOTHING UNTOWARD HAPPENS.
BUT OF COURSE DOCTOR.
GREAT, NOW'S MY CHANCE!
WHAT THE FUCK ARE YOU DOING? THERE'S BARELY ENOUGH ROOM IN HERE FOR ME!
HI RICH!

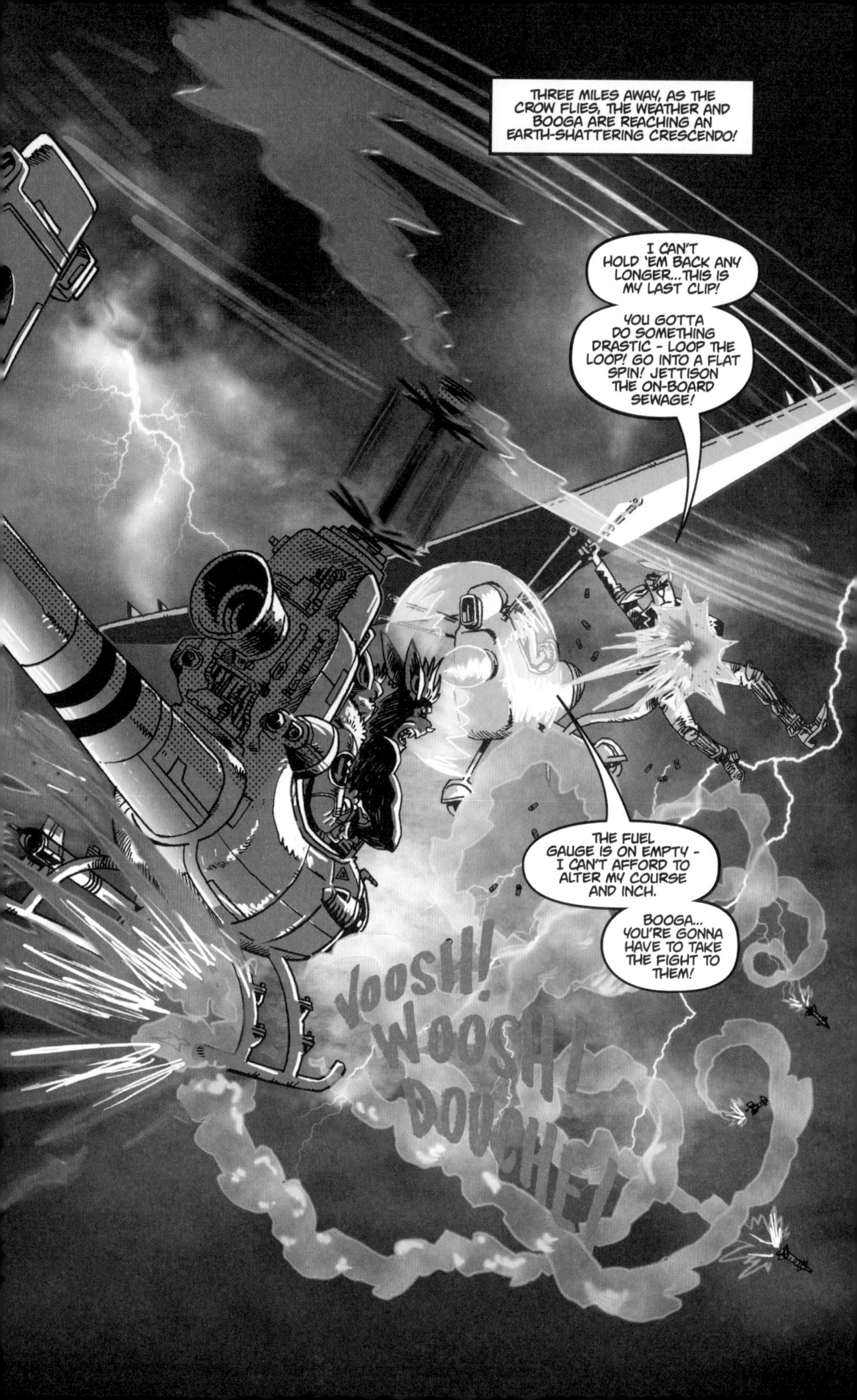
THREE MILES AWAY, AS THE CROW FLIES, THE WEATHER AND BOOGA ARE REACHING AN EARTH-SHATTERING CRESCENDO!
I CAN'T HOLD 'EM BACK ANY LONGER...THIS IS MY LAST CLIP!
YOU GOTTA DO SOMETHING DRASTIC - LOOP THE LOOP! GO INTO A FLAT SPIN! JETTISON THE ON-BOARD SEWAGE!
THE FUEL GAUGE IS ON EMPTY - I CAN'T AFFORD TO ALTER MY COURSE AND INCH.
BOOGA... YOU'RE GONNA HAVE TO TAKE THE FIGHT TO THEM!
VOOSH! WOOSH! DOUCHE!

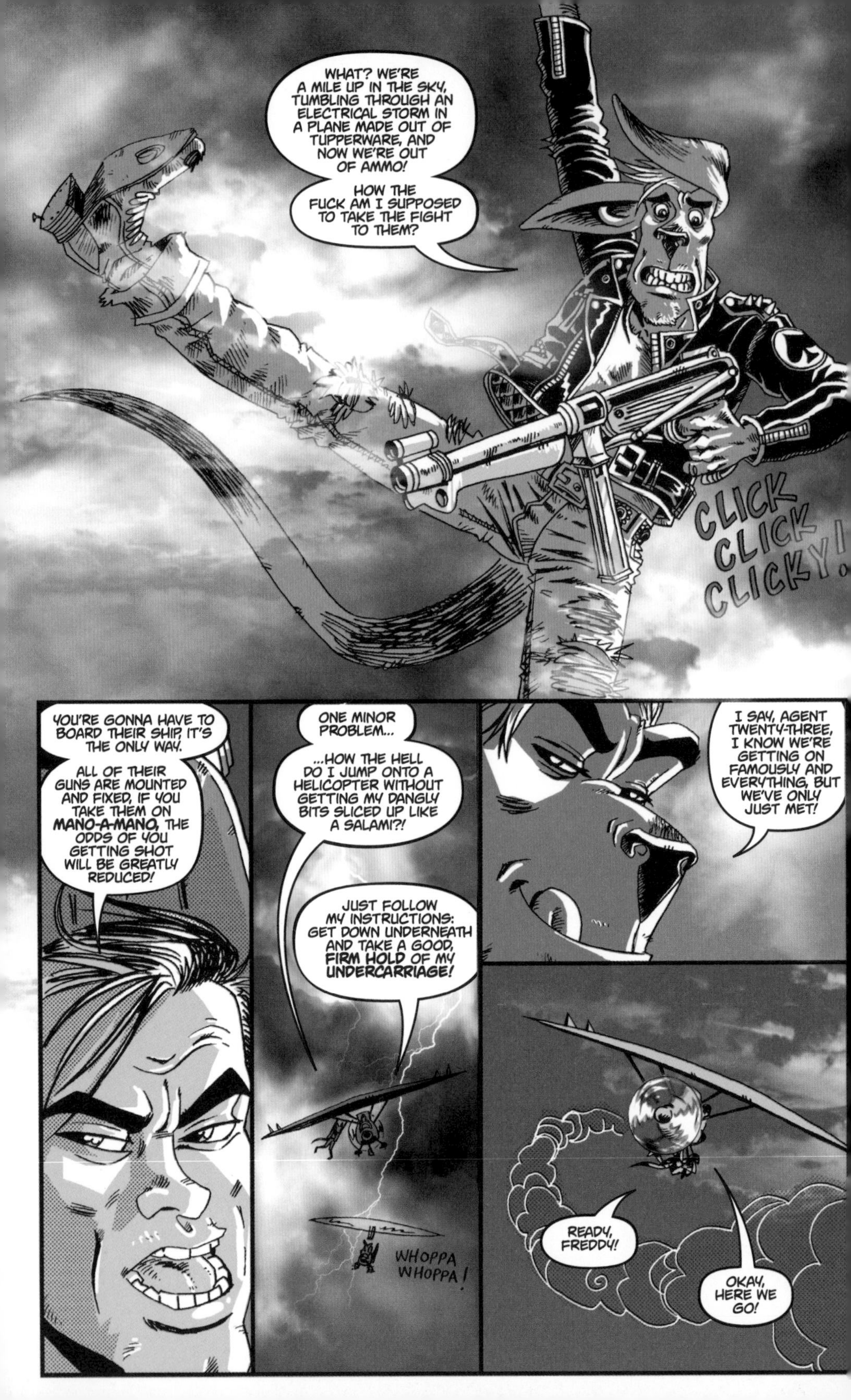
WHAT? WE'RE A MILE UP IN THE SKY, TUMBLING THROUGH AN ELECTRICAL STORM IN A PLANE MADE OUT OF TUPPERWARE, AND NOW WE'RE OUT OF AMMO!
HOW THE FUCK AM I SUPPOSED TO TAKE THE FIGHT TO THEM?
CLICK CLICK CLICKY!
YOU'RE GONNA HAVE TO BOARD THEIR SHIP, IT'S THE ONLY WAY.
ALL OF THEIR GUNS ARE MOUNTED AND FIXED, IF YOU TAKE THEM ON MANO-A-MANO, THE ODDS OF YOU GETTING SHOT WILL BE GREATLY REDUCED!
ONE MINOR PROBLEM...
...HOW THE HELL DO I JUMP ONTO A HELICOPTER WITHOUT GETTING MY DANGLY BITS SLICED UP LIKE A SALAMI?!
JUST FOLLOW MY INSTRUCTIONS: GET DOWN UNDERNEATH AND TAKE A GOOD, FIRM HOLD OF MY UNDERCARRIAGE!
WHOPPA WHOPPA!
I SAY, AGENT TWENTY-THREE, I KNOW WE'RE GETTING ON FAMOUSLY AND EVERYTHING, BUT WE'VE ONLY JUST MET!
READY, FREDDY!
OKAY, HERE WE GO!

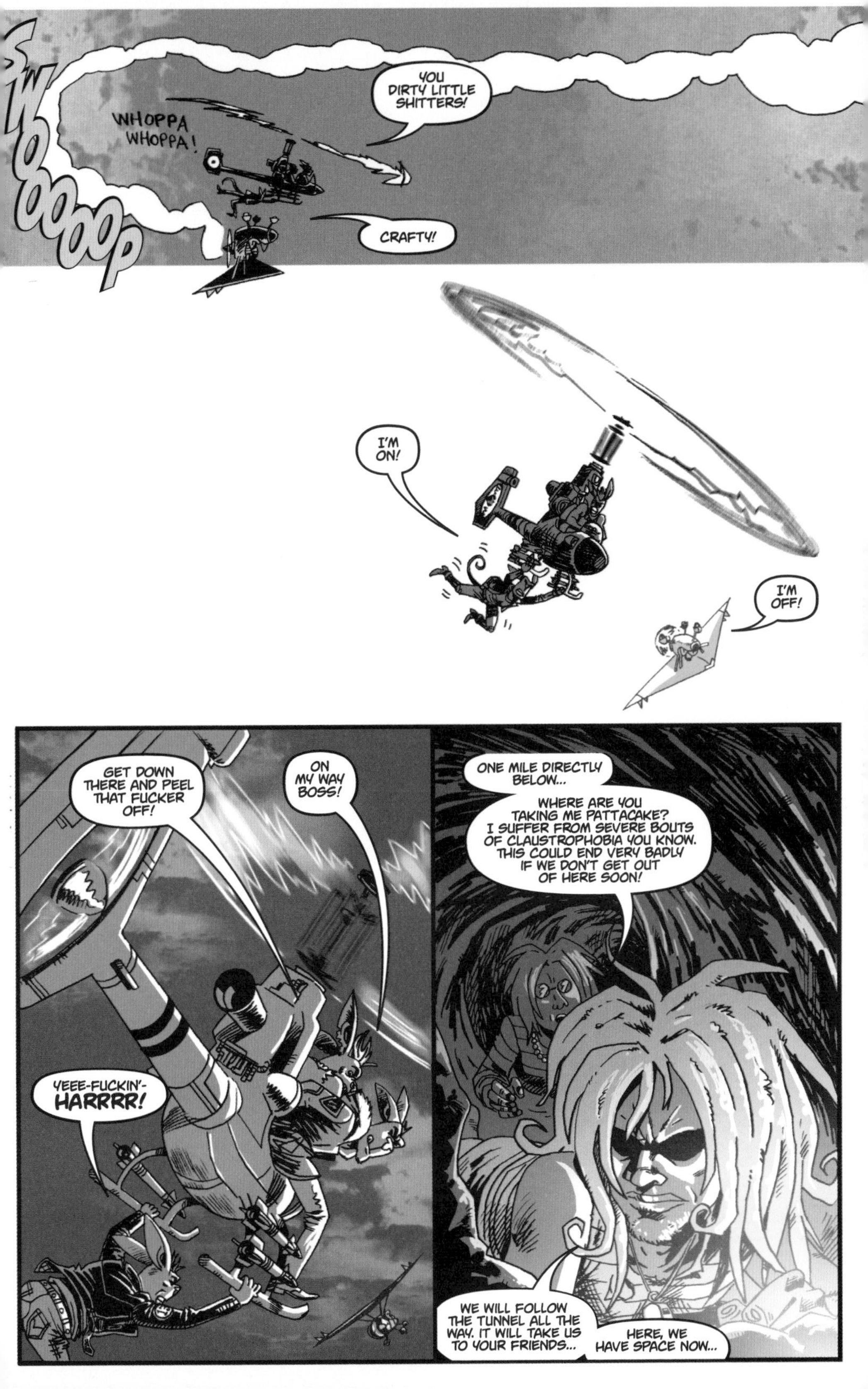
SWOOOOOP
YOU DIRTY LITTLE SHITTERS!
WHOPPA WHOPPA!
CRAFTY!
I'M ON!
I'M OFF!
GET DOWN THERE AND PEEL THAT FUCKER OFF!
ON MY WAY BOSS!
YEEE-FUCKIN'-HARRRR!
ONE MILE DIRECTLY BELOW...
WHERE ARE YOU TAKING ME PATTACAKE? I SUFFER FROM SEVERE BOUTS OF CLAUSTROPHOBIA YOU KNOW. THIS COULD END VERY BADLY IF WE DON'T GET OUT OF HERE SOON!
WE WILL FOLLOW THE TUNNEL ALL THE WAY. IT WILL TAKE US TO YOUR FRIENDS...
HERE, WE HAVE SPACE NOW...

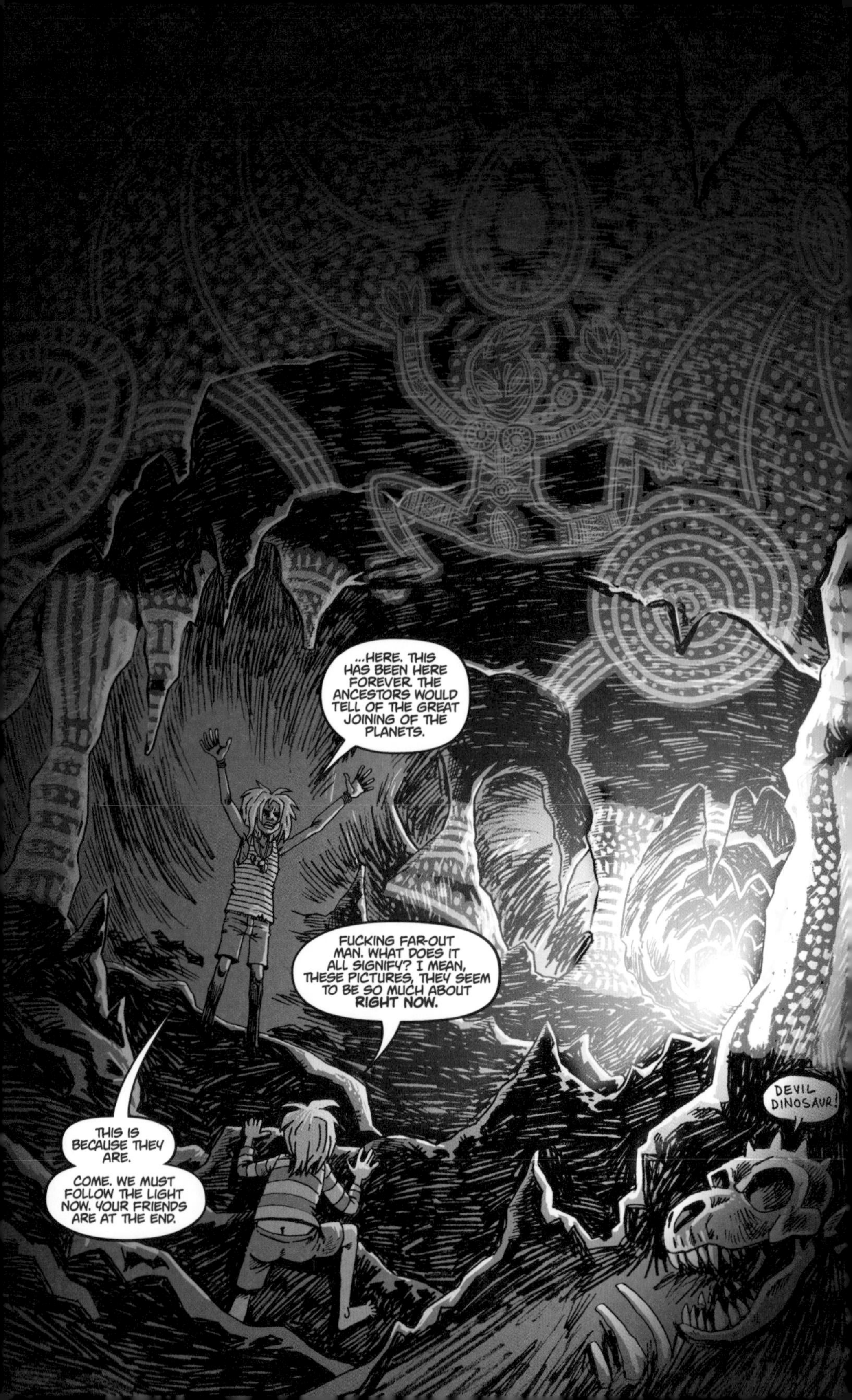
...HERE. THIS HAS BEEN HERE FOREVER. THE ANCESTORS WOULD TELL OF THE GREAT JOINING OF THE PLANETS.
FUCKING FAR-OUT MAN. WHAT DOES IT ALL SIGNIFY? I MEAN, THESE PICTURES, THEY SEEM TO BE SO MUCH ABOUT **RIGHT NOW.**
THIS IS BECAUSE THEY ARE.
COME. WE MUST FOLLOW THE LIGHT NOW. YOUR FRIENDS ARE AT THE END.
DEVIL DINOSAUR!

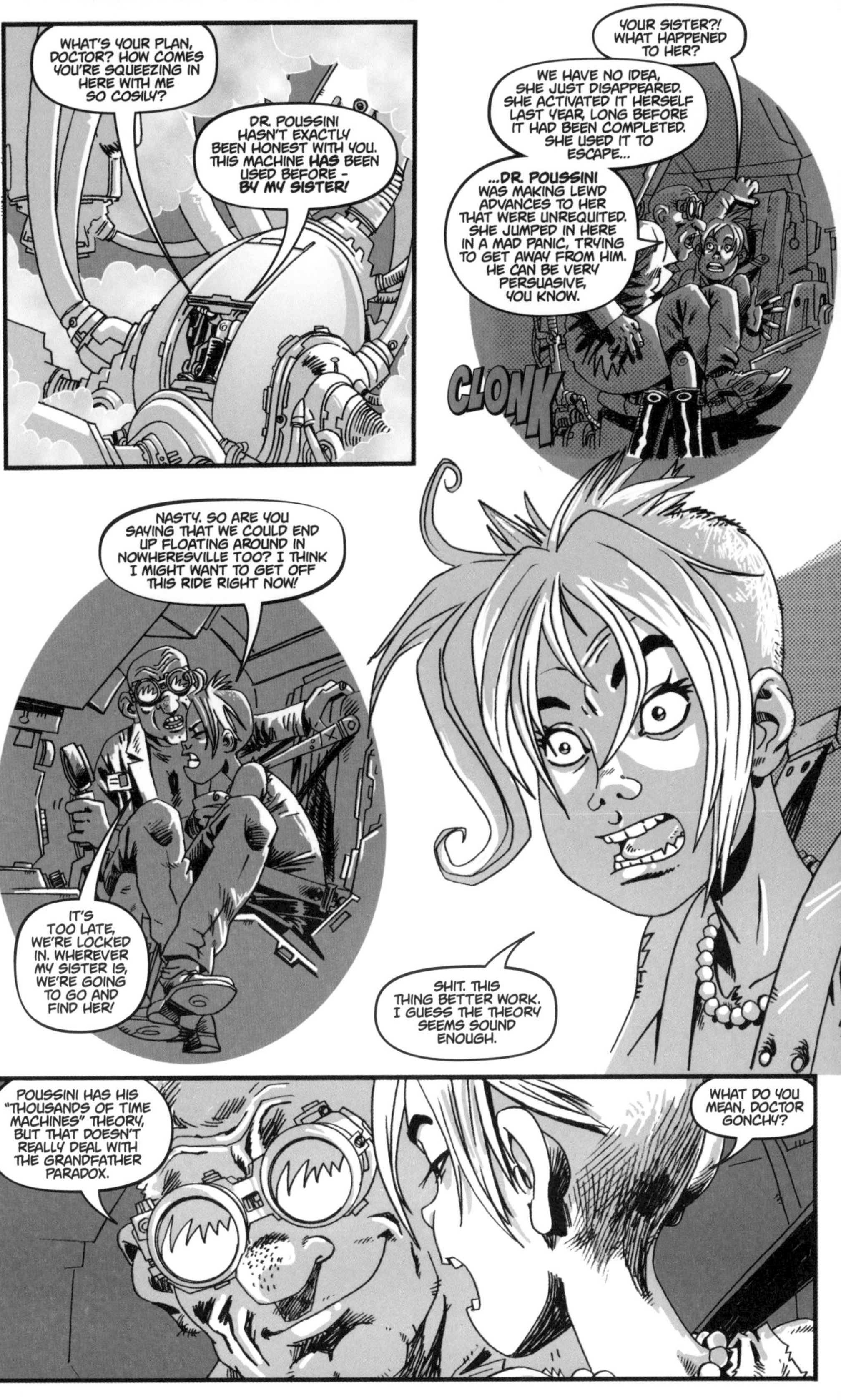
WHAT'S YOUR PLAN, DOCTOR? HOW COMES YOU'RE SQUEEZING IN HERE WITH ME SO COSILY?
DR. POUSSINI HASN'T EXACTLY BEEN HONEST WITH YOU. THIS MACHINE HAS BEEN USED BEFORE - BY MY SISTER!
YOUR SISTER?! WHAT HAPPENED TO HER?
WE HAVE NO IDEA, SHE JUST DISAPPEARED. SHE ACTIVATED IT HERSELF LAST YEAR, LONG BEFORE IT HAD BEEN COMPLETED. SHE USED IT TO ESCAPE...
...DR. POUSSINI WAS MAKING LEWD ADVANCES TO HER THAT WERE UNREQUITED. SHE JUMPED IN HERE IN A MAD PANIC, TRYING TO GET AWAY FROM HIM. HE CAN BE VERY PERSUASIVE, YOU KNOW.
CLONK
NASTY. SO ARE YOU SAYING THAT WE COULD END UP FLOATING AROUND IN NOWHERESVILLE TOO? I THINK I MIGHT WANT TO GET OFF THIS RIDE RIGHT NOW!
IT'S TOO LATE, WE'RE LOCKED IN. WHEREVER MY SISTER IS, WE'RE GOING TO GO AND FIND HER!
SHIT. THIS THING BETTER WORK. I GUESS THE THEORY SEEMS SOUND ENOUGH.
POUSSINI HAS HIS "THOUSANDS OF TIME MACHINES" THEORY, BUT THAT DOESN'T REALLY DEAL WITH THE GRANDFATHER PARADOX.
WHAT DO YOU MEAN, DOCTOR GONCHY?

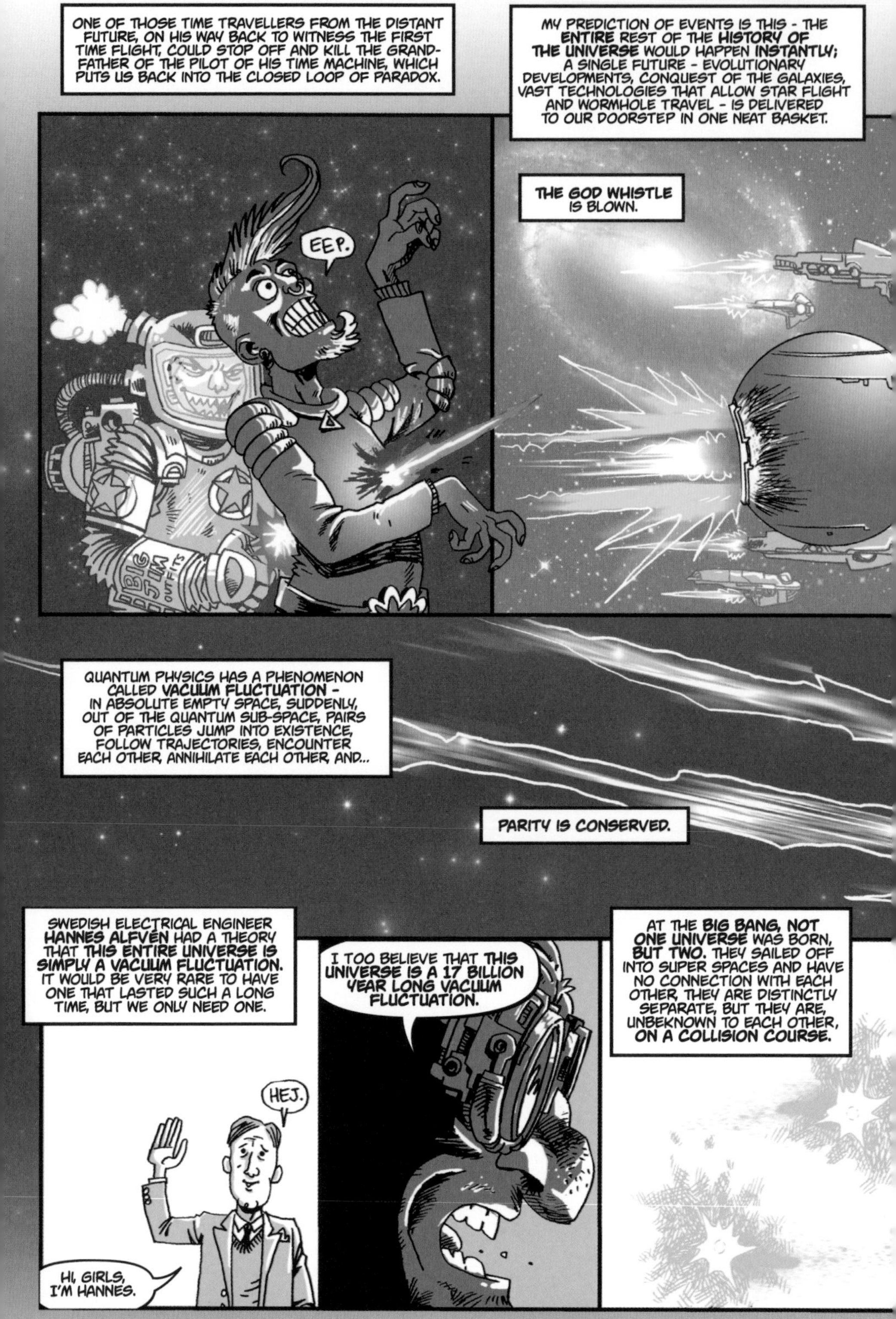

ONE OF THOSE TIME TRAVELLERS FROM THE DISTANT FUTURE, ON HIS WAY BACK TO WITNESS THE FIRST TIME FLIGHT, COULD STOP OFF AND KILL THE GRAND-FATHER OF THE PILOT OF HIS TIME MACHINE, WHICH PUTS US BACK INTO THE CLOSED LOOP OF PARADOX.
EEP.
BIG JIM OUTFITS
MY PREDICTION OF EVENTS IS THIS - THE ENTIRE REST OF THE HISTORY OF THE UNIVERSE WOULD HAPPEN INSTANTLY; A SINGLE FUTURE - EVOLUTIONARY DEVELOPMENTS, CONQUEST OF THE GALAXIES, VAST TECHNOLOGIES THAT ALLOW STAR FLIGHT AND WORMHOLE TRAVEL - IS DELIVERED TO OUR DOORSTEP IN ONE NEAT BASKET.
THE GOD WHISTLE IS BLOWN.
QUANTUM PHYSICS HAS A PHENOMENON CALLED VACUUM FLUCTUATION - IN ABSOLUTE EMPTY SPACE, SUDDENLY, OUT OF THE QUANTUM SUB-SPACE, PAIRS OF PARTICLES JUMP INTO EXISTENCE, FOLLOW TRAJECTORIES, ENCOUNTER EACH OTHER, ANNIHILATE EACH OTHER, AND...
PARITY IS CONSERVED.
SWEDISH ELECTRICAL ENGINEER HANNES ALFVÉN HAD A THEORY THAT THIS ENTIRE UNIVERSE IS SIMPLY A VACUUM FLUCTUATION. IT WOULD BE VERY RARE TO HAVE ONE THAT LASTED SUCH A LONG TIME, BUT WE ONLY NEED ONE.
HEJ.
HI, GIRLS, I'M HANNES.
I TOO BELIEVE THAT THIS UNIVERSE IS A 17 BILLION YEAR LONG VACUUM FLUCTUATION.
AT THE BIG BANG, NOT ONE UNIVERSE WAS BORN, BUT TWO. THEY SAILED OFF INTO SUPER SPACES AND HAVE NO CONNECTION WITH EACH OTHER, THEY ARE DISTINCTLY SEPARATE, BUT THEY ARE, UNBEKNOWN TO EACH OTHER, ON A COLLISION COURSE.

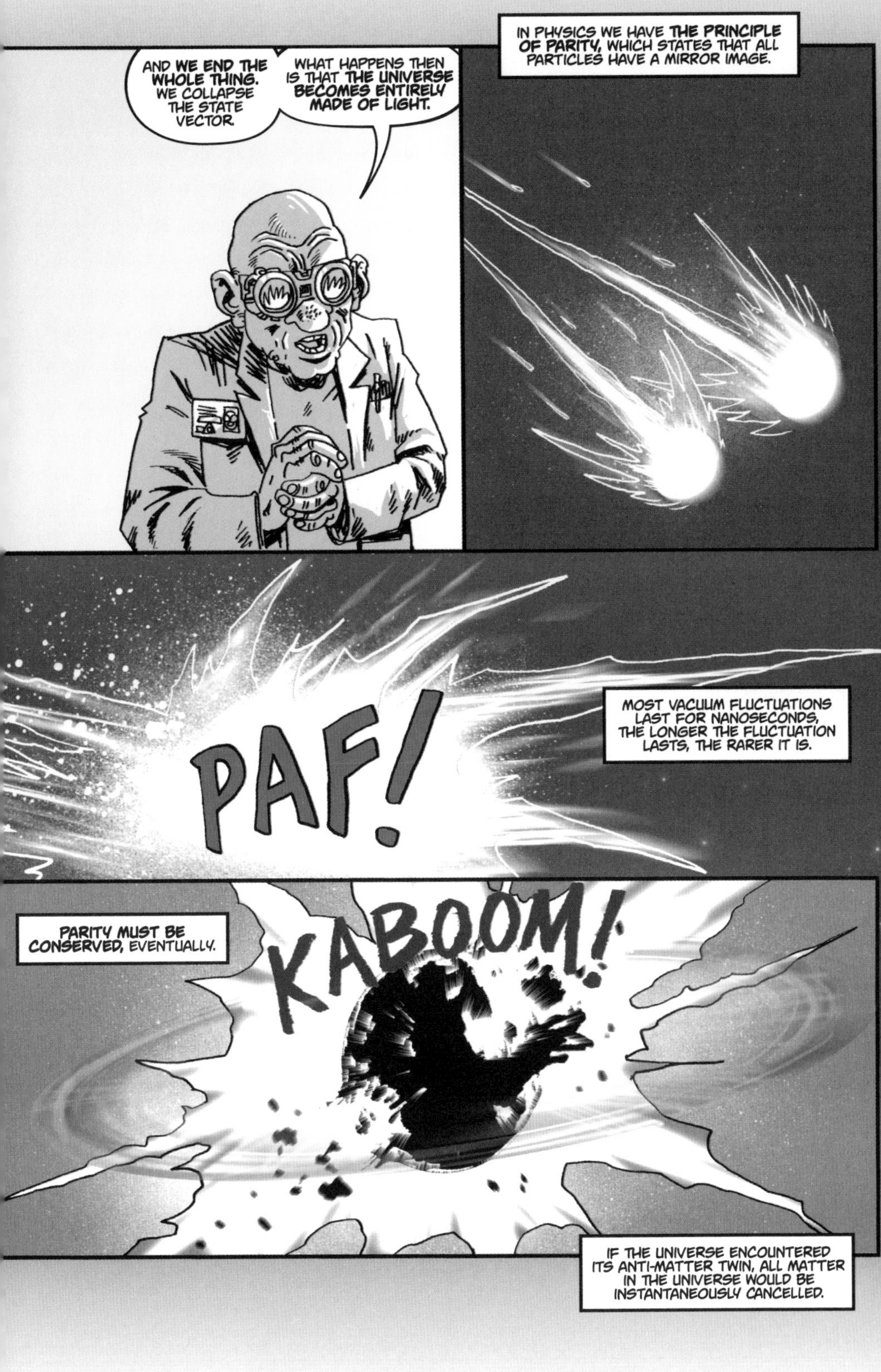
AND WE END THE WHOLE THING. WE COLLAPSE THE STATE VECTOR.
WHAT HAPPENS THEN IS THAT THE UNIVERSE BECOMES ENTIRELY MADE OF LIGHT.
IN PHYSICS WE HAVE THE PRINCIPLE OF PARITY, WHICH STATES THAT ALL PARTICLES HAVE A MIRROR IMAGE.
PAF!
MOST VACUUM FLUCTUATIONS LAST FOR NANOSECONDS, THE LONGER THE FLUCTUATION LASTS, THE RARER IT IS.
PARITY MUST BE CONSERVED, EVENTUALLY.
KABOOM!
IF THE UNIVERSE ENCOUNTERED ITS ANTI-MATTER TWIN, ALL MATTER IN THE UNIVERSE WOULD BE INSTANTANEOUSLY CANCELLED.

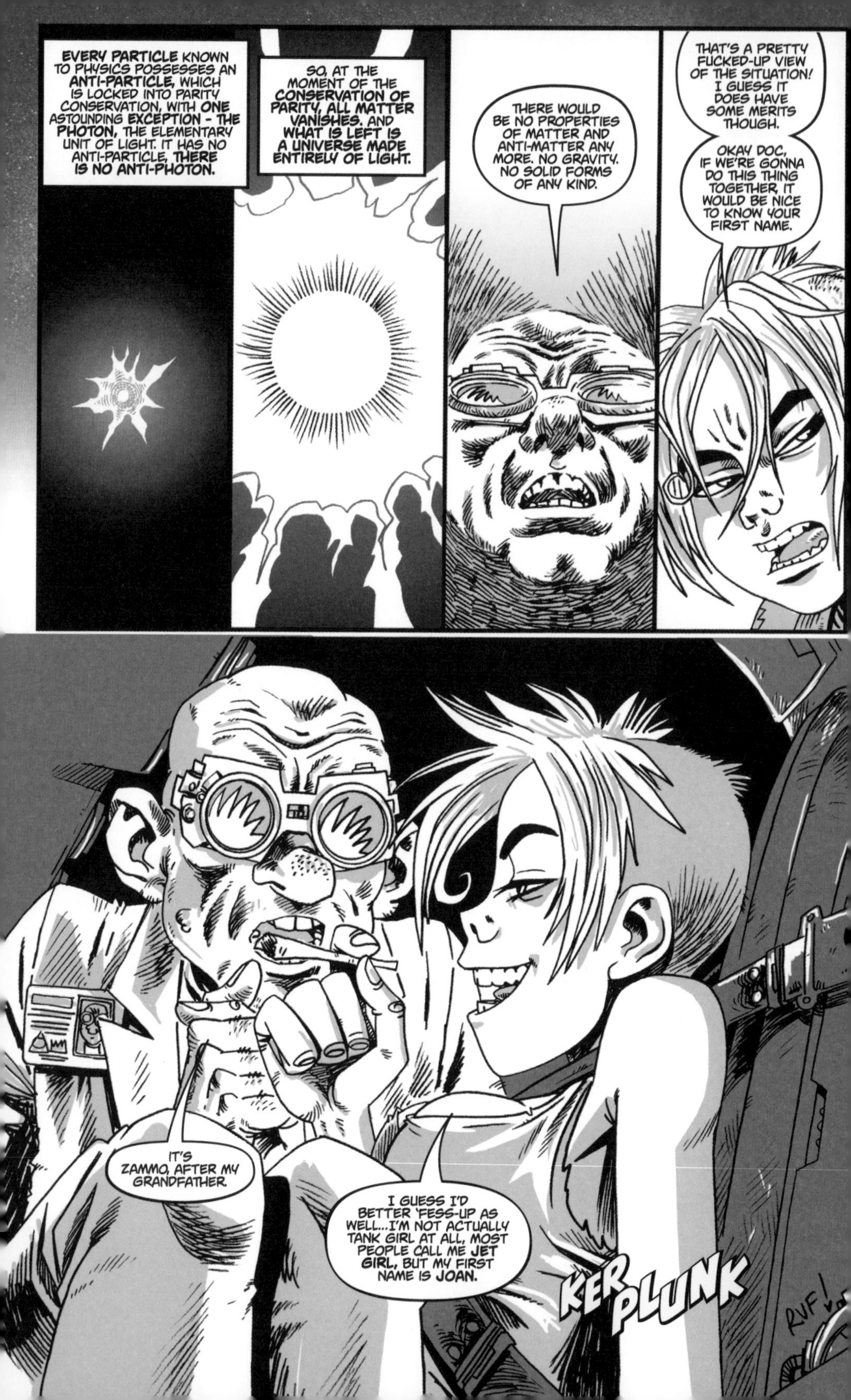
EVERY PARTICLE KNOWN TO PHYSICS POSSESSES AN ANTI-PARTICLE, WHICH IS LOCKED INTO PARITY CONSERVATION, WITH ONE ASTOUNDING EXCEPTION - THE PHOTON, THE ELEMENTARY UNIT OF LIGHT. IT HAS NO ANTI-PARTICLE, THERE IS NO ANTI-PHOTON.
SO, AT THE MOMENT OF THE CONSERVATION OF PARITY, ALL MATTER VANISHES. AND WHAT IS LEFT IS A UNIVERSE MADE ENTIRELY OF LIGHT.
THERE WOULD BE NO PROPERTIES OF MATTER AND ANTI-MATTER ANY MORE. NO GRAVITY. NO SOLID FORMS OF ANY KIND.
THAT'S A PRETTY FUCKED-UP VIEW OF THE SITUATION! I GUESS IT DOES HAVE SOME MERITS THOUGH.
OKAY DOC, IF WE'RE GONNA DO THIS THING TOGETHER, IT WOULD BE NICE TO KNOW YOUR FIRST NAME.
IT'S ZAMMO, AFTER MY GRANDFATHER.
I GUESS I'D BETTER 'FESS-UP AS WELL...I'M NOT ACTUALLY TANK GIRL AT ALL, MOST PEOPLE CALL ME JET GIRL, BUT MY FIRST NAME IS JOAN.
KER PLUNK
RUF!

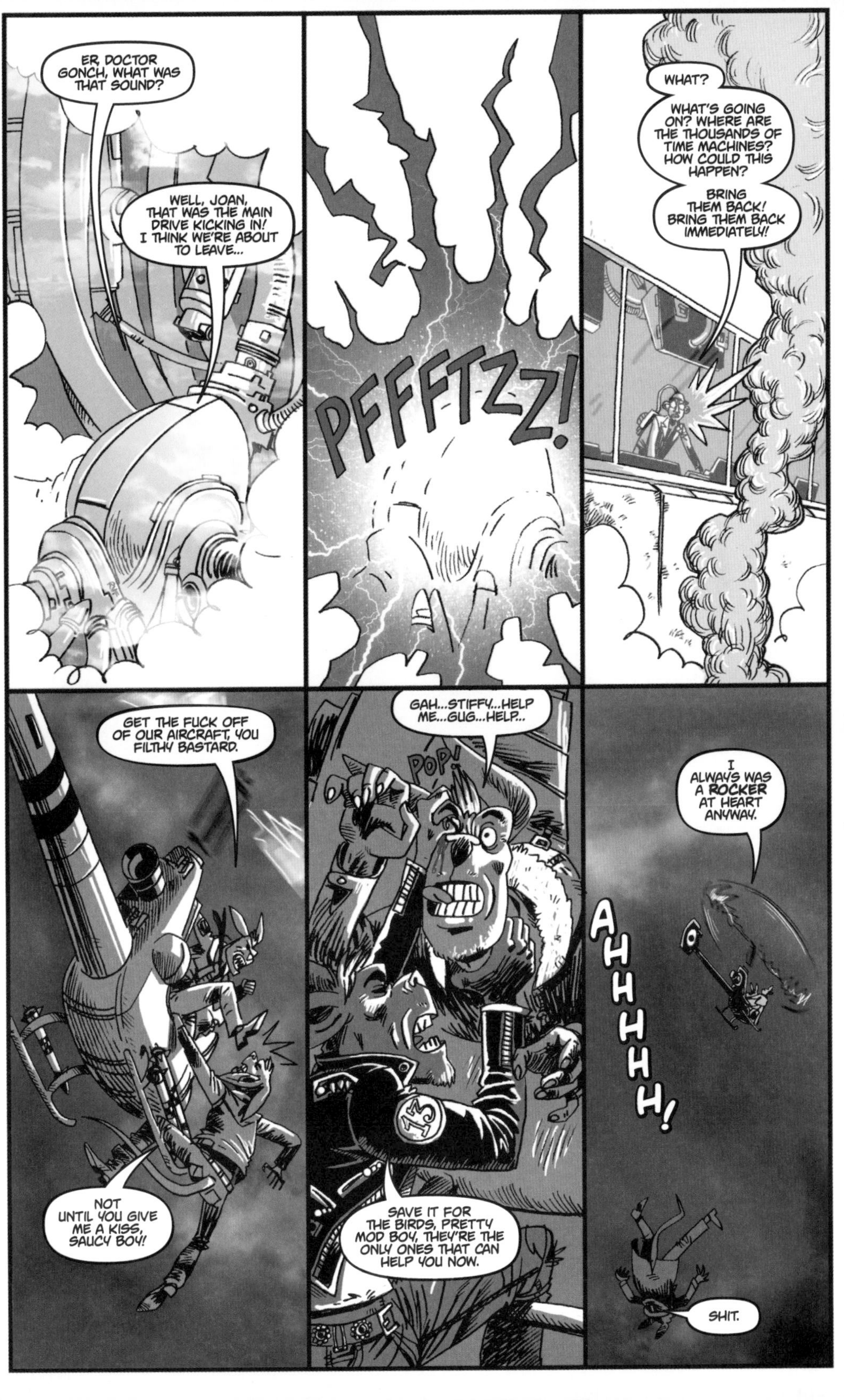
ER, DOCTOR GONCH, WHAT WAS THAT SOUND?
WELL, JOAN, THAT WAS THE MAIN DRIVE KICKING IN! I THINK WE'RE ABOUT TO LEAVE...
PFFFTZZ!
WHAT?
WHAT'S GOING ON? WHERE ARE THE THOUSANDS OF TIME MACHINES? HOW COULD THIS HAPPEN?
BRING THEM BACK! BRING THEM BACK IMMEDIATELY!
GET THE FUCK OFF OF OUR AIRCRAFT, YOU FILTHY BASTARD.
NOT UNTIL YOU GIVE ME A KISS, SAUCY BOY!
GAH...STIFFY...HELP ME...GUG...HELP...
POP!
SAVE IT FOR THE BIRDS, PRETTY MOD BOY, THEY'RE THE ONLY ONES THAT CAN HELP YOU NOW.
I ALWAYS WAS A **ROCKER** AT HEART ANYWAY.
AHHHHH!
SHIT.

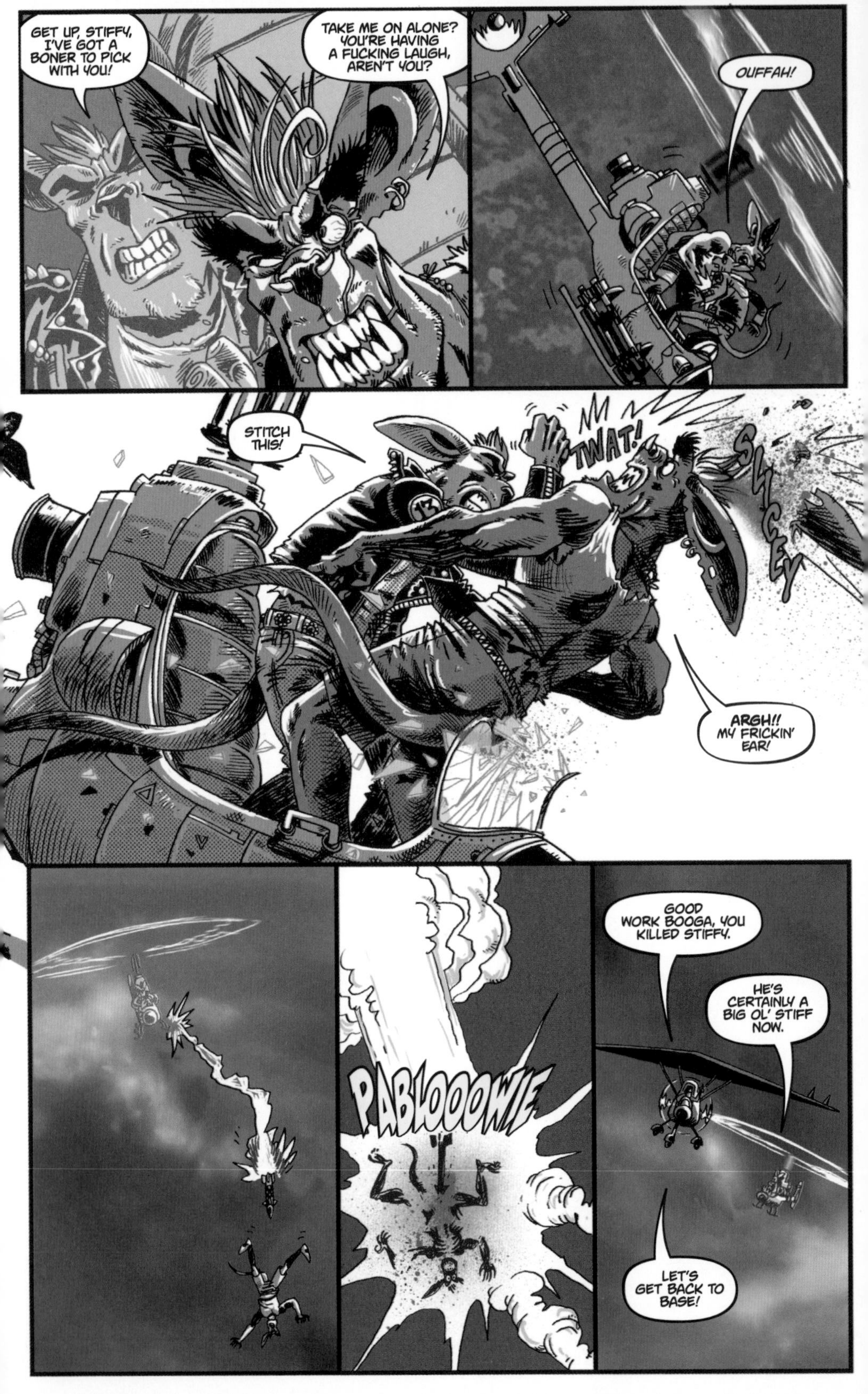
GET UP, STIFFY, I'VE GOT A BONER TO PICK WITH YOU!
TAKE ME ON ALONE? YOU'RE HAVING A FUCKING LAUGH, AREN'T YOU?
OUFFAH!
STITCH THIS!
TWAT!
SLICEY
ARGH!! MY FRICKIN' EAR!
PABLOOOWIE
GOOD WORK BOOGA, YOU KILLED STIFFY.
HE'S CERTAINLY A BIG OL' STIFF NOW.
LET'S GET BACK TO BASE!

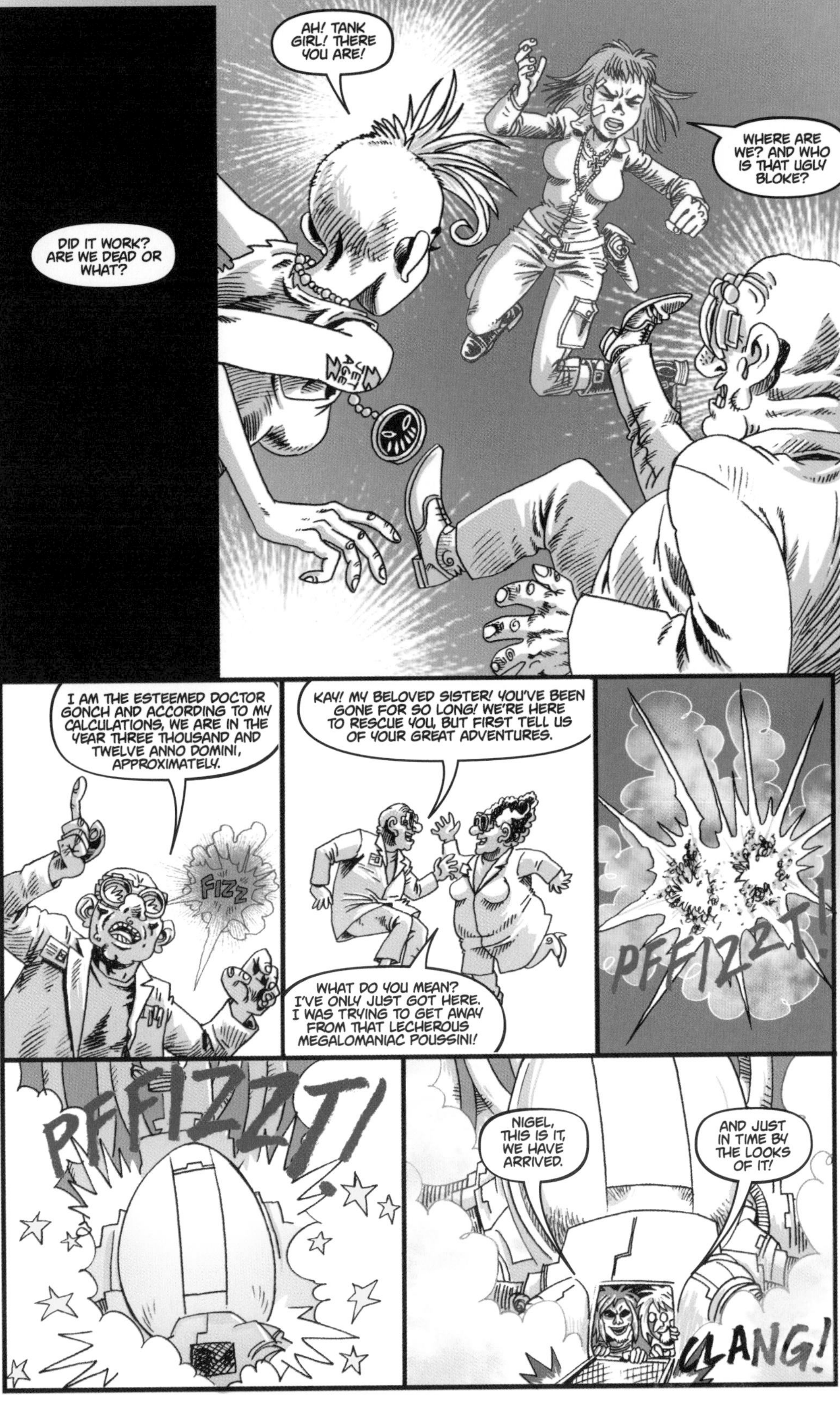
DID IT WORK? ARE WE DEAD OR WHAT?
AH! TANK GIRL! THERE YOU ARE!
WHERE ARE WE? AND WHO IS THAT UGLY BLOKE?
I AM THE ESTEEMED DOCTOR GONCH AND ACCORDING TO MY CALCULATIONS, WE ARE IN THE YEAR THREE THOUSAND AND TWELVE ANNO DOMINI, APPROXIMATELY.
FIZZ
KAY! MY BELOVED SISTER! YOU'VE BEEN GONE FOR SO LONG! WE'RE HERE TO RESCUE YOU, BUT FIRST TELL US OF YOUR GREAT ADVENTURES.
WHAT DO YOU MEAN? I'VE ONLY JUST GOT HERE. I WAS TRYING TO GET AWAY FROM THAT LECHEROUS MEGALOMANIAC POUSSINI!
PFFIZZT!
PFFIZZT!
NIGEL, THIS IS IT, WE HAVE ARRIVED.
AND JUST IN TIME BY THE LOOKS OF IT!
CLANG!

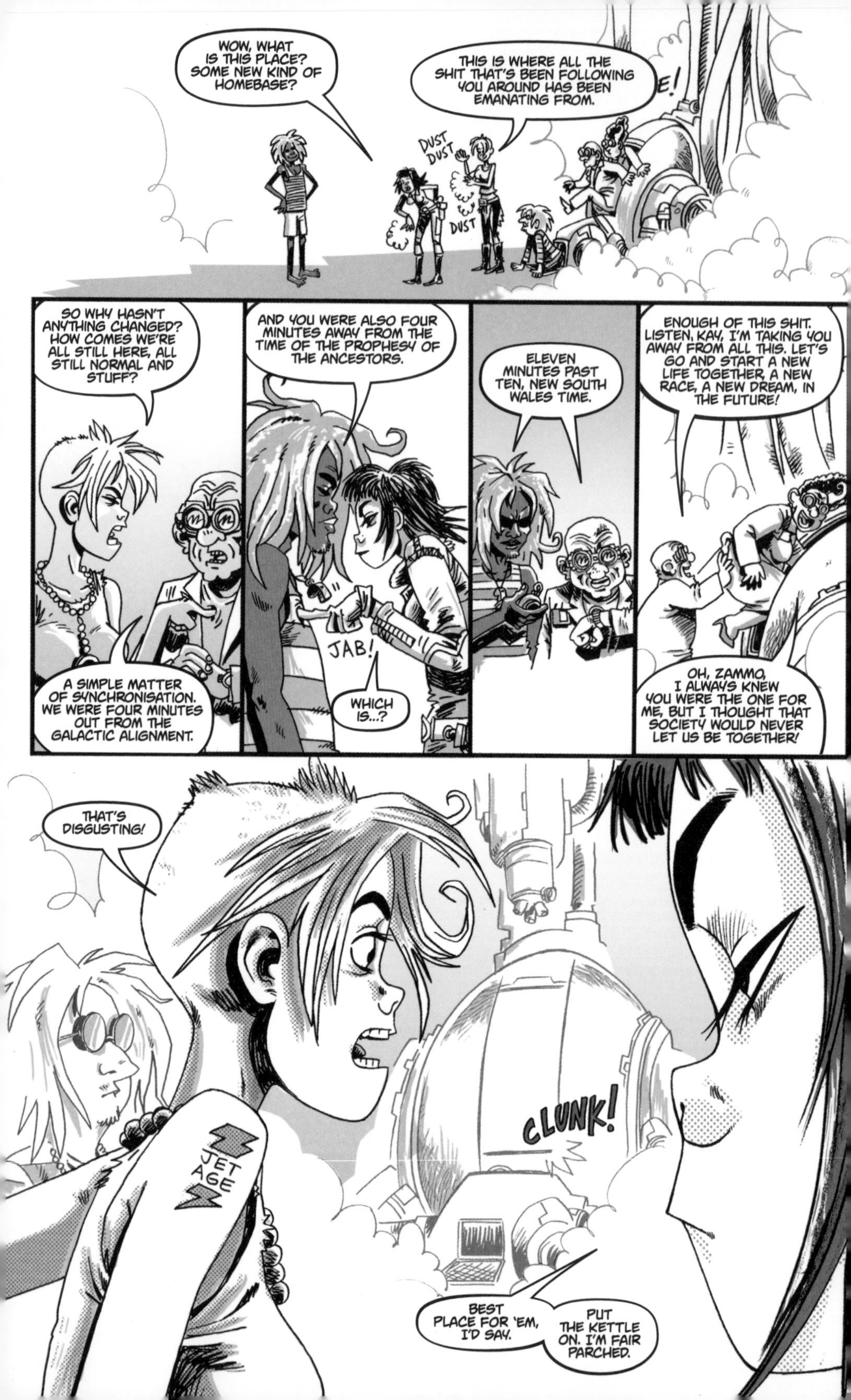
WOW, WHAT IS THIS PLACE? SOME NEW KIND OF HOMEBASE?
THIS IS WHERE ALL THE SHIT THAT'S BEEN FOLLOWING YOU AROUND HAS BEEN EMANATING FROM.
DUST DUST
DUST
SO WHY HASN'T ANYTHING CHANGED? HOW COMES WE'RE ALL STILL HERE, ALL STILL NORMAL AND STUFF?
A SIMPLE MATTER OF SYNCHRONISATION. WE WERE FOUR MINUTES OUT FROM THE GALACTIC ALIGNMENT.
AND YOU WERE ALSO FOUR MINUTES AWAY FROM THE TIME OF THE PROPHESY OF THE ANCESTORS.
JAB!
WHICH IS...?
ELEVEN MINUTES PAST TEN, NEW SOUTH WALES TIME.
ENOUGH OF THIS SHIT. LISTEN, KAY, I'M TAKING YOU AWAY FROM ALL THIS. LET'S GO AND START A NEW LIFE TOGETHER, A NEW RACE, A NEW DREAM, IN THE FUTURE!
OH, ZAMMO, I ALWAYS KNEW YOU WERE THE ONE FOR ME, BUT I THOUGHT THAT SOCIETY WOULD NEVER LET US BE TOGETHER!
THAT'S DISGUSTING!
JET AGE
CLUNK!
BEST PLACE FOR 'EM, I'D SAY.
PUT THE KETTLE ON. I'M FAIR PARCHED.

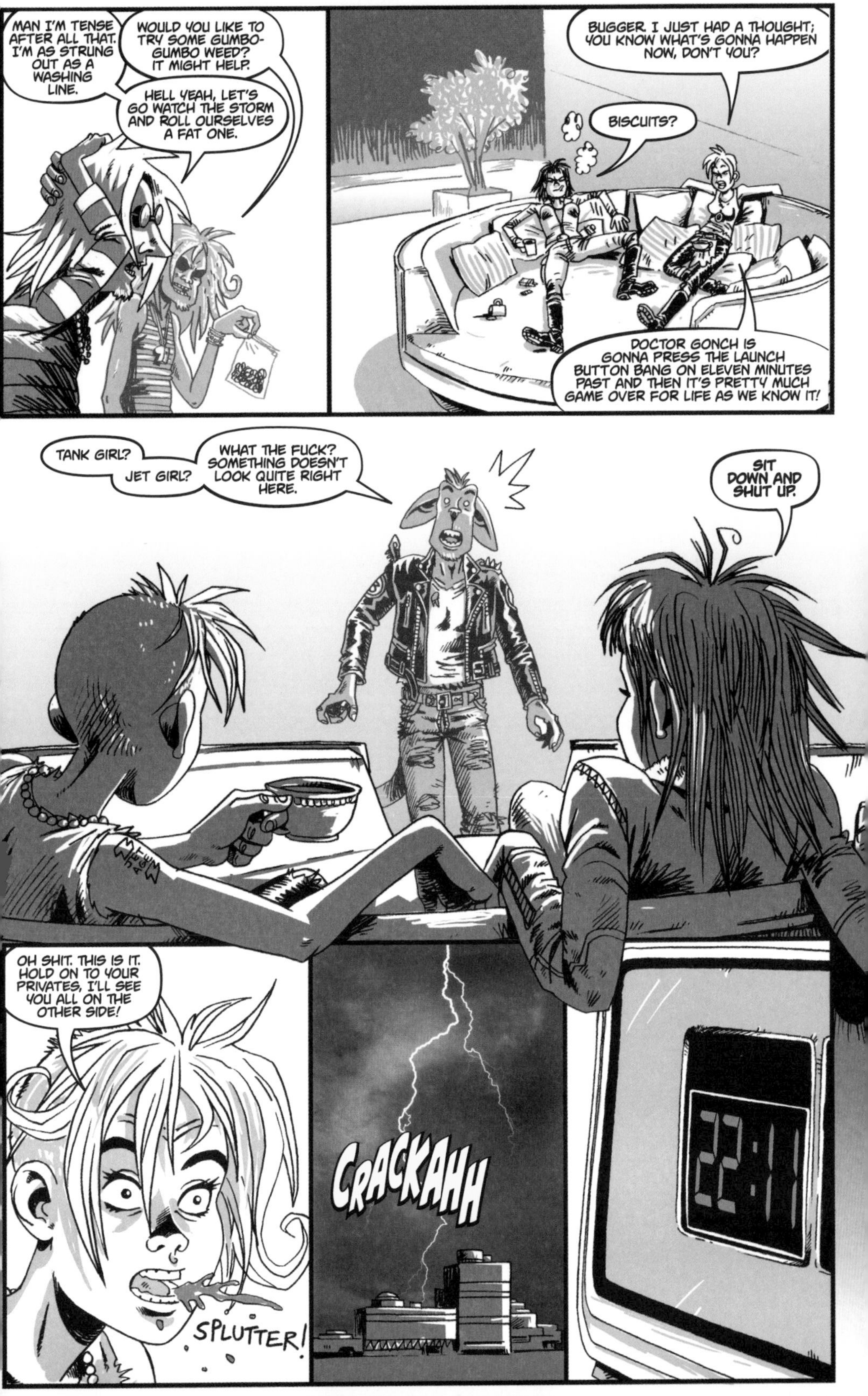
MAN I'M TENSE AFTER ALL THAT. I'M AS STRUNG OUT AS A WASHING LINE.
WOULD YOU LIKE TO TRY SOME GUMBO-GUMBO WEED? IT MIGHT HELP.
HELL YEAH, LET'S GO WATCH THE STORM AND ROLL OURSELVES A FAT ONE.
BUGGER. I JUST HAD A THOUGHT; YOU KNOW WHAT'S GONNA HAPPEN NOW, DON'T YOU?
BISCUITS?
DOCTOR GONCH IS GONNA PRESS THE LAUNCH BUTTON BANG ON ELEVEN MINUTES PAST AND THEN IT'S PRETTY MUCH GAME OVER FOR LIFE AS WE KNOW IT!
TANK GIRL?
JET GIRL?
WHAT THE FUCK? SOMETHING DOESN'T LOOK QUITE RIGHT HERE.
SIT DOWN AND SHUT UP.
OH SHIT. THIS IS IT. HOLD ON TO YOUR PRIVATES, I'LL SEE YOU ALL ON THE OTHER SIDE!
SPLUTTER!
CRACKAHH
22:11

"THIS IS IT? A UNIVERSE MADE OF ENTIRELY LIGHT? IT'S ALL GONE WHITE... JUST...WHITE..."

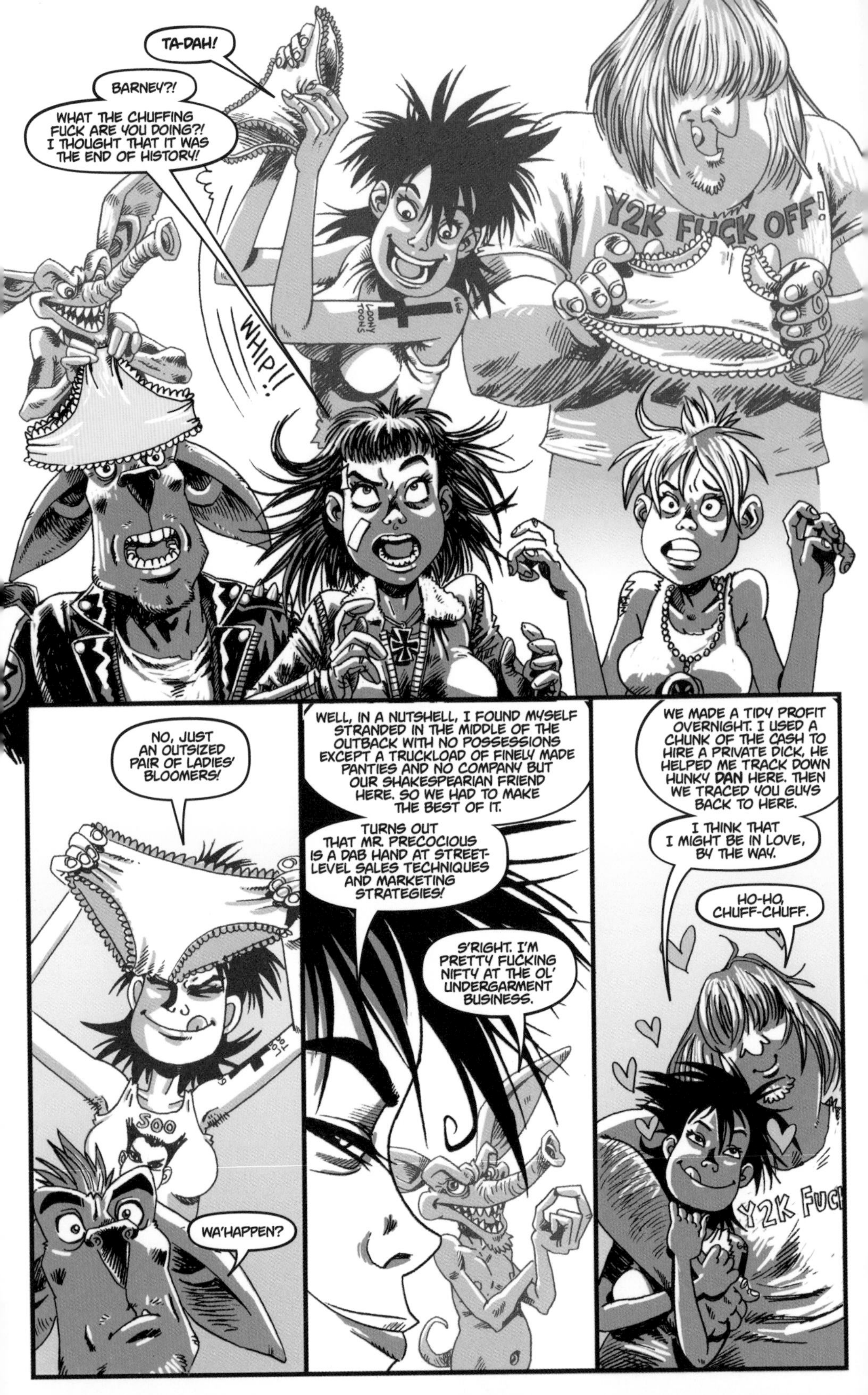
TA-DAH!
BARNEY?!
WHAT THE CHUFFING FUCK ARE YOU DOING?! I THOUGHT THAT IT WAS THE END OF HISTORY!
WHIP!!
NO, JUST AN OUTSIZED PAIR OF LADIES' BLOOMERS!
WA'HAPPEN?
WELL, IN A NUTSHELL, I FOUND MYSELF STRANDED IN THE MIDDLE OF THE OUTBACK WITH NO POSSESSIONS EXCEPT A TRUCKLOAD OF FINELY MADE PANTIES AND NO COMPANY BUT OUR SHAKESPEARIAN FRIEND HERE. SO WE HAD TO MAKE THE BEST OF IT.
TURNS OUT THAT MR. PRECOCIOUS IS A DAB HAND AT STREET-LEVEL SALES TECHNIQUES AND MARKETING STRATEGIES!
S'RIGHT. I'M PRETTY FUCKING NIFTY AT THE OL' UNDERGARMENT BUSINESS.
WE MADE A TIDY PROFIT OVERNIGHT. I USED A CHUNK OF THE CASH TO HIRE A PRIVATE DICK, HE HELPED ME TRACK DOWN HUNKY DAN HERE. THEN WE TRACED YOU GUYS BACK TO HERE.
I THINK THAT I MIGHT BE IN LOVE, BY THE WAY.
HO-HO, CHUFF-CHUFF.

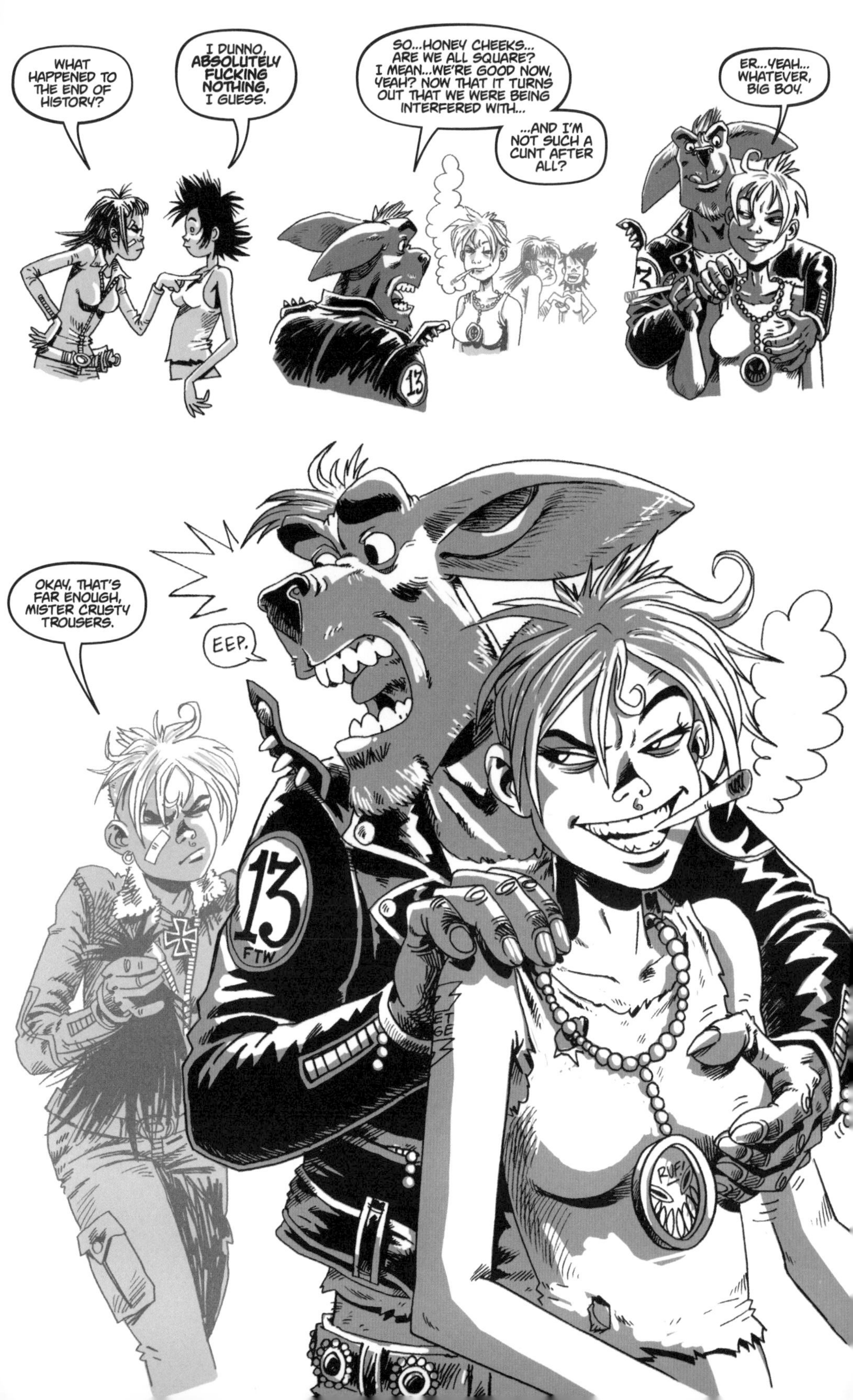
WHAT HAPPENED TO THE END OF HISTORY?
I DUNNO, ABSOLUTELY FUCKING NOTHING, I GUESS.
SO...HONEY CHEEKS... ARE WE ALL SQUARE? I MEAN...WE'RE GOOD NOW, YEAH? NOW THAT IT TURNS OUT THAT WE WERE BEING INTERFERED WITH...
...AND I'M NOT SUCH A CUNT AFTER ALL?
ER...YEAH... WHATEVER, BIG BOY.
OKAY, THAT'S FAR ENOUGH, MISTER CRUSTY TROUSERS.
EEP.
13
FTW
RUF!

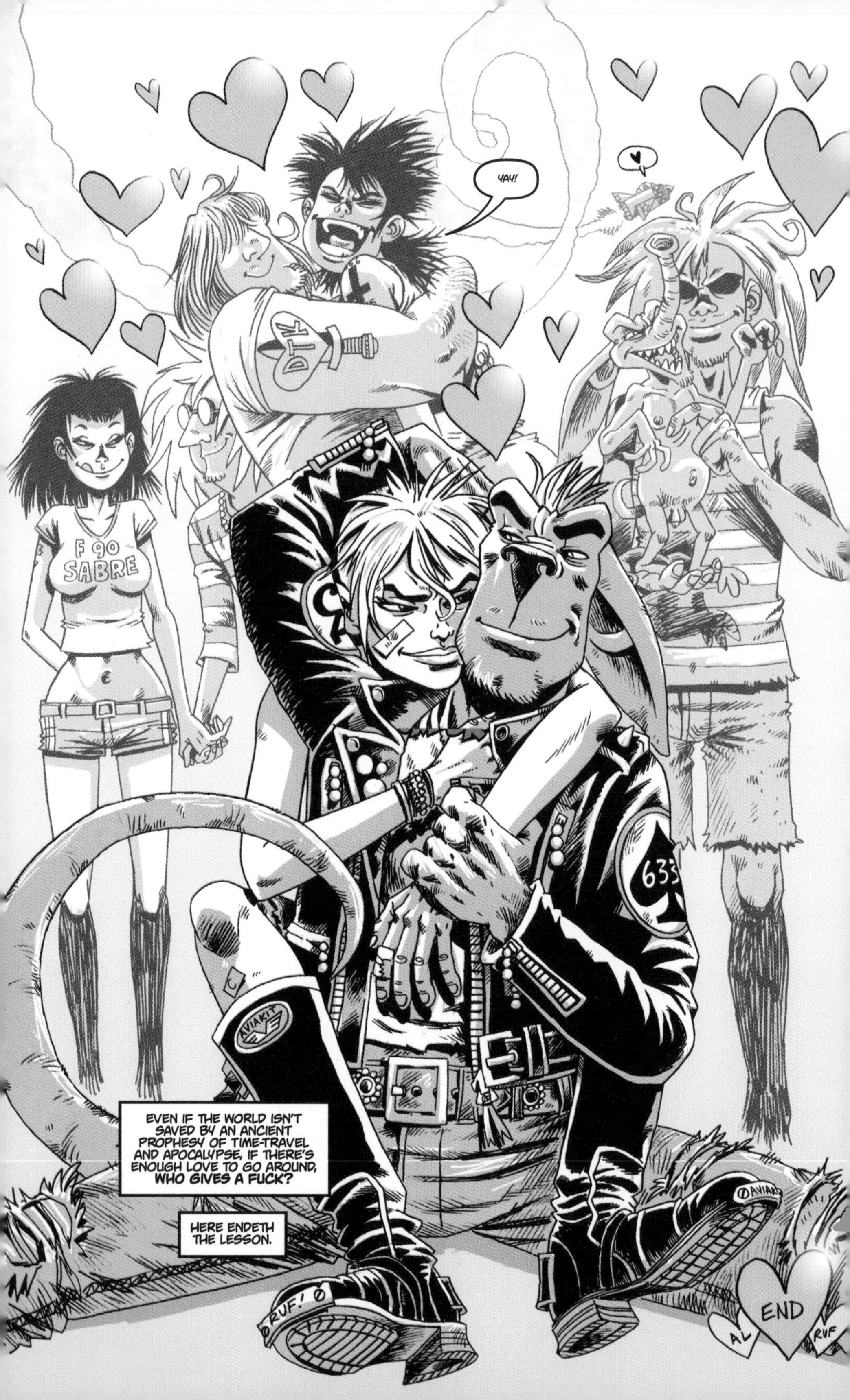
YAY!
EVEN IF THE WORLD ISN'T SAVED BY AN ANCIENT PROPHESY OF TIME-TRAVEL AND APOCALYPSE, IF THERE'S ENOUGH LOVE TO GO AROUND, WHO GIVES A FUCK?
HERE ENDETH THE LESSON.
F 90 SABRE
END
AL
RUF

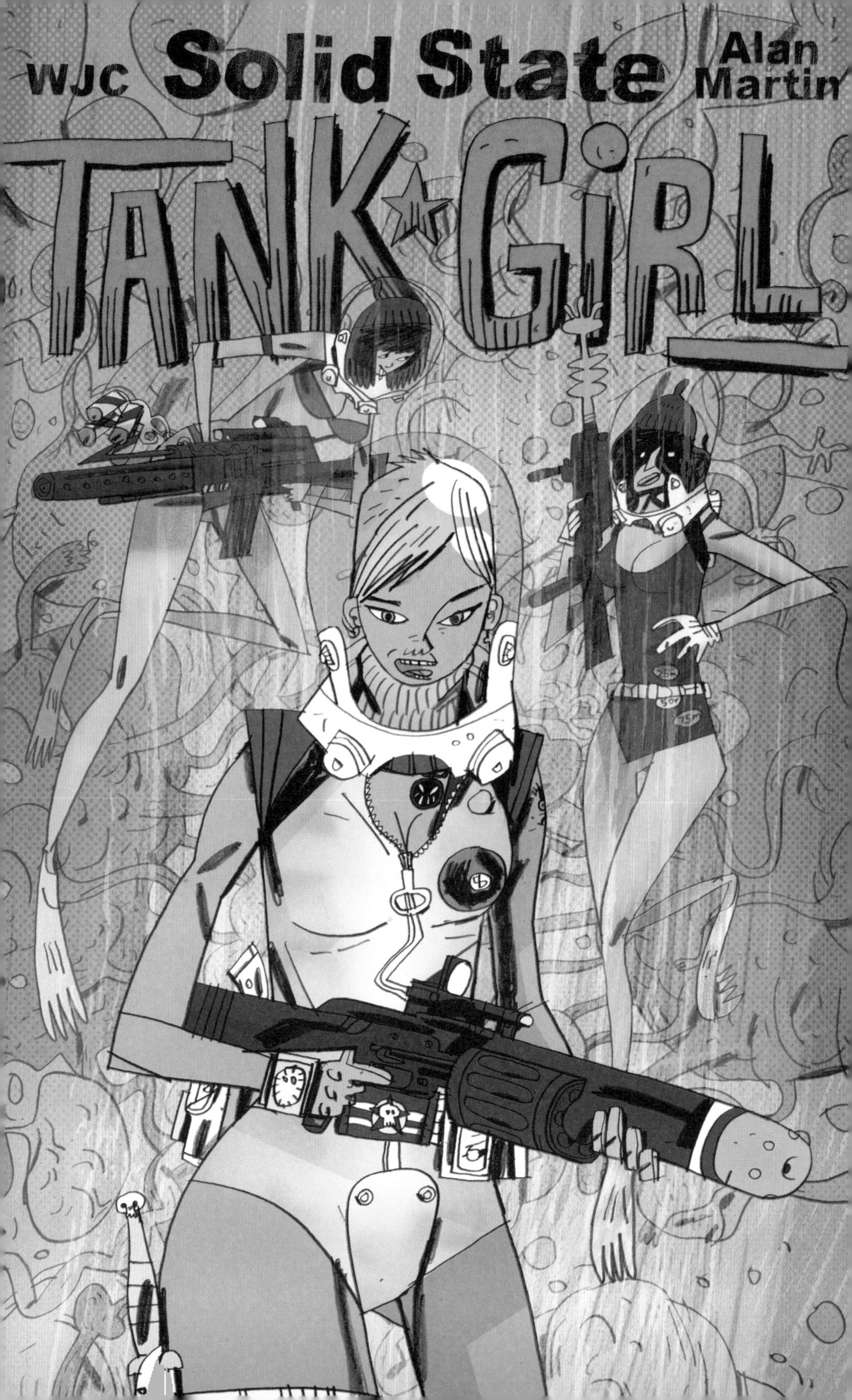
WJC
Solid State
Alan Martin
TANK GIRL

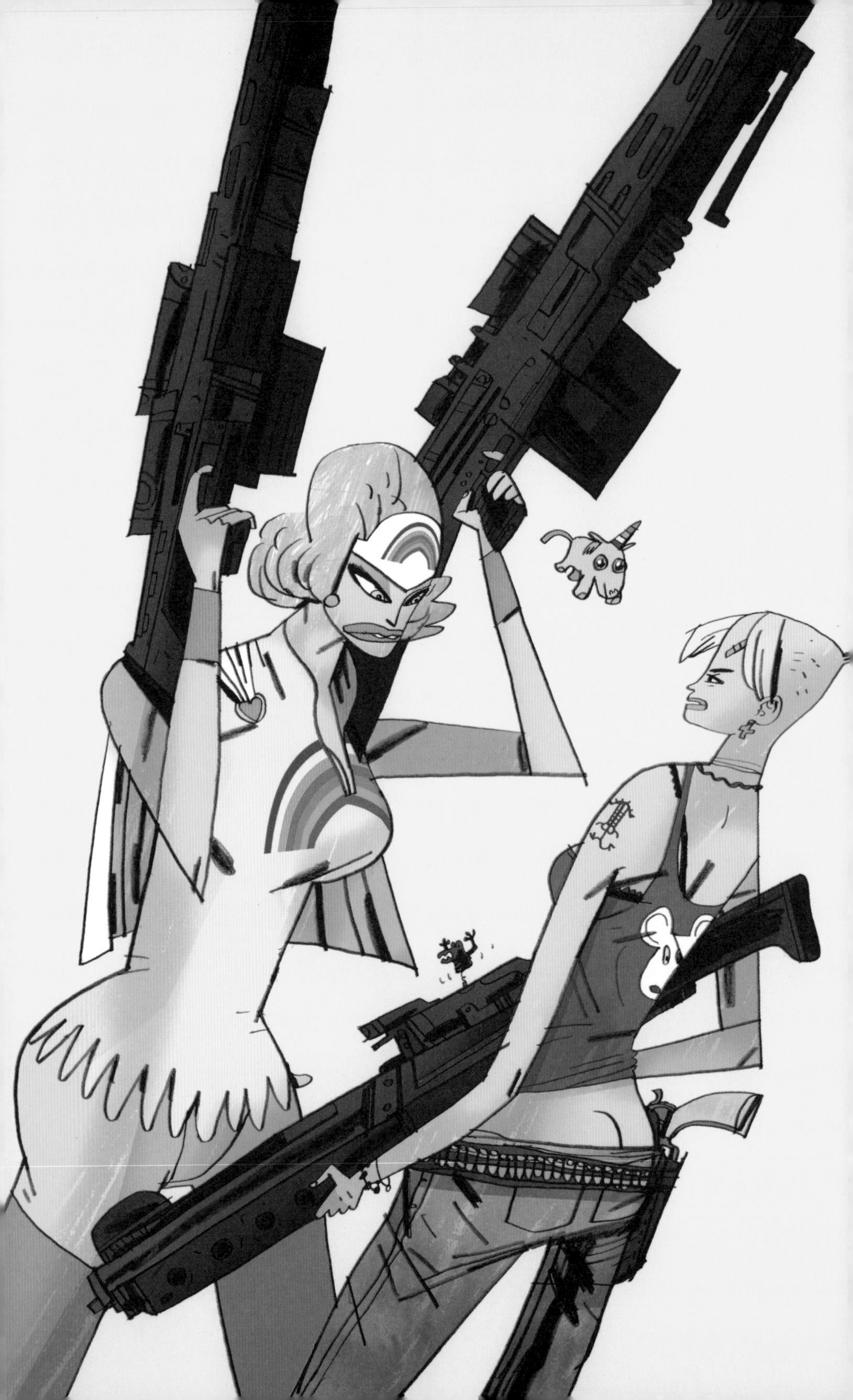

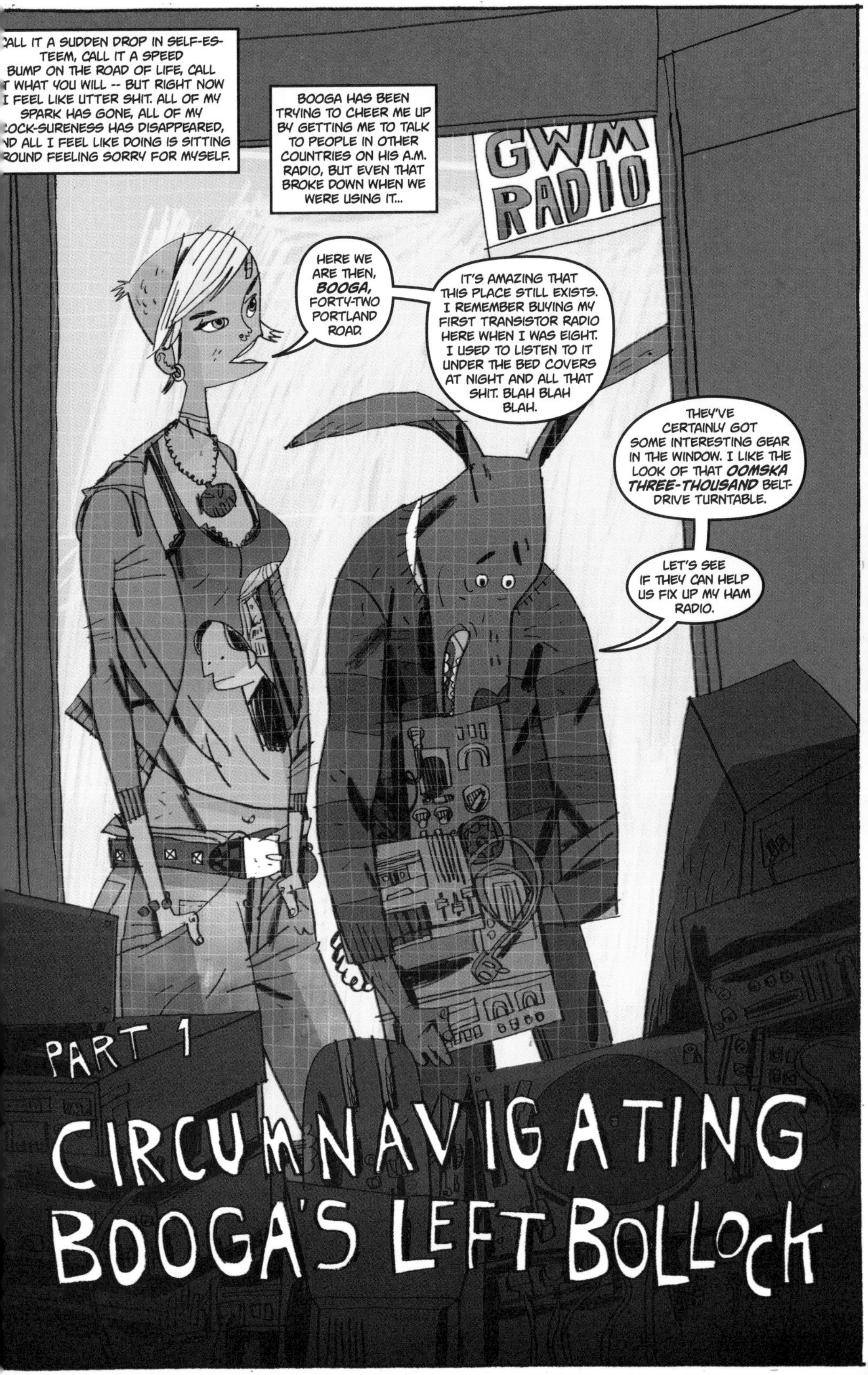
CALL IT A SUDDEN DROP IN SELF-ESTEEM, CALL IT A SPEED BUMP ON THE ROAD OF LIFE, CALL IT WHAT YOU WILL -- BUT RIGHT NOW I FEEL LIKE UTTER SHIT. ALL OF MY SPARK HAS GONE, ALL OF MY COCK-SURENESS HAS DISAPPEARED, AND ALL I FEEL LIKE DOING IS SITTING AROUND FEELING SORRY FOR MYSELF.
BOOGA HAS BEEN TRYING TO CHEER ME UP BY GETTING ME TO TALK TO PEOPLE IN OTHER COUNTRIES ON HIS A.M. RADIO, BUT EVEN THAT BROKE DOWN WHEN WE WERE USING IT...
GWM RADIO
HERE WE ARE THEN, BOOGA, FORTY-TWO PORTLAND ROAD.
IT'S AMAZING THAT THIS PLACE STILL EXISTS. I REMEMBER BUYING MY FIRST TRANSISTOR RADIO HERE WHEN I WAS EIGHT. I USED TO LISTEN TO IT UNDER THE BED COVERS AT NIGHT AND ALL THAT SHIT. BLAH BLAH BLAH.
THEY'VE CERTAINLY GOT SOME INTERESTING GEAR IN THE WINDOW. I LIKE THE LOOK OF THAT OOMSKA THREE-THOUSAND BELT-DRIVE TURNTABLE.
LET'S SEE IF THEY CAN HELP US FIX UP MY HAM RADIO.
PART 1
CIRCUMNAVIGATING BOOGA'S LEFT BOLLOCK

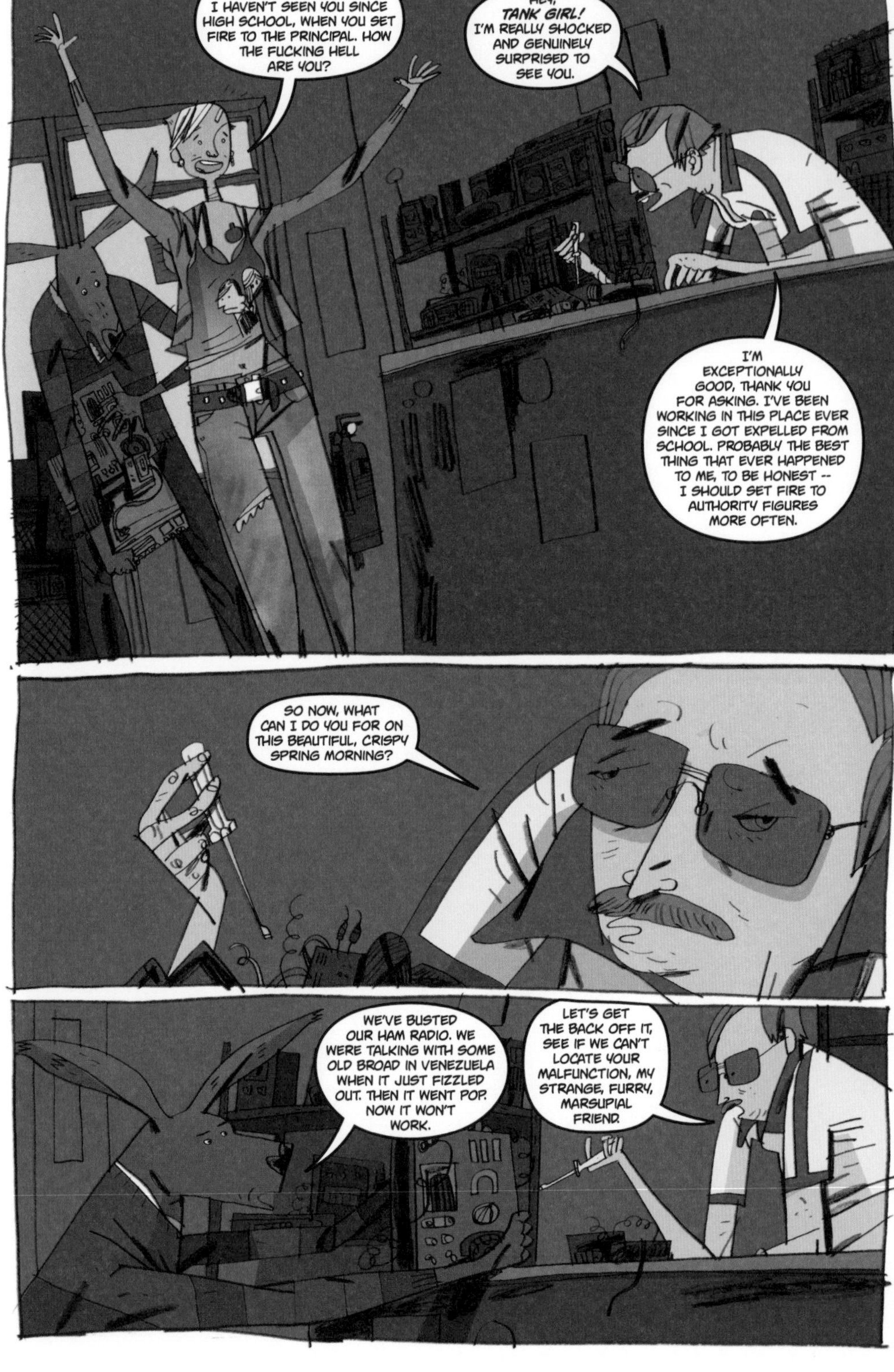
BLOW ME, IT'S CROFTY. MY OLD MATE! I HAVEN'T SEEN YOU SINCE HIGH SCHOOL, WHEN YOU SET FIRE TO THE PRINCIPAL. HOW THE FUCKING HELL ARE YOU?
HEY, TANK GIRL! I'M REALLY SHOCKED AND GENUINELY SURPRISED TO SEE YOU.
I'M EXCEPTIONALLY GOOD, THANK YOU FOR ASKING. I'VE BEEN WORKING IN THIS PLACE EVER SINCE I GOT EXPELLED FROM SCHOOL. PROBABLY THE BEST THING THAT EVER HAPPENED TO ME, TO BE HONEST -- I SHOULD SET FIRE TO AUTHORITY FIGURES MORE OFTEN.
SO NOW, WHAT CAN I DO YOU FOR ON THIS BEAUTIFUL, CRISPY SPRING MORNING?
WE'VE BUSTED OUR HAM RADIO. WE WERE TALKING WITH SOME OLD BROAD IN VENEZUELA WHEN IT JUST FIZZLED OUT. THEN IT WENT POP. NOW IT WON'T WORK.
LET'S GET THE BACK OFF IT, SEE IF WE CAN'T LOCATE YOUR MALFUNCTION, MY STRANGE, FURRY, MARSUPIAL FRIEND.

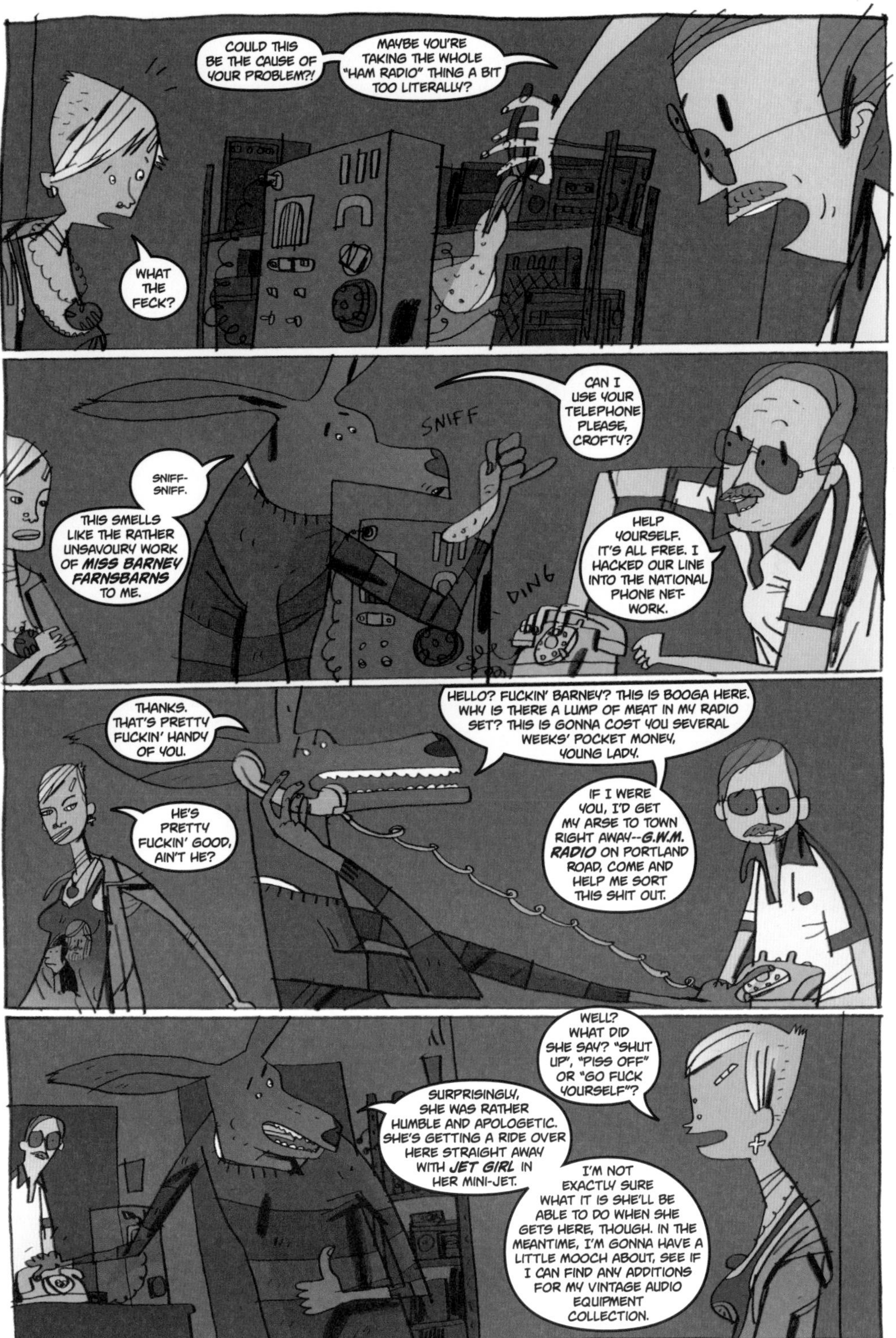
COULD THIS BE THE CAUSE OF YOUR PROBLEM?!
MAYBE YOU'RE TAKING THE WHOLE "HAM RADIO" THING A BIT TOO LITERALLY?
WHAT THE FECK?
SNIFF
CAN I USE YOUR TELEPHONE PLEASE, CROFTY?
SNIFF-SNIFF.
THIS SMELLS LIKE THE RATHER UNSAVOURY WORK OF MISS BARNEY FARNSBARNS TO ME.
HELP YOURSELF. IT'S ALL FREE. I HACKED OUR LINE INTO THE NATIONAL PHONE NET-WORK.
DING
THANKS. THAT'S PRETTY FUCKIN' HANDY OF YOU.
HELLO? FUCKIN' BARNEY? THIS IS BOOGA HERE. WHY IS THERE A LUMP OF MEAT IN MY RADIO SET? THIS IS GONNA COST YOU SEVERAL WEEKS' POCKET MONEY, YOUNG LADY.
HE'S PRETTY FUCKIN' GOOD, AIN'T HE?
IF I WERE YOU, I'D GET MY ARSE TO TOWN RIGHT AWAY--G.W.M. RADIO ON PORTLAND ROAD, COME AND HELP ME SORT THIS SHIT OUT.
WELL? WHAT DID SHE SAY? "SHUT UP", "PISS OFF" OR "GO FUCK YOURSELF"?
SURPRISINGLY, SHE WAS RATHER HUMBLE AND APOLOGETIC. SHE'S GETTING A RIDE OVER HERE STRAIGHT AWAY WITH JET GIRL IN HER MINI-JET.
I'M NOT EXACTLY SURE WHAT IT IS SHE'LL BE ABLE TO DO WHEN SHE GETS HERE, THOUGH. IN THE MEANTIME, I'M GONNA HAVE A LITTLE MOOCH ABOUT, SEE IF I CAN FIND ANY ADDITIONS FOR MY VINTAGE AUDIO EQUIPMENT COLLECTION.

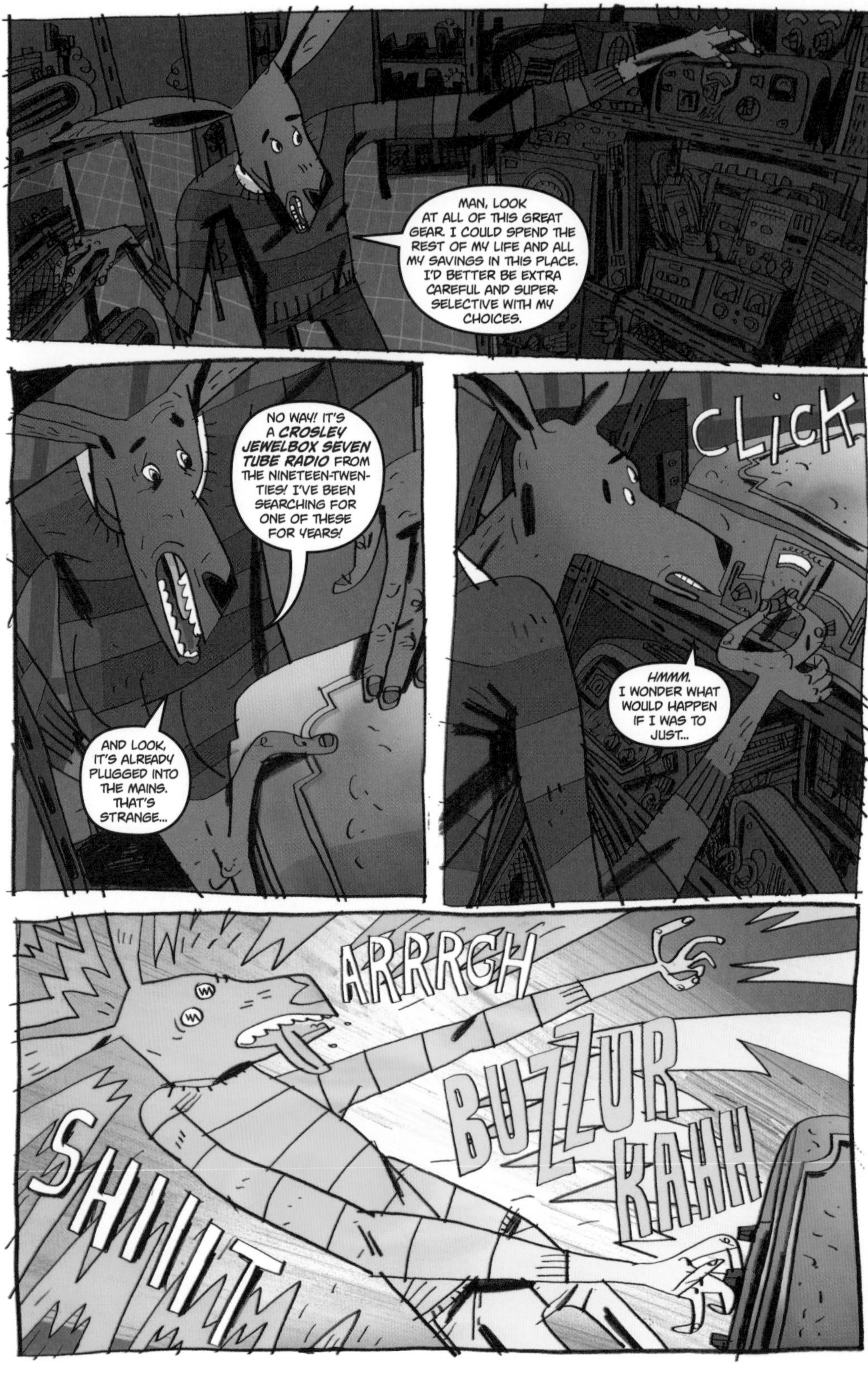
MAN, LOOK AT ALL OF THIS GREAT GEAR. I COULD SPEND THE REST OF MY LIFE AND ALL MY SAVINGS IN THIS PLACE. I'D BETTER BE EXTRA CAREFUL AND SUPER-SELECTIVE WITH MY CHOICES.
NO WAY! IT'S A CROSLEY JEWELBOX SEVEN TUBE RADIO FROM THE NINETEEN-TWENTIES! I'VE BEEN SEARCHING FOR ONE OF THESE FOR YEARS!
AND LOOK, IT'S ALREADY PLUGGED INTO THE MAINS. THAT'S STRANGE...
CLICK
HMMM. I WONDER WHAT WOULD HAPPEN IF I WAS TO JUST...
ARRRGH
BUZZUR
KAHH
SHIIIT

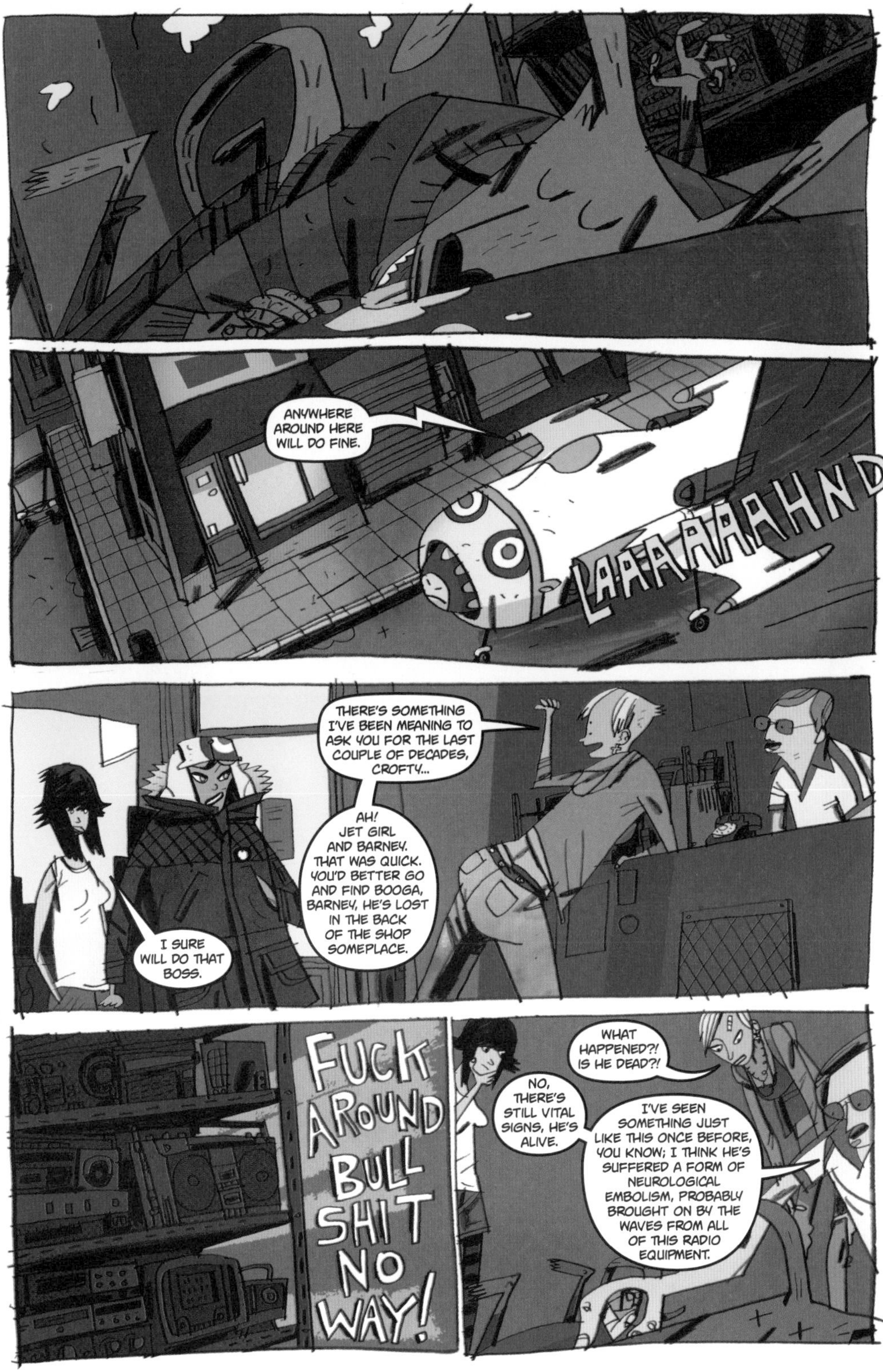
ANYWHERE AROUND HERE WILL DO FINE.
LAAAAAAHND
THERE'S SOMETHING I'VE BEEN MEANING TO ASK YOU FOR THE LAST COUPLE OF DECADES, CROFTY...
AH! JET GIRL AND BARNEY. THAT WAS QUICK. YOU'D BETTER GO AND FIND BOOGA, BARNEY, HE'S LOST IN THE BACK OF THE SHOP SOMEPLACE.
I SURE WILL DO THAT BOSS.
FUCK AROUND BULL SHIT NO WAY!
WHAT HAPPENED?! IS HE DEAD?!
NO, THERE'S STILL VITAL SIGNS, HE'S ALIVE.
I'VE SEEN SOMETHING JUST LIKE THIS ONCE BEFORE, YOU KNOW; I THINK HE'S SUFFERED A FORM OF NEUROLOGICAL EMBOLISM, PROBABLY BROUGHT ON BY THE WAVES FROM ALL OF THIS RADIO EQUIPMENT.

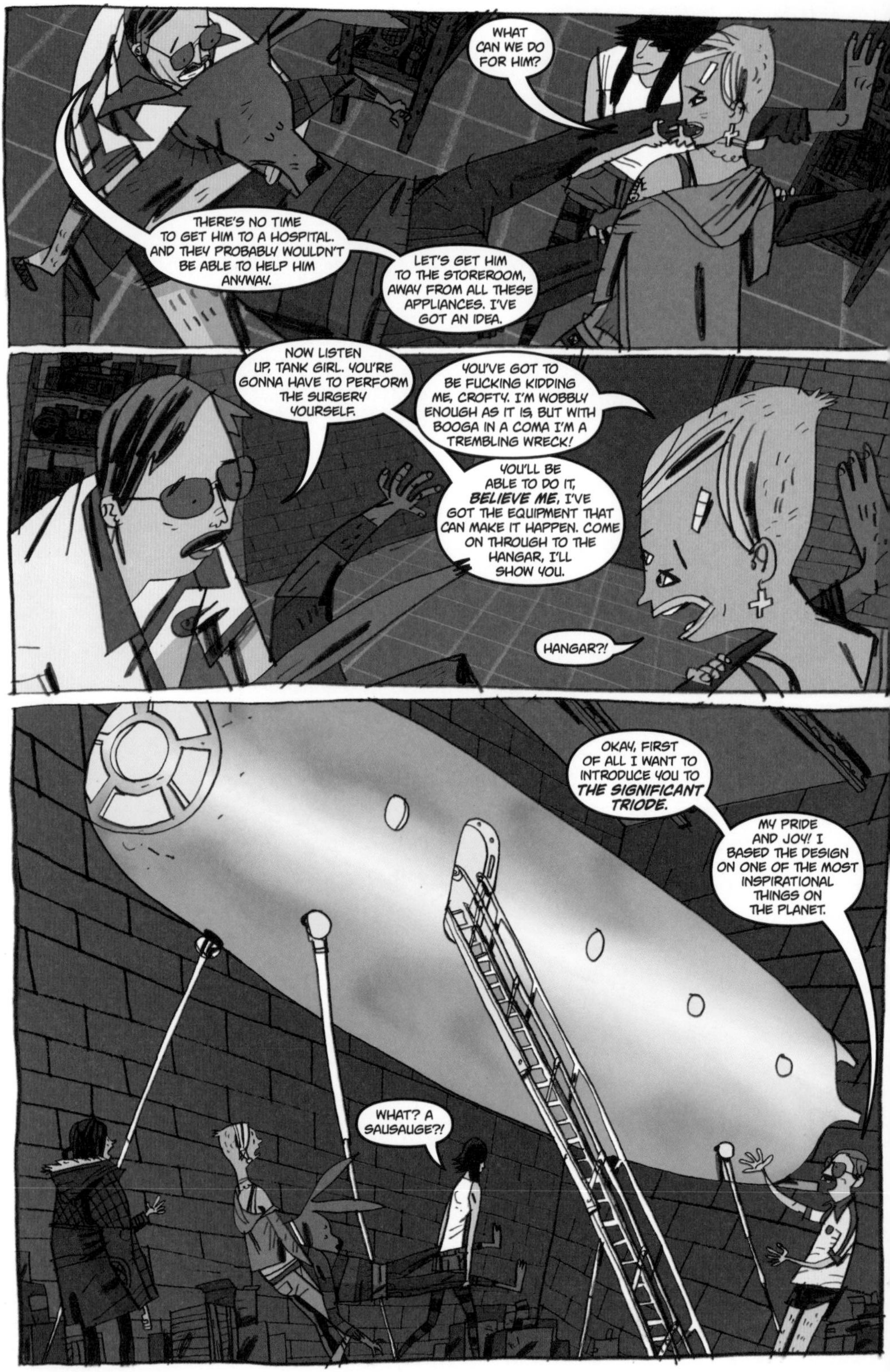
WHAT CAN WE DO FOR HIM?
THERE'S NO TIME TO GET HIM TO A HOSPITAL. AND THEY PROBABLY WOULDN'T BE ABLE TO HELP HIM ANYWAY.
LET'S GET HIM TO THE STOREROOM, AWAY FROM ALL THESE APPLIANCES. I'VE GOT AN IDEA.
NOW LISTEN UP, TANK GIRL. YOU'RE GONNA HAVE TO PERFORM THE SURGERY YOURSELF.
YOU'VE GOT TO BE FUCKING KIDDING ME, CROFTY. I'M WOBBLY ENOUGH AS IT IS, BUT WITH BOOGA IN A COMA I'M A TREMBLING WRECK!
YOU'LL BE ABLE TO DO IT, ***BELIEVE ME***, I'VE GOT THE EQUIPMENT THAT CAN MAKE IT HAPPEN. COME ON THROUGH TO THE HANGAR, I'LL SHOW YOU.
HANGAR?!
OKAY, FIRST OF ALL I WANT TO INTRODUCE YOU TO ***THE SIGNIFICANT TRIODE.***
MY PRIDE AND JOY! I BASED THE DESIGN ON ONE OF THE MOST INSPIRATIONAL THINGS ON THE PLANET.
WHAT? A SAUSAUGE?!

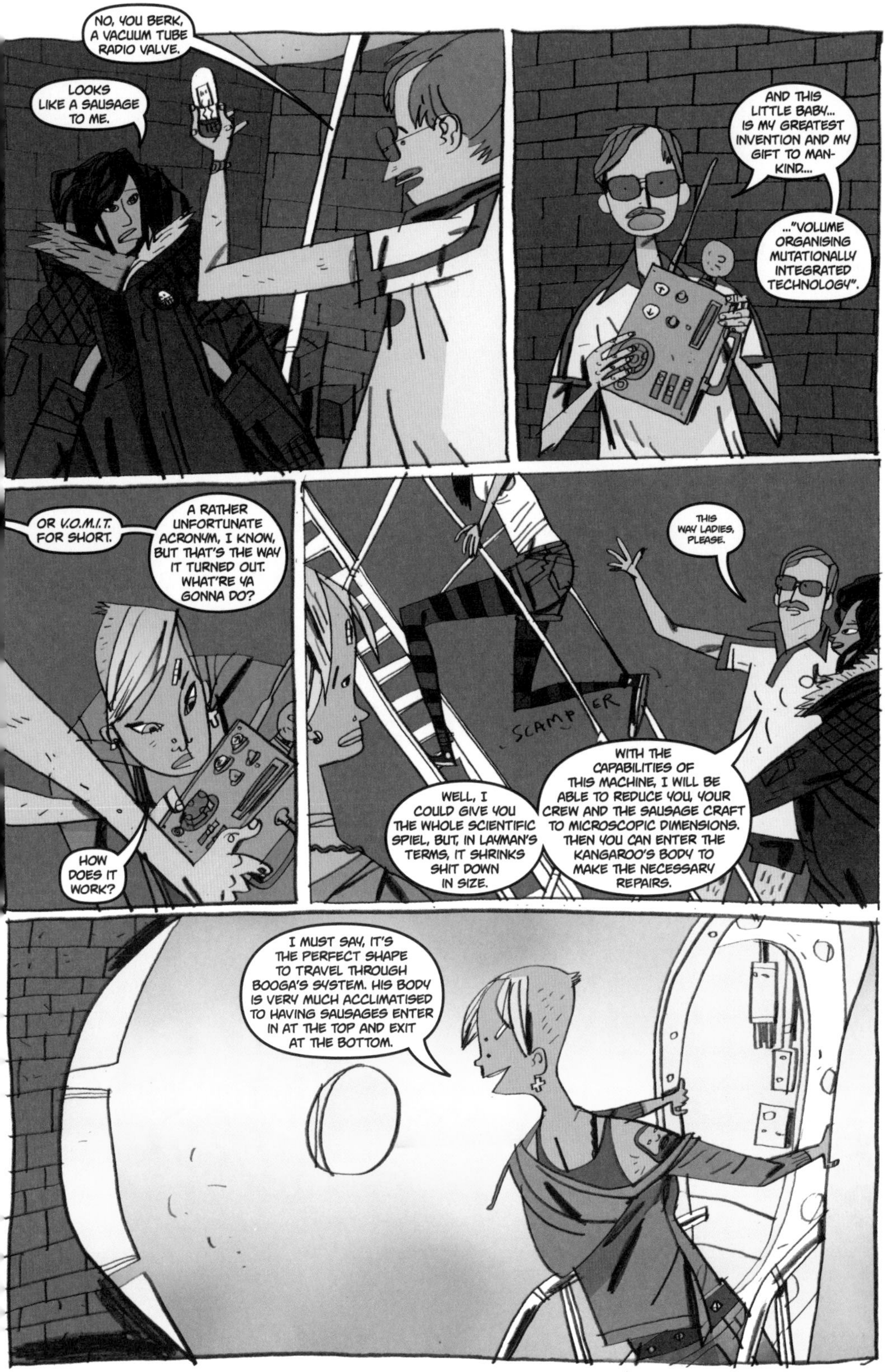
LOOKS LIKE A SAUSAGE TO ME.
NO, YOU BERK, A VACUUM TUBE RADIO VALVE.
AND THIS LITTLE BABY... IS MY GREATEST INVENTION AND MY GIFT TO MAN-KIND...
..."VOLUME ORGANISING MUTATIONALLY INTEGRATED TECHNOLOGY".
OR V.O.M.I.T. FOR SHORT.
A RATHER UNFORTUNATE ACRONYM, I KNOW, BUT THAT'S THE WAY IT TURNED OUT. WHAT'RE YA GONNA DO?
HOW DOES IT WORK?
WELL, I COULD GIVE YOU THE WHOLE SCIENTIFIC SPIEL, BUT, IN LAYMAN'S TERMS, IT SHRINKS SHIT DOWN IN SIZE.
SCAMPER
THIS WAY LADIES, PLEASE.
WITH THE CAPABILITIES OF THIS MACHINE, I WILL BE ABLE TO REDUCE YOU, YOUR CREW AND THE SAUSAGE CRAFT TO MICROSCOPIC DIMENSIONS. THEN YOU CAN ENTER THE KANGAROO'S BODY TO MAKE THE NECESSARY REPAIRS.
I MUST SAY, IT'S THE PERFECT SHAPE TO TRAVEL THROUGH BOOGA'S SYSTEM. HIS BODY IS VERY MUCH ACCLIMATISED TO HAVING SAUSAGES ENTER IN AT THE TOP AND EXIT AT THE BOTTOM.

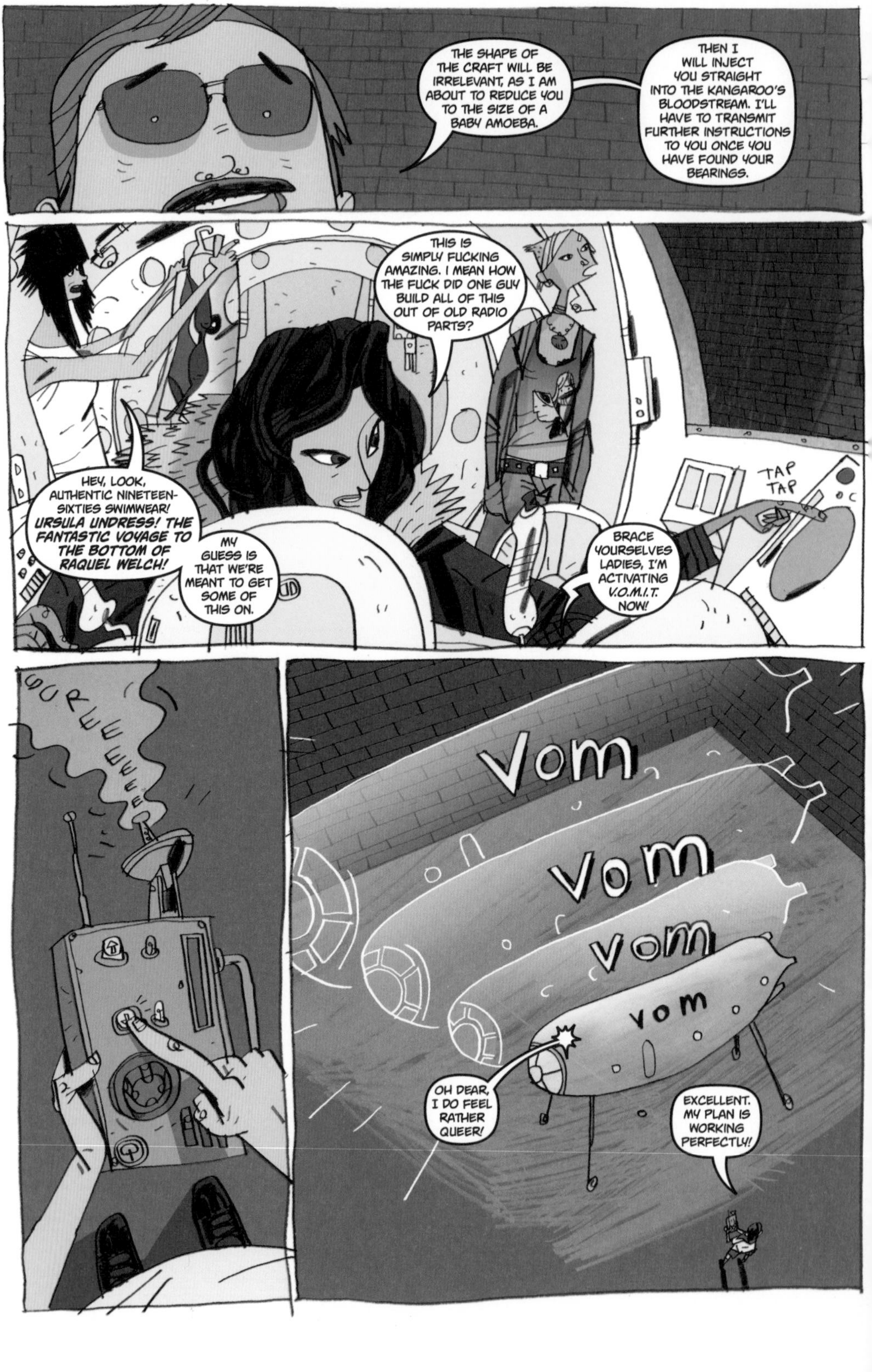

THE SHAPE OF THE CRAFT WILL BE IRRELEVANT, AS I AM ABOUT TO REDUCE YOU TO THE SIZE OF A BABY AMOEBA.
THEN I WILL INJECT YOU STRAIGHT INTO THE KANGAROO'S BLOODSTREAM. I'LL HAVE TO TRANSMIT FURTHER INSTRUCTIONS TO YOU ONCE YOU HAVE FOUND YOUR BEARINGS.
THIS IS SIMPLY FUCKING AMAZING. I MEAN HOW THE FUCK DID ONE GUY BUILD ALL OF THIS OUT OF OLD RADIO PARTS?
HEY, LOOK, AUTHENTIC NINETEEN-SIXTIES SWIMWEAR! URSULA UNDRESS! THE FANTASTIC VOYAGE TO THE BOTTOM OF RAQUEL WELCH!
MY GUESS IS THAT WE'RE MEANT TO GET SOME OF THIS ON.
BRACE YOURSELVES LADIES, I'M ACTIVATING V.O.M.I.T. NOW!
TAP TAP
GUREEEEEEEE
Vom
Vom
vom
vom
OH DEAR, I DO FEEL RATHER QUEER!
EXCELLENT. MY PLAN IS WORKING PERFECTLY!

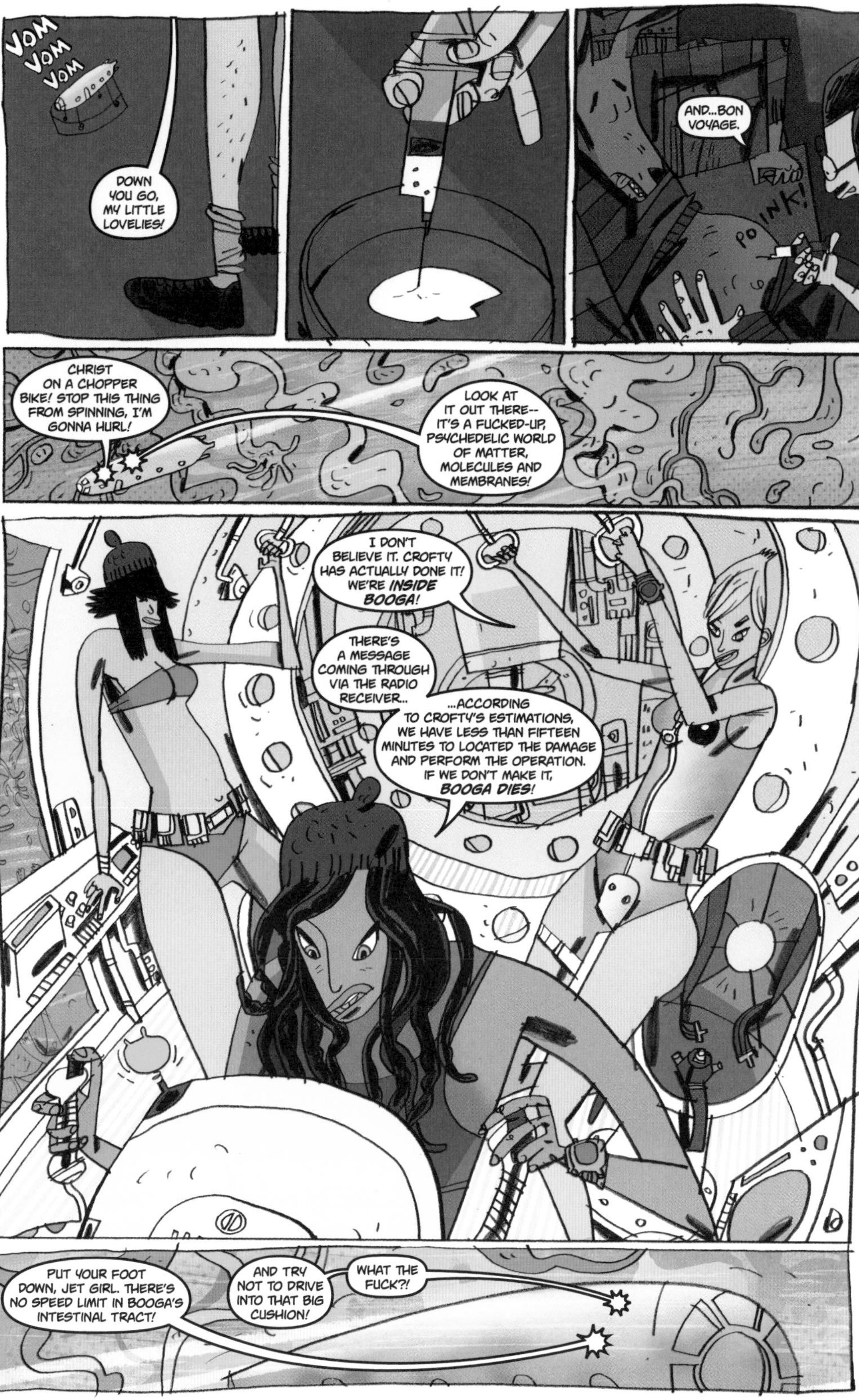
VOM VOM VOM
DOWN YOU GO, MY LITTLE LOVELIES!
AND...BON VOYAGE.
POINK!
CHRIST ON A CHOPPER BIKE! STOP THIS THING FROM SPINNING, I'M GONNA HURL!
LOOK AT IT OUT THERE-- IT'S A FUCKED-UP, PSYCHEDELIC WORLD OF MATTER, MOLECULES AND MEMBRANES!
I DON'T BELIEVE IT. CROFTY HAS ACTUALLY DONE IT! WE'RE *INSIDE BOOGA*!
THERE'S A MESSAGE COMING THROUGH VIA THE RADIO RECEIVER...
...ACCORDING TO CROFTY'S ESTIMATIONS, WE HAVE LESS THAN FIFTEEN MINUTES TO LOCATED THE DAMAGE AND PERFORM THE OPERATION. IF WE DON'T MAKE IT, *BOOGA DIES*!
PUT YOUR FOOT DOWN, JET GIRL. THERE'S NO SPEED LIMIT IN BOOGA'S INTESTINAL TRACT!
AND TRY NOT TO DRIVE INTO THAT BIG CUSHION!
WHAT THE FUCK?!

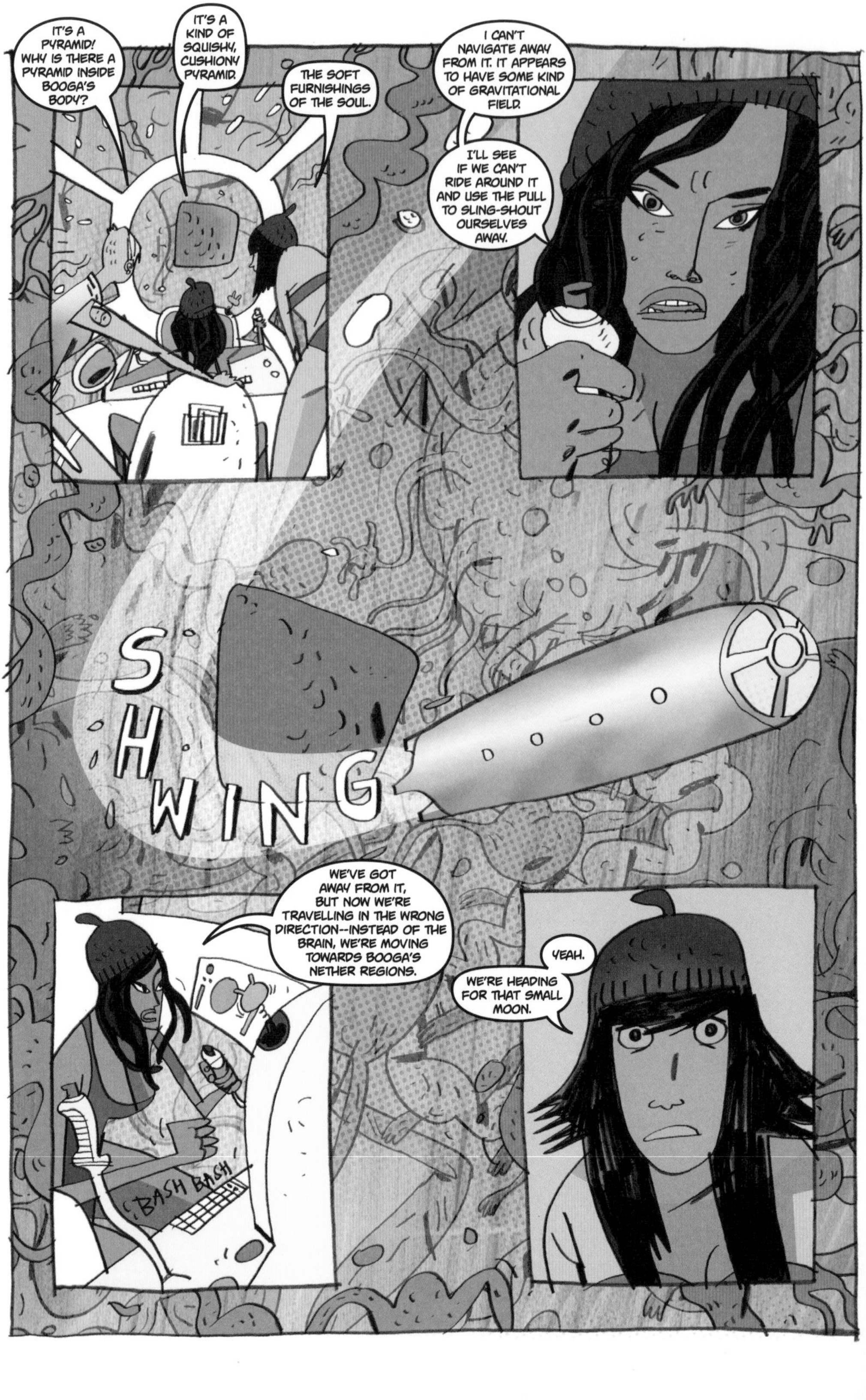
IT'S A PYRAMID! WHY IS THERE A PYRAMID INSIDE BOOGA'S BODY?
IT'S A KIND OF SQUISHY, CUSHIONY PYRAMID.
THE SOFT FURNISHINGS OF THE SOUL.
I CAN'T NAVIGATE AWAY FROM IT. IT APPEARS TO HAVE SOME KIND OF GRAVITATIONAL FIELD.
I'LL SEE IF WE CAN'T RIDE AROUND IT AND USE THE PULL TO SLING-SHOUT OURSELVES AWAY.
SHWING
WE'VE GOT AWAY FROM IT, BUT NOW WE'RE TRAVELLING IN THE WRONG DIRECTION--INSTEAD OF THE BRAIN, WE'RE MOVING TOWARDS BOOGA'S NETHER REGIONS.
BASH BASH
YEAH.
WE'RE HEADING FOR THAT SMALL MOON.

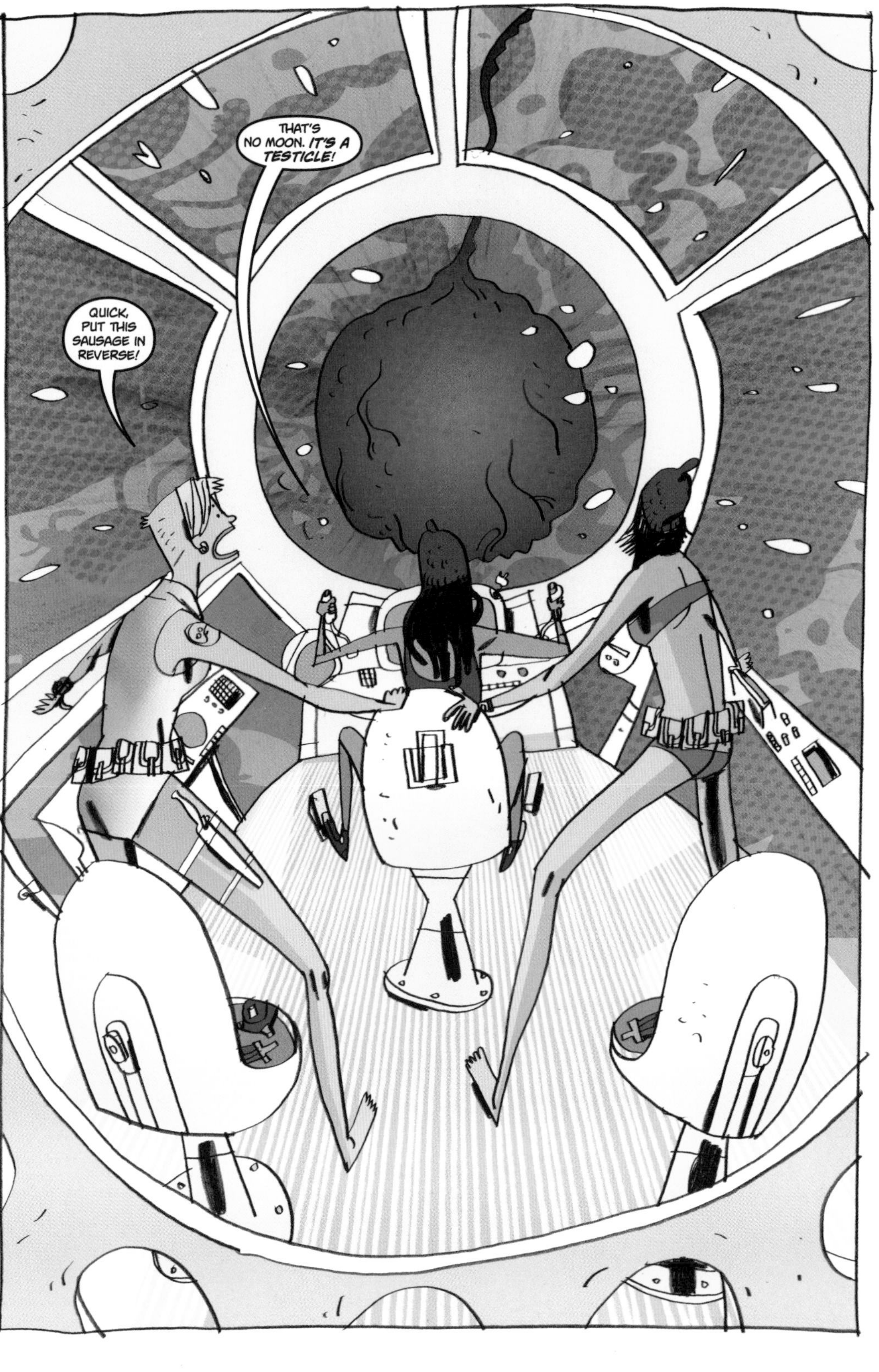
THAT'S NO MOON. IT'S A TESTICLE!
QUICK, PUT THIS SAUSAGE IN REVERSE!

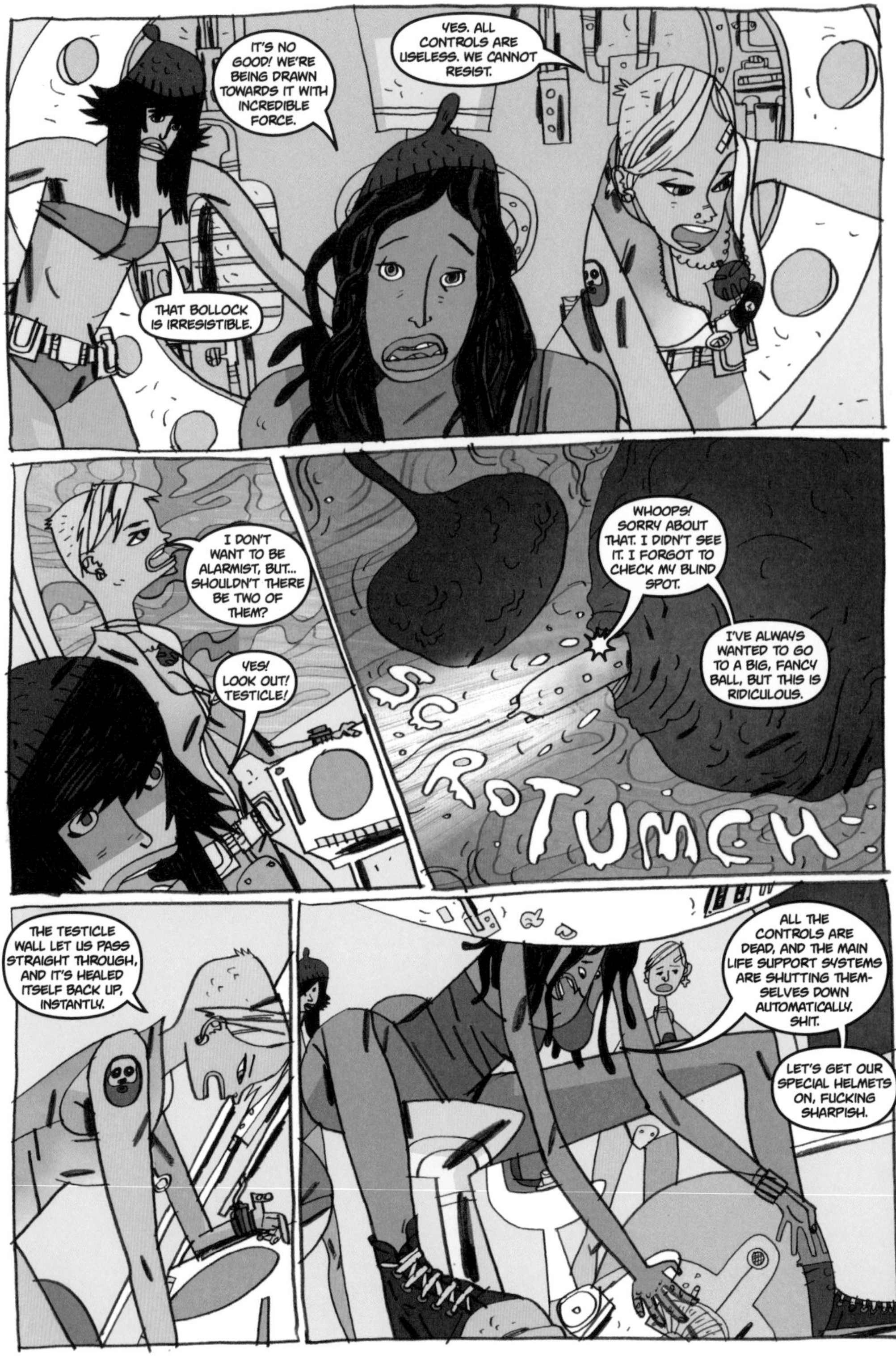
IT'S NO GOOD! WE'RE BEING DRAWN TOWARDS IT WITH INCREDIBLE FORCE.
YES. ALL CONTROLS ARE USELESS. WE CANNOT RESIST.
THAT BOLLOCK IS IRRESISTIBLE.
I DON'T WANT TO BE ALARMIST, BUT... SHOULDN'T THERE BE TWO OF THEM?
YES! LOOK OUT! TESTICLE!
WHOOPS! SORRY ABOUT THAT. I DIDN'T SEE IT. I FORGOT TO CHECK MY BLIND SPOT.
I'VE ALWAYS WANTED TO GO TO A BIG, FANCY BALL, BUT THIS IS RIDICULOUS.
SCROTUMCH
THE TESTICLE WALL LET US PASS STRAIGHT THROUGH, AND IT'S HEALED ITSELF BACK UP, INSTANTLY.
ALL THE CONTROLS ARE DEAD, AND THE MAIN LIFE SUPPORT SYSTEMS ARE SHUTTING THEMSELVES DOWN AUTOMATICALLY. SHIT.
LET'S GET OUR SPECIAL HELMETS ON, FUCKING SHARPISH.

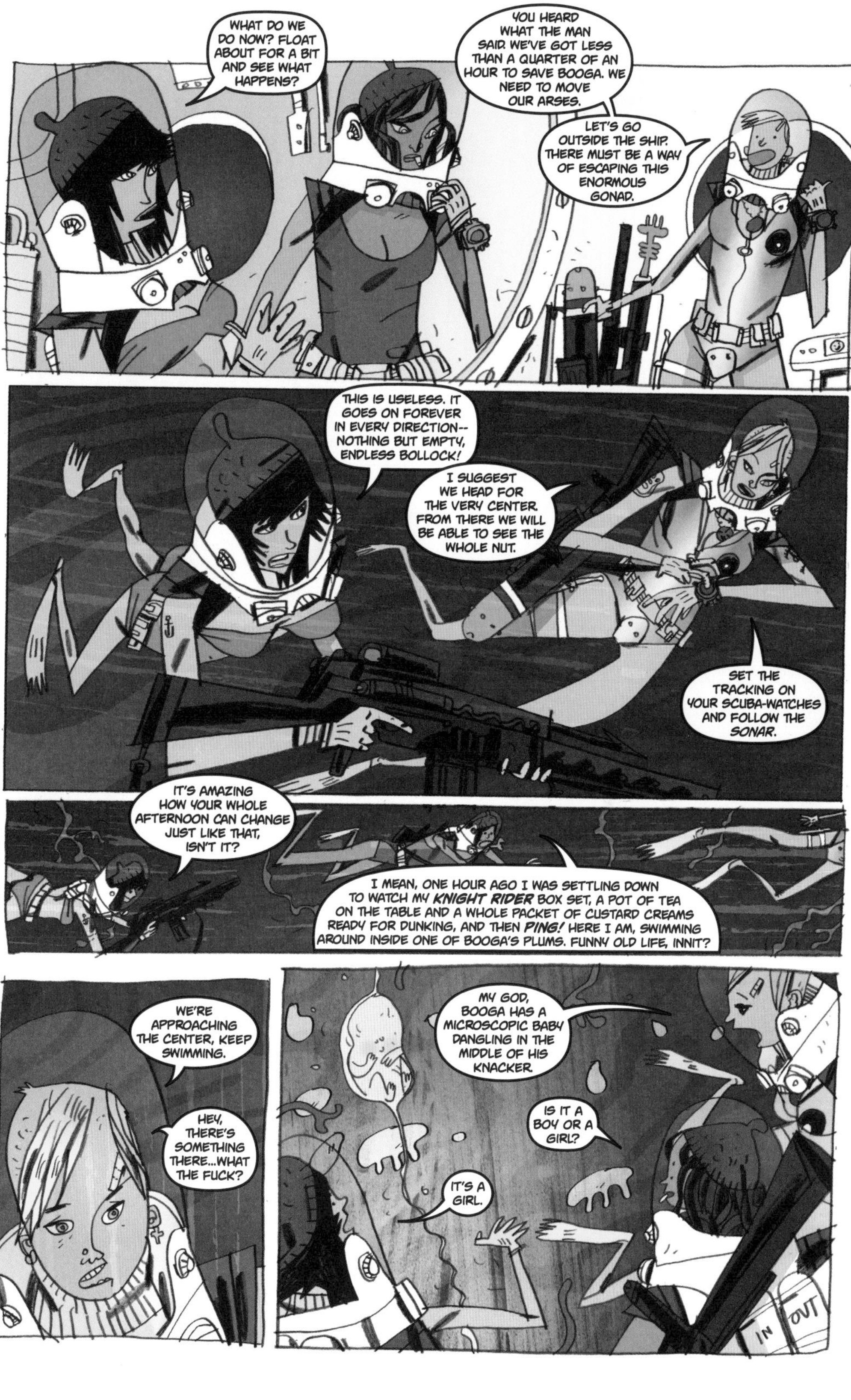
WHAT DO WE DO NOW? FLOAT ABOUT FOR A BIT AND SEE WHAT HAPPENS?
YOU HEARD WHAT THE MAN SAID. WE'VE GOT LESS THAN A QUARTER OF AN HOUR TO SAVE BOOGA. WE NEED TO MOVE OUR ARSES.
LET'S GO OUTSIDE THE SHIP. THERE MUST BE A WAY OF ESCAPING THIS ENORMOUS GONAD.
THIS IS USELESS. IT GOES ON FOREVER IN EVERY DIRECTION-- NOTHING BUT EMPTY, ENDLESS BOLLOCK!
I SUGGEST WE HEAD FOR THE VERY CENTER. FROM THERE WE WILL BE ABLE TO SEE THE WHOLE NUT.
SET THE TRACKING ON YOUR SCUBA-WATCHES AND FOLLOW THE *SONAR*.
IT'S AMAZING HOW YOUR WHOLE AFTERNOON CAN CHANGE JUST LIKE THAT, ISN'T IT?
I MEAN, ONE HOUR AGO I WAS SETTLING DOWN TO WATCH MY ***KNIGHT RIDER*** BOX SET, A POT OF TEA ON THE TABLE AND A WHOLE PACKET OF CUSTARD CREAMS READY FOR DUNKING, AND THEN ***PING!*** HERE I AM, SWIMMING AROUND INSIDE ONE OF BOOGA'S PLUMS. FUNNY OLD LIFE, INNIT?
WE'RE APPROACHING THE CENTER, KEEP SWIMMING.
HEY, THERE'S SOMETHING THERE...WHAT THE FUCK?
MY GOD, BOOGA HAS A MICROSCOPIC BABY DANGLING IN THE MIDDLE OF HIS KNACKER.
IS IT A BOY OR A GIRL?
IT'S A GIRL.
IN
OUT

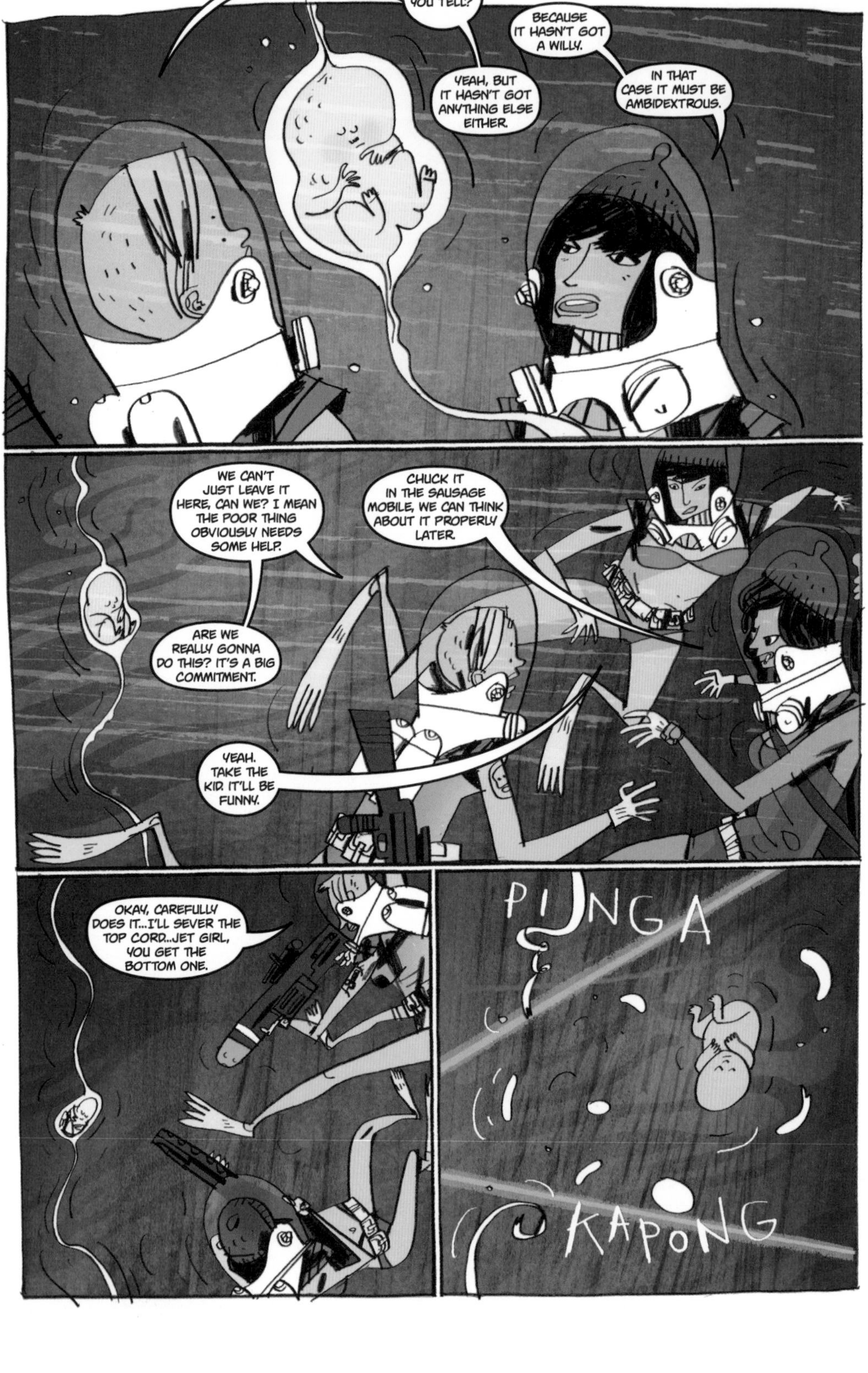
HOW CAN YOU TELL?
BECAUSE IT HASN'T GOT A WILLY.
YEAH, BUT IT HASN'T GOT ANYTHING ELSE EITHER.
IN THAT CASE IT MUST BE AMBIDEXTROUS.
WE CAN'T JUST LEAVE IT HERE, CAN WE? I MEAN THE POOR THING OBVIOUSLY NEEDS SOME HELP.
ARE WE REALLY GONNA DO THIS? IT'S A BIG COMMITMENT.
CHUCK IT IN THE SAUSAGE MOBILE, WE CAN THINK ABOUT IT PROPERLY LATER.
YEAH. TAKE THE KID. IT'LL BE FUNNY.
OKAY, CAREFULLY DOES IT...I'LL SEVER THE TOP CORD...JET GIRL, YOU GET THE BOTTOM ONE.
PINGA
KAPONG

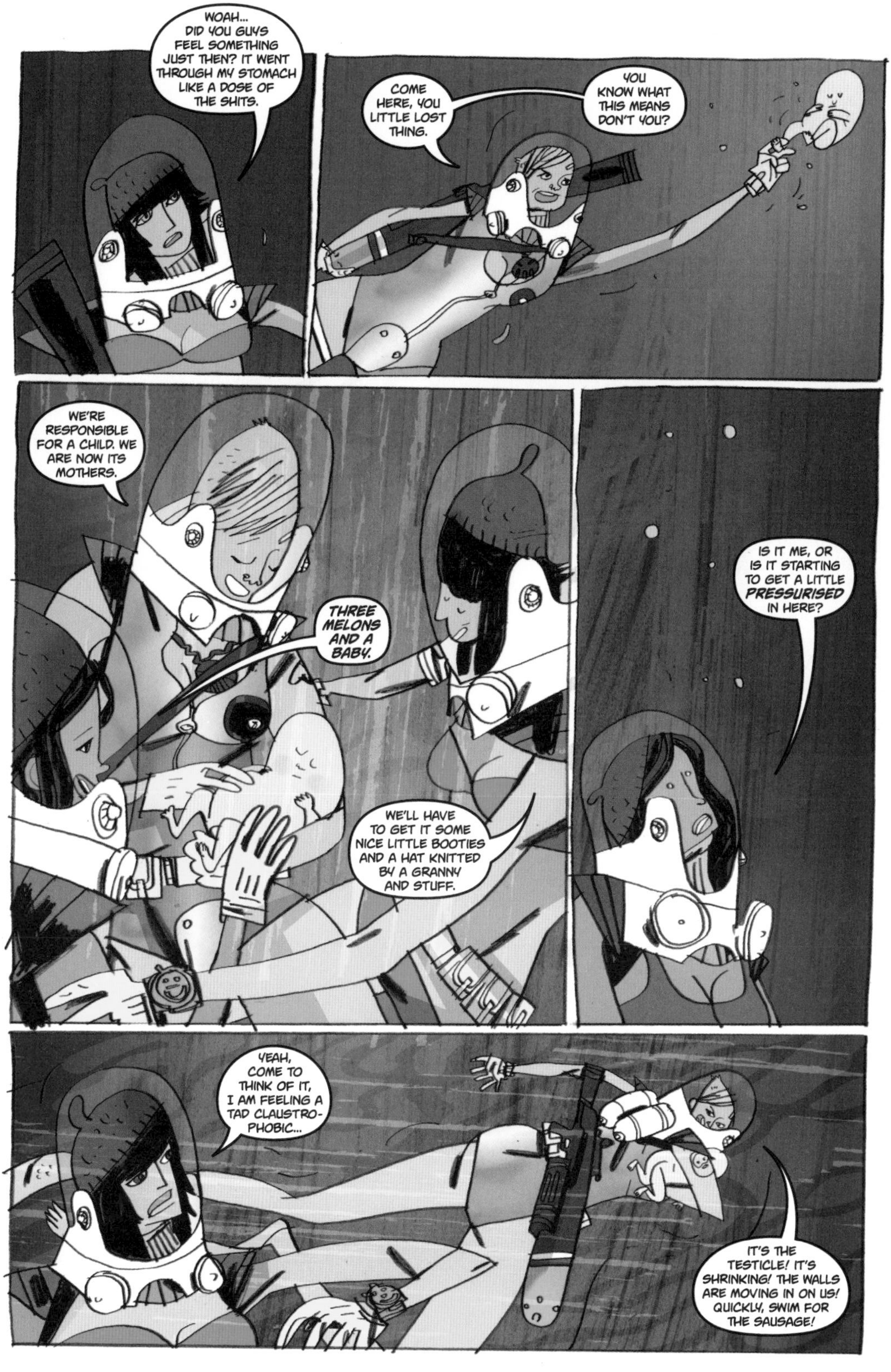
WOAH... DID YOU GUYS FEEL SOMETHING JUST THEN? IT WENT THROUGH MY STOMACH LIKE A DOSE OF THE SHITS.
COME HERE, YOU LITTLE LOST THING.
YOU KNOW WHAT THIS MEANS DON'T YOU?
WE'RE RESPONSIBLE FOR A CHILD. WE ARE NOW ITS MOTHERS.
THREE MELONS AND A BABY.
WE'LL HAVE TO GET IT SOME NICE LITTLE BOOTIES AND A HAT KNITTED BY A GRANNY AND STUFF.
IS IT ME, OR IS IT STARTING TO GET A LITTLE PRESSURISED IN HERE?
YEAH, COME TO THINK OF IT, I AM FEELING A TAD CLAUSTRO-PHOBIC...
IT'S THE TESTICLE! IT'S SHRINKING! THE WALLS ARE MOVING IN ON US! QUICKLY, SWIM FOR THE SAUSAGE!

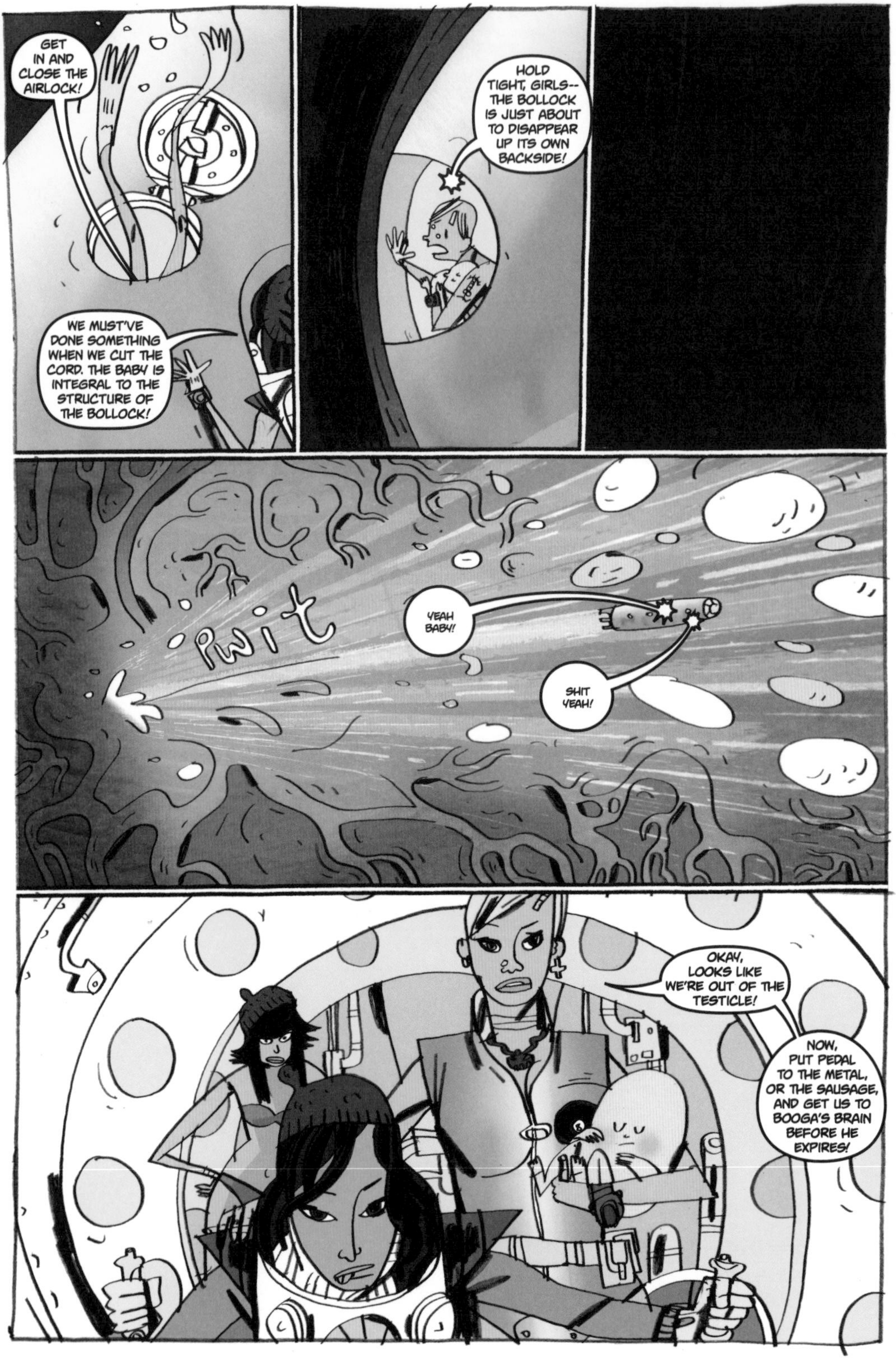
GET IN AND CLOSE THE AIRLOCK!
WE MUST'VE DONE SOMETHING WHEN WE CUT THE CORD. THE BABY IS INTEGRAL TO THE STRUCTURE OF THE BOLLOCK!
HOLD TIGHT, GIRLS-- THE BOLLOCK IS JUST ABOUT TO DISAPPEAR UP ITS OWN BACKSIDE!
PWIT
YEAH BABY!
SHIT YEAH!
OKAY, LOOKS LIKE WE'RE OUT OF THE TESTICLE!
NOW, PUT PEDAL TO THE METAL, OR THE SAUSAGE, AND GET US TO BOOGA'S BRAIN BEFORE HE EXPIRES!

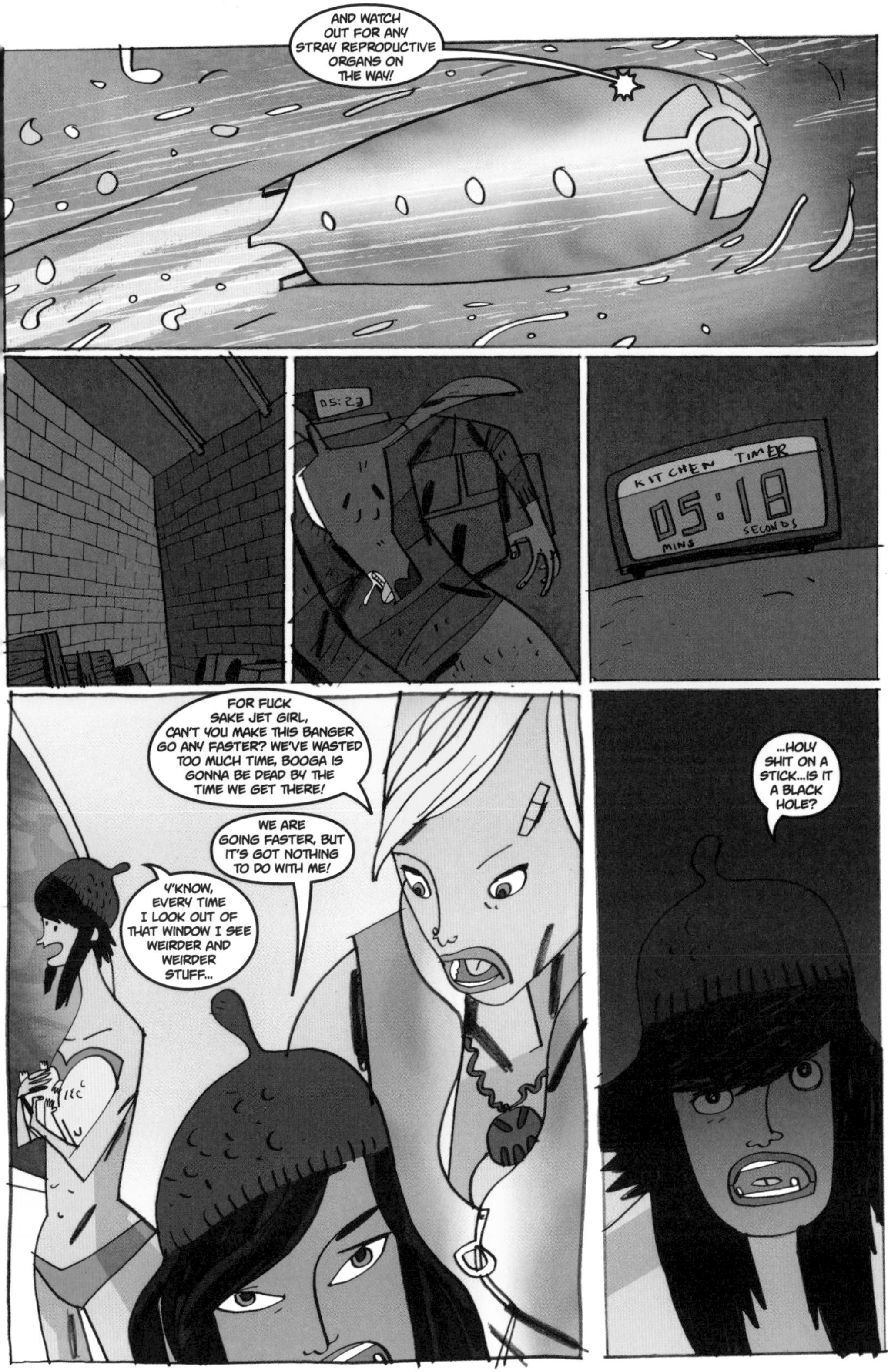

AND WATCH OUT FOR ANY STRAY REPRODUCTIVE ORGANS ON THE WAY!
05:23
KITCHEN TIMER
05:18
MINS
SECONDS
FOR FUCK SAKE JET GIRL, CAN'T YOU MAKE THIS BANGER GO ANY FASTER? WE'VE WASTED TOO MUCH TIME, BOOGA IS GONNA BE DEAD BY THE TIME WE GET THERE!
WE ARE GOING FASTER, BUT IT'S GOT NOTHING TO DO WITH ME!
Y'KNOW, EVERY TIME I LOOK OUT OF THAT WINDOW I SEE WEIRDER AND WEIRDER STUFF...
...HOLY SHIT ON A STICK...IS IT A BLACK HOLE?

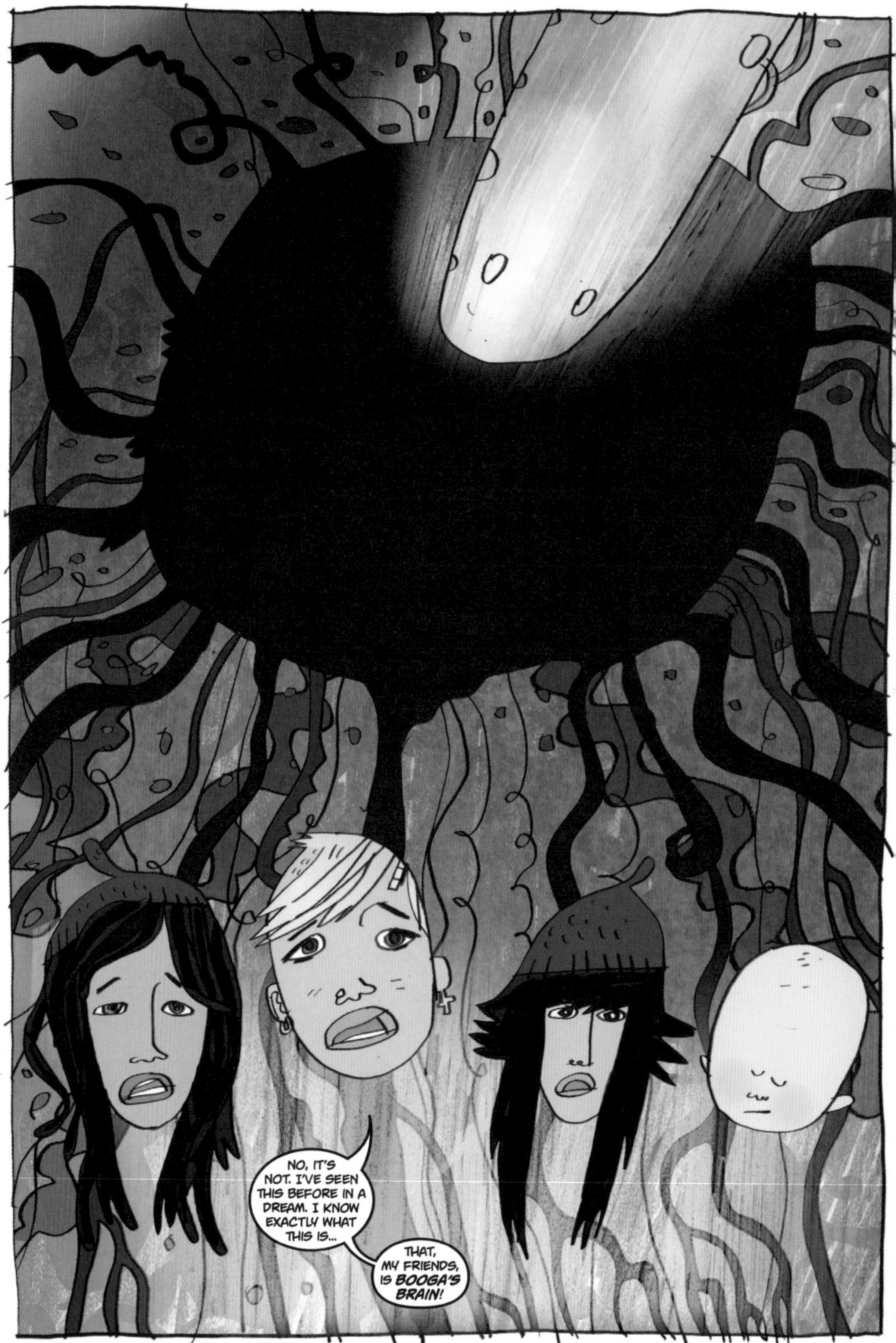
NO, IT'S NOT. I'VE SEEN THIS BEFORE IN A DREAM. I KNOW EXACTLY WHAT THIS IS...
THAT, MY FRIENDS, IS BOOGA'S BRAIN!

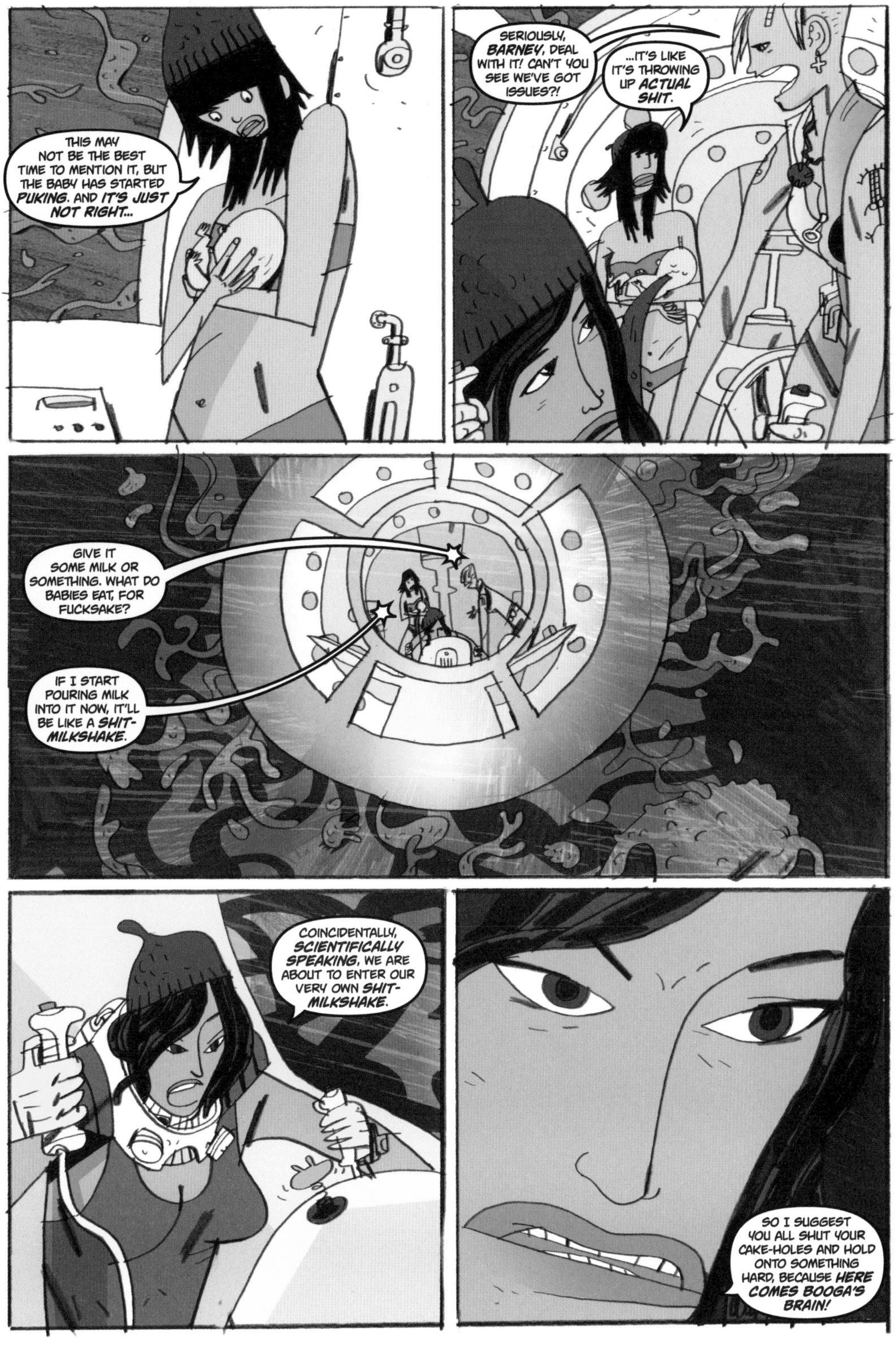
THIS MAY NOT BE THE BEST TIME TO MENTION IT, BUT THE BABY HAS STARTED PUKING. AND IT'S JUST NOT RIGHT...
SERIOUSLY, BARNEY, DEAL WITH IT! CAN'T YOU SEE WE'VE GOT ISSUES?!
...IT'S LIKE IT'S THROWING UP ACTUAL SHIT.
GIVE IT SOME MILK OR SOMETHING. WHAT DO BABIES EAT, FOR FUCKSAKE?
IF I START POURING MILK INTO IT NOW, IT'LL BE LIKE A SHIT-MILKSHAKE.
COINCIDENTALLY, SCIENTIFICALLY SPEAKING, WE ARE ABOUT TO ENTER OUR VERY OWN SHIT-MILKSHAKE.
SO I SUGGEST YOU ALL SHUT YOUR CAKE-HOLES AND HOLD ONTO SOMETHING HARD, BECAUSE HERE COMES BOOGA'S BRAIN!

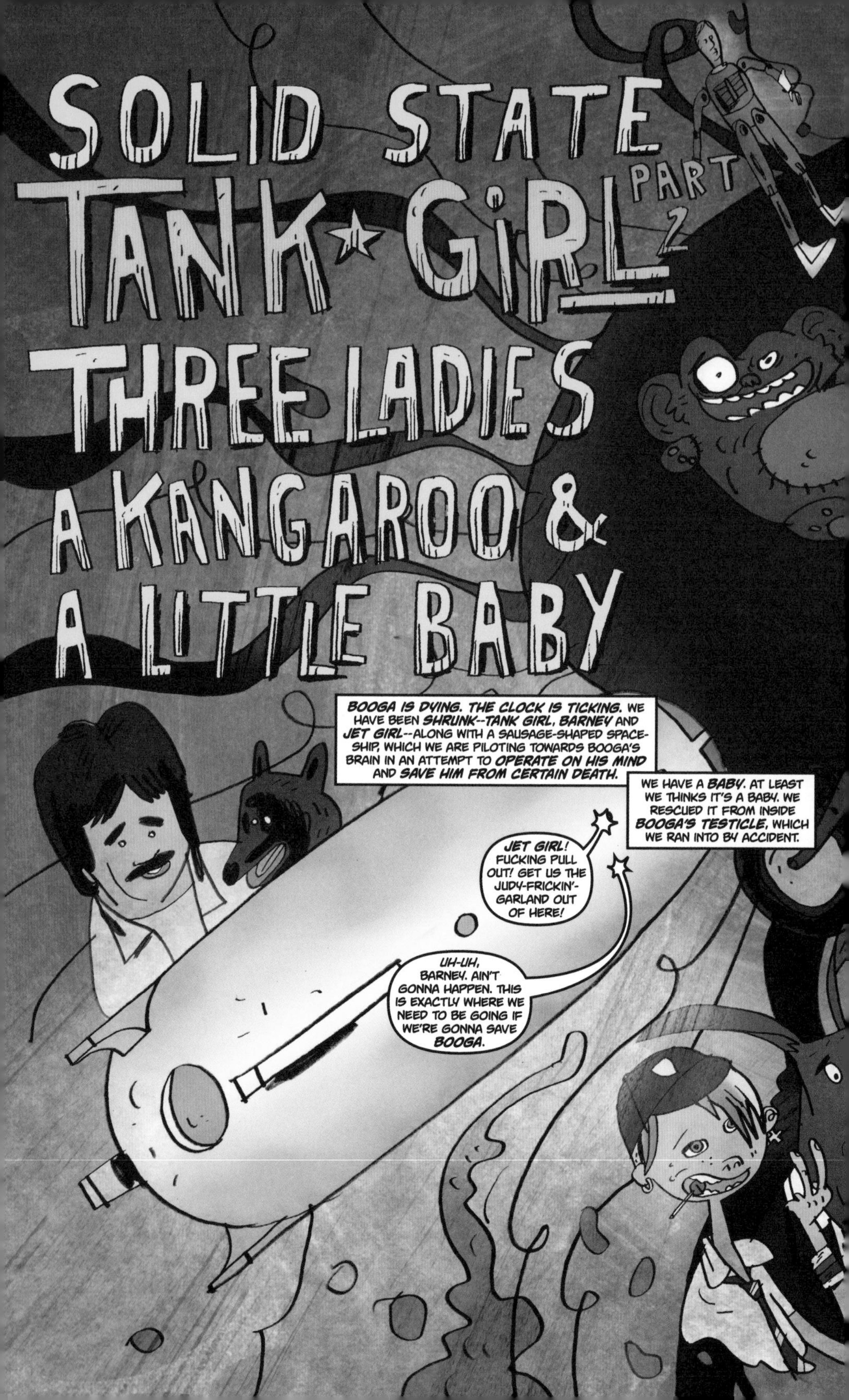
SOLID STATE
TANK GIRL PART 2
THREE LADIES A KANGAROO & A LITTLE BABY
BOOGA IS DYING. THE CLOCK IS TICKING. WE HAVE BEEN SHRUNK--TANK GIRL, BARNEY AND JET GIRL--ALONG WITH A SAUSAGE-SHAPED SPACE-SHIP, WHICH WE ARE PILOTING TOWARDS BOOGA'S BRAIN IN AN ATTEMPT TO OPERATE ON HIS MIND AND SAVE HIM FROM CERTAIN DEATH.
WE HAVE A BABY. AT LEAST WE THINKS IT'S A BABY. WE RESCUED IT FROM INSIDE BOOGA'S TESTICLE, WHICH WE RAN INTO BY ACCIDENT.
JET GIRL! FUCKING PULL OUT! GET US THE JUDY-FRICKIN'-GARLAND OUT OF HERE!
UH-UH, BARNEY. AIN'T GONNA HAPPEN. THIS IS EXACTLY WHERE WE NEED TO BE GOING IF WE'RE GONNA SAVE BOOGA.

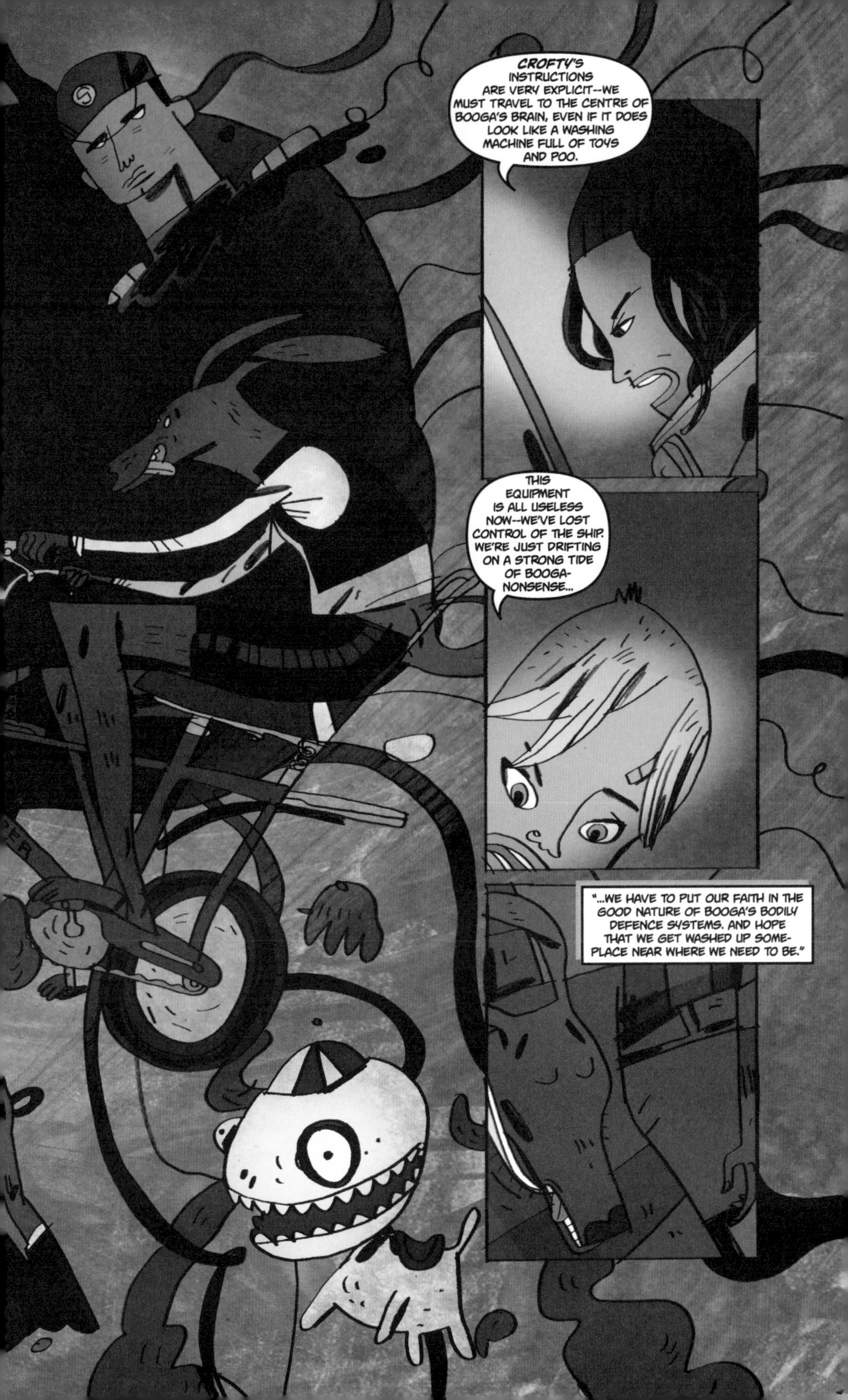
CROFTY'S INSTRUCTIONS ARE VERY EXPLICIT--WE MUST TRAVEL TO THE CENTRE OF BOOGA'S BRAIN, EVEN IF IT DOES LOOK LIKE A WASHING MACHINE FULL OF TOYS AND POO.
THIS EQUIPMENT IS ALL USELESS NOW--WE'VE LOST CONTROL OF THE SHIP. WE'RE JUST DRIFTING ON A STRONG TIDE OF BOOGA-NONSENSE...
"...WE HAVE TO PUT OUR FAITH IN THE GOOD NATURE OF BOOGA'S BODILY DEFENCE SYSTEMS. AND HOPE THAT WE GET WASHED UP SOME-PLACE NEAR WHERE WE NEED TO BE."

THAT'S NOT OUR ONLY PROBLEM--IF BOOGA EXPIRES, HIS BLOOD WILL CLOT AND HIS BODY WILL SEIZE UP. WE'LL BE STUCK LIKE SHIT IN YOUR GRIPS.

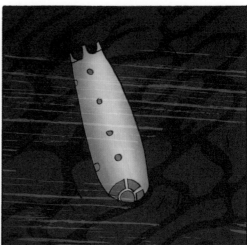

YEAH, WELL, BOOGA AIN'T GONNA DIE. I WON'T LET HIM.

CAN WE TELL IF THIS THING IS STILL MOVING?

ACCORDING TO THE MOTION DETECTORS, WE'VE STOPPED DEAD.

RIGHT. TIME TO SORT THIS SHIT OUT ONCE AND FOR ALL. I'M GOING OUT.

ALONE.

CLICK

I MAY BE SOME TIME.

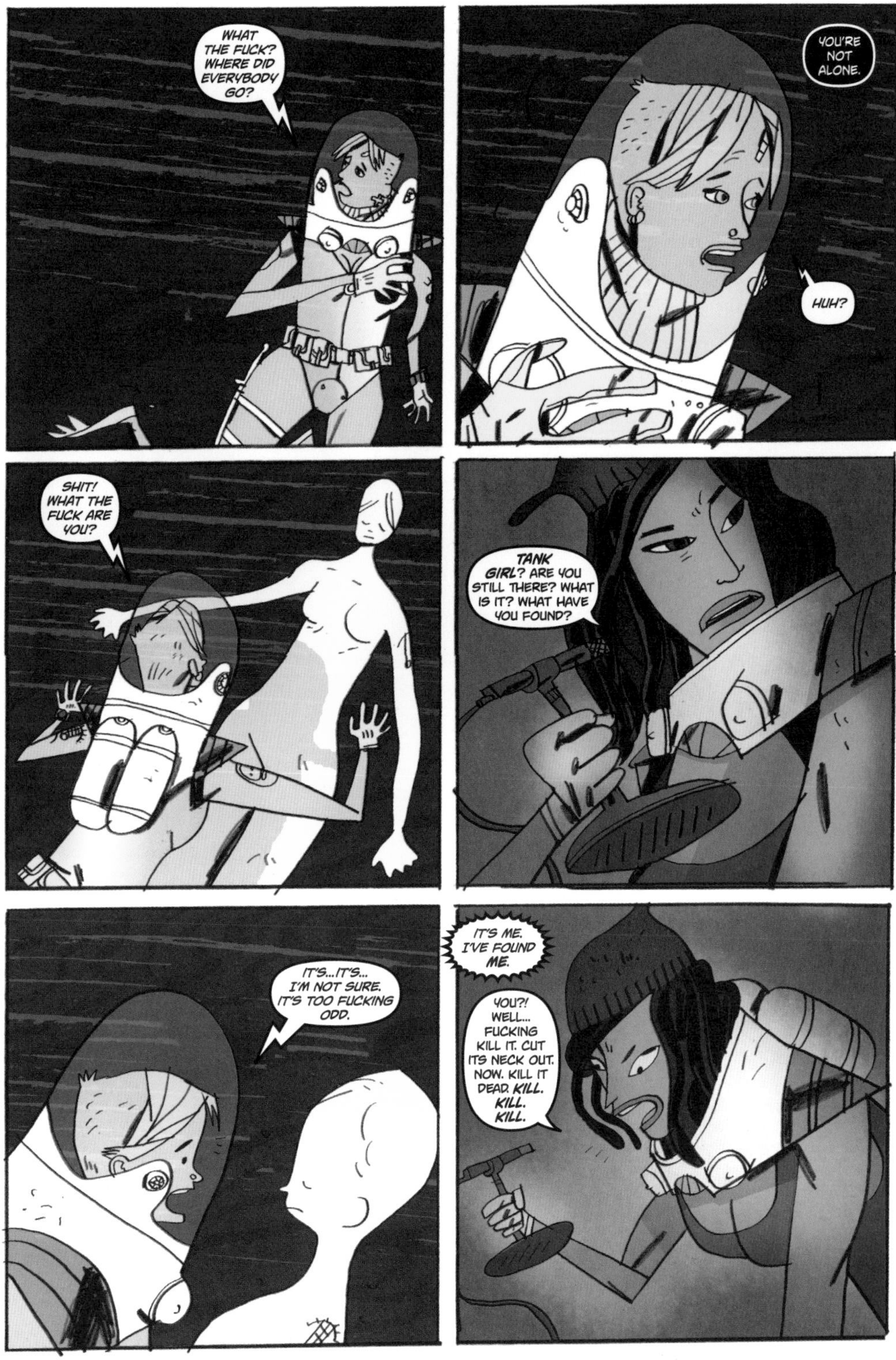
WHAT THE FUCK? WHERE DID EVERYBODY GO?
YOU'RE NOT ALONE.
HUH?
SHIT! WHAT THE FUCK ARE YOU?
TANK GIRL? ARE YOU STILL THERE? WHAT IS IT? WHAT HAVE YOU FOUND?
IT'S...IT'S... I'M NOT SURE. IT'S TOO FUCKING ODD.
IT'S ME. I'VE FOUND ME.
YOU?! WELL... FUCKING KILL IT. CUT ITS NECK OUT. NOW. KILL IT DEAD. KILL. KILL. KILL.

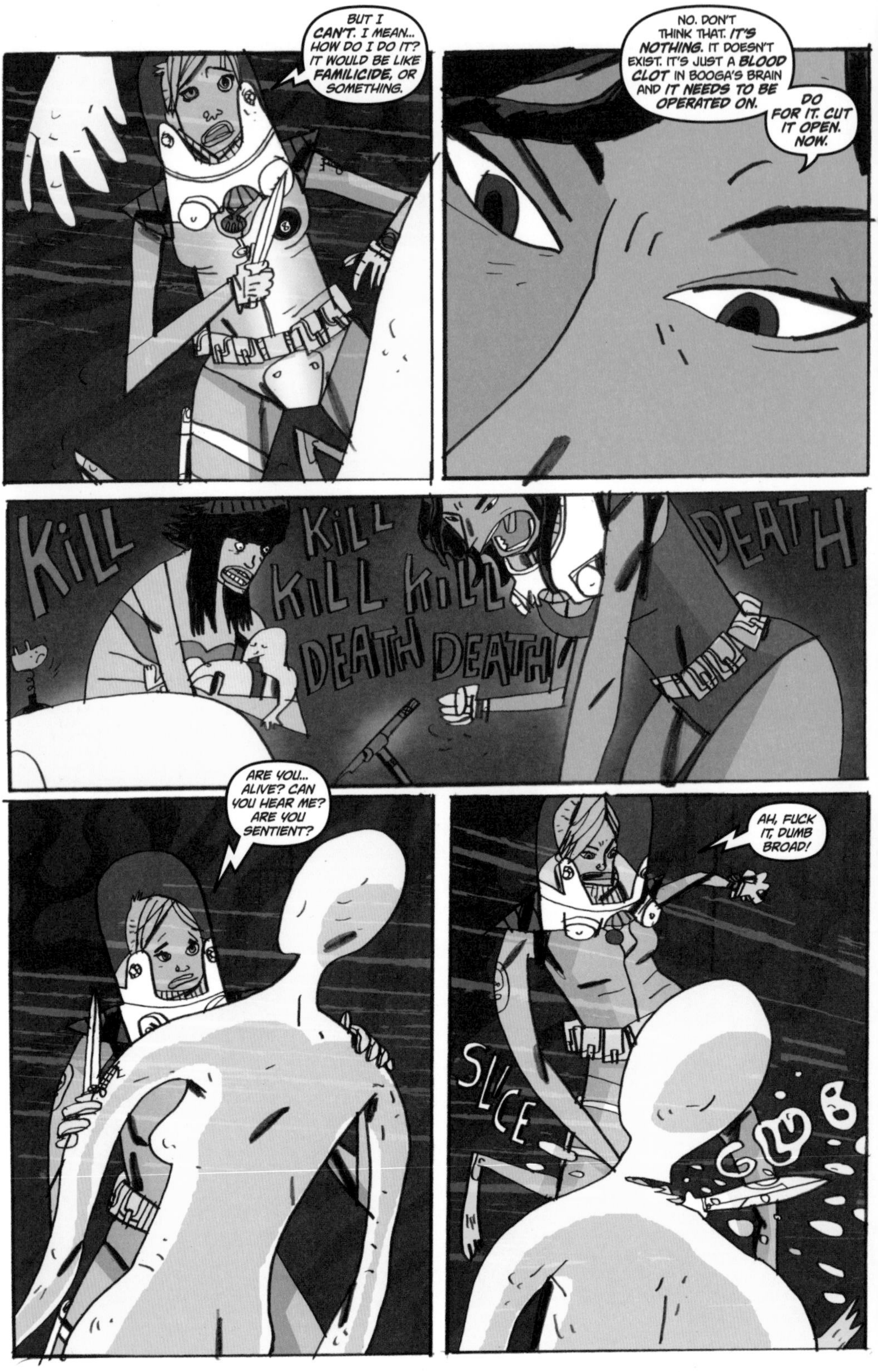
BUT I CAN'T. I MEAN... HOW DO I DO IT? IT WOULD BE LIKE FAMILICIDE, OR SOMETHING.
NO. DON'T THINK THAT. IT'S NOTHING. IT DOESN'T EXIST. IT'S JUST A BLOOD CLOT IN BOOGA'S BRAIN AND IT NEEDS TO BE OPERATED ON.
DO FOR IT. CUT IT OPEN. NOW.
KILL KILL KILL KILL DEATH DEATH DEATH
ARE YOU... ALIVE? CAN YOU HEAR ME? ARE YOU SENTIENT?
AH, FUCK IT, DUMB BROAD!
SLICE
GLUB

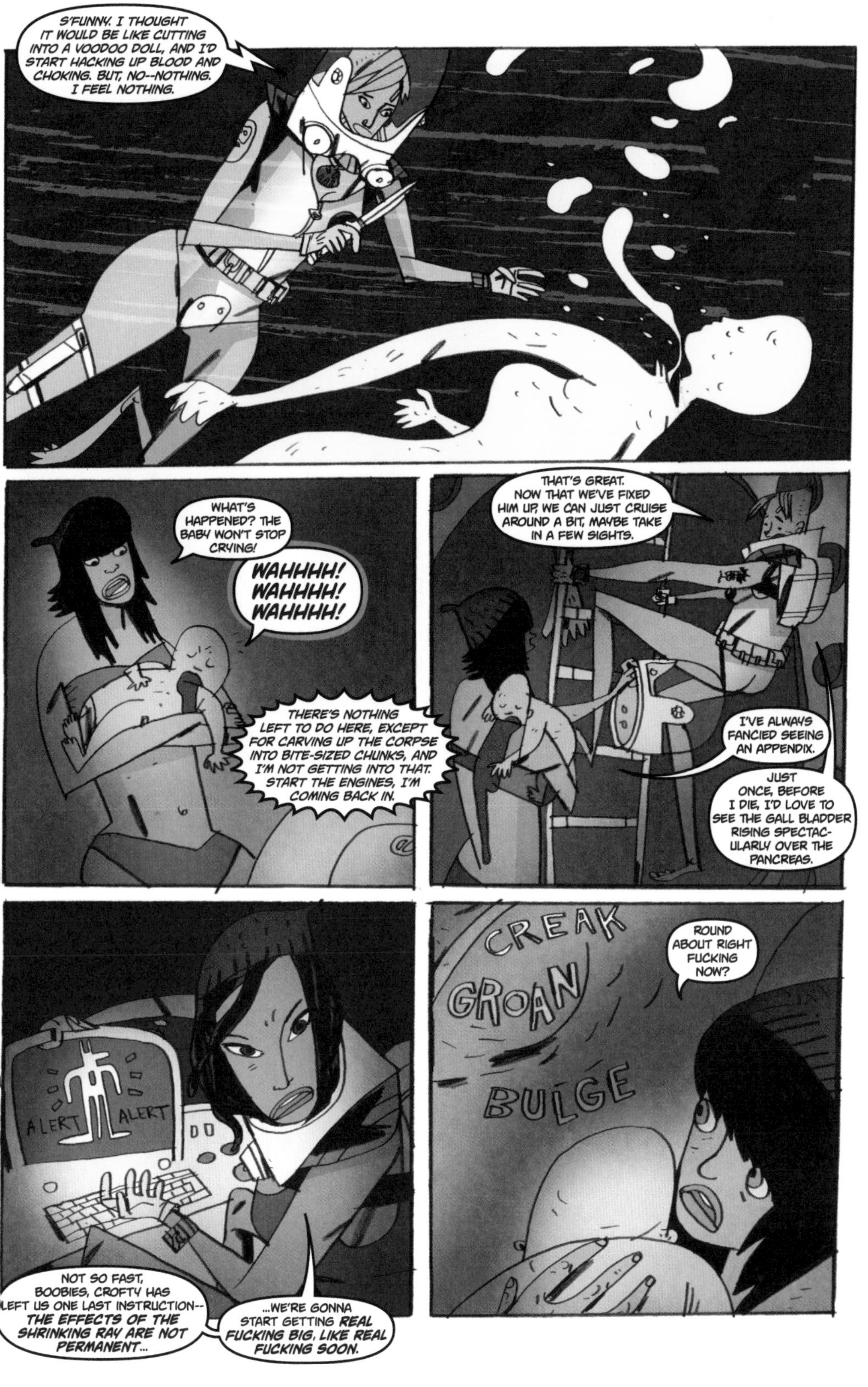

S'FUNNY. I THOUGHT IT WOULD BE LIKE CUTTING INTO A VOODOO DOLL, AND I'D START HACKING UP BLOOD AND CHOKING. BUT, NO--NOTHING. I FEEL NOTHING.
WHAT'S HAPPENED? THE BABY WON'T STOP CRYING!
WAHHHH! WAHHHH! WAHHHH!
THERE'S NOTHING LEFT TO DO HERE, EXCEPT FOR CARVING UP THE CORPSE INTO BITE-SIZED CHUNKS, AND I'M NOT GETTING INTO THAT. START THE ENGINES, I'M COMING BACK IN.
THAT'S GREAT. NOW THAT WE'VE FIXED HIM UP, WE CAN JUST CRUISE AROUND A BIT, MAYBE TAKE IN A FEW SIGHTS.
I'VE ALWAYS FANCIED SEEING AN APPENDIX.
JUST ONCE, BEFORE I DIE, I'D LOVE TO SEE THE GALL BLADDER RISING SPECTACULARLY OVER THE PANCREAS.
ALERT
ALERT
NOT SO FAST, BOOBIES, CROFTY HAS LEFT US ONE LAST INSTRUCTION-- THE EFFECTS OF THE SHRINKING RAY ARE NOT PERMANENT...
...WE'RE GONNA START GETTING REAL FUCKING BIG, LIKE REAL FUCKING SOON.
CREAK
GROAN
BULGE
ROUND ABOUT RIGHT FUCKING NOW?

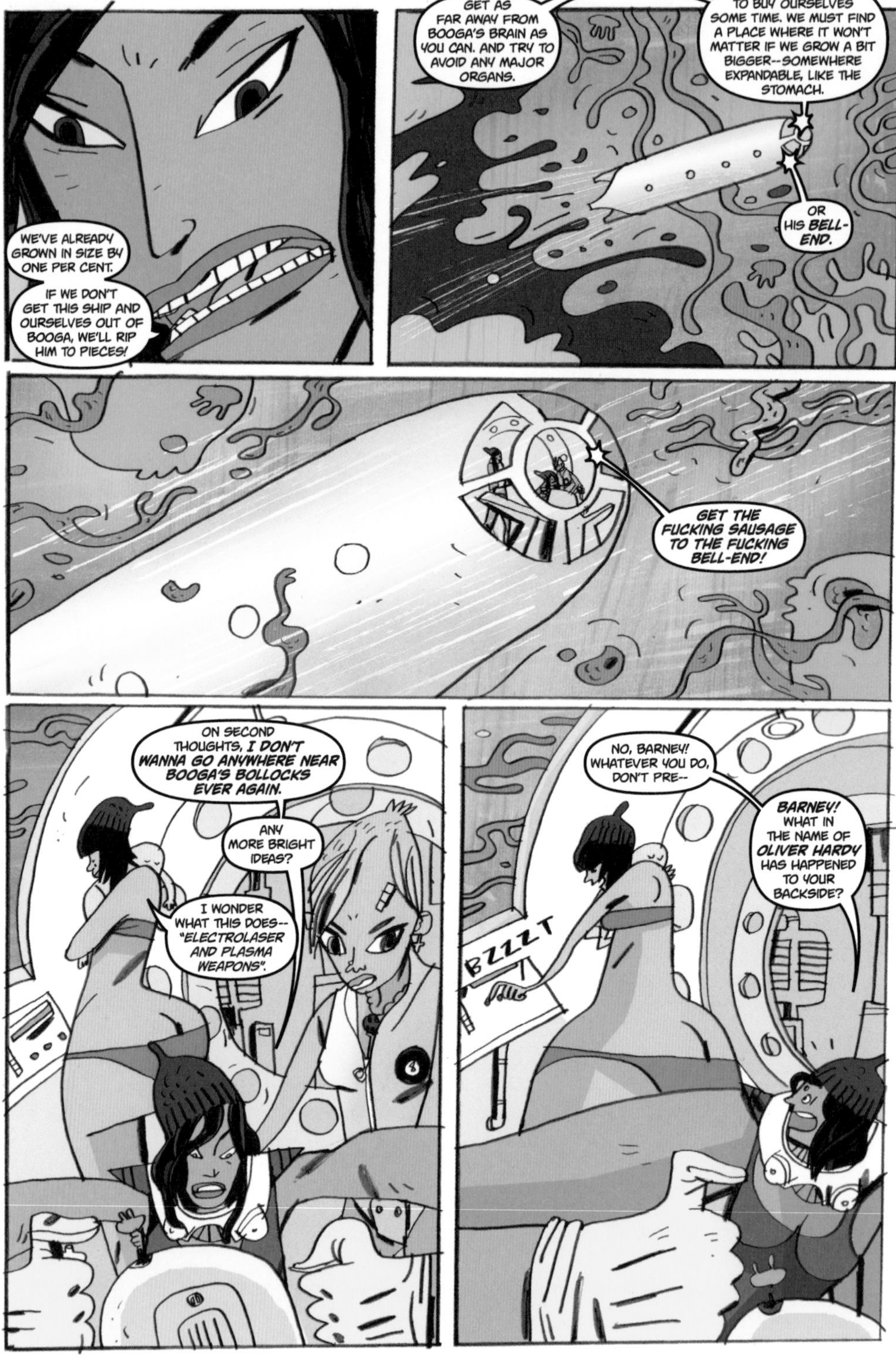
WE'VE ALREADY GROWN IN SIZE BY ONE PER CENT.
IF WE DON'T GET THIS SHIP AND OURSELVES OUT OF BOOGA, WE'LL RIP HIM TO PIECES!
GET AS FAR AWAY FROM BOOGA'S BRAIN AS YOU CAN. AND TRY TO AVOID ANY MAJOR ORGANS.
WE'VE GOT TO BUY OURSELVES SOME TIME. WE MUST FIND A PLACE WHERE IT WON'T MATTER IF WE GROW A BIT BIGGER--SOMEWHERE EXPANDABLE, LIKE THE STOMACH.
OR HIS BELL-END.
GET THE FUCKING SAUSAGE TO THE FUCKING BELL-END!
ON SECOND THOUGHTS, I DON'T WANNA GO ANYWHERE NEAR BOOGA'S BOLLOCKS EVER AGAIN.
ANY MORE BRIGHT IDEAS?
I WONDER WHAT THIS DOES--"ELECTROLASER AND PLASMA WEAPONS".
BZZZT
NO, BARNEY! WHATEVER YOU DO, DON'T PRE--
BARNEY! WHAT IN THE NAME OF OLIVER HARDY HAS HAPPENED TO YOUR BACKSIDE?

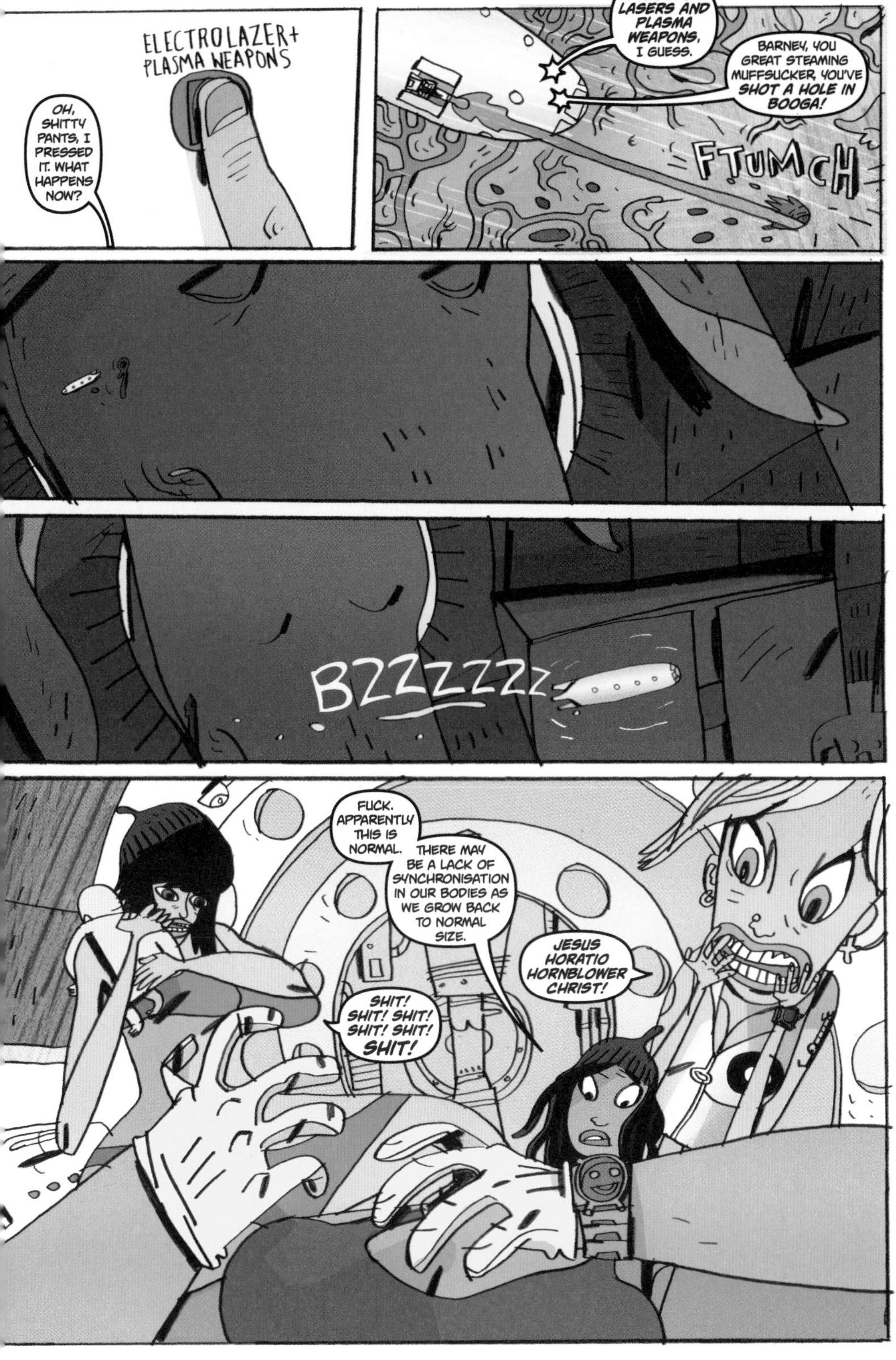
ELECTROLAZER+ PLASMA WEAPONS
OH, SHITTY PANTS, I PRESSED IT. WHAT HAPPENS NOW?
ELECTRO-LASERS AND PLASMA WEAPONS, I GUESS.
BARNEY, YOU GREAT STEAMING MUFFSUCKER, YOU'VE SHOT A HOLE IN BOOGA!
FTUMCH
BZZZZZZz
FUCK. APPARENTLY THIS IS NORMAL.
THERE MAY BE A LACK OF SYNCHRONISATION IN OUR BODIES AS WE GROW BACK TO NORMAL SIZE.
JESUS HORATIO HORNBLOWER CHRIST!
SHIT! SHIT! SHIT! SHIT! SHIT! SHIT!

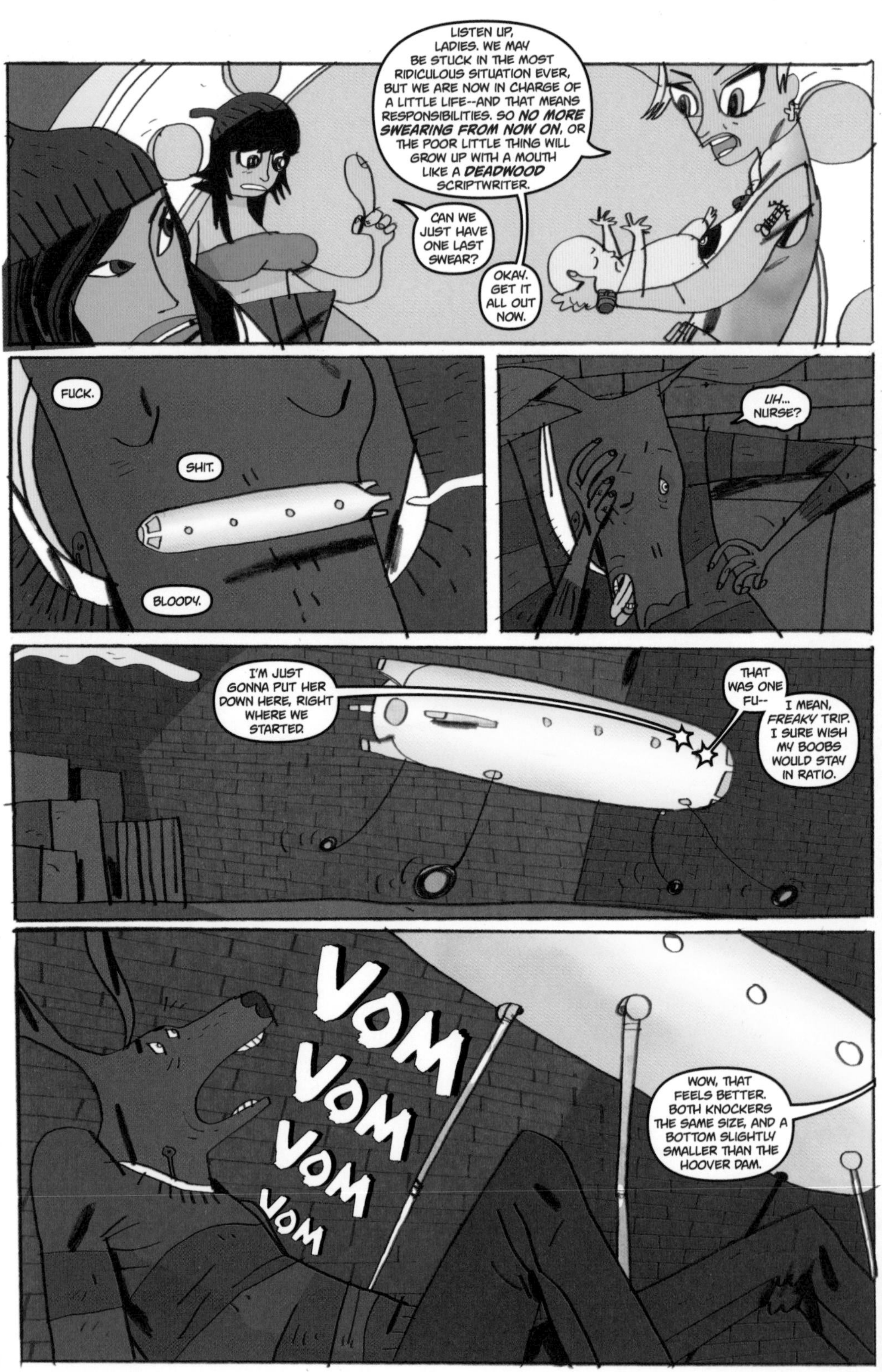
LISTEN UP, LADIES. WE MAY BE STUCK IN THE MOST RIDICULOUS SITUATION EVER, BUT WE ARE NOW IN CHARGE OF A LITTLE LIFE--AND THAT MEANS RESPONSIBILITIES. SO NO MORE SWEARING FROM NOW ON, OR THE POOR LITTLE THING WILL GROW UP WITH A MOUTH LIKE A DEADWOOD SCRIPTWRITER.
CAN WE JUST HAVE ONE LAST SWEAR?
OKAY. GET IT ALL OUT NOW.
FUCK.
SHIT.
BLOODY.
UH... NURSE?
I'M JUST GONNA PUT HER DOWN HERE, RIGHT WHERE WE STARTED.
THAT WAS ONE FU--
I MEAN, FREAKY TRIP. I SURE WISH MY BOOBS WOULD STAY IN RATIO.
VOM VOM VOM VOM VOM VOM
WOW, THAT FEELS BETTER. BOTH KNOCKERS THE SAME SIZE, AND A BOTTOM SLIGHTLY SMALLER THAN THE HOOVER DAM.

WHAT THE FUCK...?

IT NEEDS CHANGING. IT'S POOED.

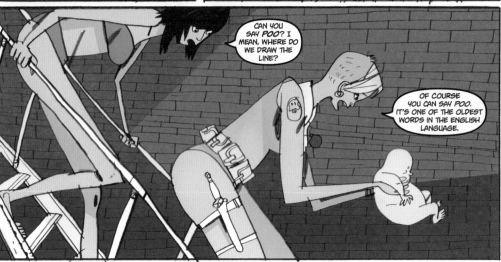

CAN YOU SAY *POO*? I MEAN, WHERE DO WE DRAW THE LINE?

OF COURSE YOU CAN SAY *POO*. IT'S ONE OF THE OLDEST WORDS IN THE ENGLISH LANGUAGE.

I MUST BE FUCKING DREAMING.

NO, BOOGA. YOU ARE NOT DREAMING. AND QUIT IT WITH THE SWEARING--IT COULD HAVE A LASTING, DETRIMENTAL EFFECT ON OUR BABY.

OUR BABY?! I FEEL LIKE I MUST BE MISSING SOME VITAL INFORMATION HERE.

JESUS FUCK, WHAT HAPPENED TO ME? IT'S LIKE SOMEONE HAS EXTRACTED MY SOUL BY KICKING ME REPEATEDLY IN THE BRAIN AND BALLS. AND WHY IS MY FUCKING NECK BLEEDING?

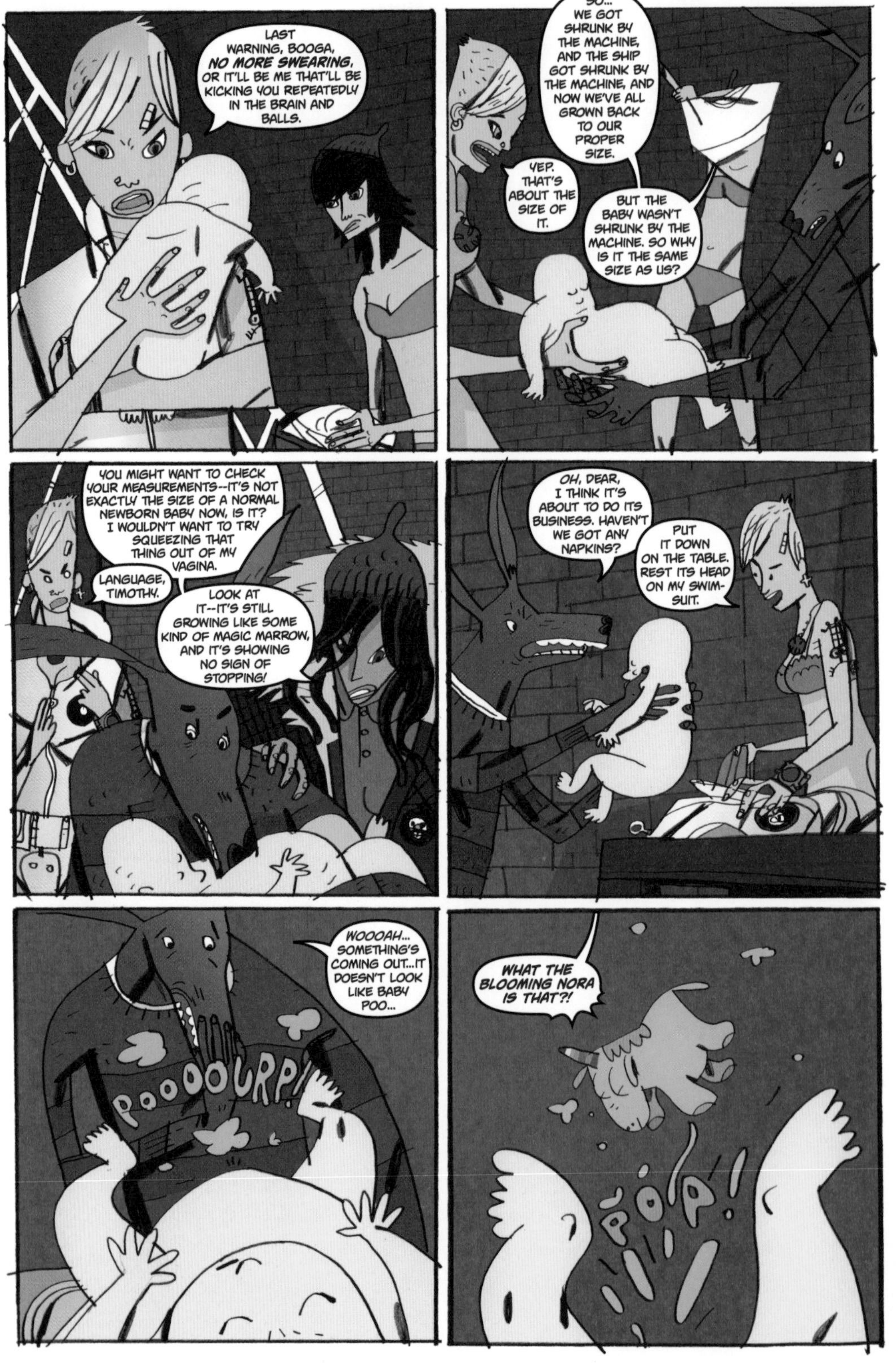
LAST WARNING, BOOGA, NO MORE SWEARING, OR IT'LL BE ME THAT'LL BE KICKING YOU REPEATEDLY IN THE BRAIN AND BALLS.
SO... WE GOT SHRUNK BY THE MACHINE, AND THE SHIP GOT SHRUNK BY THE MACHINE, AND NOW WE'VE ALL GROWN BACK TO OUR PROPER SIZE.
YEP. THAT'S ABOUT THE SIZE OF IT.
BUT THE BABY WASN'T SHRUNK BY THE MACHINE. SO WHY IS IT THE SAME SIZE AS US?
YOU MIGHT WANT TO CHECK YOUR MEASUREMENTS--IT'S NOT EXACTLY THE SIZE OF A NORMAL NEWBORN BABY NOW, IS IT? I WOULDN'T WANT TO TRY SQUEEZING THAT THING OUT OF MY VAGINA.
LANGUAGE, TIMOTHY.
LOOK AT IT--IT'S STILL GROWING LIKE SOME KIND OF MAGIC MARROW, AND IT'S SHOWING NO SIGN OF STOPPING!
OH, DEAR, I THINK IT'S ABOUT TO DO ITS BUSINESS. HAVEN'T WE GOT ANY NAPKINS?
PUT IT DOWN ON THE TABLE. REST ITS HEAD ON MY SWIM-SUIT.
WOOOAH... SOMETHING'S COMING OUT...IT DOESN'T LOOK LIKE BABY POO...
POOOOURP!
WHAT THE BLOOMING NORA IS THAT?!
POP!

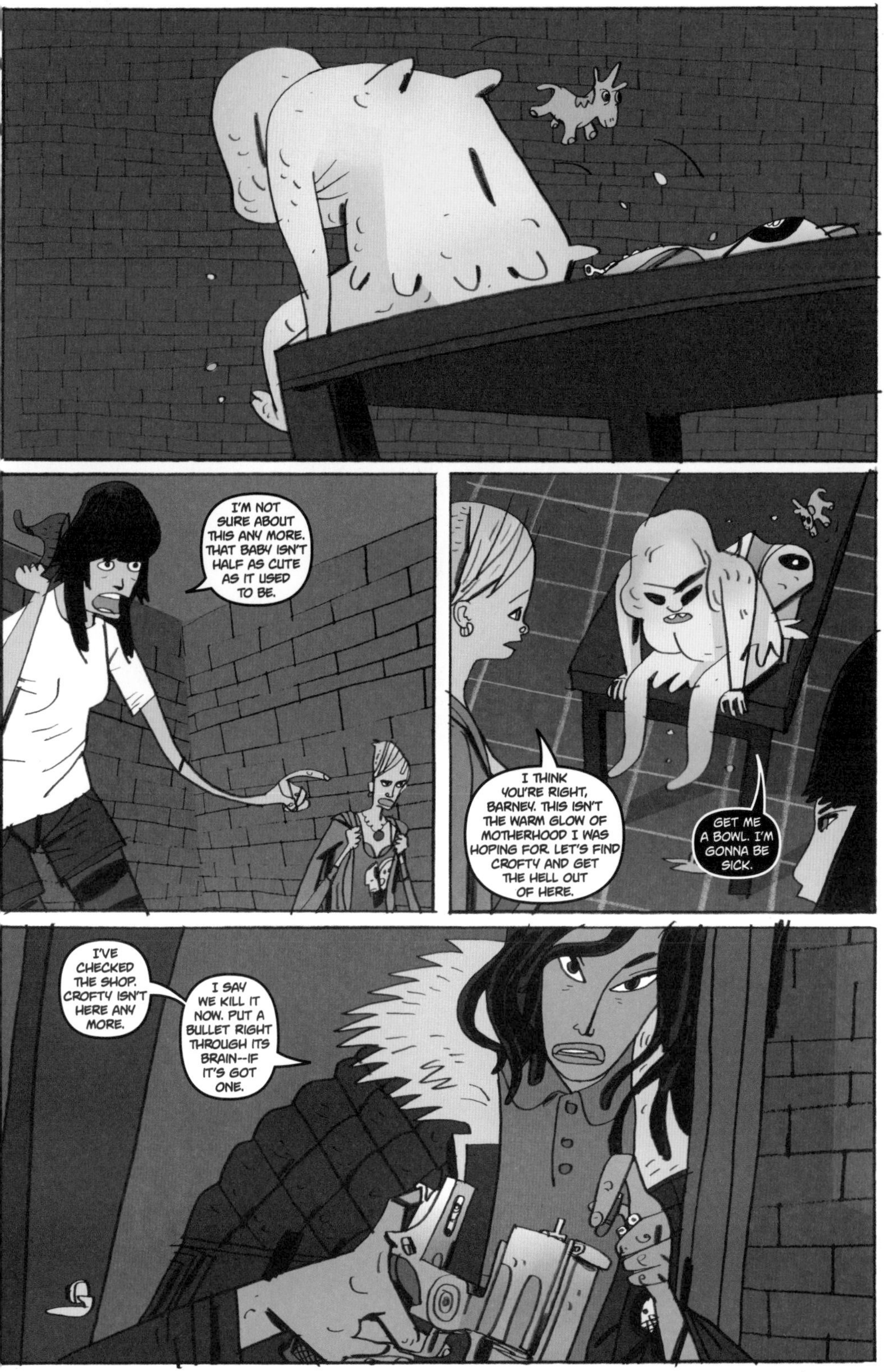
I'M NOT SURE ABOUT THIS ANY MORE. THAT BABY ISN'T HALF AS CUTE AS IT USED TO BE.
I THINK YOU'RE RIGHT, BARNEY. THIS ISN'T THE WARM GLOW OF MOTHERHOOD I WAS HOPING FOR. LET'S FIND CROFTY AND GET THE HELL OUT OF HERE.
GET ME A BOWL. I'M GONNA BE SICK.
I'VE CHECKED THE SHOP. CROFTY ISN'T HERE ANY MORE.
I SAY WE KILL IT NOW. PUT A BULLET RIGHT THROUGH ITS BRAIN--IF IT'S GOT ONE.

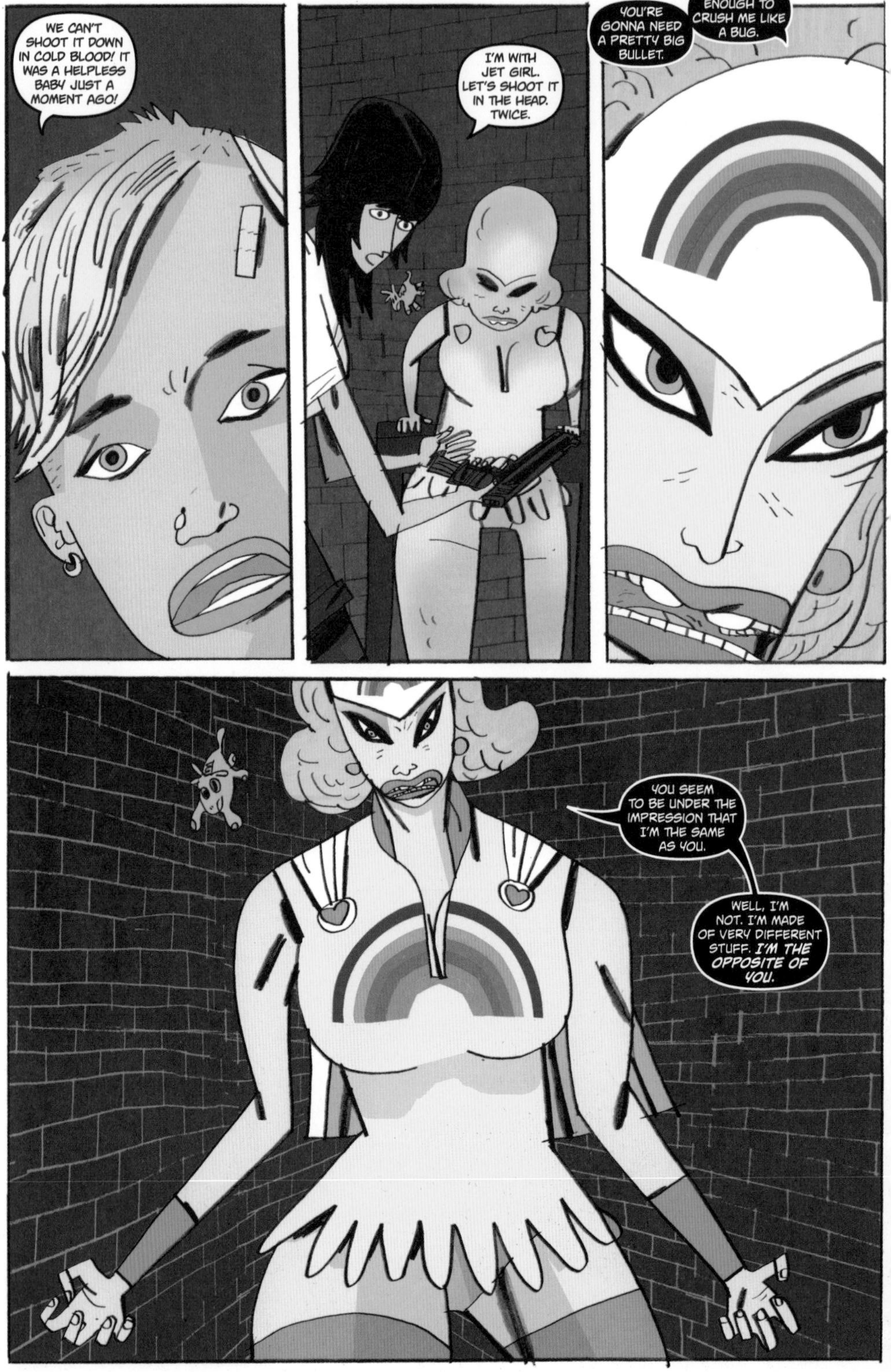
WE CAN'T SHOOT IT DOWN IN COLD BLOOD! IT WAS A HELPLESS BABY JUST A MOMENT AGO!
I'M WITH JET GIRL. LET'S SHOOT IT IN THE HEAD. TWICE.
YOU'RE GONNA NEED A PRETTY BIG BULLET.
ONE BIG ENOUGH TO CRUSH ME LIKE A BUG.
YOU SEEM TO BE UNDER THE IMPRESSION THAT I'M THE SAME AS YOU.
WELL, I'M NOT. I'M MADE OF VERY DIFFERENT STUFF. I'M THE OPPOSITE OF YOU.

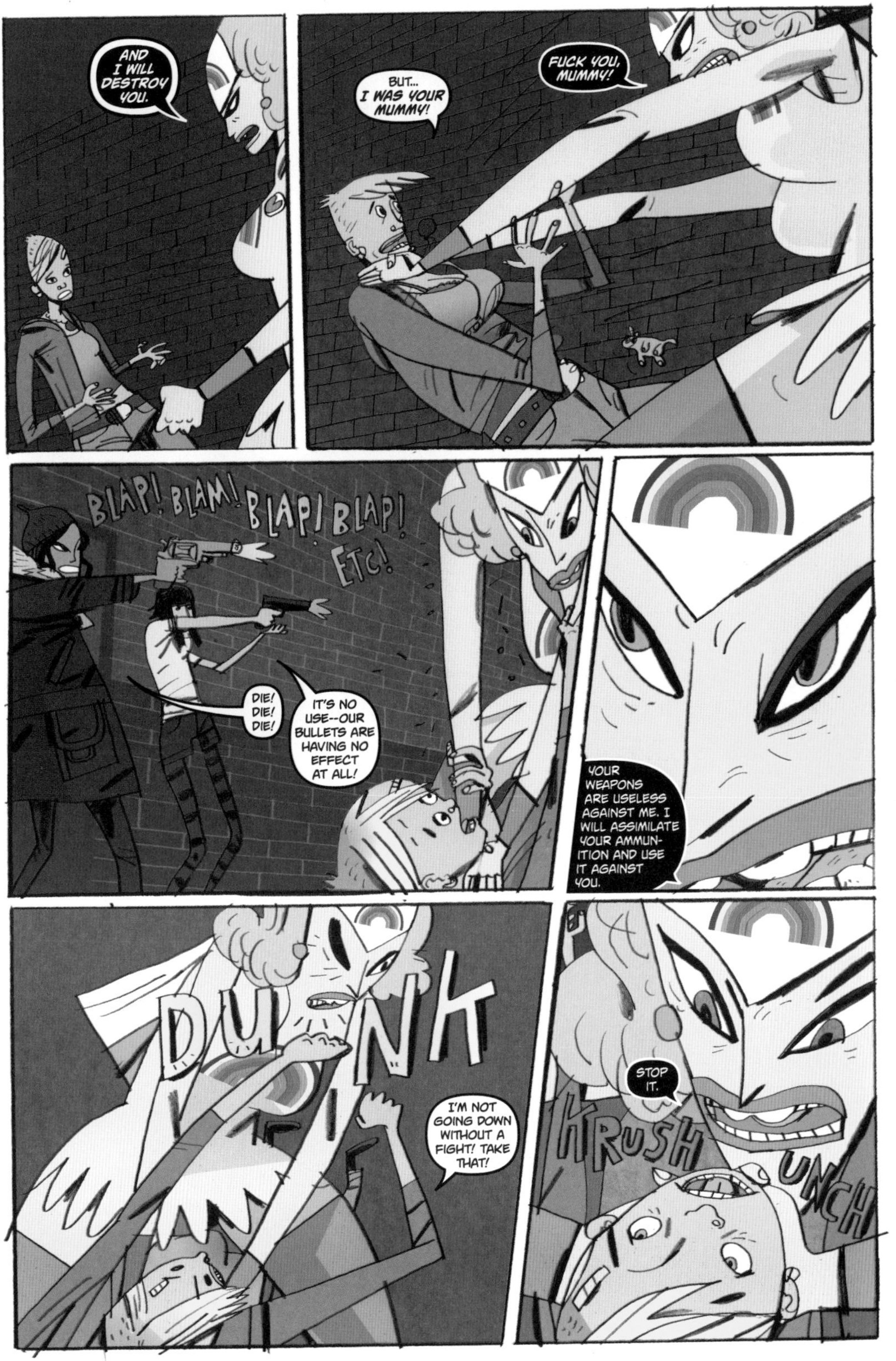
AND I WILL DESTROY YOU.
BUT... I WAS YOUR MUMMY!
FUCK YOU, MUMMY!
BLAP! BLAM! BLAP! BLAP! ETC!
DIE! DIE! DIE!
IT'S NO USE--OUR BULLETS ARE HAVING NO EFFECT AT ALL!
YOUR WEAPONS ARE USELESS AGAINST ME. I WILL ASSIMILATE YOUR AMMUNITION AND USE IT AGAINST YOU.
DUNK
I'M NOT GOING DOWN WITHOUT A FIGHT! TAKE THAT!
STOP IT.
KRUSH
UNCH

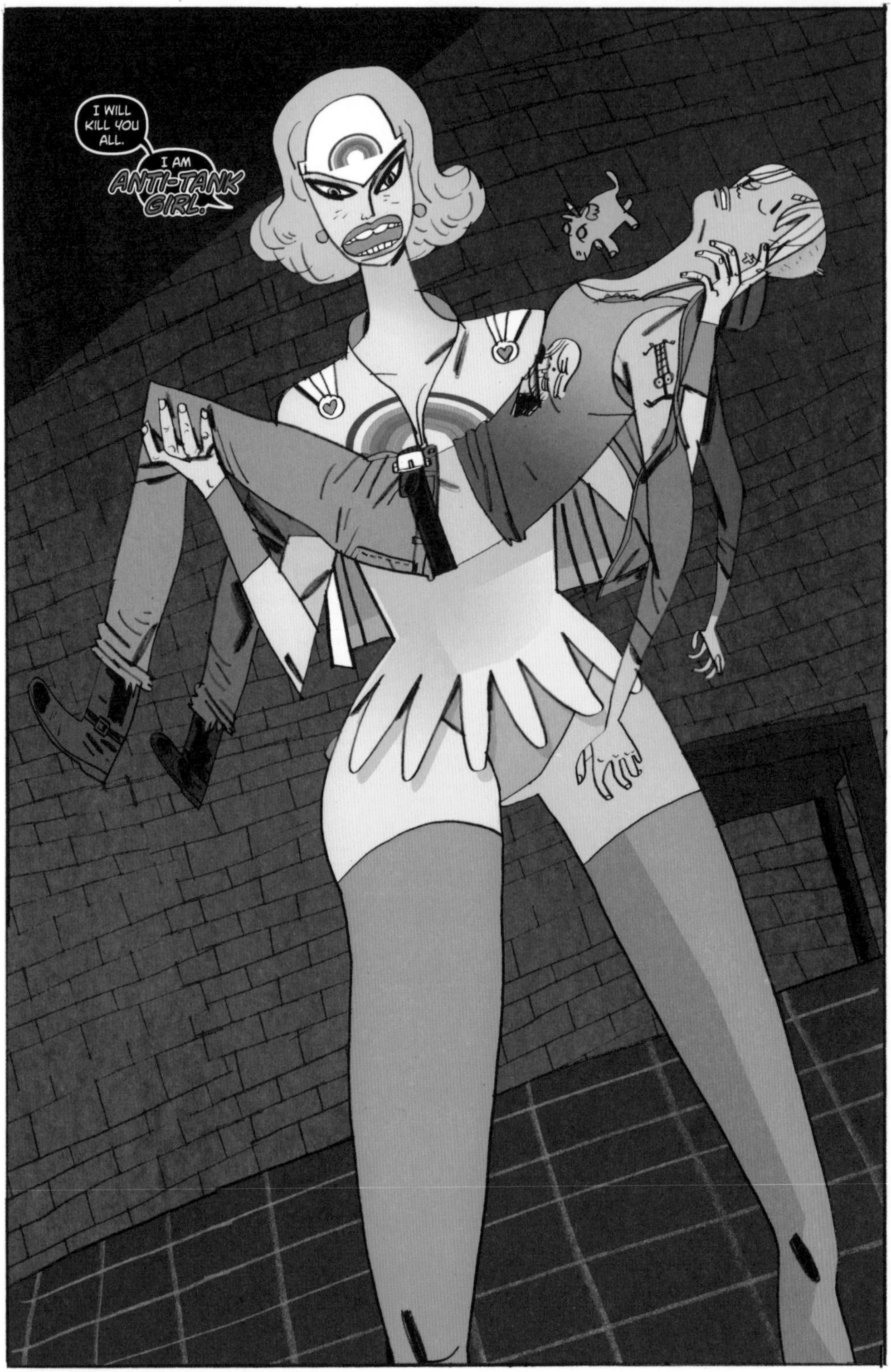
I WILL KILL YOU ALL.
I AM ANTI-TANK GIRL.

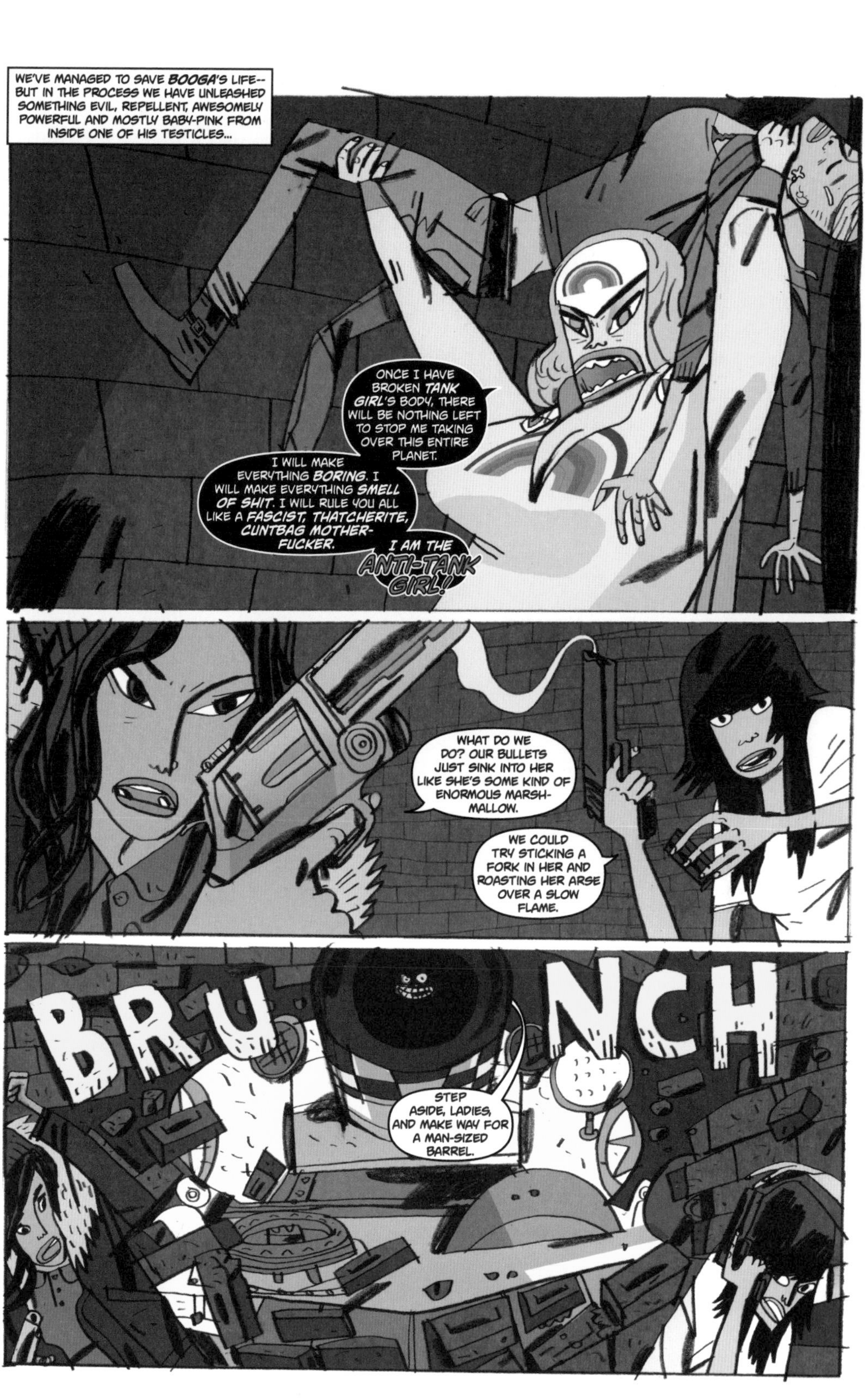

WE'VE MANAGED TO SAVE BOOGA'S LIFE-- BUT IN THE PROCESS WE HAVE UNLEASHED SOMETHING EVIL, REPELLENT, AWESOMELY POWERFUL AND MOSTLY BABY-PINK FROM INSIDE ONE OF HIS TESTICLES...
ONCE I HAVE BROKEN TANK GIRL'S BODY, THERE WILL BE NOTHING LEFT TO STOP ME TAKING OVER THIS ENTIRE PLANET.
I WILL MAKE EVERYTHING BORING. I WILL MAKE EVERYTHING SMELL OF SHIT. I WILL RULE YOU ALL LIKE A FASCIST, THATCHERITE, CUNTBAG MOTHER-FUCKER.
I AM THE ANTI-TANK GIRL!
WHAT DO WE DO? OUR BULLETS JUST SINK INTO HER LIKE SHE'S SOME KIND OF ENORMOUS MARSH-MALLOW.
WE COULD TRY STICKING A FORK IN HER AND ROASTING HER ARSE OVER A SLOW FLAME.
BRUNCH
STEP ASIDE, LADIES, AND MAKE WAY FOR A MAN-SIZED BARREL.

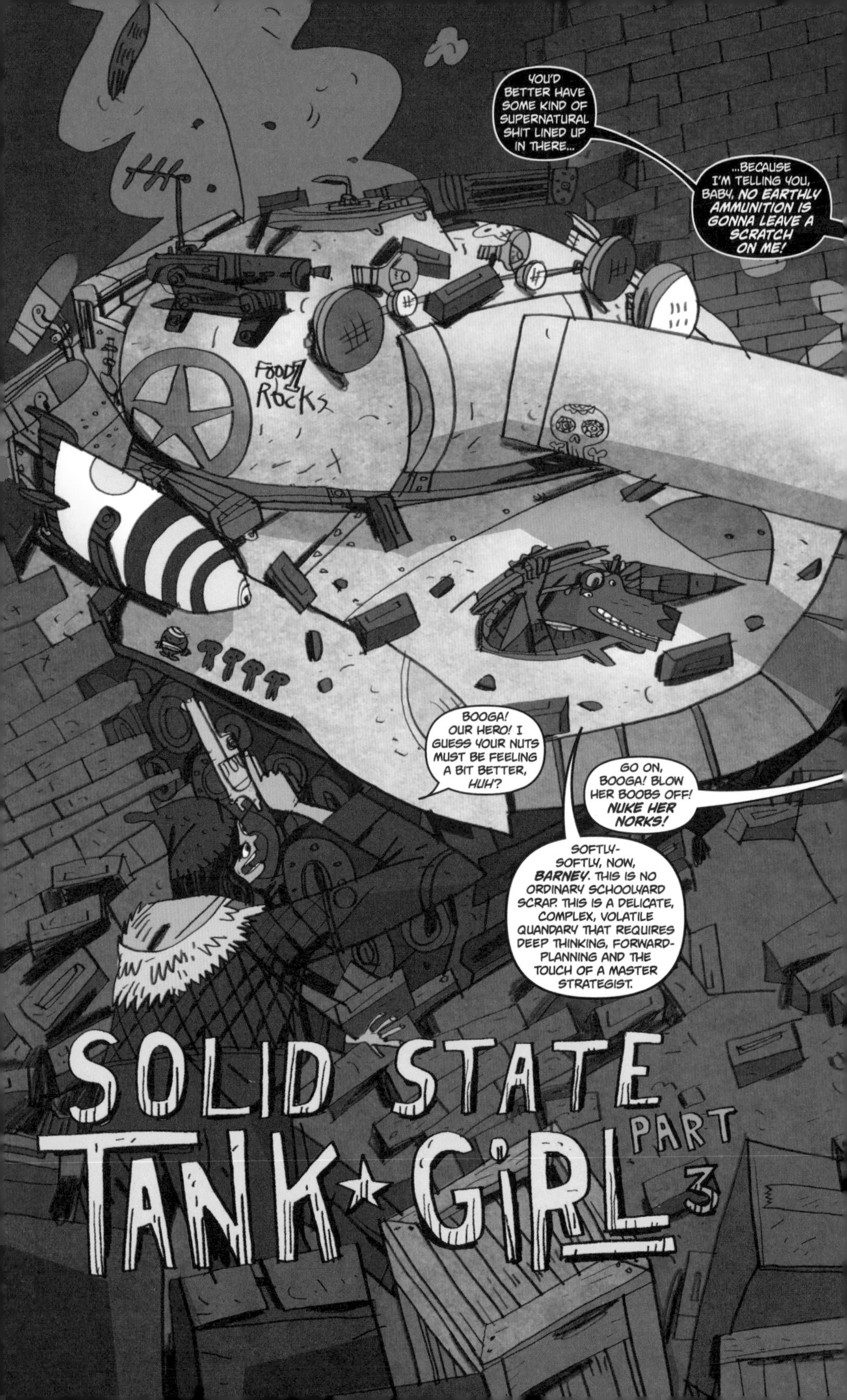
YOU'D BETTER HAVE SOME KIND OF SUPERNATURAL SHIT LINED UP IN THERE...
...BECAUSE I'M TELLING YOU, BABY, NO EARTHLY AMMUNITION IS GONNA LEAVE A SCRATCH ON ME!
FOOD 1 ROCKS
BOOGA! OUR HERO! I GUESS YOUR NUTS MUST BE FEELING A BIT BETTER, HUH?
GO ON, BOOGA! BLOW HER BOOBS OFF! NUKE HER NORKS!
SOFTLY-SOFTLY, NOW, BARNEY. THIS IS NO ORDINARY SCHOOLYARD SCRAP. THIS IS A DELICATE, COMPLEX, VOLATILE QUANDARY THAT REQUIRES DEEP THINKING, FORWARD-PLANNING AND THE TOUCH OF A MASTER STRATEGIST.
SOLID STATE
TANK GIRL PART 3

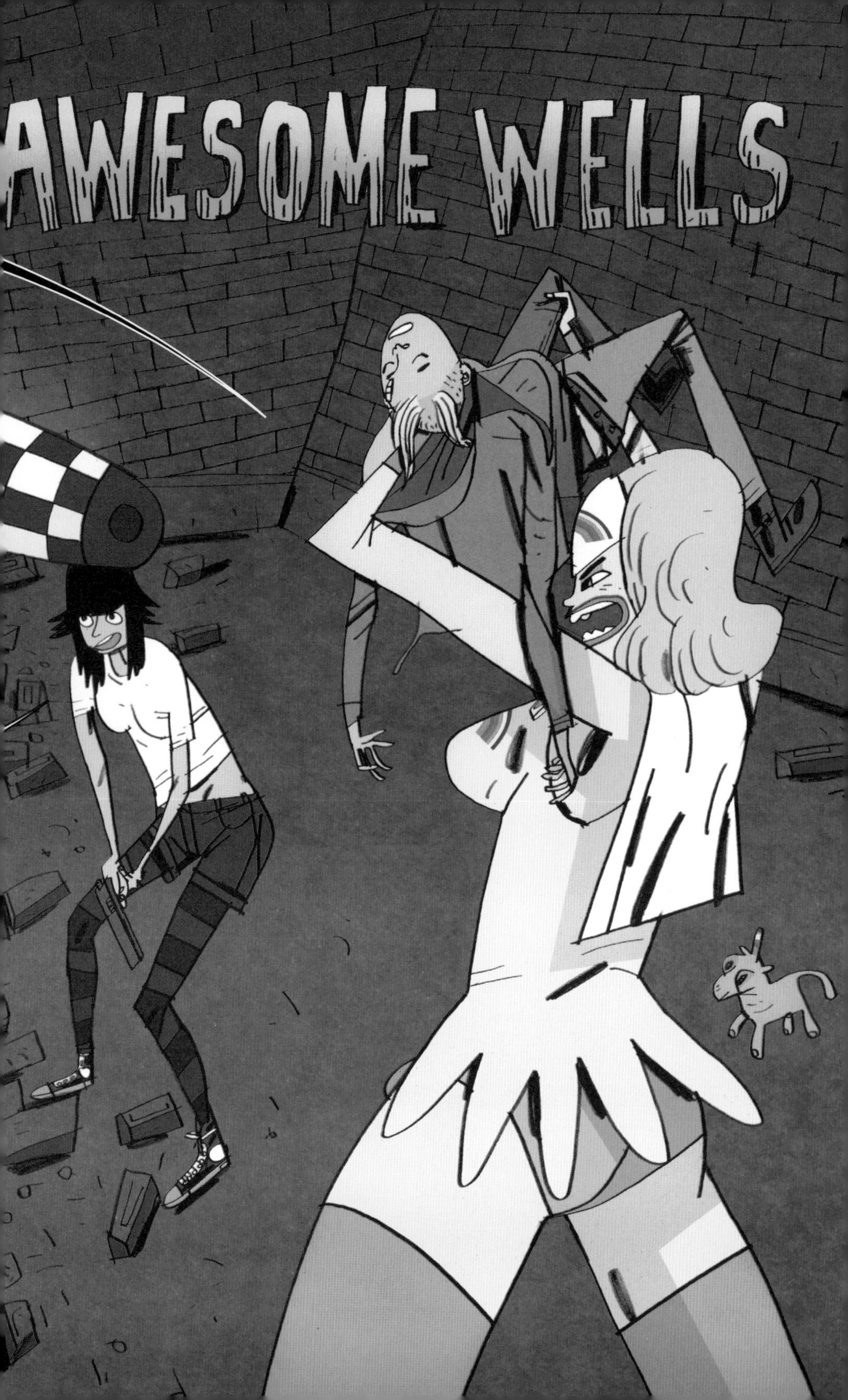
AWESOME WELLS

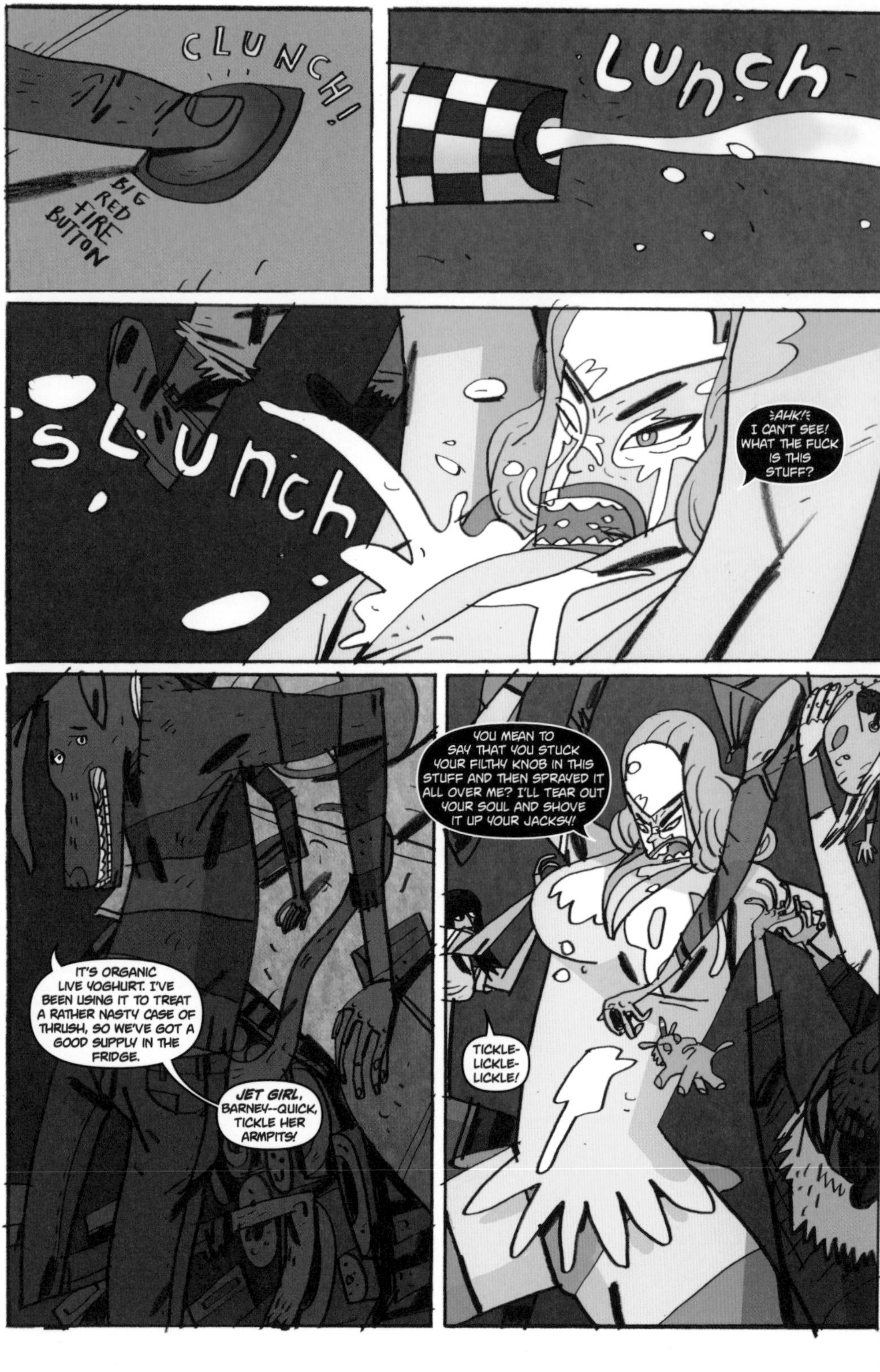
CLUNCH!
BIG RED FIRE BUTTON
LUNCH
SLUNCH
AHK! I CAN'T SEE! WHAT THE FUCK IS THIS STUFF?
IT'S ORGANIC LIVE YOGHURT. I'VE BEEN USING IT TO TREAT A RATHER NASTY CASE OF THRUSH, SO WE'VE GOT A GOOD SUPPLY IN THE FRIDGE.
JET GIRL, BARNEY--QUICK, TICKLE HER ARMPITS!
YOU MEAN TO SAY THAT YOU STUCK YOUR FILTHY KNOB IN THIS STUFF AND THEN SPRAYED IT ALL OVER ME? I'LL TEAR OUT YOUR SOUL AND SHOVE IT UP YOUR JACKSY!
TICKLE-LICKLE-LICKLE!

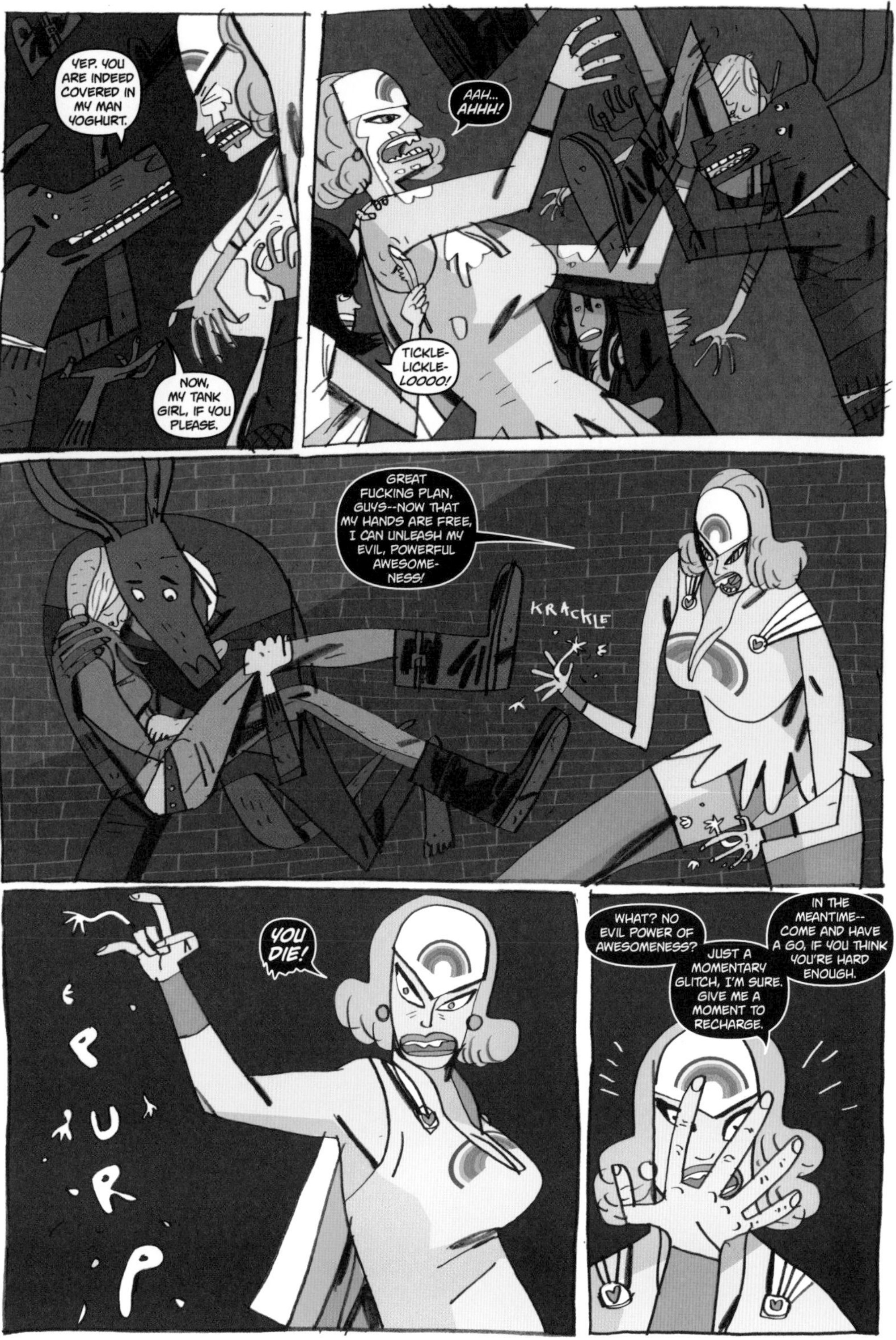

YEP. YOU ARE INDEED COVERED IN MY MAN YOGHURT.
NOW, MY TANK GIRL, IF YOU PLEASE.
AAH... AHHH!
TICKLE-LICKLE-LOOOO!
GREAT FUCKING PLAN, GUYS--NOW THAT MY HANDS ARE FREE, I CAN UNLEASH MY EVIL, POWERFUL AWESOME-NESS!
KRACKLE
YOU DIE!
PURP
WHAT? NO EVIL POWER OF AWESOMENESS?
JUST A MOMENTARY GLITCH, I'M SURE. GIVE ME A MOMENT TO RECHARGE.
IN THE MEANTIME-- COME AND HAVE A GO, IF YOU THINK YOU'RE HARD ENOUGH.

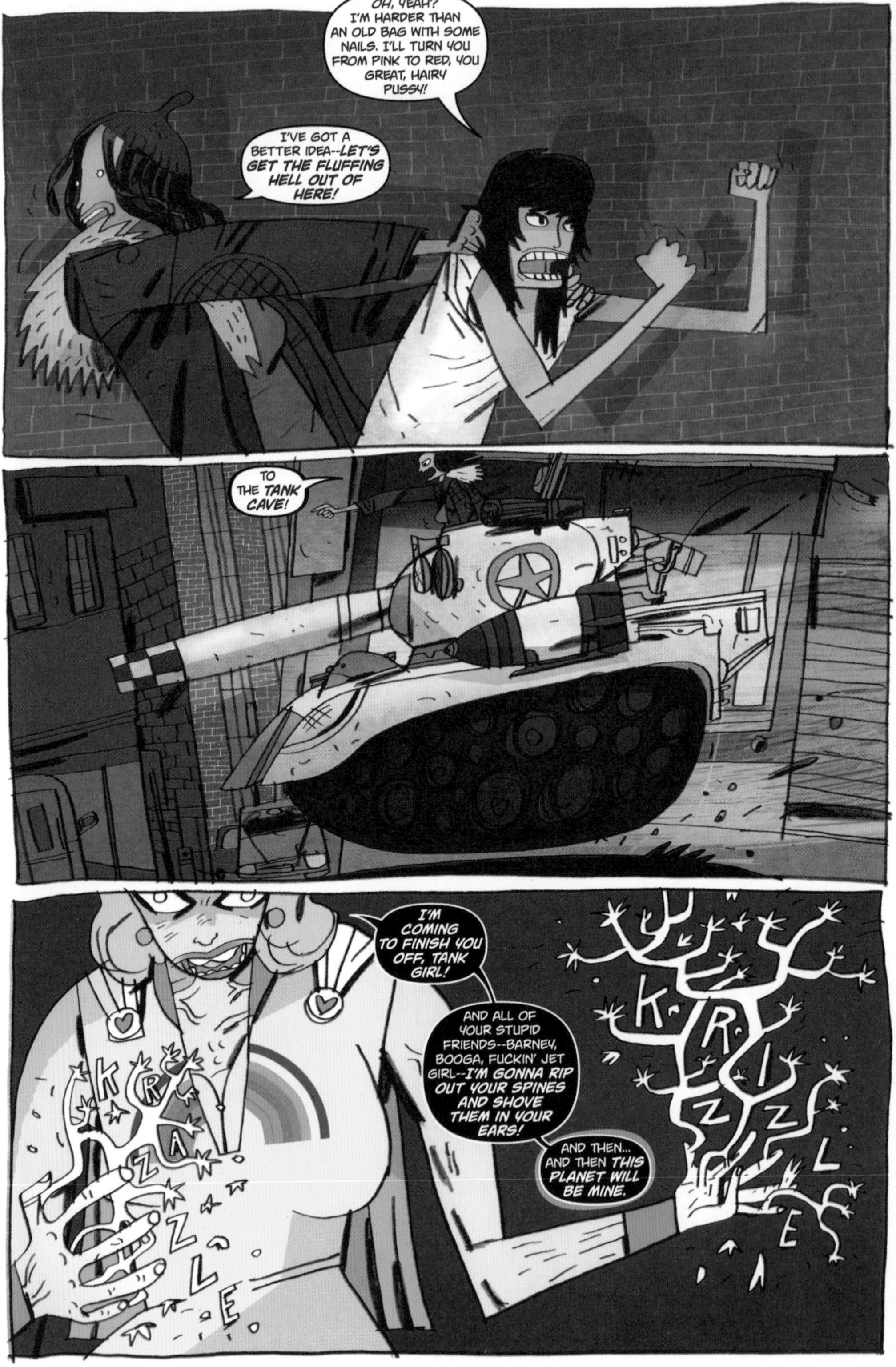
OH, YEAH? I'M HARDER THAN AN OLD BAG WITH SOME NAILS. I'LL TURN YOU FROM PINK TO RED, YOU GREAT, HAIRY PUSSY!
I'VE GOT A BETTER IDEA--LET'S GET THE FLUFFING HELL OUT OF HERE!
TO THE TANK CAVE!
I'M COMING TO FINISH YOU OFF, TANK GIRL!
AND ALL OF YOUR STUPID FRIENDS--BARNEY, BOOGA, FUCKIN' JET GIRL--I'M GONNA RIP OUT YOUR SPINES AND SHOVE THEM IN YOUR EARS!
AND THEN... AND THEN THIS PLANET WILL BE MINE.
KRIZZLE
KRAZZLE

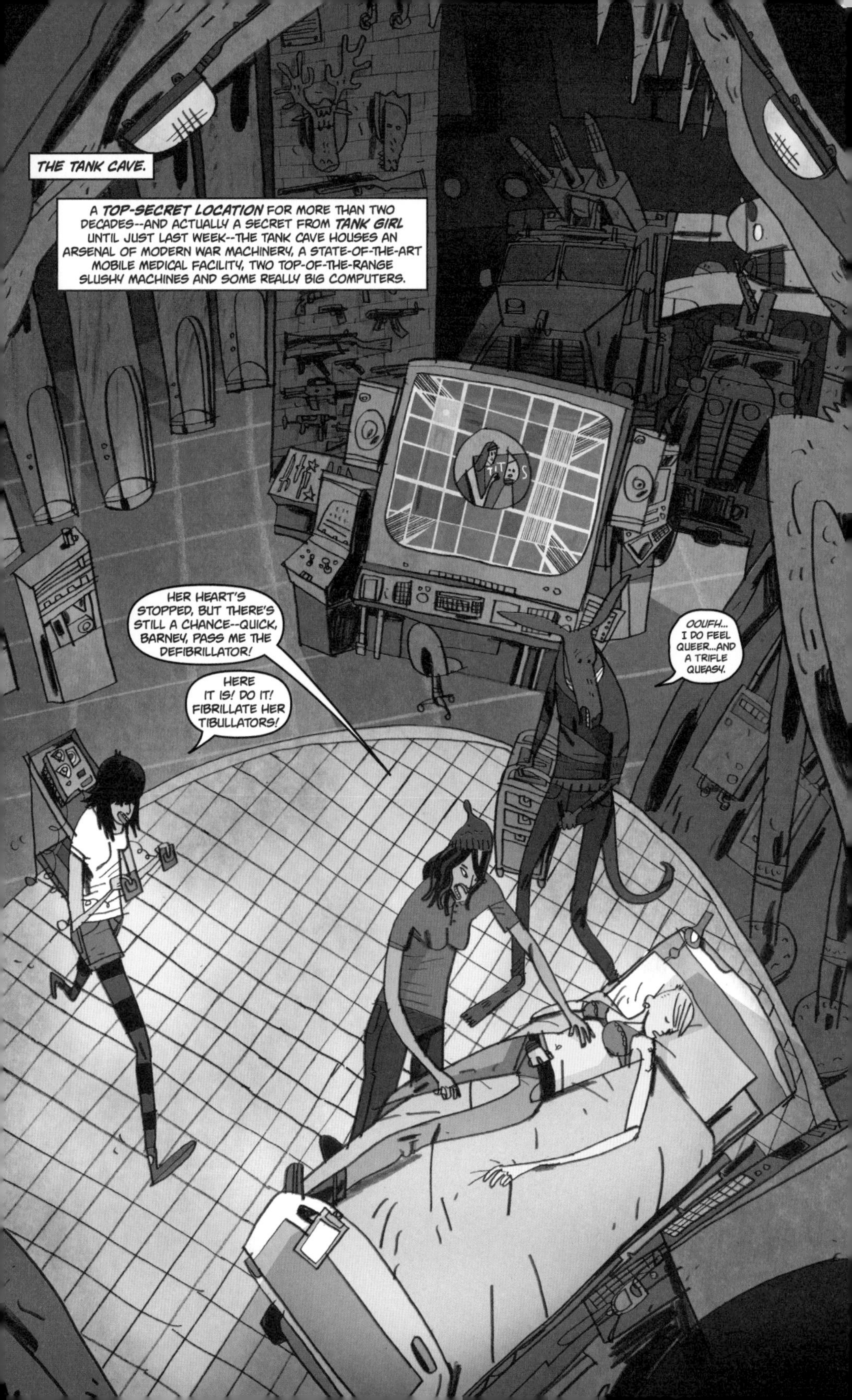
THE TANK CAVE.
A TOP-SECRET LOCATION FOR MORE THAN TWO DECADES--AND ACTUALLY A SECRET FROM TANK GIRL UNTIL JUST LAST WEEK--THE TANK CAVE HOUSES AN ARSENAL OF MODERN WAR MACHINERY, A STATE-OF-THE-ART MOBILE MEDICAL FACILITY, TWO TOP-OF-THE-RANGE SLUSHY MACHINES AND SOME REALLY BIG COMPUTERS.
HER HEART'S STOPPED, BUT THERE'S STILL A CHANCE--QUICK, BARNEY, PASS ME THE DEFIBRILLATOR!
HERE IT IS! DO IT! FIBRILLATE HER TIBULLATORS!
OOUFH... I DO FEEL QUEER...AND A TRIFLE QUEASY.

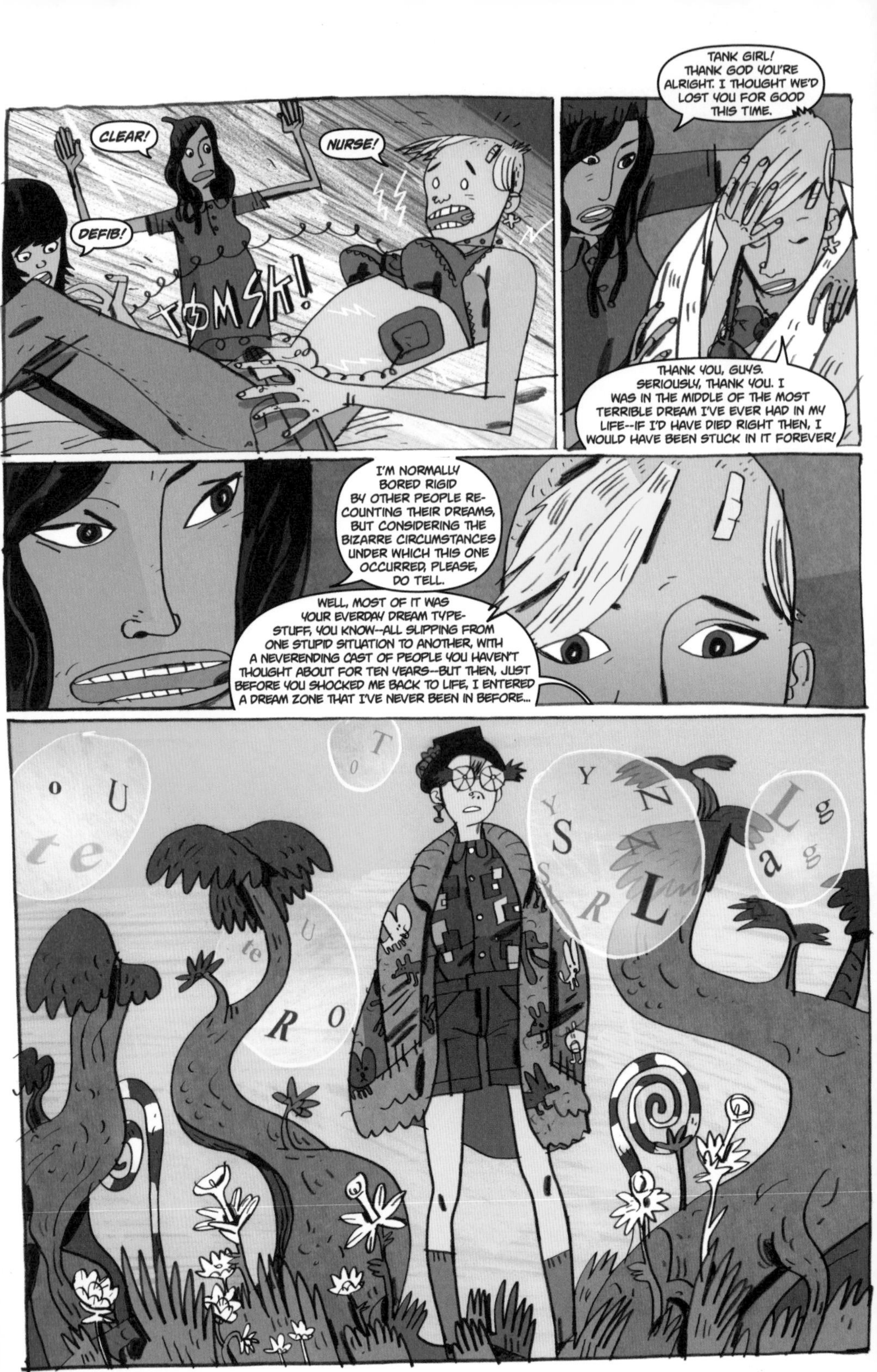
CLEAR!
NURSE!
DEFIB!
TOMSK!
TANK GIRL! THANK GOD YOU'RE ALRIGHT. I THOUGHT WE'D LOST YOU FOR GOOD THIS TIME.
THANK YOU, GUYS. SERIOUSLY, THANK YOU. I WAS IN THE MIDDLE OF THE MOST TERRIBLE DREAM I'VE EVER HAD IN MY LIFE--IF I'D HAVE DIED RIGHT THEN, I WOULD HAVE BEEN STUCK IN IT FOREVER!
I'M NORMALLY BORED RIGID BY OTHER PEOPLE RE-COUNTING THEIR DREAMS, BUT CONSIDERING THE BIZARRE CIRCUMSTANCES UNDER WHICH THIS ONE OCCURRED, PLEASE, DO TELL.
WELL, MOST OF IT WAS YOUR EVERDAY DREAM TYPE-STUFF, YOU KNOW--ALL SLIPPING FROM ONE STUPID SITUATION TO ANOTHER, WITH A NEVERENDING CAST OF PEOPLE YOU HAVEN'T THOUGHT ABOUT FOR TEN YEARS--BUT THEN, JUST BEFORE YOU SHOCKED ME BACK TO LIFE, I ENTERED A DREAM ZONE THAT I'VE NEVER BEEN IN BEFORE...

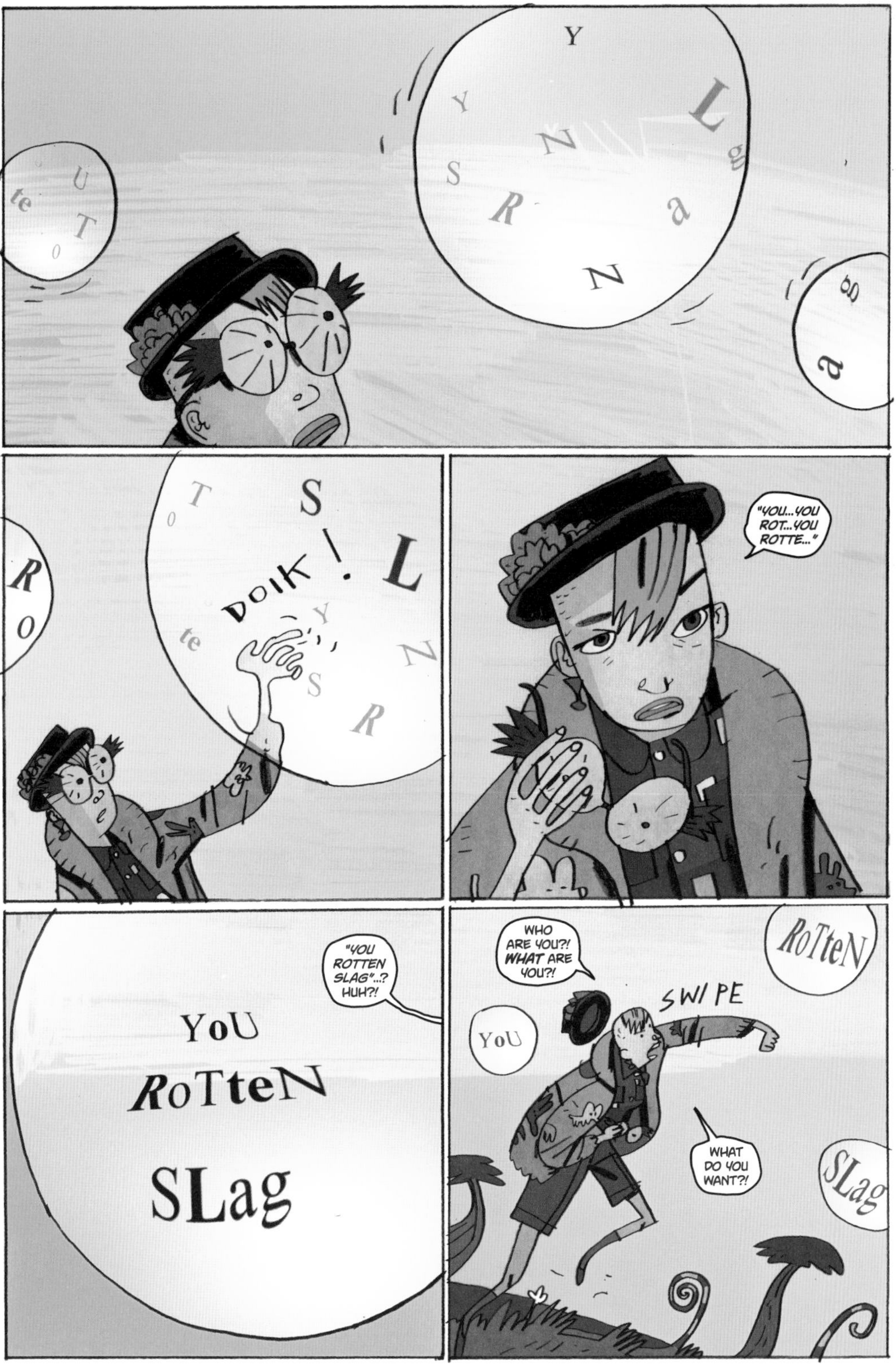
DOIK!
"YOU...YOU ROT...YOU ROTTE..."
YoU RoTteN SLag
"YOU ROTTEN SLAG"...? HUH?!
WHO ARE YOU?! WHAT ARE YOU?!
RoTteN
SWIPE
YoU
WHAT DO YOU WANT?!
SLag

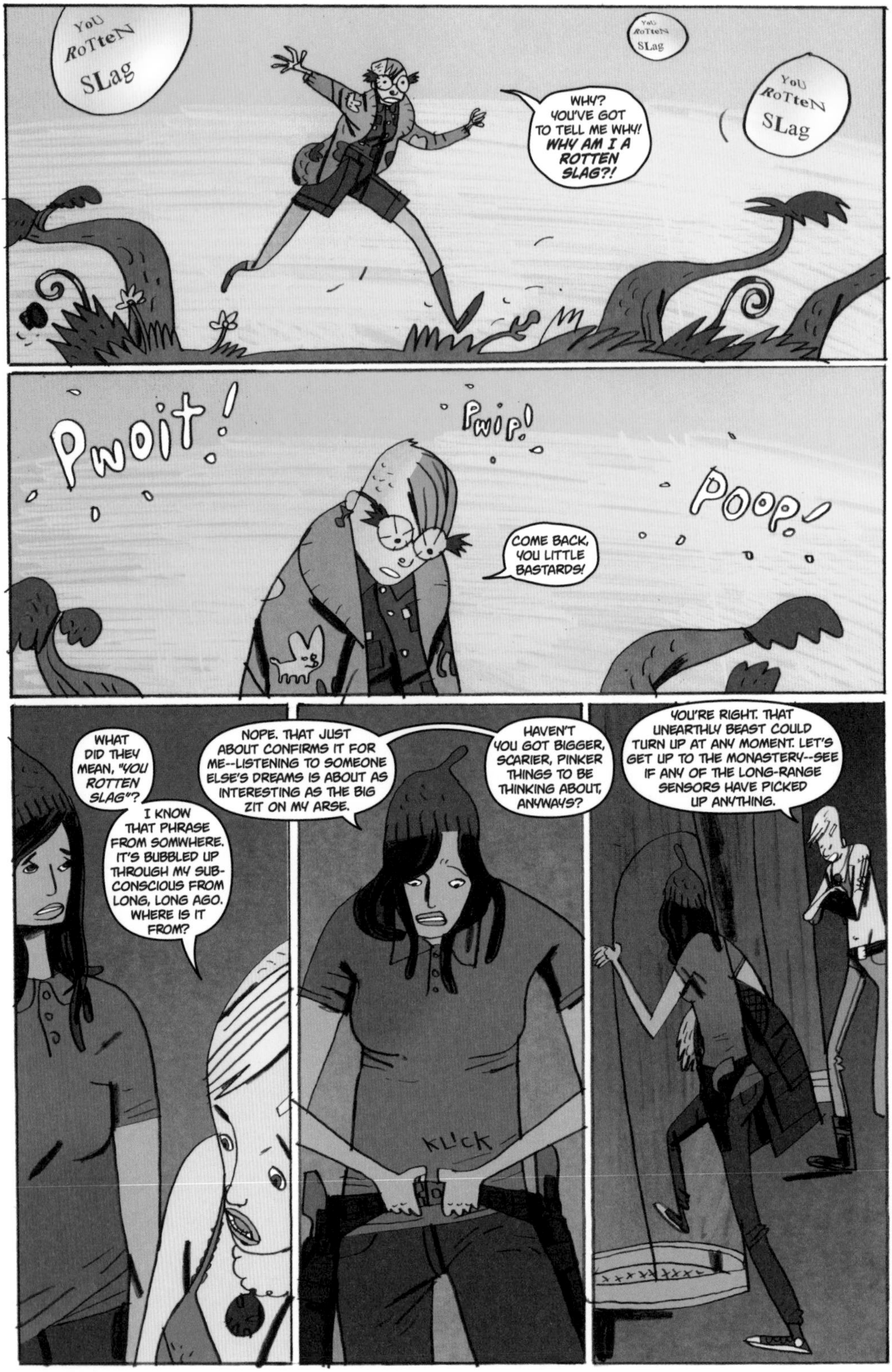
YoU RoTteN SLag
YoU RoTteN SLag
WHY? YOU'VE GOT TO TELL ME WHY! WHY AM I A ROTTEN SLAG?!
YoU RoTteN SLag
Pwoit!
Pwip!
POOP!
COME BACK, YOU LITTLE BASTARDS!
WHAT DID THEY MEAN, "YOU ROTTEN SLAG"?
I KNOW THAT PHRASE FROM SOMWHERE. IT'S BUBBLED UP THROUGH MY SUB-CONSCIOUS FROM LONG, LONG AGO. WHERE IS IT FROM?
NOPE. THAT JUST ABOUT CONFIRMS IT FOR ME--LISTENING TO SOMEONE ELSE'S DREAMS IS ABOUT AS INTERESTING AS THE BIG ZIT ON MY ARSE.
HAVEN'T YOU GOT BIGGER, SCARIER, PINKER THINGS TO BE THINKING ABOUT, ANYWAYS?
KLICK
YOU'RE RIGHT. THAT UNEARTHLY BEAST COULD TURN UP AT ANY MOMENT. LET'S GET UP TO THE MONASTERY--SEE IF ANY OF THE LONG-RANGE SENSORS HAVE PICKED UP ANYTHING.

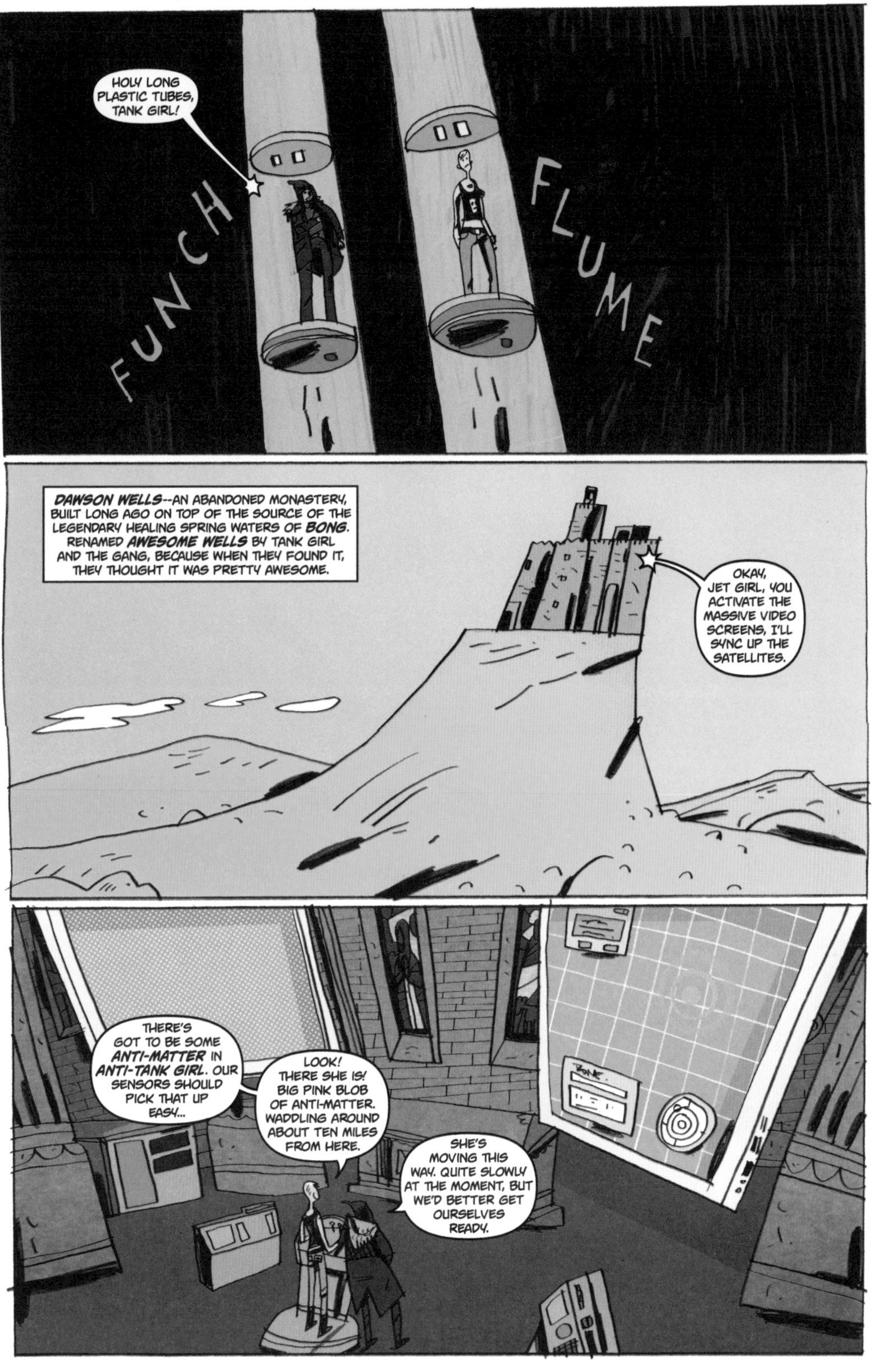
HOLY LONG PLASTIC TUBES, TANK GIRL!
FUNCH
FLUME
DAWSON WELLS--AN ABANDONED MONASTERY, BUILT LONG AGO ON TOP OF THE SOURCE OF THE LEGENDARY HEALING SPRING WATERS OF BONG. RENAMED AWESOME WELLS BY TANK GIRL AND THE GANG, BECAUSE WHEN THEY FOUND IT, THEY THOUGHT IT WAS PRETTY AWESOME.
OKAY, JET GIRL, YOU ACTIVATE THE MASSIVE VIDEO SCREENS, I'LL SYNC UP THE SATELLITES.
THERE'S GOT TO BE SOME ANTI-MATTER IN ANTI-TANK GIRL. OUR SENSORS SHOULD PICK THAT UP EASY...
LOOK! THERE SHE IS! BIG PINK BLOB OF ANTI-MATTER. WADDLING AROUND ABOUT TEN MILES FROM HERE.
SHE'S MOVING THIS WAY. QUITE SLOWLY AT THE MOMENT, BUT WE'D BETTER GET OURSELVES READY.

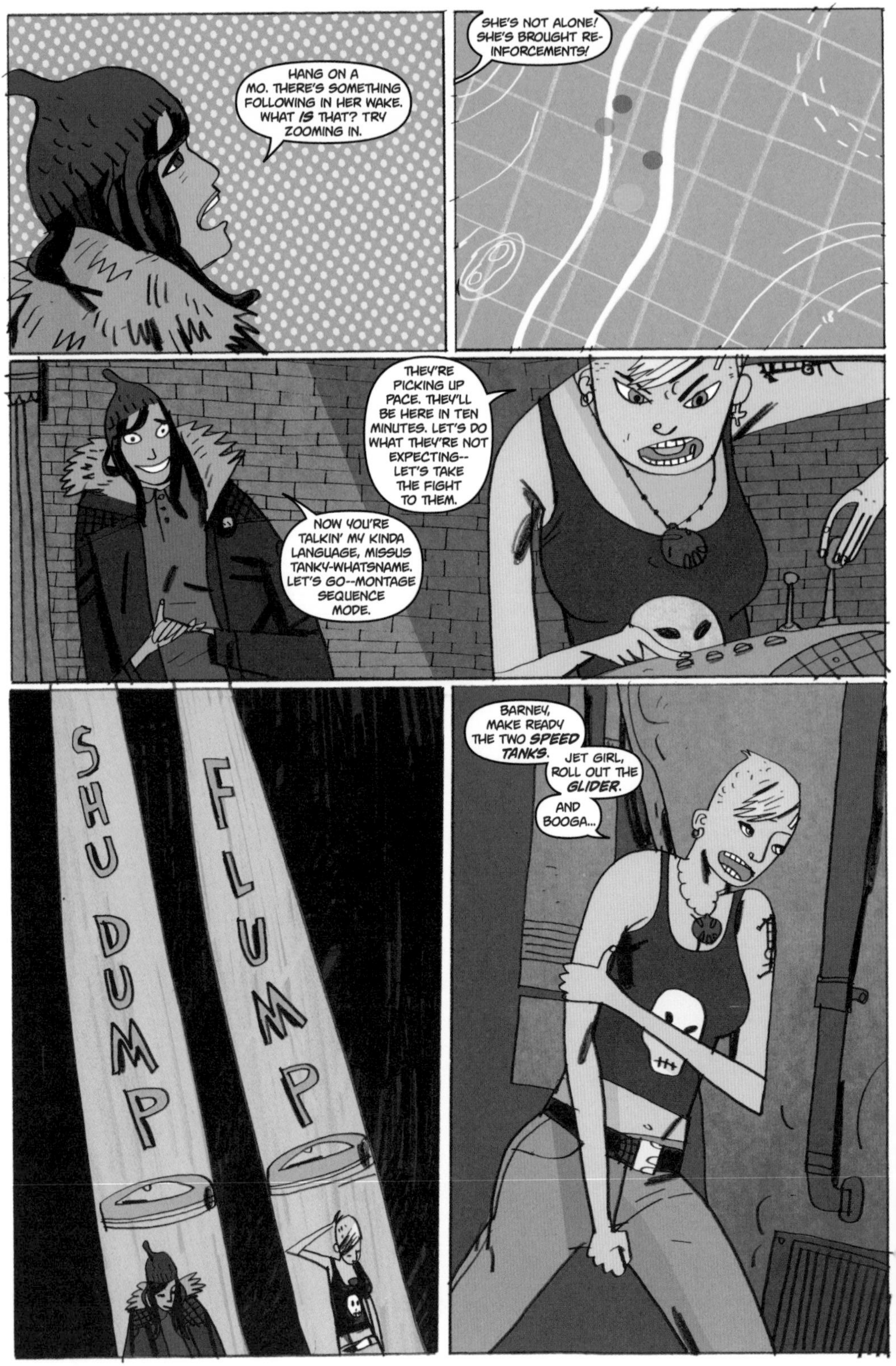
HANG ON A MO. THERE'S SOMETHING FOLLOWING IN HER WAKE. WHAT *IS* THAT? TRY ZOOMING IN.
SHE'S NOT ALONE! SHE'S BROUGHT RE-INFORCEMENTS!
THEY'RE PICKING UP PACE. THEY'LL BE HERE IN TEN MINUTES. LET'S DO WHAT THEY'RE NOT EXPECTING--LET'S TAKE THE FIGHT TO THEM.
NOW YOU'RE TALKIN' MY KINDA LANGUAGE, MISSUS TANKY-WHATSNAME. LET'S GO--MONTAGE SEQUENCE MODE.
SHU DUMP
FLUMP
BARNEY, MAKE READY THE TWO *SPEED TANKS*.
JET GIRL, ROLL OUT THE *GLIDER*.
AND BOOGA...

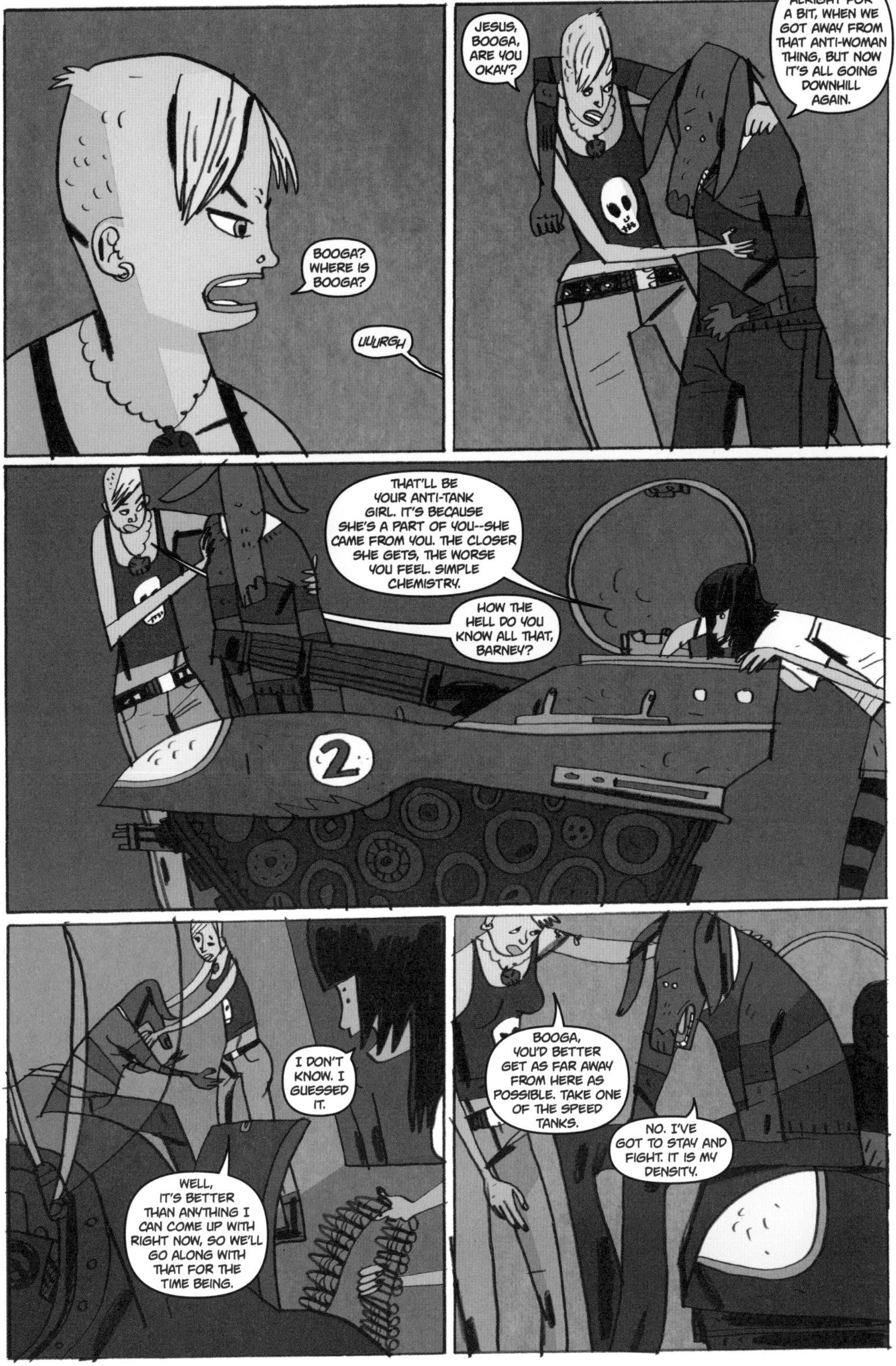
BOOGA? WHERE IS BOOGA?
UUURGH
JESUS, BOOGA, ARE YOU OKAY?
I FELT ALRIGHT FOR A BIT, WHEN WE GOT AWAY FROM THAT ANTI-WOMAN THING, BUT NOW IT'S ALL GOING DOWNHILL AGAIN.
THAT'LL BE YOUR ANTI-TANK GIRL. IT'S BECAUSE SHE'S A PART OF YOU--SHE CAME FROM YOU. THE CLOSER SHE GETS, THE WORSE YOU FEEL. SIMPLE CHEMISTRY.
HOW THE HELL DO YOU KNOW ALL THAT, BARNEY?
I DON'T KNOW. I GUESSED IT.
WELL, IT'S BETTER THAN ANYTHING I CAN COME UP WITH RIGHT NOW, SO WE'LL GO ALONG WITH THAT FOR THE TIME BEING.
BOOGA, YOU'D BETTER GET AS FAR AWAY FROM HERE AS POSSIBLE. TAKE ONE OF THE SPEED TANKS.
NO. I'VE GOT TO STAY AND FIGHT. IT IS MY DENSITY.

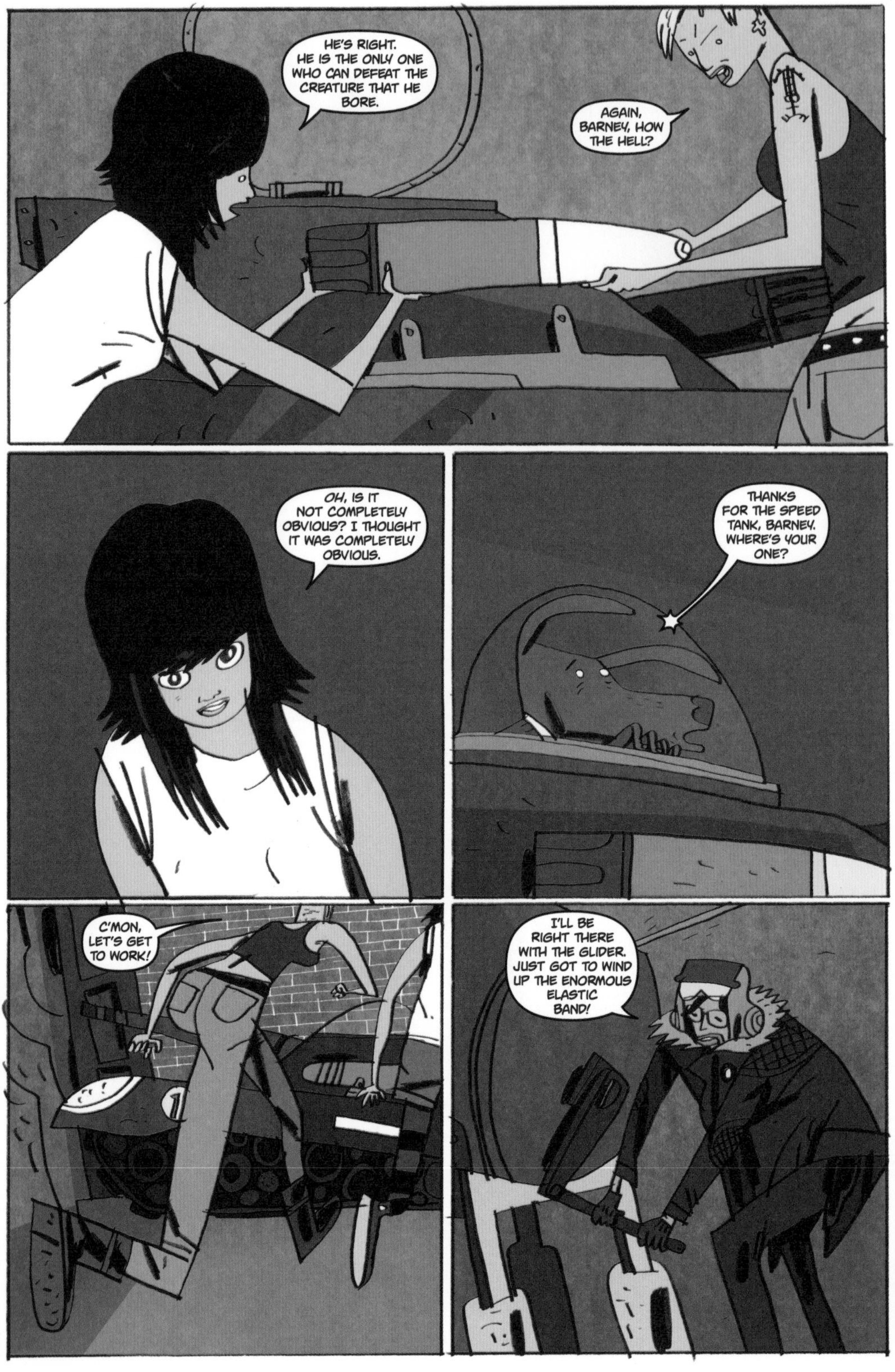
HE'S RIGHT. HE IS THE ONLY ONE WHO CAN DEFEAT THE CREATURE THAT HE BORE.
AGAIN, BARNEY, HOW THE HELL?
OH, IS IT NOT COMPLETELY OBVIOUS? I THOUGHT IT WAS COMPLETELY OBVIOUS.
THANKS FOR THE SPEED TANK, BARNEY. WHERE'S YOUR ONE?
C'MON, LET'S GET TO WORK!
I'LL BE RIGHT THERE WITH THE GLIDER. JUST GOT TO WIND UP THE ENORMOUS ELASTIC BAND!

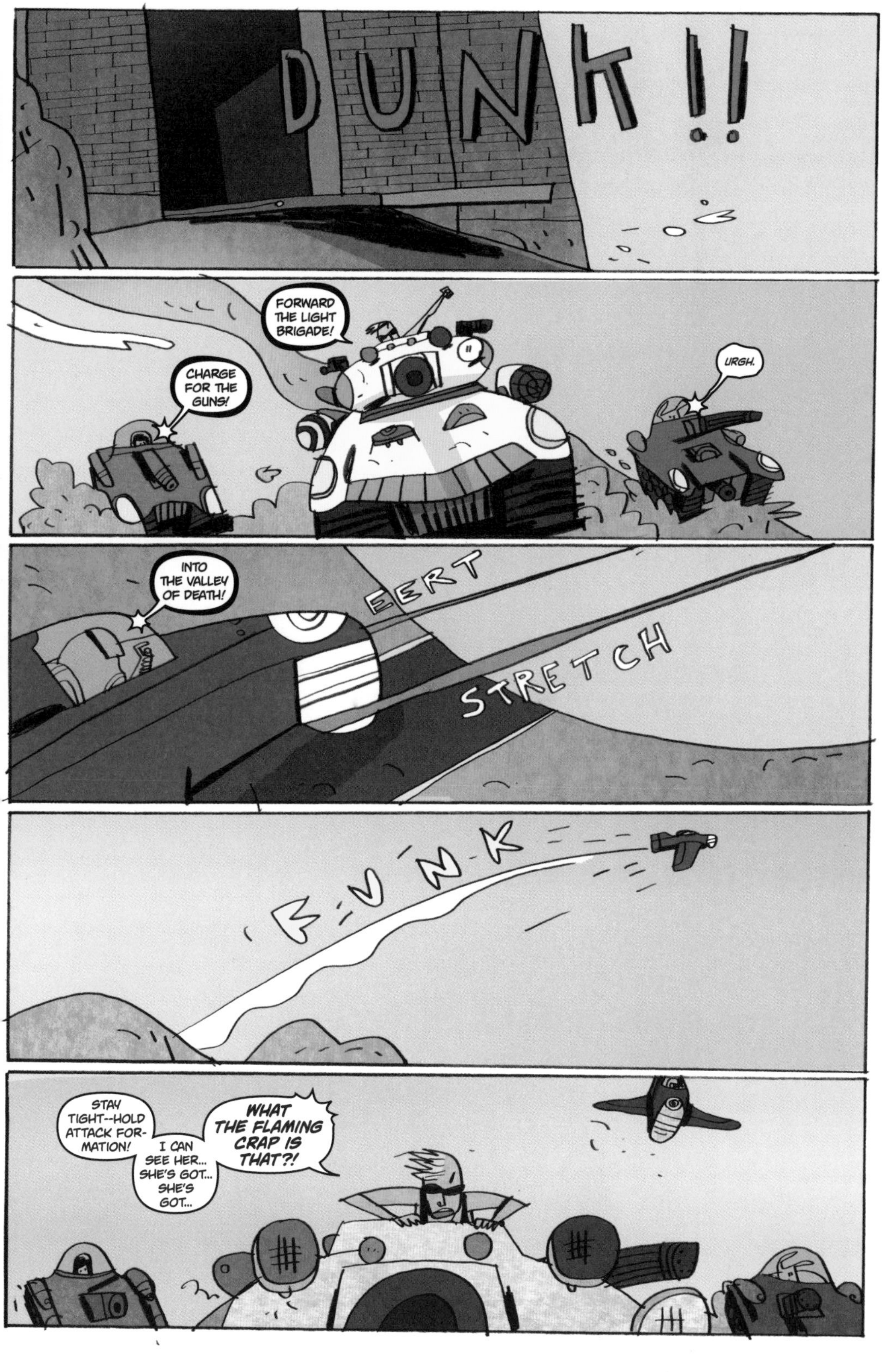
DUNK!!
FORWARD THE LIGHT BRIGADE!
CHARGE FOR THE GUNS!
URGH.
INTO THE VALLEY OF DEATH!
EERT
STRETCH
FUNK
STAY TIGHT--HOLD ATTACK FORMATION!
I CAN SEE HER... SHE'S GOT... SHE'S GOT...
WHAT THE FLAMING CRAP IS THAT?!

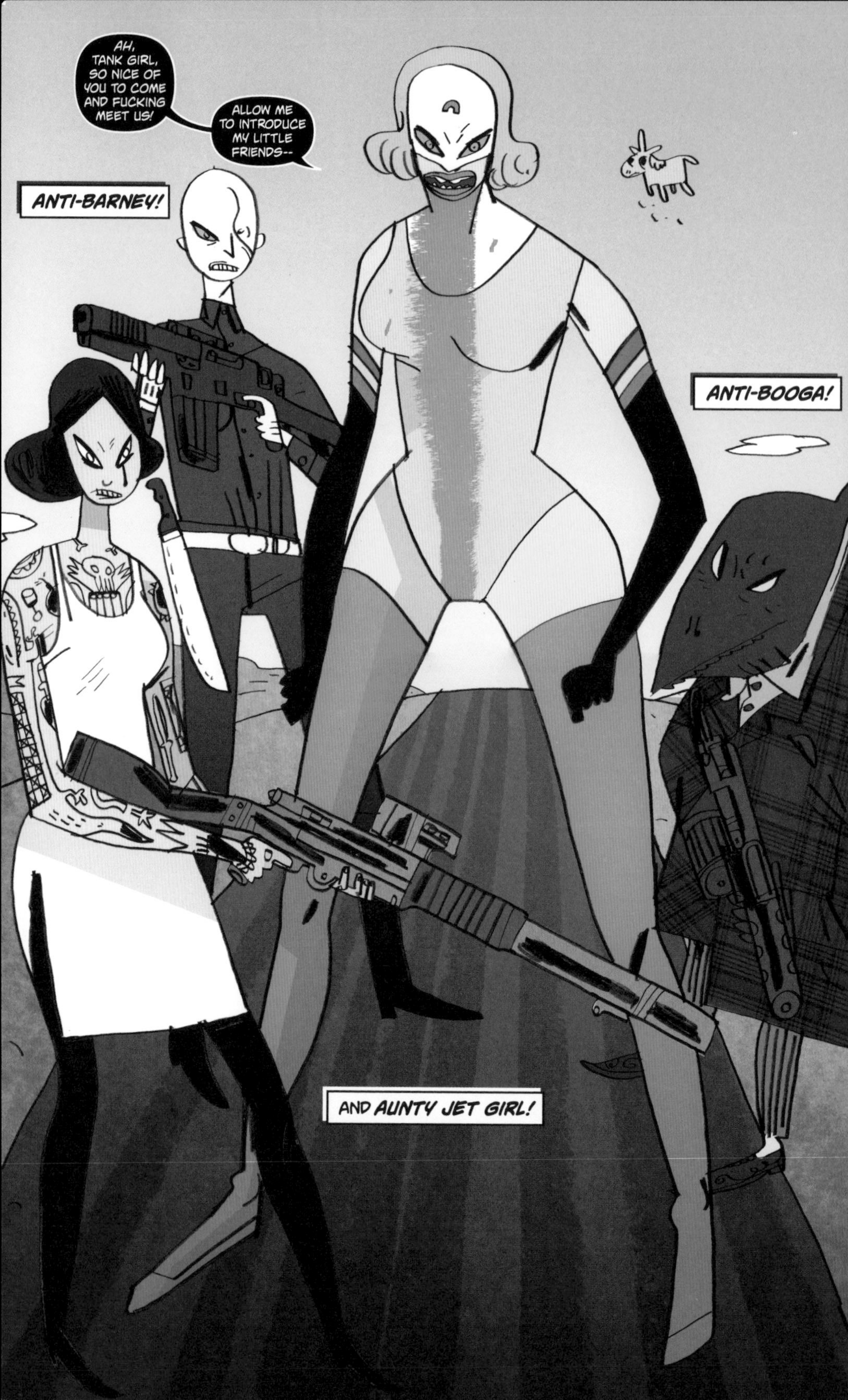
AH, TANK GIRL, SO NICE OF YOU TO COME AND FUCKING MEET US!
ALLOW ME TO INTRODUCE MY LITTLE FRIENDS--
ANTI-BARNEY!
ANTI-BOOGA!
AND AUNTY JET GIRL!

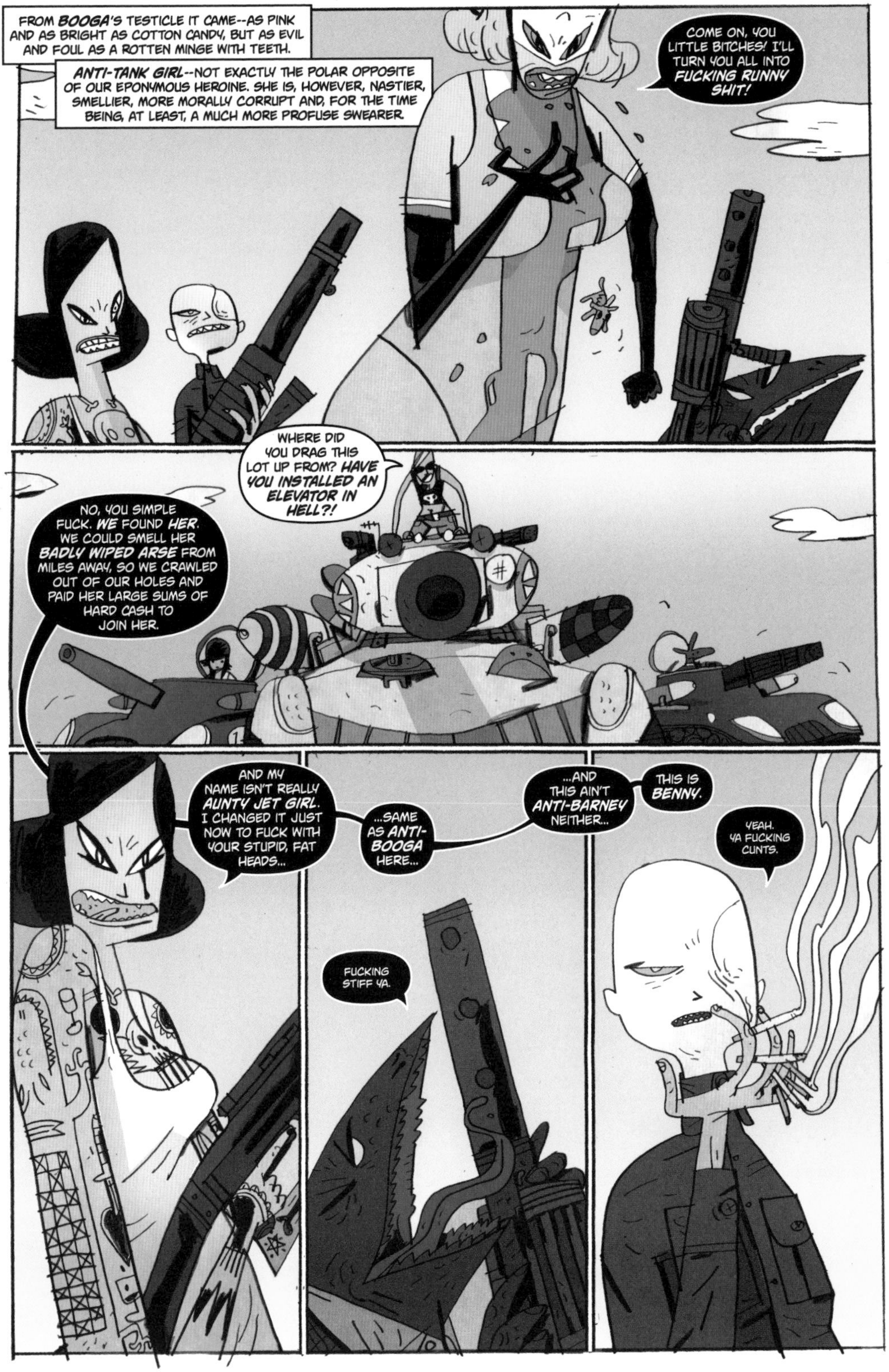

FROM BOOGA'S TESTICLE IT CAME--AS PINK AND AS BRIGHT AS COTTON CANDY, BUT AS EVIL AND FOUL AS A ROTTEN MINGE WITH TEETH.
ANTI-TANK GIRL--NOT EXACTLY THE POLAR OPPOSITE OF OUR EPONYMOUS HEROINE. SHE IS, HOWEVER, NASTIER, SMELLIER, MORE MORALLY CORRUPT AND, FOR THE TIME BEING, AT LEAST, A MUCH MORE PROFUSE SWEARER.
COME ON, YOU LITTLE BITCHES! I'LL TURN YOU ALL INTO FUCKING RUNNY SHIT!
WHERE DID YOU DRAG THIS LOT UP FROM? HAVE YOU INSTALLED AN ELEVATOR IN HELL?!
NO, YOU SIMPLE FUCK. WE FOUND HER. WE COULD SMELL HER BADLY WIPED ARSE FROM MILES AWAY, SO WE CRAWLED OUT OF OUR HOLES AND PAID HER LARGE SUMS OF HARD CASH TO JOIN HER.
AND MY NAME ISN'T REALLY AUNTY JET GIRL. I CHANGED IT JUST NOW TO FUCK WITH YOUR STUPID, FAT HEADS...
...SAME AS ANTI-BOOGA HERE...
...AND THIS AIN'T ANTI-BARNEY NEITHER...
THIS IS BENNY.
FUCKING STIFF YA.
YEAH. YA FUCKING CUNTS.

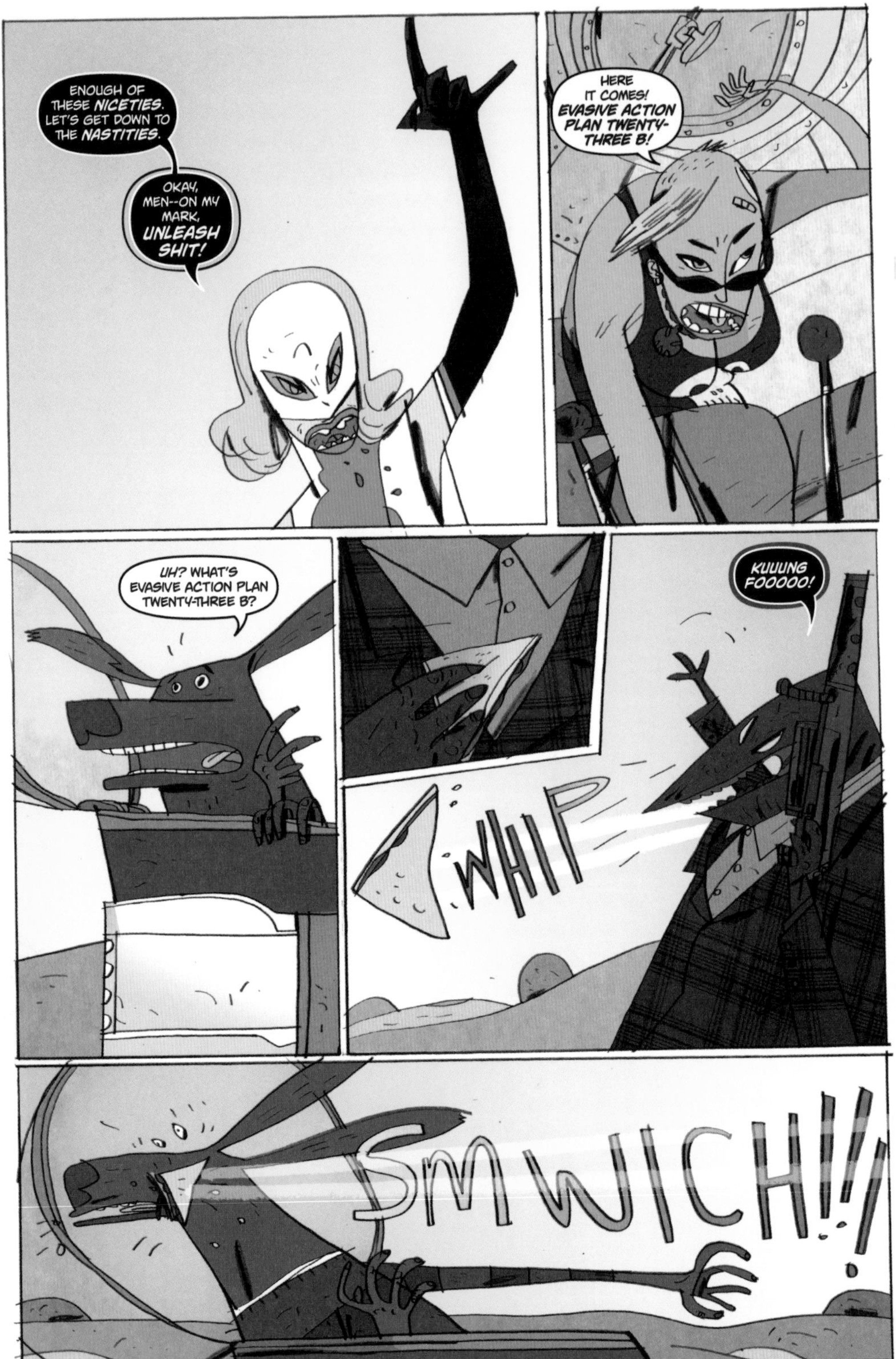
ENOUGH OF THESE NICETIES. LET'S GET DOWN TO THE NASTITIES.
OKAY, MEN--ON MY MARK, UNLEASH SHIT!
HERE IT COMES! EVASIVE ACTION PLAN TWENTY-THREE B!
UH? WHAT'S EVASIVE ACTION PLAN TWENTY-THREE B?
KUUUNG FOOOOO!
WHIP
SMWICH!!!

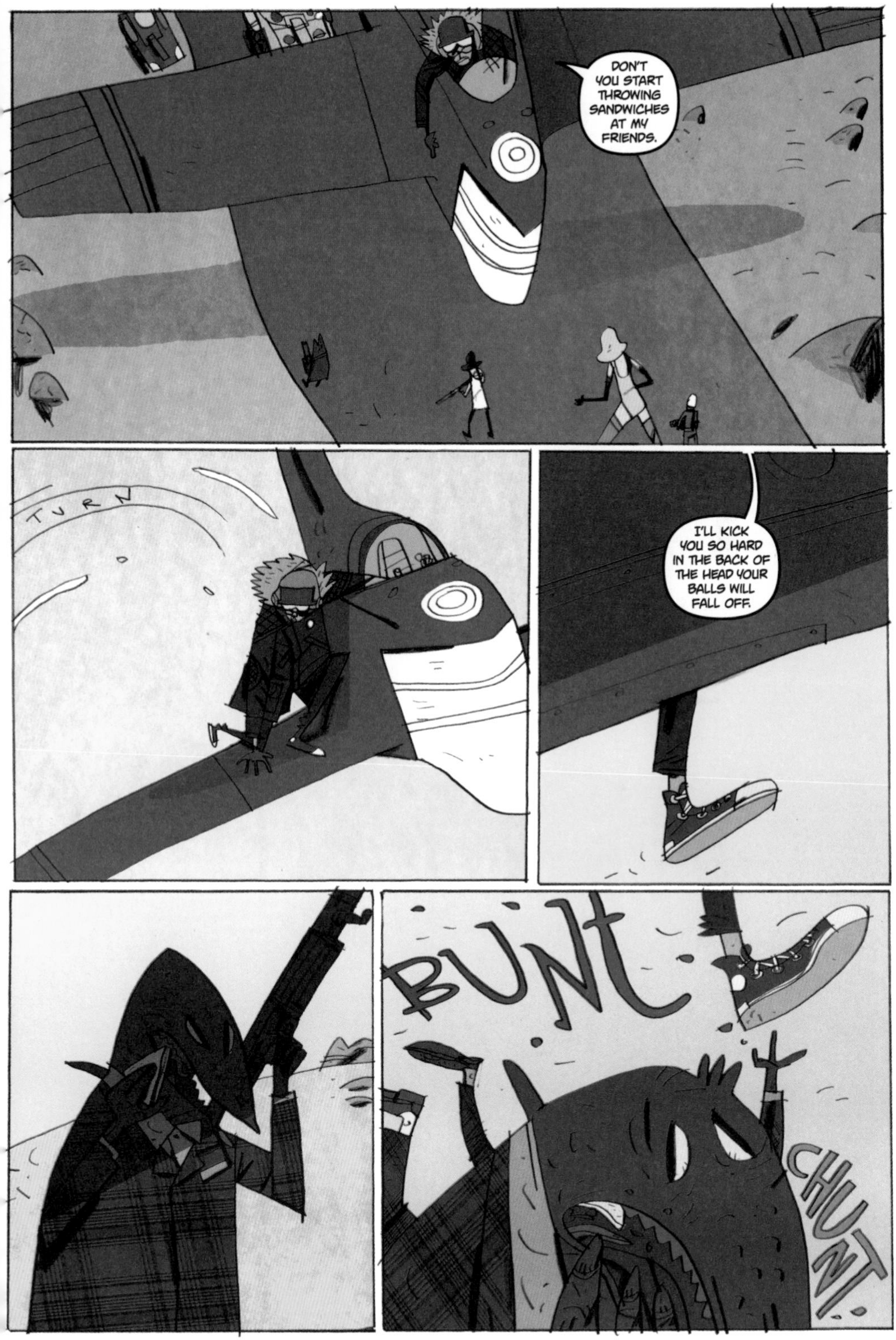
DON'T YOU START THROWING SANDWICHES AT MY FRIENDS.
TURN
I'LL KICK YOU SO HARD IN THE BACK OF THE HEAD YOUR BALLS WILL FALL OFF.
BUNT
CHUNT

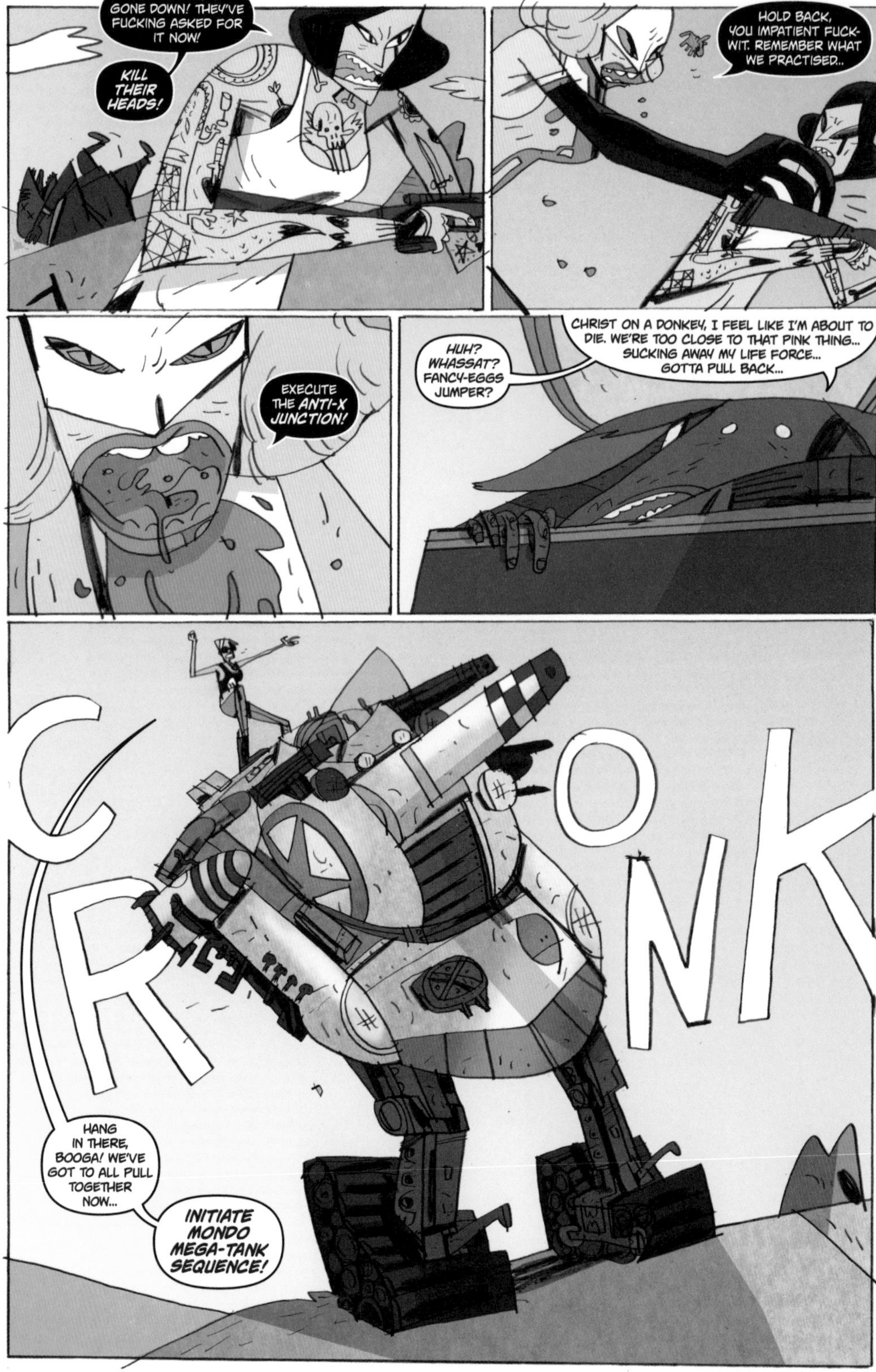
ANTI-BOOGA'S GONE DOWN! THEY'VE FUCKING ASKED FOR IT NOW!
KILL THEIR HEADS!
HOLD BACK, YOU IMPATIENT FUCK-WIT. REMEMBER WHAT WE PRACTISED...
EXECUTE THE ANTI-X JUNCTION!
CHRIST ON A DONKEY, I FEEL LIKE I'M ABOUT TO DIE. WE'RE TOO CLOSE TO THAT PINK THING... SUCKING AWAY MY LIFE FORCE... GOTTA PULL BACK...
HUH? WHASSAT? FANCY-EGGS JUMPER?
CRONK
HANG IN THERE, BOOGA! WE'VE GOT TO ALL PULL TOGETHER NOW...
INITIATE MONDO MEGA-TANK SEQUENCE!

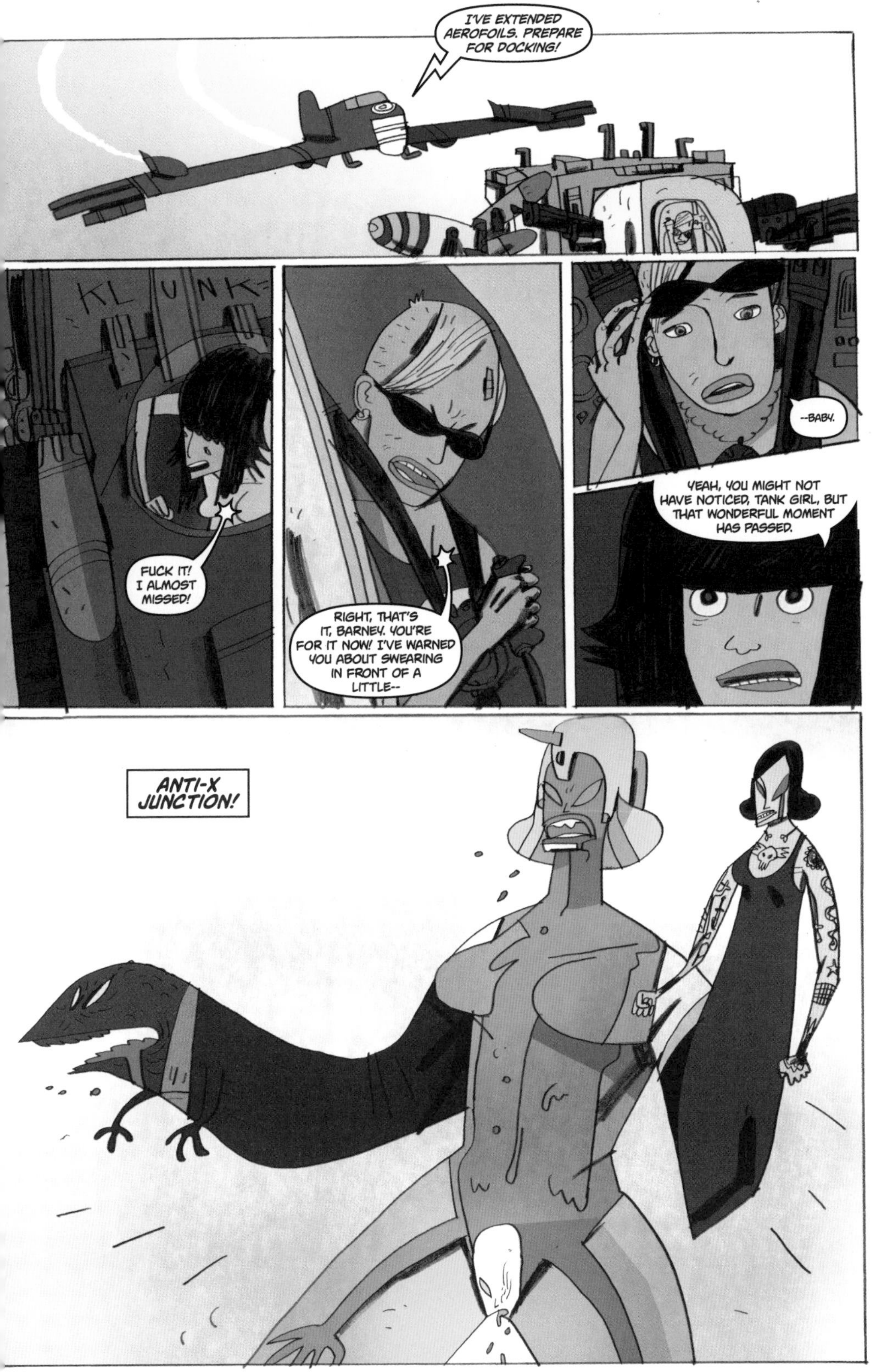
I'VE EXTENDED AEROFOILS. PREPARE FOR DOCKING!
KLUNK
FUCK IT! I ALMOST MISSED!
RIGHT, THAT'S IT, BARNEY. YOU'RE FOR IT NOW! I'VE WARNED YOU ABOUT SWEARING IN FRONT OF A LITTLE--
--BABY.
YEAH, YOU MIGHT NOT HAVE NOTICED, TANK GIRL, BUT THAT WONDERFUL MOMENT HAS PASSED.
ANTI-X JUNCTION!

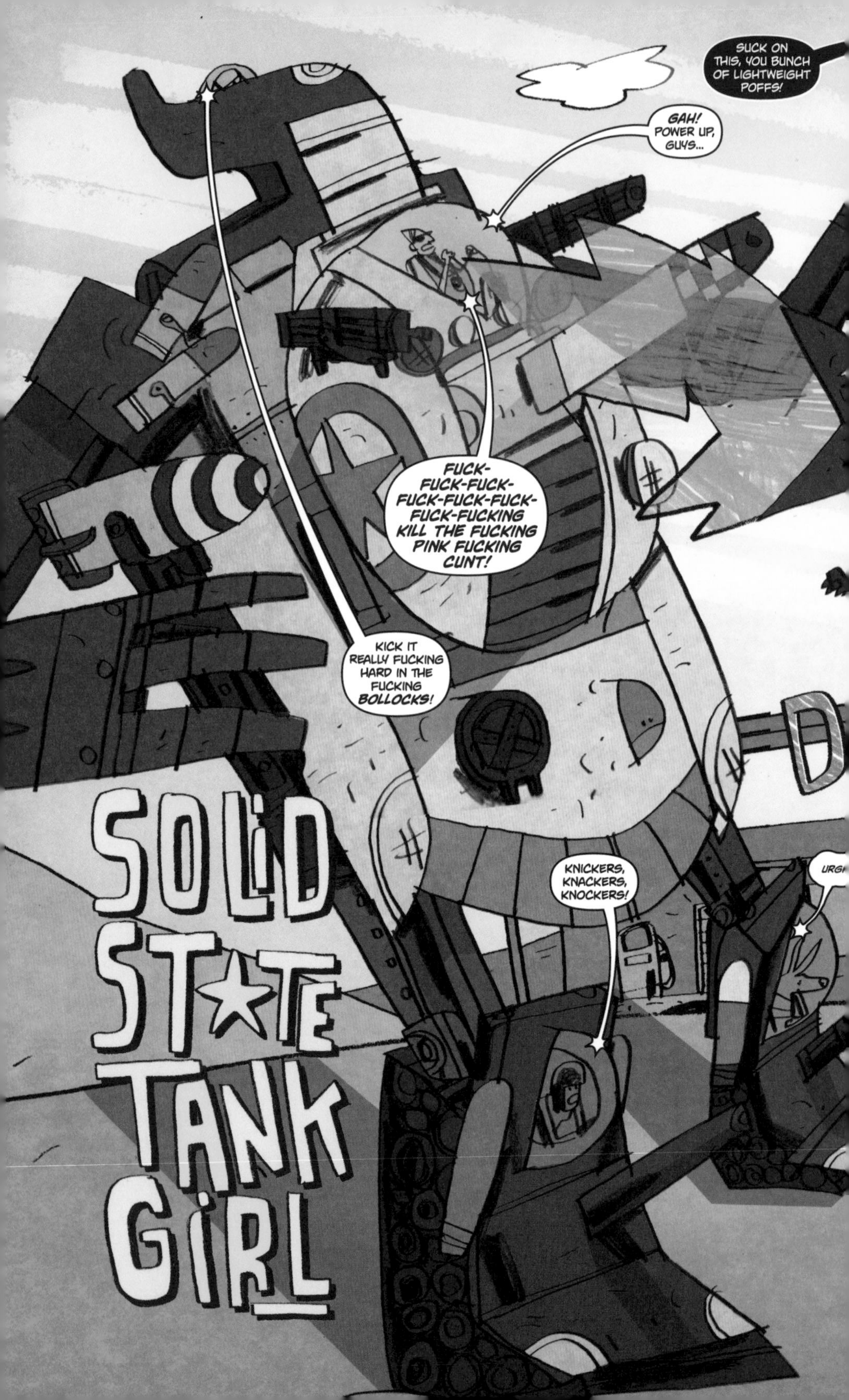
SUCK ON THIS, YOU BUNCH OF LIGHTWEIGHT POFFS!
GAH! POWER UP, GUYS...
FUCK-FUCK-FUCK-FUCK-FUCK-FUCK-FUCK-FUCKING KILL THE FUCKING PINK FUCKING CUNT!
KICK IT REALLY FUCKING HARD IN THE FUCKING BOLLOCKS!
SOLID STATE TANK GIRL
KNICKERS, KNACKERS, KNOCKERS!
URG

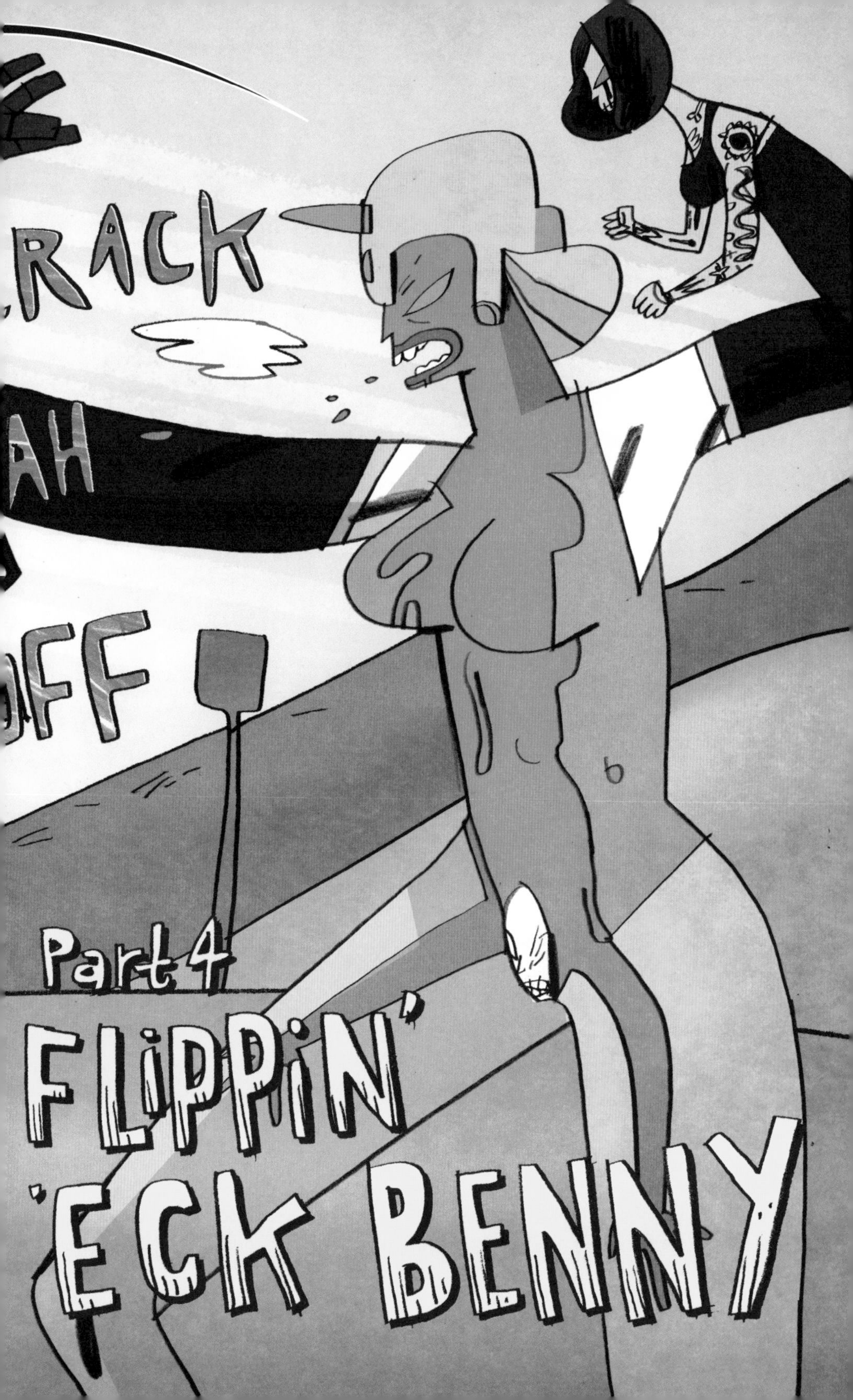

RACK
AH
OFF
Part 4
FLIPPIN' 'ECK BENNY

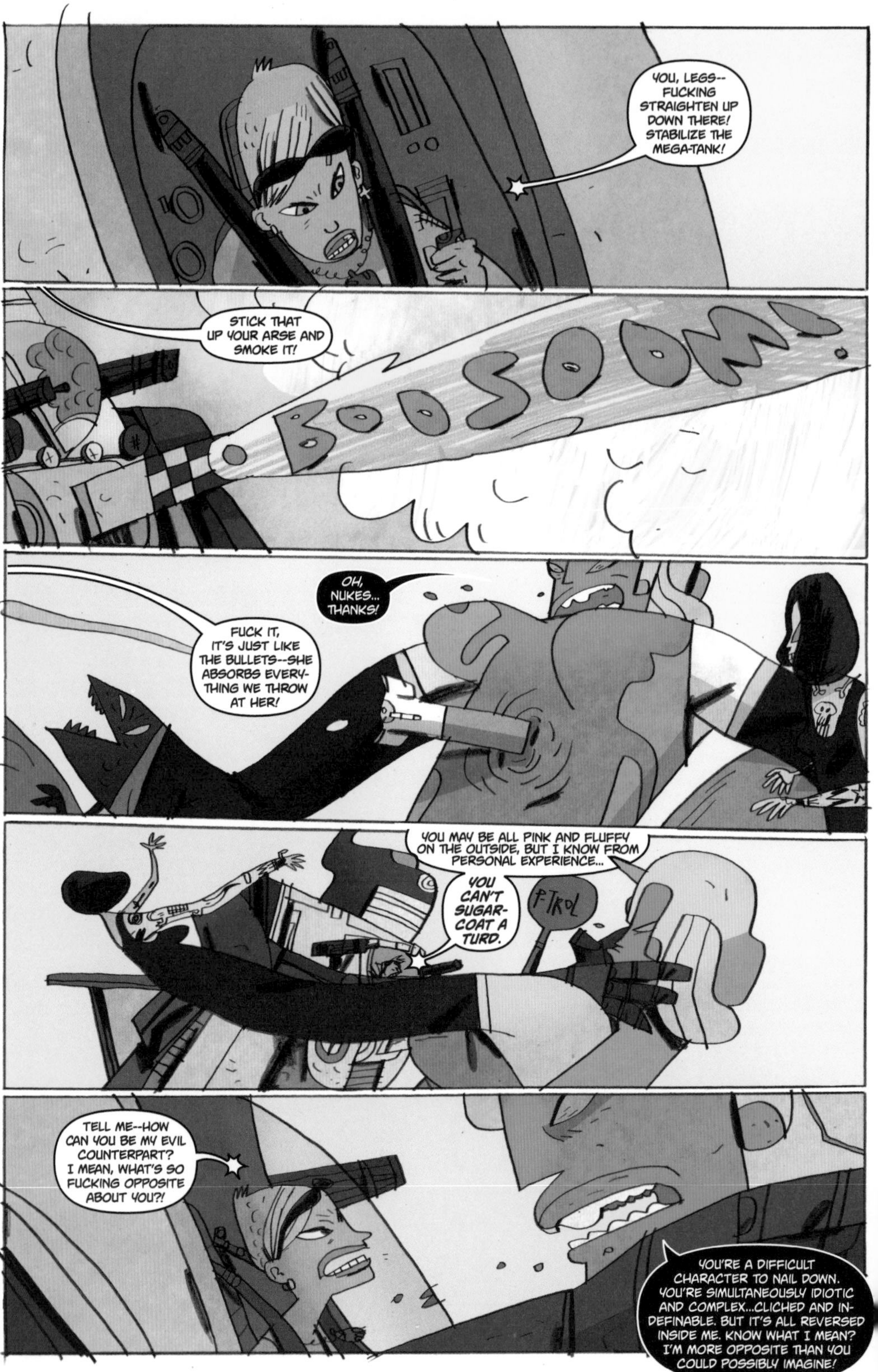
YOU, LEGS-- FUCKING STRAIGHTEN UP DOWN THERE! STABILIZE THE MEGA-TANK!
STICK THAT UP YOUR ARSE AND SMOKE IT!
BOOSOOM!
OH, NUKES... THANKS!
FUCK IT, IT'S JUST LIKE THE BULLETS--SHE ABSORBS EVERY-THING WE THROW AT HER!
YOU MAY BE ALL PINK AND FLUFFY ON THE OUTSIDE, BUT I KNOW FROM PERSONAL EXPERIENCE...
YOU CAN'T SUGAR-COAT A TURD.
TELL ME--HOW CAN YOU BE MY EVIL COUNTERPART? I MEAN, WHAT'S SO FUCKING OPPOSITE ABOUT YOU?!
YOU'RE A DIFFICULT CHARACTER TO NAIL DOWN. YOU'RE SIMULTANEOUSLY IDIOTIC AND COMPLEX...CLICHED AND IN-DEFINABLE. BUT IT'S ALL REVERSED INSIDE ME. KNOW WHAT I MEAN? I'M MORE OPPOSITE THAN YOU COULD POSSIBLY IMAGINE!

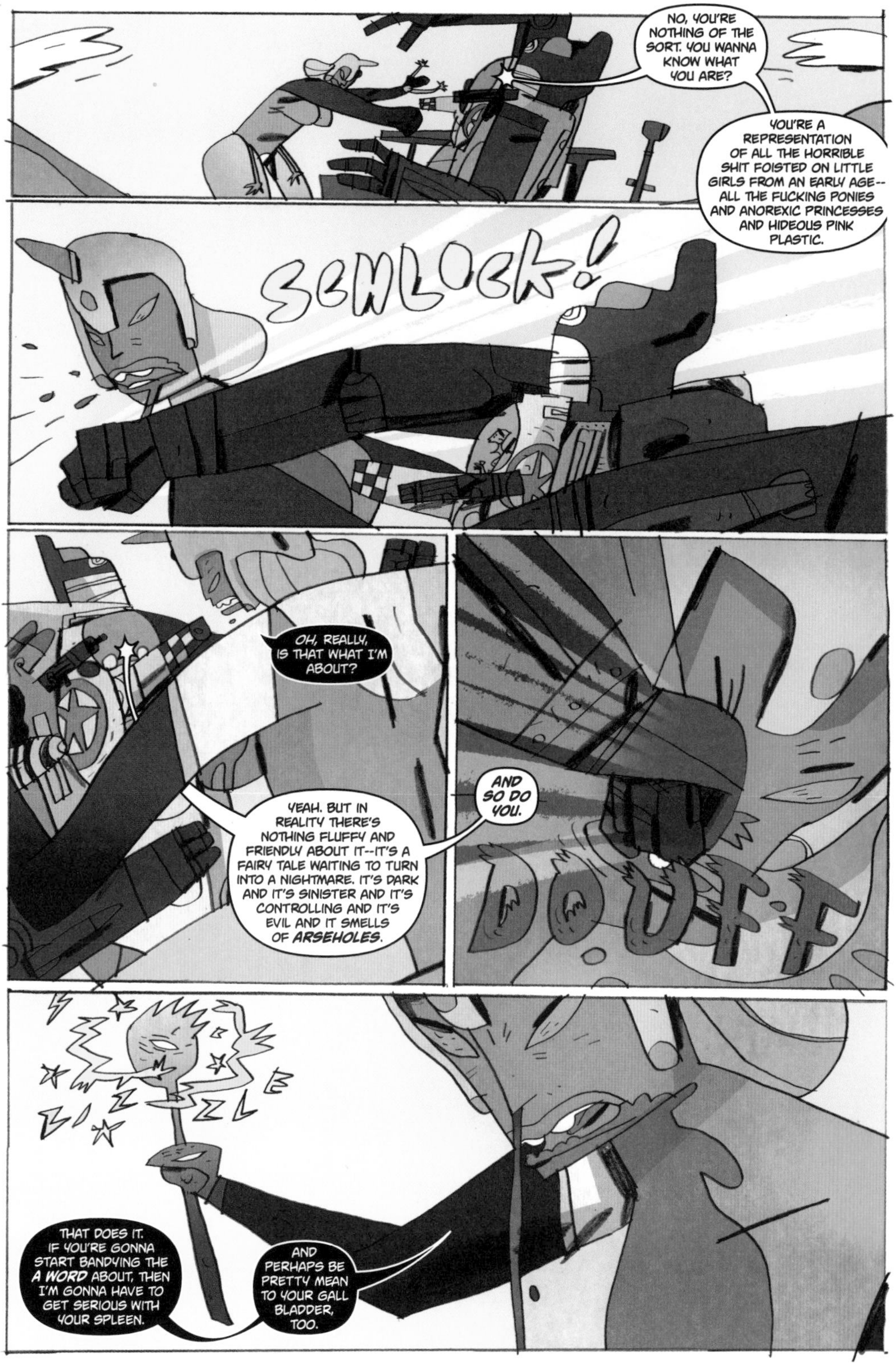
NO, YOU'RE NOTHING OF THE SORT. YOU WANNA KNOW WHAT YOU ARE?
YOU'RE A REPRESENTATION OF ALL THE HORRIBLE SHIT FOISTED ON LITTLE GIRLS FROM AN EARLY AGE--ALL THE FUCKING PONIES AND ANOREXIC PRINCESSES AND HIDEOUS PINK PLASTIC.
SCHLOCK!
OH, REALLY, IS THAT WHAT I'M ABOUT?
YEAH. BUT IN REALITY THERE'S NOTHING FLUFFY AND FRIENDLY ABOUT IT--IT'S A FAIRY TALE WAITING TO TURN INTO A NIGHTMARE. IT'S DARK AND IT'S SINISTER AND IT'S CONTROLLING AND IT'S EVIL AND IT SMELLS OF ARSEHOLES.
AND SO DO YOU.
DOUFF
BZZLE
THAT DOES IT. IF YOU'RE GONNA START BANDYING THE A WORD ABOUT, THEN I'M GONNA HAVE TO GET SERIOUS WITH YOUR SPLEEN.
AND PERHAPS BE PRETTY MEAN TO YOUR GALL BLADDER, TOO.

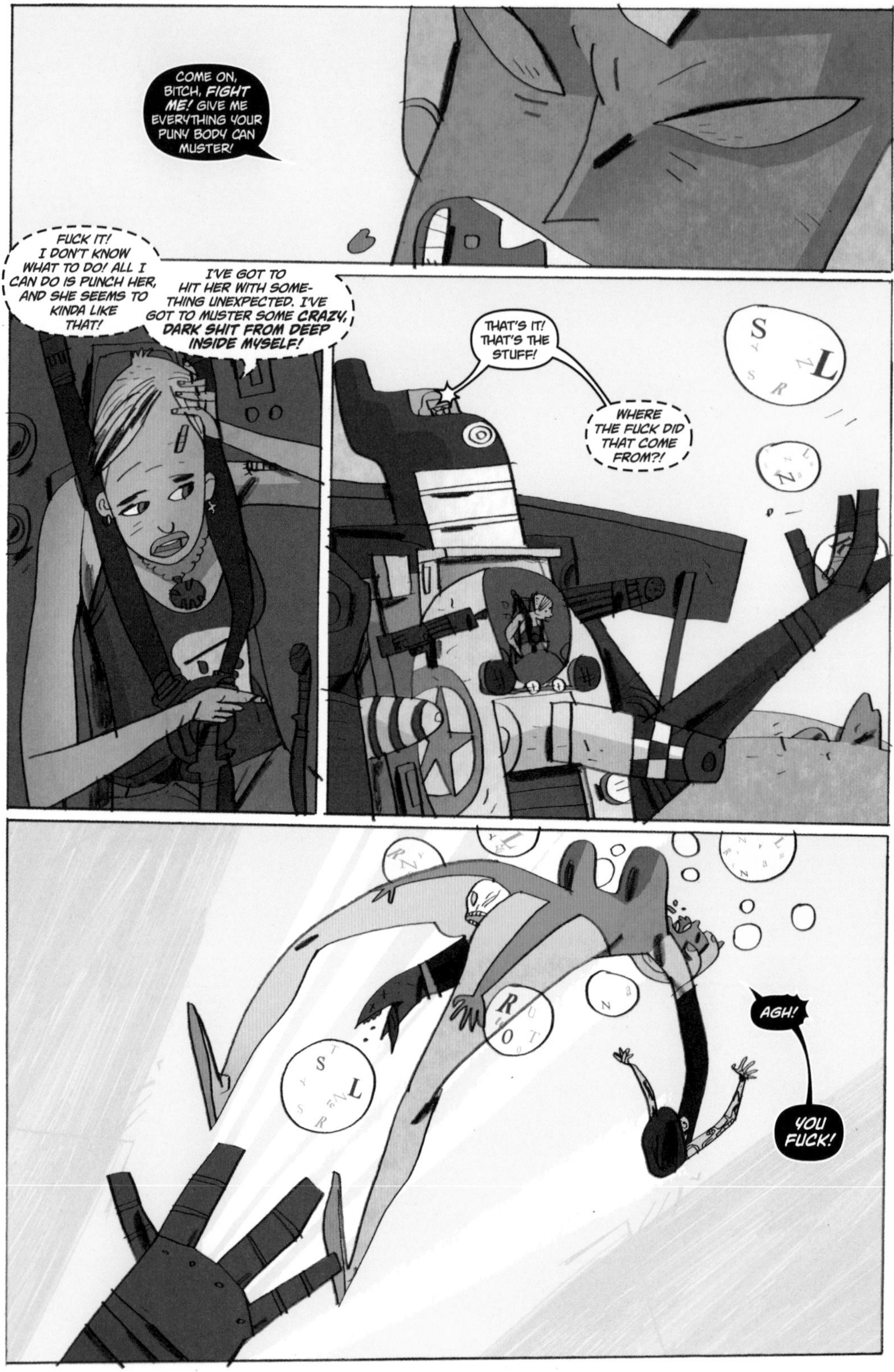
COME ON, BITCH, FIGHT ME! GIVE ME EVERYTHING YOUR PUNY BODY CAN MUSTER!
FUCK IT! I DON'T KNOW WHAT TO DO! ALL I CAN DO IS PUNCH HER, AND SHE SEEMS TO KINDA LIKE THAT!
I'VE GOT TO HIT HER WITH SOME-THING UNEXPECTED. I'VE GOT TO MUSTER SOME CRAZY, DARK SHIT FROM DEEP INSIDE MYSELF!
THAT'S IT! THAT'S THE STUFF!
WHERE THE FUCK DID THAT COME FROM?!
AGH!
YOU FUCK!

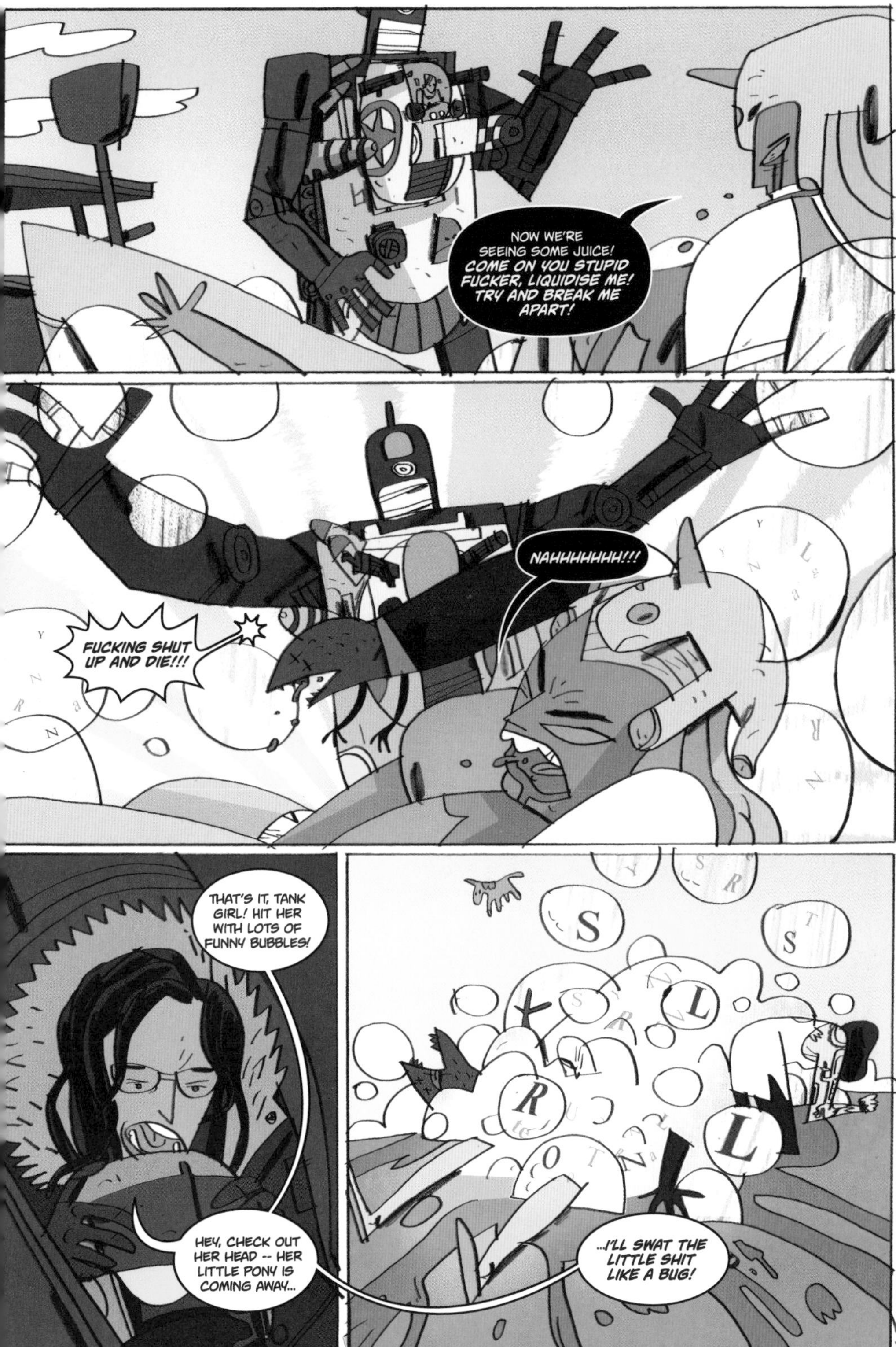
NOW WE'RE SEEING SOME JUICE! COME ON YOU STUPID FUCKER, LIQUIDISE ME! TRY AND BREAK ME APART!
NAHHHHHHH!!!
FUCKING SHUT UP AND DIE!!!
THAT'S IT, TANK GIRL! HIT HER WITH LOTS OF FUNNY BUBBLES!
HEY, CHECK OUT HER HEAD -- HER LITTLE PONY IS COMING AWAY...
...I'LL SWAT THE LITTLE SHIT LIKE A BUG!

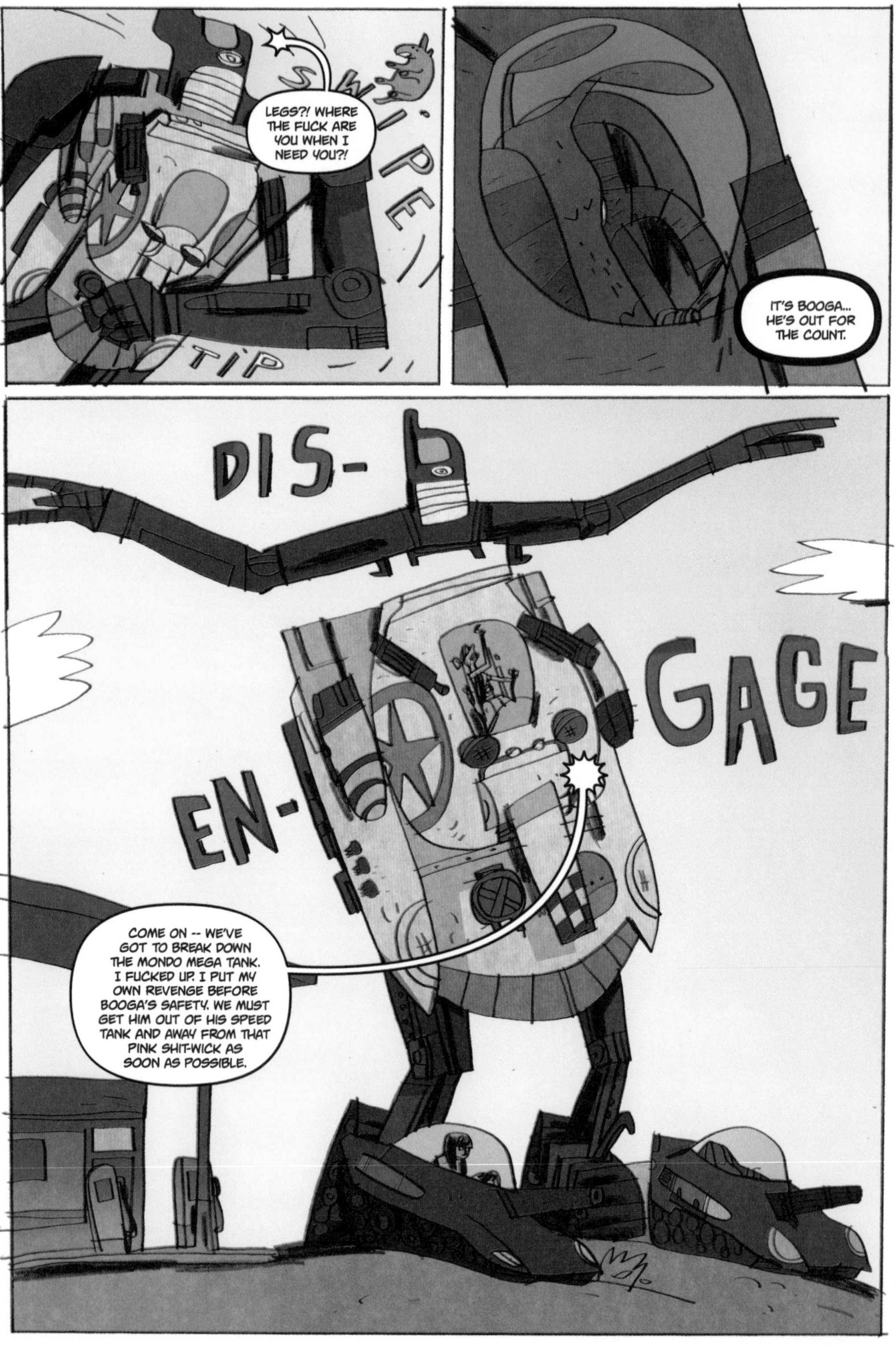
LEGS?! WHERE THE FUCK ARE YOU WHEN I NEED YOU?!
SWIPE
TIP
IT'S BOOGA... HE'S OUT FOR THE COUNT.
DIS-
ENGAGE
EN-
COME ON -- WE'VE GOT TO BREAK DOWN THE MONDO MEGA TANK. I FUCKED UP. I PUT MY OWN REVENGE BEFORE BOOGA'S SAFETY. WE MUST GET HIM OUT OF HIS SPEED TANK AND AWAY FROM THAT PINK SHIT-WICK AS SOON AS POSSIBLE.

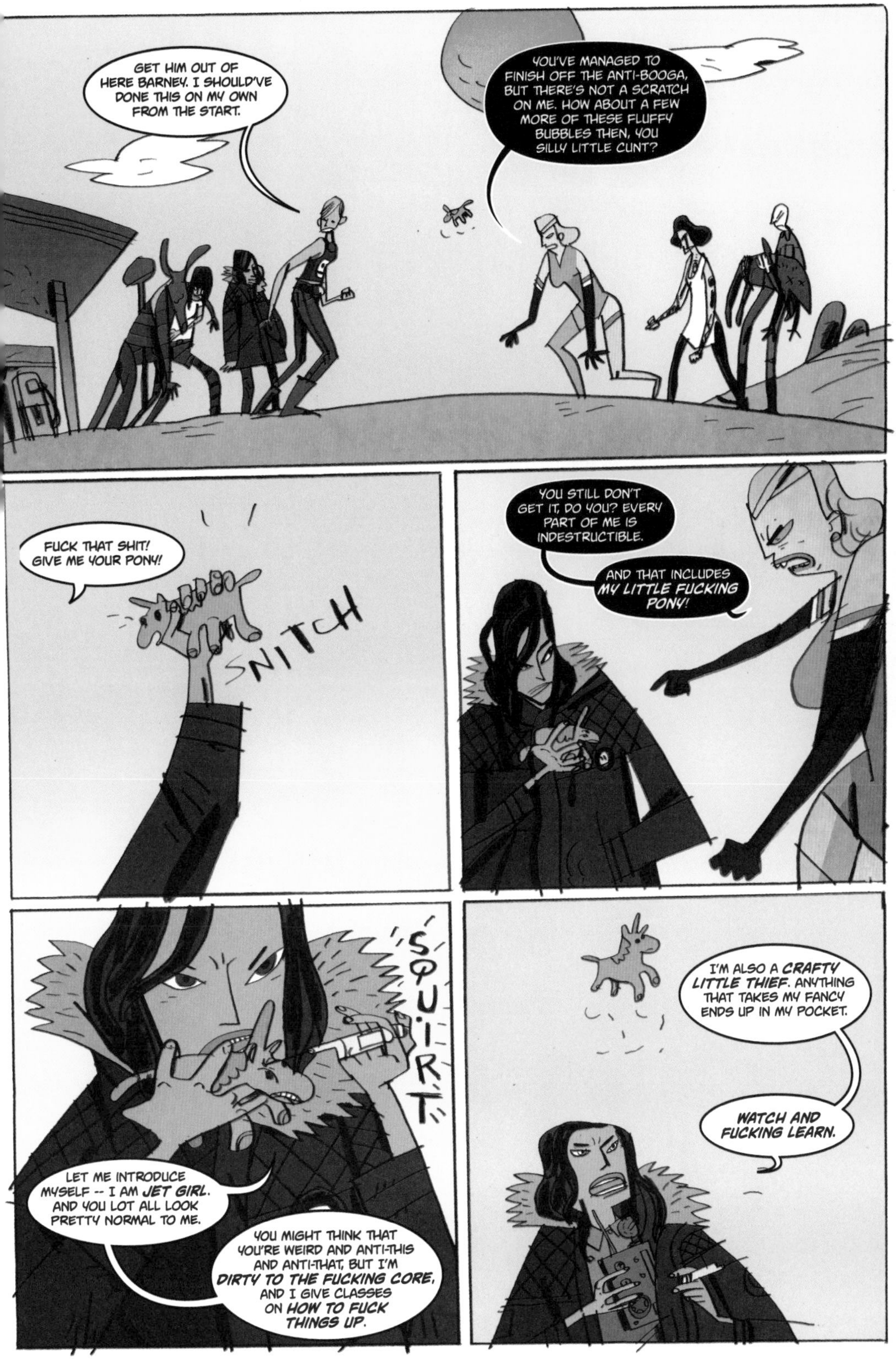
GET HIM OUT OF HERE BARNEY. I SHOULD'VE DONE THIS ON MY OWN FROM THE START.
YOU'VE MANAGED TO FINISH OFF THE ANTI-BOOGA, BUT THERE'S NOT A SCRATCH ON ME. HOW ABOUT A FEW MORE OF THESE FLUFFY BUBBLES THEN, YOU SILLY LITTLE CUNT?
FUCK THAT SHIT! GIVE ME YOUR PONY!
SNITCH
YOU STILL DON'T GET IT, DO YOU? EVERY PART OF ME IS INDESTRUCTIBLE.
AND THAT INCLUDES MY LITTLE FUCKING PONY!
SQUIRT
LET ME INTRODUCE MYSELF -- I AM JET GIRL. AND YOU LOT ALL LOOK PRETTY NORMAL TO ME.
YOU MIGHT THINK THAT YOU'RE WEIRD AND ANTI-THIS AND ANTI-THAT, BUT I'M DIRTY TO THE FUCKING CORE, AND I GIVE CLASSES ON HOW TO FUCK THINGS UP.
I'M ALSO A CRAFTY LITTLE THIEF. ANYTHING THAT TAKES MY FANCY ENDS UP IN MY POCKET.
WATCH AND FUCKING LEARN.

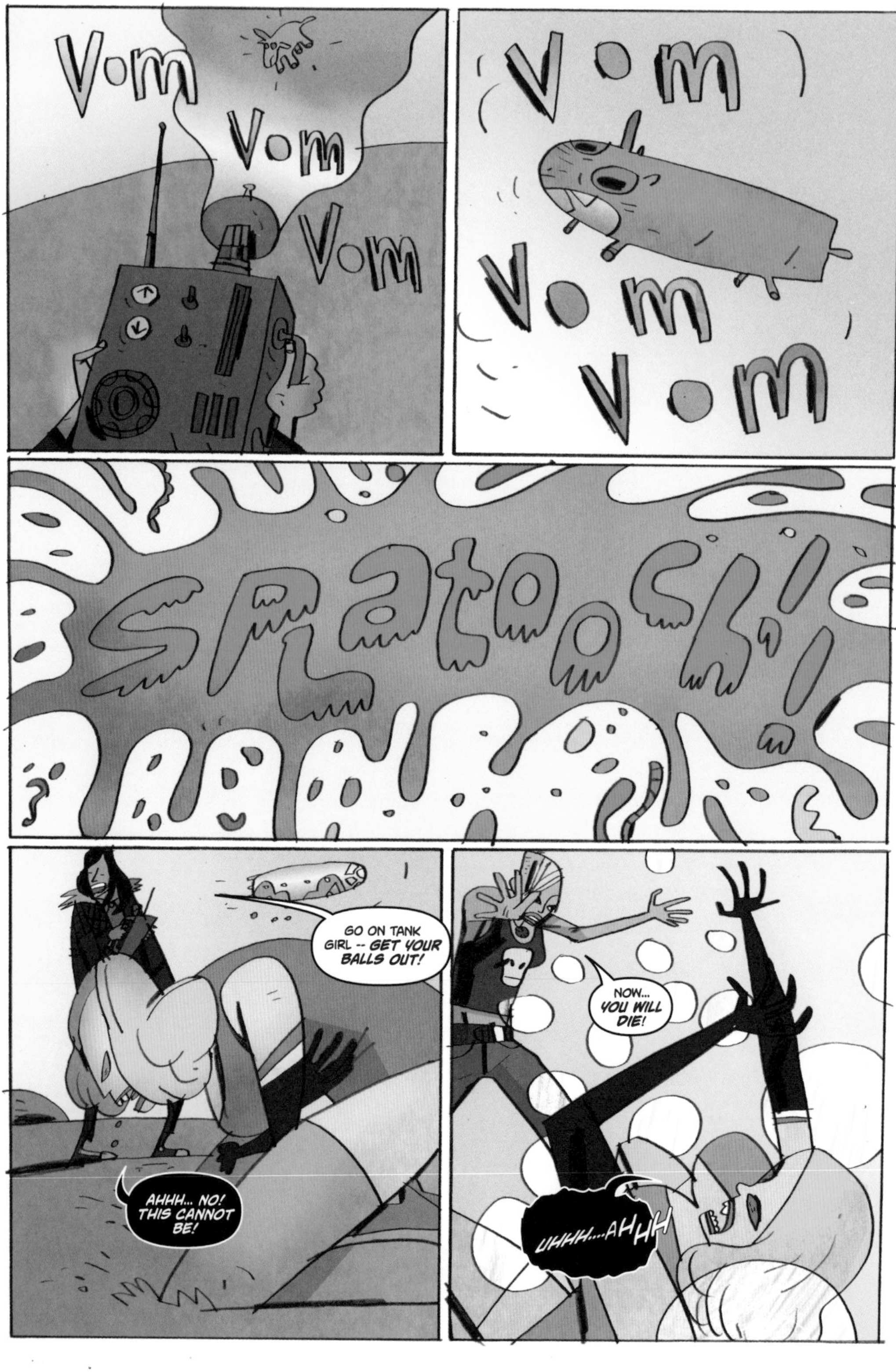
Vom
Vom
Vom
Vom
Vom
Vom
Splatoosh!
GO ON TANK GIRL -- GET YOUR BALLS OUT!
AHHH... NO! THIS CANNOT BE!
NOW... YOU WILL DIE!
UHHH....AHHH

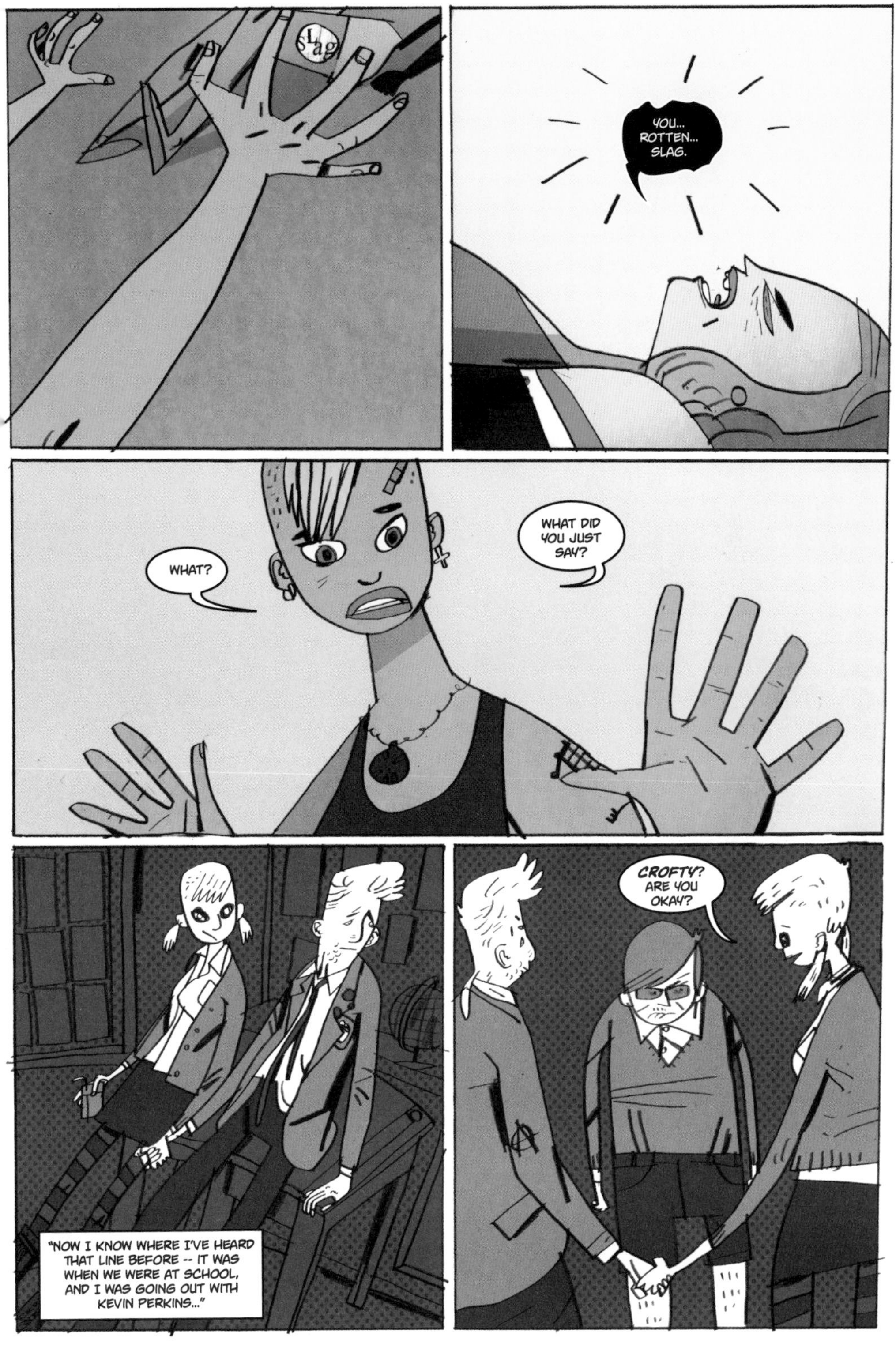
SLAG
YOU... ROTTEN... SLAG.
WHAT?
WHAT DID YOU JUST SAY?
"NOW I KNOW WHERE I'VE HEARD THAT LINE BEFORE -- IT WAS WHEN WE WERE AT SCHOOL, AND I WAS GOING OUT WITH KEVIN PERKINS..."
CROFTY? ARE YOU OKAY?

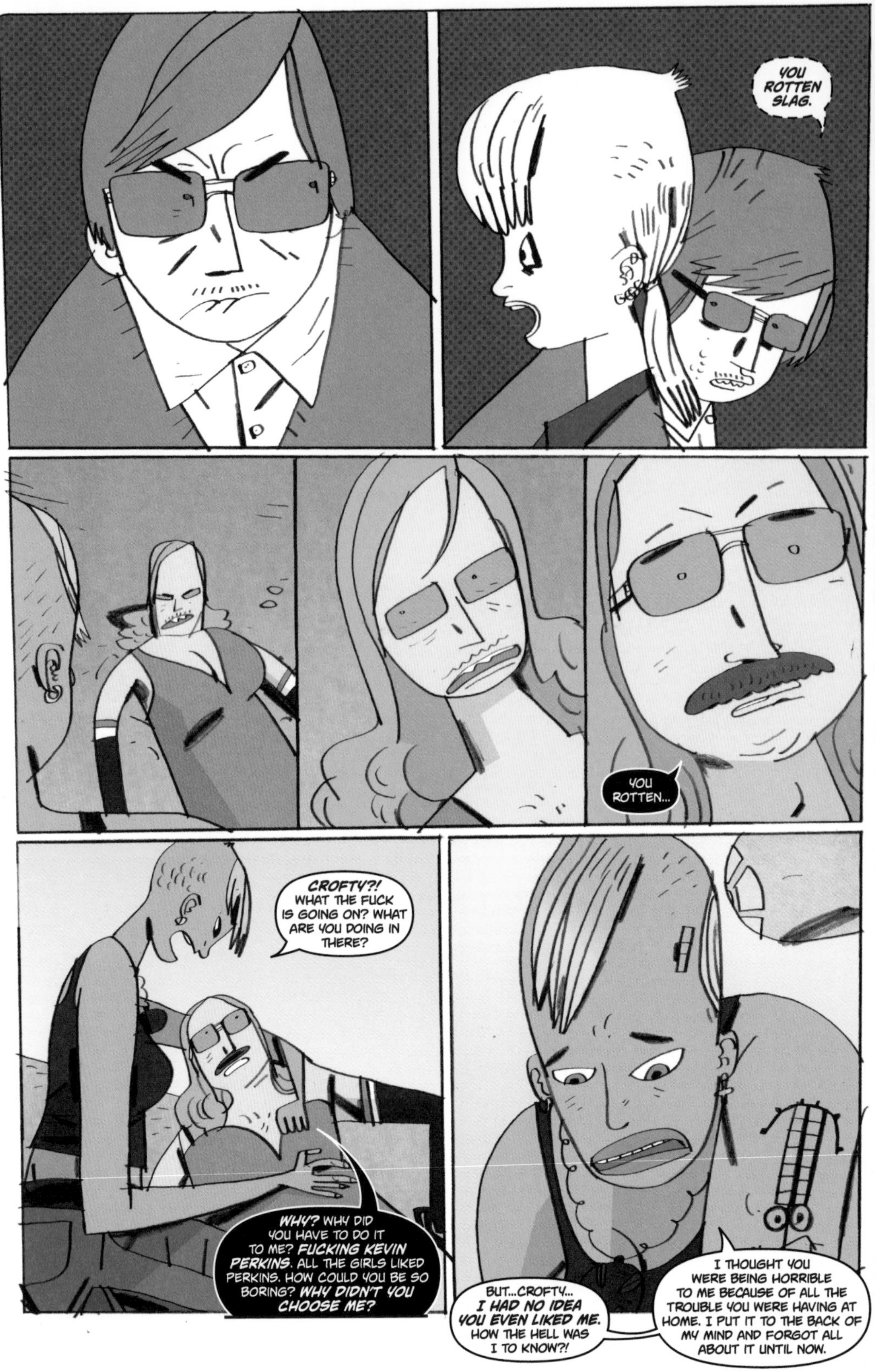
YOU ROTTEN SLAG.
YOU ROTTEN...
CROFTY?! WHAT THE FUCK IS GOING ON? WHAT ARE YOU DOING IN THERE?
WHY? WHY DID YOU HAVE TO DO IT TO ME? FUCKING KEVIN PERKINS. ALL THE GIRLS LIKED PERKINS. HOW COULD YOU BE SO BORING? WHY DIDN'T YOU CHOOSE ME?
BUT...CROFTY... I HAD NO IDEA YOU EVEN LIKED ME. HOW THE HELL WAS I TO KNOW?!
I THOUGHT YOU WERE BEING HORRIBLE TO ME BECAUSE OF ALL THE TROUBLE YOU WERE HAVING AT HOME. I PUT IT TO THE BACK OF MY MIND AND FORGOT ALL ABOUT IT UNTIL NOW.

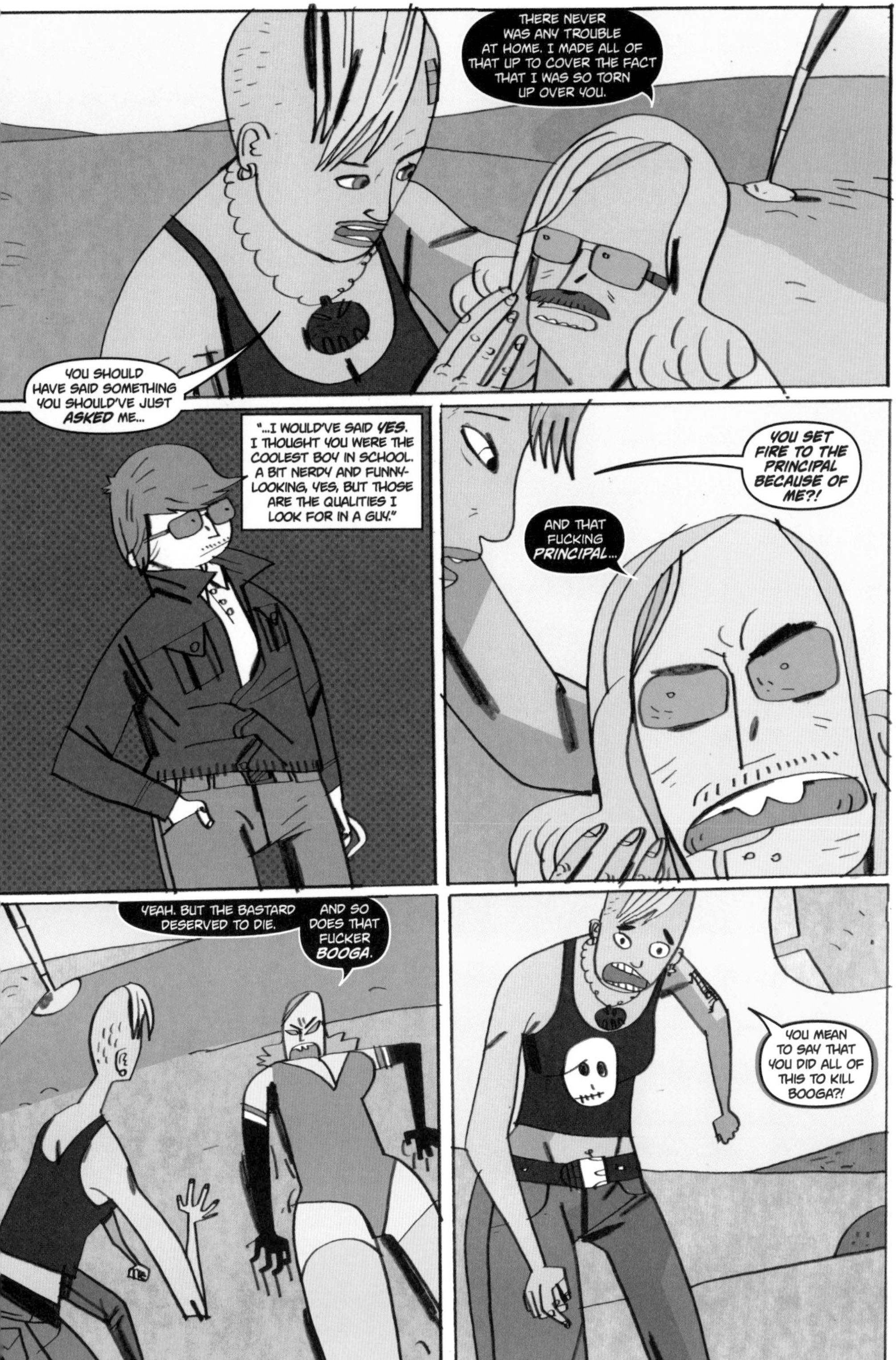

THERE NEVER WAS ANY TROUBLE AT HOME. I MADE ALL OF THAT UP TO COVER THE FACT THAT I WAS SO TORN UP OVER YOU.
YOU SHOULD HAVE SAID SOMETHING YOU SHOULD'VE JUST ASKED ME...
"...I WOULD'VE SAID YES. I THOUGHT YOU WERE THE COOLEST BOY IN SCHOOL. A BIT NERDY AND FUNNY-LOOKING, YES, BUT THOSE ARE THE QUALITIES I LOOK FOR IN A GUY."
AND THAT FUCKING PRINCIPAL...
YOU SET FIRE TO THE PRINCIPAL BECAUSE OF ME?!
YEAH. BUT THE BASTARD DESERVED TO DIE.
AND SO DOES THAT FUCKER BOOGA.
YOU MEAN TO SAY THAT YOU DID ALL OF THIS TO KILL BOOGA?!

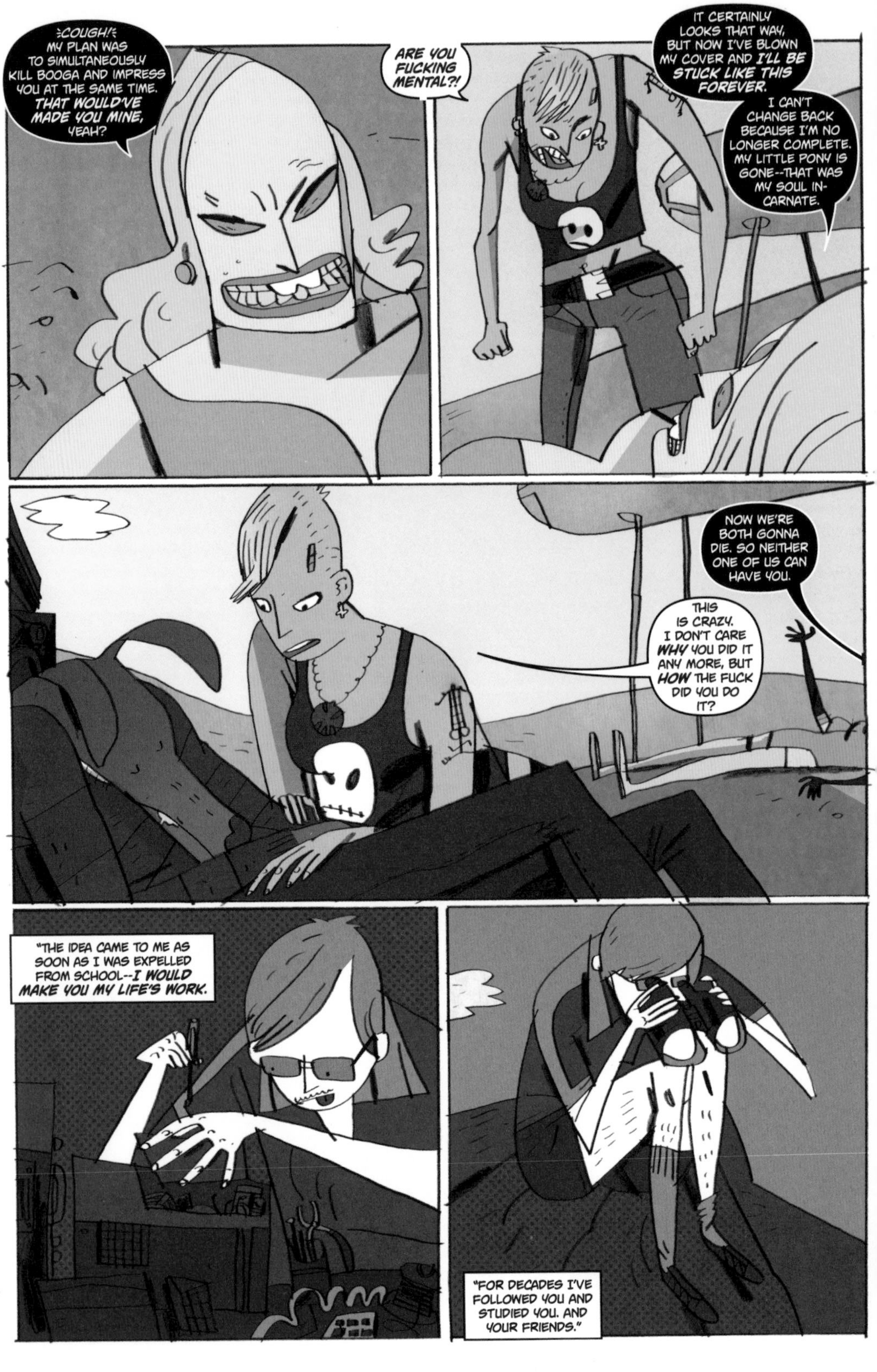

COUGH! MY PLAN WAS TO SIMULTANEOUSLY KILL BOOGA AND IMPRESS YOU AT THE SAME TIME. THAT WOULD'VE MADE YOU MINE, YEAH?
ARE YOU FUCKING MENTAL?!
IT CERTAINLY LOOKS THAT WAY, BUT NOW I'VE BLOWN MY COVER AND I'LL BE STUCK LIKE THIS FOREVER.
I CAN'T CHANGE BACK BECAUSE I'M NO LONGER COMPLETE. MY LITTLE PONY IS GONE--THAT WAS MY SOUL IN-CARNATE.
NOW WE'RE BOTH GONNA DIE. SO NEITHER ONE OF US CAN HAVE YOU.
THIS IS CRAZY. I DON'T CARE WHY YOU DID IT ANY MORE, BUT HOW THE FUCK DID YOU DO IT?
"THE IDEA CAME TO ME AS SOON AS I WAS EXPELLED FROM SCHOOL--I WOULD MAKE YOU MY LIFE'S WORK.
"FOR DECADES I'VE FOLLOWED YOU AND STUDIED YOU. AND YOUR FRIENDS."

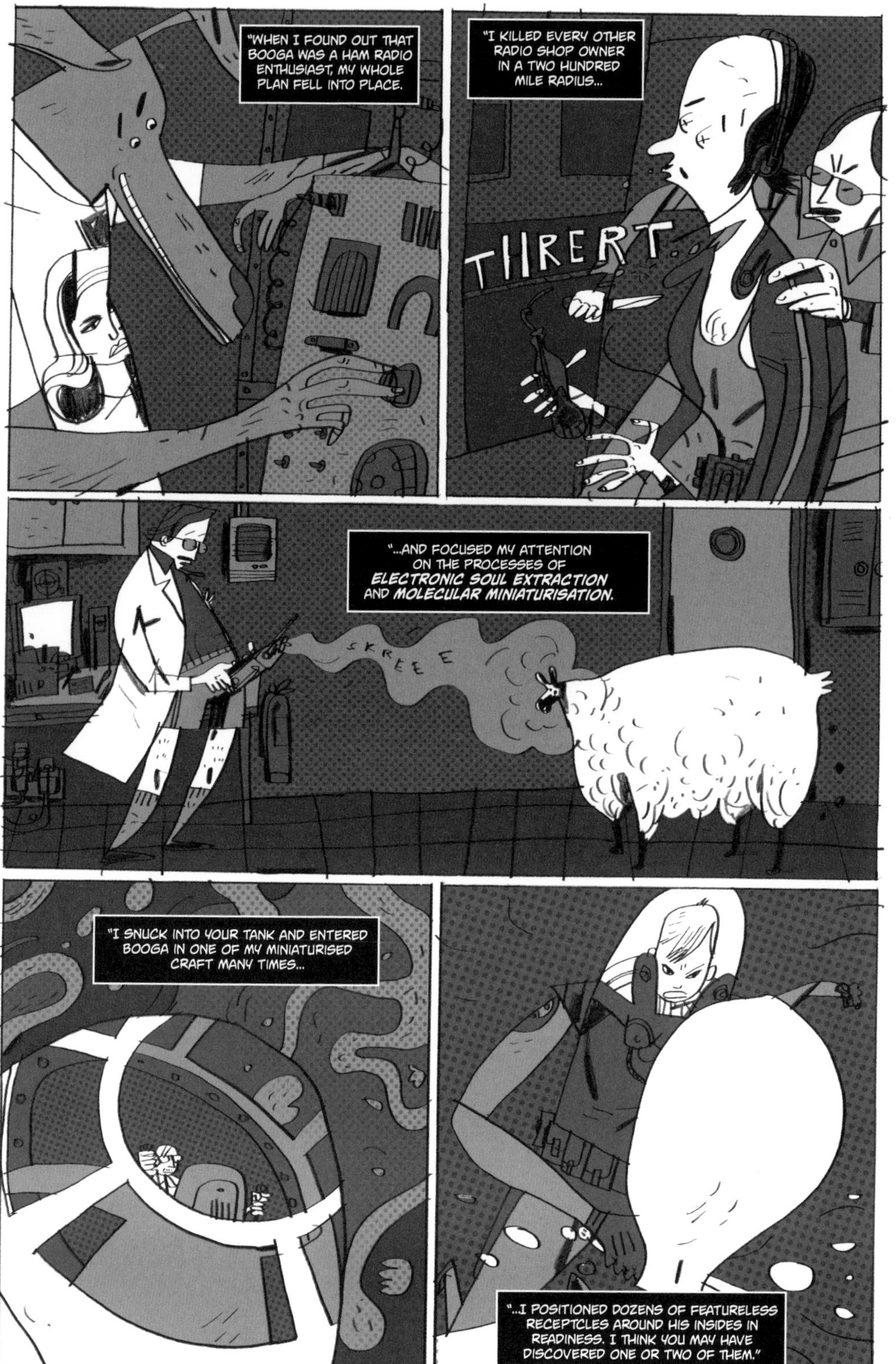
"WHEN I FOUND OUT THAT BOOGA WAS A HAM RADIO ENTHUSIAST, MY WHOLE PLAN FELL INTO PLACE.
"I KILLED EVERY OTHER RADIO SHOP OWNER IN A TWO HUNDRED MILE RADIUS...
THRERT
"...AND FOCUSED MY ATTENTION ON THE PROCESSES OF ELECTRONIC SOUL EXTRACTION AND MOLECULAR MINIATURISATION.
SKREEE
"I SNUCK INTO YOUR TANK AND ENTERED BOOGA IN ONE OF MY MINIATURISED CRAFT MANY TIMES...
"...I POSITIONED DOZENS OF FEATURELESS RECEPTCLES AROUND HIS INSIDES IN READINESS. I THINK YOU MAY HAVE DISCOVERED ONE OR TWO OF THEM."

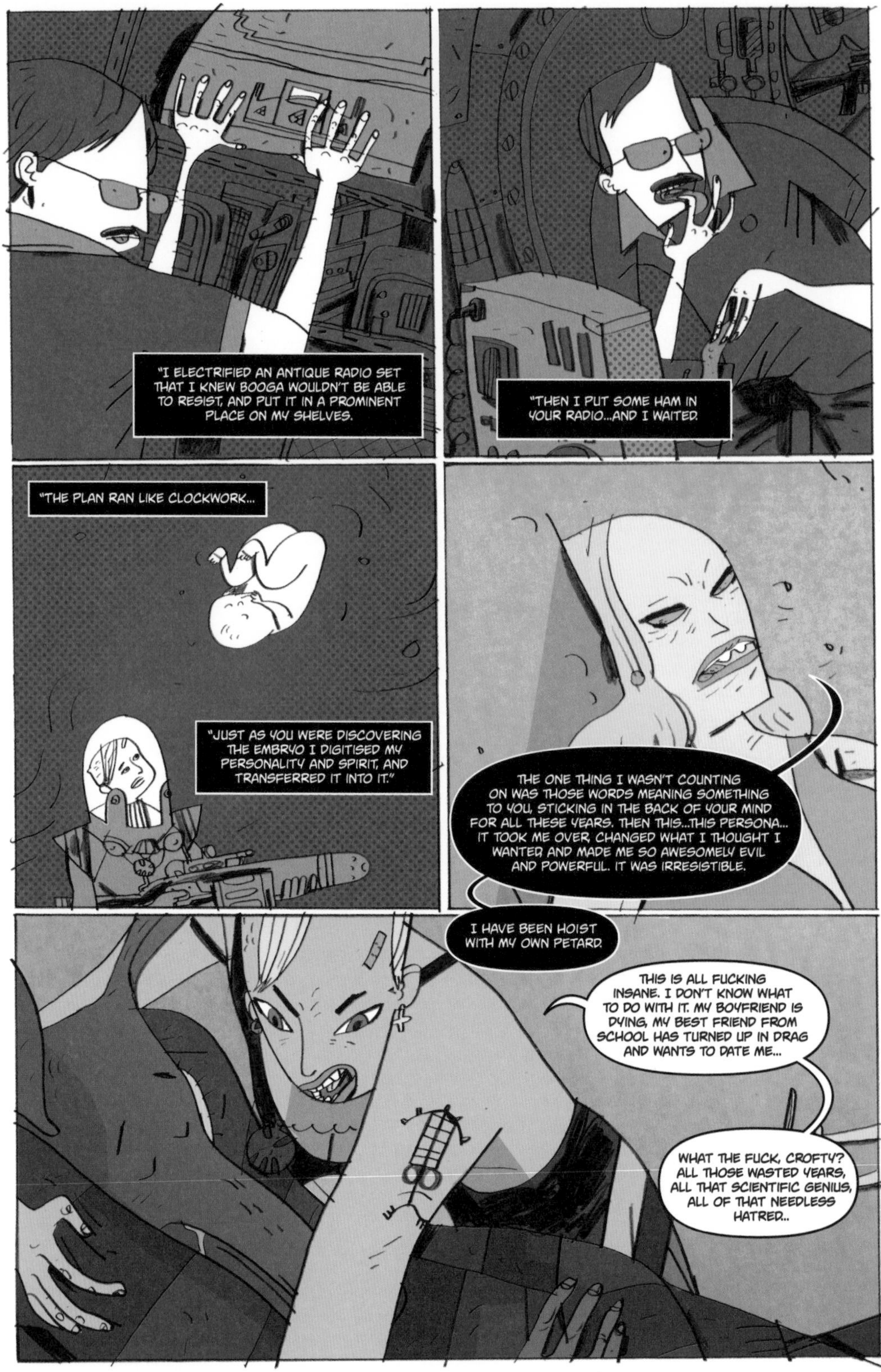
"I ELECTRIFIED AN ANTIQUE RADIO SET THAT I KNEW BOOGA WOULDN'T BE ABLE TO RESIST, AND PUT IT IN A PROMINENT PLACE ON MY SHELVES.
"THEN I PUT SOME HAM IN YOUR RADIO...AND I WAITED.
"THE PLAN RAN LIKE CLOCKWORK...
"JUST AS YOU WERE DISCOVERING THE EMBRYO I DIGITISED MY PERSONALITY AND SPIRIT, AND TRANSFERRED IT INTO IT."
THE ONE THING I WASN'T COUNTING ON WAS THOSE WORDS MEANING SOMETHING TO YOU, STICKING IN THE BACK OF YOUR MIND FOR ALL THESE YEARS. THEN THIS...THIS PERSONA... IT TOOK ME OVER, CHANGED WHAT I THOUGHT I WANTED, AND MADE ME SO AWESOMELY EVIL AND POWERFUL. IT WAS IRRESISTIBLE.
I HAVE BEEN HOIST WITH MY OWN PETARD.
THIS IS ALL FUCKING INSANE. I DON'T KNOW WHAT TO DO WITH IT. MY BOYFRIEND IS DYING, MY BEST FRIEND FROM SCHOOL HAS TURNED UP IN DRAG AND WANTS TO DATE ME...
WHAT THE FUCK, CROFTY? ALL THOSE WASTED YEARS, ALL THAT SCIENTIFIC GENIUS, ALL OF THAT NEEDLESS HATRED...

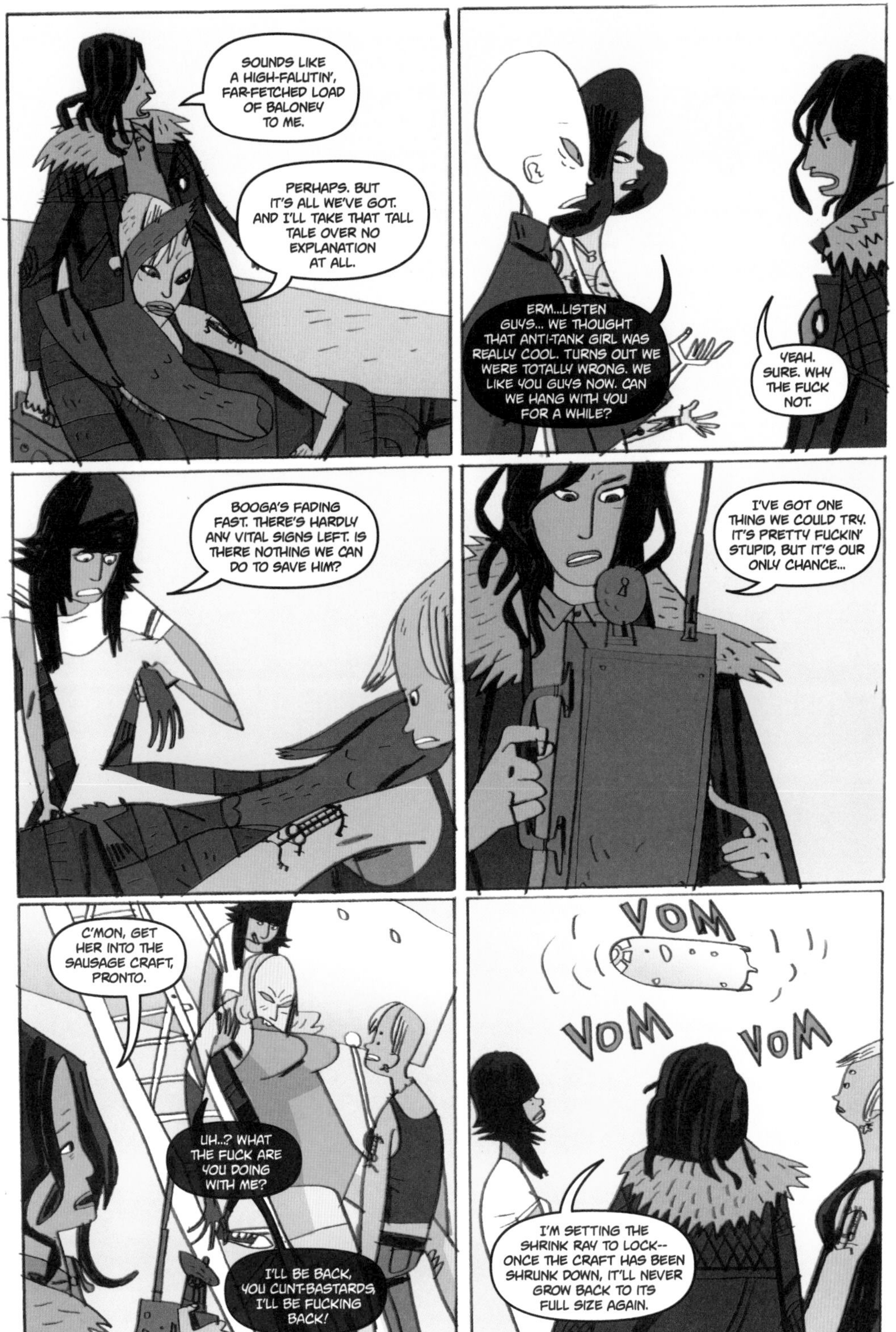
SOUNDS LIKE A HIGH-FALUTIN', FAR-FETCHED LOAD OF BALONEY TO ME.
PERHAPS. BUT IT'S ALL WE'VE GOT. AND I'LL TAKE THAT TALL TALE OVER NO EXPLANATION AT ALL.
ERM...LISTEN GUYS... WE THOUGHT THAT ANTI-TANK GIRL WAS REALLY COOL. TURNS OUT WE WERE TOTALLY WRONG. WE LIKE YOU GUYS NOW. CAN WE HANG WITH YOU FOR A WHILE?
YEAH. SURE. WHY THE FUCK NOT.
BOOGA'S FADING FAST. THERE'S HARDLY ANY VITAL SIGNS LEFT. IS THERE NOTHING WE CAN DO TO SAVE HIM?
I'VE GOT ONE THING WE COULD TRY. IT'S PRETTY FUCKIN' STUPID, BUT IT'S OUR ONLY CHANCE...
C'MON, GET HER INTO THE SAUSAGE CRAFT, PRONTO.
UH..? WHAT THE FUCK ARE YOU DOING WITH ME?
I'LL BE BACK, YOU CUNT-BASTARDS, I'LL BE FUCKING BACK!
VOM
VOM
VOM
I'M SETTING THE SHRINK RAY TO LOCK-- ONCE THE CRAFT HAS BEEN SHRUNK DOWN, IT'LL NEVER GROW BACK TO ITS FULL SIZE AGAIN.

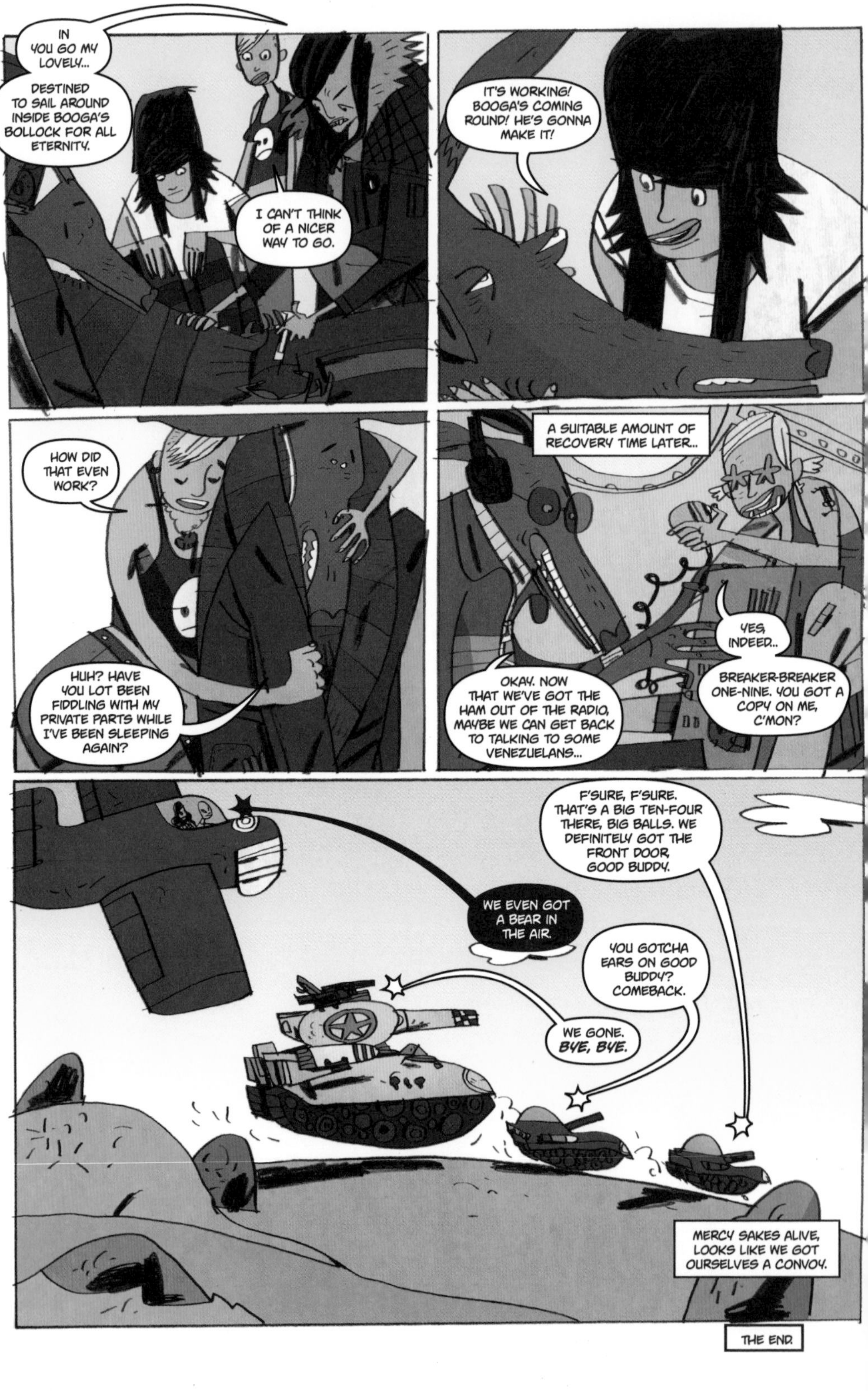
IN YOU GO MY LOVELY...
DESTINED TO SAIL AROUND INSIDE BOOGA'S BOLLOCK FOR ALL ETERNITY.
I CAN'T THINK OF A NICER WAY TO GO.
IT'S WORKING! BOOGA'S COMING ROUND! HE'S GONNA MAKE IT!
HOW DID THAT EVEN WORK?
HUH? HAVE YOU LOT BEEN FIDDLING WITH MY PRIVATE PARTS WHILE I'VE BEEN SLEEPING AGAIN?
A SUITABLE AMOUNT OF RECOVERY TIME LATER...
OKAY. NOW THAT WE'VE GOT THE HAM OUT OF THE RADIO, MAYBE WE CAN GET BACK TO TALKING TO SOME VENEZUELANS...
YES, INDEED...
BREAKER-BREAKER ONE-NINE. YOU GOT A COPY ON ME, C'MON?
F'SURE, F'SURE. THAT'S A BIG TEN-FOUR THERE, BIG BALLS. WE DEFINITELY GOT THE FRONT DOOR, GOOD BUDDY.
WE EVEN GOT A BEAR IN THE AIR.
YOU GOTCHA EARS ON GOOD BUDDY? COMEBACK.
WE GONE. BYE, BYE.
MERCY SAKES ALIVE, LOOKS LIKE WE GOT OURSELVES A CONVOY.
THE END.

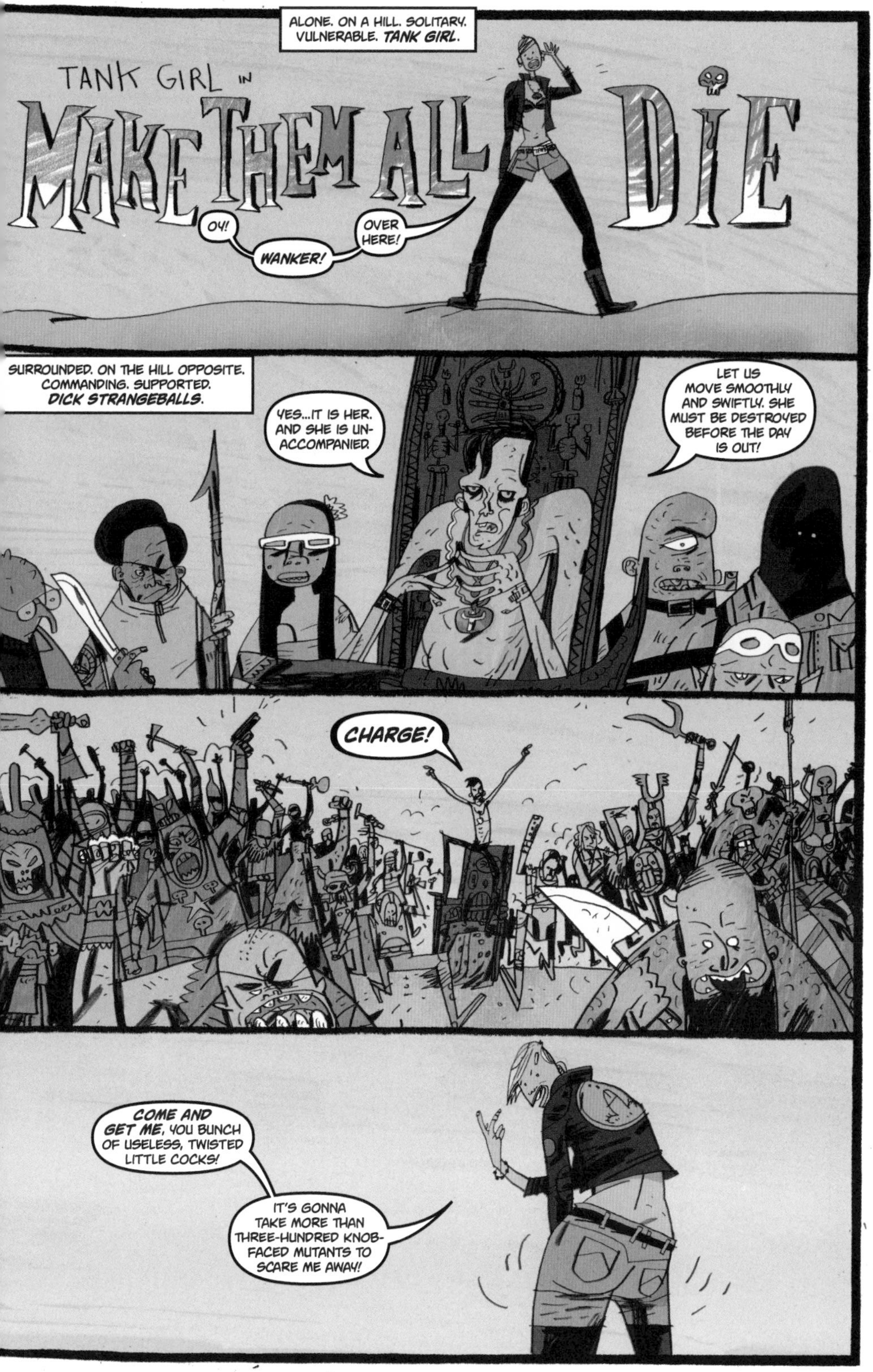

ALONE. ON A HILL. SOLITARY. VULNERABLE. TANK GIRL.
TANK GIRL IN
MAKE THEM ALL DIE
OY!
WANKER!
OVER HERE!
SURROUNDED. ON THE HILL OPPOSITE. COMMANDING. SUPPORTED. DICK STRANGEBALLS.
YES...IT IS HER. AND SHE IS UN-ACCOMPANIED.
LET US MOVE SMOOTHLY AND SWIFTLY. SHE MUST BE DESTROYED BEFORE THE DAY IS OUT!
CHARGE!
COME AND GET ME, YOU BUNCH OF USELESS, TWISTED LITTLE COCKS!
IT'S GONNA TAKE MORE THAN THREE-HUNDRED KNOB-FACED MUTANTS TO SCARE ME AWAY!

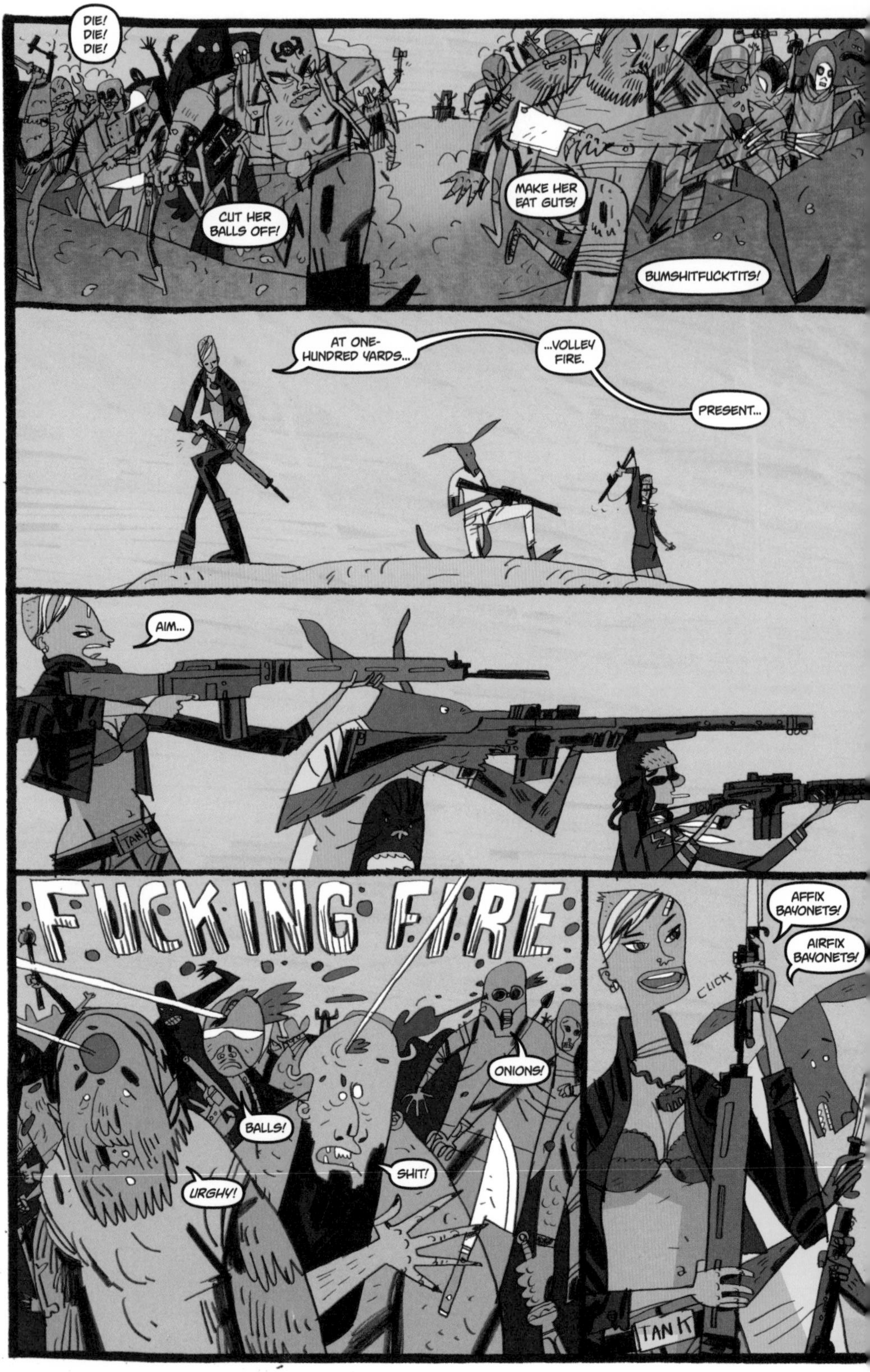
DIE! DIE! DIE!
CUT HER BALLS OFF!
MAKE HER EAT GUTS!
BUMSHITFUCKTITS!
AT ONE-HUNDRED YARDS...
...VOLLEY FIRE.
PRESENT...
AIM...
TANK
FUCKING FIRE
BALLS!
ONIONS!
SHIT!
URGHY!
AFFIX BAYONETS!
AIRFIX BAYONETS!
CLICK
TANK

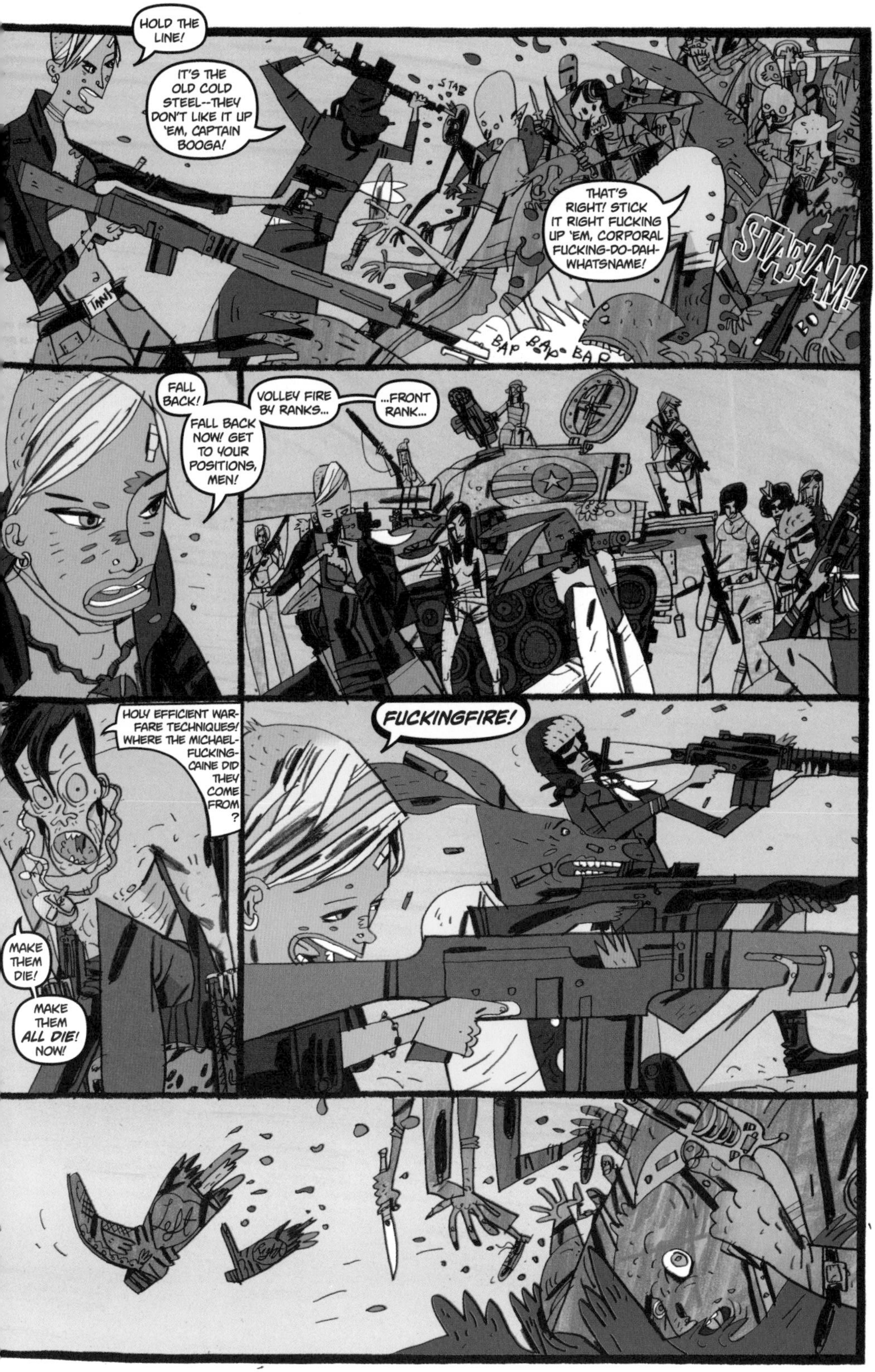
HOLD THE LINE!
IT'S THE OLD COLD STEEL--THEY DON'T LIKE IT UP 'EM, CAPTAIN BOOGA!
STAB
THAT'S RIGHT! STICK IT RIGHT FUCKING UP 'EM, CORPORAL FUCKING-DO-DAH-WHATSNAME!
STABLAM!
BAP BAP BAP BAP
FALL BACK!
FALL BACK NOW! GET TO YOUR POSITIONS, MEN!
VOLLEY FIRE BY RANKS...
...FRONT RANK...
HOLY EFFICIENT WARFARE TECHNIQUES! WHERE THE MICHAEL-FUCKING-CAINE DID THEY COME FROM?
FUCKINGFIRE!
MAKE THEM DIE!
MAKE THEM ALL DIE! NOW!

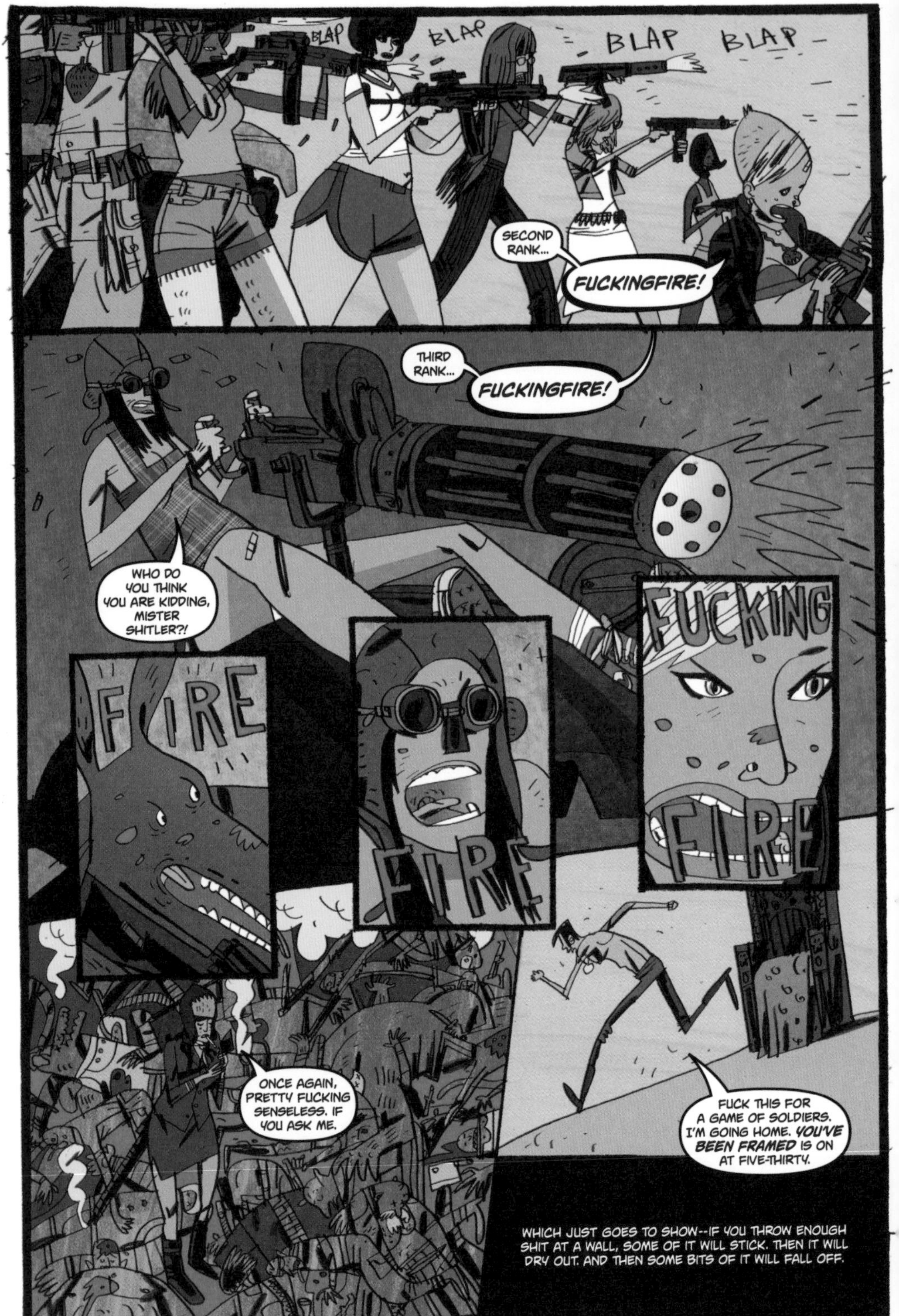
BLAP
BLAP
BLAP
BLAP
SECOND RANK...
FUCKINGFIRE!
THIRD RANK...
FUCKINGFIRE!
WHO DO YOU THINK YOU ARE KIDDING, MISTER SHITLER?!
FIRE
FIRE
FUCKING FIRE
ONCE AGAIN, PRETTY FUCKING SENSELESS. IF YOU ASK ME.
FUCK THIS FOR A GAME OF SOLDIERS. I'M GOING HOME. YOU'VE BEEN FRAMED IS ON AT FIVE-THIRTY.
WHICH JUST GOES TO SHOW--IF YOU THROW ENOUGH SHIT AT A WALL, SOME OF IT WILL STICK. THEN IT WILL DRY OUT. AND THEN SOME BITS OF IT WILL FALL OFF.

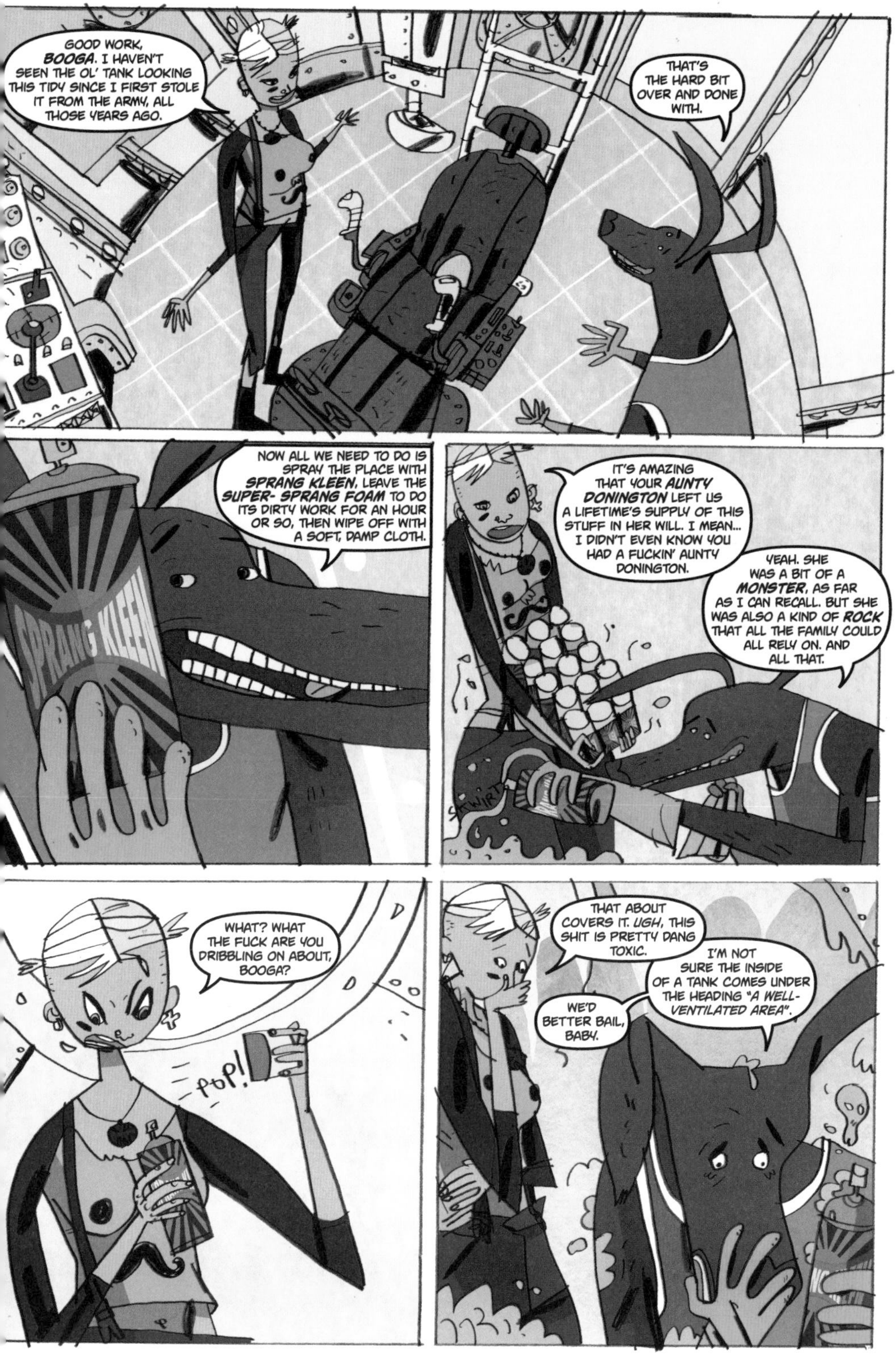
GOOD WORK, **BOOGA**. I HAVEN'T SEEN THE OL' TANK LOOKING THIS TIDY SINCE I FIRST STOLE IT FROM THE ARMY, ALL THOSE YEARS AGO.
THAT'S THE HARD BIT OVER AND DONE WITH.
NOW ALL WE NEED TO DO IS SPRAY THE PLACE WITH **SPRANG KLEEN**, LEAVE THE **SUPER- SPRANG FOAM** TO DO ITS DIRTY WORK FOR AN HOUR OR SO, THEN WIPE OFF WITH A SOFT, DAMP CLOTH.
SPRANG KLEEN
IT'S AMAZING THAT YOUR ***AUNTY DONINGTON*** LEFT US A LIFETIME'S SUPPLY OF THIS STUFF IN HER WILL. I MEAN... I DIDN'T EVEN KNOW YOU HAD A FUCKIN' AUNTY DONINGTON.
YEAH. SHE WAS A BIT OF A ***MONSTER***, AS FAR AS I CAN RECALL. BUT SHE WAS ALSO A KIND OF ***ROCK*** THAT ALL THE FAMILY COULD ALL RELY ON. AND ALL THAT.
SKWIRT
WHAT? WHAT THE FUCK ARE YOU DRIBBLING ON ABOUT, BOOGA?
POP!
THAT ABOUT COVERS IT. *UGH*, THIS SHIT IS PRETTY DANG TOXIC.
I'M NOT SURE THE INSIDE OF A TANK COMES UNDER THE HEADING *"A WELL-VENTILATED AREA"*.
WE'D BETTER BAIL, BABY.

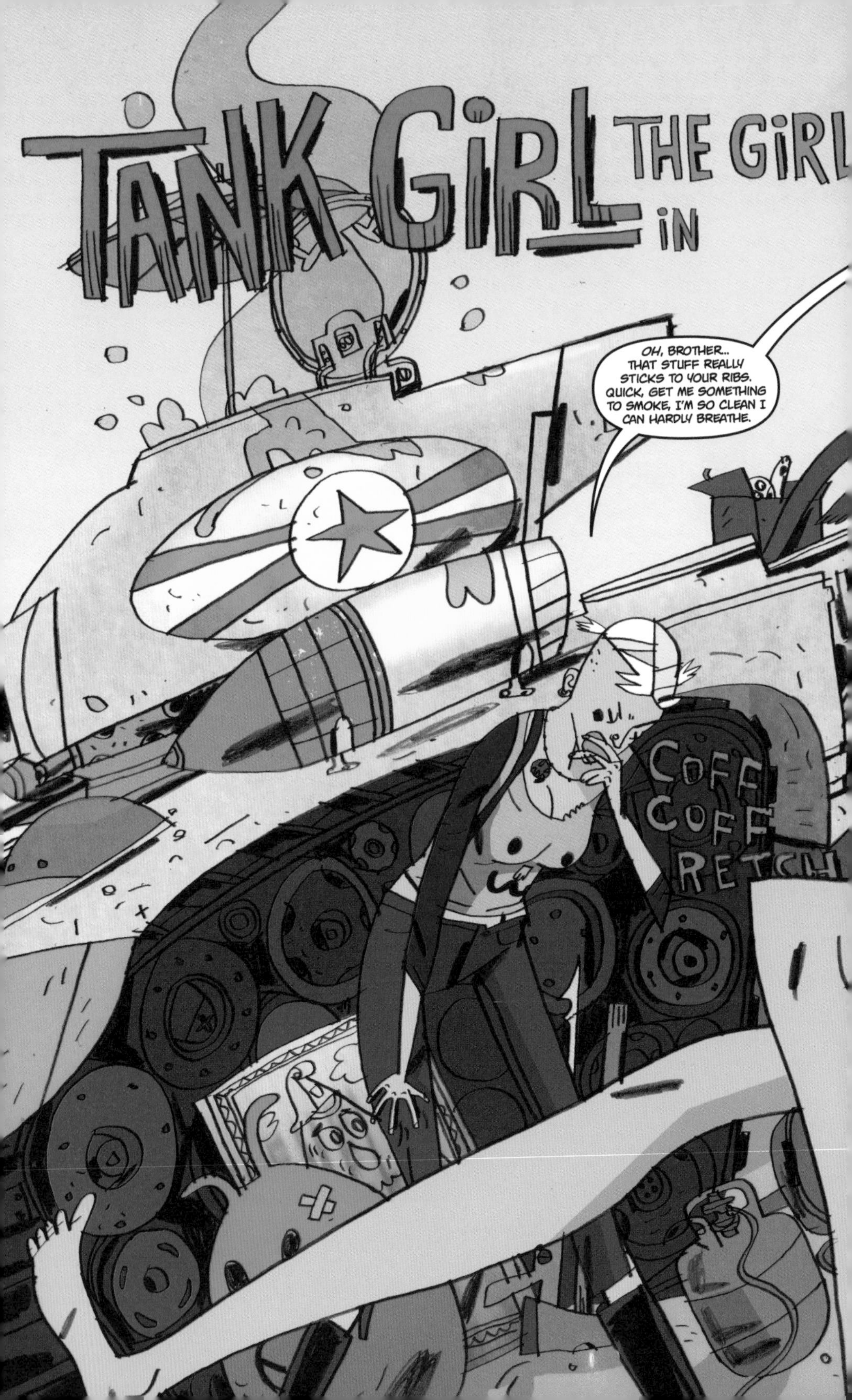
TANK GIRL
THE GIRL
IN
OH, BROTHER... THAT STUFF REALLY STICKS TO YOUR RIBS. QUICK, GET ME SOMETHING TO SMOKE, I'M SO CLEAN I CAN HARDLY BREATHE.
COFF COFF RETCH

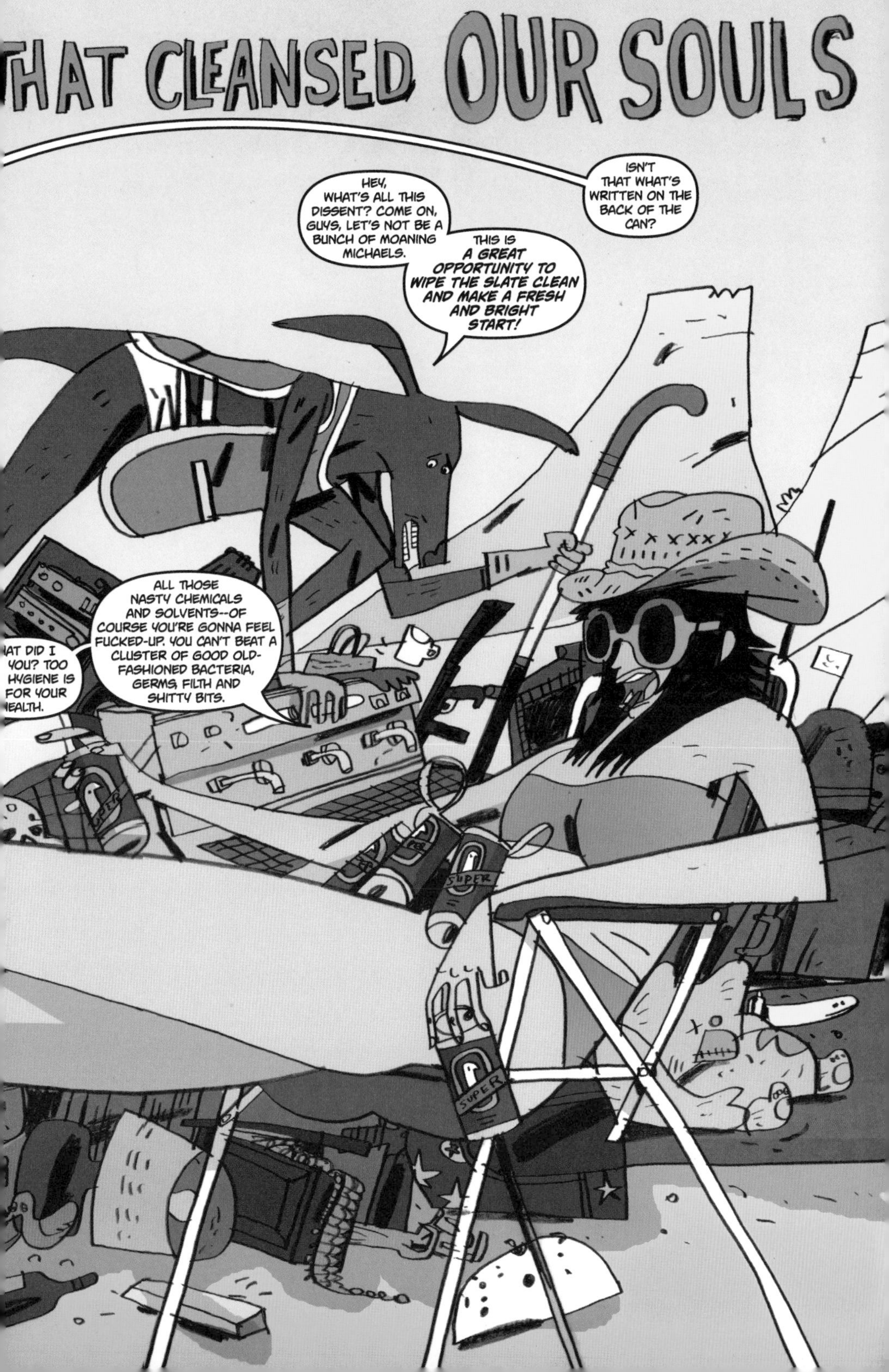
THAT CLEANSED OUR SOULS
ISN'T THAT WHAT'S WRITTEN ON THE BACK OF THE CAN?
HEY, WHAT'S ALL THIS DISSENT? COME ON, GUYS, LET'S NOT BE A BUNCH OF MOANING MICHAELS.
THIS IS A GREAT OPPORTUNITY TO WIPE THE SLATE CLEAN AND MAKE A FRESH AND BRIGHT START!
HAT DID I YOU? TOO HYGIENE IS FOR YOUR HEALTH.
ALL THOSE NASTY CHEMICALS AND SOLVENTS--OF COURSE YOU'RE GONNA FEEL FUCKED-UP. YOU CAN'T BEAT A CLUSTER OF GOOD OLD-FASHIONED BACTERIA, GERMS, FILTH AND SHITTY BITS.
SUPER
SUPER

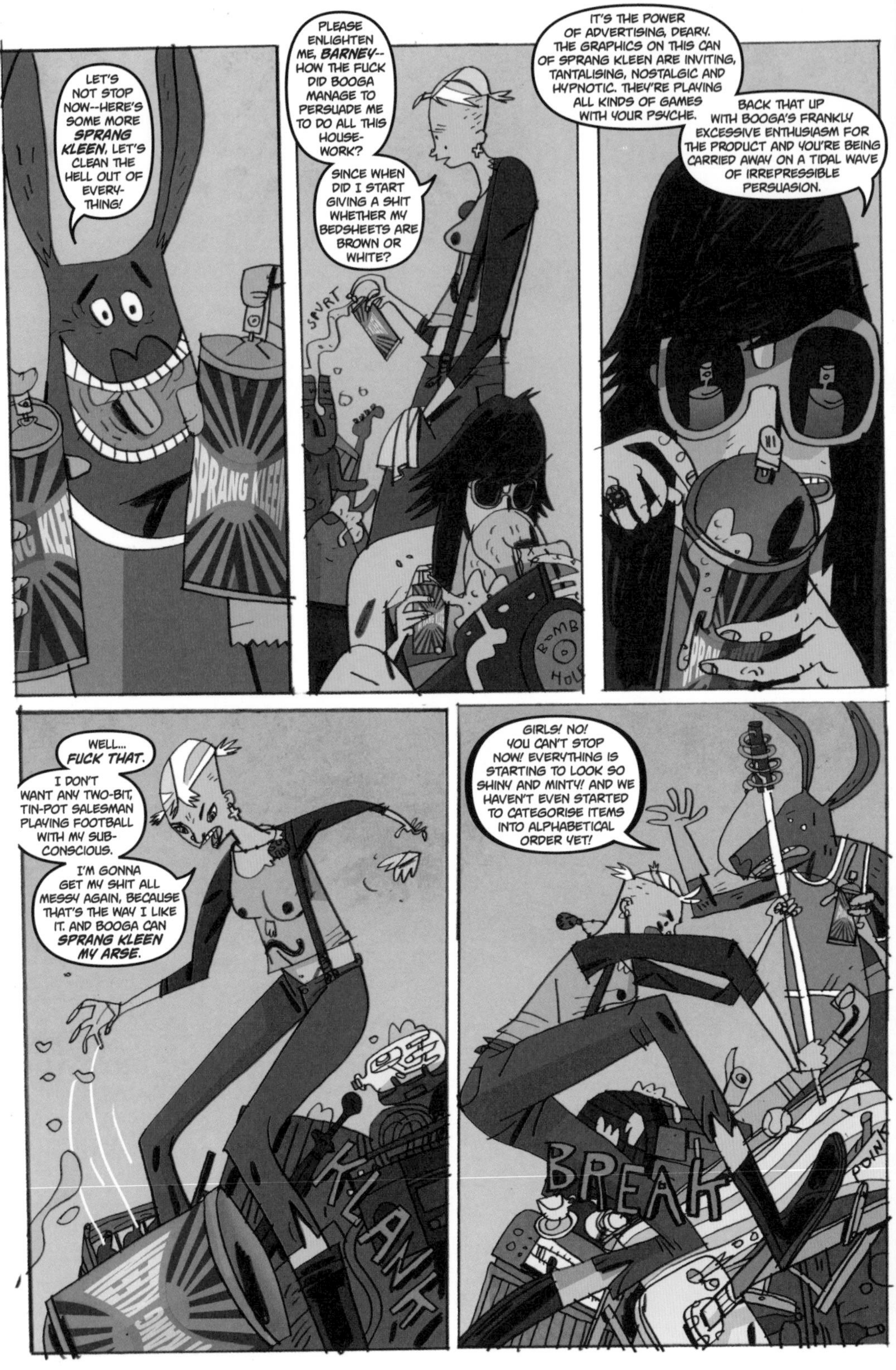

LET'S NOT STOP NOW--HERE'S SOME MORE **SPRANG KLEEN**, LET'S CLEAN THE HELL OUT OF EVERY-THING!
SPRANG KLEEN
PLEASE ENLIGHTEN ME, **BARNEY**-- HOW THE FUCK DID BOOGA MANAGE TO PERSUADE ME TO DO ALL THIS HOUSE-WORK?
SINCE WHEN DID I START GIVING A SHIT WHETHER MY BEDSHEETS ARE BROWN OR WHITE?
SPURT
BOMB HOUSE
IT'S THE POWER OF ADVERTISING, DEARY. THE GRAPHICS ON THIS CAN OF SPRANG KLEEN ARE INVITING, TANTALISING, NOSTALGIC AND HYPNOTIC. THEY'RE PLAYING ALL KINDS OF GAMES WITH YOUR PSYCHE.
BACK THAT UP WITH BOOGA'S FRANKLY EXCESSIVE ENTHUSIASM FOR THE PRODUCT AND YOU'RE BEING CARRIED AWAY ON A TIDAL WAVE OF IRREPRESSIBLE PERSUASION.
WELL... **FUCK THAT**.
I DON'T WANT ANY TWO-BIT, TIN-POT SALESMAN PLAYING FOOTBALL WITH MY SUB-CONSCIOUS.
I'M GONNA GET MY SHIT ALL MESSY AGAIN, BECAUSE THAT'S THE WAY I LIKE IT. AND BOOGA CAN **SPRANG KLEEN MY ARSE**.
KLANK
GIRLS! NO! YOU CAN'T STOP NOW! EVERYTHING IS STARTING TO LOOK SO SHINY AND MINTY! AND WE HAVEN'T EVEN STARTED TO CATEGORISE ITEMS INTO ALPHABETICAL ORDER YET!
BREAK

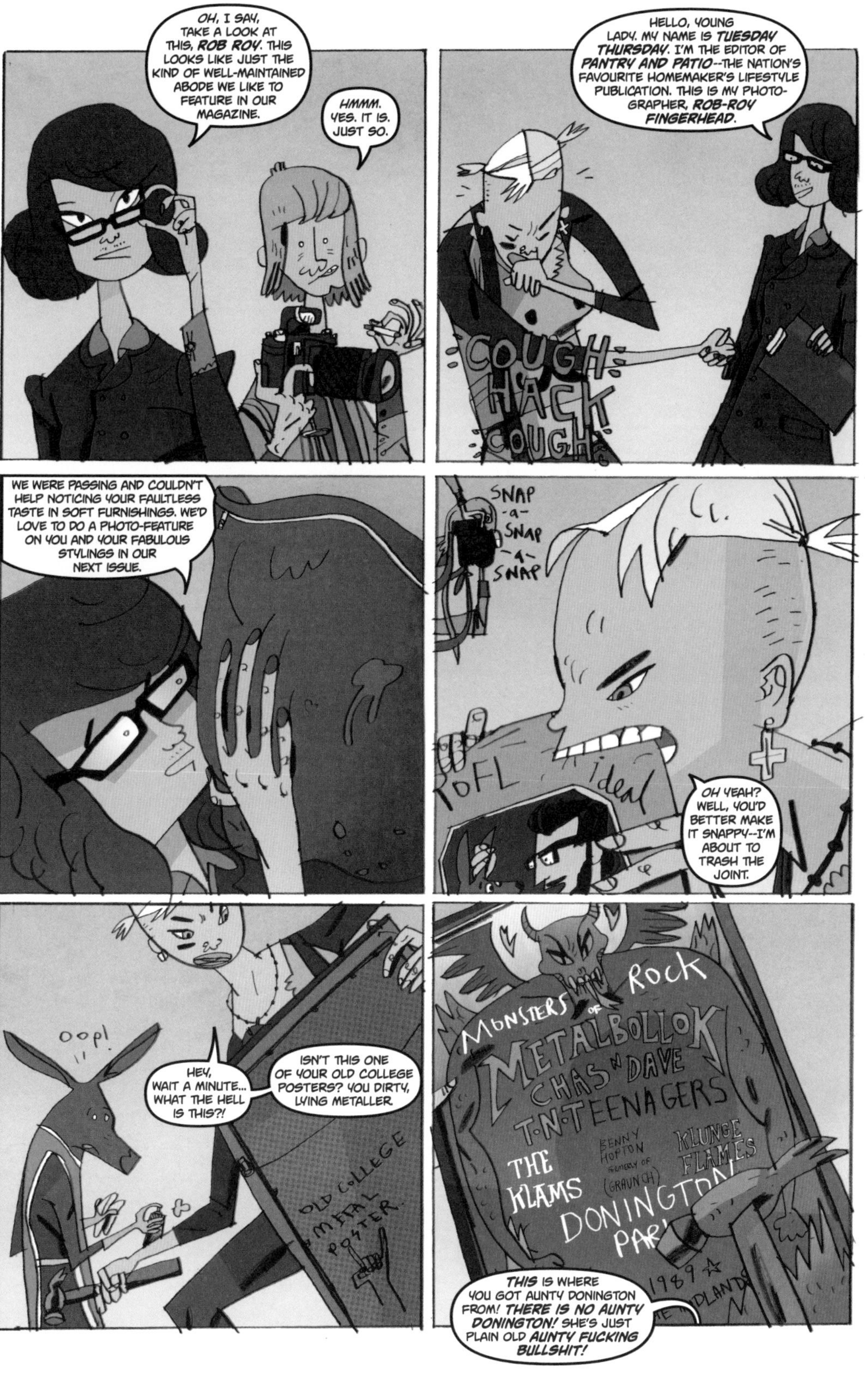
OH, I SAY, TAKE A LOOK AT THIS, ROB ROY. THIS LOOKS LIKE JUST THE KIND OF WELL-MAINTAINED ABODE WE LIKE TO FEATURE IN OUR MAGAZINE.
HMMM. YES. IT IS. JUST SO.
HELLO, YOUNG LADY. MY NAME IS TUESDAY THURSDAY. I'M THE EDITOR OF PANTRY AND PATIO--THE NATION'S FAVOURITE HOMEMAKER'S LIFESTYLE PUBLICATION. THIS IS MY PHOTO-GRAPHER, ROB-ROY FINGERHEAD.
COUGH HACK COUGH
WE WERE PASSING AND COULDN'T HELP NOTICING YOUR FAULTLESS TASTE IN SOFT FURNISHINGS. WE'D LOVE TO DO A PHOTO-FEATURE ON YOU AND YOUR FABULOUS STYLINGS IN OUR NEXT ISSUE.
SNAP -a- SNAP -a- SNAP
OH YEAH? WELL, YOU'D BETTER MAKE IT SNAPPY--I'M ABOUT TO TRASH THE JOINT.
oop!
HEY, WAIT A MINUTE... WHAT THE HELL IS THIS?!
ISN'T THIS ONE OF YOUR OLD COLLEGE POSTERS? YOU DIRTY, LYING METALLER.
OLD COLLEGE METAL POSTER
MONSTERS OF ROCK
METALBOLLOK
CHAS 'N' DAVE
T.N.T. TEENAGERS
THE KLAMS
KLUNGE FLAMES
DONINGTON PAR
1989
THIS IS WHERE YOU GOT AUNTY DONINGTON FROM! THERE IS NO AUNTY DONINGTON! SHE'S JUST PLAIN OLD AUNTY FUCKING BULLSHIT!

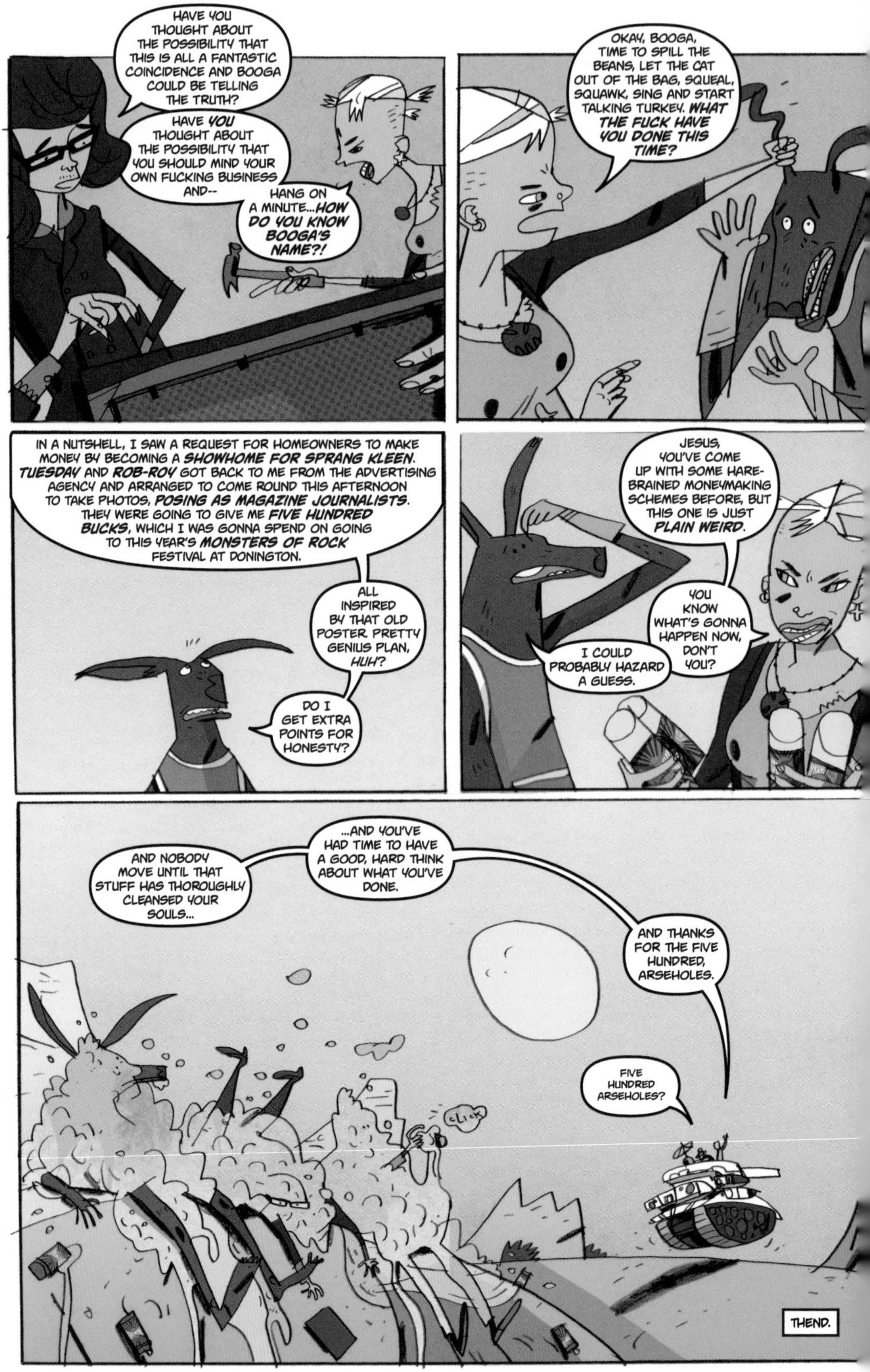
HAVE YOU THOUGHT ABOUT THE POSSIBILITY THAT THIS IS ALL A FANTASTIC COINCIDENCE AND BOOGA COULD BE TELLING THE TRUTH?
HAVE *YOU* THOUGHT ABOUT THE POSSIBILITY THAT YOU SHOULD MIND YOUR OWN FUCKING BUSINESS AND--
HANG ON A MINUTE...*HOW DO YOU KNOW BOOGA'S NAME?!*
OKAY, BOOGA, TIME TO SPILL THE BEANS, LET THE CAT OUT OF THE BAG, SQUEAL, SQUAWK, SING AND START TALKING TURKEY. *WHAT THE FUCK HAVE YOU DONE THIS TIME?*
IN A NUTSHELL, I SAW A REQUEST FOR HOMEOWNERS TO MAKE MONEY BY BECOMING A *SHOWHOME FOR SPRANG KLEEN*. *TUESDAY* AND *ROB-ROY* GOT BACK TO ME FROM THE ADVERTISING AGENCY AND ARRANGED TO COME ROUND THIS AFTERNOON TO TAKE PHOTOS, *POSING AS MAGAZINE JOURNALISTS*. THEY WERE GOING TO GIVE ME *FIVE HUNDRED BUCKS*, WHICH I WAS GONNA SPEND ON GOING TO THIS YEAR'S *MONSTERS OF ROCK* FESTIVAL AT DONINGTON.
ALL INSPIRED BY THAT OLD POSTER. PRETTY GENIUS PLAN, *HUH?*
DO I GET EXTRA POINTS FOR HONESTY?
JESUS, YOU'VE COME UP WITH SOME HARE-BRAINED MONEYMAKING SCHEMES BEFORE, BUT THIS ONE IS JUST *PLAIN WEIRD*.
YOU KNOW WHAT'S GONNA HAPPEN NOW, DON'T YOU?
I COULD PROBABLY HAZARD A GUESS.
AND NOBODY MOVE UNTIL THAT STUFF HAS THOROUGHLY CLEANSED YOUR SOULS...
...AND YOU'VE HAD TIME TO HAVE A GOOD, HARD THINK ABOUT WHAT YOU'VE DONE.
AND THANKS FOR THE FIVE HUNDRED, ARSEHOLES.
FIVE HUNDRED ARSEHOLES?
CLICK
THEND.

The Nutbag Ranger and Bonto say

"WE ARE NOT AFRAID OF YOUR SHIT"

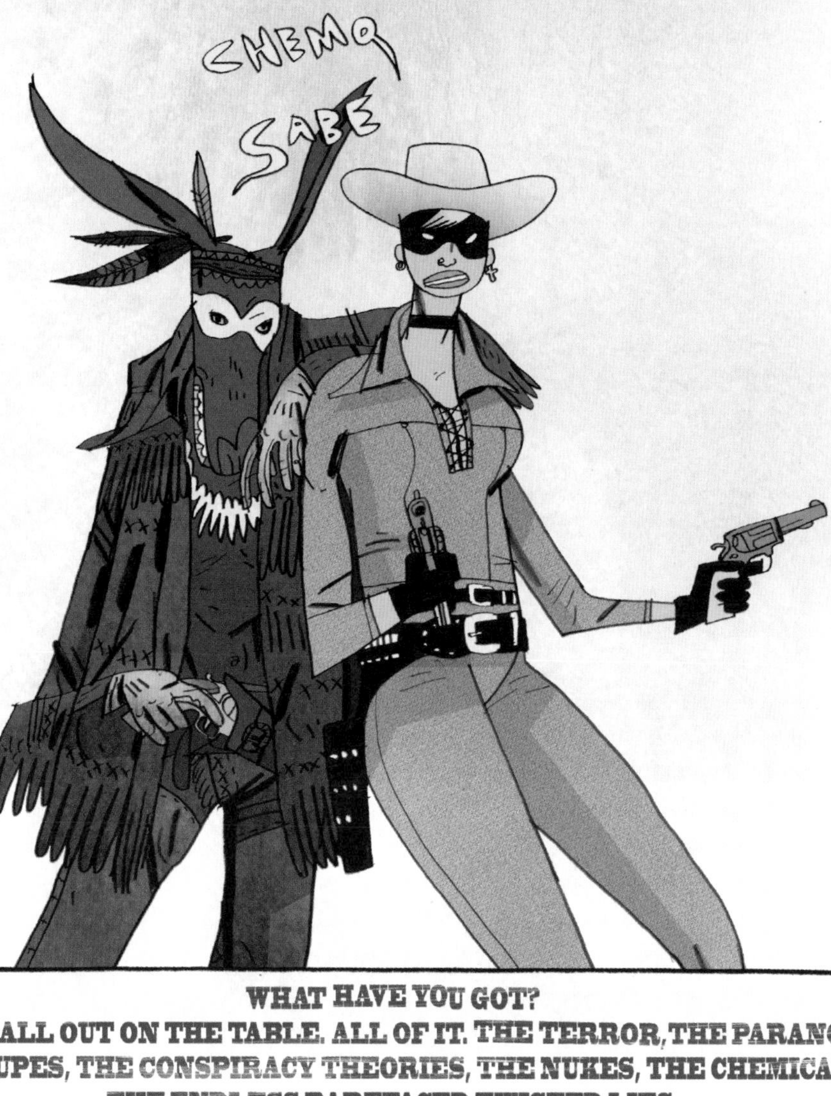
CHEMO
SABE

WHAT HAVE YOU GOT?
LAY IT ALL OUT ON THE TABLE. ALL OF IT. THE TERROR, THE PARANOIA,
THE DUPES, THE CONSPIRACY THEORIES, THE NUKES, THE CHEMICALS,
THE ENDLESS BAREFACED TWISTED LIES,
THE TINY SPYING ROBOTS THAT ARE INVISIBLE TO THE NAKED EYE.
ALL OF THIS. EVERYTHING YOU'VE GOT. SHOW US EVERYTHING.
BECAUSE WE ARE NOT AFRAID OF YOUR FUCKING SHIT.

It's 1969
I'm three years old
I'm sat in front of the black and white T.V
With my lemon curd sandwich
And my glass of Nesquick

And Davy Jones is dead

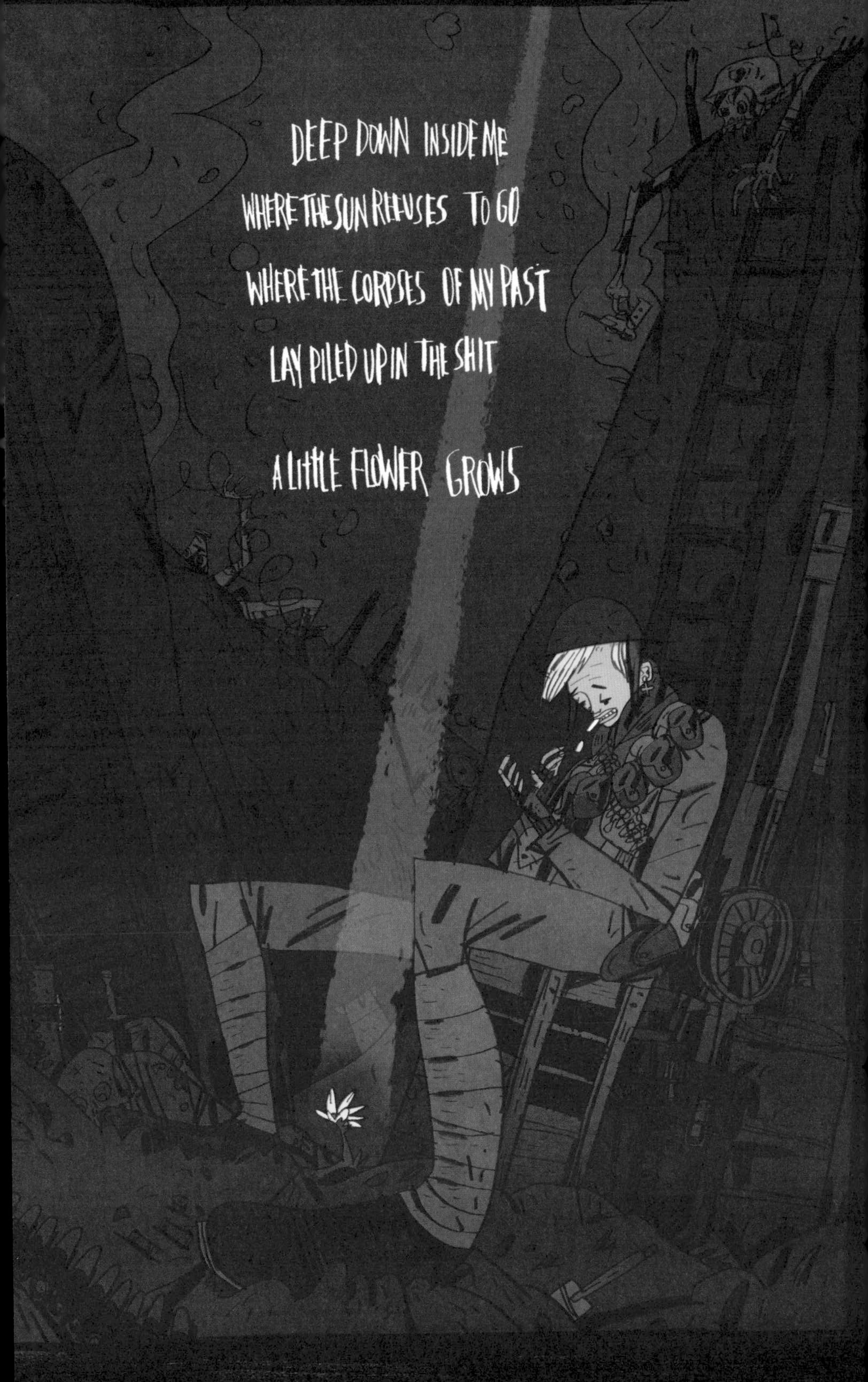

DEEP DOWN INSIDE ME
WHERE THE SUN REFUSES TO GO
WHERE THE CORPSES OF MY PAST
LAY PILED UP IN THE SHIT
A LITTLE FLOWER GROWS

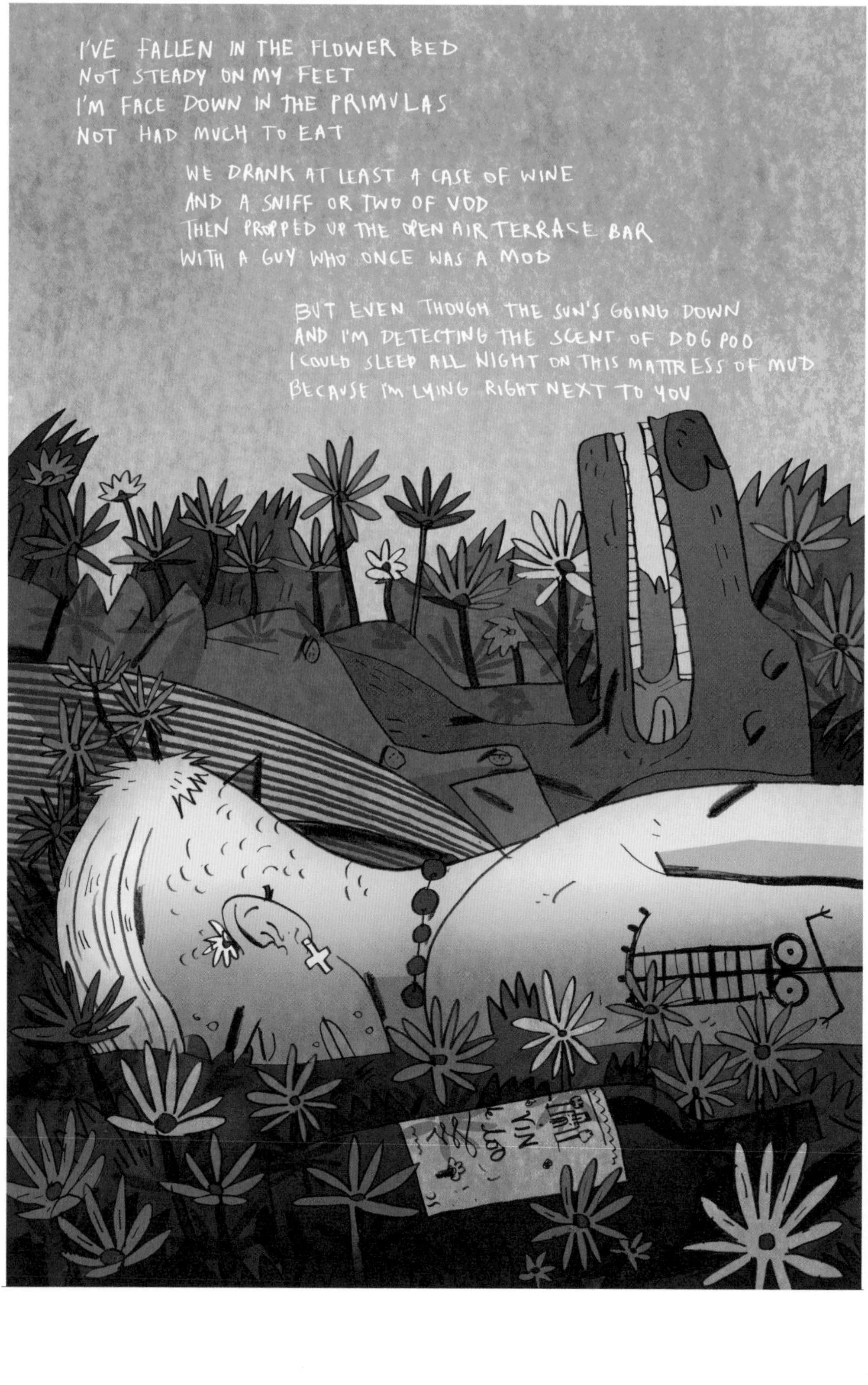
I'VE FALLEN IN THE FLOWER BED
NOT STEADY ON MY FEET
I'M FACE DOWN IN THE PRIMULAS
NOT HAD MUCH TO EAT
WE DRANK AT LEAST A CASE OF WINE
AND A SNIFF OR TWO OF VOD
THEN PROPPED UP THE OPEN AIR TERRACE BAR
WITH A GUY WHO ONCE WAS A MOD
BUT EVEN THOUGH THE SUN'S GOING DOWN
AND I'M DETECTING THE SCENT OF DOG POO
I COULD SLEEP ALL NIGHT ON THIS MATTRESS OF MUD
BECAUSE I'M LYING RIGHT NEXT TO YOU

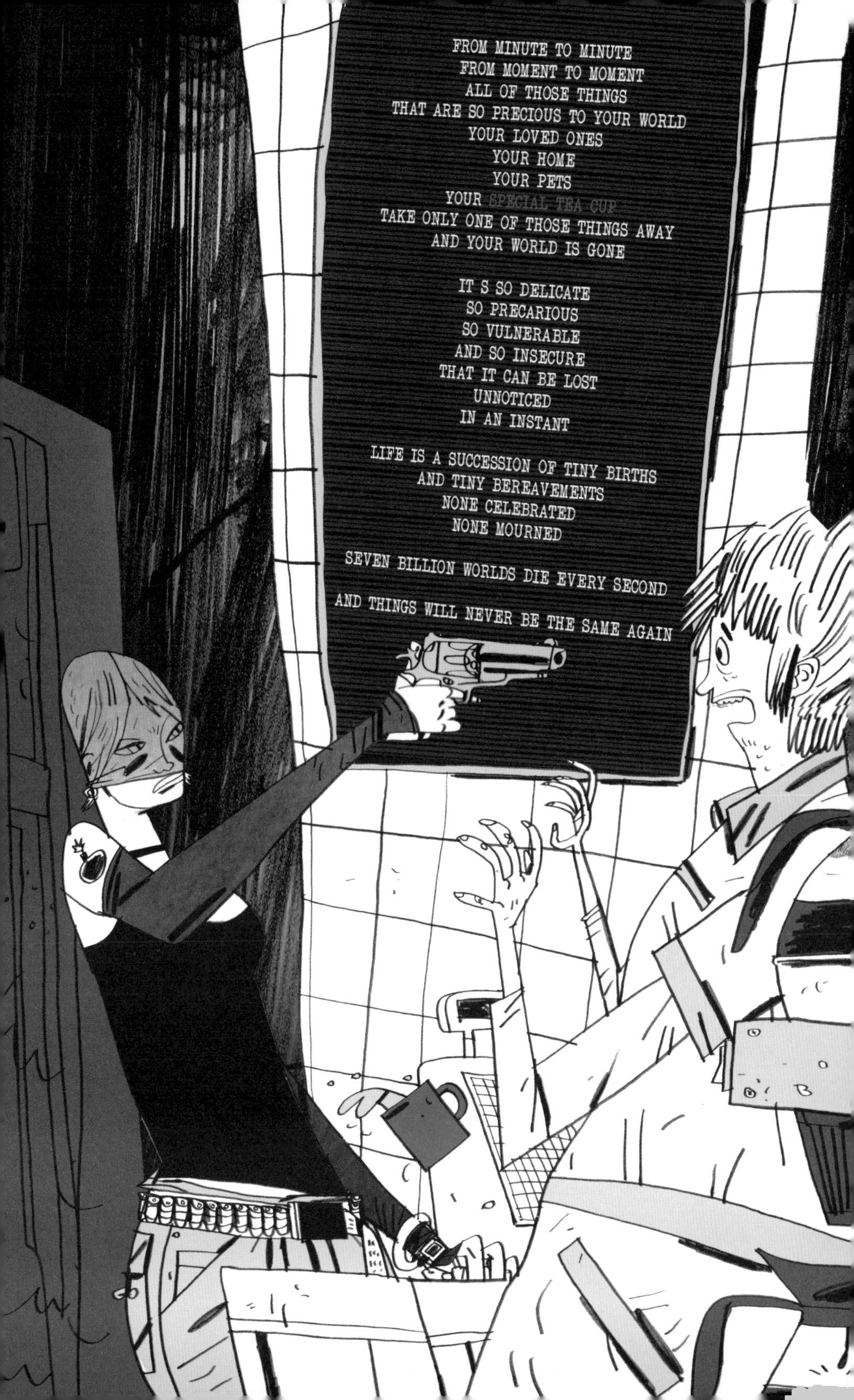
FROM MINUTE TO MINUTE
FROM MOMENT TO MOMENT
ALL OF THOSE THINGS
THAT ARE SO PRECIOUS TO YOUR WORLD
YOUR LOVED ONES
YOUR HOME
YOUR PETS
YOUR SPECIAL TEA CUP
TAKE ONLY ONE OF THOSE THINGS AWAY
AND YOUR WORLD IS GONE
IT S SO DELICATE
SO PRECARIOUS
SO VULNERABLE
AND SO INSECURE
THAT IT CAN BE LOST
UNNOTICED
IN AN INSTANT
LIFE IS A SUCCESSION OF TINY BIRTHS
AND TINY BEREAVEMENTS
NONE CELEBRATED
NONE MOURNED
SEVEN BILLION WORLDS DIE EVERY SECOND
AND THINGS WILL NEVER BE THE SAME AGAIN

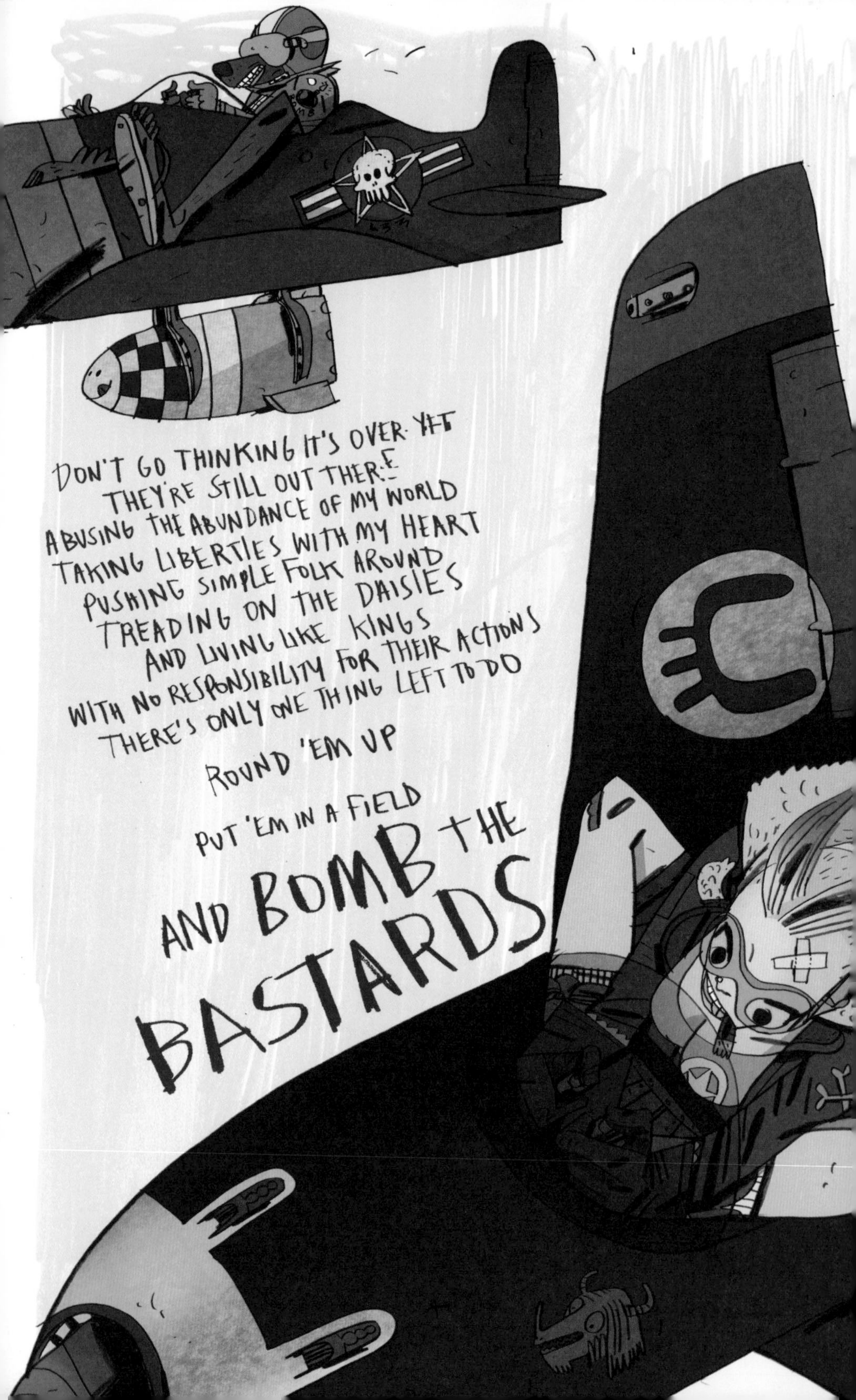
DON'T GO THINKING IT'S OVER YET
THEY'RE STILL OUT THERE
ABUSING THE ABUNDANCE OF MY WORLD
TAKING LIBERTIES WITH MY HEART
PUSHING SIMPLE FOLK AROUND
TREADING ON THE DAISIES
AND LIVING LIKE KINGS
WITH NO RESPONSIBILITY FOR THEIR ACTIONS
THERE'S ONLY ONE THING LEFT TO DO
ROUND 'EM UP
PUT 'EM IN A FIELD
AND BOMB THE
BASTARDS

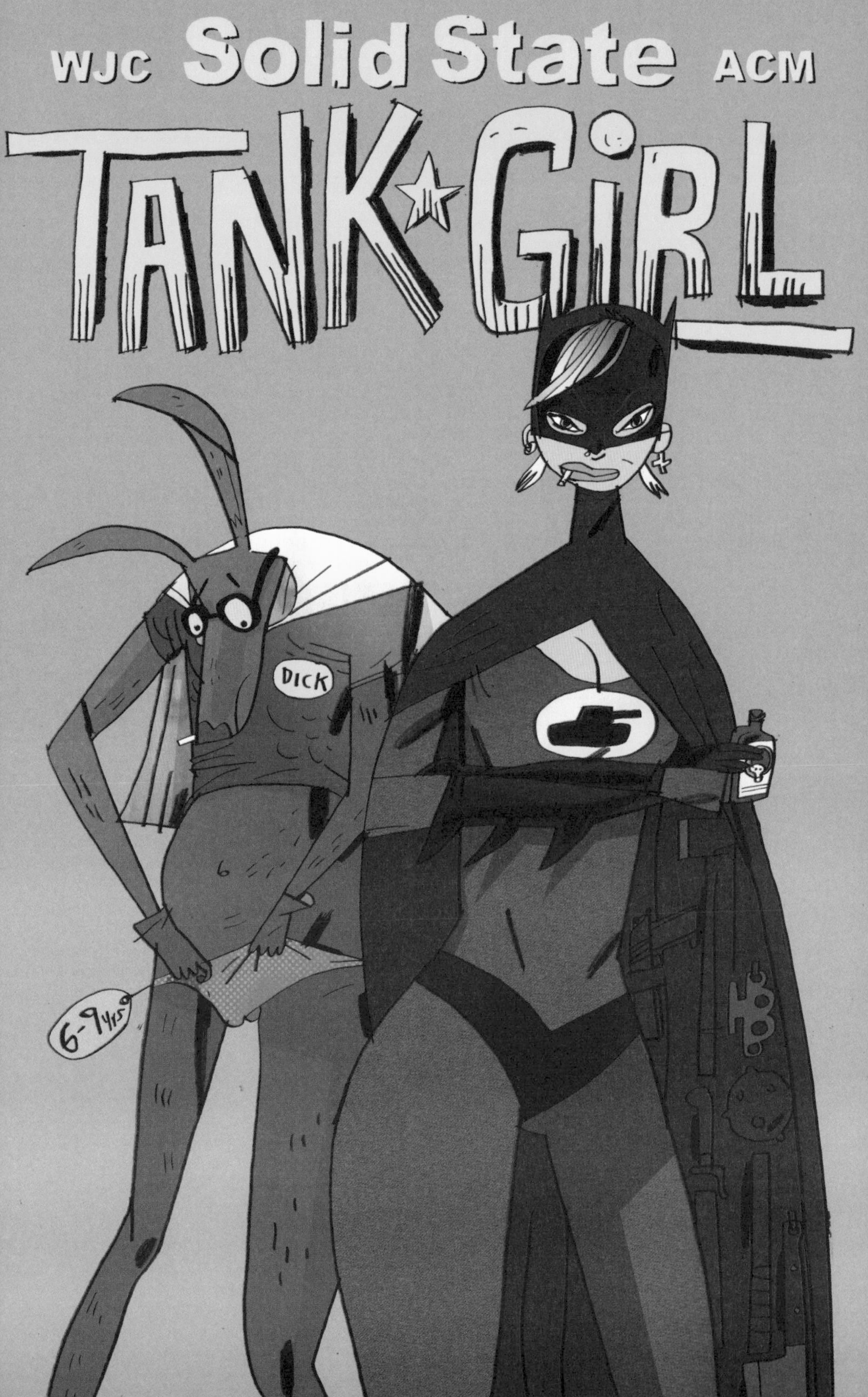
WJC Solid State ACM
TANK GIRL
DICK
6-9yrs

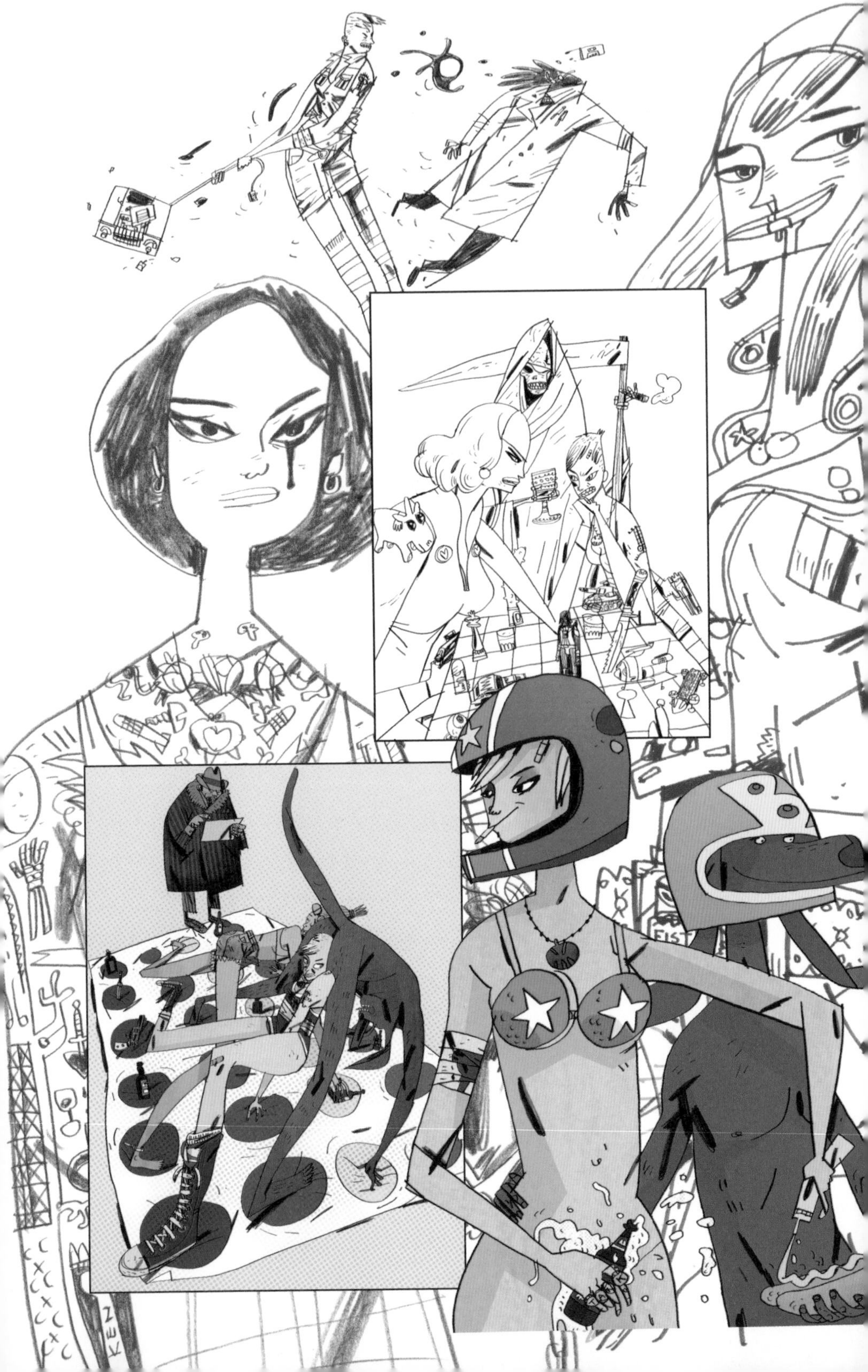
FIST

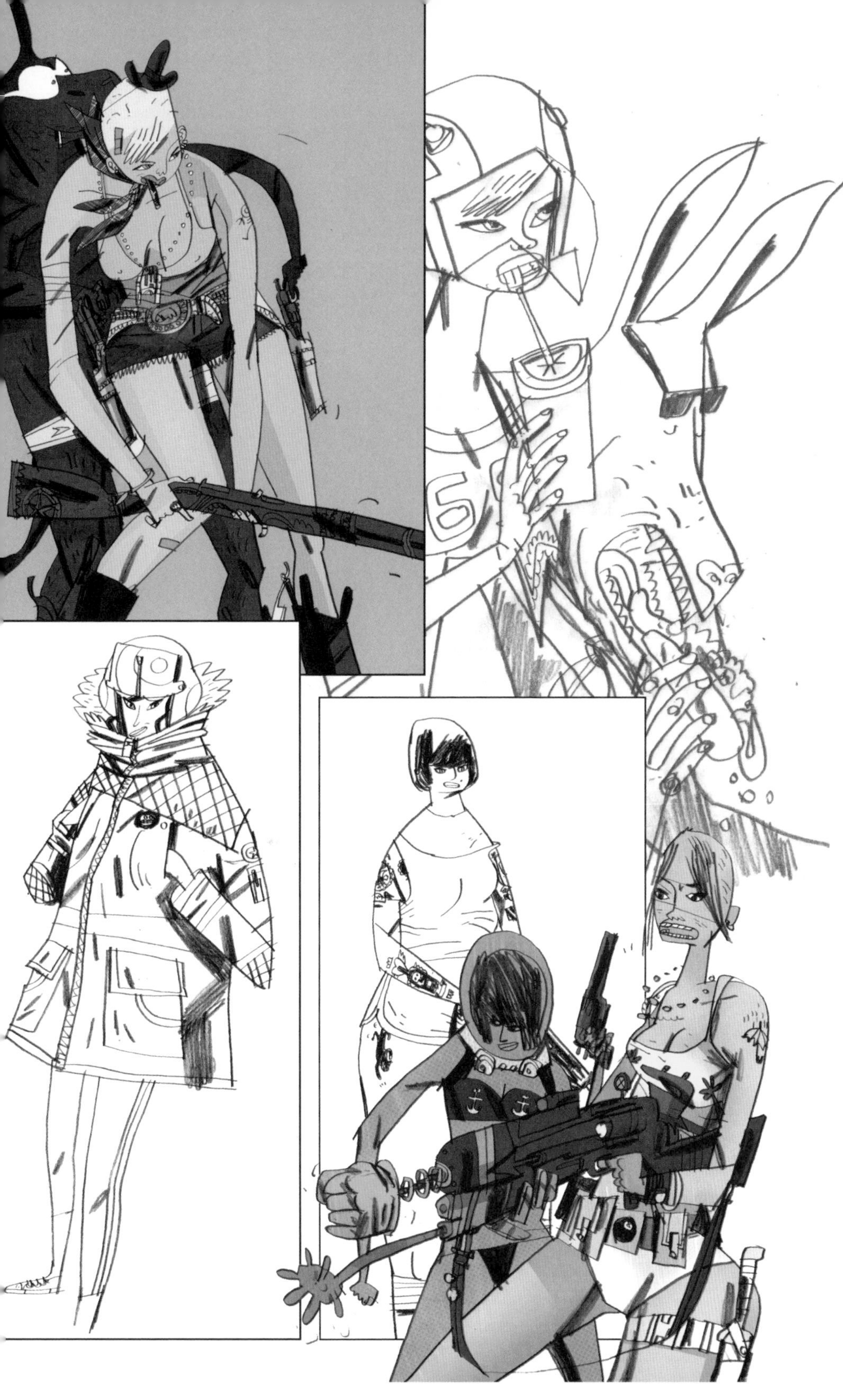

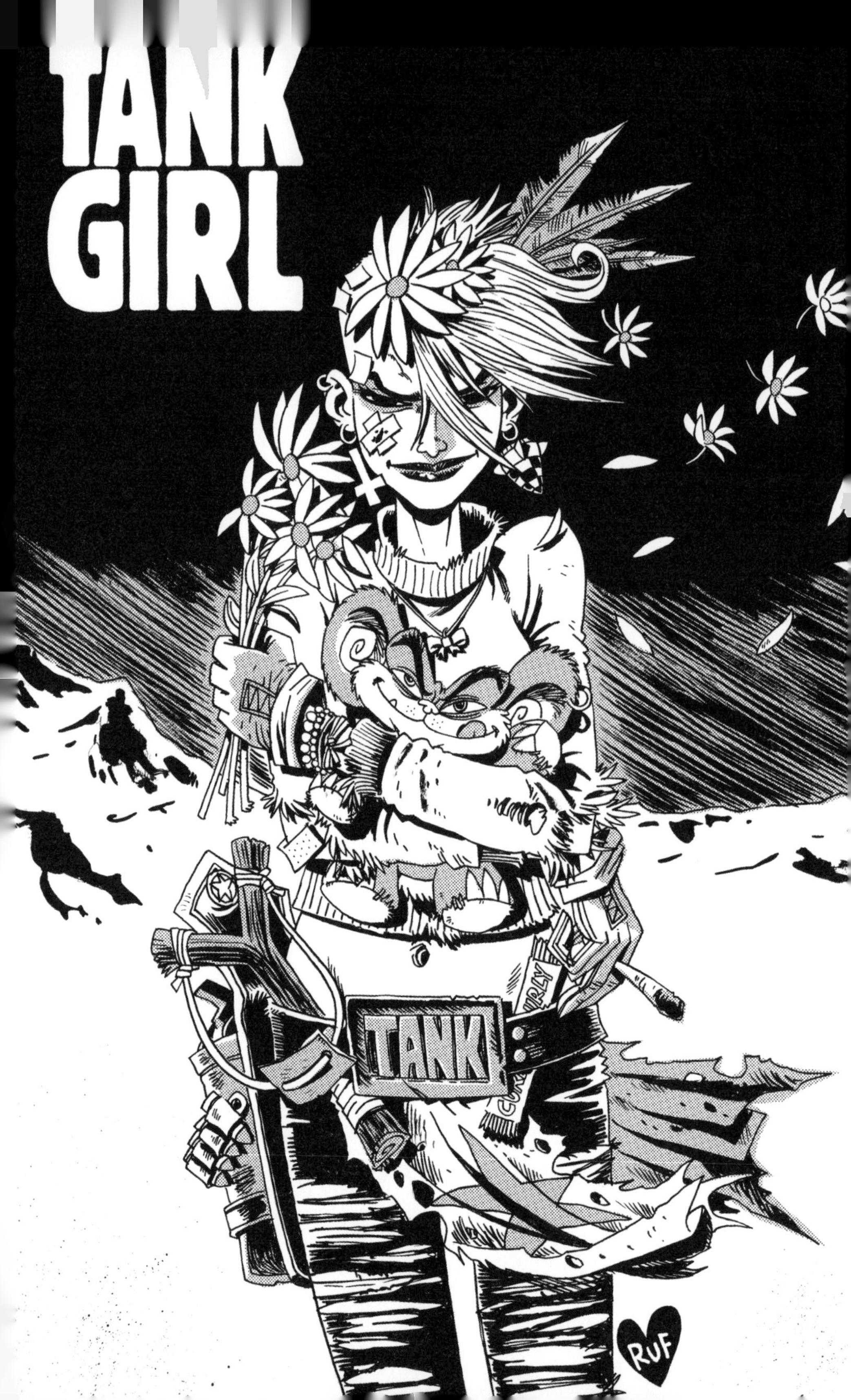
TANK GIRL
TANK
RUF

JIM MAHFOOD'S SKETCHBOOK

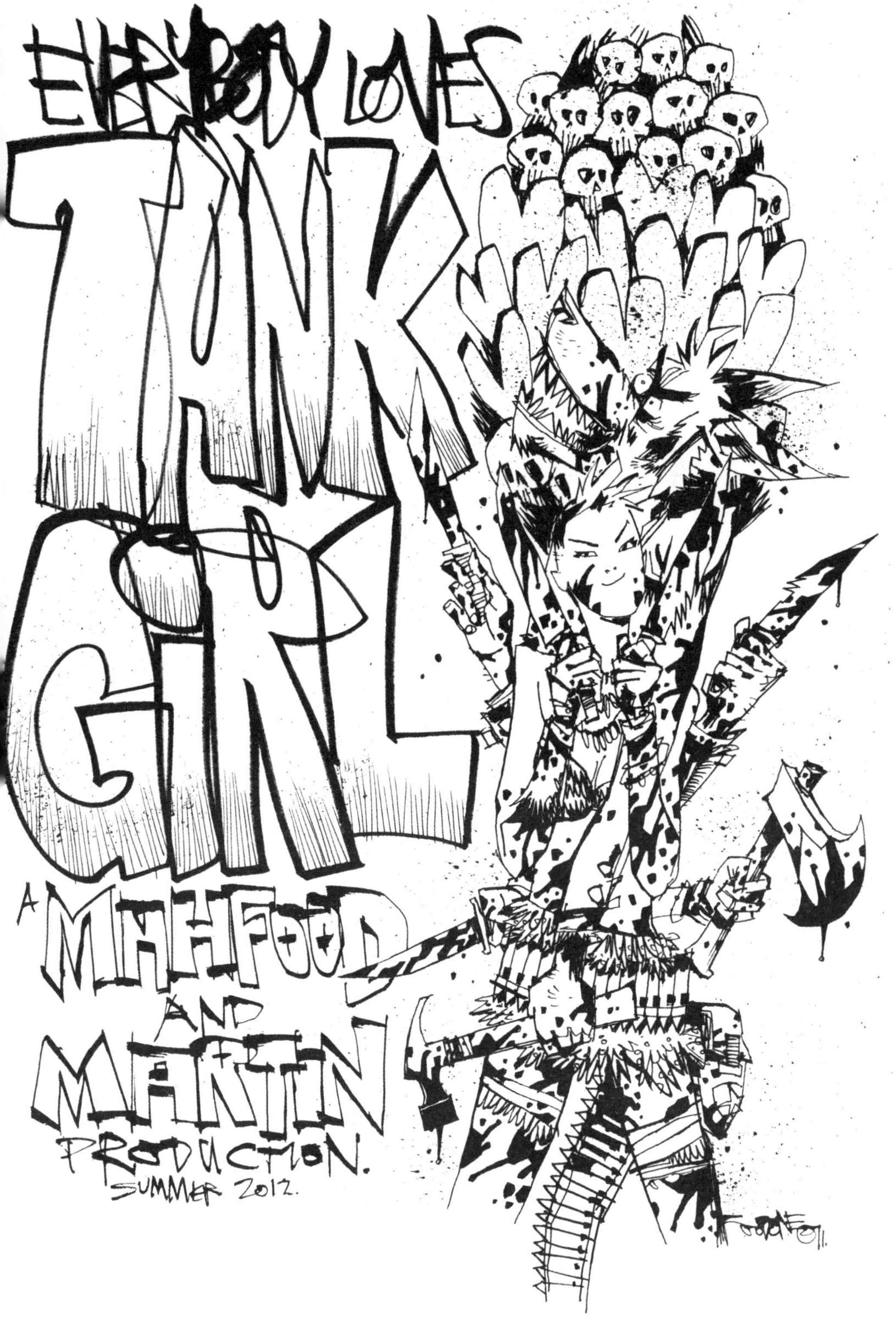
EVERYBODY LOVES
TANK GIRL
A MAHFOOD AND MARTIN PRODUCTION.
SUMMER 2012.

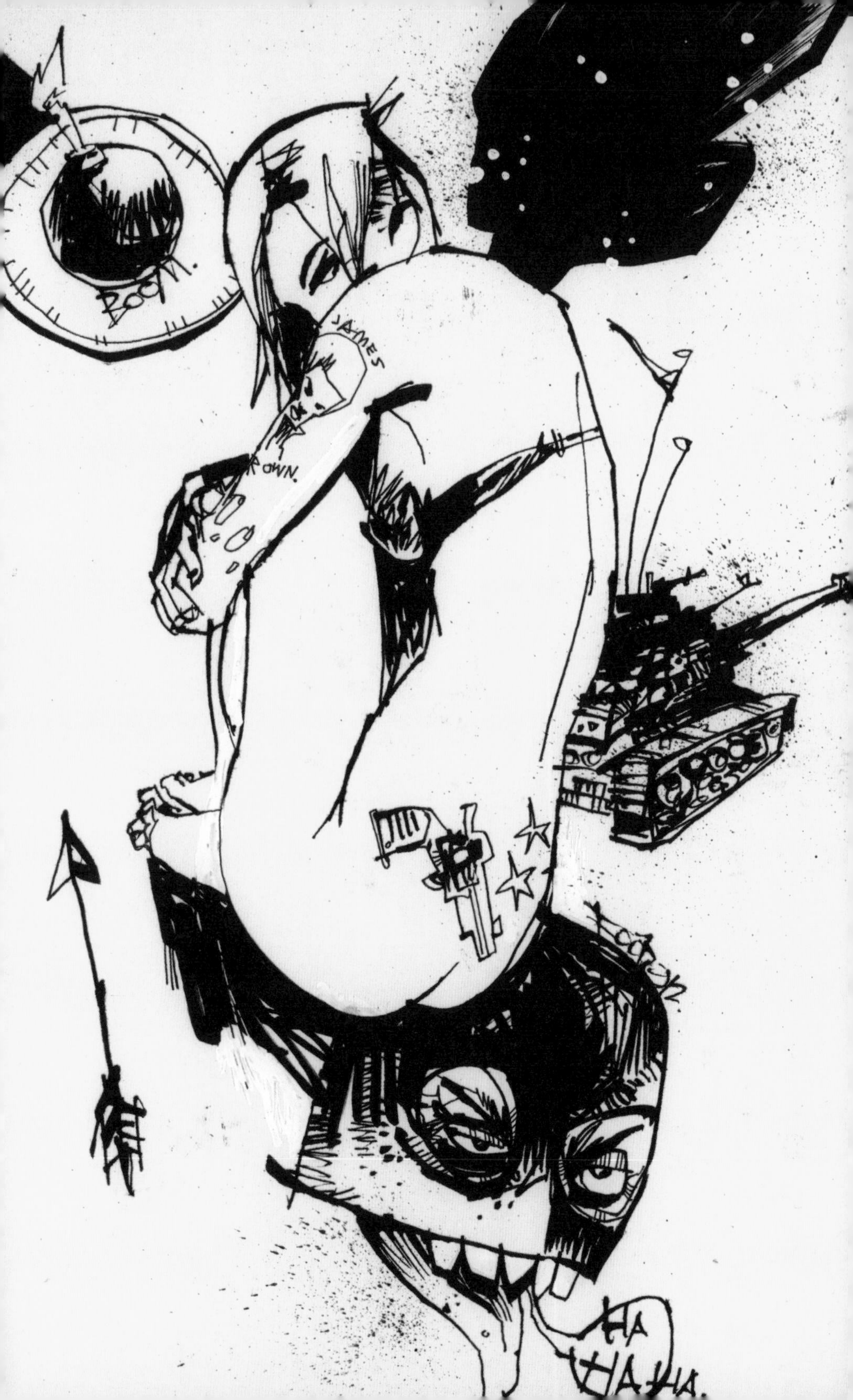
BOOM.
JAMES
ROWN.
HA HAHAHA.

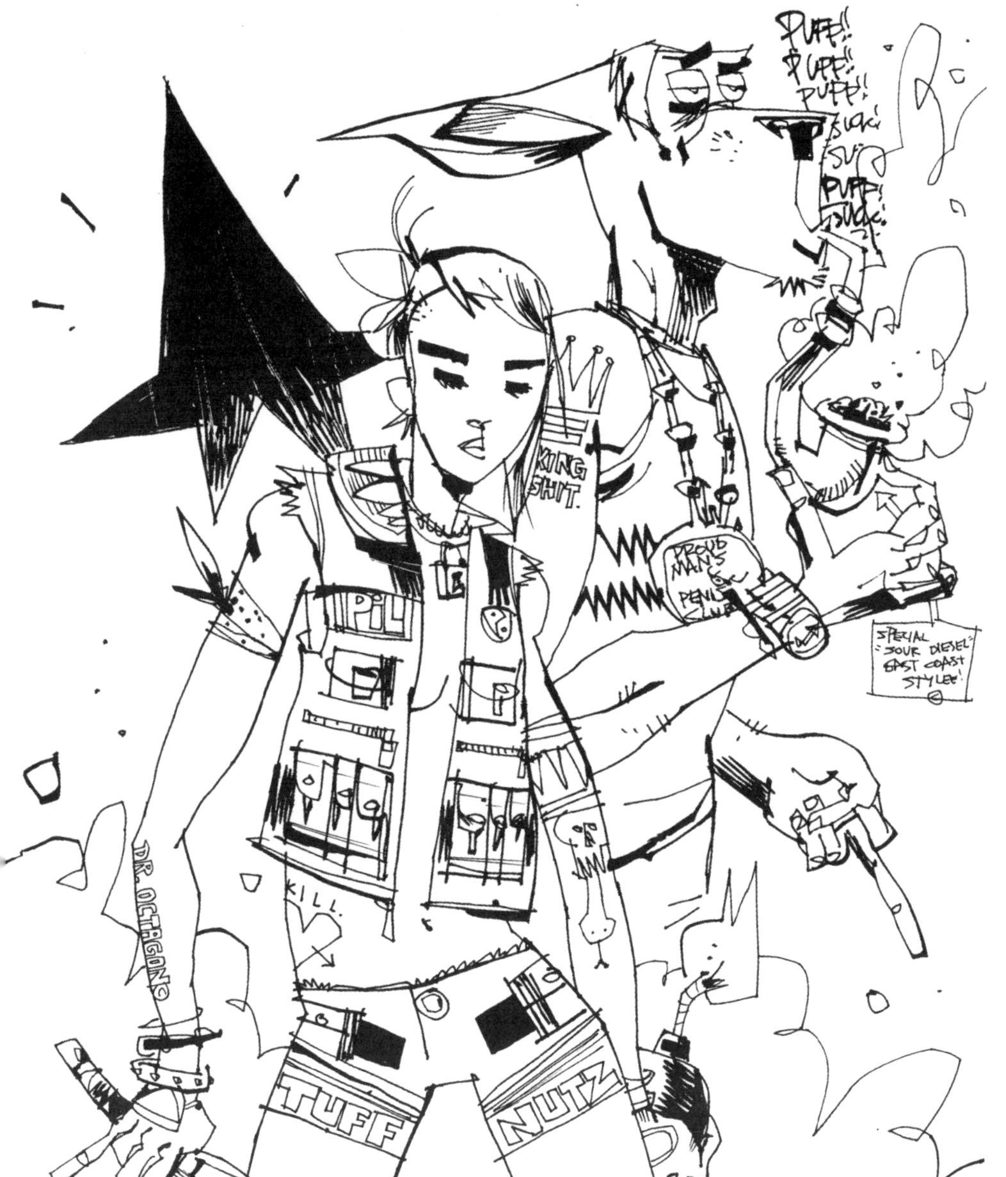
PUFF!!
PUFF!!
PUFF!!
SUCK!
PUFF!
SUCK!
KING SHIT.
PROUD MAN'S
SPECIAL SOUR DIESEL EAST COAST STYLEE!
PIL
KILL.
DR. OCTAGON
TUFF
NUTZ

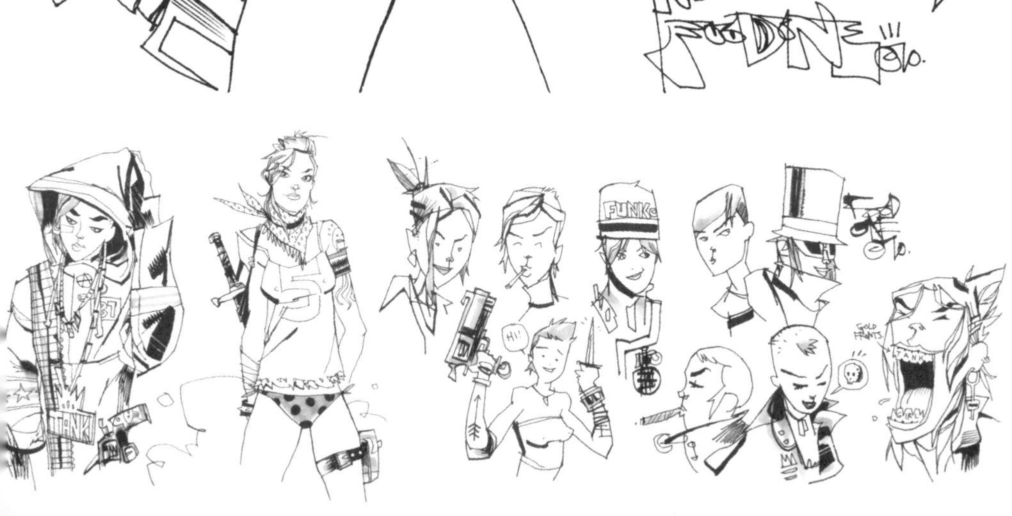
TANK
FUNK
HI!
GOLD FRONTS
TANK

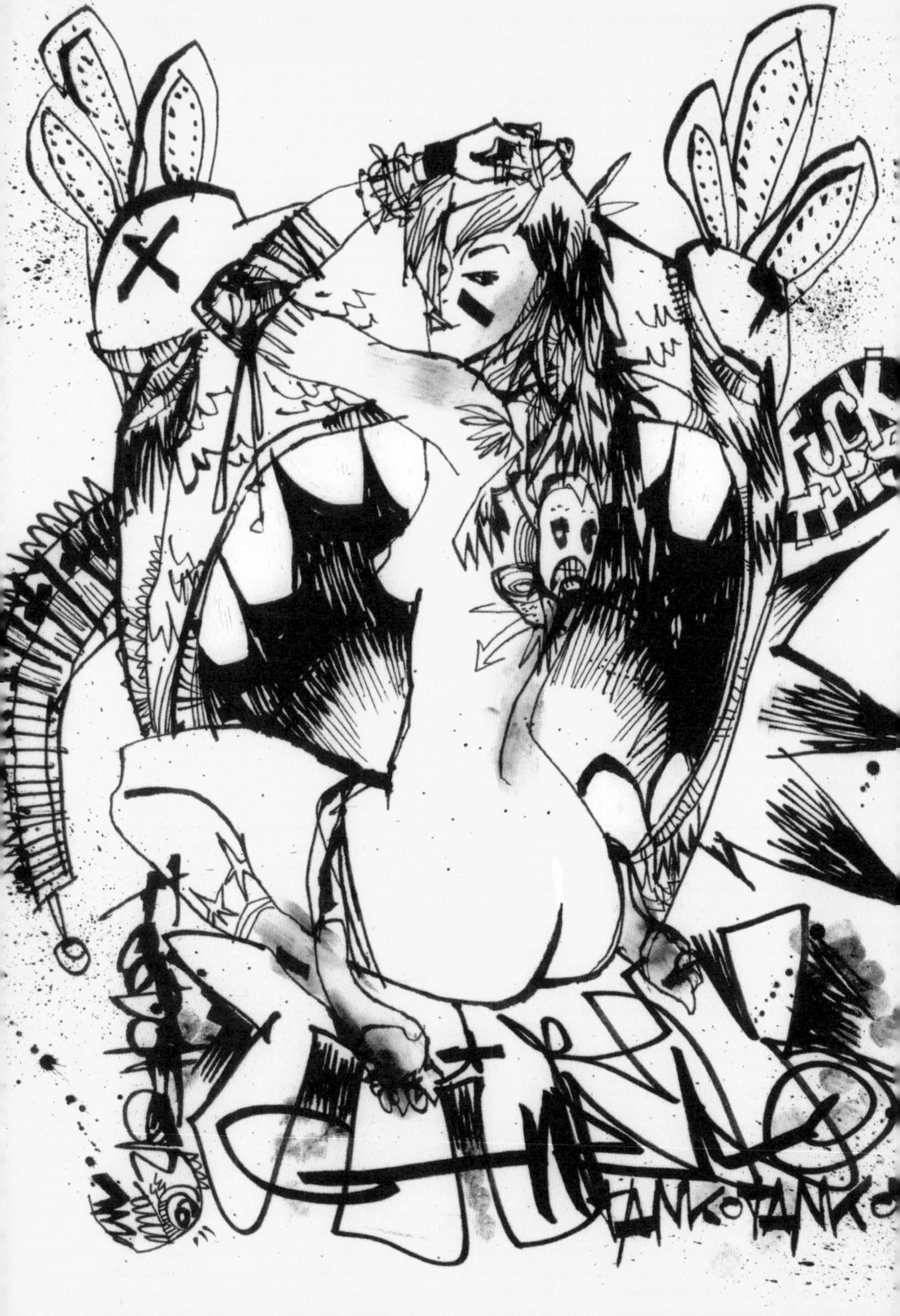
FUCK
TANKO TANKO

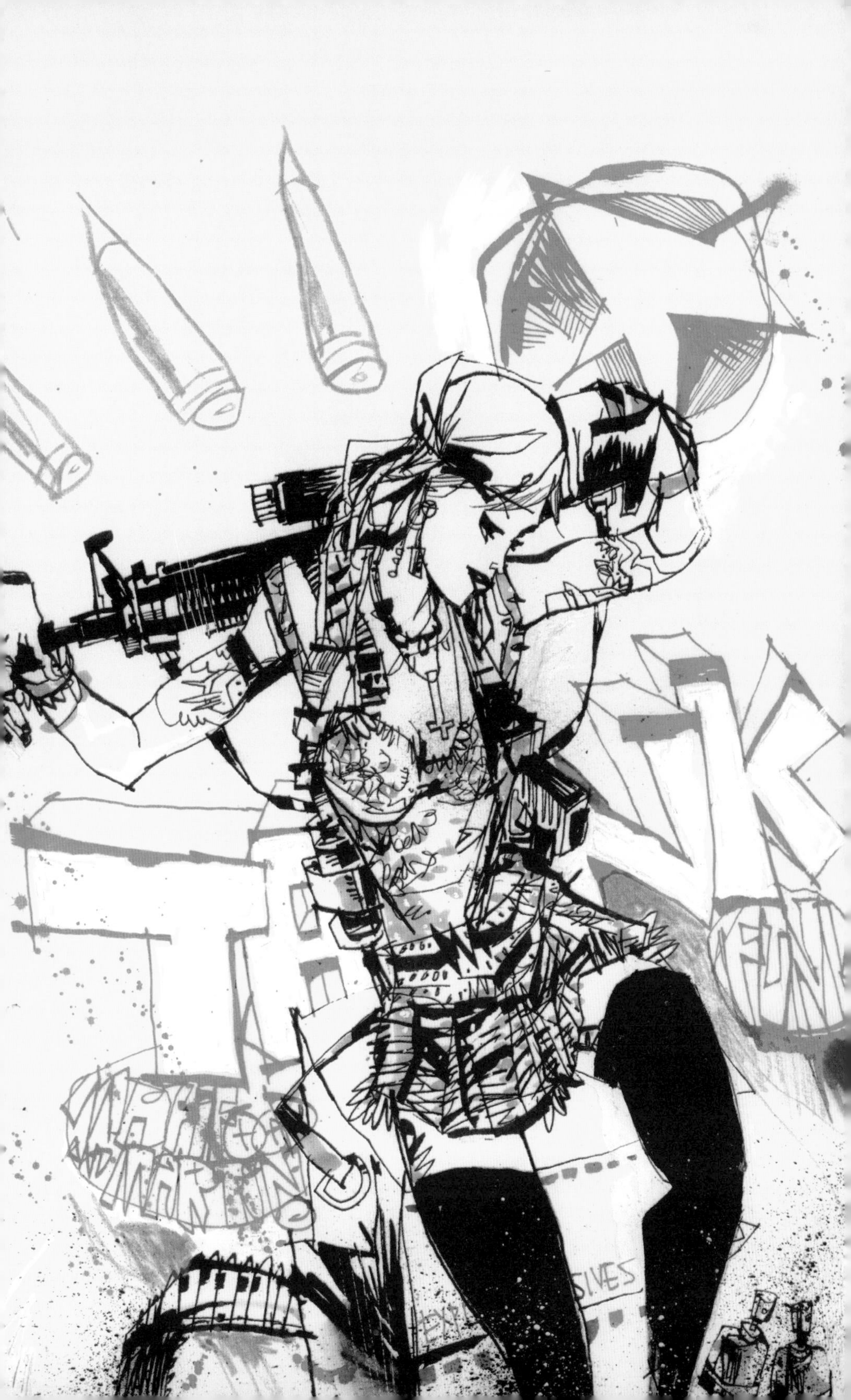
SIVES

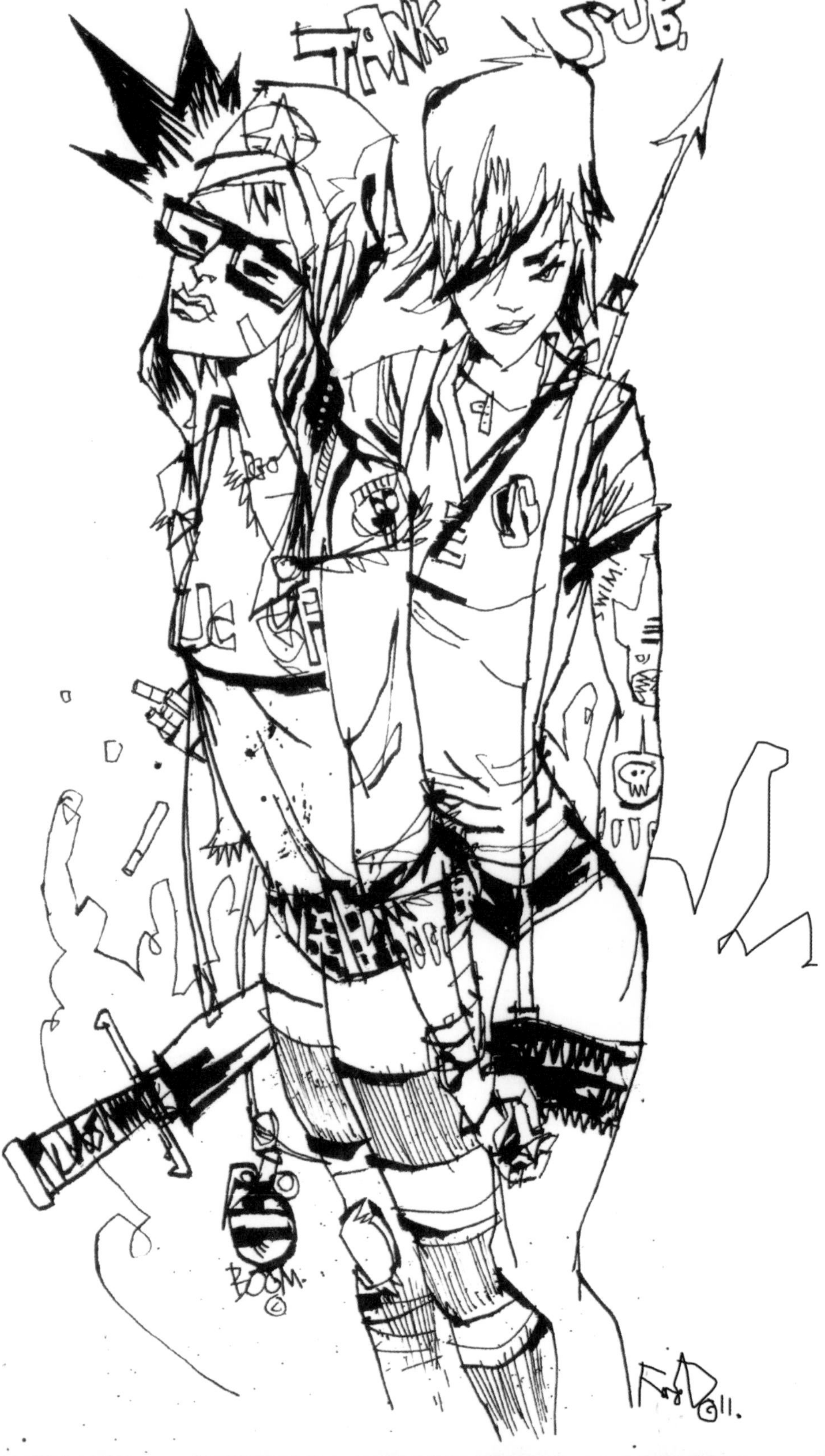
TANK
SUB.
BOOM.

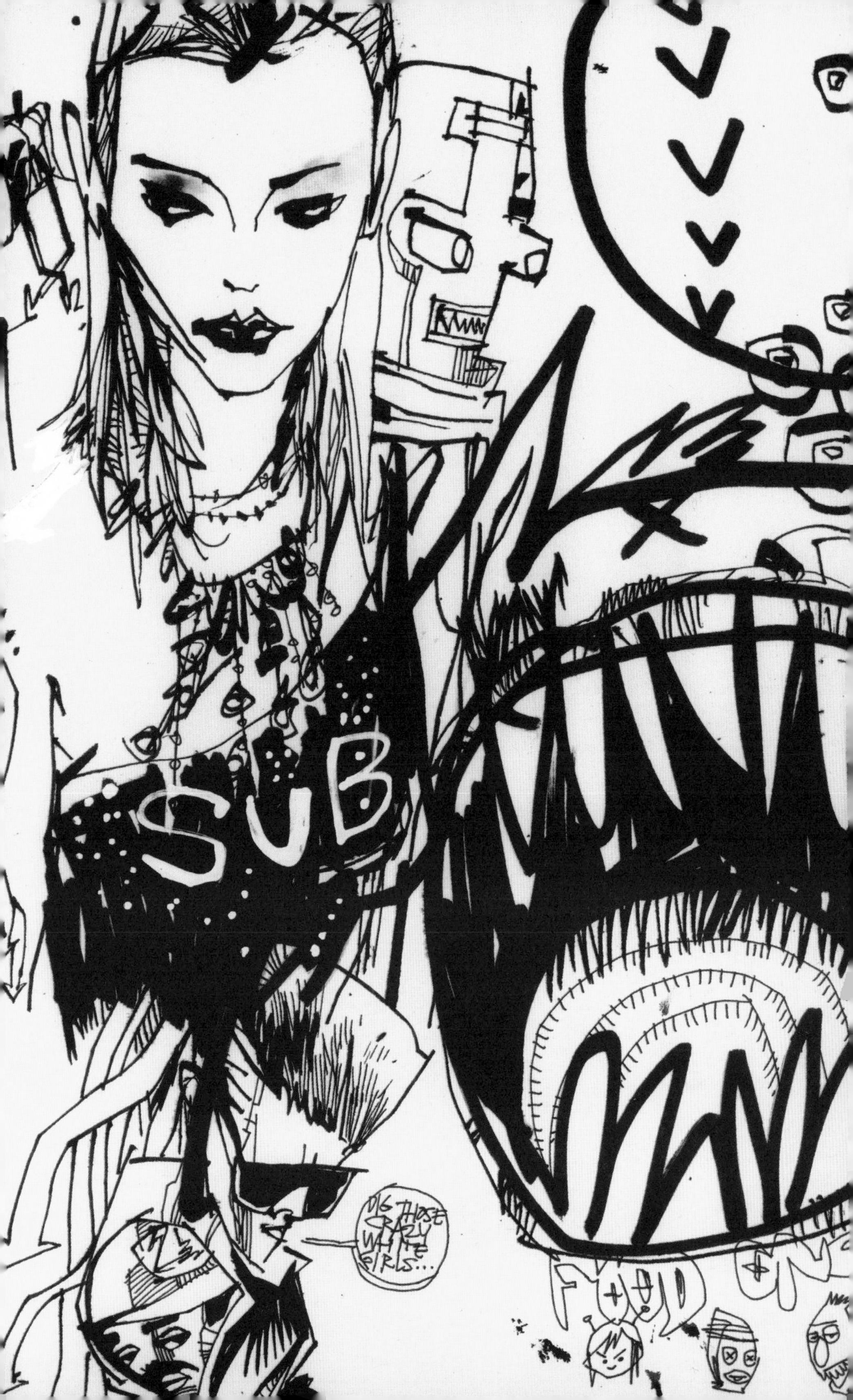
SUB
DIG THOSE CRAZY WHITE GIRLS...
FOOD

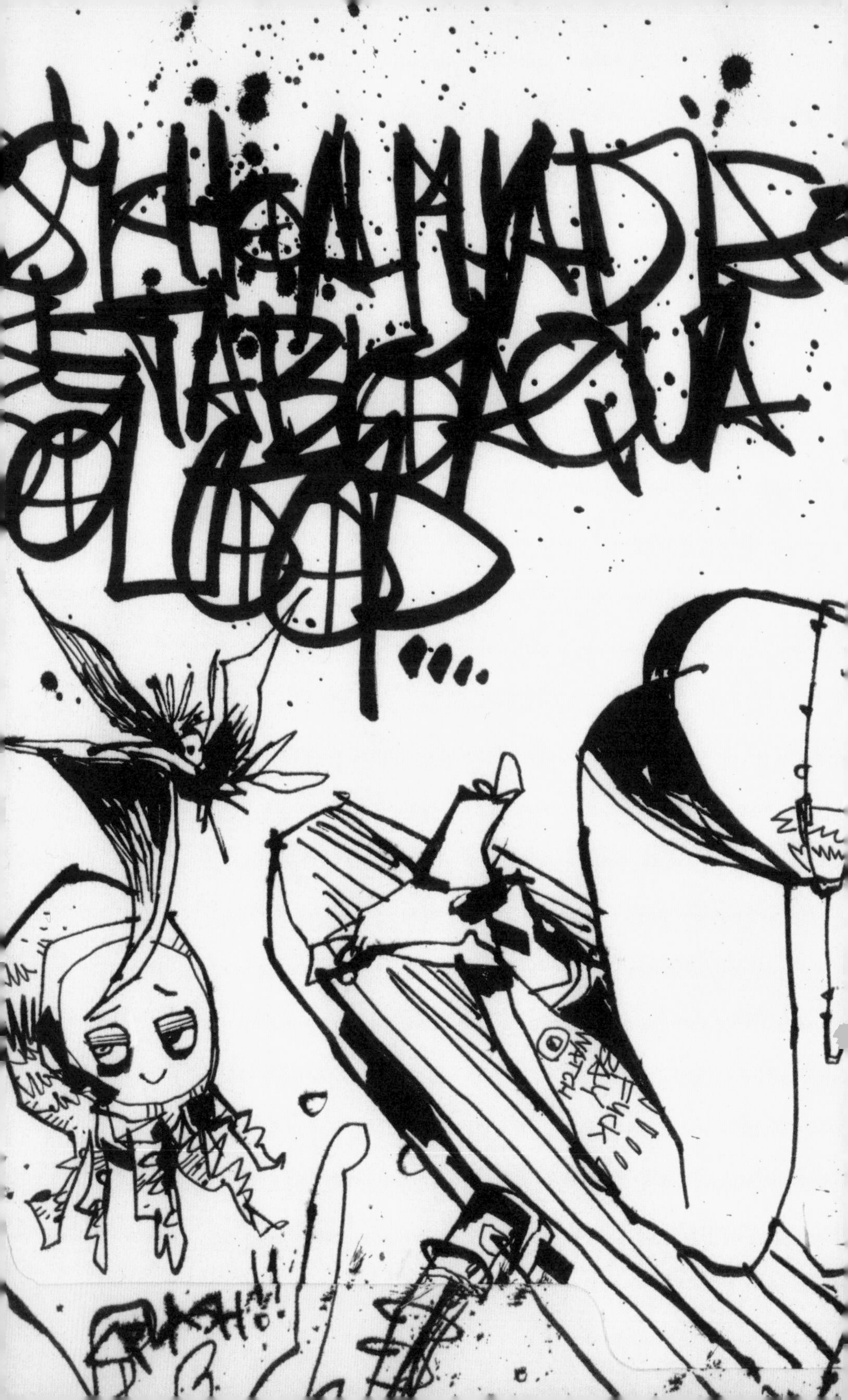
WATCH

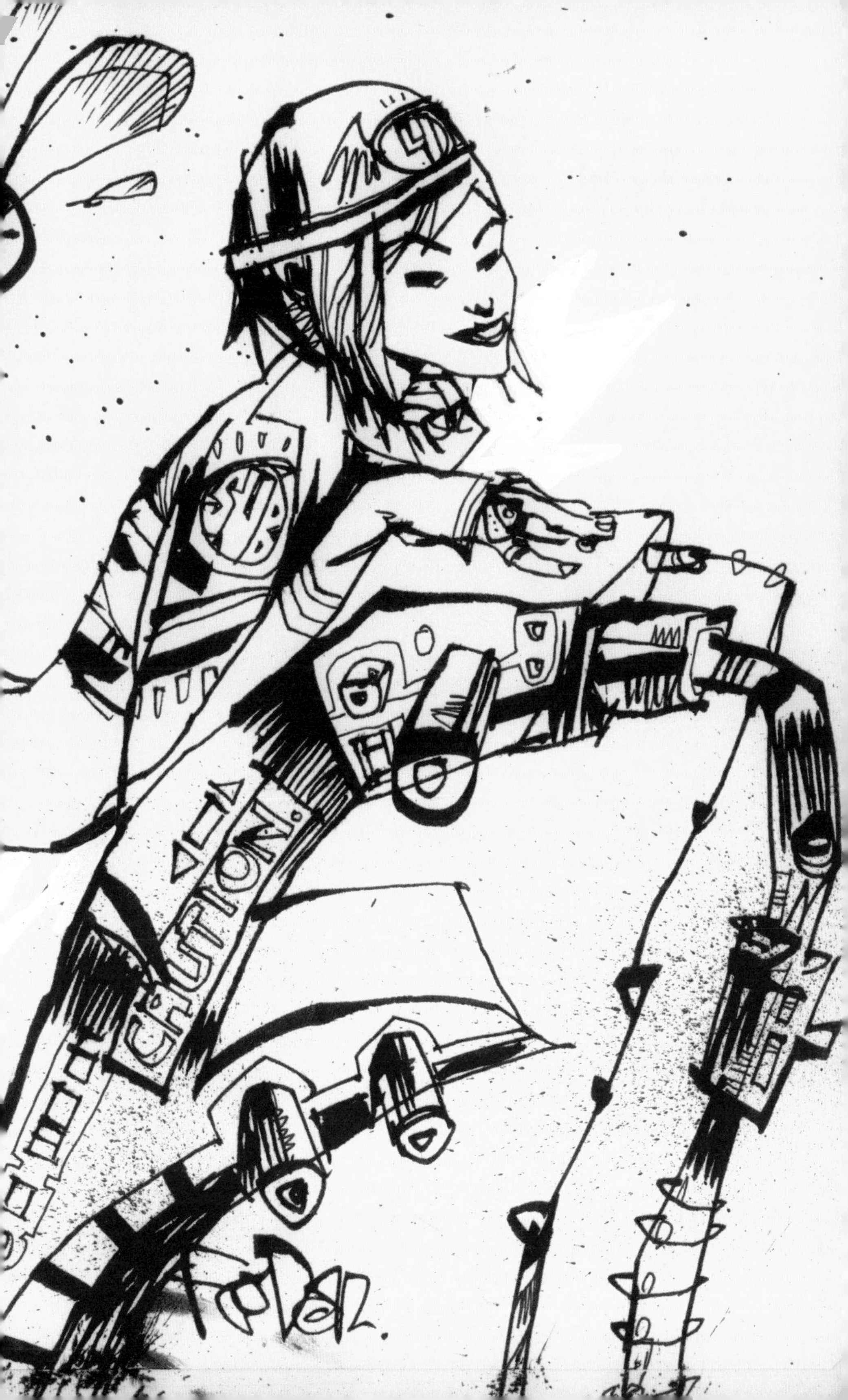
CAUTION!
CAUTION

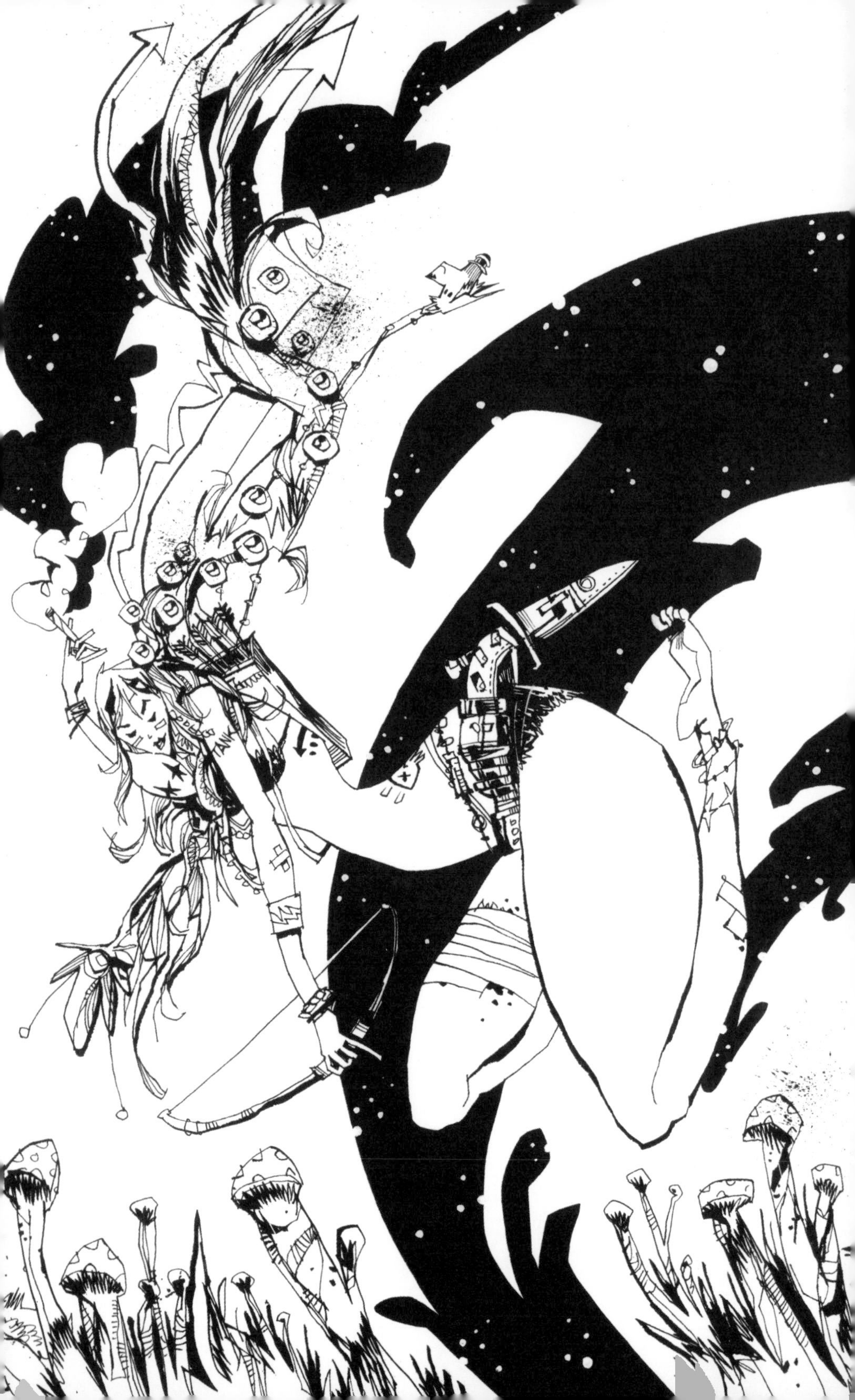
TANK

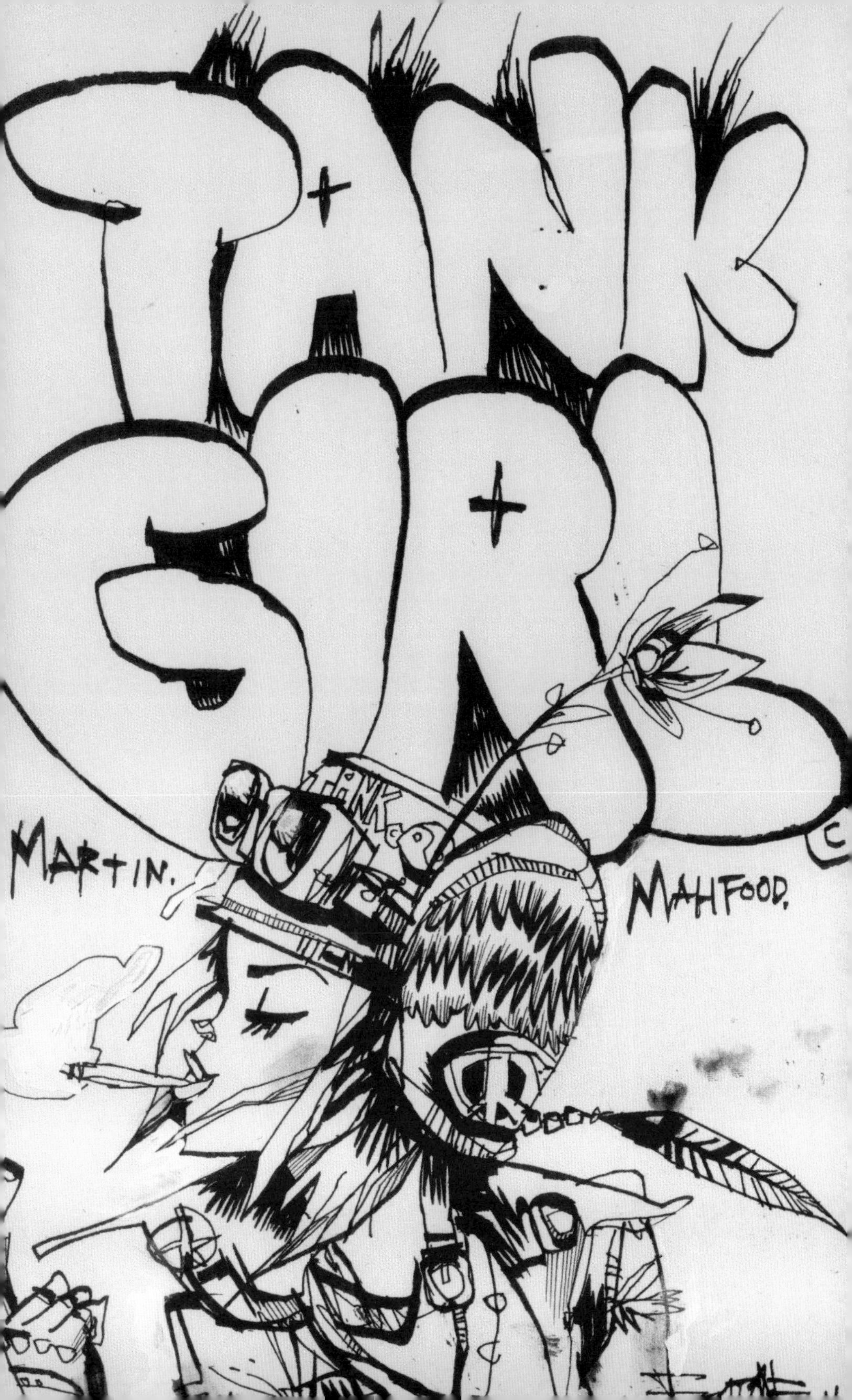
TANK GIRL
MARTIN.
MAHFOOD.

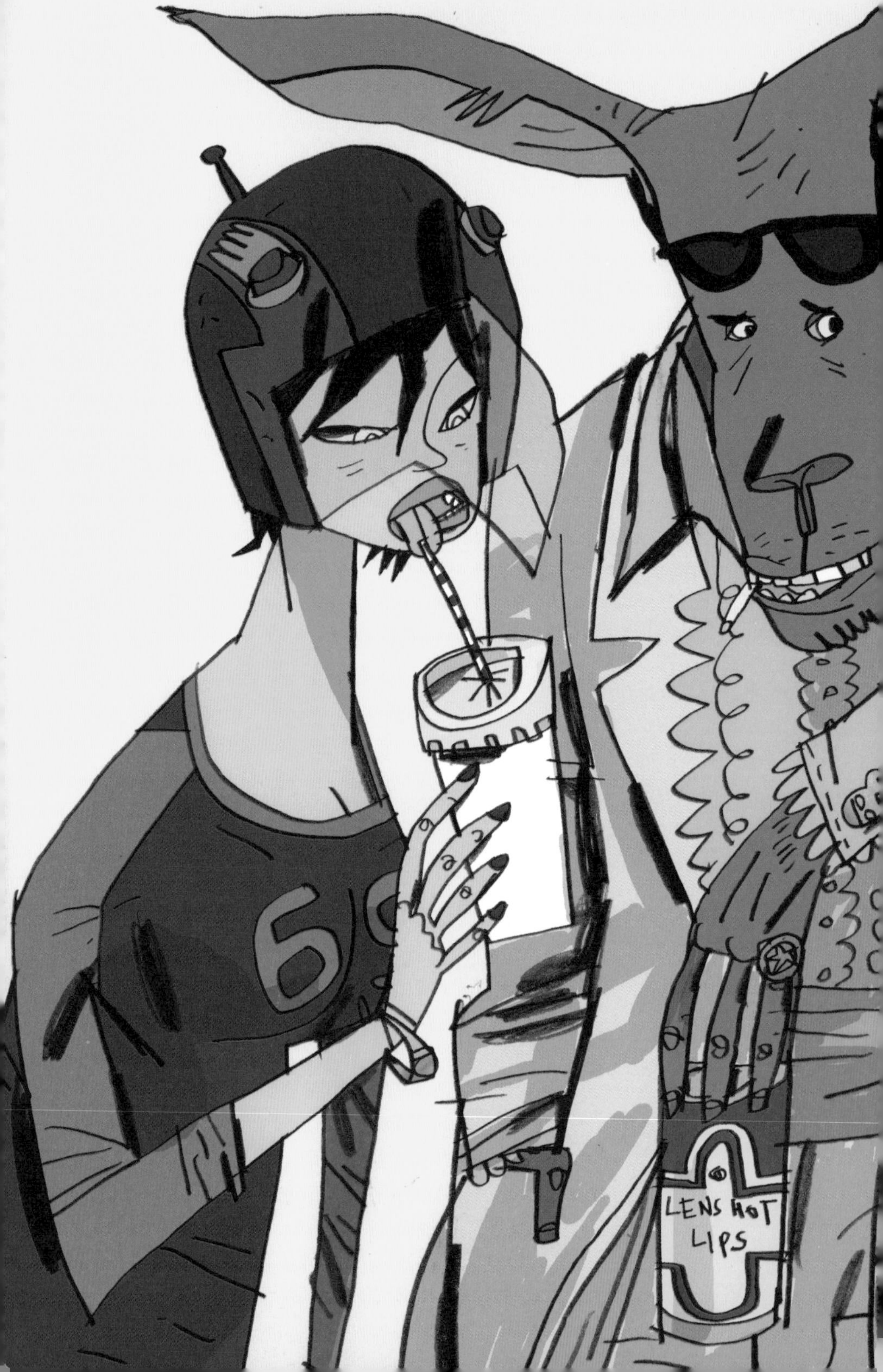
LENS HOT
LIPS

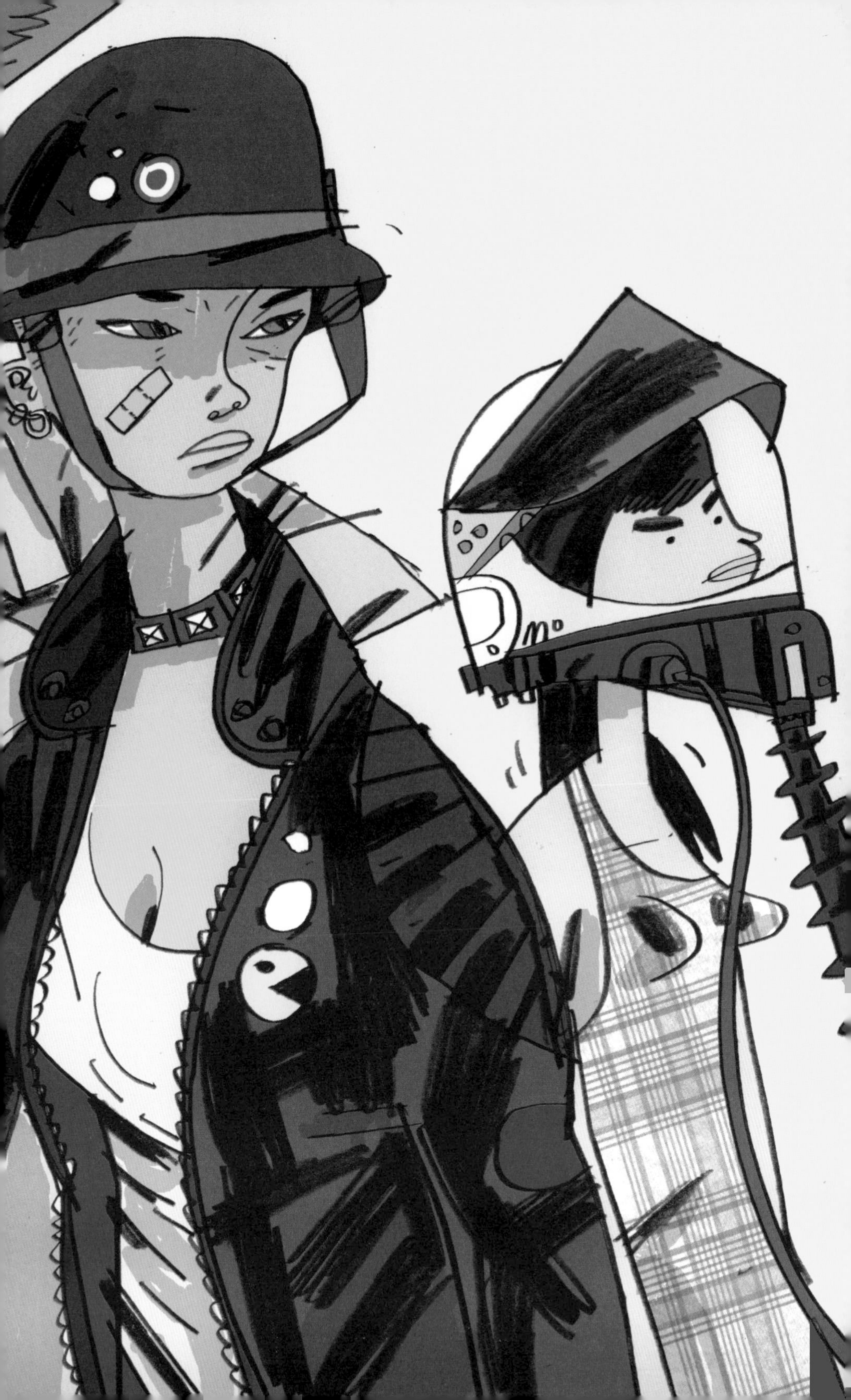

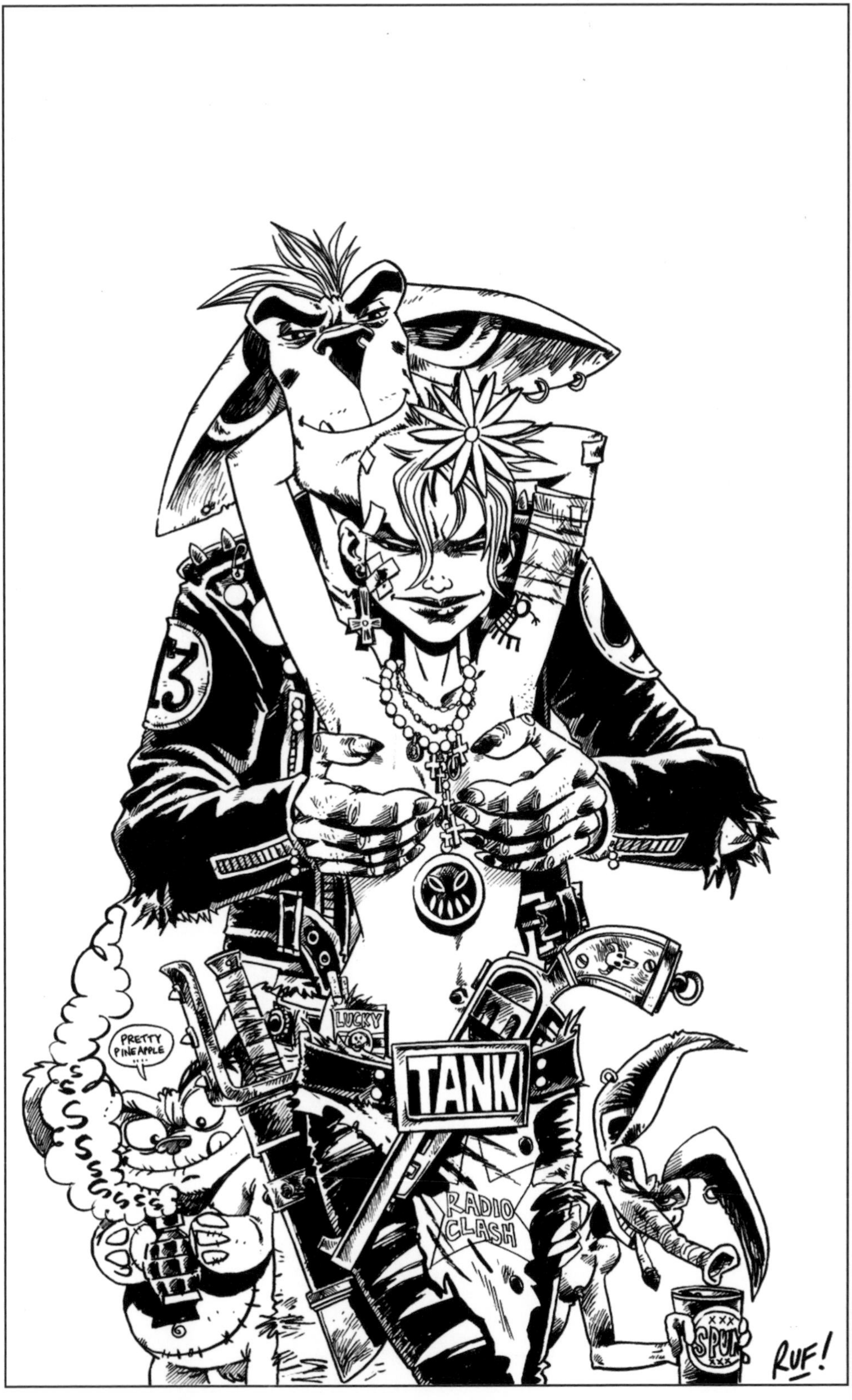
PRETTY PINEAPPLE ....
13
LUCKY
TANK
RADIO CLASH
RUF!